AFRICAN AMERICAN COMMUNICATION & IDENTITIES

To my lovely wife Ricci, again and again. I love you!

AFRICAN AMERICAN COMMUNICATION & IDENTITIES

Essential Readings

Editor

Ronald L. Jackson II
Pennsylvania State University

SAGE Publications
International Educational and Professional Publisher
Thousand Oaks ▪ London ▪ New Delhi

For information:

Sage Publications, Inc.
2455 Teller Road
Thousand Oaks, California 91320
E-mail: order@sagepub.com

Sage Publications Ltd.
6 Bonhill Street
London EC2A 4PU
United Kingdom

Sage Publications India Pvt. Ltd.
B-42, Panchsheel Enclave
Post Box 4109
New Delhi 110 017 India

Printed in the United States of America

Library of Congress Cataloging-in-Publication Data

African American communication and identities : essential readings / Ronald L. Jackson, II, editor.
        p. cm.
Includes bibliographical references and index.
ISBN 0–7619–2845–6—ISBN 0–7619–2846–4 (pbk.)
    1. African Americans-Communication. 2. African Americans-Ethnic identity.
3. Communication and culture-United States. I. Jackson,
Ronald L., 1970-
P94.5.A37A367 2004
302.2′089′96073—dc21   2003013998

Printed on acid-free paper

03 04 05 06 07 08 09 10 9 8 7 6 5 4 3 2 1

Acquiring Editor:	Todd R. Armstrong
Editorial Assistant:	Veronica K. Novak
Production Editor:	Claudia A. Hoffman
Typesetter:	C&M Digitals (P) Ltd.
Indexer:	Molly Hall
Cover Designer:	Janet Foulger

CONTENTS

ACKNOWLEDGMENTS

All honor and glory for the completion of this project goes to God.

I am grateful for each and every author whose work appears in this book and the legions of other scholars whose work is not featured here but who have worked arduously to expand the lines of inquiry reflected in this volume of readings. I owe many intellectual debts to persons who directly or indirectly guided me to this point in my career and blessed me with insights about the multitudinous communicative experiences of African Americans. Those who have done so include such intellectual giants as Molefi Kete Asante, Jack Daniel, Melbourne Cummings, Patricia Hill Collins, Geneva Smitherman, John Baugh, Lyndrey Niles, Marsha Houston, Stuart Hall, and Richard Wright. There are many others, too many to name, but you, too, are appreciated. Thanks to Veronica Novak and Claudia Hoffman at Sage, and special thanks to Todd Armstrong, Senior Acquisitions Editor at Sage Publications, for his consistency, punctuality, professionalism, and enthusiasm. Also, I appreciate the feedback of Thurmon Garner at the University of Georgia and Joni Jones at the University of Texas at Austin, peer reviewers for this book; your comments were so helpful. Finally, I am thankful for the assistance and feedback shared with me by several cherished colleagues: Carlos D. Morrison, Trina J. Wright, Shaun Gabbidon (from whom the idea for this book came), Jeffrey Lynn Woodyard, Celnisha L. Dangerfield, Jennifer R. Warren, Michael Hecht, and Bradford R. Hogue. Thanks also to the many colleagues and friends of the NCA Black Caucus and African American Communication & Culture Division who completed surveys.

INTRODUCTION

Toward Long Overdue Recognition of Research Concerning African American Communication and Identities

This collection showcases and celebrates some of the foundational and contemporary pioneering and pivotal works of scholars who have contributed to what is now known as African American Communication Studies. In presenting this volume of identity-focused approaches to African American communication of the late twentieth and early twenty-first centuries, I am in no way suggesting that this is an exclusive set of essays to which there is no equally rigorous match. However, the essays included here are quite significant for what they tell us about the distinctive confluence between communication and African American identities.

THE RESULT OF EXPORTING AFRICAN AMERICAN COMMUNICATION RESEARCH

Just as we communicologists have, for years, imported the works of other disciplines, we have also exported our works. In fact, according to a recent bibliography of African American communication research compiled by Ronald Jamal Stephens (2000), the majority of African American communication scholarship is published in interdisciplinary periodicals and small, independently run academic presses. As a result, for years there has been the presumption that African American communication scholarship primarily exists in the form of unpublished papers presented at professional conferences—such as that of the National Communication Association—or not at all. In fact, however, an exhaustive search within and among journals in other fields uncovers a significant body of published writings pertaining to this variegated research area. Because I have done so elsewhere (Jackson, 2000), I will not explore the reasons here for this cross-pollination. It is my intuition that this has not been considered a real problem because the communication literature has been, instead, richly populated with articles and books that affirm the importance of culturally homogeneous ways of knowing, and these ways of knowing supposedly have satisfied the interests of the intellectual masses. I contend that this view limits our knowledge and stunts our curiosity about communicative and cultural particularities.

My Early Academic Reflections about the Perceived Absence of African American Communication Research

I can vividly remember the brief span between the time I received my bachelor's degree and the time I began work on my master's. I began to wonder whether there were any Black communication researchers and, certainly, whether African American identities were of any real concern to those who were entrusted to study and teach about human interaction. Until my doctoral program, I had no idea that there was a vast literature replete with scholars who were dedicated to exploring African American communicative experiences. I felt invalidated, alone, devalued, and dismissed. All throughout my doctoral program, I kept those previously felt emotions in mind and committed myself to introducing a volume such as this one to the world. In centralizing the contributions of stalwart communication scholars whose works are exemplary of fine innovative research, I want all readers, especially those just now being exposed to this broad area of inquiry, to know that the intellectual legacies of those who study African American communication have not been forgotten. Furthermore, this book is a tribute to them and a direct source of inspiration to other contemporary African American cultural researchers working to expand this branch of research to represent even more African American communicative and cultural experiences. This is a venture by which we not only collectively celebrate research but also celebrate our identities and, indeed, our very humanity.

Born Out of Necessity

There is an old folk saying that necessity is the mother of invention. In other words, some things are brought forth into being by virtue of perceived absence or need. *African American Communication and Identities: Essential Readings* was born out of a need to acknowledge African American communication research and hold it in value alongside other culturally specific approaches to and studies of human interaction.

Unfortunately, within the province of communication research, scholars are both subjected to and participate in the production of a presumably panoptic—and, incidentally, hegemonic—range of insights concerning human interaction. Nearly the entire body of communication literature embraces exclusively the perspectives of European Americans and their European predecessors. This culturally myopic cognitive and intellectual set frequently devalues the cultural specificities of human communicative experiences. In doing so, the multidisciplinary field of communication has been debilitated. For this reason, the book is not called simply *African American Communication* but is, instead, called *African American Communication and Identities: Essential Readings* because it is critical to accent the constitutive aspects of African American communication behaviors as they relate to how African Americans define themselves culturally. As Collins (1990) and Asante (1987) teach us, we are no more able to separate an author from her writings than we are to isolate African Americans from their cultures and, hence, their indigenous identities.

A tremendous amount of evidence suggests that during and prior to the development of European-centered paradigms concerning rhetoric, language, and also discourses pertaining to interpersonal, group, organizational, and mass-mediated relationships, there were also African-centered, Asian-centered, Native American- and Hispanic-centered paradigms developing around these ideas. Some of this proliferation of communication-related discourses and paradigms has been uncovered gradually throughout the last fifty years. The fascinating and unfortunate implicit commentary that exists as a corollary to this absence is that these non-European discourses do not matter; this volume is testament to the fact that they do.

The Process of Selecting Essays for Inclusion

Despite the fact that this is a book of reprinted articles and essays that originally appeared in academic journals and books, it is no small task to assemble a volume of this nature. There are literally hundreds of essays that can qualify as African American communication studies. The process of selecting essays for *African American Communication and Identities: Essential Readings* began in the summer of 2000 and ended in January, 2003. To ensure that this first-of-a-kind book was reflective of an entire scholarly community's contributions to the field of African American communication, I decided to invite that community of researchers to participate in the essay selection process. It began in the largest known academic contingencies of African American communicologists, the National Communication Association's Black Caucus and African American Communication and Culture Division, comprised of over 400 members collectively. I sent members a two-page electronic survey asking them to identify works that they considered significant and foundational to African American communicology. I made additional surveys available to members at the business meetings of these two units during the 2000 NCA convention. I directly contacted several dozen scholars and asked them to complete surveys. After we received about 75 surveys, Carlos Morrison, Trina Wright, and I noted consistencies among respondents and devised a list of approximately forty scholars and their pivotal essays. Initially, I intended to feature only landmark essays, but gradually there emerged a consensus among the three of us to diversify the volume, interspersing foundational as well as recent but significant essays. After the three of us made all the selections, Carlos and I conducted additional independent searches of scholars we may have overlooked. Subsequently, we shared our findings, and I narrowed the list even further after Jennifer Warren, my graduate research assistant, and I uncovered additional sources and considered publisher limitations. The result of this extensive process is the volume you hold in your hands.

Layout of Book

To examine the micro-communicative aspects of African American communication, we've arranged the text into six parts. We begin with the theoretical and rhetorical dimensions and move outward to broader contexts, such as that of relational, gendered, organizational, and mass mediated communication.

Part I, Theoretic Approaches to African American Communication and Identity, is comprised of five essays that primarily focus on new and refreshing conceptual innovations not theorized systematically by anyone else in the communication literature. Addressing paradigmatic notions of cultural personhood, self-esteem, rhetoric, discursive continuities from Africa, and nonverbal behavior, these writings are noted for their coherent explanations of previously unstudied facets of African American communicative behaviors within the field of communication. Part I seeks to answer in what ways can we conceptualize the unique communicative experiences of African Americans. Jack L. Daniel and Geneva Smitherman's classic article, "How I Got Over" begins this section. In it, they discuss the deep structures of African American culture that permeate communicative behaviors. Molefi Kete Asante, another of the pioneers of African American communication research, wrote the next essay concerning afrocentricity, in which he expands his discussion of this conceptual brainchild in a much more explicative and systematic way than any of his other previously published essays. These heralded theoretic writings offer segue into the intellectually exciting essays that follow, essays concerned with racial complicity, Black kinesics, and theatrical improvisation, respectively. Certainly, the most unique features of these essays are their inherent cultural and communicationist posture.

Part II, African American Rhetoric and Language, includes four essays that are significant works authored by trailblazers in African American communication research. Each of them, with the exception of Eric King Watts' more recent study, is a very well-known treatment of African American rhetorical and/or linguistic nuances. Their placement in a book of this nature is indisputable. Deborah F. Atwater's exploratory thinkpiece leads this discussion of rhetoric and language with challenges to the field, ones that still confront us today. The remaining essays answer the challenge in different ways, with detailed analyses of African American ethos, culturally specific discursive devices, and a discussion of linguistic continuities and Black community preservation of ancestral linguistic norms.

Part III of the book is titled African American Communication in Relational Contexts. Within this section, four chapters cover relational dimensions of African American identities, from issues of communication satisfaction to friendship, marriage, and homosexual relationships. The essays in this section explicate communicative experiences in platonic, romantic, and family arrangements. Each chapter is innovative. Although there were many studies that predated the ones found here, this area of interpersonal communication study has only recently expanded to include such a wide range of African American communication issues, which is why so many of the studies are fairly recent. Michael L. Hecht, Sidney Ribeau, and J. K. Alberts penned the first essay in this section. They help set the tone for an ensuing discussion of conversation and relational improvement strategies that cross racial boundaries and permeate varying relational contexts, including friendship, dating, and marital relationships.

Communicating African American Gendered Identities is the name of Part IV of this collection. Although all five of the studies in this section were written in the last decade, each offers innovative conceptions of African American gendered identities that were virtually absent prior to their emergence. Marsha Houston, who many consider the pioneer of African American women's communication research, has only recently spoken specifically of African American women without reference to men or White women. It is this essay that sets the pace for coming generations of scholars who will find it appropriate to study African American women on their own. Jackson and Dangerfield's essay, the final one in this section of the book, seems on the surface to have presented the opposite perspective. We theorize about African American men and masculinities, but we do insist on introducing women into the discussion and allow for the possibility that women might also be masculine. Each of the essays in this section addresses new and refreshing aspects of African American gendered realities.

Part V, African American Communication and Identities in Organizational and Instructional Contexts, combines organizational and instructional communication studies. The four essays in this section are fairly new heuristic contributions to the study of African Americans. The section begins with Brenda J. Allen's essay, the pioneering work that has reintroduced many scholars to the significance of research on diversity in organizations. Allen's influence on research concerning Black women's organizational experiences is profound and is only hinted at in her essay, but Patricia S. Parker continues Allen's line of research while establishing her own presence in her exploration of Black women executives' communicative experiences in dominant culture organizations. Subsequently, this section shifts to include the instructional communication literature, which is particularly limited by so few studies concerning African

Americans. Katherine Grace Hendrix offers insights into issues of students' perceived credibility of their professors. Her work is monumental for the field of communication and nicely contributes to the instructional literature. My essay on identity negotiation within the institutional structure of some academic contexts rounds out this section. These new essays offer a clear set of ideas that are cogently presented and pivotal.

The final section of the book, Part VI, includes essays concerning African American identities in mass mediated contexts. With the exception of Squires' chapter, these essays are well known treatments of African Americans in the mass media. Clearly, this section, as all of the other sections, could have been much larger. There are dozens of studies on print, electronic and televisual journalism, radio, television, and film. Although this section does not include research on advertising, there are dozens of sources on African Americans and advertising (Kern-Foxworth, 1994; Turner, 1994). Nonetheless, this segment related to mass media depictions and programming offers a nice sampling of extant research in the area of African American communication.

From the conceptual frameworks presented in Part I to the media studies in Part VI, each of the essays in this book constitutes a small but very significant portion of the research on African American communication. It is important to recognize, however, that space limitations omitted several pivotal works by scholars such as Orlando Taylor, Dorthy Pennington, Teresa Nance, Terry Orbuch, Stanley Gaines, Lyndrey Niles, Keith Gilyard, bell hooks, Bishetta Merritt, Carolyn Calloway-Thomas, Marilyn Kern-Foxworth, Jeanette Dates, Mark Orbe, Aaron Gresson, William Pipes, Carter G. Woodson, Halle Quinn Brown, Chief Fela Sowande, and John Lucaites. Even this is not an exhaustive list of researchers who represent a wide range of interdisciplinary scholarship covering issues of African American identity. While I edited this book with a spirit of inclusiveness, I also regret that I could not include all of the landmark and pivotal essays in the field of African American communication.

In many ways, this book is an act of recovery. It is my sincere hope that scholars who write communication textbooks and scholarly monographs will cite these readings ad infinitum. The contributors to this volume deserve it, for they have left us an intellectual legacy of issues, challenges, needs, and paradigms that, in the end, seek to secure a space for the celebration of African Americans, their identities and their everyday lives.

REFERENCES

Asante, M. K. (1987). *Afrocentric Idea.* Philadelphia: Temple University Press.

Collins, P. H. (1990). *Black Feminist Thought.* New York: Routledge.

Jackson, R. L. (February 2000). So Real Illusions of Black Intellectualism: Exploring Race, Roles, and Gender in the Academy. *Communication Theory, 10(1),* 48–63.

Kern-Foxworth, M. (1994). *Aunt Jemima, Uncle Ben, and Rastus: Blacks in Advertising Yesterday, Today and Tomorrow.* Westport, CT: Greenwood Press.

Stephens, R. J. (2000). *Preliminary bibliography and summary report to NCA African American Communication and Culture Division.* Unpublished manuscript.

Turner, P. (1994). *Ceramic Uncles & Celluloid Mammies: Black Images and Their Influence on Culture.* New York: Anchor Books.

Part I

THERORETIC APPROACHES TO AFRICAN AMERICAN COMMUNICATION AND IDENTITY

We often discuss paradigms as lenses and frames. These metaphors are useful for explaining how people make sense of what they see. Essentially, paradigms are ways of shaping perspective. Think of perspective as a container that comes in all shapes and sizes and is capable of holding liquid. Now imagine the container as theory and the liquid as knowledge; hence, we use theory to contain what we know. Another function of theory is to shape knowledge. So, if we have two liquid-filled containers, one being a chalice and the other a test tube, the contours of those containers allow us to view knowledge differently. In other words, the container helps us shape and gain access to other perspectives. In the case of the African American communication paradigms featured here, it is clear that each is influenced by African American cultural worldviews.

The exciting thing about communication theory is that it is the entry point through which most communication scholars and undergraduate students are first introduced to the field of communication. It is very important that neophyte scholars are acquainted with culture-centered approaches to communication as well as those that appear not to be concerned with culture. Part I invites readers to explore a range of concepts and ideas that emanate from and are shaped by cultural perspectives.

To begin, Jack L. Daniel and Geneva Smitherman explicate the differences between surface and deep structures that can be found within and among Black African descendants in the United States. In postulating a traditional African world view or African diasporic perspective, Daniel and Smitherman instructively indicate several communication dynamics and patterns that they argue are carryovers from "geographically disparate Africans," such as call-and-response, rhythmic and spiritual functioning, and also two culturally specific interpretations of time: sacred and micro time (i.e., polychronic time).

In line with Daniel and Smitherman's exploration of African continuities, Molefi Kete Asante introduces his metatheory coined "afrocentricity," a term that would vibrate throughout academic circles and across the lips of everyday citizens throughout the world in a span of two decades. The paradigm is said to have begun with an essay he penned earlier entitled, "Markings of an African Concept of Rhetoric"; the essay that appears here, however, is the first to appear in one of his books, his 1987 *The Afrocentric Idea*. In this essay, he differentiates orature from rhetoric and defines orature as "the total oral tradition of Africans and African Americans . . . the comprehensive body of oral

1

discourse on every subject and in every genre of expression produced by people of African descent." The essay is significant because it is one of the first explanations of nommo to describe the use of the spoken word in African American oratory, from the homiletics employed during preaching to the anaphora evident in the fiery speeches of Marcus Garvey and the syncopation and rhythm entwined in music. Asante's theorizing of afrocentricity is founded upon a history of ideas respective of African cultural carryovers. No matter whether he is discussing the Dogon culture's quadrilectic epistemology of the "word at face value, the word off to the side, the word from behind or the clear word," Asante clarifies the imperative to retrieve understanding of orature via African ancestral legacies.

Mark Lawrence McPhail does not expend as much energy trying to uncover African sources of influence on African American communication. Instead, he devises a theory of critical discourse to which he credits Greek sophists. Complicity theory, according to McPhail, is primarily a "theory of the opposite party [that] calls into question the principle of negative difference and ultimately essentialist epistemology and rational logic." In his philosophical articulation of complicity, McPhail locates several instances in which discourses argue for the existence of some immutable essence, such as in the case of racism. Then, he pinpoints the faulty logic implicit in that immutability while contending that the discourse is fueled by both party's unwavering insistence on the correctness of their position, which only subconsciously reinvents the cycle of essentialism. Since this initial essay, McPhail has drastically shifted his position on essentialism, but I chose this essay because it remarkably diversifies the perspectives found in extant African American communication theories.

The next essay by Kenneth R. Johnson also expands conceptualizations of African American communication. Johnson accomplishes this by comparing nonverbal communication patterns (specifically, kinesic behaviors) of Blacks in the United States with other Americans. He buttresses his analysis with comparisons to kinesic behaviors of West Africans. Some of the differences Johnson notes between Blacks and Whites, for example, are eye movements and styles of walking. He concludes that educators, counselors, and community practitioners need to be aware of these kinesic differences in order to truly understand the full range of communicative behaviors of African Americans.

The final essay in Part I was written by Joni L. Jones. Titled "Improvisation as a Performance Strategy for African-based Theatre," Jones's essay is perhaps the first of its kind in the field of communication. Alongside her disciplinary colleague D. Soyini Madison (also in this volume), Jones published this essay in *Text & Performance Quarterly*. In it, she makes the case for improvisation being a performance strategy to be employed within African-based theatre. She explains that she examined use of improvisation during a Yoruba performance that centralized an Egungun masquerade, which is a ceremony that celebrates ancestors. Subsequently, she used this paradigm to develop two productions in which participant-observers selected sketches to be performed by a group of six student performers of different cultures. The performance concluded with "Free Sketches," which were improvised scenarios meant to facilitate community unraveling of painful issues. Jones' contribution here is her introduction of Yoruba performance practices to an African American theatre aesthetic.

Reading 1.1

HOW I GOT OVER

Communication Dynamics in the Black Community

JACK L. DANIEL AND GENEVA SMITHERMAN

This study is an analysis of the sacred and secular dynamics of the African-American communications system . . . *My soul look back and wonder . . .* which has served to extrapolate, ritualize, and thus preserve the African essence of Afro-American life . . . *how I got over.* We seek to develop a theoretical and conceptual framework for defining Black communication by explicating the cosmology of traditional Africa and demonstrating its continuity in both sacred and secular Black[1] life. Of necessity we have centered our search on the Traditional Black Church[2] because of its crucial and long-standing historical role in sustaining the culture and communication process of African-Americans.

In seeking to clarify the communication patterns of superficially different Black Americans, we take as our text what many a "street man" has told "young-bloods": "Beauty is only skin deep but love is to the bone." This text calls attention to the existence of two levels of reality which will be referred to here as "surface" and "deep" structures. In this context, beauty is a surface structure and love is something that resides within the deep structure—"love is to the bone."

Surface and deep structures have unique but complementary natures. Surface structures are objective, empirical, subject to relatively rapid change, constrained by time and space, and nongenerative in nature. Deep structures are intangible, subjective, archetypal, not culturally bound, and generative in nature. Consider the nature of surface and deep structures from the structuralist viewpoint: "The reality sought by structural analysis . . . is not empirical reality but reality at the level of abstract pattern, in terms of certain diagnostic features of empirical phenomena. We seek in the observed phenomena evidence of a regularity that inheres at some other level. . . . It is the set of rules—'knit one, purl two,' and so on—that is the structuralist reality, not the ribbing on Susie's new

From Daniel, J., & Smitherman, G. (1976). How I got over: Communication dynamics in the black community. *Quarterly Journal of Speech, 62*(1), 26-39.

cardigan."[3] Here we are concerned with apprehending the "knit ones, purl twos" of Black Communication. The Black communications network is actualized in different specific ways, contingent upon the socio-cultural context (e.g., "street" vs. "church"), but its basic underlying structures, being grounded in the Traditional African World View, are essentially similar. We bear witness to the cultural continuities between such seemingly disparate groups as preachers and poets, bluesmen and Gospelettes, testifiers and toast-tellers, reverends and revolutionaries.

Among these variations, the Traditional Black Church is an exemplary form of Black communication. To speak of the "traditional" Black Church is to speak of the holy-rolling, bench-walking, spirit-getting, tongue-speaking, vision receiving, intuitive-directing, Amen-saying, sing-song preaching, holy-dancing and God-sending

Church. Put another way, this Church may be defined as that in which the cognitive content has been borrowed from Western Judaeo-Christian tradition, and the communication of that content—the affective process—has remained essentially African. This specific convergence of Judaeo-Christian content and African process is found in Protestant denominations, such as Baptist, Methodist, Holiness, and Sanctified, where the worship patterns are characterized by spontaneous preacher-congregation calls and responses, hollers and shouts, intensely emotional singing, spirit possession, and extemporaneous testimonials to the power of the Holy Spirit.

The Traditional Black Church is peopled by lower socio-economic, working class Blacks—domestics, factory workers, janitors, unskilled laborers, etc. While today there is an ever increasing number of high school graduates, most "pillars of the Church" have less than a high school education. It is within the Traditional Black Church that traditional Black folk (Blacks who haven't been assimilated into the elusive American mainstream) create much of their reality. The Traditional Black Church is both a sacred and secular community whose special character, according to Joseph R. Washington, is: " . . . not its content but its intent, for the cult is a synthesis of Western

Christianity beliefs, practices, ceremonies, rituals, and theologies, with the African tradition of religion as permeating all dimensions of life, without final distinction between the sacred and the secular. The intent of the Black cult is that of traditional African religions—the seeking of the power of the spirit of God in all times, places, and things because without that power man is powerless."[4] Given these kinds of demographics, the Traditional Black Church becomes "more than a church. It is more than a community. It is a human phenomenon responding to social and economic upheavals."[5]

The essential nature of communication in that Church is an interacting, spontaneous process which has been referred to as "call-response." Briefly defined, this African-derived process is the verbal and nonverbal interaction between speaker and listener in which each of the speaker's statements (or "calls") is punctuated by expressions ("responses") from the listener. As a fundamental aspect of the Black communications system, call-response spans the sacred-secular continuum in Black Culture. In the Church, it is often referred to as the congregation's way of "talking back" to the preacher, the most well-known example of which is "A-men." But Traditional Black Church members also call and respond between themselves as well as the preacher, and Church musicians frequently will "get a thang goin" between themselves and their instruments. More than an observed ritual in Church services, call-response is an organizing principle of Black Cultural Reality which enables traditional Black folk to achieve the unified state of balance or harmony which is essential to the Traditional African World View.

In contrast to those historians, such as E. Franklin Frazier, who have held that American enslavement obliterated for the slaves "the habits and customs as well as the hopes and fears that characterized the life of their forebears in Africa . . . ,"[6] our argument is that the residue of an African heritage persists, undiminished and intact, in the call-response pattern of Black communication. A heritage that may indeed have been amputated in substance yet survives in form.

We have postulated the following two hypotheses to be dealt with in this paper:

(1) There are similarities in the world views of geographically disparate Africans which we refer to as the "Traditional African World View." This View, though possibly not distinctive to Africans, is nevertheless significant for understanding patterns of Black communication in the United States.

(2) The call-response pattern, exhibited most clearly in traditional Black worship service, is reflective of the Traditional African World View. Upon close examination, we find that it is pervasive in secular dimensions of Black Culture and communication and that it reveals not simply a surface difference between white and Black Americans, but a more profound "deep structure" difference rooted in the Traditional African World View.

TRADITIONAL AFRICAN WORLD VIEW

Our hypotheses, of course, rest on the conviction that there *is* a Traditional African World View. While there are differences in the many tribes, languages, customs, physiognomies, spirits, and deities that exist throughout the African continent, these seeming "diversities" are surface variations on the basic themes acknowledged by traditional Africans. Focusing on such surface differences as tribal customs or politically defined African boundaries may only serve to obscure the existence of the deep structure that is shared by all traditional African people.

Of importance here is the fact that basic underlying thought patterns do exist amid the unending diversity of African people, and thus it is appropriate to speak of traditional African thought as a single entity—albeit with complex and diverse manifestations. Robert F. Thompson conducted field studies of African art in nine different African cultures, and was able to identify common canons of form pervading them all.[7] Similarly, Daryll Forde's studies of African social values in various tribal cultures brought him to remark that: "One is impressed, not only by the great diversity of ritual forms and expressions of beliefs, but also by substantial underlying similarities in religious outlook and moral injunction."[8]

To be sure, students of African culture have yet to detail *all* of the salient features that transcend tribal differences and constitute what we are calling the "Traditional African World View." Yet sufficient patterns of commonality have emerged from research findings and field studies to suggest an interlocking network of cultural and philosophical synonymity in Africa.[9] We turn now to consider some of these common patterns.

UNITY BETWEEN SPIRITUAL AND MATERIAL

A fundamental tenet of the Traditional African World View is what Daryll Forde considers as the African formulation about the workings of the universe,[10] and what E. G. Parrinder referred to as the traditional Africans' perception of a "spiritual universe."[11] The conception is that of a dynamic, hierarchical unity between the spiritual and material aspects of life. Specifically, there is a unity between God, man, and nature, with God serving as the head of the hierarchy. God is followed by lesser deities, spirits, man, other forms of life, and things. Man resides in the middle of the hierarchy, and as such, he is composed of both a spiritual and material self, with, as K. A. Busia noted,[12] the fundamental sense of causation being spiritual. Fela Sowande also speaks to this basic assumption: "Here there is no room for the clear-cut separation of spirit and matter as opposites; spirit is matter at its most rarefied, while matter is spirit at its most congealed. Thus, it is that man has both a 'lower mind,' his heritage from the visible world of nature, and also a 'higher mind' equally his inheritance, but from the invisible world of spirit."[13]

John Mbiti notes the existence of a hierarchy with spiritual and intellectual determinants. He presents the following categories of traditional African religious ontology.

1. "Gods" as the ultimate explanation of the genesis and sustenance of both man and all things.

2. "Spirits" being made up of superhuman beings and the spirits of men who died a long time ago.

3. "Man" including human beings who are alive and those about to be born.

4. "Animals and plants" or the remainder of biological life.

5. "Phenomena and objects without biological life."[14]

As this hierarchy is presented by Mbiti, there are divinities ranging from God through lesser deities who number up to the one thousand and seven hundred "orisha" found among the Yoruba. Closer to man, there are the spirits of the ancestors who continue to have influence over their descendants.

The traditional African world is alive with Gods, spirits, the living dead (persons who recently died), people, animals, plants, and objects without biological life. God is omnipresent, and as Balandier and Maquet indicate, "from the supreme God to the recent dead, there stretches a hierarchy of divine or semi-divine figures who possess the vital force preeminently and whose cooperation must be sought."[15] Spirits dwell in animate and inanimate objects, and man, upon completing his development, transubstantiates into the spiritual realm. That is, the Traditional African World View assumes that man's ultimate destiny is to move on to the "higher ground" of the spiritual world. Both Sowande, a West African, and Mbiti, an East African, emphasize the common belief in the importance of man's spiritual self in the material-spiritual hierarchy. Sowande goes even further to note that when the connection to man's higher self is disrupted, man slips down to a lower level of the hierarchy—i.e., he becomes an animal. "But the senior partner must be his 'higher mind' for this is his one and only link with the world of reality, the invisible world of spirit. It is the disruption or negation of this link that results in that subtle change of attitude by which a world view degenerates into an opportunistic, hypocritical, callously inhuman view of the world, which turns man from a god-in-the-making into a hairless predatory male animal on two legs, no matter what his human pretensions may be socially, academically, or otherwise."[16]

CENTRALITY OF RELIGION

Concomitant with the African emphasis on spirituality is the centrality of religion as a pervasive, dominating force in the life of man. Throughout Africa (and the African diaspora as well), there is no dichotomy between sacred and secular life. Mbiti indicates that there are "no irreligious people" in traditional African society for to be "without religion amounts to a self-excommunication from the entire life of society . . . African people do not know how to exist without religion."[17] Religion permeates all aspects of life since every phase of life in some way relates to man's journey to the spirit world.

Traditional African people are, as Joseph, R. Washington wrote, "a people for whom religion was as common as daily bread."[18] "Religion is not a sometime affair. It is a daily, minute involvement of the total person in a community and its concerns. Indeed, the spirit will not come forth with power apart from the community emptying itself (and thus the priest), so that the power can reign without interference. . . . The heart of traditional African religions is the emotional experience of being filled with the power of the spiritual."[19] Religious beings engaged in the drama of life in a spiritual universe constitute a basic concept of the traditional African "religious configuration."[20]

And among many Blacks in America, religion plays the same active role in life. C. Eric Lincoln maintained that religion was an inextricable dimension on all levels of Black existence in America: "The black man's pilgrimage in America was made less onerous because of his religion. His religion was the organizing principle around which his life was structured. His church was his school, his forum, his political arena, his social club, his art gallery, his conservatory of music. It was lyceum and gymnasium as well as sanctum sanctorum. His religion was his fellowship with man, his audience with God. It was the peculiar sustaining force which gave him the strength to endure when endurance gave no promise, and the courage to be creative in the face of his own dehumanization."[21] Thus, religion, as a fundamental construct of the Traditional African World View, became (to borrow a term from Melville J. Herskovits[22]) the "cultural focus" of Afro-Americans.

HARMONY IN NATURE AND THE UNIVERSE

In traditional African thought, it is believed that the laws governing one's self and the laws governing the universe are one and the same. But one cannot simply hold this belief; he must be it and act it. Thus the African World View is manifested in any given individual only when he has become truly a "living witness." One becomes a "living witness" when he aligns himself with the forces of nature, and instead of being a proselytized "true believer," strives to live in harmony with the universe. That is, adherents of the Traditional African World View live as if they are microcosms of a universe that is maintained by the synergic functioning of its spiritual and material essences. Living in harmony with the nature of the universe means, as Sowande indicates, that this World View is not simply a tool for operating in and on the world. Rather, the "world view" emerges "only when the individual has lived himself into what these elements stand for; he must breed into himself the attitudes that they represent; he must turn into the laws of his own being. . . ."[23] For the traditional African, then, the universe is not an intellectual concept, but a "force field with all things interacting" in balance and harmony.[24]

In Childhood and Cosmos: The Social Psychology of the Black African Child, Pierre Erny presents an African perspective on childhood that is based, in part, on the propositions being set forth here. Erny indicated that an understanding of who the Black child is must be premised on the deeper understanding of the African Cosmos. "In the traditional African World View, being is identical with life. A vital force similar to that of man animates each object: from god to the least grain of sand the African universe is a seamless cosmos. Each living force is in necessary union with other forces if it wants to increase rather than dwindle. It is inserted in a dynamic hierarchy in which everything is interdependent. Thus, we are introduced into a universe of correspondences, analogies, harmonies, interactions. Man and cosmos constitute one single network of forces; to grasp one intellectually is to grasp the other."[25]

The complementarity of all things in the force field of the universe provides the paradigm for resolving seeming opposites in life. Just as the traditional African finds unity in the sacred and secular aspects of life, he does not dichotomize day and night, good and bad, life and death, or beginning and end. Instead of a perception of opposites, there is a perception of complementary, interdependent, interacting forces, each of which constitutes the beginning and end of the other. The two given forces are synergic in nature, and together they produce a "beat" or rhythm such as the beat of the heart. The universe moves by the many rhythms that are created by the various, complementary, interdependent forces. Thus, traditional African religious ontology constitutes a unity in which "one mode of existence presupposes all others and a balance must be maintained so that these modes neither drift too far apart from one another nor get too close to one another."[26] Put another way, "there is a time and place for everything."

AFRICAN SOCIETY PATTERNED AFTER NATURAL RHYTHMS

In traditional Africa, people pattern their social interactions after the presumed existence of natural rhythms. A traditional African community is itself a rhythm based on the synergic functioning of "I" and "We." Such a community survives on the rhythm of "I am, because we are; and since we are, therefore, I am."[27] What happens to one in some way affects the entire community, and what happens to the entire community necessarily affects all individuals within that community. Neither "I" nor "We" have meaning apart from the other. As an example of the impact of this rhythmic functioning of "I" and "We," consider the traditional attitude toward marriage.

For African people, marriage is the focus of existence. It is the point where all the members of a given community meet: the departed, the living and those yet to be born. All the dimensions of time meet here, and the whole drama of history is repeated, renewed, and revitalized. Marriage is a drama in which everyone becomes an actor or actress and not just a spectator. Therefore, marriage is a duty, a requirement from the corporate society, and rhythm of life in which everyone must participate. Otherwise, he is a rebel and a law-breaker, he is not only abnormal but 'under human.' Failure to get married under normal circumstances means that the person concerned has rejected society and society rejects him in turn.[28]

Throughout the rhythm of life there are many special events that require the participation of every member of the community. Participation is always individual and corporate, i.e., "I" and "We." There are to be no chains broken nor any rhythms stopped.

TIME AS PARTICIPATION IN EVENTS

Community participation is such a crucial element of the Traditional African World View that the African concept of time is defined in terms of participation in experienced events rather than fixed, abstract points. According to Pierre Erny, "African temporality is not lineal, going from a beginning towards an end."[29] On the other hand, as Erny states: " . . . It's not purely circular either. At each return, something remains behind, and something new is added. It is more precise, therefore, to speak of time as a 'spiral.' The peasant and traditional African has a very strong consciousness of being in a world where everything takes place in cycles, where a single life disappears only to better reappear, in a world where there is nothing new under the sun, where a fundamental continuity underlies all changes that can be perceived, where past, present, and future answer one another endlessly."[30]

In discussing the World View with regard to the concept of time, we will employ the term "phase" to steer us away from the notion of numerically fixed points so common to Western world ontology. As a conceptual term, "phase" should suggest the traditional African predisposition towards recurring, harmonic cycles, and towards series of events which occur in relation

to each other. . . . "What goes around comes around. . . ." African phase is related to natural rhythms such as the seasons of the year; it is rhythmical and cyclical rather than linear, in nature. What matters is not the exact, abstract time of the month or day, but one's participation in a wedding or harvest during a given period of the year or season. Being on time has to do with participating in the fulfillment of an activity that is vital to the sustenance of a basic rhythm, rather than with appearing on the scene at, say "twelve o'clock sharp." The key is not to be "on time" but "in time."[31]

Traditional African phase focuses on present and past experiences rather than on the future which has not been experienced. Since the World View conceptualizes a universe which is cyclical in nature, the "future" is perceived as the past recurring in a different form. Hence there is considerable importance attached to the present and its relation to the past as opposed to the "future." Phase thus is said to be "backward looking," as the traditional African is firmly rooted in the past experiences of elders and the living dead.

From our foregoing discussion of the Traditional African World View, several salient features emerge:

1. There is a fundamental unity between the spiritual and the material aspects of existence. Though both the material and the spiritual are necessary for existence, the spiritual domain assumes priority.

2. While the universe is hierarchical in nature, all modes of existence are necessary for the sustenance of its balance and rhythm. Harmony in nature and the universe is provided by the complementary, interdependent, synergic interaction between the spiritual and the material. Thus we have a paradigm for the way in which "opposites" function. Specifically, "opposites" constitute interdependent, interacting forces which are necessary for producing a given reality.

3. Communities are modeled after the interdependent rhythms of the universe. Individual participation is necessary for individual survival. Balance in the community, as in the universe, consists of maintaining these interdependent relationships.

4. The universe moves in a rhythmical and cyclical fashion as opposed to a linear progression. "Progression," as such, occurs only into the past world of the spirit. Thus the "future" is the past. In the community, then, one's sense of "time" is based on participation in and observation of nature's rhythms and community events.

5. Since participatory experiences are key to one's sense of "time," the fundamental pedagogy in the school of life becomes experience, and age serves as a fundamental basis for hierarchical social arrangements.

CALL-RESPONSE

Recall that the Traditional African World View conceptualizes a cosmos which is an interacting, interdependent balanced force field. Further, the society is based on such an assumption, and accordingly, the communications system takes on an interactive, interdependent nature. As Oliver Jackson succinctly states it:

> The moral sanctity of . . . life [in African society] derives from the idea that all is spiritual and that the Supreme Power embodies the totality of the cosmos in one spiritual unity . . . the African continuum is essentially harmonious. Men, in building their societies, endeavor to reproduce this 'divine or cosmic harmony.' This is the basis of all ethical and moral behavior in community life. This human microcosm must reaffirm the harmonious modality of the cosmic macrocosm.[32]

As a basic communications tactic, call-response seeks to synthesize "speakers" and "listeners" in a unified movement. It permeates all communication, and in the Traditional Black Church it is the basis of all other communicative strategies. Call-response reaffirms the "modality of the cosmic macrocosm."

We are talking, then, about an interactive network in which the fundamental requirement is active participation of all individuals. In this kind of communications system, "there is no sharp line between performers or communicators and the audience, for virtually everyone is performing and everyone is listening."[33] The process requires that one must give if one is to receive, and receiving is actively acknowledging another. Robert Farris Thompson refers to the antiphonal nature of Black communication as "perfected social interaction." He elaborates on this concept as follows:

> The arrogant dancer, no matter how gifted or imaginative, may find that he dances to drums and handclaps of decreasing strength and fervor. He may find, and this is damaging to his reputation, that the chorus will crystallize around another person, as in the telling of tales among the Tiv of northern Nigeria. There, we are told by Laura Bohannan, the poor devil who starts a tale without proper preparation or refinement will find the choral answering to his songs becomes progressively weaker until they ultimately reform about a man with stronger themes and better aesthetic organization. He is soon singing to himself. The terror of losing one's grip on the chorus is a real one in some African societies, a poignant dimension of social interaction that for some reason is not mentioned in discourse on singing in African music . . .
>
> Thus call-and-response and solo-and-circle, far from solely constituting matters of structure, are in actuality levels of perfected social interaction. The canon is a danced judgment of qualities of social integration and cohesion. . . .[34]

The power potential and fundamental essence of this interactive system is such that Thompson conceives of it as the "politics of perfection."

Call-response or "perfected social interaction" embodies communality rather than individuality. Emphasis is on group cohesiveness and cooperation; the collective common good and spiritual regeneration is reinforced by the visitation of the Spirit, and the efforts of all are needed to bring this about. The preacher says "Y' all ain wid me today, the church is dead," therein acknowledging that he can't make it by himself. But the existence of the "call," which is issued by a single individual in the Group, underscores the importance of individual roles within the Group. The individual is challenged to do what he can within the traditional mold, and he is reaffirmed by the infinite possibilities for unique responses. Centuries-old group norms are balanced by individualized, improvisational emphases. By taking advantage of process, movement, creativity of the moment, and emotional, intuitive, and spiritual guidance, the individual can exercise his sense of Self by virtue of his unique contribution to the Group.

The musical tradition of Black singing groups (sacred and secular) well exemplifies the call-response tradition. Characteristically, a group is comprised of a lead singer ("caller") and his background ("responders"). The leader opens the song and sets the initial mood, but from that point on, the direction and execution of the song depend on the mutual forces of the leader in spiritual combination with his background. For instance, note the opening of the well-known Gospel "How I Got Over":

Leader (Call):   How—

Background (Response):   How I got over.

Leader (call repeated with emphatic feeling):
   I said how—

Background (response building with the lead):
   How I got over.

Leader: My soul—

Background: My soul look back and wonder—

Leader: How—

Background: How I got over.

The next verse usually repeats the words of this opening but with greater feeling and emotional intensity, there by taking the song to another spiritual level. The total performance of the group is gauged by their skill in manipulating this musical interplay to move their listeners to get the "spirit in the dark."

We find the same musical tradition in the secular world of Black singing groups (who became the model for contemporary mainstream white groups). For example, note the opening lines to "Don't You Know I Love You So," a popular song from the early 1950s and the beginnings of Black "rock n' roll soul music." The song was recorded by the Clovers, a Black group that has perhaps long since been forgotten.

Leader (call):   Oh, don't you know—

Background (Response):   I love you, love you so.

Leader (call repeated):   Oh, don't you know—

Background (Response):   I love you, love you so.

Background: Oh, don't you know I

(taking over call):   love you, love you so—

Leader (responding):   And I'll never, never let you
   go—

Leader and: Ooo-dee—ooo-duu—

Background together: do-wah—I love you so.

CALL-RESPONSE IN THE TRADITIONAL BLACK CHURCH

The Traditional Black Church, it may be recalled, is that church where Blacks use drums, pianos, organs, guitars, tambourines, other musical instruments, their hands, feet, and voices for producing rhythms, guiding holy dancing, and facilitating spirit possession. In such churches, spirit possession is fundamental to the worship of Jesus Christ (who, at times, appears to be a functional substitute for an African deity). Communication in these churches involves an interactive, interdependent, spontaneous process for achieving a sense of unity in which members of the congregation obtain a feeling of satisfaction within themselves, between themselves and others, and between themselves and spiritual forces. Call-response is a fundamental communications strategy designed to bring about this sense of satisfaction.

Much of what is accomplished by call-response can be witnessed by moving through the hierarchy of the Traditional Black Church. That hierarchy is outlined below:

God (The Father, Spirit, and the Holy Ghost)

Minister, Reverend, Elder (God sent men) Mother of
   the Church

Old Folk—Elders

Deacons (Spiritual men who assist the Church Head)

Trustees (Lower in hierarchy because of their fiscal
   concerns)

Saved Adults

Adult Ushers and Nurses

Saved Young Folk

Unsaved Adults and Children

Backsliders (Former Saved people who have resorted to sin)

Sinners

God must send the man who is to lead, and, subsequently, God tells the man what to say and inspires him to say it. From the outset, Church communication takes on a degree of spontaneity since the leader must "wait on the Lord." Simultaneously, it is the beginnings of process, i.e., the *call* by God and the man's *response* by taking up the ministry. Once one acknowledges God's call and one affirmatively responds (many, to their detriment, have tried to ignore God's call), one must still await God's guidance in the daily conduct of one's affairs. Thus process and spontaneity are maintained by the calls-and-responses between God and the man.

Service in the Traditional Black Church begins with the recognition of the need for God's entrance at the outset. Because it is necessary for God to enter the service, the initial part of the service consists of everyone's making simultaneous calls-and-responses to invoke the spirit. The deacons pray, and, as they pray, the minister, the deaconesses, and elders of the church facilitate their efforts.

Deacon:	Come by here today Lord, come by here
Minister:	Yes Lord, come by here
Deaconesses:	Please Lord, Please Lord
Deacon:	Won't you enter our hearts this morning
Adult:	Here I am Lord, help me, please

The order varies in terms of who's calling and who's responding at any given moment. In addition to the above involvements, the elders are usually singing or humming, and musicians are also helping to bring God into the service.

Following this "warming up" period of invoking the spirit, and other intermediate parts of the service, the preacher gets into his sermon by issuing his initial call: "My theme for today is Waiting on the Lord." The congregation responds with "Take your time," "Fix it up, Reb.," "Come on up, now," or simply "Preach, Reb." When the preacher's calls get stronger and more emotional, you can see the Spirit moving over there in the Amen Corner, and hear the congregation urging him on with "Go head, now!" "Yessuh!" "Watch yo-self, now!" and such nonverbal responses as nodding of heads, clapping of hands, stomping feet, jumping up and down, jerking the body, holy dancing, "shouting." While the preacher is moving his congregation through the Power of the Word, the congregation's verbal and body responses are also moving him to a higher level of emotional feeling and understanding of the Magic of the Word. Many's the time the Black preacher has been heard to say, "I sho was gon take it easy today, but the folks made me preach."

In the following example of a funeral sermon from Richard Wright's novel, *The Long Dream*, note the congregation's various insistent and emotional responses which the preacher plays off of as he concretely drives home the abstract notion of death.

'Tell it! Tell it!'

'Look down on us, Lawd!'

'Mercy, mercy, have mercy, Jesus!'

'Who dares,' the reverend asked in a wild cry, 'say "No!" when that old Angel of Death calls? You can be in your grocery store ringing up a hundred-dollar sale on the cash register and Death'll call and you'll have to drop the sale and go! You can be a-riding around in your big Buick and Death'll call and you have to go! You about to git out of your bed to go to your job and old Death'll call and you'll have to go! Mebbe you building a house and done called in the mason and the carpenter and then old Death calls and you have to go! 'Cause Death's asking you to come into your *last* home! Mebbe you planning on giting married and your wonderful bride's awaiting at the altar and you on your way and old Death calls: "Young man, I got another bride for you! Your *last* bridge!"'

'Lawd, it's true!'

'Gawd's Master!'

'Be with us, Lawd!' . . .

[The Reverend demanded:] ' . . . Who understands the Divine Plan of Justice? On the Fourth of July, Gawd reared back and said:

"Death, come here!"'

'Wonderful Jesus!'

"'Death, go down to that place called *America!*"'

'Lissen to the Lawd!'

"'Death find that state they call Mississippi!"'

'Gawd's a-talking!'

'Death, go to a town called *Clinton-ville!*"'

'Lawd, Lawd, Lawd!'

"'Death, I want you to tell Tyree Tucker that I want to see 'im!"'

'Have mercy, Jesus!'

A black woman gave a prolonged scream and began leaping about; ushers rushed to her and led her bounding body out of the church.

"'Death, tell Tyree that I don't care *what* he's doing, he's got to come home!"'[35]

As the process gets more and more involved, spiritual forces "take over." Shouting breaks out all over the church. Older saved people and children with "special gifts" start speaking in tongues. The preacher moves on up to his climax, and the congregation suddenly breaks out in song. Now Reverend can't quit. The Spirit won't let him stop. He runs down out of the pulpit. Nurses are fanning those shouters who have passed out. The musicians and the choir begin to take over as the Spirit has driven the physical bodies to exhaustion. "My, my, my!" . . . "My, my, my!" . . . "Yes! yes!" . . . "oo-koo-Koombasigh!" . . . "akbaba-hunda!". . . . Thus, community is achieved. God has moved from the minister though the elders, and with the involvement of the saved, the "doors of the church are opened" to the unsaved.

CALL-RESPONSE IN SECULAR LIFE

As we have noted throughout his paper, traditional views distinguish but seek a unity between sacred and secular life. Thus not only is call-response necessary in the Traditional Black Church, it is also a basic communication strategy permeating Black secular life.

In secular style, call-response takes the form of a back-and-forth banter between the rapper (rhetor) and various members of his group, in which, for instance, group members might raise points to see how skillfully the rapper deals with them. Or the group will spur the rhetor on to greater heights of verbal accomplishment by expressions of approval, like "Oh, you mean, nigger" (said with affinity), "get down, man," or "get back, baby," and with nonverbal behavior like laughter, giving skin, hitting on the wall or backs of chairs, and rich body movements, like rocking back and forth on the heels, circular movements approximating a kind of short dance step. In the secular world, too, there is a kind of hierarchy (though not as rigidly stratified with distinct roles, as in the Church). The secular hierarchy is headed by the heroic man of words in the form of poolroom, barbershop, or street corner rapper; sharp-witted player of the Dozens; or creative narrator of Toasts and other Black folk stories.

In addition to the plain, everyday conversational sets where this pattern comes into play, it is interesting to observe it in operation in more "formal" secular settings, such as at Black political rallies and poetry performances. Just as in Church, the speaker's initial call will be punctuated by expressive responses (secularized, of course). Instead of "Preach, reverend," we hear "Teach, brother." "Amen" is replaced by "Do it, baby." And we hear many *tell the truth's, shonuff's, and yeah! yeah's!,* just as in the Church. There are gestures such as the giving of the Black Power sign (raised clenched fist), which replaces the church gesture of waving one's hand in the air ("I couldn't say nothing, I just waved my hand"). When it really gets good, and the speaker is shonuff tellin it like it T.I.IS., folk begin to holler, jump up and down in their seats (i.e., "shouting" as in church), and stomp their feet. Like the preacher and everyday Black people, poets and political rhetor-rappers thrive on audience involvement—they need to know that their audience is moved by their rap and gauge its power by the degree and extent of their responses.

Calling-responding; stating and counter-stating; acting and re-acting; testing your performance as you go—it is such a natural, habitual dynamic in Black communication that Blacks do it quite unconsciously when rapping to other Blacks. But call-response can be disconcerting to both parties in Black-white communication, presenting a real case of cross-cultural communication interference. When the Black person is speaking, the white person, because call-response is not in his cultural heritage, obviously does not engage in the response process, remaining relatively passive, perhaps voicing an occasional, subdued "mmmmhhm." Judging from the white individual's seeming lack of involvement in the communication, the Black communicator gets the feeling that the white isn't listening to him, and may repeatedly punctuate his "calls" with questions. such as "Are you listening to me?" "Did you hear me?" etc. In an extended conversation, such questions become annoying to the white, and he may exclaim, "Yes, I'm listening, of course, I'm listening, I'm standing right here!" Then when the white communicator takes over the "call," the Black person, as is customary, begins to get all into it, responding with verbal expressions, like "Dig it!" "Tell it," "I hear you," "Go head, run it down," and moving and dancing around when he hears something that he thinks is really dynamite. Judging from all this apparent "communication interference," the white person gets the feeling that the Black person isn't listening because he "keeps interrupting and turning his back on me." (There is also the possibility that the Black person will not be his natural self and respond at all: hence also preventing maximum communication.)

In the excerpt below, from Ralph Ellison's short story, "Mister Toussan," Buster and Riley exemplify a secular version of call-response. Buster is narrating the story of the Haitian General, Toussaint L'Ouverture, who, in 1791, led the only successful slave revolt in history. Note how Riley punctuates and reinforces each line of the story (i.e., Buster's call') with varied "A-men" type responses, occasionally, as he probably does in Church, repeating the exact words of the "call," other times issuing forth with exclamatory *Jesuses* and *Yeah's!*, and sometimes adding the completer to Buster's "call" statements.

Riley looked hard at Buster and seeing the seriousness of the face felt the excitement of a story rise up within him.

'Buster, I'll bet a fat man you lyin.' What'd that teacher say?'

'Really, man, she said that Toussan and his men got up on one of them African mountains and shot down them peckerwood soldiers fass as they'd try to come up . . .'

'Why good-God-a-mighty!' yelled Riley.

'Oh boy, they shot 'em down!' chanted Buster.

'Tell me about it, man!'

'And they throwed 'em off the mountain. . . .'

' . . . Goool-leeel. . . .

' . . . And Toussan drove 'em cross the sand. . . .'

' . . . Yeah! And what was they wearing, Buster? . . .'

'Man, they had on red uniforms and blue hats all trimmed with gold, and they had some swords all shining what they called sweet blades of Damascus . . .'

'Sweet blades of Damascus! . . .'

' . . . They really had 'em,' chanted Buster.

'And what kinda guns?'

'Big, black cannon!'

'And where did ole what-you-call-'im run them guys? . . .'

'His name was Toussan.'

'Toussan! Just like Tarzan. . . .'

'Not *Taar-zan,* dummy, *Toou-zan!*'

'Toussan! And where'd ole Toussan run 'em?'

'Down to the water, man. . . .'

' . . . To the river water. . . .'

' . . . Where some great big ole boats was waiting for 'em. . . .'

' . . . Go on, Buster!'

'An' Toussan shot into them boats. . . .'

' . . . He shot into em. . . .'

' . . . Shot into them boats. . . .'

'Jesus!! . . .'

'With his great big cannons. . . .'

'. . . Yeah! . . .'

'. . . Made a-brass. . . .'

'. . . Brass. . . .'

'. . . An' his big black cannon balls started killin' them peckerwoods. . . .'

'. . . Lawd, Lawd . . .'

'. . . Boy, till them peckerwoods hollered *Please, Please Mister Toussan, we'll be good!*'

'An' what'd Toussan tell em, Buster?'

'Boy, he said in his big deep voice. *I ought a drown all a-you bastards.*'

'An' what'd the peckerwoods say?'

'They said Please Please, *Please, Mister Toussan. . . .*'

'. . . We'll be good,' broke in Riley.

'Thass right, man,' said Buster excitedly. He clapped his hands and kicked his heels against the earth, his black face glowing in a burst of rhythmic joy.

'Boy!'

'And what'd ole Toussan say then?'

'He said in his big deep voice: *You all peckerwoods better be good, 'cause this is sweet Papa Toussan talking and my nigguhs is crazy about white meat!*'

'Ho, ho, ho!' Riley bent double with laughter. The rhythm still throbbed within him and he wanted the story to go on and on . . . [36]

At this point, Riley has become uncontrollably ecstatic about the story and superconfident that he knows how to "put the right stuff" to story-telling. So they switch roles, Riley becoming the "caller," Buster the "responder," and thus the moving rhythm of this story within a story is sustained to its climax.

As a communicative strategy, then, call-response is the manifestation of the cultural dynamic which finds audience and listener or leader and background to be a unified whole. Shot through with action and interaction, Black communicative performance is concentric in quality—the "audience" becoming both observers and participants in the speech event. As Black American Culture stresses communality and group experientially, the audience's linguistic and paralinguistic responses are necessary to co-sign the power of the speaker's rap or call. They let him know if he's on the right case. A particular individual's linguistic virtuosity is rewarded with a multiplicity of fervent and intense responses. Thus despite the cultural constraints imposed on individuality, skillful sacred and secular rappers can actualize their Selfhood within the community setting. Finally, as with other rhetorical strategies in Black communication, call-response is universally imbedded in the Traditional African World View, the "deep structure" of Black Culture, and we find this structure surfacing in concrete reality by witnessing the various ways individuals manipulate the strategy or deal within the ritual.

CONCLUSION

We contend that the Traditional African World View constitutes the basis, the source, the "deep structure" and indeed, the fountainhead, of Black communication in America. We find that View most carefully preserved and retained in the Traditional Black Church. Recognizing that one cannot duplicate in America *precisely* what would have existed in traditional African society, we have been concerned with demonstrating communicative *patterns*—"knit ones and purl twos"—which clearly reveal the appropriation and transformation of the Traditional African World View for the complex social situations that obtain in America. And these tasks have led us to conclude that call-response is a basic communicative strategy necessary to the social and cultural life-blood of Black America.

DISCUSSION QUESTIONS

1. What do Daniel and Smitherman mean by a "Traditional African World View"?

2. How is call-and-response reflective of what Daniel and Smitherman call a "deep structure"?

3. Compare and contrast a "Traditional African World View" with what you might call a traditional American world view.

4. Explain the role of spirits and/or the spiritual in the "Traditional African World View."

5. How do Daniel and Smitherman say that the rhythmic nature of the universe is tied to Black rhetoric?

Reading 1.2

THE AFROCENTRIC IDEA

MOLEFI KETE ASANTE

AFRICAN AMERICAN ORATURE AND CONTEXT

The study of African American oratory is intricately interwoven with the study of history; and a central aspect of African American history is the persistent public discussions related to our American experience. Having to defend our humanity, to agitate for minimal rights, and to soothe the raw emotions of mistreated fellows, our speakers have been forced to develop articulate and effective speech behavior on the platform. That a principal dimension of black history is encompassed by platform activities in the form of lectures, sermons, and agitations should stand without question from the student familiar with history.

Unable to read or write English and forbidden by law (in most states) to learn, the African in America early cultivated the natural fascination with *nommo,* the word, and demonstrated a singular appreciation for the subtleties, pleasures, and potentials of the spoken word, which has continued to enrich and embolden his history. Thus, in part because of strict antiliteracy laws during slavery, vocal communication became, for a much greater proportion of blacks

than whites, the fundamental medium of communication. Orature, the total oral tradition of Africans and African Americans, provides a comprehensive corpus of work for examination.

Of *chirologia* and *chironomia;* in most cases, the speaker transforms his audience through the spontaneous exaggeration of sounds combined with the presentation of vital themes. This is in some ways analogous to the African view that the power of transformation can never be in things that depend on men to control them, but must reside in *bantu,* or human beings. Argument, because it is formulated and arranged by humans, has no power of itself, except as it is expressed by humans. As a fetish has no power of its own but can only be efficacious when the word is spoken, so the proper expression by the right person of an argument or song may bring results. In this sense, therefore, black gospel preachers and blues singers are sharing in the same experiential spontaneity when they rely on vocal creativity to transform the audience.

With an African heritage steeped in orature and the acceptance of transforming vocal communication, the African American developed a consummate skill in using language to produce

From Asante, M. K. (1980). *Afrocentricity*. Philadelphia: Temple University Press.

communication patterns alternative to those employed in the American situation. These channels remained rhetorical, even as they consciously or subconsciously utilized linguistic changes for communicative effectiveness. During slavery, communication between different ethnic and linguistic groups was difficult, but the almost universal African regard for the power of the spoken word contributed to the development of alternative communication patterns in the work songs, Ebonics, sermons, and the spirituals with their dual meanings, one for the body and one for the soul. It is precisely the power of the word, whether in music or speeches, that authentically speaks of an African heritage. Thus to omit orature as manifest in speeches and songs from any proper investigation of African American history is to ignore the essential ingredient in the making of our drama.

The Power of *Nommo*

Let us look at this more closely. To understand the nature of African American communication means that one must understand the *nommo* continues to permeate our existence. This is not to say that all or even most of us, given the situation, can immediately identify the transforming power of vocal expression. It is apparent when a person says, "Man, that cat can rap." Or one can identify it through the words of the sister leaving a Baptist church, "I didn't understand all those words the preacher was using, but they sure sounded good." Inasmuch as the *nommo* experience can be found in many aspects of African American life, one can almost think of it as a way of life. Therefore, the scholar, rhetorician, or historian who undertakes an analysis of the black past without recognizing the significance of vocal expression as a transforming agent is treading on intellectual quicksand.

What is clear is that the black leaders who articulated and articulate the grievances felt by the masses have always understood the power of the word in the black community. This is the meaning of the messianism I speak of in regard to Nat Turner, Martin Luther King, and others. Their emergence has always been predicated upon the power of the spoken word. Indeed, it is

extremely difficult to speak of black leaders without speaking of spokespersons in the elemental sense, who were vocally brilliant and could move audiences with sudden tears or quick smiles. It is no fluke of history that persons who only had letters after their names or organizational talents have seldom been acclaimed "black leaders"; it is rather a fact, intricately related to the eminence of the spoken word within the black community. The able historian, Carter G. Woodson, understood this most clearly, as indicated in his 1925 work *Negro Orators and Their Orations.* Other black historians have given more than passing attention to the influence of black orators on the black community. In books by Eppse, Quarles, Ferris, and others, significant commentary is devoted to the oratorical gifts of black leaders. Discussing orature therefore becomes, for the serious student of our culture, an attempt to interpret the preeminence of the spoken word.

Slavery and Rhetoric

The central fact of black history in America is slavery and antislavery, which stands astride every meaningful rhetorical pathway like a giant elephant. That black speakers before and after the abolition of slavery are concerned with it is immensely important in the development of eloquence. However, it is not only physical slavery that dominates the history of America but the exploitation of the African through ideological impositions. Europe is insinuated into every aspect of black existence, even the sacred process of naming. Black discourse, therefore, to be healthy discourse, is resistance. While the stated theme of a speech may be white racism, black pride, American hypocrisy, freedom, crime, poverty, desegregation, poor housing conditions, and voting rights, the underlying issue to be dealt with is always the slavery experience. What shall be made of it? How shall we more adequately deal with the residual effects of slavery? And how can we regain our pre-slavery—indeed, pre-American—heritage?

What is more demonstrative of a people's proud heritage than the pre-American values and attitudes of Africans? When the Yoruba, Fanti, Efik, Congo, Asante, Dahomeans, and Mandingo arrived in America, they had no past of family instability, disrespect for elders, and juvenile insurrection. So when the contemporary warrior-orators express the belief that white racism has been the chief obstacle to black psychological and physical liberation, they are speaking of the central position of slavery in our history. They are taking an antiapartheid, antislavery, antiracist position and are becoming in the process the embodiment of the resistance. It is this psychological-political resistance that constitutes a universe of alternative discourse.

As human slavery is the central fact of African history in America, so antislavery is the crucible of black rhetorical expression. Although there had been African protest, vocal and physical, to slavery, a steady stream of orators against slavery did not spring forth until the turn of the nineteenth century. The pressure upon blacks to defend themselves as human beings while agitating for equal rights, combined with the need to correct false and demeaning characterizations of Africans, provided constant practice on the platform. Many of the leading speakers gravitated towards the seminaries, learning the rules of homiletics and exegesis. Once out of school, they often applied practical lessons in public speaking and analysis to their natural gifts and were soon on their way to becoming accomplished orators. Not a few African American speakers learned the rudiments of the "proper rules" of rhetoric from seminary training; others learned form the Quaker abolitionists. All of them used *nommo,* the productive word, to the advantage of their eloquence.

The early African speeches in America dealt with the institution of slavery. By the nineteenth century, Peter Williams, James Forten, and Theodore Wright were using their rhetorical abilities to state grievances and to chart future directions for the race. In 1808, Peter Williams spoke on the "Abolition of the Slave Trade" and expressed hope that Africans would soon be free. But the slave trade continued beyond the constitutional deadline in many instances, like a runner past the designated finish line, and slavery draped its misery more completely over its African subjects. However, Williams' speech expressed the universal optimism of a people who knew that things had to get better, because nothing was more horrible than slavery.

Although black spokespersons have been priests, they have more often been prophets. Subsequent to Williams' 1808 address, other speakers spoke optimistically of deliverance in both a practical and a mystical sense. One might refer to this phenomenon as messianism (as I discuss elsewhere in this volume). Characterized by prophetic visions, it is often present in the rhetoric of oppressed people. The orators voiced their opposition to the oppressing agent and simultaneously looked for some type of manifestation, either in person or process, capable of alleviating their suffering, thereby bringing in the millennium. In their speeches, messianism was manifest on two levels: (1) black salvation and (2) world salvation. Many orators saw the black "saints" liberating the world. The orators, like poets, spoke of "strong men coming," but unlike the poets, they were often the embodiment of their rhetoric, or at least they and others thought so. When Marcus Garvey stormed out of the West Indies in the first quarter of the twentieth century with his doctrine of psychic and physical migration to Africa, he became the sum total of black salvation to millions. In fact, the psychological implications of the cult orators are that they believe, and their votarists believe them to be, the fulfillment of the rhetoric. One thinks immediately of the language of Daddy Grace: *"The Bible says you shall be saved by Grace, I'm Grace."* Nat Turner saw himself as the vicar of God upon the earth. And in 1914 the mother of Father Divine's church, Lorraine, stood on the grounds of the White House saying, "The Lord has come."

In such a psychological climate, the name Moses grew as important in Africans' minds as the person had been in Israel's eyes, and dominated the future of blacks as Moses had dominated the history of Jews. "Go down, Moses, Way Down in Egypt's Land, Tell Ol' Pharaoh to Let My People Go," was symbolic of the Africans' hope. It was this kind of optimism that had swept over blacks in the North on January 1, 1808, the day slave trading was to be abolished. While the Northern blacks leaped with joy, the Southern whites put sharper thorns under the feet of the slaves. Blacks who were not enslaved could see a new day dawning that had neither the blemish of the trade nor the dark spot of the institution on its horizon, and their speeches reflected this optimism. Williams says:

> *But let us no longer pursue a theme of boundless affliction. An enchanting sound now demands your attention.* Hail! Hail! glorious day, whose resplendent rising disperseth the clouds which have hovered with destruction over the land of Africa, and illumines it by the most brilliant rays of future prosperity. Rejoice, oh! Africans! No longer shall tyranny, war and injustice, with irresistible sway, desolate your native country. Rejoice, my brethren, that the channels are obstructed through which slavery, and its direful concomitants, have been entailed on the African race.

Such optimism is born of a people obsessed with the future, particularly when the past had been so terrible.

The antislavery speeches of black abolitionists soon came to have a discernible structure. The rhetor spoke of slavery's history and horrors, eulogized white philanthropists (mostly Quakers), and appealed to God for deliverance. Every black orator knew the institution of slavery from beginning to end, which was necessary knowledge for public speeches. And many black speakers worked closely with white philanthropists and abolitionists and therefore could speak easily of white contributions. The radical Quakers, who were often in the middle of public discussions on the issue of slavery, endeared themselves to black orators. Their exploits became incentives for blacks who agitated for the liberation of their enslaved brethren. Actually tailored for the times, the speeches almost always ended with some method of mythication. Invocations, poems, and religious expressions, calling on God to intervene in one way or another, were prevalent in the speeches of black antislavery orators. Thus the black antislavery speakers contributed to the heightening of contradictions within the pre–Civil War American society by constant use of religious symbolism to express their position and their redefinition of cultural heroes by honoring white abolitionists. A Eurocentric critique of the discourse of this period often casts the black speakers in the role of reactionaries when,

in fact, they often defined the grounds of discourse.

After the Civil War, vocal expression did even more to mold the ideas of Afro-Americans who could now assemble with relative ease. Their heroes and heroines were antislavery fighters, midnight runners, and underground railroad "conductors." Although laws were quickly enacted against loitering, black religious assemblies were permitted and several capable speakers appeared between 1865 and 1920 with various proposals and programs for black salvation. But of the parade of "orators" who marched across the stage in full view of the destitute black masses, Marcus Garvey possessed an awesome combination of force and form to electrify millions. His bombastic oratorical performances, played out with sensitive and dramatic understanding of a cultural phenomenon, made him the most widely acclaimed black spokesman of any generation. From Garvey's time onward, black oratory would simultaneously contain something of his political and social opinion as well as a portion of his cultural and ethnic responsiveness. Garvey drummed his message to the quickening intellectual and emotional pace of the African audience. Democracy and freedom were in the air and the rhythm of the time was: Wake up, black man!

Despite this fact, the extensive implications of *nommo* are not clearly sensed in sole concentration on the political and social rhetoric of Afro-Americans. Probably only within the religious experience, when worshippers and leaders—including preachers, deacons, and church mothers—interact, does the concept blossom into its full communicative significance. The complexities of the religious interactive event, which can involve from one person responding to a preacher to nearly the whole congregation caught up in continuous response, ranging from weeping to shouts of joy, are indicative of the several interlocking communication networks that may be set off when the preacher gives the word.

Such response configurations are not begun automatically; every speaker does not possess the assurance that he will be successful in provoking a total response. In fact, some preachers never succeed in moving an audience to the total interactive event, which is necessary for them to consider their speeches successful. These preachers must be satisfied with the occasional feedback expressed by an "Amen" or a "Lord, help," offered by several members as the sermon is presented. Other preachers, through a delicate combination of vocal manipulations, characterized by rhythm and cadence, and vital thematic expression, usually developed in narrative form, can easily produce a creative environment when message is intensified by audience response.

Understanding the oral emphasis within the traditional African American churches, one becomes aware of the close relationship between speech and music. The antiphonal pattern, where the speaker presents a theme that is answered by respondents, pervades our speech as it permeates African music. Writing of the relationship of African music to Afro-American music in *Blues People,* LeRoi Jones (Amiri Baraka) observes: "The most salient characteristics of African, or at least West African, music is a type of song in which there is a leader and a chorus; the leading lines are sung by a single voice, the leader's, alternating with a refrain sung by the chorus." While this pattern in music may be African in origin, it is not uncommon to Afro-American religious singing. The leader "lines" the song and the congregation responds, thus fulfilling the *antiphony.*

Speech and music, as manifestations of *nommo,* relate in still another manner within black churches. As mentioned earlier, a speaker is not assured of a totally interactive audience unless he blends the proper vocal rhythms and thematic interests. In addition to these elements, the communicative situation can be made more productive by audience conditioning through singing. In this sense, singing sets the stage or mood by preparing the audience emotionally and physically for the preacher, whose communication task is made easier because of the audience receptivity. Singing, then, in the black religious audience, although instructive, is much more palliative; it soothes the emotions and draws the congregation together. Not having to concentrate on rhetorical means to encourage cohesiveness, the preacher inherits an attentive audience by virtue of the choir's work. In mounting the platform to speak to a religious audience, the black preacher does not

challenge *nommo* but uses it, becomes a part of it, and is consumed in the fire of speech and music. The perfect force of the moment is sensual, giving, sharing, generative, productive, and ultimately creative and full of power. Hallelujah!

The sermon, as the principal spoken discourse during the religious service, can reflect the preacher's awareness of the audience's responsiveness. His voice proves extremely significant as he alternates stressed and unstressed syllables, giving even the pauses rhythmic qualities. Witnessing the mixed outpouring of breathing and syllabic patterns, it is clear to the observer that the preacher initiates and sustains a tension between an audience and himself through vocal expression. The basic vocal pattern is established by the preacher and is accompanied by a secondary pattern emanating from the audience. Thus the spoken word, as a sermon, appears to maintain the essential unity of the interlocking communication networks in its role as the main event of the religious service.

The socio-historical perspectives of black orature, whether African or American based, share certain common grounds. Central to the understanding of the role of vocal expressiveness within the African American community are *nommo,* the generative and dynamic quality of vocal expression, and slavery, the primary fact of black existence in America. *Nommo* has continued to manifest itself in the black community, notably within the church; and slavery's role in American history, while providing a common reference point, has made all black speeches relative. Historically, black oratory, both sacred and secular, has been collective in the same sense that most artistic productions are created for and meant to be shared by entire audiences. To understand the nature of discourse in the African American community, we should examine African conceptions of communication, inasmuch as the connection has been well established.

The philosophical basis of communication in Africa was celebrated in the West when Father Placied Tempels, a Belgian monk whose first language was Flemish, published *Bantoe-Filosofie* in 1945 and in 1946 brought out the French edition. In 1956, this work was translated into German and then became available to a wide European audience. What makes Tempels' work important is the fact that, as a Franciscan missionary in the Congo (now Zaire) since 1933, he had meticulously recorded his observations of the Baluba people. His presentation of Baluba thought as an integrated system of philosophy provided a refreshing portrait of the complexity of African thought.

Marcel Griaule's research among the Dogon people of Mali was published in 1947. Griaule, an ethnologist, had spent years studying the behaviors, social and economic, of the Dogon. His interest in their metaphysical system led him to seek out a great priest and hunter named Ogotommêli. In October 1946, Ogotommêli, who had been accidentally blinded, summoned Griaule to his house for a conversation on Dogon philosophy. For thirty-three days, Ogotommêli expounded to Griaule the world system, the religion, the metaphysics, and ethics of the Dogon people, invalidating many of the negative conceptions of Europeans held about African genius. Ogotommêli's language was elaborate, symbolic, and eloquent. His images were full and his meanings precise. Griaule recorded Ogotommêli's conversations in the Dogon language and translated them into French, then published a book (translated in English) as *Conversations with Ogotommêli.*

The significance of Griaule's interaction with the Dogon is that he became a student. Marcel Griaule, anthropologist, found that it took sixteen years of meetings and discussions with the Dogon before he could understand the abstract knowledge eventually presented to him. Indeed, there are four stages to knowledge in Dogon culture: (1) the word at face value, (2) the word off to the side, (3) the word from behind, and (4) the clear word. The eight levels of the clear word are reserved for the highest priests who have shown evidence of many years of study. Griaule reached only the first level of the clear word!

A collaborator and colleague of Griaule, Germaine Dieterlen, worked among the Bambara, neighbors of the Dogon, to produce "An Essay on Bambara Religion." Of course, Rattray had done work in English on the Asante (Ashanti), and the Yoruba had been studied by both British and Yoruba scholars, but the intense interest produced by Tempels' and

Griaule's books reasserted the philosophical richness of African thought for the European mind.

African American thought, as expressed in religion and myth, may be seen as an extension of the African foundations. Paul Carter Harrison writes in *The Drama of Nommo* that even "the popular dance of African/Americans is a continuation of the African sensibility." African American spoken discourse continues the sensibilities expressed as orature on the continent. Oswald Spengler once wrote of the African as demonstrating "not a purposed organization of space such as we find in the mosque and the cathedral, but a rhythmically ordered sequence of spaces." While it is often difficult to tell what Spengler thought of the "rhythmically ordered sequence of spaces" that constitutes the African frame of mind, clearly he understood, even in his unwillingness to appreciate the richness of the African culture, that its rhythms were different. In the movements and spaces, the circles and curves, and the artistic sensibilities of the ancient traditions, one still finds the allegiance to transcending rhythms.

MYTHOFORMS IN AFRICAN AMERICAN COMMUNICATION

Myth, conventionally defined as a traditional story or tale that has functional value for a society, usually serves as a way of dealing with mystery. For example, all known cultures have creation myths that relate humans to nature, explaining where we came from and where we are going. In the modern Western world, myth has become synonymous with fallacy and superstition and is associated with an escape from, rather than an immersion in, reality—its original purpose. In industrialized societies, science denies mystery and technology replaces mythmaking. In the information age, Western culture is intent on demystification and deconstruction. But while science and technology seem to have answered some basic questions about life on the planet, they have also contributed greatly to human uncertainty. Anxiety, accompanying the possibility of nuclear holocaust, mars children's lives and Western technological society lacks the words with which to build an interposing myth.

Lévi-Strauss claims that myths operate without our knowledge. In conventional thinking, a myth is normally considered a story or tale of a traditional nature that has functional value for a society. However, *mythos,* the Greek word from which we derive "myth," actually meant "utterance." When *mythos* was connected to *logos,* "the study of," we were able to achieve *mytho-logia,* "mythology," the study of myth or analytical utterance. So it is precisely because these "deep utterances" operate at unconscious levels that they maintain our symbolic life at a conscious level.

We are no longer victims of an alien nature that threatens to subdue us; we are, as the continental Africans would teach us, structured by the symbol, *nommo,* that makes us one with nature. In the mind of the African sages, we are of the same essence as the cells of trees and plants. We are, quite honestly, not humans separated from other matter; we are, more correctly, as the physicists now understand, of the same nature. Within this context, myth is an organizing principle in human symbolic discourse. What is it that we speak of if it is not life or death?

Myth is most pervasive as a mythoform, the all-encompassing deep generator of ideas and concepts in our living relationship with our peers, friends, and ancestors. A productive force, it creates discourse forms that enable speakers to use cultural sources effectively. Mythoform is different from the universal principle that Armstrong seeks by an exposition of the creative works of Yoruba artists. I am not convinced that what he seeks exists. He is correct to challenge Jung, Lévi-Strauss, and others for exalting Western cultural concepts to universality, but Armstrong overreacts by seeking the underlying patterns that give rise to all of the myths of all cultures. This is unnecessary and indeed impossible, unless of course one sees life itself as the essential generator, the mythoform, for all concepts.

The Nigerian critic and theorist of myth, Isidore Okpewho, attempts to set the Ijo creation myth of Woyengi within its context, only to be beguiled by the overarching symbolism of Lévi-Strauss.[20] Okpewho chooses to use Lévi-Strauss as a starting point for his critique of the Woyengi myth, without consideration of the sharp criticism of Lévi-Strauss by Armstrong. This is unfortunate, because he falls completely into the Western structuralist trap, which gives him no way to escape. Okpewho is directed by the same "constraining structures of the mind" that he found in Lévi-Strauss. Thus, he writes that he will try to discover "by means of structural analysis and the aid of ethnographic inquiry the informing matrix of thought and concern in the tale." What he discovers, in spite of his structuralist endeavor with the Woyengi tale and his rather acerbic aside against the position of Cheikh Anta Diop on the place of matriarchy in Africa, is that static structuralism, tied to Western frames, cannot inform dynamic, polyvalent mythic possibilities that are meta-Western. Between the beginning of consciousness and the unknown is a great amount of human philosophical discussion and activity about the prior-to-consciousness and the after-consciousness; rhetoric is therefore the discussion of life and death, consciousness and unconsciousness, being and nonbeing. Every act that exists in the realms of deliberation, forensics, or panegyrics is an act in the conscious. To act philosophically is to act mythologically. Rhetoric becomes mythological action when it considers the prior-to and the after-consciousness, even while they occur in consciousness.

African American Mythmaking

These analytical utterances, or rather utterances with imbedded messages, can be found in most contemporary speeches of African Americans. In the most passionate rhetoric and actions of African Americans we still find that *pathos* accompanies *mythos* into the twentieth century. Therefore, a discussion of the nature of myth in African American thought is a way to discover the values of a spiritual, traditional, even mystical rhetoric as it confronts a technological, linear world and to provide us with ideas for an Afrocentric alternative to apocalyptic thinking. I have chosen to consider the evidence of African American culture alone, an Afrocentric view, to say that the context of the mythoform is such that it adapts to the circumstances to history. In this respect, the myths I examine have nothing to do with the general concept of universality. They represent the African's response in the Americas to a historical moment. (Now it is true that other cultures have similar responses to similar conditions, but these must be seen in their own, fundamental contexts.) The utterances are not mythoforms themselves; they are only enactments of the mythoforms. Thus, mythoforms are the basal psychic patterns by which we organize our experiences. These are reported in various existential enactments.

In the language of the African American speaker, myth becomes an explanation for the human condition and an answer to the problem of psychological existence in a racist society. This is not different from the myths of Oduduwa among the Yoruba or Okomfo Anokye among the Asante—or a hundred other African ethnic communities. Creation myths of the type found in traditional African and European cultures are not present in the African American cultural experience, if we take the formal arrival of Africans in the Virginia colony in 1619 as a point of departure. The creation myths of Africa remained intact for most Africans, and therefore the practical myths dealt with questions of geographical and cultural alienation, conflict with a hostile society, and the separation of technology and nature. What is more significant is that myth is connected to life and its social functions. Relationships between family members and relationships to outsiders are at the heart of a functional doctrine of the myth. We act mythically. But functionalism alone cannot dictate what myth is or should be. How can a mythoform be used?

One use of mythoforms is to preserve links to the past—that is, a cultural history. Let us be clear that we understand the ever-presence of the ancestors. When we speak of the African community, we are speaking of the *living* and the *dead.* Recall the earlier explanations of the nature of libation among the Ga celebrations of community throughout African societies, and of *nommo* as a collective experience; in fact, without the participation of the ancestors, *nommo* cannot be completed since the dead are the agents who continue to energize the living. They assure us that the discourse of life will not be chaotic, and we take this, in whatever society we live, as a permanent expression of rebirth.

Perhaps the African American version is truncated by Christianity or Islam or some other non-African mythic expression, but even in modified form we see how ancestral myths are a part of our communicative sense.

The ability to recognize ancestral myths is often left to the older members of the black community. They recall the traditional songs and the oral reports that refer to certain myths imbedded in verbal expressions. For example, the admonition frequently heard in south Georgia, "Call me like you gon' call me when I am dead," had as much imbedded continuity as the passed-down banjo or the hot irons used to press clothes. The elders find a connectedness with their past when they hear such a direct reference to the adoration given to the dead. However, beyond what appears to be a metaphysical attachment is the continuation of practices that find their source in the traditions.

The work of Melville Herskovits in *The Myth of the Negro Past* still stands as a monument to the powerful presence of the African ancestors in the Americas. What Herskovits and others have demonstrated is the abundance of cultural memory in African American societies. Indeed, the ghost tales are often nothing more than the modification of ancestor tales and relate to the near as well as remote past. As a child in Georgia, I often heard my relatives speak of "seeing" great-grandfather or great-grandmother. The folklore often gives the stories to us with expressions such as "This actually happened," "Use to be years ago when we first come here," "Way back there in them days gone by," "This man I know, he was an old, old man," or "My grandpa once told me that he seed his daddy."

Various manifestations of the role of ancestors have occurred in African American society, and there have been special observances at cemeteries where certain types of material possessions have been placed on the graves to appease the ancestors. Libations are still poured in some places in the American South as an indication of respect for "those who are not with us," and despite the Christian religion, much of African American religion is devoted to the idea of transition from life to death to life eternal. "Life eternal" has a special ring to believers because it is easily connected to the belief in reincarnation, the ever-presence of dead spirits, and the fact that the dead are often reborn in the children. We use these concepts as anchors for the mythoforms, or rather the mythoforms find their materiality in the relationship to ancestors.

When we examine the nature and utility of myth in African American discourse, we see that it is about ancestral heroes and heroines. The African American myth is the highest order of symbolic motifs. Furthermore, the myth emerges as a story with a basis in historical or indefinite time, but in all cases the story is of triumphs and victories, even if it is considered in the suffering-myth genre or is found in Ananse or Brer Rabbit–type tales.

A significant function of the African American myth in discourse is the demonstration of control over circumstances, as opposed to control over nature. It is the heroine's or hero's mission, sometimes messianic in nature, to surmount any obstacle in the cause of peace, love, or collective harmony. African American myths are set in the inexact past—unless, of course, they are historic, legendary myths, such as Harriet Tubman's. In such cases they are set in a specific time and place, although they may be of anonymous origin. If we use Stagolee, John Henry, Harriet Tubman, Shine, or John Jasper as examples of some African American myths, we can see how myth also functions as a proto-science. It can provide solutions to crises in the collective life of the people. In this way it is not aetiological—that is, merely offering causes for conditions and circumstances—but rather poignantly eschatological. What we notice when we examine African American myths is that they possess a kind of epistemological maturity, unlike the traditional African myth, which may be seen as an interpretation of reality. The idea of hope and possibility rises on the shoulders of an African American imaginative mythology that sees the future as brighter than the present. Social situations molded the ultimate form of this myth. A story may demonstrate the myth but is not the myth.

Hope is typified in the mythological character called Shine. This version of the ballad appeared in Georgia in the 1950s:

> Shine, little Harlem boy blacker than me,
> Sailed the wrong ship in the wrong sea.

> Old *Titanic* hit a iceberg block,
> Shook and shimmied and reared from shock.
> Shine come up from the engine floor
> Running so fast he broke down an iron door.
> Captain told Shine, "Get on back downstairs!"
> Shine told the Captain. "You better say your prayers."
> Captain's daughter hollered, "Lord, the water's up to my neck."
> Shine said, "Baby you'd better swim, by heck."
> Captain said, "Boy I got pumps to pump the water down."
> Shine said, "Pump on, I want be around."
> Shine jumped overboard into the sea
> Looked back at the white folks and said, "Swim like me."
> And he swam on.
> Captain's daughter hist her dress over her head
> Shine said, "You'll catch pneumonia baby and be stone cold dead."
> And he swam on.
> Captain's daughter cried, "Shine, Shine, save poor me and I'll give everything your eyes can see."
> Shine said, "There's plenty on land baby, waiting for me."
> And he swam on.
> Captain yelled, "Shine, my boy, I got a bank account.
> Save poor me and you'll get any amount."
> Shine said, "More banks on land than on sea."
> And he swam on.
> White headed millionaire, aged eighty five,
> *Titanic* deck yelling, "I want to stay alive.
> Shine, Shine, hear my plea!"
> Shine said, "Jump in the sea Grandpa, and swim like me."
> And Shine swam on.
> Five o'clock in the morning in Harlem and daybreak near.
> Shine said, "How come they close up these bars so early when Shine just got here?"
> And he walked on.
> Newsstand on the corner, brought the *Daily News.*
> Nothing on the front page but *Titanic* blues.
> He walked on.
> Got to his girl friend's house,
> She cried, "How can it be?"
> Shine said, "Yes baby it's me."
> And they got it on.

"Shine" is preeminently a myth of self-discovery in the midst of chaos. This is one of the moments of crisis that African American mythic figures like to enter. Harriet Tubman, with slavery and human bondage; John Henry, with the challenge of a mountain; High John de Conquerer, with any and every conceivable personal difficulty; and Shine, with the sinking of the *Titanic,* are self-discovery myths.

Melvin Dixon writes that "the moment of self-discovery has been one of the more dramatic turning points in the personal history of every black American." In the moment of crisis, Shine recognizes that his condition was normally one of second-class status but that *he* could swim. This discovery gives him power over the white and wealthy that he would never have achieved if it had not been for the sinking of the *Titanic.* The moral is not lost on the African American community: Crisis has a way of equalizing everyone.

There are some aspects to the use of myths in African American discourse that are filled with slaveship pathos. The fact that myth functions means only that it is recognized as having certain positive capabilities, and the managing of myths in discourse could lead to a renewed emphasis on deep style in orature and, quite correctly, introduce another uniquely African American element on the public platform. Contemporary African American myth contains the powerful suffering genre. Even in the most victorious myths, one frequently finds the suffering genre. Perhaps this is because victory, in a political sense, is often based upon suffering in the minds of African Americans. How to turn the suffering genre into a positive, victorious consciousness occupies a whole Afrocentric literary school of thought.

Baldwin and Richards have written extensively on the cultural question, with direct reference to the crisis in African American motifs. Baldwin sees the psychology of oppression as giving birth to the complex mental confusion besetting the African American. On the other hand, Richards, after Karenga and Diop, has analyzed the extent of the cultural malady that afflicts a whole generation of thinkers and artists incapsulated by European cultural domination. Out of the cauldron has come the suffering genre in African American myths. There is

an implicit belief that suffering brings redemption. In fact, it is the peculiarly African American emphasis, similar to the Christian myth, that gives its potency in contemporary society. Black speakers have frequently allied themselves (or the masses) with this suffering Christ, who would save humanity. In the speeches of Booker T. Washington one can see the myth of suffering redemption at work: God has a great purpose for a people whom he allowed to suffer so much. Like Jesus Christ, the African race was going through the Valley of the Shadow of Death to rise again at the new dawn, having saved the world through its substantive, creative experience of pain.

Akin to the suffering genre is the suckling genre, mainly (but not entirely) identified with the mother-earth, which relates everything to the motif of caring. We care for the world, not just for our own children, and in our myth the suckling mother is a multimammarian who gives milk to all, equally. Our speakers speak of "the brotherhood of man and the fatherhood of God" and move on to illustrate that if God will not take care of others, then our mothers will mop the sweat off the brows of all. Martin Luther King Jr. called such individuals "men and women who will be as maladjusted as the prophet Amos, who in the midst of the injustices of his day would cry out in words that echo across the centuries. 'Let justice roll down like waters, and righteousness like a mighty stream.'" Nearly seventy-five years earlier, Joseph C. Price, the outstanding orator and educator of the nineteenth century, had said, "There is no true freedom that does not give full recognition and assent to that cardinal principle of humanity—the fatherhood of God and the brotherhood of man." In many respects, the suckling myth establishes the African American as responsible for the world. Somehow we will purge the world of its sins through our suffering; we will teach the brotherhood and sisterhood of the earth. This becomes a suckling mythology, as befits a redemptive or messianic idea.

Harriet Tubman is a extraordinary mythic figure in our rhetorical consciousness because she is symbolic, that is, an expression of our epic journey. Tubman's transformation from birth to self-imposed exile, to rites of initiation, to triumphant return to the South to deliver her brothers and sisters represents all of us. In that sense, she is more than symbol, she is enactment. Within the African American cosmos, Tubman is a combination of intense secular and sacred power. She established her credibility; that is, she became a heroic character by carrying out her professed actions. The deliverance of more than three hundred slaves from bondage during the most difficult period of slavery indelibly wrote her name in the mythology of African American discourse. Children are often taught to sing "I love Harriet Tubman because she first loved me." Tubman embodies the care and concern of a mother figure; she is the Great Mother.

She is also what Armstrong calls an "affecting presence," because her enactments occur in a special way: "by presentation and celebration, the existential and generative germ of the culture." We call her name in the secret hours of the night when we lay our children down to sleep, when we fly in airplanes over the seas, when we reach into our psychic lives for strength to overcome stress, when we seek guidance and courage. Armstrong declares that "this is why the affecting presence in all cultures is sometimes venerated, sometimes credited with the power to work good or evil, and is nearly universally valued greatly and accorded distinctive treatment." Tubman is the embodiment, even in her death-life, of a cultural principle, a myth, without precise substance, but a pattern, an enactment of history, profound in its impact upon a community that has known significant epic journeys.

This pattern occurs every time one person reaches back to bring another alongside. Within the Afrocentric culture one sees a distaste for individual achievement that is not related to collective advancement. Harriet Tubman's classic historical action becomes the mythoform for all such patterns of behavior. Any analysis of African American culture must consider the caring mythoform represented in the Tubman example as a possible pattern of behavior. We are confronted by it in the daily interactions of our lives, from the extended-family philosophy to the assistance to the needy in our churches. How can you be well to do and not care about the poor around you? is a particularly Tubman mythoform question. She is heroine, not as an individual, but as a caring, assisting person.

The hero myths that occupy significant places in the African American mythology are, as we've said, John Henry, Stagolee, Shine, John Jasper, Harriet Tubman, and a host of religiously related myths, such as the story of Job. They are hero or heroine-centered myths because they extend the ordinary to the totality of our cultural existence. John Henry is the strong, powerful steel driver who is capable of drilling a tunnel through a mountain quicker and cleaner than power-driven drills. His ability to use muscle power and physical stamina to overcome the mountain is indicative of the deep reality of the African American's reliance on physical strength during the epic sojourn in America. Use of the John Henry myth is usually confined to instances of physical confrontation or maintenance of philosophical positions. There are instances when the John Henry myth shares some of the characteristics of the Stagolee myth; this is true mainly as each myth regards physical prowess.

Stagolee is the radical impulse to challenge an authority that seeks to repress freedom, improvisation, and harmony. The direct-action orientation of Stagolee is found in Marcus Garvey, Fannie Lou Hamer, Malcolm X, and Martin Luther King Jr. But Stagolee does not have King's religious emphasis; he is a symbol of uncensored, unselfconscious force, pulsating with unpredictability. This mythoform is a recurring pattern in every aspect of African culture in America. The musician who improvises, the basketball player who follows his own rhythms to demonstrate his skill, or the maverick who refuses to have her art suppressed; these are the heroes of the cultural pattern.

Stagolee was the prototype bad man in the sense that no-body bothered him, not even the devil. He is the embodiment of a myth that emphasizes toughness. Known for his supranatural skill at surviving the worst personal tragedy and emerging victoriously, Stagolee is the ultimate projection of the black phallus into the white belly of America. The myth's persistence within the African American community is testimony to its appealing characteristics. What is especially interesting is that Stagolee, unlike John Henry, does not represent the Protestant ethic. John Henry is perceived as the good man who works hard to achieve victory through sweat. Stagolee is his opposite, who will achieve victory by any means necessary. Both are authentic myths of the African American experience and both represent specific characters in the historical and contemporary community; Stagolee, however, retains the fundamental attitude of resistance of the slave revolts.

Stagolee, the representative enactment of the deep-seated and strongly felt sentiment for justice and emancipation, is widely believed by African Americans to be the thorn in the side of a white, hypocritical government. Out of this intellectual and social context is born a man-child in the promised land, as Claude Brown saw it, or a Malcolm X, who preached acid theses, asserted without compromise, against the flailing and anguished figure of an insane political society. As John Illo says, "Indirection is not workable, for the state has stolen irony; satire is futile, its only resource is to repeat the language of the administration." Only then must the Stagolee myth step forward to demonstrate again how alien we are in this culture and society. But Stagolee is only a presentation, a presence, an enactment, often made symbolic, of the uniqueness that is our experience in America. Such a position in society invites defiance and resistance. In *Die, Nigger, Die,* H. Rap Brown said that when whites say talk low, African Americans should say talk loud; when they say don't play the radio then play it. Brown's reasoning during the Ebony Explosion of the 1960s was that whites tended to disregard the premises of African American discourse and, consequently, did not deserve to have their way, particularly since what they wanted was often contrary to our natural response to the environment. Similarly, the intellectual posture of the black scholar or orator is often based on the attitude of rebellion.

The artist or speaker who uses these myths may never call explicitly upon the names John Henry or Stagolee to express the truth of the myth. However, the myth is so implicit in the culture that its use is impossible to avoid if one engages in any type of discourse. The real mythical essence of these heroes occurs with regularity in the discourse of the African American orator. For example, it was to Stagolee that Robert C. Weaver, former Secretary of Housing and Urban Development in the United States,

referred when he said in a speech before the challenge to democracy of the Fund for the Republic Symposium (June 13, 1963) that "Negroes who are constantly confronted or threatened by discrimination and inequality articulate a sense of outrage. Many react with hostility, sometimes translating their feelings into antisocial actions." Weaver's use of the Stagolee complex was perfect for delivery to a largely white audience, for it did not explain anything about the will of blacks to change the conditions. It was wild, outrageous, hostile, and antisocial behavior in response to a more calculated, wilder, more hostile, and more outrageous discrimination. Weaver knew the Stagolee myth so deeply in his soul that he was able to frame his mouth to say that, in some parts of the community, "a separate culture with deviant values develops." Weaver was talking Stagolee; everything he said described a mythoform well known in the black community, and it was presented by Weaver to his white audience as an explanation of our militant side. Although Weaver used the pejorative language of the white culture to speak of us, he spoke from the deep wellspring of African American historical experiences. To understand Weaver's blacks who "articulate a sense of outrage" is to touch the very source of Stagolee's power. Stagolee is not just bitter; he is outraged at discrimination, paternalism, and bigotry. Thus, when Robert Weaver used the "sense of outrage" term, he was speaking the language of a black community become Stagolee.

Stagolee is the myth that allows the African American to rail against evil with violence, to shoot, to cut, to maim, to kill—if that is necessary to restore a sense of human dignity. Thus, any speaker who uses the appeal to Stagolee, directly or indirectly, is addressing one of the principal hero myths of the community. A classic use of the myth was in Malcolm X's "Black Revolution" speech. In 1964, before a packed crowd at the Militant Labor Forum in New York City, Malcolm said that "you've got 22,000,000 black people in this country today . . . who are fed up with taxation without representation, who are ready to do the same thing your forefathers did to bring about independence." Much of Malcolm X's image as a dynamic orator came from his embodiment of the Stagolee myth in his oratory, and not so much in his personal history. Before his conversion to the teachings of the Honorable Elijah Muhammad, he may have been the personification of Stagolee. However, as a Muslim minister, he was righteous and rather conservative in habits; it was his oratory that carried the Stagolee myth to its highest degree. Malcolm talked outrage and the possibility of violence in the defense of this dignity.

To get beyond the notions of myth as legends of gods, esoteric themes, and aetiological tales, I chose to demonstrate how certain cultural-specific forms are enacted through living celebrations and presentations of being in everyday African American life. Quite frankly, I am not sure one can understand concrete discourse without an appreciation of mythoforms. When I spoke of Harriet Tubman, I mentioned that she was an enactment of our epic journey. I think, however, her historical nature ought to be made plain. In this way we neither confuse history with myth nor myth with specific enactments of mythoforms.

Harriet Tubman is not typical as an expression of myth since she is a legendary but historical mythical character; I mean that there are historical records to attest to her life. Nevertheless, she is perhaps the most salient mythical character in African American history. It is from her that we get the numerous leaders who arise to deliver the people from bondage to salvation. She is not messianic in either the sense of Moses of the Old Testament or Jesus of the New; she is, rather, the spirit-mother, protecting, suckling, and leading her children. The Harriet Tubman enactment of the salvation myth manifests itself in how we relate the stories of the Bible to our everyday realities. Those stories are not real because of the lives of Moses and Jesus; they are real because the experience of Harriet Tubman lives within the hearts of every African American person. That is why people find it difficult to accept the appellation "Moses of her people" for her. She was more than Moses; she was life and love. She performed not out of duty to her people but out of love for them. This is the myth that is found in much of the language of Martin Luther King Jr. In the "Eulogy to Dr. King," Benjamin Mays, himself a celebrated orator, said that there was no element of compulsion in the dying of Martin Luther King. "He was acting on an inner urge that drove him on, more courageous than those who advocate violence as a way out, for they carry weapons of destruction for defence." Not in his nonviolence was King in keeping with Harriet Tubman, but in the "inner urge" to deliver the people. According to the Tubman presentation, she once told a slave who was reluctant to escape, "I'll see you buried and in your grave before I'll see you a slave." Needless to say, the man followed her to freedom.

Myth in its artistic frame and in its Afrocentric reinterpretation elevates and sustains African American culture. Ultimately, Stagolee must be seen as the oratorical or verbal symbol of resistance. We seek to effect the great opposition in discourse by calling upon this major mythoform. Stagolee is an archetype of the rebel, the protest speaker, the revolutionary. And Stagolee is indeed the discourse metaphor for the rhetoric of resistance. . . .

DISCUSSION QUESTIONS

1. According to Asante, what is the function of *nommo*?

2. How does Asante differentiate orature and oratory?

3. Asante suggests that some preachers never succeed in "moving" an audience. Is it necessary to move an audience in order to be effective in the African American oral tradition?

4. What is meant by the claim that African- and American-based socio-historical perspectives on Black orature share common grounds?

5. Explain the four stages of knowledge in the Dogon culture and their relationship to the word.

Reading 1.3

COMPLICITY

The Theory of Negative Difference

MARK LAWRENCE MCPHAIL

It's astounding the first time you realize a stranger has a body—the realization that he has a body makes him a stranger. It means you have a body too. You will live with this forever, and it will spell out the language of your life.

—James Baldwin

This excerpt from Baldwin's novel, *If Beale Street Could Talk* (pp. 64–65), succinctly describes the material manifestations and linguistic implications of *the other,* a figure that has become a central concern in contemporary radical criticism. The heroine of the novel is a young woman named Tish, and, in a short section in which Baldwin describes the recognition of the other as stranger, Tish confronts the social and physical realities of negative difference, the complicity it engenders, and its impact on human communicative interaction. Although Tish lives in a fictional world, her insights have important implications for critical discourse. The other illustrates the problem of language in Western culture in its most extreme form, as a figure made flesh that reifies the existence of an essential reality, a reality "out there," separate and distinct from the human agents that interact within it. This belief in separateness has, indeed, made us strangers, and has created a language of negative difference that manifests itself in the social and symbolic realities of race, gender, and rhetoric.

The calling into question of this language of negative difference has become a key strategy in many feminist, afrocentric, and rhetorical theories of discourse. Scholars in these areas have explicated various indictments of the phallocentric, eurocentric, and essentialist linguistic strategies defined and perpetuated by dominant population groups, and some have begun the difficult task of addressing the complicitous nature of critical discourse. This essay explores the problem of complicity as it is manifest in critical discourses that converge at the juncture of gender, race, and rhetoric. By focusing on this juncture, it illustrates how racism and

From McPhail, M. L. (1991). Complicity: The theory of negative difference. *The Howard Journal of Communications, 3*(1 & 2), 1-13.

sexism are products of a conceptualization of language peculiar to essentialist epistemology, and prefigured by the historical conflict between rhetoric and philosophy. It further suggests that contemporary race, gender, and rhetorical studies provide the foundation for an epistemic stance that situates critical self-reflection within a context that makes possible a more positive approach to linguistic definition.

COMPLICITY AND NEGATIVE DIFFERENCE

Herein, the term *complicity* simply means "an agreement to disagree," and *negative difference* refers to the principle of critical analysis that undergirds essentialist epistemology. This analysis of complicity as a theory of negative difference is rooted in the linguistic theories articulated by the ancient Greek sophists, particularly Thrasymachus of Chalcedon, whose *theory of the opposite party* clearly illustrates the problem of complicity as it functions in argumentative discourse. Thrasymachus observes that individuals "who are at variance are mutually experiencing something that is bound to befall those who engage in senseless rivalry: believing they are expressing opposite views, they fail to perceive that their actions are the same, and that the theory of the opposite party is inherent in their own theory" (Freeman, 1977, p. 141). This theory of the opposite party calls into question the principle of negative difference, and ultimately essentialist epistemology and rational logic. Essentialism, which is the dominant epistemological position articulated in Western culture, posits a reality in which material and symbolic processes exist in and of themselves. This results in linguistic practices which legitimate argumentative and critical discourse, precisely because such discourse is aimed at the discovery of *essential* truths.

It also results in social practices that perpetuate the principle of negative difference in human interaction. For example, racism is "one of the most blatant and potentially evil forms of essentialist thought," notes Crapanzano (1985) in *Waiting: The Whites of South Africa.* Crapanzano explicates the connection between complicity and negative difference with which

this study is concerned when he explains that often racism's "critical consideration masks other classifications that have the same epistemological roots and permit the same social and psychological tyranny" (p. 20). The isolation of racism as an object of critical analysis obscure: the underlying epistemological foundation, essentialism, which also undergird: problems of gender, class and classification. In his discussion of the *rhetoric of domination and subordination,* Crapanzano connects essentialism with the problem of complicity when he argues that although racist and other essentialist social categories—when they exist—enter the rhetoric of domination and subordination in hierarchical societies, they are not as freely manipulated by the dominant, the possessors of power, status, and wealth, as is popularly thought, (p. 20)

Following Memmi and Mannoni, he argues that the belief that individuals can respond to oppression without recognizing their complicity in its perpetuation fails to consider the political and linguistic complexities that circumscribe the system: "Such a view fails, of course, to recognize the constraints of the dominant. To be dominant in a system is not to dominate the system" (pp. 20, 21). Crapanzano's analysis provides a starting point for a discussion of complicity precisely because it isolates and illustrates the essentialist presuppositions of language that undergird the theory of negative difference.

Plato's Phaedrus

Those presuppositions are deeply rooted in Western conceptualizations of language, and provide a common point of reference for our understanding of the relationship between race, gender, and rhetoric. Gates (1984) illustrates the connection between race and the theory of negative difference in "Criticism in the Jungle": "Ethnocentrism and 'logocentricism' are profoundly interrelated in Western discourse as old as the *Phaedrus* of Plato, in which one finds one of the earliest figures of blackness as an absence, a figure of negation" (p. 6). Blackness as a figure of negation points to an *essential* difference, one intimately connected to the assumptions of knowledge in Western discourse. Whitson (1988) explicates how negative difference functions in relation to both rhetoric and gender in "The *Phaedrus* Complex." He argues that, in the *Phaedrus*, Plato has "relegated rhetoric to the negative pole of binary oppositions that privilege a particular truth claim: presence/absence, light/dark, man/woman, truth/appearance, and philosophy/rhetoric. The term for this kind of metaphysics is phallogocentricism: the primacy of the phallus and the philosopher's word as law" (p. 18). These epistemological assumptions of both racist and sexist language can also be traced to the essentialist presuppositions of language clearly evident in the debate between rhetoric and philosophy.

These presuppositions are explored by Lanham (1976) in his examination of the "serious premises" of epistemology that underlie Western discussions of style as it relates to rhetoric. The significance of Lanham's essay as regards race and gender is its explication of the essentialist presuppositions of *serious* reality and the resulting historical disenfranchisement of rhetoric by philosophy. The relationship between rhetorical and philosophical reality is grounded in, and perpetuated by, the same assumptions concerning language and reality that create the social divisions of race and gender. What Lanham call "the Rhetorical Ideal of Life" constantly calls into question the assumptive grounds of serious reality in much the same way that race and gender studies have challenged the legitimacy of eurocentric and phallocentric discourses. Contemporary rhetorical theory, like radical critical theory, has witnessed a re-emergence of the primacy of language that necessitates a consideration of how the principle of negative difference functions in argumentative and critical discourse.

Indeed, this re-emergence of the primacy of language in radical critical studies has confronted critics of race, gender, and language with the problematical possibility that they have, through argumentative discourse, participated in the creation of the realities of racism, sexism, and logocentrism. This is the problem of complicity, and it is rooted in the tendency of critical discourse to privilege itself even as it calls privilege into question. Baudrillard (1988) explains complicity in terms of seduction: "This is what happens initially when a discourse *seduces itself;* the original way in which it absorbs meaning and empties itself of meaning in order to better fascinate others: the primitive seduction of language" (p. 150). In attempting to privilege itself, radical criticism has been seduced by the very "abduction of meaning" that it attempts to oppose. Baudrillard continues: "Every discourse is complicit in this abduction of meaning, in this seductive maneuver of interpretation: if one discourse did not do this, then others would take its place" (p. 150). Confronting radical criticism, then, is *the distinct possibility that it represents a mere replacement of one oppressive discourse for another and a reproduction of the very principles and practices that it ostensibly rejects.*

Marxist Considerations of Hegemony

Laclau (1977) discusses complicity in Marxist considerations of hegemony in terms of the concept of *articulation.* According to Laclau, the problem of radical antagonism emerges within discursive structures in such a way as to undermine the practical possibilities inherent in discourse. Within this context, hegemony can be seen as an agreement to disagree, which re-articulates itself in the collaborative nature of hegemonic praxis. To the extent that critics of race, gender, and language oppose hegemonic discourses based upon positions that subscribe to this rhetoric of negative difference, they become complicitous with those discourses, and in effect reify them. Laclau and Mouffe (1989) explicate the concept of articulation as it applies to the complicitousness of feminist and antiracist struggles:

> The political space of the feminist struggle is constituted within the ensemble of practices and discourses which create the different forms of subordination of women; the space of the antiracist struggle, within the overdetermined ensemble of practices constituting racial discrimination. But the antagonisms within each of these relatively autonomized spaces divide them into two camps. This explains the fact that, when social struggles are directed not against objects constituted within their own space but against simple empirical referents—for example, men or white people as biological referents—they find

themselves in difficulties. For, such struggles ignore the specificity of the political spaces in which the other democratic antagonisms emerge. (p. 132)

Both feminists and antiracist theoretical struggles are in difficulty when they ignore the assumptive grounds of the linguistic spaces in which epistemic antagonisms occur, and, thus, complicitously re-articulate the problem of negative difference in their own critical discourses.

Complicity thus manifests itself in terms of an adherence to the problematical ideological assumptions of position and privilege inherent in critical discourse. Radhakrishnan (1987) makes the point powerfully clear in "Ethnic Identity and Post-Structuralist Difference": "The assumption that there exists an essence (African, Indian, feminine, nature, etc.) ironically perpetuates the same ahistoricism that was identified as the enemy during the negative/critical or 'diconstructive' phase of the ethnic revolution" (p. 208). Radhakrishnan then asks the question most central to the problem of complicity of the linguistic level: "Doesn't this all sound somehow familiar: the defeat and overthrow of one sovereignty, the emergence and consolidation of an antithetical sovereignty, and the creation of a different, yet the same, repression?" (p. 208). His analysis of feminist historiography suggests some strategies for critics of language sincerely committed to transcending, and not simply reconstructing, the problem of negative difference.

Feminist and African American Literary and Political Theory and Practice

Indeed, it is within the arena of feminist literary and political theory that the problem of complicity has become increasingly evident and problematical, perhaps because it is within this space that issues of gender, race, and classification most clearly converge. Dobris and White (1989) suggest that this complicity is most evident in terms of the inconsistencies of feminist discourse in regard to women of nondominant populations:

Exclusivity, ignorance and blaming the victim all contribute to a feminist discourse that is devoid of

the experiences of non-dominant women. Thus, while the dominant discourse of feminism presents itself as all-inclusive, it is clear that members of non-dominant groups construct images of feminism that project a white, Christian, heterosexual, middle-class identity, leaving most other women excluded from its purview. (p. 17)

Their insights provide an important point of departure for the consideration of how complicity is problematized within contemporary feminist theory.

hooks (1984) explicitly recognizes the problem of complicity and its articulation in feminist theory and practice in *Feminist Theory: From Margin to Center:*

Women must begin the work of feminist reorganization with me understanding that we have all (irrespective of race, sex, or class) acted in complicity with the existing oppressive system. We all need to make a conscious break with the system. . . . We cannot motivate [other women] to join a feminist struggle by asserting a political superiority that makes the movement just another oppressive hierarchy. (pp. 161–162)

hooks suggests that contemporary feminist praxis contains within it the possibility of perpetuating the same type of privileges legitimated by the oppressive system from which it must break, and argues for a recognition of complicity as a first step in transcending that possibility.

Christian (1987), in her critique of French feminism, illustrates how critical discourse, ostensibly aimed at transcending the hegemonic dialectic, reifies it. She registers her concern that this particular school of feminist scholarship "has become authoritative discourse, monologic, which occurs precisely because it does have access to the means of promulgating its ideas" (p. 60). Christian confronts the same problem in black feminist literary criticism. "Since I can count on one hand the number of black feminist literary critics in the world today, I consider it presumptuous of me to invent a theory of how we *ought* to read" (p. 53). Like hooks, Christian's analysis of the complicitous privileging of discourse enables her to transcend the problematical dualities of race, gender, and identity and confront the underlying epistemological concerns that are problematic in feminist theory and practice.

Christian generalizes her analysis of these concerns when she contends that many "critics do not investigate the reasons why that statement—literature is political—is now acceptable when before it was not; nor do we look to our own antecedents for the sophisticated arguments upon which we can build in order to change the tendency of any established Western idea to become hegemonic" (1987, p. 55). One way to facilitate the type of change that Christian and many other critics of race and gender are attempting is to recognize that our complicity with hegemonic discourse begins with the very language we use to call that discourse into questions: critical, argumentative language. Christian's observations that "the new emphasis on literary critical theory is as hegemonic as the world which it attacks" and that "the language it creates is one which mystifies rather than clarifies our condition, making it possible for a few people who know that particular language to control the critical scene" (p. 55), must be extended to a general discussion of the epistemological presuppositions of argumentative language. In contemporary radical criticism the problem of negative difference is manifest in an adherence to principles of essentialist epistemology and the problematical divisions in constructs in terms of symbolic and social action.

Awkward concurs, and returns us to the juncture of race, gender, and language in his discussion of the essentialist presuppositions of justificatory positions taken by contemporary African American and feminist literary critics concerning cross-gender/racial critical abilities. Using principles of psychoanalytic criticism, he responds to the assertion that men are incapable of doing feminist criticism, and compares the assertion to the arguments presented by black critics during the 1960s regarding the abilities of whites to analyze African American literature. Awkward (1988) suggests that psychoanalytic theory deconstructs traditional feminist criticism by exposing its essentialist presuppositions in terms of its "problematic appeals to an authority of female experience,"

and calls into question "the neither biologically nor culturally justified nature of feminist criticism's practice of a whole reverse discrimination." He concludes: "To simply reverse the binary opposition man/woman, when we are painfully aware of its phallocentric origins, is to suggest complicity with the male-authored fiction of history. No feminist should be comfortable with such a suggestion, despite the potential institutional gains." One can easily extend Awkward's analysis to the practice of criticism itself, which is a privileged discourse in the mouths of its practitioners that is rarely, if ever, turned back upon itself.

Indeed, no critics should be comfortable with such a simple reversal of any of the binary oppositions that criticism so eloquently calls into question. And yet, within the context of essentialist epistemology, critical discourse is often limited to perpetuating just this type of dialectical binary opposition. Criticism, whether or not it calls into question privileged discourse, *is itself a privileged discourse, and thus must strive to perpetuate one position at the expense of another.* This is the rhetoric of what Lanham calls *serious* reality, the rhetoric of dialectical critical discourse that becomes little more than an ideological discourse of self-legitimating privilege. This is the discourse that radical criticism calls into question, but which at the same time legitimates the theories and practices of critics who would oppose eurocentric, phallocentric, or other discourses of negative difference. This is the problem of complicity, which demands a self-reflexive reassessment of the underlying assumptions of critical inquiry and their reification of *serious* reality, and calls forth a coherent rhetoric of judgment.

This, I believe, is precisely what Valesio attempts in *Novantiqua: Rhetorics as a Contemporary Theory.* Valesio (1980) concurs with Lanham's observation that "rhetoric's real crime, one is often led to suspect, is its candid acknowledgement of the rhetorical aspects of 'serious' life" (p. 7), and argues that

the real "enemy" of rhetoric is: not logic but ideology. If the struggle has been between rhetoric and logic, it would not have raged with such a continuity and force; but is did, and still continues to do so, because rhetoric is more or less clearly perceived as a threat to the assurance that any ideological system requires and confirms—and this perception is quite correct. (p. 61)

Valesio reconstructs the debate between rhetoric and philosophy by arguing that rhetoric is not a counterpart to dialectic, but *is* dialectic, when he asserts that dialectic is "*the dominant form in which rhetorical structure manifests itself*" (p. 113). This reconstruction of the relationship between rhetoric, dialectic and ideology transcends the problem of negative difference that historically has circumscribed symbolic and social interaction.

Valesio suggests that rhetoric, in its capacity to call into question privileged discourses, transcends the principle of negative difference by its insistence that all discourses are "at every point shaped and slanted according to specific argumentative structures" (p. 62). The implication of this insistence cannot be simply dismissed, for it suggests that when critics of race, gender, and language engage in argumentation they risk re-articulating—being seduced by—the very ideological structures that they are attempting to transcend.

Radhakrishnan (1988), in his analysis of feminist historiography, concurs: "Could it not be the case that we are either flogging a dead horse or that our interest is not in achieving a 'break,' but in the eternal and timeless maintenance of a 'tradition of opposition' that has perforce to keep alive the very tradition it questions?" (p. 201). The challenge for feminist criticism, Radhakrishnan suggests, is to transcend the problem of negative difference embedded in the language of gender, and this challenge, I believe, is applicable to all practitioners of radical criticism concerned with issues of gender, race, class, and classification.

Although complicity is evident in contemporary feminist theory and practice, to isolate this one arena of discourse would be to ignore the extent to which the same issues exist in terms of race, class, and classification, and merely to allow "one weasel term [to] substitute for another" (Crapanzano, p. 20). Complicity arises out of a failure to acknowledge and call into question the essentialist presuppositions of critical discourse. The underlying principle of essentialism is the principle of negative difference, which is central to argumentative and critical discourse and, thus, a basic element of our linguistic and symbolic interaction. This raises an important theoretical question that confronts scholars in women's studies, communication, and contemporary black thought: To what extent are nondominant population groups, through their participation in the prevailing essentialist linguistic system, complicitous in constructing oppressive social realities? As critics we are confronted by an important epistemological dilemma, in the sense that breaking with the system is reifying the system in its most basic form: negation. This paradox points to the underlying problem of complicity.

To the extent that we all participate in discourse—practical and theoretical—presupposed by essentialist assumptions, we participate in the construction of oppressive social realities. As scholars and social critics we are privileged by ontological and epistemological principles of negative difference that we readily use to participate in the argumentative and antagonistic symbolic systems that sustain and perpetuate the problem of negative difference. If criticism is to be radical in terms of its own presuppositions, it must look to its own assumptive ground for an epistemic stance that transcends the tradition of opposition of which Radhakrishnan (1987) speaks: "The task for radical ethnicity is to thematize and subsequently problematize its entrapment with these binary elaborations with the intention of 'stepping beyond' to find its own adequate language" (p. 216). In order to step beyond the binarity of essentialism, I believe it is necessary to step into it: that is, to confront it on its own terms, in its own language, to call into question the necessity of negation by legitimating it through affirmation.

COMPLEMENTARY DIFFERENCES

Such a view goes beyond essentialist conceptualizations of reality by positing the possibility of articulating a social reality in which differences might be complementary, and not merely antagonistic. The possibility of such an affirmative transformation is perhaps best articulated within the context of the narrative paradigm, in the rhetorical realm of literature. Woolf (1978) indicates the impact of subscribing to the discourse of negative difference on human consciousness in the final chapter of *A Room of One's Own:* "Perhaps to think, as I had been thinking these two days, of one sex as distinct from the other is an effort. It interferes with the unity of mind" (p. 145). The challenge for contemporary critics is to remove this interference, to begin to give voice to that element of the other that is within each of us, and find within discourse the possibility of achieving a unity of mind and method that transcends and transforms negative difference.

Certainly, this is what Baldwin (1974) does with the character of Tish: he transcends the reality of gender in order to live within the space of *the other,* and this is a rhetorical move. Lanham (1976) amplifies the possibility of making such a move when he writes that rhetoric "provided a training in tolerance, if by that we mean getting inside another's skull and looking out," and goes on to explain that rhetoric teaches what is perhaps the most important lesson of being human: forgiveness. "For what is forgiveness but the acknowledgement that the sinner sinning is not truly himself, but plays a misguided role? If always truly ourselves, which of us shall scape hanging?" (pp. 7, 8). If we can make this rhetorical move in the realm of fiction, perhaps we can learn to make it in the realm of critical theory and eventually in the realm of social praxis as well.

The rhetoric of which Lanham speaks seems peculiarly different than the traditional view of rhetoric that we have inherited, defined by philosophy and limited to the "forms and mannerisms" of persuasive discourse. The traditional view, Lanham suggests, is in opposition to the actual practice of rhetoric, and this opposition "goes far to explain the two persistently puzzling facts about the history of rhetoric: why it has been so deplored and why it has so endured" (p. 5). Philosophy for centuries has denigrated rhetoric in a fashion similar to the way Europeans have denigrated Africans and men have denigrated women, through critical discourses that have focused on, and reified, *essential* differences. "Such criticism," writes Lanham, "points to differences so fundamental they indicate a wholly different way of looking at the world" (p. 5).

Certainly, this is what contemporary critics in race, gender and language studies are suggesting, and many have focused the reconstruction of rhetoric on articulating afrocentric, female, and non-persuasive linguistic strategies. Arthur Smith (Asante, 1974) suggests that "*Rhetoric as concept is foreign to the traditional African ethos,*" primarily because of its emphasis on persuasion (p. 139). Gearhart (1979), in "The Womanization of Rhetoric," equates rhetoric as persuasion with violence. "My indictment of our discipline of rhetoric springs from my belief that any intent to persuade is an act of violence" (p. 195), she declares. Young, Becker, and Pike (1970) have pointed to the importance of Rogerian rhetoric as an alternative to persuasive discourse, and echo Gearhart's concerns by observing that "users of this strategy deliberately avoid conventional persuasive structures and techniques because these devices tend to produce a sense of threat," which is precisely what users are trying to avoid (p. 275).

In order to understand this concern with persuasion we might begin with the Platonic dialogue *Gorgias.* In this dialogue, Socrates questions Gorgias and his two students. Callicles and Polus, and induces them to admit that rhetoric has to do with persuasion. Using dialectic, the question and answer method of philosophy that emphasizes definition and through which an understanding of *true* reality can be achieved. Socrates questions Gorgias until he admits that rhetoric is "a creator of persuasion." At this point Socrates goes on to argue that rhetoric is, in face, not an art, but a mere set of techniques used to pander to an audience. This argument has shaped definitions or rhetoric from that time forward.

However, it seems unlikely that Gorgias would have defined rhetoric as persuasion when he stated in the *Encomium of Helen* that "persuasion by speech is equivalent to abduction by force" (Freeman, 1977, p. 132). Gorgias, who readily admitted to being a teacher of rhetoric, called into question the Platonic assertion of the primacy of dialectic, and this is the basis of Socrates' attack on rhetoric. Pirsig (1985), in *Zen and the Art of Motorcycle Maintenance,* concurs: "Socrates is not using dialectic to understand rhetoric, he is using it to destroy it, or at least to bring it into disrepute, and so his questions are not real questions at all—they are word traps which Gorgias and his fellow rhetoricians fall into" (p. 333). Pirsig sees the debate between philosophy and rhetoric in terms of the conflict between *classical* and *romantic* reality, and arrives at a conclusion similar to Lanham's: "What you have here is a conflict of *visions of reality*" (p. 49).

Pirsig's character Phaedrus counters the definition of rhetoric as persuasion with the concept of rhetoric as quality, and in his discussion of the "classic-romantic dichotomy" points out the underlying logic that separates the two: "Persons tend to think and feel exclusively in one mode or the other and in doing so tend to misunderstand and underestimate what the other mode is all about. But no one is willing to give up the truth as he sees it." Pirsig's insights touch on the problem of complicity in terms of the agreement to disagree, which points toward the importance of the philosophical definition of rhetoric as persuasion. When viewed as persuasion, rhetoric is used to impart the knowledge of a pre-existent reality, one arrived at through dialectical attenuation and understanding. This is the conceptualization of rhetoric that we have inherited from Aristotle, who defined rhetoric as "the faculty of discovering in the particular case the available means of persuasion," and conceptualized it as "the counterpart of dialectic." It is also the definition of rhetoric articulated in the Platonic dialogue, *Phaedrus.*

The *Phaedrus* initially seems to be a reversal of Socrates's earlier condemnation of rhetoric, but actually it is an explanation of the hierarchical relationship between rhetoric, dialectic, and knowledge. In the *Phaedrus,* Socrates suggests that rhetoric can be an art of persuasion, but only when used by the dialecticians, who alone have an understanding of *true* reality. Socrates equates dialectic with love, and argues that the dialectician understands the true nature of human souls and uses rhetoric accordingly to lead each soul toward the light of truth. The philosopher, who is the consummate dialectician, is the guardian of the knowledge of *true* reality, which is arrived at through the process of definition and which distinguishes things in terms of their natures. This is the underlying logic of essentialist epistemology, or *serious*

reality, and it attempts to free us from rhetoric in the same way that the Socratic charioteer attempts to free us from the dark horse of the soul that would lead us from the singularity of *true* reality.

This dark horse is the same figure of negation that Gates and Whitson explicate, and it is at this juncture that the relationship between rhetoric, race, and gender becomes quite clear. The rhetoric of contemporary race, gender, and literature goes beyond a rhetoric of persuasion—one which reflects a pre-existent reality—and offers the possibility of a *rhetoric of coherence,* one that defines and constructs reality in such a way as to resolve the problem of privileging one position at the expense of another. Coherence allows us to consider seemingly competitive positions as complementary, offers an excellent metaphysical system for a reconceptualization of essence, and emerges in rhetoric in two ways: metaphysically and epistemologically.

Metaphysically, coherence represents the tendency of rhetoric, as Lanham observes (1976), to offer itself as "a coherent counterstatement to 'serious' reality" (p. 6), and, epistemologically, coherence theory provides the foundations of knowing, within which rhetoric can assert itself as a legitimate science of symbolism. Coherence theory synthesizes alternative possibilities by focusing on their shared and mutually dependent foundations, and views all propositions as contingent upon, and thus inseparable from, one another. Coherence theory, which is characterized by an epistemic stance, as Chisolm (1966) observes, posits "a being for whom all truths are evident, but also, that each of us is identical with that being, and therefore with each other" (p. 113). It transcends essentialist conceptualizations of knowing and being by positing that the truth of a given proposition must be measured in terms of its context, i.e, in relation to its assumptive presuppositions and to all of the other propositions with which it is consistent *and* inconsistent.

Coherence theory reconstructs the traditional relationship between rhetoric and philosophy precisely because it points to the underlying complementariness of any ontological or epistemological stance. Philosophy can no longer distinguish or separate itself from rhetoric without reference to the extent to which they are interrelated and contingent upon one another. This reconstruction transforms the debate between rhetoric and philosophy, and, through implication, our conceptualization of the negative difference of race and gender as well. The debate between philosophy and rhetoric has two purposes closely aligned with those that circumscribe antagonisms of race and gender: first, to privilege one position at the expense of the other by constructing an arbitrary distinction between the two; and, second, to reify the first position by using the second to legitimize the first as essentially real. *Real* reality must invent *the inferior other* in order to remain real, in order to survive. This is best achieved by harnessing the power of the word to disempower the word and by articulating in language an argumentative discourse that fails to apply its own principles to itself.

Criticism is that discourse. And to the extent that radical critics, too, engage in critique and assert the existence of essential differences through that critique, they participate in the discourse of negative difference. Therein lies their complicity. Radical criticism cannot escape that complicity as long as it attempts to

> ignore the simple fact that no case can be argued, no proposition stated—however radical in its intent—without falling back on the conceptual resources vested in natural language. And that language is in turn shot through with all the anthropocentric "metaphysical" meanings which determine its very logic and intelligibility. (Norris, 1987, p. 22)

When critics participate in argumentative critical discourse they are grounded in the very epistemological sensibility that they hope to transcend. They are privileged by the theory of knowledge that, ostensibly, they are calling into question.

Radical criticism, seduced by the very epistemic stance that it has called into question, is merely another manifestation of essentialism's articulatory power. This seduction—this re-articulation of the discourse of negative difference—poses an important challenge in terms of radical criticism's ability to articulate a method that transcends the simplistic negativity of merely rejecting the language from which it arises. Radical criticism, in short, must acknowledge its complicity before it can transcend the discourse of negative difference in which it is grounded and recognize that the sociological realities of race, gender, and language are deeply rooted in the common ground of *human* consciousness and its classification and symbol systems.

A reconstruction of the insights of Kress and Hodge (1979) suggests directions for further theory and practice.

> The basic system of classification is itself abstract, and isn't manifest until it is made actual by human agents engaged in social interaction. This abstract character is its source of strength, in that the system itself is never scrutinized, so it is not usually open to criticism's weakness, because it is constantly being subtly renegotiated by individuals who are responding to forces outside the language system. Classification only exists in discourse, and discourse is always at risk. (p. 64)

Rhetoric allows us to call discourse into question, and a rhetoric of coherence will allow us to renegotiate the risks of interaction and perhaps transform our classification systems so that we might emphasize similarity and affirmation.

In constructing a coherent theory of rhetoric, we need to recognize the complicity that is created by negation, both in symbolic and social interaction. As Kress and Hodge observe, "Negatives can create a universe of alternative meanings, which the speaker formally renounces but which exist as a result of his renunciation. His relationship to his meaning is peculiarly ambivalent" (p. 145). As we begin to scrutinize, reconceptualize, and reconstruct out classification system, we will find forces within the language that will formulate a discourse devoid of domination; one which, in its affirmative approach to language, thought, and action, will be both radical and revolutionary. Such an approach to language will enable critics to engage in a rhetoric that actively recognizes and seeks to transcend the illusory black and white divisions of race, gender, and the language of negative difference.

Discussion Questions

1. When considering issues of race, what does McPhail claim is the principal challenge asserted through complicity theory?

2. In McPhail's complicity theory, what does complicity mean?

3. How is essentialism tied to racial and/or cultural identity?

4. Give a recent example of how the "language of negative difference" is used by the media.

5. What does McPhail say is the danger of a "criticism based off of binary oppositions"?

Reading 1.4

BLACK KINESICS

Some Non-Verbal Communication Patterns in the Black Culture

KENNETH R. JOHNSON

Although much research has been written on *verbal* communication patterns of Black People, little research has been directed toward their non-verbal communication patterns. The research of Bailey, Baratz, Dillard, Fasold, Kochman, Labov, Shuy, Stewart, Wolfram and others on the verbal communication patterns of Black people has demonstrated that many Black people speak a variety—or dialect—of English that differs from other varieties of English. The existence of Black dialect or Black English or Nonstandard Negro dialect (it has been given these labels) has been conclusively demonstrated; thus, it can be expected that non-verbal communication patterns in the Black culture, too, differ from those in the dominant culture or other American sub-cultures. Indeed, many of those who have researched verbal patterns (particularly Kochman and Stewart) have commented on this difference. The purpose of this paper is to describe some of these non-verbal communication patterns of Black people and the meanings these patterns convey.

Bailey, Dillard and Stewart have suggested that Black dialect did not evolve from a British or American variety of English, but that it evolved through a pidginization-creolization process. Further, they suggest that its evolution has been influenced by the African languages Black people originally spoke. Turner's monumental study of the dialect of the Gullahs, or Geechies, demonstrated the survival of "Africanisms" in the Gullah dialect. (The Gullahs—or Geechies, as most Black people call them—are a group of Black people who live mainly on the islands off the coast of South Carolina and along the coasts of South Carolina and Northern Georgia and who speak what is clearly a creolized variety of English which, most likely, is the prototype of Black dialect.) Black dialect, however, is much more like standard English (and other varieties of English) than the Gullah dialect. Still, its

From Johnson, K. (1971). Black kinesics: Some nonverbal communication patterns in black culture. In L. Samovar & R. Porter (Eds.), Intercultural communication: A reader (pp. 181-189). Belmont, CA: Wadsworth.

evolution—according to some researchers—has been influenced by the former African languages Black people originally spoke.

The hypothesis that Black dialect has a different base of development from other varieties of American English (even though it is similar to other varieties of American English and it shares many common features) can be extended to non-verbal communication patterns. That is, non-verbal communication patterns in the Black culture that are not commonly exhibited by other Americans possibly have their origins in African non-verbal communication patterns. This does not mean that all non-verbal communication patterns of Black people differ from those of other Americans. As with language patterns, Black people share many non-verbal patterns with other Americans. On the other hand, those unique non-verbal patterns of Black Americans don't necessarily have to be identical to African non-verbal communication patterns in order for them to have an African origin. Years and years of separation of Black Americans from their original African cultures could have produced alterations in these original non-verbal patterns, and separation could have produced entirely new patterns unrelated to African patterns.

Some support for the hypothesis that Black non-verbal communication patterns have an African base can be gained through observing Africans. For example, the non-verbal patterns—specifically, body movement—of a touring dance troupe from a West African country which visits the United States periodically are remarkably similar to those of Black Americans. This dance troupe includes a street scene in its repertoire and except for the props and, to a lesser extent, the costumes, the spirited talk ("lolly-gagging," "jiving," "signifying" and "sounding") accompanied by body movements (especially walking) and gestures is not very different from what can be seen on any busy ghetto street during a hot summer evening. The similarity is too great to be due to chance.

Much research to support this hypothesis needs to be done. The purpose of this paper is not to establish the link between African non-verbal communication patterns and those of Black Americans. Instead, the hypothesis is suggested to provide a possible theoretical base

to explain the differences between Black non-verbal communication patterns described here and the non-verbal communication patterns of other Americans.

A second hypothesis is that the isolation of the Black population from other Americans produced some differences in non-verbal communication patterns within the Black culture. Perhaps research will establish the validity of both hypotheses—that is, non-verbal communication patterns in the Black Culture could be a result of former African patterns and also a result of patterns that have evolved out of the indigenous conditions of Black Americans.

The focus of this paper will be on those non-verbal patterns that have been labeled *Kinesics* by Birdwhistell. Specifically, kinesics refers to how people send messages with their bodies through movement, expressions, gestures, etc. Birdwhistell has pointed out that these non-verbal patterns are a learned form of communication which are patterned within a culture, and that they convey a particular message. Some of these patterns that are unique to the Black population and the messages they convey are described below.

Not every Black person exhibits every feature in his non-verbal behavior. However, these features occur with such great frequency in the Black population that they can be considered patterned behavior. (The same is true of Black dialect features. Not every Black person who speaks Black dialect will have all the features of this dialect in his speech.)

In stress or conflict situations, particularly when one of the participants is in a subordinate position (for example, a conflict situation involving a parent and child or a teacher and student), Black people can express with their eyes an insolent, hostile disapproval of the person who is in the authority role. The movement of the eyes is called "rolling the eyes" in the Black culture.

"Rolling the eyes" is a non-verbal way of expressing impudence and disapproval of the person who is in the authority role and of communicating every negative label that can be applied to the dominant person. The movement of the eyes communicates all or parts of the message. The main message is hostility. The movement of the eyes—rolling the eyes—is performed in the following way. First, the eyes are moved from one side of the eye-socket to the other, in a low arc (usually, the movement of the eyes—that is, the rolling—is preceded by a stare at the other person, but not an eye-to-eye stare). The lids of the eyes are slightly lowered when the eye balls are moved in the low arc. The eye balls always move *away* from the other person. The movement is very quick, and it is often unnoticed by the other person, particularly if the other person is not Black. Sometimes, the eye movement is accompanied by a slight lifting of the head, or a twitching of the nose, or both. Rolling the eyes is more common among Black females than it is among Black males.

This movement of the eyes is different from the movement of the eyes which is called "cutting the eyes" in the dominant culture. In "cutting the eyes" the movement of the eyes is always *toward* another person. Furthermore, after the eyes are focused on the other person (following the cutting) they usually remain focused in a stare. In other words, the stare follows the cutting action.

Black people (particularly females) will often roll their eyes when being reprimanded or "lectured to" about some infraction of a rule. After the person who is in the authority role has continued the lecture for a while, the Black person in the subordinate role (the "receiver" of the lecture) will roll the eyes. Rolling the eyes can also be used to express a kind of general disapproval. For example, if two Black women are together and a third woman enters their social sphere wearing a dress that the other two Black women know costs $5.95 and obviously giving the impression that she not only looks good but that the dress is much more expensive, then one of the two Black women will roll her eyes. In this situation the message communicated is "She sure think she cute but she don't look like nothing, 'cause that dress cost $5.95."

Rolling the eyes is probably partly responsible for the saying used by many Black people: "Don't look at me in that tone of voice." In fact, one of the indications that rolling the eyes is a hostile impudent non-verbal message is that when it is done the Black person in the authority role will stop lecturing and say, "Don't you roll your eyes at me!" (The implied meaning of this command is, "I know what you're thinking and I know the names you're calling me.")

Sometimes, this command is punctuated by a slap "up-side the head."

Often, white teachers (who are in an authority role and who have contact with Black children) will miss the message communicated by Black children when they roll their eyes. It's just as well, because rolling the eyes gives the Black child an opportunity to non-verbally release his hostility and endure the reprimand with a minimum amount of conflict. Black teachers, on the other hand, usually recognize the action and properly interpret the message. As mentioned before, this sometimes causes them to punish the child, thus escalating the conflict and worsening the situation.

It is not known whether or not rolling the eyes is a non-verbal pattern in Western African cultures. It would be interesting and also a test of the hypothesis presented above if this could be determined.

Another eye behavior used by many Black Americans is found in many West African cultures. I am referring to the "reluctance" of Black Americans to look another person (particularly, another person in an authority role) directly in the eye.

Thus, the stereotyped view of many whites (particularly in the South) has some truth. That is, many Blacks (especially Black males) don't look another person in the eye, if the other person is in an authority role. To look another person in the eye (in the context of the dominant culture) is a non-verbal way of communicating trustworthiness, forthrightness, masculinity, truthfulness, sincerity, etc. In the Black cultural context, avoiding eye contact is a non-verbal way of communicating a recognition of the authority-subordinate relationship of the participants in a social situation.

Many Black children are taught not to look another person (particularly older persons) in the eye when the older person is talking to the younger person. To do so is to communicate disrespect.

In the South Black males were taught—either overtly or covertly—not to look a white male in the eye because this communicated equality. Thus, not to look white males in the eye was really a survival pattern in the South.

Note how "culture clash" can occur because of the avoidance of eye contact: in the dominant culture, eye contact is interpreted one way, while it is interpreted in another way within the Black culture. Avoidance of eye contact by a Black person communicates, "I am in a subordinate role and I respect your authority over me," while the dominant cultural member may interpret avoidance of eye contact as, "Here is a shifty unreliable person I'm dealing with."

Avoiding eye contact to communicate respect and acknowledgement of one's being in a subordinate role is a common pattern in Western Africa. (This pattern is also found in other cultures for example, in the Japanese culture.) It could well be that this particular pattern within the Black culture has its origins in former African cultures of Black Americans.

Reinforcing the avoidance of eye contact is a stance that young Blacks take in a conflict situation (this stance sometimes is taken by adult Blacks, too). Often, in a conflict situation Black youngsters (particularly, males) will slowly begin to take a limp stance as the reprimand from the person in the authority role goes on and on. The stance is as follows: the head is lowered, the body becomes extremely relaxed and the Black person stands almost as if he is in a trance. The stance is not taken immediately, but slowly evolves as the reprimand proceeds.

Young white males usually stand very rigid, with their legs spread and their arms extended stiffly down the sides of their bodies (fists balled up) as the reprimand is delivered.

The limp stance is a defense mechanism which non-verbally communicates: "I am no longer a person receiving your message of reprimand; I am only an object." Or, it communicates: "My body is present, but my mind is completely removed from the present encounter." In any case, when a Black person adopts this stance in a conflict situation, the best thing to do is to terminate the reprimand—the Black person is not receiving the message. The person in the authority role—the person delivering the reprimand—can be sure whether or not this is the non-verbal message if he notices the way the Black person walks away from him after the reprimand.

Before describing the walk away from a conflict situation, it is necessary to describe the "Black walk." It communicates non-verbal messages in other situations besides conflicts.

Young Black males have their own way of walking. Observing young Black males walking down ghetto streets, one can't help noticing that they are, indeed, in Thoreau's words "marching to the tune of a different drummer." The "different drummer" is a different culture; the non-verbal message of their walk is *similar* to the non-verbal message of young white males, but not quite the same.

The young white males' walk is usually brisk, and they walk on the balls of their feet with strides of presumed authority. Both arms swing while they walk. The non-verbal message is: "I am a strong man, possessing all the qualities of masculinity, and I stride through the world with masculine authority."

The young Black males' walk is different. First of all, it's much slower—it's more of a stroll. The head is sometimes slightly elevated and casually tipped to the side. Only one arm swing at the side with the hand slightly cupped. The other arm hangs limply to the side or it is tucked in the pocket. The gait is slow, casual and rhythmic. The gait is almost like a walking dance, with all parts of the body moving in rhythmic harmony. This walk is called "pimp strut," or it is referred to as "walking that walk."

The walk of young Black males communicates the same non-verbal message as that of young white males. In addition, the Black walk communicates that the young Black male is beautiful, and it beckons female attention to the sexual prowess possessed by the walker. Finally, the Black walk communicates that the walker is "cool"; in other words, he is not upset or bothered by the cares of the world and is, in fact, somewhat disdainful and insolent towards the world.

The young Black male walk must be learned, and it is usually learned at quite a young age. Black males of elementary school age can often be seen practicing the walk. By the time they reach junior high school age, the Black walk has been mastered.

The description of the walk is a general description, and it includes all the components that can be present in the walk. All the components are not always present in each individual's walk, because each individual must impose a certain amount of originality onto the general pattern. Thus, some young Black males will vary the speed or swing of the head or effect a slight limp or alter any one or a number of the components of the Black walk at achieve originality. The general "plan" of the walk, however, is recognizable even with the imposed originality. This imposed originality also communicates the individualism of each young Black male.

The Black walk is used for mobility (as any walk is) and to arrive at a destination. Sometimes, however, one gets the feeling that *where* the young Black male is going is not as important as *how* he gets there. There is a great deal of "styling" in the walk. The means are more important than the end.

The walk is also used as a hostile rejection of another person in a conflict situation. For example, after a person in authority role has reprimanded a young Black male, the person with authority can tell whether his reprimand has had positive effects (e.g., the young Black male follows the dictates of the reprimand, he is sorry for the offense, etc.) by the way the young Black male walks away from the authority figure. If the young Black male walks away in a "natural" manner, then the reprimand was received positively; if he walks away with a "pimp strut" it means that the young Black male has rejected the reprimand and in fact is non-verbally telling the authority person to "go to hell."

Young Black females communicate the same non-verbal message when walking away from a person in an authority role after a conflict situation by pivoting quickly on both feet (something like the military "about face") and then walking briskly away. Sometimes the pivot is accompanied by a raising of the head and a twitching of the nose.

When either the young Black male or the young Black female walks away from the authority person in the above manners, the knowledgeable authority person (particularly if he or she is Black) will angrily tell the young Black person to "come back here and walk away right." To walk away "right" means to walk away without communicating the negative, disrespectful, insolent message. This is proof that these walks are sending a message.

The Black walk is reflected in the stance young Black males take while talking in a group. For example, when talking in a group, the participants (say, four or five young Black males) will often adopt a kind of stationary "pimp strut." This means that while the young Black males are talking, they stand with their hands half-way in their pockets, and they move in the rhythmic, fluid dance-type way (without actually walking) to punctuate their remarks. The arm that is free will swing, point, turn and gesture as conversation proceeds. It's almost as if they are walking "in place." This kind of behavior always accompanies a light or humorous conversation, or a conversation about masculine exploits. It never accompanies a serious discussion about more general topics (planing something, difficulties with parents, political issues, etc. However, if these kinds of topics are discussed in terms of the young Blacks' masculinity or if they are "styling" while discussing these topics, the stationary "pimp strut" stance *will* be taken).

Often, when this stance is taken, *how* one says something—the style—is more important than *what* one says.

Another interesting thing that happens when a group of young Black males talk in a group is that the periphery of the group continually fluctuates. That is, the group moves in and out toward and from the center. (Young white males, when they are talking in a group, usually maintain a tight circle during the discussion.) When something particularly interesting or funny is said (if the statement reflects a use of language that is unique, creative and "styled") one or more of the participants will turn his back to the center of the group and walk away— almost dance away—with great animation to non-verbally communicate his confirmation of what has been said and his recognition of the creative way in which it was said. In other words, when young Black males are discussing a "light" or humorous topic, the observer can expect a great deal of movement and fluctuation in the periphery of the circle of discussants.

Another non-verbal behavioral pattern easily noticed in Black male group discussion is the way males punctuate laughter. Often, when something especially funny is said by a Black, the audience (either one or more other Blacks who are in the audience or group) will raise a cupped hand to the mouth and laugh. The hand is not actually placed over the mouth; instead, it is held about six inches away from the mouth as if to muffle the laugh. Sometimes this action is accompanied by a backward shuffle. This action—the cupped hand in front of the mouth—is common among West Africans. The non-verbal message is that the audience has acknowledged the particularly witty statement of the speaker.

The above description of Black group discussion always applies to a topic being discussed that is not serious. When a serious topic is being discussed, these behavioral patterns are not present in the group's behavior. Thus, we know that the topic is light when the group is "jiving" or "styling" or just playing verbal games. (Blacks play a verbal game of using language in a unique, creative, humorous way for the purpose of seeing how they can "mess up" the English language for comical effects.)

The Black walk is also carried over into the "rapping stance" of young Black males. A "rapping stance" is the stance a young Black male takes when talking romantically to a young Black female. (The word "rap" originally referred only to romantic talk to a female. When it was adopted by the young white population, the word took on an added meaning, to refer to any kind of aggressive talk on any topic.) The "rapping stance" of young Black males is a kind of stationary "pimp strut." When young Black males are talking romantically to young Black females—particularly when they are making the initial "hit," or when they are making the initial romantic overtures to a Black female that preludes a romantic relationship—they stand a certain way that non-verbally communicates: "Look at me. I am somebody you can really "dig" because I am beautiful and I am about to lay my 'heavy rap' on you and you can't resist it. Now listen to my 'rap' and respond."

The "rapping stance" is as follows: first, the Black male does not stand directly in front of the Black female but at a slight angle; the head is slightly elevated and tipped to the side (toward the female); the eyes are about three-fourths open; sometimes, the head very slowly nods as the "rap" is delivered; the arms conform to the "pimp strut" pattern—one hand may be half-way in the pocket, while the other arm hangs free; finally, the weight of the body is concentrated on the back heel (in the "rapping stance" the feet are not together but are positioned in a kind of frozen step). The Black female will listen to this "rap" nonchalantly with one hand on her hip.

The young white male "rapping stance" is different: the female is backed up against the wall, white the young white male extends one arm, extends the fingers and places his palm against the wall to support himself as he leans toward the female with all his weight placed on the foot that is closest to the female. Sometimes, both arms are extended to support his weight, thus trapping the female between his two extended arms.

It has been pointed out that Black males often turn their backs to another participant in a communication situation. This action always communicates a very friendly intimate message. This action—turning one's back to another—can be observed when Black males greet each other. One of the most friendly greetings that can be given to another Black is to walk up to him and verbally greet him with a warm statement (often, this verbal statement is delivered in a falsetto voice, the friendly level or "game" level) and then, after the verbal greeting is delivered, one (or both) of the participants will turn his back to the other and walk away for a few steps. This is probably the friendliest greeting Black males can give to each other. The non-verbal message is probably: "Look, I trust you so much that I unhesitatingly place myself in a vulnerable position in greeting you."

Another pattern that is common when Black males greet each other is for one to approach the other person, verbally greet him, and then stand during the initial stages of the greeting with the one hand cupped over the genitals. This stance is sometimes maintained throughout the subsequent conversation, particularly if the subsequent conversation pertains to sexual exploits or some kind of behavior which is particularly masculine.

This stance—the cupped hand over the genitals—can even be observed, sometimes, when the young Black male is in his "rapping stance." The non-verbal message here is not clear; perhaps, the young Black male is communicating non-verbally that he is so sexually potent that he must subdue or "rein in" his sexual potential.

The action of turning one's back on another person in a group discussion or greeting always non-verbally communicates trust or friendliness. It also non-verbally communicates confirmation of what another Black has stated. For example, when one Black makes a statement that another Black particularly confirms, the Black who wants to non-verbally communicate his confirmation will turn his back to the other. Often, this action is preceded by a "slap" handshake—that is, both Blacks will execute the "soul" handshake that consists of one Black holding his palm in an upward position while the other Black slaps the palm with his own, usually in a vigorous manner.

Turning the back can often be seen in a Black audience. When listening to a speaker (a preacher, teacher, etc.) members of the Black audience will often shift their positions in their seats to slightly turn their backs to the speaker to non-verbally communicate confirmation and agreement with the speaker's remarks (before this action, members of the Black audience will slightly bend forward in their seats to non-verbally communicate that they are concerned about or perhaps not quite sure of what the speaker is saying. At that moment when they understand what the speaker is saying or they agree with the speaker, they will shift in their seats to slightly expose their backs).

It was indicated that when listening to a "rap" of a Black male a Black female will often stand with one hand on her hip. Whenever a Black female places one hand on her hip, it non-verbally communicates an intense involvement with or concern about the situation. But the hand-on-hip stance non-verbally communicates a more specific meaning in other communication situations: it usually communicates intense aggression, anger, disgust or other hostile negative feelings toward the speaker.

In a conflict situation, or when a Black female delivers a hostile verbal message, the verbal message is often accompanied by the hand-on-hip stance. This is the most aggressive stance that Black females take, and it is executed in the following manner: first, the feet are placed firmly in a stationary step, with the body weight concentrated on the heel of the rear foot; the buttocks are protruded; and, one hand is placed on the extended hip (the hip is extended because of the weight concentration on the rear foot and the protrusion of the buttocks); the hand either rests on the hip supported by the fingers being spread, or it is supported by making the hand into a fist and resting the knuckles against the hip. Sometimes, the body of the Black female will slowly rock to and fro during the stance, particularly while she is listening to the other person. If the stance is not taken while the Black female is listening, it is quickly taken when she delivers her hostile verbal message. The stance can also be accompanied by a rolling of the eyes and a twitching of the nose to further punctuate the hostility of the Black female. (Flip Wilson, in his Geraldine characterization, often assumes this stance. In fact, Flip Wilson is a very good illustrator of Black female non-verbal aggressive behavior because the behavior is distorted for comical effects and easily noticed.)

Most Black people know to "cool it" when Black women take this stance. The non-verbal message communicated when a Black female takes this stance is: "I'm really mad, now. You better quit messing with me." (Chicano females often stand with both hands on their hips with their feet spread wide and their heads slightly raised to non-verbally communicate a similar message.)

The non-verbal behavior described in this paper provides some illustrations of the non-verbal communication patterns of Black people that are different from those of white people and other cultural groups in this country. *Why* they are different is a question that must be answered by research. The purpose here, again, has not been to explain the *why,* but to describe some of these patterns that are different. Hypotheses were presented to provide a basis on which this research can be conducted.

It is important (particularly, for people who work with Blacks—school teachers, social workers, industry personnel) to recognize these patterns and the messages they convey because it helps one to better understand the communications of Black people. In some ways, non-verbal communication patterns are more important than verbal communication patterns because they are often unconscious—a person cannot easily hide his true feelings when this is the case. The importance of non-verbal communication is indicated in the adage: "Your actions speak so loudly, I can hardly hear what you say."

DISCUSSION QUESTIONS

1. What is kinesics?

2. In what ways are kinesic behaviors of Blacks culturally particular?

3. Johnson suggests that Black women "roll their eyes" to show disapproval. Can you identify other kinesic behaviors specific to Black women?

4. Being that this article was written in 1971, do you think that deferential kinesic behaviors, such as Black children not looking at elders in the eye, still exist or would you say such examples are passé?

5. According to Johnson, how does Flip Wilson's variety show character Geraldine exemplify Black kinesics?

Reading 1.5

IMPROVISATION AS A PERFORMANCE STRATEGY FOR AFRICAN-BASED THEATRE

JONI L. JONES

African-American theatre has, for the most part, imitated dramaturgical models offered by commercially successful European-American theatre. In doing so. African-American theatre has nurtured a specific set of theatrical traditions at the expense of African-based traditions. The fact that many contemporary African-American playwrights use linear plot construction and proscenium production techniques, devices that are not well represented among indigenous African performance practices, suggests that African-American theatre might be reinvigorated by an infusion of African aesthetics. Ultimately, an immersion in African performance practices could yield the formation of a decidedly new theatrical aesthetic, one that borrows, reshapes, and discards various cultural practices, in order to create a more uniquely African-American dramaturgy. The ground-breaking work of Pearl Primus and Katherine Dunham in dance pushed African-American dance specifically, and American dance in general, toward what is now an African-American dance aesthetic. Similarly, in music, the stretching of jazz into bop by Thelonious Monk, Miles Davis, and Charlie Parker established a recognizable African-American musical idiom. African-American theatre artists who actively used African-based aesthetics can help in creating theatre traditions as original as those in dance and music. In this essay, I explore improvisation as a performance strategy based in Yoruba practices and developed as an African-American aesthetic in two productions. In a final section, I specify unresolved tensions and offer directions for continued exploration that emerged in developing improvisation as African-based performance.

African-American theatre scholars and practitioners have been interested in African-based dramaturgy at least since the Black Arts Movement of the 1970s when directors such as Barbara Ann Teer, Robert Macbeth, and Paul Carter Harrison consciously examined African

From Jones, J. L. (1993). Improvisation as a performance strategy for African-based theatre. *Text & Performance Quarterly, 13*(3), 233-251.

performance as a way of developing an African-based theatrical aesthetic for African-Americans. Each of these directors developed her or his own unique brand of African-based theatre. Teer and Macbeth created unscripted theatricalized rituals while Harrison retained linear plot construction within an African participatory and communal frame. In order to begin the process of offering African-American playwrights dramaturgical alternatives to Scribean-based dramaturgy with its single author, scripted linear plot construction and throughline of action, land its separation of participants into actors and audience, I examined the performance practices of the Yoruba of Southwestern Nigeria and incorporated the salient features of those practices into two productions.

THREE YORUBA PERFORMANCE PRACTICES

To understand the complexities of Yoruba performance, I studied a variety of Yoruba performance practices using the schema offered by Yemi Ogunbiyi (10–11). Ogunbiyi divides traditional Yoruba performance into three categories: Dramatic Ritual, The Popular Tradition, and The Yoruba Travelling Theatre. Ogunbiyi's work challenges John Pepper Clark's (58) classification of Yoruba performance by suggesting that Clark has created an unworkable dichotomy when he distinguishes "traditional," meaning nontext-based performance, from "modern," meaning scripted performance. Such a classification system leaves the important nontext-based yet contemporary work of Hubert Ogunde and Duro Ladipo straddling two categories. Ogunbiyi has addressed this problem by placing Yoruba performance on a continuum that moves from the non-scripted religious performance of Dramatic Ritual to the scenario-based secular performance of the Yoruba Travelling Theatre with The Popular Tradition existing between these two categories.

Within Ogunbiyi's classification, I examined *Egungun* masquerades as Dramatic Ritual, *Apidan* Theatre as The Popular Tradition, and Ogunde Theatre as The Yoruba Travelling

Theatre. The *Egungun* masquerades are communal ceremonies for honoring ancestors. The general structure of an *Egungun* masquerade, or festival as they are also known, varies widely from one Yoruba town to another; however, most of the masquerades include community preparations, a processional, dancing drumming, singing *oriki* or praise poems, prayers, and the offering of gifts and feasting.[1] Dance is the central activity of an *Egungun* masquerade, and it is the richly costumed *Egungun* dance that Robert Farris Thompson calls "African art in motion" (224). The spirit-possessed dancers may rid the community of accumulated evil, bring blessings to each house in the compound, or accept gifts from the ancestor's children in this ceremony designed to maintain peace between the ancestors and the living.

The *Apidan* Theatre developed from the *Egungun* masquerades as one classification of *Egungun* dances. In the seventeenth century the *Apidan* separated from the religious *Egungun* to become a professional company of court, then public, performers.[2] *Apidan* performances included a processional, salutes and pledges to deities and natural forces, tragic and comedic sketches, drumming, singing, dancing, and a recessional. During the improvised sketches, which serve as the core of an *Apidan* performance, the performer may transform himself into an animal, imitate members of the society, or illustrate a situation. Here, the use of the male pronoun is deliberate as women were members of the singing chorus but not dancers performing sketches. Both the *Egungun* masquerades and the *Apidan* theatre are performed outdoors in a circular performance area.

Ogunde Theatre was begun in 1944 by Hubert Ogunde when he left the Nigerian Police Force to produce and direct his first theatrical production.[3] Of the three types of performance practices examined in this research. Ogunde theatre is the most Westernized in its dramaturgy and staging. While an Ogunde production would include indigenous Yoruba performance practices such as an efficacious intent, a processional, a recessional, drumming, song, dance, and praise songs to ancestors, deities, or natural forces, Ogunde also included a drama with a throughline of action based on the Scribean model with exposition, rising action, crisis, climax, and denouement. The dramas were most often based on critical political issues of the day and, though scripted, were advanced through improvisation among company members and with commentary from participant observers. Ogunde performances were frequently indoors, and, as proscenium staging was typically used, there was a separation between the performers and the participant observers.

After comparing the characteristics of performances in each category, I identified nine essential commonalities that constitute a Yoruba-based performance: sketch, seriation, improvisation, monologue with choral support, the Black vernacular, simultaneity, efficacy, the fusion of dance/music/*nommo,*[4] and the active involvement of the participant observers, or audience in Western terminology.[5] A feature of Yoruba performance that provides ample resonance with African-American life is improvisation.

Improvisation Among
African-Americans and the Yoruba

Improvisation is a fundamental survival strategy and artistic technique for African Americans. In a society which systematically bars African Americans from hegemonic positions of power and constrains the development of an African-American cultural and political reality, learning to improvise in a hostile environment over which one has little control becomes a survival tool of the highest order. This maneuverability, which helps African Americans endure the devastation of dislocation and thwart the continued colonization of our minds, is the basis for African-American verbal artistry and musical traditions.

Margaret Thompson Drewal argues that improvisation among African Americans is a formal manifestation of the African tradition of play. For Drewal, play refers to "a whole gamut of spontaneous individual moves" (18) and is not to be confused with Western connotations of play which include frivolous and unimportant activity. Similarly, Henry Louis Gates, Jr. notes the importance of "signifying," a form of improvisation, to African Americans when he

writes: "Signifyin(g) is so fundamentally black, that is, it is such familiar rhetorical practice, that one encounters the great resistance of inertia when writing about it. By inertia I am thinking here of the difficulty of rendering the implications of a concept that is so shared in one's culture as to have long ago become second nature to its users" (64). Improvisation in church services is seen as African-Americans might testify to the greatness of God in spontaneous speeches, participate in the call-and-response of a sermon, or offer a happy-dance, demonstrating their union with the Holy Spirit.[6] Improvisation in African-American music is best known in jazz. In discussing the signifying tradition in African-American literature, Gates repeatedly uses jazz references. He describes the ways in which one artist offers a revision of another's composition. This sort of signifying, or improvisation, can also be seen in rap compositions, like those of Kool Moe Dee when he incorporates James Brown's music into his own.

Improvisation is connected to an African sense of time which gives primacy to now. What is occurring in the present takes precedence over future events which do not exist on the conscious plane. The activity in which one is engaged governs time, rather than time governing the activity. John S. M'biti describes how the flow of African life is centered on what is occurring rather than on when it occurs when he writes that "time is meaningful at the point of the event and not at the mathematical moment (19)." Similarly, Dorothy Pennington says that for Africans, "the event is the essence" (131). Improvisation is the performance mode best suited to this world view because it privileges the experience of now, allowing the performers to imaginatively embellish the moment with their *iwa,* or personal life force. Through spirit-possession and improvisation Yoruba performance is created. In an *Egungun* masquerade, the performers are usually spirit-possessed, receiving their impulses from deities or ancestors. The performers in *Apidan* sketches and Ogunde productions use improvisation. Because improvisation occurs when the performer spontaneously allows her or his *iwa* to come forth, I place spirit-possession and improvisation on a continuum of spontaneously derived performance.

Using the performance practices of the Yoruba as a foundation, I fashioned a dramaturgical/performance paradigm that relied heavily on improvisation in the development of a production. Although the focus of this article will be on the use of improvisation in that production, it is important to note that improvisation is intimately related to other features of Yoruba-based drama, notably efficacy and the active involvement of the participant observers.

Efficacious performance need not be thought of in baldly educational terms, but should include increasing the spirit of a community, replenishing the community's *ase,* or life force, Richard Schechner places efficacy and entertainment on a continuum which acknowledges that performance may be more heavily weighted at one pole and still display elements from the other pole. In Schechner's, usage, efficacy is associated with collective creativity, which resonates with both the improvisational and participatory elements of Yoruba performance practices. Victor Turner addressed the issue of efficacy in his discussion of social dramas which attempt to redress a breach that has been committed in the society. The idea of breach works especially well with *Egungun* masquerades because they occur after the death of a member of the society. Death, for Turner, is a "life-crisis ritual" that constitutes a breach that must be redressed (11). In my productions, I chose to begin healing the wounds that exist between African-American men and women. African-American women and men have barriers between them that prevent the development of healthy interpersonal relationships. This breach is the result of a history plagued by racism and economic oppression. The pain between the groups was made glaringly apparent with the recent publication of incendiary works like Shahrazad Ali's *The Black Man's Guide to Understanding the Black Woman* and the media histrionics surrounding the Anita Hill-Clarence Thomas hearings.[7] The healing I sought to stimulate was akin to Turner's redressive stage in that the rift between African-American men and women was the breach that needed healing through performance. Performance as healing is an essential feature of the African-based productions with

which I have worked: the healing is the way in which such performances achieve efficacy.

Improvisation as practiced by the Yoruba and in the African-American contexts cited allows for the active involvement of the participant observers. Yoruba theatre scholar Ovin Ogunba refers to this involvement as the "imaginative collaboration" (22) of the participant observers. The participant observers are as important to a Yoruba performance as they are to a performance orchestrated by Augusto Boal. Boal's directorial intent is congruent with my own: we both seek to create a people's theatre that empowers all the participants by offering them an opportunity to actively explore their own solutions to social problems. In this way, performance can begin to heal the wounds of a community by allowing all present to physically participate in the examination of those wounds.

Kenyan writer and director Ngugi wa Thiong'o created his own theatre which was founded on a philosophy similar to Boal's. Wa Thiong'o included the participant observers in every stage of his theatre's development from rehearsals, to performance, to post-production discussions. His productions were collaboratively generated between the participant observers and the performers in much the same way that Boal's improvised scenarios require the participant observers to continually offer alterations to the progression of the performance. Guided by the work of the Yoruba, Boal, and wa Thiong'o, I designed two productions to explore the effectiveness of improvisation in public performances and the usefulness of improvisation for the development of an African-American theatrical aesthetic.

A Test of Yoruba-Based Dramatic Structure: "The University Show"

As a way of refining my understanding and usage of the Yoruba-based dramatic structure, I first tested the improvisation structure with graduate student performers enrolled in the course Styles of African and African-American Performance at the University of Texas at Austin.[8] Six of the performers were European Americans and one was Puerto Rican. The intended participant observers were predominantly European-American students and staff and faculty from the Department of Speech Communication and the Department of Theatre and Dance. "The University Show" was presented on March 9, 1992, in the atrium of the Theatre and Dance building. The participant observers were seated or standing in a wide semi-circle around the performance space with the company member guitarist at the apex of the circle. Several participant observers walked around throughout the performance, and some stopped only momentarily en route to classes or offices. The performers presented a series of randomly chosen sketches connected by chanted seques. This particular performance happened to end with "Free Sketches," which consisted of three improvisations suggested by the participant observers.

Improvisation in the "Free Sketches" was used to actively involve the participant observers in the creation of the performance and to serve the efficacious aims of Yoruba-based performance by allowing the participant observers to grapple with their own issues. For the Yoruba, traditional performance is not solely for entertainment but also carries spiritual and educational value as *well*. In general terms, performance is designed to replenish the community *ase* through gathering and sharing. Performance can more specifically engender harmony with ancestors as with the *Egungun* masquerade, or it can arouse public dissent about political issues as in Ogunde Theatre. A way to increase a community's life force is to help that community address painful issues and to stimulate healing the wounds those issues expose. The simple coming together in a performance event can begin a healing that the sketches themselves can deepen with provocative ideas and circumstances. Unlike the Yoruban for whom improvisation is culturally ingrained, the participant observers with whom I worked had to be encouraged, even prodded, into their role as co-creators. This cultural difference meant that I could not rely solely on the Yoruba's brand of improvisation in which participant observers—without instruction—directed, joined, or critiqued the performance. In our effort to accommodate the needs of participant observers more accustomed to a

separation between performers and "audience," I modified Boal's "Joker" techniques.

Boal uses the "Joker" as a narrator or commentator who analyzes the action and even joins it if doing so will help to wring more options from the scene. I first gave the graduate students objectives to fulfill and circumstances under which to operate. We began with two-person scenarios that could include more characters as the scenario progressed. A third student served as the "Joker," or director, who explained the scenario at its beginning and interrupted the action either when she or he felt the scene was not probing the complexities of the issue at hand or when the participant observers had recommendations about the direction of the scene. But unlike Boal's "Joker," the director in "The University Show" did not join the action. This choice left the director free to attend simultaneously to the action of the scene and to the responses of the participant observers. In performance, two undergraduate students solicited possible scenarios from the participant observers during a pre-performance "feast" of snacks contributed by the participant observers in lieu of an admission charge. These students gave me the scenarios they had gathered and I determined which ones might be the most stimulating for this diverse group of participant observers.

In one of the three scenarios performed, an African-American woman (Character I) told her European-American roommate (Character II) that the roommate's boyfriend (Character III) had hurled a racial epithet at her the previous night. A European-American woman played Character I, a Puerto Rican woman played Character II, and a European-American man played Character III. When the situation for the scenario was announced, the involvement among the participant observers increased. Some nudged one another, some laughed, and others gave that long "oo" sound that is the recognition that something risky is about to take place. Two African-American male students were sitting close to the scene and talked with one another throughout this improvisation. Although their involvement with one another increased, they did not overtly contribute to the development of the scene. The director stopped the scene to ask for suggestions, yet these two obviously engaged participant observers did not share their ideas. Several other participant observers, mostly the handful of African-Americans in attendance, suggested that Character I be more aggressive in her confrontation with her roommate. Someone suggested that the boyfriend be added to the scene, and the director granted this request. The director chose one of the performers to play the boyfriend and the scene continued with three characters. After the production, the director of this scenario said she wanted to directly ask the two excited African-American students to share what they were saying, but she was worried that doing so would violate their privacy, and perhaps bring attention to another set of tensions not specifically connected to the scenario. She did not feel she knew the men well enough to single them out. In addition, she was concerned about making them token representatives of African Americans and she did not know an effective strategy for bringing them into the scene. Not only were we were all stumbling through the formation of the most effective rules for this highly interactive style of improvisation, but we were also made aware of the differences between Yoruba aesthetics (where participation in the communal event of performance can be assumed) and the separation, relative passivity, and privacy norms of European-American audience aesthetics.

In fact, all three directors of the improvised scenarios had the option of adding participant observers to the scene, but none of them made use of this option. These participant observers did not know that it was permissible to join the performance so the directors had to make this possibility clear. The participant observers have to be taught their role in a way that the Yoruba do not. Adding participant observers to the performance encourages them to actualize the solutions they are offering, thereby solidifying their role as participants and intensifying their commitment to their suggestions and the goals of healing. Yoruba aesthetics assume that wounds heal best through living the solution in performance, not only through suggesting solutions to others.

In written critiques of "The University Show," the graduate students described their frustrations with improvisation in the "Free Sketches." Some of those frustrations were born of their own immediate work with the process, and other frustrations were generated from the participant observers' feedback. The performers' criticisms of the improvisations focused on clarifying the role of the director, giving some general shape to the structure of the improvisations, and allowing more rehearsal time for the performers to develop the skills necessary to engage in effective improvisation. One of the graduate student performers suggested that a production with this seriate sketch structure should always end with "Free Sketches" rather than having "Free Sketches" be one of the randomly chosen sketch options. In this way, the production ends with a maximum amount of involvement from participant observers, reinforcing their role a co-creators and underscoring the sense of healing that can occur as they examine their own choices through improvisation.

WILD WOMEN AND ROLLING STONES: YORUBA-BASED DRAMATURGY IN AN AFRICAN-AMERICAN CONTEXT

With these ideas in mind I began rehearsals for *Wild Women and Rolling Stones,* a production which further explored Yoruba-based dramatic structure and techniques for improvisation developed in "The University Show." *Wild Women and Rolling Stones* was also intended to begin healing interpersonal wounds between African-American women and men. Five African-American women and five African-American men comprised the core company; an African-American drummer and an African-American percussionist provided a rhythmic foundation for the production. *Wild Women and Rolling Stones* was performed in a gymnasium in East Austin, a predominantly African-American part of Austin, Texas. Food was contributed as admission and a local African dance company performed before and after the production. The jump ball circle in the center of the gymnasium floor served as the performance space. Most participant observers sat in chairs or on the floor in a semi-circle around the performance while others stood or walked about. Drumming accompanied much of the performance. Thus, the entire context was an important way to help the participant observers understand their relationship to the African-based production. The participant observers, who were coming to an event that was billed as a "play," were encouraged to adjust their expectations and their behavior to this different theatrical event.

Wild Women and Rolling Stones consisted of five scripted seriate sketches that closed with the improvised "Free Sketches," as recommended by the graduate student performers from "The University Show." The scripted sketches were either created during rehearsals from extended improvisations or used improvisation in performance to display an individual's *iwa* (personal power).

The sketch entitled "Boy Meets Girl" grew out of improvisations during rehearsals. For this sketch, the company engaged in an extended improvisation as five-year-old playmates. Children's songs were played on a tape recorder and the company was placed in cross-gender pairs. For approximately twenty minutes, each pair created a relationship as they shared or fought over toys, sang songs, told lies, hit, cried, hid, teased, flirted, or sulked. Performers were then told that they were teenagers at a high school dance, and contemporary popular music was played. They had to maintain their same cross-gender partner and sustain the character they had begun to develop. The pairs found all manner of stories to live, including one in which a girl threatened to shoot a boy for talking about her mother. This improvisation lasted approximately fifteen minutes. At a separate rehearsal, one of the graduate students in "The University Show" and the dramaturg for the production, taught the company traditional Puerto Rican dances. For an hour, the company vigorously danced to Puerto Rican rhythms and embellished the steps to suit their own style. Through these improvisations they came to develop personalities, dances, and fragments of dialogue that were later used in the performance of "Boy Meets Girl."

Although the improvised work in "Boy Meets Girl" served the performance well, this type of improvisation was only minimal preparation for the completely improvised "Free Sketches" that had generated so much confusion

and concern in "The University Show." To prepare for the performance of "Free Sketches," I selected a company member and gave her or him a scenario dealing with relationships between African-American women and men. The company was told that as directors they were to explore options for examining the stated issue of the scenario, and as performers they had to follow the suggestions of the director. There was much discussion about how best to incorporate participant observers in the improvisation and how to initiate the scene. We decided that regardless of the number of suggestions made by participant observers, the director could choose those the performers would bring to life. One company member developed an effective method in rehearsals of quickly naming the various suggestions offered by the participant observers and then telling the performers they could choose whichever ones they liked. This technique gave the performers some flexibility and allowed the directors to share control.

The rapport the director established with the participant observers had a critical impact on the amount and quality of the comments they would receive. One director tended to speak very slowly when describing the issue to performers and would take suggestions from all of the participant observers who had comments. This strategy slowed the pace of the "Free Sketch;" hence, I instructed the directors to describe the scenario succinctly and apologize for only recognizing a few of the participant observers. Another director gave the performers detailed psychological realities complete with motivations and past histories. This technique was pared down to simple statements so that performers were able to carry out the suggestions in their own ways. Yet another director unintentionally chided the participant observers with comments like, "Oh, come on, you can do better than that," or "No, I don't want that idea." This director was told to thank each participant observer for her or his comment and to move on without evaluating the responses.

We decided that it was best not to directly reject any suggestion, but that it would be helpful to remind the participant observers that the intention of the performance was to begin healing relationships, not to win power struggles.

The director also had to be sensitive to the restlessness of the participant observers and the pace of the scene; these signals would help the director determine when it was time to interrupt the scene to solicit suggestions or to add a new character. The director would start the scene with the command "begin," and would interrupt with the command "pause." After stopping the scene to receive ideas, the director would resume the scene with the command "begin." The director determined when she or he felt the issue had been sufficiently examined. At this point, the director, would command "end," and all the performers in the scene, the director, and all the participant observers who had offered any comments would gather in the center of the performance space to embrace. It was important that the participant observer who had created the scenario be recognized and included in this closing embrace. This closing was a direct result of the discomfort the graduate students felt in preparing the "Free Sketches" for "The University Show." After sharing so much of themselves in performance, the graduate students wanted a way to show appreciation to all those who participated and a way to psychically move out of the characters they had inhabited and back into themselves. The closing hug was yet another way of making the participant observers co-owners of the production.

On each night of performance, I selected three company members to serve as directors. They gathered issues from the participant observers before the performance began while the participant observers listened to the drumming and mingled in the crowd. The directors picked one of the scenarios suggested by a participant observer, and when "Free Sketches" began, they described the scenario, chose two performers from among the company, gave the performers instructions, and stopped and started the action to add recommendations from the participant observers. Before the "Free Sketches" began, the chosen performers asked the participant observers for simple props like a tie, pen, or scarf. These objects were used in the scene and returned at its conclusion. The props were another way of increasing the participant observers' involvement in the performance. The directors encouraged comments from the participant observers and asked one or more to join in

the scene. Unlike Boal's "Joker," they did not spend much time analyzing the scene for the participant observers; with hindsight, this analysis might have yielded even more varied possibilities from the participant observers.

Even though the use of improvisation was in its developmental stages for this production, the improvisations generated a great deal of audience participation. During one scenario, a director was announcing the scene in which an African-American woman with natural hair was talking with a friend whose hair had been chemically straightened. The interchange proceeded as follows:

Director: Ok, now, uhmm, there's these two friends. One has straight hair and, you know, one has kinky hair—

Participant Observers: (*shouting from around the gymnasium*) *Natural* hair! Don't say no kinky! Naw, uh uh!

Director: Ooop! Ooop! (*slowly and reverently bowing to the participant observers with hands in prayer*) Yes, yes! Natural hair! Excuse me! Marilyn, you be the one with straight hair (*the performer stands and tosses her hair from side to side; the participant observers laugh at this action*). And Jewell, you be the one with, with uh, *natural hair* (*the participant observers cheer and applaud the director for using the terminology they suggested*).

The spontaneous involvement of the participant observers suggests that they had begun to have a sense of ownership with the production. *Wild Women and Rolling Stones* did not belong solely to the performers and the director/playwright; it signalled a shared communal event for which everyone was responsible. The playfulness with which the participant observers were able to voice a serious objection to the director's language, and the respect with which the director accepted it, suggests that the separation between the participant observers and the performers had decreased. For examples, later in the same scenario, the performer with the straight hair broke the fourth wall performance convention by turning away from the other performer, looking directly at the participant observers and saying "Girl, you know how this hair thing is!" The participant observers laughed, applauded, and cheered at this direct inclusion of their own experiences.

Eventually, the participant observers did not have to be prompted by the director to offer suggestions on the course of the scene. During the same scenario, one participant observer seated on the floor called out. "Have a brother and a white man decide who's the prettiest! Bring them up there and let them pick!" The director acknowledged the comment and took the suggestion. He asked a Hispanic participant observer and a company member to be the added characters. The company member he chose was an African-American with very light skin who entered the performance space with his arms uplifted asking "Which one do I play? The white guy or the brother?" The participant observers exploded into laughter at this spontaneous and potent humor which underscored the issue of ethnicity that was central to the scenario. Improvisation allows the performer to acknowledge that she or he is playing a character, not becoming one; this constructed and reconstructed identity and reconstructed requires the performer to consciously participate in a matrix of complex realities.

The improvisational nature of the production generated dialogue among the participant observers. In one scenario, a woman did not want to dance with the man who had just asked her to join him on the dance floor. One participant observer standing at the edge of the circle with her baby in a carrier on her back cupped her hands and shouted, "I think you should dance with him!" Another participant observer seated in the circle responded. "Yeah! That's right! You *should* dance with him! You came to the party. Why you want to stand there? There's nothing wrong with him! You should go ahead and dance with him! That's what's wrong now! Just go ahead and dance with the man!" This participant observer used the other participant observer's comment as a springboard for her own commentary. The gymnasium filled with cheers of encouragement as her speech progressed; in this way, the participant observers were simultaneously creating a dialogue among themselves and between the performers.

The power of improvisation was amply demonstrated during a scenario in which a man wanted to approach a woman about having a sexual relationship. Initially, the woman was resistant until a participant observer said "What happens if she wants it too?" The female performer then turned to the participant observers and asked for a condom. Immediately, the participant observers began groping in their pockets, wallets, and purses in search of the desired prop. Couples were turning to one another quickly negotiating the appropriateness of sharing their birth/disease control preferences publicly. One of my students who was among the participant observers looked embarrassedly at me, tugged on her date's elbow, and then laughed as he tossed his condom into the performance space along with the other condoms that were flying to the center from all directions. The performer then searched among the variety of condoms on the floor, found several she wanted to use, placed them in her purse, and continued with the scene amid much laughter and a heightened sense of participation.

TOWARDS AN AFRICAN-AMERICAN THEATRE AESTHETIC

In describing jazz improvisation, Jerry Coker states that "when we ignore the given melody and build new melodies over the chord progression of the given melody (called *lyricism*), we are improvising at the highest level" (3). Coker's description implies that there is a known melody and that one has the skill to create new melodies in response to the known one. Developing African-based improvisation for an African-American aesthetic was itself an improvisation between "given" and "new" melodies. In this work, the given melodies were grounded in Scribean-based dramaturgy of Western performance practices such as linear plot construction and proscenium production techniques, while the new melodies were the performance practices of the Yoruba. In this section I reflect on the two productions described above to identify six challenges that emerged in developing improvisation as a performance strategy for an African-American theatre aesthetic, including unresolved tensions that arise between African-based and European-American-based aesthetics.

The Scenarios

The first challenge in developing an African-American theatre aesthetic is the generation of scenarios for improvisation, including the topics and structure of the scenarios. The scenarios in both productions were typically conflict-driven, particularly in *Wild Women and Rolling Stones* which offered scenarios such as the following: a women tells her partner her job is asking her to relocate, a man must explain to his date why he was flirting with another woman, and a European-American man is having a relationship with an African-American woman unbeknownst to his European-American girlfriend. These melodies tended to be flat and reminiscent of standard soap opera fare. The scenarios begged for cliché melodramatic options and performances with little opportunity for creativity, complexity, and multiple solutions. The conflict so central to the scenario required attention, making it difficult to "ignore the given melody" of a predictable and pat resolution of conflict. The challenge was to state scenarios in such a way that the conflict, if any, emerged during the improvisation rather than imposing the conflict on the improvisation. In "The University Show" the scenario involving the racial slur displayed this structural emergence because the performers could decide whether or not there would be conflict between them and then develop its directions. The woman whose boyfriend verbally abused her friend could have opted to become outraged and confront the boyfriend about it. The victim of the verbal abuse could decide if it was trivial. Presenting the scenario without immediate and direct conflict between the characters allows for the exploration of multiple and complex options, defining conflict from within the community, rather than battling out the single conflict attached to the scenario. In *Wild Women and Rolling Stones,* the scenario in which a man wanted to begin a relationship with a woman was also stated so that the performers could choose whether or not there would be conflict. The conflict-driven scenarios tend toward linear plot construction complete with a climatic confrontation and an amicable resolution.

Among the Yoruba, conflict was most often seen in the scenarios and scripts of The Yoruba Travelling Theatre, that portion of Yoruba performance most heavily influenced by linear plot construction, a throughline of action, and a separation of the participants into actor and "audience." In the *Egungun* masquerades an event occurs, such as a dance at the doorstep of the members of the compound, and in *Apidan* Theatre, typically a character-type is imitated. Neither of these performance practices relies on the resolution of a conflict.

Viola Spolin's work, much of which establishes characters within a conflict situation, is fundamental improvisational training in many United States theatre institutions.[9] This structure was so ingrained in my previous work with improvisation, it became difficult to break away from it. In addition to the strategies suggested above, one option is to explore improvisation that is advanced through a synchronous relationship between the performer of the spoken word and the drummer. This scenario structure is more akin to the Yoruba performance in which the drummer and the dancer improvise playfully with one another. This performance strategy would dispense with conflict and the potential need for linear plot construction.

Performance Style

A second challenge in developing an African-based theatre aesthetic concerns performance style and characterizations. The two productions yielded very little internal reflection, silent contemplation, or subtleties of performance. Characterizations and performance styles were frequently exaggerated. In the scenario that dealt with hair texture, for example, the two performers proceeded with predictable rhetoric about the politics of hair, addressed directly to the participant observers, rather than trying to explore and deeply understand their hair choices in dialogue with each other. This performance style may have grown from the rather stereotypic and conflict-driven scenarios that were suggested. However, there were two notable exceptions to these broad performance styles. In "The University Show" the scenario involving the racial slur had quiet moments as the victim of the verbal attack tried to determine how to respond to her roommate's insistence that this could not have happened. The performer was feeling her way through the moment in what appeared to be a sincere exploration of her responses instead of offering glib, artificially angry one-liners to her roommate's challenge. In *Wild Women and Rolling Stones,* one scenario involved a mother confronting her son about his drug use. The woman playing the mother stood quietly several times during the scene as if she were sincerely trying to decide what to do next. Here, the performers seemed to be working to understand their problem rather than impress the participant observers with their wit.

My efforts to steer the improvised performances away from theatrical effect and achieve a style that reflects the aesthetics of naturalism in acting may actually be counter to the style of performance among the Yoruba, however. The *Apidan* performances are detailed yet broadly drawn characterizations. Ogunde performances similarly appear to be based on broad characterizations rather than psychological realism. The company members' performance style may have actually used Yoruba-based performance techniques while I was still encouraging a kind of realism that is not found widely in Yoruba performance. Unwittingly, I may have been responding to years of training in Western theatrical realism that appears to be at odds with the broad character strokes found in much Yoruba performance. The development of an African-based theatre aesthetic invites further exploration of the tensions between "broad" and "natural" performance styles within contemporary African-American cultures.

Participant Observes

Although the use of public improvisation is fraught with problems, improvisation creates a vitality, spontaneity, and participation not commonly found in scripted texts. Improvisation also chips away at barriers that exist among the participant observers and between the participant observers and performers. The barriers themselves may hinder healing because they represent some of the very wounds all are gathered to heal. These barriers are also hierarchies: the social roles and the internalized cultural definitions that determine who is a performer and who is not, who should speak and who should not, who can have power and who cannot. The

role of participant observers is especially critical to developing an African-based theatre aesthetic. The suggestions from the participant observers in both productions came from a wide variety of participant observers, to the extent that in *Wild Women and Rolling Stones* a teenaged participant observer played the father in the scenario about the son using drugs. In a scripted production, that teenager would not have had an opportunity to live out the role of father and discover its complexities; instead, he would have been told what the role of father is through the performance of that role by a designated performer.

Although African Americans are accustomed to engaging in improvisation in socially restrictive situations as a means of survival and to utilizing improvisation in dance and music, African Americans are less familiar with improvisation in theatrical performance. Unlike the Yoruba who expect improvisation in their performance practices, African Americans as well as other participant observers must learn how to use improvisation as a dramaturgical device. The participant observers for the two productions examined here were given instructions for improvising scenes and those instructions were modified as the participant observers worked through the improvisations. In "The University Show," the participant observers didn't know the extent to which they could engage in the performance. The result was that they never physically entered the performance space as one of the characters. In *Wild Women and Rolling Stones,* the directors were explicit about asking the participant observers to take on character roles because we learned that the participant observers needed more direct information as they experienced an unfamiliar theatrical form. The parameters for the improvisations were generated solely by the company members; eventually those parameters can be more actively shaped by the participant observers. As more participant observers become comfortable with improvisation, they will create rules that meet their needs and the demands of the form.

Training

Training for improvisation as an African-American performance strategy also persents specific challenges to performers and directors. Ideally, the company would work closely together over a long period of time. The six-week rehearsal period for *Wild Women and Rolling Stones* was not sufficient for developing the necessary expertise with improvisation. In some ways, the close-knit group structure used by Hubert Ogunde with Ogunde Theatre would be a useful model for this work. Having a dedicated group of performers with whom to work, Ogunde was able to rigorously explore his theatrical philosophies with persons who had a visceral understanding of those philosophies. Such a structure would increase the intimacy and allow for the development of respect, appreciation, and friendship that makes improvisation powerful.

Within the parameters of our two productions, we developed some strategies for training directors in improvisation. For example, the director for the "Free Sketches" must be clear with her or his instructions. Too many directions can stifle creativity, and too few can leave everyone confused. It is important that the director make explicit the kind of involvement that is permissible from the participant observers to that their suggestions reflect their desires for the scene and not the rules they believe they are to follow. The participant observers for such productions have to be trained to understand and negotiate their role in a way that the Yoruba do not.

Performance Space

The context for an African-based performance requires careful consideration. The more the context deviates from traditional theatre, the more likely the participant observers will dispense with traditional notions of theatre and enter into the participatory improvisational world being created. Ogunba feels that the involvement of the participant observers goes beyond laughing, clapping, or commenting to extend to "the creation of the right atmosphere, that it is more conceptually based than the general run of drama in, say, the western tradition" (22).

The Yoruba frequently perform outdoors encircled by participant observers. White the circle was easy to duplicate, the communal feeling of Yoruba performance must be given greater consideration. The gymnasium used for *Wild Women and Rolling Stones* served this function better than the theatre and dance building used for "The University Show." I attempted to create "the right atmosphere" as a conceptual space by asking for food rather than money as admission, opening the production of *Wild Women and Rolling Stones* with an African dance company, and offering a feast after the performance. Locating *Wild Women and Rolling Stones* in a gymnasium and asking for food as admission helped the participant observers anticipate that whatever was going to happen would be out of the ordinary; therefore, their relationship to the performance would likewise be out of the ordinary. Carefully selecting and shaping the performance setting and context can guide the participant observers to responses more congruent with African-based theatre.

Efficacy

A final challenge for developing an African-American theatre-aesthetic focuses on efficacy, or the collective creativity and power of performance to heal a community's spirit. The specific wounds I had hoped to begin healing centered around the interpersonal relationships between African-American women and men. As a springboard for performance, this design was actually working with a generalized problem rather than, like the Yoruba, responding to a local community incident. In some ways the breach I identified between African-American men and women was an artificial device to address the larger issue of community-building. Among the Yoruba, the performances grow out of particular community events. In my productions, the performances were not directly linked to a specific community event. This shifted the nature of the efficacy from the issue at hand, relationship between African-American men and women, to the more broad issue of replenishing the community *ase*.

Healing requires time and an understanding of the parameters of the performance by all participating. For the Yoruba, performance is woven into daily activities, and is often connected to a community event such as a funeral, an initiation, or the dedication of property. In such a situation, performance is a form of redress or continuity; performance heals a specific breach or it prevents one by providing protection. One production is merely a beginning in that direction, and the community-building generated from the production suggests that the groundwork has been established for the long hard work that lasting healing demands. Even without empirical evidence demonstrating that healing occurred, I am encouraged by the fact that at the end of one performance two police officers on duty stopped to see what was going on in the gym, and they stayed to eat and play drums while everyone danced. On another night, two participant observers spontaneously joined the circle or performers when the performers introduced themselves and said farewell. The two participant observers followed suit by introducing themselves, hugging the performers, and leaving the performance space dancing along with the performers. The freedom that is at the heart of improvisation gives space for this communal interaction, and it is this interaction that is a step toward healing community wounds.

CONCLUSION

The development of an African-American theatrical aesthetic is a long range objective of this work. The performers, participant observers, and I were pulled between competing aesthetics in which we improvised our parts between "given" and "new" melodies. For example, I had to reconsider my own internal psychological performance style to see the ways in which the broad characterizations typically found in Yoruba performance might be more appropriate to improvisation. The structure of the improvisations seemed linked to the conflict-laden work of Viola Spolin rather than the character explorations of the *Apidan* theatre. The generally accepted four-to-six week rehearsal period was insufficient for the intimacy required for skillful improvisation. For the Yoruba, the context is understood from a lifetime of acquaintance with the form; for Western participant observers the appropriate context for this work must be constructed so that they anticipate a participatory improvisational event, with efficacious rather than only entertainment goals.

The tensions between my newly acquired understanding of African-based performance and my previous work in traditional Western theatre practice were addressed by guest critic and Executive Director of the National Black Theatre, Barbara Ann Teer when she wrote. "I think Ms. Jones needs to choose whether she wants to do Western theatre forms or African ones. . . . I would strongly suggest taking more risk with the style and the structure. Break out of the Western, linear mode completely" (372). In fact, I hope to discover what the creolization of African and Western performance traditions might be by becoming immersed in African performance practices and then selecting and adapting the Western traditions which best support the African-based values.

As African-American theatre artists immerse ourselves in alternatives to linear plot construction and proscenium production techniques, we may forge dramaturgical structures born of the varied cultures in which we live and work. In the Yoruba-based dramatic structure I am devising, improvisation is a core element; therefore, the problems public improvisation present must be tackled if such a structure is to be created. Margaret Thompson Drewal equates *ere*, "serious play," with improvisation among the Yoruba (6). For Drewal, *ere* is "an engaging, participatory, transformational process" that is "integral to the practice of everyday life" (14). Not to include improvisation in Yoruba-based dramatic structure is to omit an essential feature of Yoruba performance and a vital aspect of African-American life. The theatre practitioner's challenge is to discover how to harness the obvious power of improvisation to meet the structural demands of performance that seeks to heal wounds. The improvisational strategies employed so spontaneously among African-Americans in every-day life must find an analogue in theatre practice. In this way, improvisation becomes as common and as comfortable a strategy of performance as the single authored scripted text.

DISCUSSION QUESTIONS

1. How do African American-based theatrical performances differ in structure from African-based traditions?

2. Compare and contrast *Dramatic Ritual* from *The Popular Tradition*.

3. How do Yoruban *Egungun* masquerades differ from *Apidan* theatre? How is *Apidan* theatre informed by *Egungun*?

4. Why is improvisation an important discursive strategy for African Americans?

5. Is signifyin(g) a form of improvisation? Justify your response.

Part II

African American Rhetoric, Language, and Identity

There is an old Zen *koan* or teaching about a Buddhist priest and his monks. There are multiple versions of this narrative, one of which I present here.

One day, several Buddhist monks waited patiently on the side of a hill for their teacher to arrive. After an extraordinarily long wait, they saw their teacher walking slowly toward them with his hands behind his back. When he got closer, he placed his hands in front of him. He had a flower in one hand, and held the flower up for everyone to see. He remained inexpressive. He held the flower there for about ten minutes without saying a word. He made eye contact with one of the monks with whom he shared a smile. The monk understood. After the time had expired, the teacher slowly lowered the flower and looked at each of the monks and said, "This is your lesson for today." He then placed his hands behind his back and walked away.

One interpretation of this parable is that the monk who smiled understood the power of language. A flower is just a flower until it is translated using one's own universe of discourse. It is precisely that constructed universe of discourse that constricts the possibilities and confines the range of discourse. There is a link between giving something a name and bringing something into being, which is why there are many indigenous groups that try to give newborns names that will bespeak their futures or their character. Naming is only one facet to language and discourse. Rhetoric is another. Often when scholars speak of rhetoric, they refer to some attempt to use the word to persuade or to strategically center certain ideas in a given context. In the essays that follow, there is a distinct call to consider the discursive codes and strategies inherent in African American rhetoric.

Part II begins with Deborah F. Atwater's essay, which issues a challenge to develop new rhetorical paradigms to encase the culturally particular rhetorical practices of African Americans. She initiates her discussion with findings from her brief content analysis of communication journals. She reveals that, within a two-year time span, only ten articles related to "Black Communication" were published in the five journals she examined, which were *Quarterly Journal of Speech* and the four regional communication journals. Few of these articles employed new conceptual approaches to Black communication. Most used "traditional, acceptable modes of criticism." Atwater concludes her assessment of the intellectual condition of communication studies with a call to develop community-engaged approaches to Black rhetoric that not only respond to the voids contributing to tenure-track Black faculty attrition but also to the inability of "traditional, acceptable modes of criticism" to properly account for cultural differences in Black rhetorical practice.

Although he does not adopt or advocate an entirely new rhetorical approach, Eric King Watts does present a heuristic encapsulation of Alain Locke's rhetoric as discovered in his anthology of African American art and criticism, *The New Negro: An Interpretation,* by tending to its hermeneutic tendencies. In a close reading of Locke's "aesthetic praxis," Watts explores how the work of this Harlem Renaissance artist challenged the establishment to embrace political, social, and emotional dimensions of Black life. One immediate effect of this emotive condition in which the aesthetic was confined was the elevation of the African American ethos.

Indeed, all of the essays in Part II encourage the pursuit of alternative ways of analyzing African American rhetoric and identities. Yet, the next essay by Thurmon Garner could be said to be his magnum opus, especially with respect to African American rhetoric; it is certainly an important contribution to the field of African American rhetoric. Garner demonstrates that playing the dozens is more than a discursive activity; it is rhetorical practice for coping with real life conflicts. It is not that, in the absence of playing the dozens, one is unequipped for conflict management, but that "the game is an important rhetorical device which promotes community stability and cooperation by regulating social and personal conflicts." Anyone who has ever played this folkloric game understands its competitive edge, requisite quick wit, and communal nature. An interesting feature of play is the potential rotation of audience members into the position of player. Garner also notes that the game instills a "strategy of cool" that promotes clear and intentional articulation, concise directness, and an image of composure.

Articulation is one among many components of John Baugh's research concerning *Black Street Speech.* Baugh, who is now known for his coinage of the term *linguistic profiling*, grounds his exploration of Black dialect using 200 hours of interviews he recorded with African Americans throughout the United States. The principal conundrum African Americans encounter, Baugh explains, is the devaluation and dismissal of their identities. Many African Americans are reared to accept and use a nonstandard dialect outside of school and in everyday talk. Then, as they mature, they come to realize the standard or "mainstream English" takes precedent over their learned linguistic form; hence, they must learn to code switch as a survival tool. Baugh describes stylistic variations among English speakers and proposes that those who have limited contact with English speakers of different varieties are likely to be unpracticed in that variety; yet, he contends that speakers of "Black street speech" have access to the standard and are discouraged from retaining access to their dialectical code. Rhetoric and language are two significant facets to African American communication and identities. Later in this volume, contributors present several other facets of African American communication, from personal and gendered relationships to organizational, instructional, and mass mediated contextual issues.

Reading 2.1

A DILEMMA OF BLACK COMMUNICATION SCHOLARS

The Challenge of Finding New Rhetorical Tools

DEBORAH F. ATWATER

According to Florence Ladd, Dean of Students at Wellesley College, "Escalating retrenchment virtually guarantees that no substantial gains in the number of Black faculty will be realized in the future" (quoted in the *Chronicle of Higher Education,* May 18, 1981). To be sure, the retrenchment process entails increasingly detailed scrutiny of faculty credentials in tenure/promotion reviews. In a recent study of the Urban League, it is reported that over 45% of the surveyed Black faculty members without tenure rated their chances of obtaining tenure as limited. To further substantiate the preceding point, a recent comparative study of minority and nonminority faculty perceptions of career opportunities at Penn State (1982) found that no Black faculty on the tenure track indicated they "thought tenure is possible" or "expect to get tenure and make a career at Penn State." It is within this tenuous academic environment that

the search for new rhetorical tools by Black communication scholars will be discussed.

Black communication scholars must have a commitment to the field as well as a commitment to the community. The purposes of this article are to analyze the dilemma of Black communication scholars and to explore possible resolutions of this problem. The article addresses the following areas:

(1) a brief review of the literature

(2) the need for new rhetorical tools in the Black experience

(3) the use of traditional methods to evaluate new rhetorical tools

(4) possible ways to meet both community and personal goals

(5) a Black communication impact model

From Atwater, D. F. (1984). A dilemma of Black communication scholars: The challenge of finding new rhetorical tools. *Journal of Black Studies, 15*(1), 5-16.

REVIEW OF THE LITERATURE

Perhaps one of the most significant and comprehensive contributions to the literature on Black rhetoric is Cummings and Daniel's (1980) "Scholarly Literature on the Black Idiom." In this paper, the authors provide the following:

(1) a review of Black communication scholarship specifically dealing with Black American public address

(2) Black communication similarities resulting from colonialism, racism, and oppression

(3) a comprehensive bibliography relating to Black rhetoric and rhetorical criticism

The following journals were scrutinized for recent (1980–1982) and relevant articles on Black communication (any articles dealing with Blacks): *Central States Speech Journal, Communication Quarterly, Quarterly Journal of Speech, Southern Speech Communication Journal, and Western Journal of Speech Communication.*

Of the ten pertinent articles found, four appear in the *Southern Speech Communication Journal.* McFarlin (1980) discusses the remarkable, but little known, accomplishments of elocutionist Hallie Quinn Brown. Braden (1980) discusses the persuasive strategies to defend white supremacy in a closed society in Mississippi from 1954 to 1964. James (1980) provides an in-depth analysis of the influence of Black orality on contemporary Black poetry and its implications for performance. Calloway-Thomas and Smith (1981) suggest that differences in communication images of leadership do indeed exist for Blacks and whites.

The *Quarterly Journal of Speech* provides three pertinent articles. Stanbeck and Pearce (1981) discuss the communication strategies used by members of "subordinate" social groups when talking to "The Man." Logue (1981) focuses on the communication strategies of Black slaves on the plantations. Brown (1982) discusses attention and the rhetoric of social intervention.

Of the final three articles, one appears in *Communication Quarterly*—Haskin's (1981) article on the southern Black press during Reconstruction. Brummett's (1980) article on Burkean scapegoating and the "Zebra" murders appears in the *Western Journal of Speech Communication,* and in the last article, in the *Central States Speech Journal,* Zarefsky (1980) discusses Lyndon Johnson and the beginnings of affirmative action.

On the whole, most of the articles deal with Black communication in the traditional, acceptable modes of criticism, although James (1980), McFarlin (1980), and Calloway-Thomas and Smith (1981) provide additional insight into the Black experience by offering new and practical information on Black orality, Black speakers, and Black perceptions. However, all of the articles appear in mainstream journals. There is also a need to publish in other nontraditional journals. I will address this issue and why it is crucial to Black communication scholars in a later section.

NEW RHETORICAL TOOLS/BLACK EXPERIENCE

According to Cummings and Daniel (1980), "Until we come to grips with what is essentially Black about Black communication, we cannot develop a culturally valid rhetorical criticism. The whole history, culture, experiences of Black people must be dealt with in order to make valid critical assessments." For example, a suitable model for Afrocentric communication theory would be the Nhiwatiwa Wheel of Involved Communication, for there is no source or audience everyone is involved in except the complementary relating of experiences unified by Nommo (Blake, 1981; quoted in Simmons, 1982: 55). The Nhiwatiwa Wheel differs from the traditional models of communication, but it should if it is truly to represent the Black communication experience.

Many of the articles on Black rhetoric do not always take an Afrocentric perspective and consequently generalizations are made by those who have viewed one small segment of the Black experience (for example, see Stanbeck and Pearce's "Talking to 'The Man,'" 1981).

To be sure, Black rhetoric concentrates on Nommo, rhythmical patterns, and audience assertiveness. James (1980) discusses extensively the influence of Black orality on contemporary Black poetry. According to James (1980: 250), the distinguishing characteristics of Black orality are the following:

(1) linguistic and stylistic features of Black language

(2) supplemental elements of Black blues, jazz, and spirituals

(3) gesture, bodily movements, and dance

Black orality produces a dynamic, sound-oriented, action-oriented rhythmic mode of communication.

Sidran (1971: 3) says of the oral personality: "He is forced to behave in a spontaneous manner, to act and react (instantaneous feedback) simultaneously. As a consequence of this perceptual orientation oral man is, at all times, emotionally involved in, as opposed to intellectually detached from, his environment through his acts of communication." For this reason, the language in Black poetry is different from that generally found in white poetry. If you alter the language, you change the communicative style. Hence, if you use only traditional methods of criticism you may miss the deep structure of the language, the message. In addition, Black music and dance complement each other in the Black oral tradition, for music is the emotional basis of Black experience.

How do traditional methods of criticism affect Black communication? The following example illustrates a point.

TRADITIONAL MODES OF CRITICISM

Ritter (1980) discusses the modern jeremiad in presidential nomination acceptance addresses, 1960–1976. According to Ritter (1980: 169), "The modern jeremiad helps Americans to find a common cultural memory which unifies past and future. It allows Americans to celebrate their glorious heritage and their ultimate destiny even as they lament their present shortcomings." Even though Ritter explains that this (modern jeremiad) applies to the major parties in power, he is astute enough to realize that *all* Americans, Blacks in particular, do not share in the American Dream myth. Such speakers, according to Ritter, adopt what Bercovitch calls the rhetoric of the *anti*-jeremiad, which is a denunciation of American ideals as hypocrisy. Ritter uses Malcolm X as a representative speaker to illustrate the point. With this particular example, one cannot help but notice that the modern jeremiad (white) represents what is good and positive, whereas the anti-jeremiad (Black)

represents what is bad and negative. There are numerous examples of such dichotomies—traditional/non-traditional, superior/subordinate, standard/nonstandard—in the literature discussing and /or analyzing Black communication. We, as Black communication scholars, should not foster artificial dichotomies, for the African world view allows something to be two things at the same time. We have a responsibility to weigh carefully the methods used to analyze Black communication, so that we do not continue to contribute to those existing dichotomies.

Pennington (1980) speaks to the use of guilt-provocation as a strategy in Black rhetoric and how the traditional concept of guilt must be modified for Black speakers. Pennington (1980: 112) argues that "representative Black speakers using the same concept (guilt) employ a basis of application structurally different from the traditional notions provided by theorists on guilt." To illustrate, the provocation of moral guilt is based upon the assumption that the other has a conscience. Not all Black speakers share this assumption. Malcolm X was one black speaker who strongly believed that America had no conscience, no morals. White America is moved by economic and political threats, not by conscience. Hence the use of guilt-provocation as a strategy becomes futile.

Pennington's article is significant because she clearly defines what guilt-provocation as a strategy is to Black speakers, but, more important, she indicates that not *all* Black speakers operate under the same assumptions about guilt and may employ different strategies.

TRADITIONAL METHODS FOR EVALUATION

Why should Black communication scholars be concerned with the traditional tools of rhetorical criticism, if these do not meet their needs? Richards (1980) succinctly speaks to this issue. Although she is an anthropologist rather than a communications scholar, her view has merit: "We, as people of African descent, need to understand the nature of European culture, history, and behavior in order that we might be in a better position to deal with it, reject it, and to comprehend the dimension of its effect on us" (Richards, 1980: 59).

In the communication field there are those who would argue that classical rhetorical theory has no impact on Black communication. However, Niles (1980) states that Black rhetoric varies not in the basics, but in the conceptualization, perspective (world view), and sociocultural influences on the rhetoric. Others would argue (Ben-Jochannan, 1978) that the Greeks "borrowed" from African culture, so in essence *it is* applicable. As long as we view the tools/methods from an Afrocentric (Asante, 1980) perspective, they may aid in our analysis of Black communication.

Apparently, now is an opportune time to discuss and to proffer new paradigms. Booth (1979: 7) defines criticism as a humanistic discipline in which no one individual interpretation of a phenomenon dominates, but in which various assessments of a phenomenon exist compatibly, both simultaneously and over time. Becker (1974: 12–13) says that this is clearly a time to test new paradigms, but there is little or no sign of our relinquishing the old ones. He sees the discipline of rhetorical theory as large enough to accommodate those who would revise or replace existing theory and those who would reinterpret theory.

Oravec (1982: 70) concludes that new forms of theorizing may result from subtle shifts in criteria between the activities of theory and criticism. Even more problematic is the possibility of confusion among the principles and standards.

African people should be able to draw from several approaches to and perspectives on social scientific theorizing and to make practical and applied decisions based on the demands of the situation (Nwankwo, 1982: 52). Furthermore, the principles and standards that we adopt must be grounded in our history and culture.

Community/Personal Needs (Academic Survival)

Earlier, I discussed the need to publish in other journals. This section deals with the issue of academic survival and community involvement.

Scholarly publishing is one essential of every institution of higher education because it represents the research and intellectual discovery that continues to reinforce and establish the new basis for professional work in that area. To be sure, publishing is the *primary* evaluation for promotion and tenure and salary review of faculty. McWorter (1981) argues that "one of the general tasks of all intellectuals is research and Publishing." The other two tasks, teaching and service to the community, are "applied tasks."

Professional journals are normally mechanisms that give coherence to a specific academic profession. Blacks generally tend to be underrepresented in the mainstream publications. I contend that the publishing criterion can be met if we publish in the mainstream journals (*Quarterly Journal of Speech, Central States Speech Journal, Communication Quarterly,* and so on), but, more important, we should reevaluate the "mainstream" and change it to include the professional journals in Black Studies. The following is a topical list of 26 major Black professional journals in Black Studies.

Humanities

Black Art

Black American Literature Forum

Black Perspectives in Music

CLA Journal

Callaloo: A Black Southern Journal of Arts and Letters

Obsidian: Black Literature in Review

Social Science

Black Law Journal

Black Sociologist

Howard Law Journal

Journal of Black Psychology

Journal of Negro Education

Journal of Negro History

Journal of Non-White Concern in Personnel and Guidance

Negro Educational Review

Review of Black Political Economy

Urban League Review

General

Black Books Bulletin

Black Scholar: Journal of Black Studies and Research

First World; An International Journal of Black Thought

Freedomways: A Quarterly Review of the Freedom Movement

Journal of Black Studies

Phylon: The Atlanta University Review of Race and Culture

Review of Afro-American Issues and Culture

Studia Africana: An International Journal of Africana Studies

Umoja: A Scholarly Journal of Black Studies

Western Journal of Black Studies

McWorter's *Guide to Scholarly Journals in Black Studies* provides all background information as well as submission information.

In addition to publishing, we need to participate in and have an impact on national and international Black conferences. The annual conference of the National Council for Black Studies provides and excellent opportunity for the cross-fertilization of ideas among Black scholars from different disciplines. The World Congress on Black Communication is an excellent international forum for Blacks in the diaspora. One of the most innovative and productive conferences was the National United Black Fund held in Boston in the summer of 1979. It was significant because it made a concerted effort to combine theory with a practical community approach.

By participating in Black conferences, publishing in Black journals, and participating in community activities, the Black communication scholar can contribute to both the community and the field, and hence begin to resolve the dilemma of academic survival and community commitment.

A Communication impact model is presented in Figure 1.

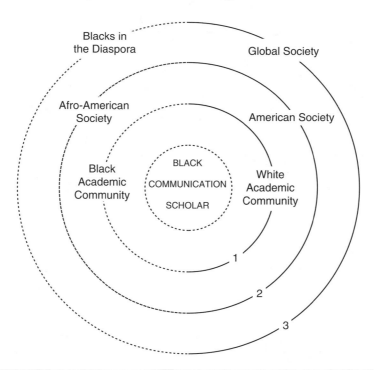

Figure 1   Communication Impact Model for Black Communication Scholars

Note: The model depicts the potential impact that Black communication scholars can have on Blacks in the diaspora. The dotted lines indicate a free flow of information between the circles.

Impact Strategies: (1) Black Academic Community/white Academic Community: publish in both mainstream and Black Studies journals: participate in professional meetings of both communities. (2) Afro-American Society/American Society: community work: political activism. (3) Blacks in the Diaspora/Global Society: participate in the World Congress on Black Communication and other International conferences.

CONCLUSION

In this article, I have provided a brief review of the literature, compared traditional rhetorical methods and tools with the need for new rhetorical methods and tools, discussed academic survival, and offered a communications impact model.

In the next decade, we *must* continue to do research, but the results of our research endeavors must ultimately reach Blacks in the diaspora.

Black communication scholars cannot make an impact on the community, cannot communicate with authenticity, if we are not true to our African heritage. In these times of increasing retrenchment, we must continue to have a commitment to our community as well as a commitment to our field. We must extend, go beyond our academic walls, permeate our total existence in our efforts to resolve our dilemma and find new and relevant rhetorical tools.

DISCUSSION QUESTIONS

1. What three constituent parts of Black rhetoric does Atwater identify as important?

2. How do "traditional modes of criticism" limit understanding of Black communication?

3. How does Black rhetoric differ from European classical rhetorical theory?

4. What is the *Diaspora*?

5. How does the Communication Impact Model of Black Communication Scholarship demonstrate the importance of reaching Blacks throughout the Diaspora via scholarship?

Reading 2.2

AFRICAN AMERICAN ETHOS AND HERMENEUTICAL RHETORIC

An Exploration of Alain Locke's The New Negro

ERIC KING WATTS

During the early part of the 20th century, Harlem was a home and a Mecca for African Americans.[1] The migration of black folk into the North in general and into upper Manhattan in particular during and after World War I helped to provide the ideological and material resources to launch the artistic explosion known as the Harlem Renaissance. Being at home in Harlem, however, meant more than one's residence or geographic location or psychological comfort; it specified an African American *ethos,* "dwelling place"[2] or "spirit house."[3] Despite a dizzying array of ideological, political, and philosophical alliances and factions among an intellectual elite promoting conflicting forms of social action for black Americans, Harlem was buoyed by the potential for powerful black collective action.[4] Spatially, Harlem occupied the center of frequently contradictory activities aimed at the construction of black community.[5] Harlem also was the site of diverse experiments in the constitution of African American communal consciousness. From this perspective, much Harlem Renaissance writing concerned the cultivation of blackness as an authentic and empowering element of Black Nationalism and U.S. democracy.[6]

As the "World's Greatest Negro Metropolis,"[7] Harlem came to signify the horizon of possibilities for an African American *ethos.* It was a dynamic forum for deliberations about the appropriate norms, premises, and practices of a distinct black culture; thus, it made available to black intellectuals the symbolic and material resources for the rhetorical invention and the articulation of a black public voice. The very idea of an African American

From Watts, E. K. (2002). African American ethos and hermeneutical rhetoric: An exploration of Alain Locke's *The New Negro. Quarterly Journal of Speech, 88*(1), 19-32.

ethos was a rhetorical and an aesthetic dilemma because Harlem Renaissance artistry was asked to serve the ends of civil rights by dramatizing the social injustices of black life and, paradoxically, it was impelled by Romantic Modernism to pursue aesthetic purity and transcend the particulars of black life.[8] Conflicting philosophies and conceptions of art and culture exacerbated the aesthetic dilemma faced by black artists and intellectuals. Accordingly, Harlem Renaissance artistry has received sharply deviating assessments over the years, praised as groundbreaking,[9] or denigrated as exotic and inferior to Anglo-European art,[10] or dismissed as imitative, "white-like" and, thus, "inauthentic."[11]

The history of the Harlem Renaissance includes an array of histories, customs, and traditions: Harlem was situated at the nexus of Black Nationalism, civil rights integrationism, Marxism, literary capitalism, and cultural elitism.[12] Various organizations, movements, and groups placed claims on Harlem writers and pressured literary magazines to advance their interests.[13] Such conflicts make the Harlem Renaissance an intriguing rhetorical situation and a particularly thorny and complex cultural milieu. No single work can reflect the diversity of the Harlem Renaissance. I, therefore, focus on the ways in which a hermeneutical rhetoric brought an African American *ethos* into being. A chief concern for Harlem elite was an interpretive discourse that could draw from the conflicting perspectives on black culture of the period to constitute an African American collective identity. In the opening section of the essay, I explore what is meant by hermeneutical rhetoric, thereby making clear how such rhetoric can bring about alternative understandings of race, culture, and community. Then, I offer Alain Locke's anthology *The New Negro: An Interpretation* as a case study. Described as the bible of the Harlem Renaissance,[14] Locke's text demonstrates the ways in which diverse cultural traditions can be topics for hermeneutical application and through rhetorical practice can be orchestrated into new forms of cultural knowledge. *The New Negro* is an instance of hermeneutical rhetoric that treats black folk tradition, African artistry, and modern pragmatism as *topoi* for rhetorical invention. Alain Locke's anthology orchestrates the transformation of the

"Old Negro" into the "New Negro" through a series of evocative reinterpretations of U.S. cultural beliefs. In the end, the New Negro emerges as a hero for a new era, embodying a transgressive notion of "race" and culture. Moreover, the New Negro is a topical resource for ongoing rhetorical invention and *praxis*. By being sensitive to how the emotions help to constitute interpretive acts, Alain Locke demonstrates an African American aesthetic *praxis* that offers up civic commonplaces and premises important to safeguarding the civic good. Locke's philosophy of cultural pluralism provided a non-essentialist perspective on the discursive character of race and identity politics that is relevant to our 21st century culture wars.

On Hermeneutical Rhetoric and an Aesthetic Praxis

Hermeneutical rhetoric involves the location and development of appropriate topics to shape public understanding. In their introduction to *Rhetoric and Hermeneutics in Our Time,* Walter Jost and Michael J. Hyde suggest that such *topoi* should be recognized as "places" at which understanding and persuasion come together.[15] Rather than conceive of knowledge as objective and given to our senses, Jost and Hyde use the writings of Martin Heidegger, Emmanuel Levinas, Kenneth Burke, M.M. Bakhtin, and others to posit that what we come to know are interpretations framed by a history of interpretations. This is not to say that interpretations can be dismissed as post-modern fictions. Hyde and Craig R. Smith argue that hermeneutics involves the "'basic mode' of 'human understanding'" and that this mode exhibits an "ontological (primordial) structure constituting the nature of human being (*Dasein*)."[16] This structure is temporal and is less a formation than a forming, changing, or becoming. Hermeneutical knowledge is predicated on our capacity to make sense of our shifting lived experiences, a capacity that, though ontological, is mediated by language.

Hermeneutics is an interpretive activity that begins and ends with the essential questioning of our everyday being with others.[17] This questioning is about how best to conduct one's personal affairs within a field of conflicting and fluid relations and is instigated by one's social world and shaped by it. The ways in which we go about our interpretive acts are constitutive of the norms of a given community and of our understanding of how they affect our goal-oriented activity, composing what Hyde and Smith refer to as our "hermeneutical situation."[18] A community's values, then inform our on-going interpretive acts that, in turn, reconstitute our collective understanding.

In *The Aesthetic Understanding,* Roger Scruton also observes that a community's values situate us hermeneutically. Scruton asserts a distinction familiar to rhetoricians, a cleft between theoretical and practical knowledge. By theoretical knowledge, he refers to an abstract, absolute domain of principles produced by Western metaphysics. When he discusses practical knowledge, he delineates two forms of "know-how": the technical and the ethical. Technical knowledge involves possessing the skills to complete a task or an awareness of the proper strategies to achieve a goal.[19] Ethical Know-how is conceived by Scruton in terms of Aristotelian virtue and is grounded in a hermeneutic practice: "I know what to do not just by knowing what a person answering to a certain description should do . . . but (typically) by making up my mind and acting accordingly."[20]

An important ethical *praxis* is posited here. By knowing what to do Scruton refers to a set of ethical precepts defining what on *ought* to do. From Scruton's perspective, hermeneutic understanding is demonstrated by a proper *application* of interpretive skill.[21] In other words, the interpretive acts that are fundamental to hermeneutic understanding necessarily involve the enactment of ethical propositions in what Bakhtin refers to as life's "once-occurrent concrete actuality."[22] For Scruton, it is not enough to *believe* oneself to be committed to a set of intellectual propositions concerning the meaning of public utterances and texts shaping our collective consciousness, to think, for example, that the words "all men are created equal" include African Americans and women. One's public conduct must manifest that belief in order for that understanding *to be as such.*[23] Hermeneutic understanding is, thus, public and

constitutive of the emotional entailments of everyday lived experience.

As a public activity, hermeneutic understanding is "a matter of communication in which the task of understanding is to find a common language so that the one who speaks can be heard by the other."[24] An interpretation is a productive act that expresses communal values and interests while displaying the rhetorical competence of the one who speaks the "truth" of the thing interpreted. Thus, we have arrived at the intersection of hermeneutic and rhetoric, the place at which the oratorical art is more than a dimension added to hermeneutic understanding, but is part of its foundation.[25] The ideas that make up interpretive acts are themselves rhetorical topics. Lest we become too distracted by the fixed spatial metaphor of place, Jost and Hyde remind us that topics should be conceived of as "places or evocations but not as irrefutable arguments or transparent symbols of a transcendent order."[26] As such, topics reflect human generative capacities:

They are inventional re-sources for persuasion or identification that generate or open onto a *range* of materials: from concepts and arguments at one end, whose purpose is to support claims persuasively and whose excellence is *prudentia* or *phronesis;* to images, tropes, and figures at the other end, whose purpose is to "disclose," "evoke" or "show forth" (*epi-deixis*) the topical first principles of all thought and action rather than to argue, and whose excellence is not rational *phronesis* . . . but an unrationalizable *kairos* (timeliness, appropriateness) attuned to the situation that one encounters.[27]

From a rhetorical perspective, one's competence can be assessed in terms of propriety or prudence; interpretive competence is similar. "In this regard the single, historical common term that brings invention and application together is the 'appropriate.'"[28] Both rhetoric and hermeneutic are oriented by one's sense of the proper orchestration, characterization, and articulation of topical material in accordance with one's lived experience. If topics are best located and enacted through intimate contact with social life, however, then our sense of decorum is conditioned at the outset by a complex and contingent set of social relations.[29] Our commitment to significant relations may not be adequately explained by Martin Heidegger's notion of "resolute choice," an essentially personal moment.[30] What is needed is our conscientious participation in public culture, the sort of involvement that ushers the subjective into the material world.[31] Moreover, this public activity is a form of civic training. According to Scruton, our emotions are educated about what a given community deems as good or worthwhile through our participation in community rites and rituals. This hands-on experience with the topical materials of speech suggests that our common sense is both perceptual (what we perceive to be true) and *sensual* (what we *feel* to be true). "It is now widely accepted that all emotion involves both understanding and activity."[32] Indeed, Smith and Hyde argue that the *pathé* are critical to orienting us toward one another during the work of *sensus communus.*[33] Importantly, Scruton's notion of emotional education parallels what classical rhetoricians recognize as *imitatio.*

The generative relationship between rhetoric and hermeneutic can be linked to classical *imitatio.*[34] Michael C. Leff argues that hermeneutics draws our attention to "interpretation as a source of invention and suggests how traditions can be altered without destroying their identity." Rather than conceive of *imitatio* as replication, as some modern scholars have done, Leff asserts that classical oratorical training stressed the speaker's capacity for judging the practical requirements of any given case and for providing the "linguistic resources" called for by the situation. Instead of modeling speeches, students learned how a text managed historical exigencies and constraints, becoming sensitive to how the particularities of time and place were mobilized by the orator. Within the framework Leff provides, "*imitatio* functions as hermeneutical rhetoric that circulates influence between past and present. As the embodied utterances of the past are interpreted for current application, their ideas and modes of articulation are reembodied, and old voices are recovered for use in new circumstances."[35]

Such a hermeneutical rhetoric is at the heart of my critical approach here. Leff contends that history is not cold storage for remote and abstract concepts awaiting redistribution; the past speaks to us with a voice; however, in order for voice to emerge, the emotional and ethical entailments of speech are in need of public acknowledgement.[36] Hermeneutical rhetoric is capable of facilitating voice because it specifies speech with a "strong political and ethical tendency."[37] Also relevant are the ways that idioms, styles, and premises from the past are made meaningful in cultural practices, offering up emotional values that function as rhetorical capacities and constraints. The emotions attune us to the character of communal relations and to the significance of others and of their pursuits. Practical wisdom requires more than calculative thinking; it demands a sort of reflective openness to the possibilities for placing oneself in a productive relation to others. In other words, hermeneutical rhetoric may be well suited to achieving propriety because it has a sensual dimension; it works through an aesthetic *praxis* that moves people to the places in which to "find the right word" to touch others.[38] In *The New Negro,* Alain Locke repositions the meaning of and the relations among black folk expression. African artistry, and U.S. pragmatic modernism so as invent an African American *ethos* during the Harlem Renaissance.

"HOME TO HARLEM": LOCATING THE *TOPOI* FOR AN AFRICAN AMERICAN *ETHOS*

Only a few claims regarding the Harlem Renaissance are uncontested; that *The New Negro* stands as the "keystone,"[39] the "revolutionary" advertisement,[40] and the "first national book"[41] of African America is one of them. As Harlem writers like Langston Hughes, Jean Toomer, and Claude McKay were gaining greater fame and because "some white writers had already found the Afro-American [to be] a salable commodity in the literary world,"[42] momentum was building for a cultural movement that tapped into post-WWI progressivism.[43] Black soldiers who returned from the war infused Harlem and other urban areas with optimism about race relations and black nationhood. Increasingly, great white hunters in search of the exotic made excursions into its underbelly after dark.[44] The rhythm and swing of Harlem began to set the tempo for the Broadway stage as musicals like *Shuffle Along* played to sold-out crowds.[45]

By 1924 Harlem had become a place where jubilant hedonists like white essayist Carl Van Vechten rubbed elbows with black poets like Countee Cullen. The venerable W.E.B. Du Bois, editor of the NAACP's *Crisis,* sought to "press black artists into service for the civil rights movement. They were asked to counter negative stereotypes fostered by white artists and propagandists who sought to maintain white supremacy and instigate contempt and hatred for blacks."[46] Sociologist Charles S. Johnson used the Urban League's *Opportunity* aggressively to manipulate Manhattan literati and to open doors for young black writers by putting them in contact with white patrons. Locke, a Harvard Rhodes scholar in philosophy, teamed up with Johnson and *Opportunity* to promote social enlightenment. Harlem was "in vogue,"[47] and in early 1924, the *Survey Graphic,* a magazine dedicated to "topics of intellectual and humanitarian concerns,"[48] commissioned Locke to edit a special issue on black culture. In March, "Harlem–Mecca of the New Negro" appeared and sold more than 30,000 copies in less than two weeks. The issue collected many disparate elements of Harlem artistry–poetry, fiction, and illustrations–under the banner of black art and officially signaled the beginning of the Harlem Renaissance.[49] Almost immediately thereafter, publisher Albert Boni asked Locke to begin work to transform the issue into an anthology. Following negotiations with Boni Brothers and various artists and essayists about contributions and layout, *The New Negro: An Interpretation* was published in December 1925. Like the special issue, the anthology bears Locke's distinctive philosophical and aesthetic imprint; the book ranges from critical commentary on the status of black art and culture to vivid poetry, fiction, and music. *The New Negro* does more than represent black artistry; it gathers "fugitive"[50] elements of African American history and culture and, through a reinterpretation of their relations, fosters the "forward motion" of an emerging racial consciousness.[51] The anthology received rave reviews, and Locke was established as the impresario of the "New Negro Movement." Even detractors

like Du Bois, a featured contributor to the anthology, could not deny that *The New Negro* was the Harlem Renaissance's most momentous development.[52]

Locke penned the anthology's forward and four key essays. These writings, "The New Negro," "Negro Youth Speaks." "The Negro Spirituals," and "The Legacy of the Ancestral Arts," characterize his hermeneutical rhetoric. They are interdependent and philosophically complex. Locke's Harvard training was in the philosophy of value, and he, like Du Bois, was influenced by the works of William James.[53] Jamesian pragmatics justifies the life of the mind in practical terms. That is, pragmatism grounds intellectualism because of its utility in solving social problems.[54] Pragmatism, therefore, warrants intellectuals as moral agents in the world. Jamesian philosophy tended to treat racial strife, however, as the result of misinformation that focused on transmission rather than misunderstanding and meaning. Locke and Du Bois altered Jamesian pragmatics to suit their rhetorical needs, focusing on black culture and subjectivity.[55] Locke viewed pragmatism as "anarchic pluralism and relativism," and he substituted for this atomism his own sense that cultural values have both distinctive and universal significance.[56] In the anthology, Locke marshals the tension between these two positions, channeling it into his reinterpretations of the relations among race, culture, and social policy.

"The New Negro" begins with Locke calling attention to the failure of conventional wisdom to understand black life; he blames outmoded relations among the "Sociologist, the Philanthropist, the Race-leader" for poor social studies and race relations.[57] Rather than pay tribute to the "watch and guard of [race] statistics," traditional policy makers who are accustomed to seeing black life as a "problem," Locke argues that these people misapprehend the "new psychology," the "new spirit" among "the younger generation," perceiving it to be the result of a sudden "metamorphosis" (3). This popular misunderstanding, Locke asserts, results from a persistent fiction; that is "the Old Negro had long become more of a myth than a man. The Old Negro, we must remember, was a creature of moral debate and historical controversy. His had been a stock figure perpetuated as historical fiction partly in innocent sentimentalism, partly in deliberate reactionism" (3).

Locke's rhetorical strategy begins to become apparent here. He distinguishes between the Old Negro and the New Negro by appropriating and revising the idioms of modernism and black folk culture through a series of hermeneutic moves. Modernity is called on to warrant the *ethos* of the New Negro even as it undergoes critical reconceptualization. Locke first demonstrates that the modern progressive alliance of social science and social policy does not illuminate black social development; it sustains a deception. From this perspective, the Old Negro is "something to be argued about, condemned or defended, to be 'kept down,' or 'in his place,' or 'helped up,' to be worried with or worried over, harassed or patronized, a social bogey or a social burden" (3). What is remarkable about this opening passage is that Locke also reveals and criticizes a black folk discursive strategy called masking.[58] "The Negro himself has contributed his share to this [misperception] through a sort of social mimicry forced upon him by the adverse circumstances of dependence" (3) In the tradition of black folktales, the trickster is a hero who beguiles the white imagination and subverts white supremacy by projecting a mask of ignorance, stupidity, or innocent naiveté.[59] Houston Baker has maintained that verbal misdirection is a distinctive strategy of African American folk heroes.[60] Because the race relations that fostered this discursive strategy are reinterpreted as outdated, Locke transforms the Old Negro into a tragic hero who is forced by a worn formula to wage an obsolete war with outdated weapons. The Old Negro must continue to pretend to be something other than who she really is, a mere shadow of herself (4).

Even as Locke discloses the Old Negro as a ruse, however, he maintains that this folk strategy was once functional because it masked and, thus, enabled "the actual march of development" of the New Negro (4). Locke measures this progression in terms of how the children of sharecroppers migrated from the rural South to the urban North. The march of black folk allowed them to "hurdle several generations of experience at a leap" and to behold "a new vision of opportunity . . . to seize . . . a chance

for the improvement of conditions" (6). Locke describes the migration as more than relocation; rather, "[w]ith each successive wave of it, the movement of the Negro becomes more and more *a mass movement* . . . from medieval America to modern" (6, emphasis added). In the trek from the pre-modern to the modern world, the New Negro developed "self-understanding," "self-respect," and is in the midst of "shaking off the psychology of imitation and implied inferiority" (4). The Great Migration takes on epic proportions; in its wake the New Negro becomes a cosmopolitan, like those responsible for "the Irish Renaissance" (51).

By casting aside the mask of the Old Negro, Locke's "changeling" (3) not only appears new, but also is endowed with a modern voice. Locke's distinction between the Old and the New continues in the essay, "Negro Youth Speaks." "Youth speaks, and the voice of the New Negro . . . accents the maturing speech of full racial utterance" (47). Locke has two key goals in this essay; to legitimize Harlem's "truer, finer group expression" (47) through further appropriations of the language of modernism and to revise the tenets of modernism by characterizing the racial expression of the New Negro as offering universal value. In contrast to New Negro expression, the writing of the Old Negro was "racially rhetorical rather than racially expressive" (48). Constrained by a system of Jim Crow paternalism and confronted with hideous caricatures of blackness in popular culture, black folk "felt art must fight social battles and compensate social wrongs" (50). This impulse led to the normative practice of representing the race with "the better foot foremost" (50). Locke contends that such public performances were deceptive and defensive. Artists were "posing" rather than exhibiting "poise" (48). They were necessary fabrications because they sustained black folk community, but as an inaccurate reflection of race relations and black self-concepts, they were unrealistic, not in touch with the actual march of development. Locke brings to light the effects of racism on cultural expression; masking reifies what it seeks to deconstruct; as a strategy for liberation, it is an "unstable concept."[61]

Conversely, New Negro artists have "achieved an objective attitude toward life"

(48). They "take their material objectively with a detached artistic vision" (50). The New Negro proudly voices a "new aesthetic and a new philosophy of life" that is in "alignment with contemporary artistic thought, mood, and style." The Harlem Renaissance writers are "thoroughly modern, some of them *ultra-modern,* and Negro thoughts now wear the uniform of the age" (50, emphasis added). Locke reinvents black folk as modernists, and warrants his claim by reinterpreting race as "an idiom of style" and a "contribution to the general resources of art" (51). Two senses of time operate in Locke's discourse. First, there is the sudden temporal displacement that accompanies a metamorphosis of black folk. Second, there is the actual march of time. Locke's hermeneutical rhetoric preserves both temporal movements. As a timeless icon, the Old Negro veiled the actual march of time from remote viewers. Thus, the sudden appearance of the New Negro "in his poetry, his art, his education, and his new outlook" warrants a radical reorientation of thought and social practice (5). New social methods are needed to comprehend this unknown entity. A true understanding of the New Negro "requires that the Negro of to-day be seen through other than the dusty spectacles of past controversy." Locke not only appropriates linguistic resources from the language of modern social thought, but he also transforms them;[62] the New Negro is *ultra-modern,* and therefore, "he must *know himself and be known for precisely what he is,* and for that reason he welcomes the new scientific rather than the old sentimental interest" (8, emphasis added). In place of the conventional propensity to treat black folk as a problem to be worried over, which is easily manipulated by the trickster, Locke suggests that the New Negro is a kind of (post) modern subject with an authentic viewpoint of his own. New Negroes *see themselves* with a "vigorous realism" (50). The Old interest undergoes a dual transformation–from sentimental to scientific, and from paternalistic to self-interested.

This distinction between the Old and the New compels black folk to know themselves, and it demands that whites and blacks become reacquainted with one another through new race relations and practices. Locke understood art to have such an ethical function because it disclosed alternative (and perhaps better) ways of being with others.[63] Unlike conventional cultural practices that masked the actual moods, desires, and motivations of black folk, New Negro cultural expressions are grounded in lived experiences, rooted in the actual march of time. Because these experiences are made up of the struggles of black folk to achieve common goals, "race" becomes a discursive element of modern art. Rather than a category used to identify persons by color, "race" is derived from cultural practices that can reasonably be grouped together.[64] Conventional wisdom understood "race" as biological;[65] thus, "race" conceived as an idiom or a style had not received proper treatment heretofore; it was a fixed feature of the Old Negro. The New Negro, on the other hand, seeks to "evolve" from the racial substance something technically distinctive . . . [i]n flavor of language, flow of phrase, accent of rhythm in prose, verse and music, color and tone of imagery, idiom and timbre of emotion and symbolism . . . The newer motive, then, in being racial is to be so purely for the sake of art" (51).

Locke's reformulation of modernism continues. Although he claims that this motive is new, it is best exemplified in the universality of the Old Negro sorrow songs. This is precisely why the Old Negro is not erased in what appears to be a radical disjunction with the past. Because discursive practices like masking *sustained* black folk through time, Locke brings forward folk tradition and a Southern cultural legacy as *topoi* for the New Negro. In the essay "The Negro Spirituals," the sorrow songs are treated as emotional reservoirs with great pragmatic value. The sentiment and functions of these songs demonstrate the need for further study of folk tradition. As "a classic folk expression," the Spirituals are a sign of black folk "genius" that can only be appreciated as "deeply representative of the soil that produced them" (199). Given his constitution of the New Negro as an ultra-modernist who depicts race "purely for the sake of art," Locke's hermeneutical rhetoric hinges on his ability to characterize the Spirituals as giving rise to distinctive racial expressions that contribute to an array of universal values. His reinterpretation of the Spirituals allows him to treat them as "classical" and as possessing a "peculiar quality" that is due to their emotional content and their pragmatic nature (208). Speaking broadly, Locke's education encouraged him to envision diverse cultural practices as having an integrity and authenticity that can only be apprehended through a careful analysis of how such practices sustain specific ways of life. The value of such practices is directly related to how important they are to the preservation and perpetuation of elements of a particular social system. From this perspective, no group's values and beliefs can be asserted over another group's based solely on abstract principles. The distinctiveness of "concrete human experience" warrants cultural pluralism.[66]

This sense of grounded cultural activity, bounded by common interests, is a conduit to universalism. The Spirituals are "artistically precious things" that "stand the test of time" because they embody black folk's appropriate responses to a situation (199). As a means for the Old Negro to express the grief of the dispossessed and the faith of a people looking toward a horizon of possibilities, moreover, the Spirituals redeem the soul of the trickster because masking had great propriety in localized practice. Similarly, the Spirituals empower singers to find ways to make something out of nothing. As a case in point, Locke recounts the adventures of the Fisk Jubilee Singers, who are credited not only with bringing the Spirituals to the world, but also with raising enough money to save Fisk University (202–203). Locke's narrative about the utility of the Spirituals transforms them into "culture-goods"[67] that circulate within specific cultural boundaries to maintain the health of a black folk life world.

Locke explains that it is the character of the Spirituals as life-affirming emotional utterances working effectively within specific lived conditions that allows them to be "fundamentally and everlastingly human" (199). "Indeed," he writes, "they transcend emotionally even the very experience of sorrow out of which they were born; their mood is that of religious exaltation, a degree of ecstasy indeed that makes them in spite of the crude vehicle a classic expression of the religious emotion. They lack the grand style, but never the sublime effect" (200–201). Locke brings into sharp relief the important tension between the distinctive and

the universal. Although the Spirituals have been widely recognized by virtue of their universal value, they also have been transplanted out of the black church into the theater. "And the concert stage has but taken them an inevitable step further from their original setting," away from the lived experiences that constituted them (202). As classical and universal expressions, impersonations are inevitable, but as the Spirituals are distorted with "formal European idioms and mannerisms" on the concert stage, purists double the damage by removing them from their vital places and cramming them into the "narrow confines" of "arbitrary style or form" in the name of preserving tradition (207–208).

Locke invokes the "vision and courage" of the New Negro to address this cultural dilemma. The New Negro is both an ultra-modern artist and a "sensitive race interpreter" (200, 205). Embodying this hermeneutist, Locke sketches the problem that the New Negro solves. The Spirituals are pushed and pulled in different directions because universalism is misperceived as a form of *sameness,* and cultural pluralism is misunderstood as rigid or pure identification.[68] Within this flawed logic, universal values are treated as a-historical and abstract, while cultural difference stands in opposition, privileging distinctive group identity. This kind of dialectic results in arbitrariness and relativism instead of "relative and functional rightness" because it extracts the spirituals from lived experience.[69] In exploring the Spirituals, however, the New Negro would avoid either extreme through "the most careful study of the communal life as it still lingers in isolated spots" (205). By highlighting the need for understanding the situated performance of the sorrow songs, Locke, like Du Bois and James Weldon Johnson before him, asserts social function as a criterion for cultural criticism. "We should always remember," he argues, "that [the Spirituals] are essentially congregational, not theatrical, just as essentially they are a choral not a solo form" (202). The Spirituals are returned to the group life that generated them so that "modern interpretation [can] . . . relate these songs to the folk activities that they motivated, classifying them by their respective song types" (205). Because these folk activities are responses to lived experience through time, "there is and can be no set limitation" (208). Neither universal categories nor group identity is a *priori;* each is an interpretation framed by a history of interpretations. What is at stake here is not the right absolute, but an interpenetrating set of interpretive acts.

Importantly, the outline for an aesthetic *praxis* emerger here. Locke's argument authorizes the New Negro as a principal investigator; it also posits that the proper treatment of the Spirituals and other African American cultural forms is realized by experiencing their emotional content (204). Rather than perceive the joy and pain and dialect of the Spirituals as corruptions of abstract concepts of piety, Locke's discussion discloses their sublimity and propriety. In the Spirituals, eloquence is a form of reverence; "for all of their inadequacies, the words are the vital clues to the moods of these songs. If anything is to be changed it should be the popular attitude" (204). For Locke, public opinion reflects how people feel about objects and ideas. These "emotional judgments" are "rooted in modes or kinds of valuing."[70] Locke suggests that as one's emotions are educated in close proximity to cultural practices (a mode of valuing), rather than from a remote distance (a different mode of valuing), one can achieve a greater range and depth of understanding. "The role of feeling can never be understood nor controlled through minimizing it; to admit it is the beginning of practical wisdom in such matters."[71] The New Negro characterizes such wisdom because her modern pragmatism, her understanding of cultural expression, is cultivated through close contact with black folk cultural traditions. This orientation is not so much a loss of objectivity as an acquisition of insight.

Locke is not just interested in conceiving of a New Negro; he seeks to establish his mode of invention; thus, he argues for a form of New Negro training: "We cannot accept the attitude that would merely preserve this music, but must cultivate that which would also develop it. Equally with treasuring and appreciating it as music of the past, we must nurture and welcome its contribution to the music of to-morrow" (210). Locke continues to enact his hermeneutical rhetoric through an aesthetic *praxis* in the essay "The Legacy of the Ancestral Arts," which reinterprets the character of African art and Africa's relation to black folk. Because "the American Negro brought over [from Africa] as an emotional inheritance a deep-seated aesthetic endowment," the U.S. social climate produced a black art that is "free, exuberant, emotional, sentimental and human." In contrast, African art is "rigid, controlled, disciplined, abstract, heavily conventionalized" (254). This distinction has two related purposes: first, it transforms a long history of African creativity into a formal tradition. Indeed, Locke details the ways in which the well-defined aesthetic discipline of African art has influenced the progression of European form (258–260). Second, it offers African art as a classic model that can be the basis for New Negro *imitatio.* "Then possibly from a closer knowledge and proper appreciations of the African arts must come increased effort to develop our artistic talents in the discontinued and lagging channels of sculpture, painting and the decorative arts" (255).

Locke's point is that a New Negro *ethos* should inhabit a place of antiquity, making black cultural expression both Old and New; thus, Locke's hermeneutical rhetoric infuses the future with the past. What Africa offers here is not romance nor "cultural inspiration or technical innovations, but the lesson off a *classic background,* the lesson of discipline, of style, of technical control pushed to the limits of technical mastery" (256, emphasis added). African norms and practices are not called on in reaction to European hegemony; rather, they are to be African American *topoi,* "the guidance of a distinctive tradition" (266). The course for New Negro artistry, then, is clear: "We ought and must have a school of Negro art, a local and a racially representative tradition" that will fulfill "the" promising beginning of an art movement instead of just the cropping out of isolated talent" (266). This fulfillment cannot be assessed in terms of bricks and mortar; it occurs through an on-going process in which the New Negro artists draw from distinct cultural traditions always already reinventing themselves and their voice. Throughout the *New Negro,* Locke's hermeneutical rhetoric is a demonstration of just such a practice.

Conclusions

The New Negro: An Interpretation is aptly titled. The anthology exhibits an anatomy that coordinates a diversity of places and perspectives from which an African American *ethos* may be cultivated. These places are populated with voices that can be encouraged to engage in a kind of dialogue. As Leff has said, hermeneutical rhetoric "circulates influence"[72] among these places, manufacturing "argosies of cultural exchange and enlightenment" (14). Such a practice lives at the intersection of rhetoric and hermeneutic, self and other. "In the end a philosophical hermeneutics is about self-understanding; but this . . . has little to do with a philosophy of subjectivity. Rather, it has to do with our *being at home in the world* that we are awakened to in the voice of the other."[73] In addition to the other issues that Locke takes up in the *New Negro,* the constitution of an African American dwelling places calls attention to the ways that his discursive practice revitalizes traditions—conjures them—even as he offers up those traditions for public critique and revision.

I have argued that Alain Locke enacts a hermeneutical rhetoric that exhibits an aesthetic *praxis.* Locke's rhetoric is intriguing because it provides a clear case study of the ways that rhetorical topics mediate public conversations about their own nature as ideas and practices. It reminds us of how important it is to release ourselves toward the experiences that, at the outset, make understanding possible. This knowledge is not superficial simply because we conceive of it discursively. Indeed, the meaning of our lived experiences is itself oriented by these interpretive acts. Such knowledge is transfusional and emotive. Being at home in the world does not refer only to finding a resting place; it also means *being welcomed into a place* by other dwellers. It requires the *desire* to establish community. Locke's aesthetic *praxis* is attuned to articulating the means for sharing feelings regarding our most basic fears and desires. It attends to the character of the practices that influence how our needs are met or frustrated. It also provokes dialogue about the cultural habits that are most at stake at any given moment.

As I have shown, the facticity that must be granted human life and work offers pragmatic ills and remedies for social thought about race and culture. Locke clearly understood that his notion of cultural pluralism could promote false loyalty and false divisions based on "*superficial difference*" (60). Locke was wary of the ways in which "race" and culture have been conceived as permanent values, reifying each. As derivations of the biological, race and culture are essentialist concepts that structure hierarchies of civilization. Thus, "civilized" groups rationalize the imposition of their identities on others, erasing the other's cultural distinctiveness. Such an imposition does not constitute an invitation to dwell in a common place; rather, it signifies the maintenance of abstract categorical schemes of rightness. Locke's notion of universalism is quite different from the instantiation of such arbitrary universals, based on ignorance, fear, or a thirst for power.[74] "What the contemporary mind stands greatly in need of is the divorce of the association of uniformity with the notion of the universal, and the substitution of the notion of equivalence."[75] Cultural pluralism arises out of a fundamental respect for human struggle and action. Arbitrary universals do not correspond to any on–going human experience, except possibly by fiat.

Arbitrary universals, however, produce worldly effects; they spark counter-offensives in the name of nationalism.[76] To Locke, such moves undermine the power of cultural pluralism because they promote practices that are impious, improper, and imprudent—cordoned off from a people's lived experiences. "Race," in Locke's conception, is neither an abstract category nor the prized possession of the nationalist. It is descriptive of community practices and public activity. "Blackness," then, becomes an achievement that requires public critique and commitment. "Race" does not become irrelevant; rather, it is made significant by the public recognition that it is *not* a given. Moreover, "race" in this sense becomes an ethical topic for public deliberation. We cannot speak of its conservation or dissolution without opening up for discussion the kinds of interests that would be supported or undermined. By the same token, "whiteness" becomes subject to public critique.

It is particularly urgent that such public conversations take place. The 21st century promises many advances, but it is also fostering the proliferation of hate groups. The Internet has made hate accessible and anonymous. Whiteness is often posited as a birthright and a kind of property that is being stolen, or, worse still, hate groups warn of the impending death of whiteness and circle the wagons preparing for W.A.R. (White Aryan Resistance).

Locke was familiar with this form of fear and hatred. Spurred by anti-immigrant sentiment and scientific racism, white supremacists bemoaned the possibility of whiteness being washed away in a "rising tide of color" (14). Locke's hermeneutical rhetoric affirms a group's rights to conceive of its own cultural practices; but his aesthetic *praxis* promotes a search for commonality across cultural enclaves, frustrating the nationalist (and supremacist) tendency toward isolation. Furthermore, his reinterpretation of race and culture as topics makes them mobile. It is instructive that the New Negro's search for home results in expanding the circumference of commonplaces through an affirmation of local difference. The lesson Locke teaches us is that *the principle of identification breeds contempt* Locke's hermeneutical rhetoric cultivates the authority of persons to constitute distinctive but equivalent forms of living. It also habituates practices that resist their reification. The process is both useful and healthy because rhetoric's "universal" turn necessarily involves the construction of a place in which we can all feel at home.

Discussion Questions

1. What does Watts identify as the two major challenges to the African American ethos during the Harlem Renaissance?

2. What is *hermeneutics*?

3. What is the function of hermeneutical rhetoric?

4. How was Alain Locke's philosophy indicative of pragmatism?

5. What does it mean to be a modernist and how did Alain Locke reformulate this idea?

Reading 2.3

PLAYING THE DOZENS

Folklore as Strategies for Living

THURMON GARNER

This study is an analysis of an obscene folkloric speech event popularly known in Black communities as "playing the dozens."[1] The game is an important rhetorical device which promotes community stability and cooperation by regulating social and personal conflicts. This expressive game influences, controls, guides or directs human actions in ways consistent with community norms. Like riddles, jokes, superstitions, and folklore generally, the dozens engineers solutions to recurring social problems of a group.[2] It does this through strategic forms of suggestion, persuasion, legislation, justification, social pressure, play or instruction.

Previous analyses have focused on the psychological functions the game serves in the Black community. John Dollard's pioneering essay reported that the game was a pattern of interactive insult which functioned as "a value for aggression in a depressed group."[3] He concluded that White oppression and social neglect have given rise to the game. Although the dozens is a form of displaced aggression, it is an in-group phenomenon directed toward Blacks rather than Whites. Consequently, no racial overtones exist in the game. Roger D. Abrahams focused on identity problems of Black males and reasoned that the dozens functioned as exorcism which liberated Black males from the dominant influence of strong mothers in matriarchal families. According to Abrahams, not only are Black men subordinated in a life dominated by women, but they are Black men in a White man's world.[4] In Abrahams' view the dozens game also is an in-group phenomenon that relieves racial tensions because it helps boys become men so they can face the problems of a household dominated by women and created by slavery. Although one might disagree with conclusions reached by both researchers, it is difficult to dismiss their interpretations, for the maternal figure is a predominant theme in the ritual of the dozens and the use of obscenity is an effective rhetorical technique for channeling anger in an oppressed group.[5]

Yet, important questions remain, and neither researcher answers them. For example, why do girls play the dozens if males have the

From Garner, T.E. (1983). Playing the dozens: Folklore as strategies for living. *Quarterly Journal of Speech, 69*, 47-57.

identification problem? Why do contestants also vilify males if they want to cut mother's apron strings? How does the dozens reflect the cultural norms and values of a group? The author's present research and experiences suggest that answers to these questions lie in viewing the dozens as a rhetorical device which serves the Black community by promoting attitudes, modes of action, and solutions to recurring social problems. The dozens is a pedagogic device that instructs citizens in communication strategies for the resolution of conflict in routine daily interactions.

This essay is an updated version of the author's larger field study of the daily routines among Blacks in an actual urban community fictitiously named "Tattler."[6] The community is a mixture of lower, middle, and upper-middle class Blacks who share a history dating back to the 1930s. Tattlerites also share admiration for a good story teller, a teller of lies, a frank discussion, and entertaining conversations. The effective talker is valued, not only for his ability to entertain, but for his capability to get along with others. One community member felt that communicative accommodation contributed to the stable and cooperative character of the community. He said that when he was growing up people solved their problems by "talking them out," indicating that talk also had a practical function. Viewed from this perspective, the dozens is a highly visible form of talk found in public places where social problems occur.

Material for the present study was collected over a period of eighteen months. The researcher lived in Tattler and employed participant-observer techniques for gathering firsthand information about patterns of communication. Data were gathered from the places adolescents and adults "hang out." Adolescents and young adults provided the examples. In addition, older adults shared insights about the game's value. "Up on the corner" is the phrase that Tattlerites used to denote the places where adults gathered. The corner consisted of the poolroom, its parking lot, a field behind the poolroom, and the parking lot of a small market. Younger Tattlerites met at locations where they played basketball, football, and baseball.

A follow-up study determined how older adults viewed the game. Subjects were a group of twelve men, all over forty-five, members of the Veterans of Foreign Wars (VFW) and retired, and who held regular morning breakfast in one section of a building next to the poolroom. The technique of unstructured interviewing was used to gather information.

The theoretical framework which governed the analysis of data was based on Abrahams' delineation of a rhetorical theory of folklore.[7] Essentially, Abrahams' approach views folkloric items as expressions of recurrent societal problems which articulate conflict and provide a temporary means of resolution in order to promote community. Each *item* of folklore is viewed as an implement of argument or tool of persuasion which seeks to affect the audience in some way. A rhetorical approach to folklore centers on understanding the relationship among the folkloric item as performed, the problem it articulates, and the solutions it proposes. To analyze that relationship "is to understand what the strategy of the piece is: of what it wants to convince the hearer, and how it goes about convincing."[8] Strategy for Abrahams is "argument" or "method of attack."[9] By viewing events as strategy, one begins to understand how an item of folklore attacks antisocial behavior by attempting to direct and guide people's actions. The central concern here, then, is to understand the influential function of the dozens in Tattler by determining its method of attack on personal and societal problems in the community.

The dozens game as played in Tattler has characteristics like those described by previous researchers.[10] The game is an aggressive contest which makes use of obscene language to ridicule and vilify an opponent's family, particularly the mother. The game is played by adolescents and young adults in group settings. There is a "clean" and a "dirty" version of the game. In the former, a player uses language devoid of obscene or sexual references. Examples of the clean dozens are "Your mamma looks like the Hulk" and "Your sister wears high heel sneakers." The latter version is predominant and in it a player uses derogatory sexual references about one's mother, father, sisters, or brothers, such as, "I fucked your mama in the middle of the night; that's why your sister is an ugly sight."

Adolescents used a rhyming version: "Your daddy's a fag and your mama is on the rag; Your sister needs busting before she becomes an old hag." Adults are less prescriptive and more creative; they improvise lines suitable for the occasion. One respondent, whose father was a source of ridicule because his name was Porkchop responded: "They call him Porkchop because he pokes your mamma and chops your daddy." Adults did not play the game with adolescents, but males played with females.[11] In public settings, the game is played across class lines. On occasions fighting was perceived as inevitable, but fighting, according to residents, was the recourse of a "loser." As a folkloric event, Tattlerites have recognized the dozens game as part of their culture since the 1930s.

THE DOZENS AS ARTIFICIAL CONFLICT

"Expressive folklore," writes Abrahams, "embodies and reflects recurrent social conflicts, thus giving them a 'name,' a representative and traditionally recognizable symbolic form. To handle the materials of this representation is to reveal the problem situation in a controlled context."[12] In the Tattler community playing the dozens "names" a public conflict situation in which members of a small group deliberately antagonize each other, but under significant but subtle constraints. The game, referred to as a contest, sets up an artificial interpersonal conflict situation, provides it with an adversary relationship and attempts to establish a sense of identification between the artificial forms and the real forms of conflict which it represents.

The people of Tattler are quick to recognize similarities between the dozens game and "real life" conflicts. They note that "real" life is composed of a series of "personal conflicts," of "oppositions," and "ups and downs." For Tattlerites conflict is, among other things, "getting on someone's case" (antagonizing), "going to fist city" (collision), or "going after the same man or women" (competition). Informants expressed the feeling that real everyday conflicts are easily recognized by the uneasy feeling or tensions that are created. While the game is a form of play, here the dozens becomes functional. Tensions are created, experienced, and coped with.

The dozens game in Tattler has an appearance of hostility, rather than of play. The talk is often nasty and dirty. Players use verbal insults to antagonize, confront, and "best" an opponent. The linguistic strategy is to attack. The themes are designed to provoke since they address female sexual promiscuity, male homosexuality, and immorality of other kin. In Tattler I heard players of the game say, "Your mama eats elephant dicks," "Your daddy licks red cow pussy" or "Your sister sits on corncobs." These would be fighting words under conditions other than those of the dozens game. A player's objective is to devastate an opponent verbally through ridicule and vilification. Opponents smile, but only so as to leave an impression of ill will; players stand facing each other as if locked in deadly oral combat. Although they don't, no one is sure if contestants will lose control and fight. The game's structure is such that opponents become upset and feel uncomfortable. The dramatic form is of individuals in conflict.

The dozens, as played in Tattler, is essentially a form of group conflict. When there are three or four interactants, the contest sometimes becomes a free-for-all in which each member talks about the other, or they pair-off or almost all gang up on one person. When a large audience is present, it characteristically tries to remain neutral. To keep the contest alive, the group switches its support between contestants. On-lookers are necessary to inspire competition between contestants and to reward the winner with a reputation of a "man of words."[13] On occasion, the audience ridicules players to the point that the artificial conflict situation almost becomes real conflict.

But the dozens is a contest. Because it is also viewed as a form of entertainment, the game works its rhetorical magic by suggestion. Through an entertaining format, solutions to social conflicts are articulated. For individuals in conflict, the game promotes an understanding of self and the adoption of a guarded attitude toward others.

RHETORICAL RESOLUTION OF CONFLICT

The dozens game in Tattler articulates interpersonal conflict and offers strategic solutions to the problems posed. The game does not use language which is instructive but promotes through involvement several attitudes which a speaker may adopt in conflict situations. The rhetorical power of the game resides in the fact that performers project conflict but resolve it without fighting. Because the game is brought to a conclusion, players create the illusion that heated conflicts can be solved in daily life by the same techniques. Ultimately the dozens game functions to regulate relationships among community members. The game suggests, to Tattlerites, rhetorical options for handling interpersonal conflicts. That the dozens game strategically promotes the adoption of an attitude toward conflict resolution and then guides behavior accordingly is supported by information gleaned from informants in the Tattler community. The most pressing and recurring social problem for residents of Tattler is "getting along." The game casts its advice for "getting along" through rhetorical techniques based on a *strategy of cool* and a *strategy of measured response.*

"Cool"

The dozens game helps to resolve social conflicts by encouraging communicative self-control. A central function of the game is to regulate personal behavior so that it conforms to community norms. The game does so through a two-part *strategy of cool.* One aspect of cool means to be in control of the information one transmits. Players are expected to act aggressively and attempt to direct the exchange of ideas. The second part of cool is based on projecting an image of composure by appearing detached or otherwise in possession of one's mental and emotional capabilities. To be effective the speaker must remain "poised."

The game suggests that control is necessary to the resolution of interpersonal conflicts. One method for controlling others is to dominate them rhetorically. Significantly, this attitude is implied in the terms "screaming," "downing," and "sounding." To "scream on" an antagonist is to verbally attack, and to "down" or "put-down" an opponent is to attempt to subdue or master the relationship. Young Tattlerites also

"sound on" or speak unkindly of another player. On-lookers agree that a contestant is getting the worst of an exchange, or "blown away," if continuously "screamed on," "downed," or "sounded on." To win grandly is to crush an opponent with insults and to humble him before the group. The symbolic trophy of winner goes to the player who verbally "bests" an opponent. All these terms symbolize control, albeit through ritualized conflict.

Young Tattlerites develop their own methods of attempting to control a dozens encounter. Young but inexperienced players known for well-placed one liners, are labeled "stingers." They know how to demoralize an opponent with a few over-powering statements. Other players are able to control because they are "witty" and retaliate without hesitation. My observation revealed that players in control of situations were also commanding the direction and flow of events and enjoyed the most success in building reputations. Dominant and aggressive players attacked and kept opponents on the defensive. Thus, the less aggressive opponents constantly responded to the attackers' definition of the situation. Groups favored and supported with laughter those participants who attacked; those who constantly responded to the attacker earned markedly less applause. According to informants, if a player is successful in his attack, an opponent "won't have no comeback."

The counterpart to an aggressive rhetorical attack is an aggressive verbal counterattack. Young Tattlerites felt that aggressive and dominant players can be put on the defensive. Even the "Greatest," Muhammad Ali, has had to react to punch. But a lucky punch calls for an authoritative counterpunch. Tattlerites use the term "comeback" to denote such a response to a punch or a "put-down." A "comeback" may be weak or strong but if one is to control the situation his "come back" must be strong and aggressive. "Topped," "capped," or "excelled" name those responses which are stronger than the "put-down" they respond to. The most effective "come-back" uses the theme of the "put-down," but frames it creatively. For example, the comment, "Mr. Rufus is older than dirt" got a hearty response from the group. The enthusiasm of on-lookers apparently was a result of a change of themes, from smell to age, and a creative way of framing age. The "comeback," "Ms. Mae is older than dirt" was mildly rewarded, possibly because the reply lacked creativity and the "put down" had provided closure since nothing was older than dirt. In another context and with a slightly older group of males around the age of fifteen, a similar "put-down" was made. The initial insult used the theme that a father was older than the beginning of time. The "comeback," which was received favorably by the group, centered on the themes that the attacker's mother was older than his father, was Father Time's great grandmother, and her age could be seen in the long hairs growing out of her nose. This "comeback" used the original theme of age, embellished it, and restated it creatively as an aggressive and forceful rejoinder.

If put in the position of defending oneself, the dozens game suggests that responses or comebacks should take the initiative from the attacker. The dozens game also suggests that in conflict situations gaining control means to "take charge." Older Tattlerites agree that control in interpersonal conflict situations is based upon being dominant and aggressive. To them, the marks of a man or a woman are that they protect themselves physically and verbally. An aggressive verbal stance is necessary for three reasons. First, an aggressive stance demonstrates that the speaker is committed to a position. Second, Tattlerites believe one's public image is enhanced if a player demonstrates the ability to influence others with superior verbal "firepower." Third, to "put up a fight" signals that the attacker will not have an easy prey and will suffer. They do not always attribute their rhetorical position to the dozens, but their tales and their stories are loaded with references to "screaming," "cracking," "signifying" and "jumping in someone's shit."

The game suggests that control and personal power are gained by a rhetorical strategy of dominance based on verbal aggressiveness and forcefulness. The audience's response reinforces that impression by reacting favorably to the players attack and whose "comebacks" are forceful. Moreover, players are seen as symbolically giving up or "falling apart" when they fail to respond verbally.

The rhetorical intent of "screaming" is to unedge an opponent and make him or her "blow his cool." If a player is successful, he or she stigmatizes an opponent, damages his or her public image, and causes the person to lose face. But a speaker adopts a passive rhetorical position as a means of influencing an antagonist's behavior. Tattlerites observe that persons who assume impassive stances for effect are "cool, calm, and collected," "tight" or "poised." This rhetorical tactic of appearing detached, aloof, and in control of one's wits and emotions can be successful if perceived *as a tactic.* "Poise," then, refers to the ability of a speaker to maintain composure in a crisis situation.

A player's strategy is to abuse an opponent orally until the opponent loses control, becomes hot tempered or "falls apart." To become "rattled" and make noticeable verbal mistakes are signs of weakness and imply that a player is "upset"and is "losing composure." To "freeze" by failing to respond to a challenge implies that a player has "lost" his or her wits completely. Visible changes in posture, gestures, facial expressions, and any unnecessary movement can signal that a player is agitated and indicate loss of composure. Fighting, informants note, is a complete loss of "cool."

Adults recognize that the dozens game promotes composure or poise. They give credit to its influence both consciously and unconsciously. A discussion of the value of the game revealed some men felt the dozens influenced them directly in the way they handled themselves in hostile situations. An elderly member of the group who failed to see value in the game except to "cause trouble" told the story of a friend of the group who was hospitalized after responding physically to verbal abuse. This gentleman said, "That's the same *Q* who smiled at us years ago and never got upset when we talked about this mother. And you know how bad we stayed on his case." His comment indicates that the game has alleged value the permanence of which is not always readily acknowledged or recognized.

Tattlerites believe that conflicts are not to be resolved for long periods of time but are to be negotiated and won through aggressive rhetorical techniques in an ongoing fashion. Conflict resolution or "getting along" requires that antagonists bring their hostilities into the open by "telling it like it is." Consequently, presentations in conflict situations are emotional, tense, and threatening. Telling others "like it is" contributes to highly charged interpersonal relationships. Yet, it is in these charged situations that interpersonal conflicts are negotiated, reaffirmed, and community is restored. Out of these intense emotional encounters can emerge a refreshed cooperative interpersonal spirit. Abrahams refers to this type of interaction as a special Afro-American *aufheben*. The sense in which he uses the term is "the means by which opposition is transformed into affirmation."[14] Similarly Tattlerites believe that a method for resolving interpersonal conflicts is to "get it out into the open." Antagonists have the option to sit and talk it out in a subdued fashion, but the method Tattlerites follow is to dramatize the conflict. Their actions appear aggressive because their approach is to escalate rather than de-escalate tensions. Emotional intensity increases the level of interaction so that participants' "true feelings" are immediately projected. Residents view such intense communicative interactions as rewarding because true feelings are expressed and therefore, they believe subsequent communicative interactions will be open and honest. Opponents will know that to expect. So, through a dramatization of opposing forces community is affirmed.

This perspective helps to place the folkloric event of the dozens in the Tattler community as a cultural mechanism for providing solutions for conflict. Each player attempts to make his opponent fall apart. The strategy is to escalate the encounter and increase the tension between the parties. Players are not searching for true feelings, but they are learning a useful technique by which they can express true feelings in future, real life situations. As a speaker attacks, the listener seeks to remain composed and poised; he has to "take it" or find himself in an awkward position in which his friends can see him emotionally disintegrate.

The end result of dozens game is that participants acquire at least outward self-control in interactions that are very intense. It seems significant that adults in Tattler expect exchanges in conflict situations to be verbally aggressive so that "feelings" come to the surface. But they also expect that, at least in public settings, participants in conflicts should have the ability to handle increased emotional pitch in exchanges. Looked at in this light the dozens serves as an instructive process calculated to bring out in future but real conflicts true feelings, increase ability to handle, "pressure" and to encourage better communicative relationships.

MEASURED RESPONSE

Tattlerites believe that in real life situations they can handle emotionally intense communicative encounters without resorting to physical abuse. They expect antagonists to maintain control over their own feelings, and demand that a speaker's responses fit the intensity of the occasion. The *strategy of measured response* is a process found within the dozens game which forces upon participants audience awareness and cognitive discovery of themes. The strategy of the game functions to guide Tattlerites in their selection of emotional responses appropriate for the occasion.

Tattlerites view an audience as central and necessary for the game to transpire. The game, as played in the community, is a public speech event and no one remembered ever playing with only one other person present. So, at least three people are necessary for initiating and playing the dozens. During the dozens sessions I observed in Tattler, as few as four and as many as fifteen people participated in the game. The dozens game suggests that listeners will interact with the speaker in predictable ways, as catalyst, judge, and regulator.

Rhetorically, players want to make points with the audience. Listeners react to contestants as do audiences for other sporting contests. They yell support or voice disapproval. Approval is demonstrated orally be encouraging remarks and nonverbally by enthusiastic movements. But unlike spectators in other sporting events, the audience for the dozens not only voices support or disapproval but it judges contestants as well. Players get instant reading of who is the audience's favorite and which player scores the most points. Participants recognize that in some cases the audience acts as judge and that it will award a symbolic prize of "winner."

Players recognize that the audience has the ability to move contestants in directions they do not always wish to go. The actions of on-lookers keep the game going or allow it to die away. Usually, however, the audience lifts the spirits of the contestant receiving the worst of an encounter. Through statements such as "Hang in there," "Hold tight," or "You'll get it together, keep pushing" the group inspires. If there is need, new contestants are drawn from on-lookers. This happens when one player is much superior to his opponent or when the opponent needs to save face. On-lookers who are most zealous in their support for a particular contestant are the first to be drawn into the contest. According to informants, audiences in Tattler have been known to agitate participants and move them to fighting, with challenges such as "I wouldn't let him talk about my mama that way," or "If you don't hit him you ain't a man." Tattlerites call this type of behavior "instigating." Ultimately, players become cognizant of the capabilities of the audience in its role as catalyst.

At times the role of audience is to defuse a potentially hostile situation. When abuses become personal and participants, "blow their cool" to the point of wanting to fight, group members may remind contestants that the event is only a game and should be played as such. In one such episode a fight seemed inevitable, but members of the audience cautioned antagonists that they were not leaving Tattler and would face each other on another day. The audience may also disperse or remain silent as methods of defusing hostility. "If you can't stand the shame don't play the game" is the standard warning. As catalyst or peace makers, the audience regulates the interactions between players of the dozens.

Adults in Tattler recognized the important role on-lookers played. They observed that when listeners were very supportive, players became inspired; when the audience was less supportive a player searched for themes he hoped would hit a responsive chord. A good player, they noted, had a repertoire of sayings, kept one eye on the audience, and used his verbal skills to win them over. Some players were better than others, informants observed. This was not because they had more stock arguments but because they had the "good sense" to "figure out" the "mood" of the audience and play to it.

Normally the audience for the dozens game assumed the role of judge, viewing the game as a contest and players as "contenders" for the title of "winner." To them, "contending" meant having the ability to verbally "hold one's own" in a dozens face-off. Players could not "contend" if they failed to find appropriate topics to use against an opponent. "Contending" for players was not a formal method of argumentation: it was the ability to discover and use themes and topics to fit the occasion. Those players who are good at "contending" are alert to events around them. During an episode of the game one contestant observed that his opponent's mother would be rounding the corner in a minute. At that moment, an elderly woman bent with age, wrinkled, and walking with a cane appeared at the corner. Everyone laughed with such forcefulness that the speaker's opponent could not contend since he failed to "comeback." "Contending" in playing the dozens puts severe demands on players' rhetorical invention.

Contestants in the dozens game drew their material for insulting from several general topics. The dominant references were to sexual activities of one's family. But, physical features such as age yield standard claims: "Your mama was George Washington's slave." Appearance is another topic: Your sister is so uugly (yougly) my dogs wouldn't go out with her." Likewise, a condition such as poverty: "Your family is so poor that roaches starve to death." Other attributes such as smell, food, weight, and clothes become *topoi* from which material for claims is drawn.

Contestants used stock responses against an opponent. One such verse heard in the Tattler community was:

> I fucked your mama
> She's a good old soul
> She's got a ten-ton pussy
> And a rubber asshole
> She's got hair on her pussy
> That sweeps the floor
> She's got knobs on her titties
> That open the door.

This response was used by adolescents; teenagers used longer and complicated toasts.[15]

This verse and similar ones have been passed along to be memorized by younger players. Older informants remembered using it in the forties and fifties and the same verse can be found in other works on the dozens.[16]

Players in the dozens game also made use of special topics. Young adults drew their themes from community, local, state, and national events. Presidents Nixon, Ford, and Carter were mentioned in some of the games observed, but the most numerous references were to local characters. In Tattler, references to Ms. *W* the community drunk and *R* the local vagrant served as special topics. Insults based on community events and characters often drew applause, but personalized attacks were considered inappropriate.

Members of the VFW attributed some of their interpersonal successes in conflict situations to having the ability to "contend" with an opponent. The dozens game was influential in that respect. One member claimed that in his youth his tactic centered around "playing along with the audience" rather than "playing against an opponent." Consequently, he drew his themes from local events because he believed that everyone possessed knowledge about the community. He testified that the dozens game taught him to "watch and wait." In adopting that position, he claimed to have gained insights about his opponent which allowed him to select themes to fit the occasion. In interpersonal conflict situations he guards his responses until he "figures out" the attitude of his listener. Other adults summed up their methods of handling people and the rhetorical positions they take by, in one way or another, applying the same principle that one "figured out" the power relationship between himself and others. The object in real life conflicts is to discover appropriate themes based on the role relationship between antagonists. So, in everyday life, residents felt conflicts could be managed providing the speakers "watched what he said."

The dozens game, by creating a rhetorical situation, teaches participants to measure their communicative responses. In real life, analogous conflicts arise; then, the elders of Tattler believe, players of the dozens are likely to have learned indirectly that the entire community becomes audience. And like the audience of the dozens game, this larger group will relate to individuals as catalyst, judge, instigator or regulator. Armed with knowledge of the audience the speaker may adopt themes which help him draw out his opponent's "true feelings." To get an opponent to "say what he means" involves escalating the emotional climate. And to get to the point where antagonists "let it all hang out" relies on maintaining open lines of communication. The proper reply keeps communication channels open. Antagonists used themes and topics strategically to help move interactants to higher levels of emotional intensity. They gradually escalated the tension so that interactants would continue to talk. As a rhetorical device for conflict resolution, the strategy of the dozens game is to force participants to become aware of the delicate relationship between speaker, audience, and message so that responses can be measured to fit the occasion and preserve community order.

CONCLUSION

Folklore, especially the dozens, is among a community's way of rhetorically influencing its members. This paper argues that Blacks in the Tattler community use techniques of the dozens game to guide and control interpersonal behavior when confronted later in more traditional conflict situations. The dozens game provides individuals with an artificial conflict situation and suggests rhetorical options for escalating or repairing situations similar to one encountered in real life.

The present analysis neither suggests that the game has racial overtones or that the dozens is a psychological baptism into manhood as concluded by Abrahams. Dollard is not entirely correct either. Given his interpretation, any aggressive, hostile, or unruly acts of an oppressed minority group are reactions to White society and less a result of the groups' cultural influences. The findings here are that the game is an in-group phenomenon and it is directed at Blacks, but, those who play are rewarded with communicative competency useful in Black and White society.

Strategically, the dozens game proposes communicative tactics helpful in day-to-day living. The game recommends that a sense of power is obtained through information control and personal poise. Tactically, the game helps a player develop the ability to recognize the attitudes of a group of on-lookers and advise him or her of a method of handling emotional situations appropriately.

The dozens is note-worthy for two other reasons. First, as a traditional form of folklore, the dozens is future oriented. The game illustrated ways of behaving in social conflicts yet to come. Young people play the game and it is they who are the initial benefactors; but adults look back upon the game as a form of training. Through the folkloric event of the dozens, young Tattlerites learn the norms of their own community and how society-at-large works. Secondly, the dozens speech event relies on the "strategy of indireciton"[17] for rhetorical impact. Personalized attacks are considered a low form of retaliation so the language, although explicit, must be impersonal. Indirection thus taught provides both listener and speaker with a socially approved mechanism for avoiding conflict. This indirect way of challenging indicates an important interpersonal axiom which states, that the more you know someone personally, the more impersonal and indirect your language will be in attempting to control and guide their behavior.[18]

More studies are needed to determine how folkloric speech events such as the dozens influence community interactions. Systematic examination of "practical wisdom" may show us that there are close parallels between "folk wisdoms" and "formal" textbook logics,[19] that folklore has a philosophical base, that folklore is a traditional form of argument, or that folklore is an area to which the critics, qualitative, and quantitative researchers may turn to gather deeper understanding of communicative behavior. Conversely investigating folklore as part of the rhetoric of everyday life or as the organized techniques of social control and persuasion can yield new understanding of communicative experiences in groups, organizations, and even the family.

Discussion Questions

1. What does it mean to play the dozens?

2. How can playing the dozens be understood as a rhetorical device?

3. Garner claims that the dozens is folkloric. How so?

4. Explain the process of playing the dozens. How does it become a communal activity?

5. How does one's public image get enhanced via the dozens?

Reading 2.4

BLACK STREET SPEECH

Its History, Structure, and Survival

JOHN BAUGH

Everywhere in the world, people are sensitive to language, especially to their local dialect. All of us know when we are in the presence of strangers, of anyone who is foreign to our native customs. It is largely for this reason that we tend to judge people, often harshly, by their linguistic skills or by their lack thereof. Our concepts of eloquence may therefore vary greatly, depending on our cultural point of reference. When people share linguistic and social norms, we think of them as comprising a homogeneous group. The specification of group boundaries is nevertheless a complicated task. I have consequently chosen to examine one small slice of black American culture, namely, the common dialect of the black street culture. My remarks are not limited to my personal experience or to fleeting visits to the ghetto: I have conducted over two hundred hours of tape-recorded interviews with black Americans across the United States.

Although there can be no question that significant numbers of black Americans still speak some of the most nonstandard dialects of English found in the world today, it would be erroneous to associate the language of black street culture with black Americans. The men and women who provided me with gifts of their time and conversation have only one thing in common: they are members of the same race. Their social backgrounds, education, regional history, and shades of skin span the broadest spectrum.

My years of recording in Los Angeles, Philadelphia, Chicago, and Texas have taught me that many people are emotionally involved with the topic of black American dialects. Some people argue that a nonstandard dialect is essential to cultural identity, while others see vernacular black speech as an impediment to success. A few even argue for both positions at the same time—as being complementary. In this context black Americans are no different from any other Americans who disagree about a common issue. In order to examine black American dialects with the clearest possible focus, let us first consider certain historical parallels to another nonstandard English dialect. Cockney has been spoken by the lower working classes in London for centuries. The upper classes in England, on the other hand, speak a standard dialect known as received pronunciation. Through the years

From Baugh, J. (1983). *Black street speech: Its history, structure and survival* (pp. 1-22). Austin: University of Texas Press.

Cockney has survived in the face of sporadic abandonment and various social pressures, but the dialect endures as a testament to the cohesion and survival of the Cockney speech community. One need only look to the linguistic dilemma in *Pygmalion* to appreciate the different social forces that operate on the way we speak:

HIGGINS [*in despairing wrath outside*] What the devil have I done with my slippers? [*He appears at the door*].

LIZA [*snatching up the slippers, and hurling them at him one after the other with all her force*] There are your slippers. And there. Take your slippers, and may you never have a day's luck with them!

HIGGINS [*astounded*] What on earth—! [*He comes to her*]. Whats the matter? Get up. [*He pulls her up*]. Anything wrong?

LIZA [*breathless*] Nothing wrong—with you. I've won your bet for you, haven't I? Thats enough for you. *I* don't matter, I suppose.

HIGGINS You won my bet! You! Presumptuous insect! *I* won it. What did you throw those slippers at me for?

LIZA Because I wanted to smash you face. I'd like to kill you, you selfish brute. Why didn't you leave me where you picked me out of—in the gutter? You thank God it's all over, and that now you can throw me back again there, do you?

HIGGINS [*looking at her in cool wonder*] The creature is nervous, after all.

LIZA [*gives a suffocated scream of fury, and instinctively darts her nails at his face*]!!

HIGGINS [*catching her wrists*] Ah! would you? Claws in, you cat. How dare you show your temper to me? Sit down and be quiet. [*He throws her roughly into the easy-chair*].

LIZA [*crushed by superior strength and weight*] Whats to become of me? What's to become of me?

Liza clearly placed a lot of importance on learning the standard received pronunciation, at least initially. Most readers are familiar with the scene where she offers to pay Higgins for his service, but she did so as an adult—an adult with strong social aspirations. She felt that mastery of the language could pave the way to greater personal success. In doing so, however, she eventually realized that her new linguistic skills would be unacceptable to those who valued Cockney in the community where she was raised.

Many black Americans face a similar linguistic paradox; although they grow up surrounded by peers who value the nonstandard dialect, when they enter a professional society another style of speaking is demanded. Without drawing too many analogies to Cockney, let us say that isolation from the standard dialect and, perhaps, active resistance to acquiring the dialect of the social elites may help explain the survival of black street speech. Just as some native speakers of Cockney have learned received pronunciation, many blacks have mastered standard English. Such people are a minority within a minority, and they usually revert to their first (that is, nonstandard) dialect when the appropriate situation arises. The practical problems of using "improper" speech occur when a speaker needs to know how to speak "properly." (Minorities, by virtue of being minorities, have been isolated from the social environments where the "majority" dialect thrives.) It is largely due to this plethora of social, psychological, historical, and linguistic reasons that educators have encountered so much difficulty teaching minority children in the public schools.

Again, because of the emotionally evocative nature of this topic, my decision to concentrate on analyzing speech is based, in large measure, on scientific grounds. Linguistics has occasionally been referred to as the physics of social science, because spoken utterances can be recorded and analyzed as physical commodities. This physical measurement can in turn be controlled under laboratory conditions with high levels of accuracy. That is not to suggest that linguists have solved all their theoretical problems, we can, nevertheless, trace the speech patterns of people who share the same languages and dialects, and through this analysis we can begin to understand more about each group. Because language is a by-product of human evolution, the dominance and use of languages in our modern time tell us a great deal about ourselves and our history. Thus, while I acknowledge the direct influence of social, political, and other forces on black Americans as a group, I have chosen to study language because it represents one of the more tangible keys to understanding the social dynamics of any people.

To switch analogies, time-lapse photography represented a major advancement in the study of movement and erosion. Similarly, the tape recorder gives us a time-lapse perspective on speech that our spontaneous senses cannot detect. Many of my recordings have been conducted with the same individuals over a period of years in a variety of social circumstances. I also obtained permission to conduct the recordings from each consultant. Thus, by comparing the speech of the same individuals on different occasions, I began to see systematic alternations. These linguistic adjustments were made to meet specific conversational and functional needs. In much the same way that still photography cannot capture movement, isolated observations about black speech or the occasional overhead sentence will not provide adequate evidence to examine dialect style shifts. The tape recorder is therefore a vital instrument in my analysis; over the years people have come to expect to see me with my recorder in hand. It was only through such a long-term procedure that I was able to record continuous conversations, thereby capturing dialect adjustments as circumstances changed.

Linguists have introduced a variety of new terms to account for black American dialects, but most of these terms have been rejected or criticized for one reason or another. My research on the subject illustrates a volatile linguistic picture, where a series of speaking styles is common to different black Americans. This fact should not be surprising since all speakers, regardless of language, have their personal range of formal to informal styles of talking. The reason that this phenomenon is more complicated for black Americans to do with the breadth of speaking styles that are actively used. Speakers with different backgrounds will possess ranges of styles that reflect their personal history and social aspirations. It should

therefore come as little surprise that most blacks who speak standard English also hold professional jobs or are the children of professionals. There are, of course, the noteworthy exceptions, yet they are few when compared to the general pattern. I therefore, like to think of black American dialects as dynamic entities which, as does the chameleon, adapt to blend in with the immediate setting. This position contrasts with the image of the "Black English" community described by J. L. Dillard:

> If Black English is not identical to Southern white dialects—although it has influenced the latter over a period of two centuries or more—there remains the problem of who speaks it. The best evidence we have at the present time—and it is admittedly incomplete—indicates that approximately eighty percent of the Black population of the United States speaks Black English. (*Black population*, in this case, would mean all those who consider themselves to be members of the "Black" or "Negro" community.) (1972:229)

Dillard's observations set the stage for understanding black street speech, and we are now in a better position to specify the styles of speaking that are used by the 80 percent whom he refers to. There can be no question that a majority of black Americans share some aspects of what is commonly thought of as street speech, although different aspects may appear with different frequency for various speakers. This is the natural result of the social diffusion of black America. In much the same way that Professor Higgins and Eliza Doolittle tried to replace her Cockney dialect, black Americans have gradually come to make systematic and measurable adjustments in their speech to fit more formal situations. However, racial boundaries in the United States complicate the *Pygmalion* analogy, because black Americans will still stand out in a predominantly white group, even if they have mastered standard English.

The mass media have demonstrated that blacks are quite capable of mastering standard English: it is often difficult to identify the ethnicity of announcers without the corresponding video support. As mentioned, these individuals are nevertheless a minority within a minority, the dialects that are used by highly educated black Americans would provide material for another book. My analysis is based on the speech of blacks who have had limited contact with whites. It would be wrong to imply that all my consultants are uneducated; rather, their training needs to be viewed within their own ethnographic context. For example, some of the more "successful" blacks whom I have interviewed, say, those who have completed college and now hold professional positions, are likely to be heavily in debt with mortgages and car payments. Several other consultants, although they did not have a college education, owned their homes, and their used cars were purchased with cash. Because of cultural differences, where street speech reinforces group boundaries with every intercultural exchange, many whites at first glance would consider these people to be destitute.

American blacks have long been aware of dialect differences within the racial group; in fact, such folk terms as "city rap," "country talk," and "talking proper" distinguish different types of black speech. My research was concentrated in urban areas. Most of the data were collected in Los Angeles, but I have gathered additional data in Philadelphia, Chicago, Austin, and Houston. It is largely for ethnographic reasons that I have adopted the term "black street speech," because it conveys a similar meaning to most of the black consultants whom I have interviewed, regardless of their social or regional background. Street speech is the nonstandard dialect that thrives within the black street culture, and it is constantly fluctuating, as new terminology flows in and out of colloquial vogue. I would therefore suggest that we need to think of street speech as a flexible dialect; this is not a conservative standard dialect where archaic forms are preserved by prescriptive tradition. Street speech survives because there is a population of speakers who use it in their daily lives and know that it is the appropriate style of speaking for their personal needs.

In the past I have characterized black street speech on linguistic and interactional grounds, because the nature of the dialect is fluid. The styles of speech that are used on the street may, or may not, be used at home or on the job, depending on the corresponding linguistic values or demands.

The social networks of street consultants have served my purpose, because we can trace the parameters of the speakers' linguistic worlds, and through their contacts we can come to know the special pressures that different cultural values place on their speech (compare Milroy 1980). My consultants are clearly at a disadvantage in a white society that views street speech as an ignorant dialect. The social distance between the groups has been sufficient to drive perceptual wedges between blacks and whites. As a consequence of this linguistic dilemma, many street speakers remain silent when standard English is the dominant dialect. The perceptions of "appropriate speech" and "dominant dialect" are relative to the social realities of different individuals. My research reinforces a fact that seems almost too obvious to mention—namely, people tend to adopt styles of speaking that are suited to their social needs and personal aspirations. In a white-dominated society that has traditionally tried to relegate blacks to the lowest social stratum, access to standard English has always been a tremendous battle.

It is also important for blacks to appreciate why many whites are insensitive to their linguistic plight and heritage. When a child begins to speak, the first language is learned with the greatest ease. In fact, it is the miracle of child language acquisition that represents the keystone of modern linguistic theory. The problem if insensitivity to black street speech is clouded because standard English speakers naturally find their own dialect easier to speak. And, because of the negative values that are associated with street speech, there is very little motivation for whites to learn nonstandard black speech. Whites most typically imitate black speech when they mock minority accents, which are often part of racist jokes and therefore restricted to limited social contexts. Also, street speakers become particularly sensitive when whites try to adopt black speech patterns; this is usually viewed as patronizing because the whites are perceived as talking down to the blacks. Therefore, what is natural to the standard English speaker, because it was acquired with the ease of any first language, translates

Shared Linguistic Characteristics

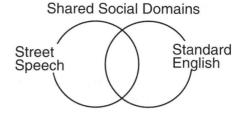

Shared Social Domains

1. Street speech bidialectalism

Figure 1   Street Speech Bidialectalism

into a much more complicated situation for street speakers, who face the more difficult problem of trying to acquire a second dialect.

The issue at hand is consequently not one of genetic or intellectual inferiority, resulting in linguistic deprivation; it is more properly a reflection of the difference between acquiring a first language versus the more difficult task of acquiring a second dialect of the first language. The standard English speaker in America is not usually required, at least on social grounds, to learn another dialect of English. Similar problems are faced by some whites who speak ethnic or regional dialects that are judged negatively outside of their group and/or area (for example, Appalachian Mountain speech. They too have witnessed the difficulty of mastering a second dialect, and many of these people reflect their loyalty to their group by maintaining the dialects of their ancestors. For blacks as a whole, the question of dialect loyalty has been cast against a backdrop of poverty and other isolating cultural factors. For many the first steps out of the ghetto came in the form of adopting the norms of more successful Americans. The negative attitudes toward black speech are largely responsible for the stylistic variation that thrives in all black American communities, but it would be wrong to suggest that most street speakers exhibit identical styles. All the consultants whom I have interviewed adopt more standardized speech while simultaneously eliminating aspects of street speech in very formal circumstances (for example, court appearances or conferences with teachers at public schools), albeit with varying degrees of proficiency. It is

this chameleon quality that is the primary object of my work.

Linguistic behavior is a vivid indicator of black survival for several reasons. Sociological insights can be gained from the (dis)use of street speech, and educators will be better equipped to implement successful pedagogical policies for students who bring street speech to the classroom as their native dialect. This practical utility can be realized only when we appreciate two fundamental differences between standard dialects and their nonstandard counterparts.

Haugen (1972) described the contrast in the following way. A standard dialect is characterized by a minimum amount of linguistic variation. Nonstandard dialects of the same language exhibit a greater range of linguistic variation. From a social perspective, however, the utility of these styles is inverted. The standard dialect can be used with the broadest social scope and acceptability, whereas the nonstandard dialects are acceptable only in a limited number of circumstances. This important contrast is illustrated in Figure 1.

Like Cockney, street speech survives in the face both of active opposition and of the increasing numbers of blacks who need to adopt standard English as part of their professional training. At this point the question of linguistic schizophrenia would seem to be logical, after all, if there are pressures for group loyalty and pressures to stop using street speech, how does the individual cope with this constant tug-of-war? This is actually less of a problem than might be expected, because the various dialects seldom overlap in the same speaking context.

Thus, when I went with one of my consultants to a court hearing, his linguistic behavior was formal; when we returned to his house and recounted the ordeal to his wife and brother-in-law, he used black street speech. Again, the issue here is not so much the fact that speakers possess formal and informal styles—everyone has experienced this phenomenon—rather street speech covers a greater range of linguistic styles, which is why it persists as a boundary for social demarcation.

If street speakers face a dilemma, it is one not so much of being torn between two forces but of learning how to move from one extreme to the other with ease and proficiency. Most of the early educational programs to help blacks learn standard English began with the objective of eliminating street speech; this was seen as a dialect that should not be tolerated. This practice reinforced the negative impression of black speech that was already held by the dominant culture. Sensitivity to the special problems surrounding the acquisition of a second dialect was not built into these early programs. In fact, the general practice was to try to teach standard English to blacks using foreign-language techniques, which often resulted in more confusion than clarification for street speakers.

On a global scale, then, we find that street speech is much like many other socially stigmatized dialects, which thrive in societies where other "prestigious" dialects are spoken by highly educated people. In Northern Ireland, England, France, Belgium, and Germany, for example, there are strong attitudes associated with various regional and social dialects. In some of these countries, critical social consequences are linked with these stereotypes. Yet, in much the same manner that Vulgar Latin came to influence changes in Classical Latin, the life of a dialect and language is dictated by the population that preserves it through use. Indeed, the birth and spread of languages have historically reflected the changing trends of human domination. Just as some species have become extinct with the encroachment of both natural and synthetic disasters, so too have some languages become extinct as the numbers of their speakers dwindled. While social attitudes play a major role in the life of languages and their dialects, political domination still remains one of the strongest motivational forces affecting language. In most cases the nonstandard dialect are seen as inferior to their standardized counterparts, but this, again, will depend on the vantage point of the observer. Without question, we find that speakers of nonstandard dialects have been relegated to marginal positions in their societies. As observed, their dialects have minimal social utility, especially in the face of strong negative opinions.

This minimal social utility has a direct impact on individuals. During the years that I have studied this topic, I have talked to black college students who felt an urgent need to acquire standard English so that they would be treated as equals in their classes. Others have expressed the frustration of knowing that they were qualified for advanced positions, only to be rejected because they didn't speak "properly." It is on this personal level that the tragedy of dialect insensitivity takes its greatest toll. The difficulty of acquiring a second dialect cannot be underestimated here, especially for those who wait until they are young adults. For example, certain wealthy families in Texas send their children for speech lessons at an early age to help them get rid of their twang. A great deal of time and money has been invested for this purpose. Most average black college students, on the other hand, may have used street speech with their peers before entering college, thereby delaying the point in their lives where they began to make an active effort to learn standard English. We now find many black children who are learning standard English as their native dialect, but these are the children of blacks who have frequent access to nonblacks, and often these black children have very limited—if any—contact with their poorer street culture counterparts.

Because of the numerous stereotypes about blacks, which tend to be exaggerated in the media, most nonblacks assume that blacks who speak standard English have overcome tremendous personal barriers, but, like so many second- and third-generation immigrants from Europe, some blacks have acquired standard English as their native dialect. We are therefore faced with a complex situation where a variety of personal decisions can directly influence the dialects that are learned and used by blacks in America.

Opinions on "bad" English abound, but there is comparatively little in the way of hard linguistic evidence to support early pronouncements on the subject. The taped interviews that I have collected represent the documentation for my observation that street speech is comprised of several flexible styles of speaking. One of the main reasons why my orientation differs from that of other researchers results from the unique practice of repeatedly interviewing the same adults under different social circumstances. Most of the early studies examine isolated black youths on a single occasion; with the newer advantage of long-term study, the true nature of vernacular street styles is exposed with greater clarity.

Regardless of how we feel about minority dialects and the negative values that are so often associated with them, they are part of the cultural fabric of our society, and it is in this context that children come to adopt the personal values which they will carry into adult life. Like those who have studied this subject before me, I recognize that historical evidence can clarify the nature of contemporary speech, and this historical evidence may, in turn, be beneficial to street speakers. It is largely for this reason that I have chosen to focus on the language of the black street culture, because this is the dialect that thrives among urban blacks who have minimal linguistic contact with those outside their community.

THE BIRTH OF BLACK STREET SPEECH

At first glance the birth of black street speech seems to be a fairly straightforward topic, where historical records would be examined to reconstruct the early stages of dialect development. But several factors, including strong prejudices among scholars, have restricted the scope of these studies, to say nothing of their quality. And, once the questions of racial difference and inequality are added, the topic becomes even more complex. The best historical studies of street speech have been completed during this century, as interest in the general topic of black studies has matured.

Understanding the question of racial equality-inferiority is essential to a full appreciation of the early investigations, because much of the

historical research was designed to address this question directly. With the proper historical insights, social scientists and educators presumed that they would be in a better position to know why modern street speakers did so poorly in school. In recent times the debate has focused on two opposed positions: street speech was considered to be either *different* or *deficient* when compared to standard English. Depending on how this question is answered, the contemporary consequences for street speakers could be severe. The sociopolitical climate at different points throughout American history has greatly influenced the objectivity of our early social science.

It will therefore be useful to maintain a distinction between the research on the history of street speech and its *actual* history, because different opinions are common. Four noteworthy trends have evolved over the years regarding the development of street speech, and, depending on where one stands, these may be seen as either helpful or detrimental. The earliest writings, going back to the birth of the nation, were, quite simply, racist. Advocates of white supremacy would point to "Negro speech" as definitive evidence of the intellectual inferiority of blacks. The first serious scholarship was produced by American dialectologists, who stressed the English foundations of street speech. The dialectologist position has been challenged more recently by students of creole languages, who looked primarily at African languages and slave trade jargons as the basis of street speech. The creolist hypothesis is still very popular among many scholars and laypersons, because it provides supportive evidence that reinforces black pride and nationalism, moreover, the creole position emphatically views black speech as being different from standard English—not inferior. The creolists were subsequently among the first legitimate scholars to establish strong links between American blacks and the African continent. However, in the fertile climate of popular support, a balanced historical picture did not emerge until very recently. The most current historical studies suggest a combined hypothesis, where aspects of the creole and dialectology positions interact to create street speech; this seems to be quite logical, since Africa and England have both left linguistic impressions on Afro-American English throughout the Americas.

Because all black Americans ultimately have their roots in Africa, where oral linguistic traditions prevailed, modern historians face a special problem due to sparse—and often questionable—data. Unlike the conservative standardized languages in Europe, where centuries of written traditions influence educated speakers, oral languages tend to change to suit the needs of each living generation of speakers. Those who are familiar with English writing and colloquial speech know that we no longer pronounce the /k/ in *knight* or the /b/ in *climb,* but we accept these archaic spellings to preserve the conventions. The dilemma facing the linguist who is interested in street speech is somewhat more cumbersome, because the "standard" for nonstandard speech is shaped through day-to-day conversations—and not by teachers or grammarians.

I will be concentrating on how these historical analyses reflect on the debate about black intelligence. And, more important, I will focus on why this unique linguistic past has given rise to *flexible* styles, where speakers tend to adapt their speech patterns to suit each situation.

To start at the beginning, then, when slaves first came to America they were considered to be property by nearly everyone. The abolitionists debated this point, but the humane dimension of the topic was quashed by the more pressing need for cheap—and reliable—labor. As beasts of burden the slaves were relegated to positions of inferiority, and racial differences made it easy to perpetuate the gap between black and white societies.

The only voices of moderation that could be heard during this early period of slavery were white voices. Slaves had no rights, it was even illegal to teach them to read and write. During this time the racist literature flowed like a swollen stream. Few voices cried out to protest the rising tide of racist opinion, as the human tragedy of slavery thrived. Contacts between blacks and whites differed in the North and South. In the North very few whites had extended exposure to blacks, that is, in a broad range of social circumstances. The southern experience, by contrast, was very different. Slave overseers, who were among the lowest social class of whites, as well as wealthy plantation owners, who had house slaves and "mammies" for their children, lived and worked in close proximity to black people. In spite of these regional differences, both areas practiced racial discrimination in one form or another. The racism that lingers today has been born from the stereotypes and prejudices that were imposed—although centuries ago—to keep the races apart.

Unfortunately, one does not have to go too far back in American history to find accounts of these distorted and self-serving opinions. The following quote is just such a painful reminder:

> Collectively, the untutored Negro mind is confiding and single-hearted, naturally kind and hospitable. *Both sexes are easily ruled,* and appreciate what is good under the guidance of common justice and prudence. Yet where so much that honors human nature remains—in apathy the typical wooly-haired races have never invented a reasoned theological system, discovered an alphabet, framed a grammatical language, nor made the least step in science or art. They have never comprehended what they have learned, or retained a civilization taught them by contact with more refined nations as soon as that contact had ceased. They have at no time formed great political states, nor commenced a self-evolving civilization. (Campbell 1851:172)

The entire statement is wrong—emphatically so from a linguistic point of view.

To concentrate, once again, on the true history of street speech, one major distinction logically accounts for the dialect differences that falsely supported the assumptions that blacks were inherently inferior to whites. Black slaves coming to this new world were systematically isolated from other speakers of their native language. Slave traders engaged in this practice, thereby deliberately planning the death of African languages, to restrict possible uprisings during the Atlantic crossing. As we shall see in greater detail later, most white immigrants—although poor—were able to keep the language of their homeland until their children and grandchildren learned English as their native language. Slaves, on the other hand, did not have the advantage—and the communicative luxury—of being able to use their mother tongue. This linguistic isolation is unique to American blacks: with the possible exception of Hawaiian natives, no other American minority has faced this type of linguistic isolation through involuntary capture.

Minstrel shows and the early portrayals of blacks in films and on the radio tended to give popular credence to racist scholarship, passing myths and stereotypes from one generation to the next. At this point in history, however, we have made sufficient strides to dismiss this biased literature as an embarrassment to American scholarship. White American racists were not the first to engage in self-serving ethnocentric writing—the foundations of British anthropology, for example, have long been criticized for similar false notions of supremacy—but America needed slaves to help build the nation, resulting in ethnoncentricity in our own backyard.

The racist literature about blacks and black speech in particular should, of course, be dismissed in any serious analysis of the subject, but we must appreciate that the opinions expressed by the white supremacists—while often absurd—reflected the feelings of a majority of white Americans. This resulted in a social climate, after the Civil War and beyond the turn of the century, where more liberal thinkers tried to present "Negroes" in a better light. Frederick Douglass did much to retard blatant racism among intellectuals, but American dialectologists were among the very first linguists to treat blacks as equal to other Americans. In fact, the dialectologists contended that it was unfair to analyze the speech of black Americans differently from that of other groups (compare Williamson and Burke 1976).

Upon close reflection, we now know that the dialectologists overstated their case, but it would be wrong to suggest that these oversights were motivated by racism. In fact, the opposite really holds true. In the social climate of America from the 1920s to the 1940s, when the dialectologist position was prevalent, there were pervasive racist attitudes toward anything that was associated with Africa. The portrayal of blacks in films from this period has been analyzed extensively by movie critics, who have observed that false impressions—while

historically inaccurate, for example, the Tarzan films—nevertheless influenced the real impressions of the average American viewer.

It was against this rigid backdrop of negative opinion that dialectologists began to raise their voices, claiming that "American Negroes" were not exotic primitives but Americans like any other immigrants. In turn they argued that efforts to view "Negroes" as a special (that is, inferior) group would only accentuate public opinion that the races were in fact unequal. The noteworthy exceptions to emerge during this period can be found in the writings of Melville Herskovits and in the work of his student Lorenzo Turner, who wrote *Africanisms in the Gullah Dialect.*[1] These writers were viewed quite skeptically when their work first appeared; but with the eventual rise of black nationalism, from the 1960s through the present time, the stature and popularity of their work have grown.

In the 1980s it is all too easy to criticize the efforts of the dialectologists, who are still quite active, because they failed to stress the African side of the issue. But this is an unfair criticism when the historical and sociological climate is taken into account. From the 1920s through the 1940s dialectologists represented the voices of moderation, and they—nearly alone—maintained the position that black Americans were linguistically equal to their white counterparts. I am compelled to stress this point, because the polemic that saturates most recent writings on this subject tends to be extremely harsh on the dialectologist practice of looking primarily at English influences.

To recap the main thrust of their position, then, dialect differences between whites and blacks were examined in much the same manner as other regional dialects. This practice assured that no group would be treated differently from any other. Nevertheless, this procedure alone proved to be inadequate as far as the history of black street speech is concerned.

By contrast, the creolist hypothesis emerged with primary emphasis on African languages, and this position is still strongly advocated by several scholars who study black American dialects. In order to fully appreciate the nature of this research, however, we need first to look at some of the factions within the linguistic profession itself.

The most advanced linguistic research focuses on analyses of educated dialects of the "classic" Romance and Germanic languages, extending to other language families with strong written traditions. The historical reconstruction of each of these languages, say, of those that grew out of Latin, is a precise enterprise, where evidence from centuries of written documentation is carefully pieced together. These reconstructions provide historical depth to the contemporary studies, where the most common practice leads modern linguists—as native speakers of their own (educated) dialects—to create their own data based on personal intuitions. Because other scholars typically speak, or are extremely familiar with, these well-documented languages, the intuitions of one scholar can be checked by the informed intuitions of another.

However, there can be no question that the practice of using oneself as a source of "scientific" evidence will have severe restrictions, once analysts encounter a language and/or dialects for which there is little or no existing documentation. In short, this is the very situation that faced analysts of black speech in the United States, and it is still a major factor affecting the quality of historical research on black street speech. Whereas most European immigrants came to America from a homeland with a strong written tradition, African slaves were taken from a land where elders memorized oral histories (see Alex Haley's *Roots*).

For my purpose here, analyzing (educated) dialects—with their long-standing prescriptive traditions and their inevitable retention of archaic forms—differs considerably from reconstructing the indigenous oral languages of Africa. With this distinction in mind, we are in a much better position to view the role of creole studies within linguistics as a general field of study. First, to clarify the relevance of this distinction, some basic terminology needs to be defined.

When slave traders first went to Africa, they obviously did not know how to speak the native African languages. In much the same way that Pilgrims tried to communicate with native Americans, new contact languages were born. Such contact languages—called pidgins—are not native to their speakers. The pidgin results from the need to communicate with people who do not speak your same language. And a pidgin represents the emergence of a new language, which is specifically born out of the contact of two—or perhaps more—other languages. In social terms pidgins tend to be stigmatized, trapped under a shroud of social domination. They usually hold a deferential position compared to the language of those who control political power, which is typically a source of influential linguistic contact.

Once speakers of the pidgin have children, and these children learn the pidgin as their native language, a transformation takes place: the pidgin becomes a creole. In other words, a creole is a nativized pidgin that can usually be distinguished from the original parent languages on several linguistic grounds, including grammatical, lexical, and phonological distinctions, among other (compare Hall 1966). This is why creoles are so easy to detect in the Caribbean islands or in any other place where new languages are born from the collision of two or more other languages.

For obvious historical reasons, the documentation regarding the birth and growth of creole languages does not compare, even modestly, with the excellent documents that have been used in the reconstruction of Indo-European languages. And it is largely for this reason that creolist scholars were not taken too seriously by linguists who were working with more "classic" languages. This was especially true when linguistics was trying to become an autonomous social science in the early 1920s. Such a situation was, of course, very troublesome to creolists, who felt—with ample justification—that their work was being neglected.

There can be no question that the isolation of creolist scholars among other linguists influenced the nature of their research. In much the same manner that the social sciences have tried to imitate the rigors of physical science methodology, however falsely, creolist scholars attempted to imitate the successful efforts of their colleagues in "classic" historical linguistics. Creolist scholars likewise came to spend tremendous amounts of time locating obscure documents from the slave trade, in the case of street speech, many of these documents were records of people who were directly involved with the capture, transportation, and sale of slaves.

Some disturbing problems arise from this situation, because far too many creolists tried to make strong historical statements based on highly questionable evidence. In fact, it is not uncommon to find historical discussions of street speech that selectively cite documents that concur with preconceived hypotheses, while contradictory evidence of equal (poor) quality is dismissed (see Dillard 1972). This problem is beginning to subside because creole studies have advanced greatly over the past two decades, and the work of several scholars has substantially improved the overall quality of research on contact languages. But the traces of the early biased research tradition have left strong impressions on contemporary analyses of street speech, and, as I have indicated previously, the creolists' hypothesis received its strongest support in the popular (black) milieu, because of the African foundations of the position. In fact, Dillard wrote the following statement about "Black English" and its history:

> Undoubtedly, the proponents of the East Anglian origins theory and of purely geographic variation (except for the complications of "archaism") have not realized that in their account of the Negro as an archaizing speaker the picture which emerges is that of a racial archaism—a Negro who just can't catch up or keep up. This is surely the most blatantly racist position which could be presented, if all of its implications are intentional. Since similar linguistic forms occur in the West Indies, on some parts of the West Coast of Africa, and even in Afrikaans, only the kind of historical explanation which scholars like Whinnom, Thompson, Stewart, and Valkoff give could possibly provide a basis for linguistic dignity for the Negro. The idea is so new—and terms like pidgin are subject to such general misunderstanding—that even Black leaders are sometimes resentful of what may seem like a less favorable presentation of Negro language history but one which, upon close examination, turns out to be the only one consistent with Black self-respect. (1972: 10–11)

It is my personal contention, as a scholar and a black man, that black self-respect will be enhanced by the truth—even though it is riddled with painful reminders of the social consequences of racism, poverty, and exploitation. Biased scholarship, no matter how it masquerades as a psychological panacea, will only continue to provide a partial image. The history of street speech is not a unilateral issue, either from Anglican or from African sources. I do not mean to imply by this that neither position is correct; rather, the best historical evidence shows that a combined hypothesis is the most accurate, at least at this time.

In order to illustrate this point, we can look at a single example of a street speech dialect feature and review the corresponding assumptions that intersect with the various historical positions. The example that I would like to consider is the use of *is* in street speech or, more specifically, the three variables involved in sentences like "He is coming" > "He's coming" > "He coming," which are all used in street speech.

As American dialects continue to merge through the gradual erosion of once rigid class, regional, and racial barriers, the dialect differences that remain provide—in a very real sense—a half-life cycle as important to linguists as carbon dating is to archaeologists. The rate of subcultural osmosis (that is, the mainstreaming of American subcultures) can be measured by the distribution of dialect differences. For reasons that are still obvious, black Americans have not overcome these barriers with the speed and ease of white immigrants. The racial barriers are less important to my observations than is a full appreciation of the corresponding influence on the development of black and white dialects.

Is, almost more than any other linguistic characteristic, has been examined in great detail to determine the absence of the verb to *be* in black street speech. It would be wrong to imply that street speech does not use *is;* rather, it is used very differently in standard English. Labov (1969) observed that street speech could omit *is* in the same linguistic environments where standard English uses contractions. The typical speaker of the black street vernacular uses all three possibilities and therefore produces a complex pattern of alternation that is influenced by linguistic and social forces alike. There has been a tendency for dialectologists and creolists to disagree on the use of *is.* As might be expected, both positions are plausible, but both start from completely different points of departure; the main difference lies in the direction of historical change assumed for black street speech. Do speakers have *is* as an underlying aspect of their dialect, or does the vernacular have a vacuous (that is, Ø) form that gradually gives way to the intrusion of *is* as speakers gain more exposure to standard English? I am, of course, simplifying the issue tremendously for the sake of illustration. The historical oppositions are as follows:

Dialectologists is > 's > Ø
Creolists   Ø > 's > is

Both positions hold some validity, and it is the combination of hypotheses that reveals the most feasible explanation to date. This debate among linguists, which is far too technical for the discussion at hand, is secondary to the fact that nonstandard black speech can be distinguished from all white dialects of American English based on *is* usage alone (compare Wolfram 1974). It is largely for this reason that such a small word has received so much scholarly attention. Yet, in spite of the good intentions of every linguist who has ever worked on this topic, significant distortions of the facts abound in popular books on the subject.

An example quoted to illustrate black English appears in Dillard's major work on the subject:

The standard example is

(1) My brother sick . . .

The child who said

(7) My brother's sick

probably was indulging in some kind of code-switching under the influence of Standard English. *Proof* [emphasis my own] of this is that he also says

(11) They's sick

(12) I's sick . . .

Dillard then goes on to illustrate another example of code switching which, as we will see, is pronounced quite similar to number 1 above and therefore is undetectable in speech:

(18) My brother be's sick [for a long time]

where (18) carried over the basically meaningless (in Black English)' s of *They's*

sick, He's sick, etc. (1972: 52, 54)

My observation is a simple one: these examples are different in print only.

Recalling that these examples have been drawn from books written by linguists, most readers would accept them at face value. However, upon close examination we can see that the quoted sentences are very misleading. To illustrate this point, I need you to perform a brief experiment. Please read the following sentence aloud: "He sick." It's important to say the sentence aloud. Now, please read "He's sick" aloud, taking care to say it as you normally would in conversation. If you repeat this process a few times, again making sure to say both sentences at your normal rate of speech, you will notice that they sound identical. Thus, from the standpoint of conversation, this is an example of phonological neutralization which is not immediately apparent from the written comparison of "He sick" versus "He's sick." I should be quick to point out that a sentence where the verb did not begin with /s/ would serve to illustrate Dillard's point better (for example, "He coming" or "She pretty").

If linguists can, albeit unintentionally, mislead their readers in this way, imagine the difficulty for those who rely on the linguists' judgment for educational or other social purposes. The preceding example stands out here because it focuses on *is*, but it is by no means special when compared to the vast oversimplification of black speech in most of the historical literature. Returning, then, to the significance of *is* within a historical survey, I have suggested that we are looking at complementary hypotheses. The reader might properly wonder how this could be; after all, how could *is* and the lack of *is* exist as historical renditions without direct opposition? The answer lies in the gradual

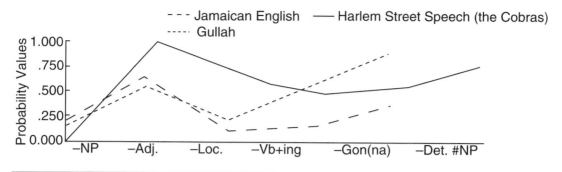

Figure 2   Variation for *is* absence in Jamaican English, Gullah, and Harlem street speech

historical changes that have occurred.[2] Elsewhere (Baugh 1980), I demonstrate that *is* usage in street speech has ancestral ties both to the Gullah dialect of the Sea Islands and to Jamaican English. Recalling my observation that many of the early creolist scholars searched for monographs from the slave trade in their efforts to reconstruct the protolanguage of slaves, it occurred to me that a new procedure might benefit from a direct comparison of contemporary oral linguistic behavior in disparate black English communities. This is exactly what I did; by comparing the speech of Harlem teens, the Gullah dialect, and Jamaican English, a parallel pattern for the deletion of *is* was revealed. This is illustrated in Figure 2.

The categories at the bottom of each graph identify specific linguistic environments that were measured for *is* usage in these three communities—and the similarities are much too great to reflect only historical coincidence. This is especially true when white American dialects are compared to this pattern. The best evidence that is now available subsequently suggests that a complex pattern of historical, social, and linguistic forces has influenced ongoing changes in black street speech. My own research suggests historical linguistic roots that link black street speech with Jamaican creole and Scots-Irish dialects.

For years educators hoped that linguists could solve the historical riddle of black street speech, but, considering the diversity of opinion that exists, practitioners were torn between two highly plausible extremes. I tend to agree with Wolfram's observation (1974) that an accurate historical picture is not necessary to formulate a clear analysis of street speech today. While it made good sense twenty years ago to consider this historical debate as part of the educational picture, the final analysis shows that contemporary speech patterns are only part of an intricate pedagogical picture. I would argue that, in spite of the benefits that historical reflection can give us, the evidence is still quite scant. In addition, we have already access to the street speech that thrives in our own inner cities, and it is from these cities that my study draws its life.

DISCUSSION QUESTIONS

1. What is meant by *Black street culture* in Baugh's essay?

2. What are the social implications of "speaking proper" in Black street culture?

3. In what ways do Blacks do linguistic or dialect style shifting?

4. According to Baugh, do Blacks need to be bidialectical? Why or why not?

5. What is the primary critical stance of creolist scholars?

Part III

African American Communication and Identity in Relational Contexts

T he quality of human lives is influenced by our relationships with others. One of the most interesting things about relationships is that they must be coordinated to be effective. They do not simply become effective without some effort. This is due in part to differences in backgrounds, interests, and ideas. Every cultural group has socially constructed its sense of self vis-à-vis its relationships with others, because we do not typically live in isolation of other groups. With this difference come challenges and sometimes conflict. When most people think about communication breakdowns, they often think of relationships. This section covers issues pertaining to communication within interpersonal, interracial, intercultural, and gendered relationships.

Michael L. Hecht, Sidney Ribeau, and J. K. Alberts authored the first essay presented in Part III. They were among the first to systematically examine perceptions of "satisfying communication" within interethnic relationships between Blacks and Whites. A spin-off from social identity theory, ethnolinguistic vitality, and mindfulness research, communication satisfaction studies were implemented as a means of developing intercultural conversational improvement and relational alignment. In many ways, this was a continuance of communication competence models developed in the late 1970s through the late 1980s. Hecht, Ribeau, and Alberts report results from four studies. The methods were triangulated, and the data yielded several salient issues and strategies that African Americans found necessary for enhancement of intercultural interactions with Whites. Perhaps the most enlightening result from the research was the fact that speech divergence continued to hold serious relational consequences for those who chose to avoid White assimilative behaviors within Black-White relationships.

Tina M. Harris and Pamela J. Kalbfleisch, authors of the next essay, further elaborate upon Black-White relationships with an accent on romantic relationships. Limiting their focus to interracial dating, the authors elucidate issues pertaining to the history of oppression experienced by Blacks and the influence this history has had on relational development. With this in mind, the study was designed to address the communication strategies used when initiating a date. By employing the Q-Sort method, Harris and Kalbfleisch were able to examine any race and gender-based differences in emergent communication strategies. The results from their open-ended surveys collected from 120 Black and White college students revealed active resistance to seeking interracial dating situations and much more of an inclination to maintain social distancing strategies.

In the relational communication literature, a logical graduation from successful dating relationships is marriage. One does not have to read many popular magazines to stumble upon an article or two about how to have a successful marriage. Linda K. Acitelli, Elizabeth Douvan, and Joseph Veroff conducted a longitudinal study in which they tracked marriages during their first three years. Of primary concern to them was whether the 373 newlywed Black and White couples' interpersonal perceptions of their relationship changed over the first three years of their marriages and whether any such perceptions had an effect on marital well being. The authors found that interpersonal perceptions were very consistent in the first three years of marriage with the exception that Black wives perceived increased similarity with their spouses while White husbands experienced increased understanding of their spouses. In both situations, "constructive behaviors" facilitated a climate of positive growth. Interestingly, Black wives' sensitivity to their husbands' feelings and needs led to increased marital happiness, but White wives' sensitivity to their husbands' feelings and needs had the reverse effect of decreased happiness. Acitelli, Douvan, and Veroff offer speculation regarding the rationale for this shift. This 7-year NIMH grant-supported investigation is a major heuristic contribution to conflict and communication style research.

The final essay in Part III concerns church involvement of African American men who have sex with men (MSM). Rarely do we find open scholarly discussions of homosexuality in the context of communication research; however, Jeffrey Lynn Woodyard, John L. Peterson, and Joseph P. Stokes present the results of their interviews with 76 18-to-20-year-old MSM in Atlanta and Chicago. Certainly one of the most intriguing facets of this study is that the authors did not simply choose to interview 76 MSM; instead, they interviewed 76 MSM who were active participants in Black churches, which have been sites of controversy with regard to homosexuality. In fact, the authors contend that the Black church "encourages sexual secrecy and is associated with decreased frequencies of same-sex contacts." Woodyard, Peterson, and Stokes's investigation is primarily centered on not just MSM's church involvement, but also how that involvement in such a climate of hostility has affected their self-esteem and sexual behavior. The results indicated that MSM either go to church openly expressing their gayness, conform by masking expressions of gayness or refusing to claim their gayness, or detach themselves from church. Those who maintain Black church involvement seldom received complete affirmation. Some of the participants belonged to churches that reject homosexuality, and, consequently, most of these men have internalized "feelings of guilt, condemnation, embarrassment, and alienation." The effect has been, in most cases, decreased same-sex contacts.

Reading 3.1

AN AFRO-AMERICAN PERSPECTIVE ON INTERETHNIC COMMUNICATION

Michael L. Hecht, Sidney Ribeau, and J. K. Alberts

News reports of ethnic strife highlight the fact that ethnic differences remain a salient issue in contemporary American society. This issue poses a challenge to scholars, for they are faced with the need to discover a means to help bridge these differences, some of which arise out of each ethnic group's distinct culture. Communication scholars particularly are in a position to help meet this need because one of the important areas in which ethnic cultures differ is in their approach to conversational interaction.

Cultural distinctiveness, and its attendant differences, may be most notably expressed in communication rules and style. A study of interethnic communication which examines cultural uniqueness and perceptions could yield insight not only into a specific culture but also promote understanding of ways to improve interethnic communication effectiveness.

A study of such interethnic communication could profitably begin with an analysis of Afro-American-white communication interaction.

Such a study is essential because Afro-Americans are an important ethnic co-population in the United States. They represent a numerically large group, and the influence of Afro-American culture on our common culture can be traced in numerous ways, including music, dance, sports, literature, and virtually all areas of the American lifestyle.

Despite this influence, institutional barriers historically have minimized interpersonal contacts between Afro-Americans and whites and thus have inhibited social relationships. In the recent past a change has begun to occur in the nature of ethnic or race relations in the United States, as the civil rights movement documents. However, increased contact has not necessarily led to improved or effective interpersonal interactions.

INTERETHNIC COMMUNICATION

Social scientific research helps explain the forces which promote and deter effective

From Hecht, M. L., Ribeau, S., & Alberts, J. K. (1989). An Afro-American perspective on interethnic communication. *Communication Monographs*, *56*, 385-410.

interethnic communication. Among those forces are cultural differences themselves. While culture is only one of the influences on communication and communication but one of the manifestations of culture, the interplay of the two can strongly affect relations between ethnic groups. An understanding of cultural differences and attendant communication differences can lead to the development of strategies for managing interethnic interaction. Certainly these strategies will not eliminate interethnic communication barriers, but they can provide skills for managing these differences more effectively.

One explanation for ineffective conversational interactions is provided by Kochman (1982), who asserts that Afro-American and white cultural differences contribute to communicative breakdowns. Contrary to the assumption that Afro-Americans and whites share identical speech and cultural conventions, Kochman describes differing norms and social styles, pointing to divergent patterns of intonation, expressive intensity, spontaneity, aggressiveness, and argument.

These differences are mirrored and elaborated in other studies. Asante and Noor-Aldeen (1984) found a pattern of indifference between Afro-American and white interactants when interracial dyads were observed, as well as a general pattern of racial isolation. Ickes (1984), however, notes that whites with more positive racial attitudes display more other-orientation cues, while the opposite applies to whites with negative attitudes.

Duncan (1978) and Jones (1971) found differences in the proxemic behavior of Afro-American and white school children, and Bachman and O'Malley (1984) report that Afro-Americans are more extreme in their responses. Hecht & Ribeau (1984) report differences in the kinds of intra-ethnic communication Afro-Americans and whites find satisfying. Afro-Americans focus more on intimate topical involvement, trust, and other-orientation while whites place greater stress on emotions and future commitment.

Also, Gudykunst and Hammer (1987) report that while Afro-Americans and whites are similar in certain aspects of uncertainty reduction, they differ in fundamental respects. Among Afro-Americans, uncertainty reduction does not necessarily lead to liking and interrogation does not reduce uncertainty. These findings cast serious doubt on the generalizability of the theory across ethnic groups.

Finally, LaFrance and Mayo (1976) report differences in interaction management between Afro-Americans and whites. Afro-Americans were found to gaze at their interactional partners more during speaking turns than during listening turns. This pattern is the opposite of that observed among white Americans (Kendon, 1967) and may lead to situations of mutual staring during Afro-American speaking turns and apparent inattentiveness during white speaking turns.

These studies demonstrate the potential tension involved in interethnic interaction and the ways ethnic differences can diminish prospects for effective communication. Effective communication requires that interactants have the requisite communication skills, be motivated to communicate, and have knowledge of self, other, situation, and topic (Spitzberg & Cupach, 1984; Spitzberg & Hecht, 1984). Ethnicity manifests itself in each of these areas and as well influences the ability of interactants to adjust to and accommodate one another (Ball, Giles, & Hewstone, 1985; Gallois, Franklin-Stokes, Giles & Coupland, 1988; Giles, Bourhis & Taylor, 1977; Giles, Mulac, Bradac, & Johnson, 1987). Also members of different ethnic groups do not share a common set of communication rules (Collier, Ribeau & Hecht, 1986) and are dissimilar in their willingness to shift their rules in order to adjust to the ethnicity of their dyadic partners (Collier, 1988).

It appears that of the many factors which influence communication effectiveness, none may do so more than ethnic culture. These differences make it important to study both the obstacles to effective inter-ethnic communication and strategies for communication improvement. A starting place for such an analysis is the identification of ethnic perspectives on communication effectiveness. Though Afro-Americans and whites may have differing styles, it is possible they still could communicate effectively if they were able to adapt their conversational patterns in order to adjust to or accommodate one another's styles.

Generally, interactants modify their messages in response to their conversational partners: speech converges (moves toward the other's style) or diverges (moves away from the other's style). These adjustments have been reported for variables such as pronunciation (Giles, 1973), vocal intensity (Natale, 1975), talk and silence sequences (Capella & Planalp, 1981), pause and utterance length (Jaffe & Feldstein, 1970) and speech rates (Webb, 1972). In general, these studies show that people coverge toward each other's presentation linguistically when the costs are less than the rewards, there is a desire for communicative efficiency, and the social norms do not dictate alternative strategies (Beebe & Giles, 1984; Bourhis, 1985). However, divergence is likely to occur when the encounter is defined in intergroup terms and there is a strong desire for group identity or when there is a desire to disassociate the self from the other (Beebe & Giles, 1984; Bourhis, 1985).

Thus, ethnic differences can influence the adjustment process. Strong ethnic group identity can promote divergence, as can peer group pressures. When dyadic partners do not share the same ethnic culture, it is more difficult to know how to adjust to each other and the adjustment process may require a communication style that is not a frequently-used aspect of the cultural repertoire (e.g., fast speaking rate among Southern Afro-Americans).

RESEARCH DIRECTIONS

With the great power differential in United States society, members of the mainstream culture have often been able to assume that other groups will adjust to their style. In fact, earlier speech accommodation research has repeatedly examined and verified the presence of code-switching in cross-cultural interactions (Giles, Bourhis & Taylor, 1977). Low power groups often shift to the mainstream style to accommodate cultural differences. However, rising controversies over issues such as bilingual and bicultural education suggest that social norms may be changing as emerging co-populations assert their own influence. Therefore, dominant groups may no longer be able to depend upon other groups' adapting to the dominant style.

These studies suggest problems inherent in Afro-American-white communication interactions. If interactions do not share common knowledge, motivation, and styles then conversational effectiveness is problematic. Such speech divergence can be viewed as a 'failure event.' Failure events occur when interactions do not run smoothly, violate rules, violate expectations and preferences, or are somehow inappropriate (Cody & McLaughlin, 1985; McLaughlin, Cody, & O'Hair, 1983; Morris, 1985; Schonbach, 1980). In other words, communication has been unsuccessful. If the interactants wish to improve the situation, they must 'align' the interaction. Alignments are conversational improvement strategies for achieving accommodation once a failure event has been encountered, and the identification of alignment specifies those processes which tune the interaction to meet the interactants' preferences (Ball, Giles, & Hewstone, 1985; Giles, 1987; Morris, 1985). Alignment research emphasizes "cooperative efforts to guide the activity rather than efforts of 'offenders' to account for admittedly deviant behavior" (Morris, 1985, p. 70). Thus, alignment research is concerned with restorative processes in problematic situations.

Much of the work on interethnic communication and failure events has been conducted at the "micro-level" of analysis. These studies focus on specific speech acts. While these studies are useful, it is important to complement this level of analysis with more macro-level studies. One such level is that of the conversational strategy.

It has been suggested that communicators often make predictions about the direction and outcomes of their interactions and design strategies to actualize their preferences (Miller & Steinberg, 1975). While it seems clear that much communication occurs 'mindlessly' or outside of awareness (Berger & Douglas, 1982; Folkes, 1985; Kitayana & Burnstein, 1988; Langer, 1978), when communicators are faced with atypical events outside of their scripted sequencing they become more aware and strategic (Douglas, 1983). Since difficult interactions should make strategic behavior more salient, it is important to examine issues in effective communication and communication improvement strategies.

Based on the presence of these differing conversational styles and Hecht and Ribeau's (1984) finding that Afro-Americans and whites differ in what constitutes satisfying intra-ethnic communication as well as the apparent difficulty the ethnic groups experience in accommodating their styles to one another, two studies were designed.

In these studies, we attempt to utilize an interpretive, cultural perspective. Cultures exist on a variety of levels—nations (Dodd, 1982), regions (Andersen, Lustig, & Andersen, 1987), relationships (Baxter, 1987, Wood, 1982) and even organizations (Smith & Eisenberg, 1987). Here we examine an ethnic culture seeking to capture an Afro-American view of the world through examining how members of this group construct and interpret their experiences (Baxter, 1987; Carbaugh, 1988; Geertz, 1973, 1983; Katriel, 1988; Katriel & Philipsen, 1981; Leiter, 1980). An interpretive, cultural perspective such as this focuses on the idioms, metaphors and themes which distinguish a group and guide its communicative experiences. This perspective requires a "thickness" of description which enables one to articulate the group's communicative experiences more clearly. The cultural approach assumes that communication and culture are mutually related, with communication expressing culture and culture framing communication (Hecht, Ribeau, & Sedano, in press; Wolfson & Pearce, 1983). An intersubjective reality emerges out of the cultural experience of group members and is expressed in an implicit perspective on communication. A cultural approach to ethnicity is established in the work of Collier (1988), Collier, Ribeau & Hecht, (1986) and Hecht, Ribeau, and Sedano (in press) with Mexican Americans and of Hecht and Ribeau (1987, in press), Kochman (1982), and Levine (1977) with Afro-Americans.

The primary goal of this work is to articulate the view of an ethnic culture. Just as the preponderance of previous work examines only a white perspective on communication, here we seek to give voice to Afro-American perceptions of interethnic communication. From a cultural perspective it is not necessary to compare this perspective to other groups. Rather, the identification of a perspective is assumed to

have utility in its own right. Further, such comparisons are not meaningful without first articulating the view of the ethnic community. The focus, then, is on describing the perspective, and future researchers and other research perspectives will be needed for comparative work which explores the similarities and differences among the perspectives of the various ethnic cultures. With these purposes in mind, the following studies were conducted.

STUDY ONE

Research Questions

Study One sought to address an aspect of this larger question by examining the issues Afro-Americans perceive as most salient to their satisfying and dissatisfying conversations with whites. In a sense, we sought to identify an Afro-American interethnic relational agenda or implicit theory of communication by examining the issues members of this ethnic culture see as most salient to their communication satisfaction. While these issues constitute only a portion of effectiveness, they provide a complement to previous research which does not address questions of effective communication directly. Since research on mainstream culture suggests that typical communication and effective communication are not isomorphic (Hecht, 1984), the effectiveness orientation is an important one. Further, since most studies of communicative effectiveness are limited to mainstream culture, this extension to Afro-American culture is promising.

In order to focus this study effectiveness was defined as satisfying communication. Previous research shows satisfaction to be the emotional response to effective interpersonal encounters (Bochner & Kelly, 1974; Maslow, 1954; Rogers, 1961; Spitzberg & Hecht, 1984; Thibaut & Kelley, 1959). Thus a type of effectiveness, satisfying communication, is explored.

Accordingly, the following two research questions were asked:

Q1: What issues do Afro-Americans perceive in satisfying and dissatisfying conversations with whites?

Q2: What conversational improvement strategies do Afro-Americans believe could improve conversations with whites?

Having identified the issues and improvement strategies in Study One, we wished to replicate the findings and examine the relationships among the issues, improvement strategies and satisfaction. As part of this process we sought to determine if the relationships among the issues, improvement strategies, and satisfaction were independent of individual difference variables. Ickes (1984) suggests that ethnicity should override demographic variables such as sex in most situations, and previously cited literature suggests ethnicity is particularly salient during intercultural interactions. Thus, we posed the following questions:

Q3a: What is the relationship between the issues and satisfaction?

Q3b: Is this relationship independent of individual difference variables?

Q4a: What is the relationship between conversational improvement strategies and satisfaction?

Q4b: Is this relationship independent of individual difference variables?

Q5a: What is the relationship between the issues and the improvement strategies?

Q5b: Is this relationship independent of individual difference variables?

As a subsidiary purpose, we explored the relationships between the issues and individual difference variables, and between improvement strategies and individual difference variables. Previous research suggests that variables such as ethnic identity (Hecht & Ribeau, 1987, in press), geographic region (Andersen, Lustig, & Andersen, 1987; Hecht, Andersen, & Ribeau, in press), sex (Pearson, 1985; Tavis & Wade, 1984), income (Pettigrew, 1981), and age (Dodd, 1982) may play a role in interethnic communication. Ethnic identity is conceptualized as that part of the self-concept that is associated with self-perceived membership in an ethnic group (Hecht & Ribeau, 1987, in press). Afro-Americans who associate different labels with

themselves also differ in what those labels mean to them (Hecht & Ribeau, in press). Research questions 3 through 5 focused on the possibility that these variables intervene in the relationships among the issues, the improvement strategies, and satisfaction. Here, in this secondary analysis, we are concerned with the direct relationship between the issues and the individual difference variables, and the improvement strategies and the individual difference variables.

Q6: Do the issues vary with the individual difference variables of ethnic identity, age, sex, geography, and income?

Q7: Do the improvement strategies vary with the individual difference variables of ethnic identity, age, sex, geography, and income?

STUDY ONE: DEVELOPMENT OF CODING SCHEME

Initial Development

Respondents

The respondent group was composed of 31 Afro-Americans (15 males and 16 females) who were student volunteers from a large, multi-sectioned, introductory speech communication course at a university in the southwestern United States. Most of the volunteers were from working class families (the majority with incomes below $25,000 per year) and ranged from 17 to 33 years old, with an average age of 25. As the course is required of all students, respondents are representative of this large, urban multi-ethnic campus but may not be representative of non-students, other geographic areas, and different socio-economic groups.

Procedures

Participants completed a questionnaire which asked them to recall two recent conversations with acquaintances of a different ethnic group which took place in a social situation. Respondents indicated their age, sex, and family income. Each participant then recounted both a satisfying and dissatisfying conversation (not necessarily with the same conversational partner), with the order randomly determined. We used only those questionnaires ($N = 31$) in which Afro-Americans recounted a conversation with a white acquaintance.

For both the satisfying and dissatisfying conversation, the participants responded in detail to a series of open-ended questions: (1) describe the location and topic of the conversation; (2) describe and explain what you did or did not say that was satisfying or dissatisfying; (3) describe and explain what your conversational partner did or did not say that was satisfying or dissatisfying; (4) describe and explain anything else in the conversation that was satisfying or dissatisfying; (5) indicate what you or your dyadic partner could have done to improve the conversation.

Detailed, 2-4 page accounts of each conversation were provided by respondents, many of whom were able to recall exact dialogue. We used self-reports of recalled conversations here and throughout this project because we sought to understand how Afro-Americans perceive their interactions. Objectivist descriptions of observed conversations provide a different sort of data. As van Dijk (1987) notes, self-reports provide insight into the content, strategy, and structure of social interaction. In justifying the method, this author notes that self reports provide "insight into the ways people subjectively recall, transform, and reproduce information from previous personal experiences" (p. 19) and that the "biases" or "unreliability" of such accounts are "precisely the elements in which we are interested" (p. 20). Further, research shows that interactants adjust to their perceptions and interpretations of communication rather than toward "actual" behavior (Beebe & Giles, 1984; Gallois, Franklin-Stokes, Giles, & Coupland, 1988). Accounting also forms the basis for a vast amount of communication and social research (e.g., Antaki, 1981; Baxter, 1986; Baxter & Bullis, 1986; Fisher, 1986; Harré, 1979; Rawlins, 1983).

Analyses

The data from questions 1-4 were analyzed by the first two authors: then the resulting lists of issues were discussed and formalized into a master list. First, the reports of each satisfying and dissatisfying conversation were read and the salient communication behaviors recorded on separate index cards. Second, the cards were sorted into themes by each investigator. Third, consensus was reached. Any differences were discussed and resolved by returning to the original questionnaire, re-reading the descriptions and interpretations, and exploring possible interpretations. In one instance an entirely different theme emerged which incorporated elements of all analyses. On another occasion a change in the wording of one investigator's theme eliminated the disagreement. Since this is a synthetic, emergent process, the extent of initial agreement is not relevant.

In the second stage, the reports (open-ended question 5) of each satisfying and dissatisfying conversation were read and salient conversational improvement strategies recorded. Then the strategies were sorted into themes by each investigator. Finally, the sortings of each investigator were combined as before.

The themes were intended to reflect the issues and improvement strategies raised by Afro-Americans respondents which constitute an agenda for satisfying and dissatisfying interethnic conversations. This agenda can be said to tap an "implicit theory of effective communication." This list is not intended to be exhaustive. Future research is needed for elaboration and development.

The interpretive themes (issues or improvement strategies) are not meant to be mutually exclusive categories (Agar & Hobbs, 1982). Since communication is multi-functioned, we believe that any act can and often does fulfill more than one function. Thus we expect the themes to overlap, with a single act simultaneously indicative of multiple themes. Examples are quoted from respondents' descriptions in order to demonstrate and explain the issues. These quotations do not verify the issues but rather clarify the conclusions derived from intensive analyses of respondents' descriptions of their conversations. Reliabilities for each system are provided in Study Two.

Results, Communication Issues

The content analyses produced a set of seven issues related to satisfying and dissatisfying communication. These seven were: Negative Stereotyping, Acceptance, Emotional Expressiveness, Authenticity, Understanding, Goal Attainment, and Powerlessness. The analysis also produced five conversational improvement strategies: Asserting a Point of View, Open Mindedness, Avoidance, Interaction Management, and Other-Orientation. Each of the strategies was observed in at least 20 per cent of the questionnaires, and two contained subcategories.

Negative stereotyping involved conversations in which the communication partner racially categorized the respondent and ascribed characteristics of his/her ethnic group to the respondent rather than treating the person as an individual. For example, an Afro-American female reported dissatisfaction when her conversational partner "seemed to say to me that she (a third party) was black and you know how they are."

In addition, several of the responses discussed a form of negative stereotyping which could be labeled "indirect stereotyping." This type of stereotyping occurred when the white dyadic partner talked to the Afro-American about those topics which were believed to be "Afro-American" topics (such as sports or music) and occurred during dissatisfying conversations. Conversely, an Afro-American female was satisfied because she "didn't feel put on the spot to speak for the whole of the Black race." And yet another Afro-American female was satisfied when her partner spoke to her "as another person and didn't let my color interfere with the conversation." Negative stereotyping, when present, is a source of dissatisfaction and, perhaps because of the pervasiveness of prejudice, is a source of satisfaction when absent.

Many respondents reported that their satisfaction was predicated on *acceptance,* a feeling that another accepts, confirms and respects their opinions. An Afro-American female remarked that she was satisfied with one conversation because there was "mutual respect for each other's beliefs." These respondents commented on feelings of equality/inequality, mutual interest, liking, and communication barriers, with the expressed interpretation that the other person accepted them. Most instances of acceptances were recorded for descriptions of satisfying conversations.

The third issue was *emotional expressiveness,* which referred to the communication of feelings. One respondent was dissatisfied because she did not express her own emotions: she reported, "I was dissatisfied that I maintained control and did not curse her out." Emotional expressiveness can refer to both one's own and one's partner's expression, with lack of expressiveness on either one's part seen as dissatisfying. Expressiveness manifests itself verbally and nonverbally. While focusing on emotions, expressiveness also includes verbalizations of ideas and opinions. This issue was present more often in descriptions of satisfying than dissatisfying conversations.

Authenticity is the label applied to genuineness, with open disclosure the positive instance and evasiveness the negative. One respondent derived satisfaction from a conversation because he "disclosed information about myself which I usually can't do with someone I don't know well." Another person was dissatisfied because she "was not direct about what I wanted to discuss with this person and did a lot of beating around the bush." Authenticity was inferred from discussion of private and personal information, and truthfulness. In addition, respondents who felt they could "be themselves" or who perceived the other as expressing opinions openly and freely attribute authenticity to the conversation. The issue of authenticity was observed more often in descriptions of dissatisfying conversations than satisfying conversations.

Feelings of *understanding* were also important to interactants' satisfaction. Satisfaction for many respondents was keyed to the feeling that their meaning was successfully conveyed. For example, one respondent reported that "there was a genuine exchange of thinking, feeling, and caring." Responses suggesting that information was exchanged and learning took place fall into this theme as well. Cues that the other person did not believe the respondent were taken as signs of lack of understanding. A greater proportion of these instances were represented in satisfying conversations.

Achieving objectives or obtaining desired ends from the communication effort constitutes the issue of *goal attainment.* Afro-American respondents seemed to desire a feeling of accomplishment, feeling satisfied when this was obtained and dissatisfied when it was not. One respondent noted dissatisfaction because "no information was exchanged in terms of what I was seeking." Goal attainment referred to the respondent's ability to achieve a desired end, whether that be solving a problem, exchanging information, or finishing a project. Goal attainment was observed more frequently in discussions of satisfying interactions than in dissatisfying interactions.

The final issue was labeled *powerlessness* and described feelings of being controlled, manipulated, and trapped. Conversely, satisfaction was manifested when interactants felt they had some control or influence over the conversation. One female explained her dissatisfaction by saying that the other interactant was "trying to persuade me using subtle tactics and assertiveness." An Afro-American male described a dissatisfying conversation in which he did not get an adequate chance to express himself. He said that the other communicator "tried to carry on the conversation all by himself . . . he would keep talking and interrupted me whenever I tried to say something." Respondents felt powerless if they were interrupted and did not get a chance to complete their thoughts, or believed that the other person controlled the topic. These conversations occurred among peers as well as in the presence of higher status others. This issue was most prevalent in descriptions of dissatisfying conversations.

Results, Conversational Improvement Strategies

Asserting a Point of View was found exclusively as a response to a dissatisfying conversation. Respondents felt that conversations could be improved by arguing their own position and convincing their conversational partner. One male said that a dissatisfying conversation could have been improved if he could "convince him [the conversational partner] to give the benefit of the doubt" to other people, whereas a female wanted to educate her partner about slavery in order to help him understand. This was mainly seen as a strategy for the respondent to employ, not the conversational partner.

A sub-group in this category not only wanted to be more assertive, but also believed that they should be more detailed, factual, and specific. For example, one female wrote that "if I had more facts I could have continued in my point of trying to make him realize these people need help."

The second theme, *Open-Mindedness,* was recommended most frequently as a strategy for improving dissatisfying conversations. Respondents expressed a desire to have people consider their ideas or opinions, rather than dismiss them without giving them sufficient consideration. For example, a male wanted the other person to be "more open-minded" and a second male said the other person should "be more patient, not assume anything, find out first." This strategy was a desired change in the conversational partner.

A sub-theme derived from improving dissatisfying conversations through open-mindedness was labeled *Treating as an Equal.* Examples included a female who wanted the other person to "not take a self-righteous position" and a second female who would have been more satisfied if her partner "had been less inclined to a superior attitude."

The third theme was called *Avoidance* and was suggested as a strategy for improving dissatisfying conversations. Those who responded with this strategy felt the only successful resolution was to either avoid the topic or end the interaction. For example, one respondent said she could have improved the situation by "not bringing up the subject," while another female said the other person could have improved the situation "by leaving my house politely." These instances were very clear-cut and obvious. Respondents felt that certain conversations should not take place and that certain topics would just have to be avoided with specific people.

The fourth strategy, *Interaction Management,* occurred exclusively among descriptions of satisfying conversations. Respondents most often mentioned regulating the amount of talk and the rate. For example, one female wrote that a satisfying conversation could have been improved by "just talking a little more," and another female reported that her conversation could have been improved by "more time" together, or a longer conversation. Others discussed turn talking. The conversation can be improved if either interactant adopts this strategy.

The final strategy, *Other-Orientation,* occurred most frequently in descriptions of satisfying conversations. These descriptions related attempts to involve the other person, find common ground, and create identification. A female said she and her partner could have "talked about something he could have related to," while a male noted that he could have "asked better questions." Either interactant can improve the conversation by being more other-oriented.

Replication I

Respondents

Intensive interviews were conducted with 20 members (10 Afro-American females and 10 Afro-American males) of this ethnic group in order to provide an initial replication of the issues and improvement strategies. Participants were recruited as key informants from the community at large in southern California and Arizona. Informants were chosen based on their ability to comment on ethnic relations, and varied in age and socio-economic status. Respondents were interviewed individually.

Procedures

First, each respondent was provided with examples of each of the issues and improvement strategies and was asked to explain what was occurring and to provide a label for the situation. Second, each respondent was provided with a list of issues and asked for examples from their personal experiences and subjective estimates of frequency of occurrence and importance. These estimates were provided in verbal, not quantitative, terms. Next, each was asked if anything could be done to improve each situation. Finally, each was provided a list of the improvement strategies and asked for examples and subjective, verbal estimates of frequency and importance.

Results

These interviews generally supported our choice of the issues and improvement strategies as well as the labels assigned. Respondents indicated that expressiveness should not be limited to the emotional arena. In fact, it was suggested that some Afro-Americans try to project a particularly "tough" or "cold" exterior in order to be seen as "cool."

It was also interesting to note that respondents were particularly sensitive to the indirect forms of stereotyping. These aroused a great deal of emotion. With the one modification to expressiveness, the themes were accepted as appropriately named and representative.

Summary

The themes developed in this study provide an initial identification of how Afro-Americans perceive interethnic communication. Some of the issues are observed primarily in descriptions of satisfaction (acceptance, authenticity, and goal attainment) or dissatisfaction (powerlessness and negative stereotyping). Some of these themes ultimately may need to be combined. Further research is needed to clarify this.

This study also indicates that there is a discernable set of strategies that Afro-Americans believe can improve their conversations with whites. Five such strategies where identified in this study. These were: Asserting a Point of View, Open-mindedness, Avoidance, Interaction Management, and Other-Orientation. Interaction management and other-orientation were suggested as strategies for improving already satisfying interactions whereas the remaining categories were recommended for improving dissatisfying conversations. In addition, interaction management and asserting a point of view were seen as strategies for oneself whereas open-mindedness was suggested for the other conversational partner. Other-orientation and avoidance were seen as appropriate for either self or other.

Given the difficulties of interethnic communication, conversational improvement strategies are important for the effective practice of interethnic relationships. We expect that such conversations often diverge and require alignment, and even effective interactions can be improved. The competent communicator must be aware of these strategies in order to overcome the inevitable problems posed by cultural differences. Our research suggests that participants in interethnic interaction have a repertoire

Table 1   Percentages of Conversations by Themes

Issues

Acceptance	Emotional Expressiveness	Understanding	Negative Stereotyping	Authenticity	Attainment	Goal Powerlessness
38.1%	24.8%	14.3%	13.3%	13.3%	13.3%	10.5%

Communication Improvement Strategies

Nothing	Interaction Management	Assertiveness	Open Minded	Avoidance	Other Orientation	Given In
36.8%	21.8%	17.2%	13.8%	12.6%	11.5%	8.0%

of strategies for such alignment work. Further research should test the efficacy of the strategies suggested by participants in this study and attempt to compare those strategies to those used in intra-ethnic communication.

Replication II

Respondents

A third group of respondents was used to test the reliability of the coding scheme and to examine research questions 3 through 7. This group consisted of 71 Afro-American respondents (23 males, 48 females) recruited from college campuses and community groups in California (37), New York (13), and Arizona (21). The average age was 31.3 ($SD = 12.6$) and the average family income was \$28,792 ($SD = \$16,310$).

Procedures

Respondents completed a questionnaire in which they provided individual difference information (age, gender, income, geography) as well as recalled and described satisfying and dissatisfying conversations with a white acquaintance in a social situation. For each type of conversation, respondents were asked the same series of questions participants were asked in the Study One questionnaire. First, they described the location and topic of conversation. Locations included at work (46%), in public (19%), at home (14%), at school (13%), and other (8%). Topics included personal lives

(34%), jobs and work (19%), politics/news/ current events (14%), race (12%), school (7%), and other (14%). Second, they indicated what they did or said that was satisfying or dissatisfying; third, they explained their answers. Then respondents described what the other participant said or did that was satisfying or dissatisfying and explained their responses. They also indicated anything else in the conversation which was satisfying or dissatisfying and explained that response. Next, they indicated what they or their dyadic partner could have done to improve the conversation. As not all respondents could recall both types of conversation, a total of 125 conversations were described. Thus, 125 was the *N* for all analyses. Finally, respondents were asked to provide the label which they use to described their ethnic identity, and additional demographic information.

Analyses

In this study, two independent coders were trained on the category system and coded the questionnaires. Interrater reliability was .79 for the issues (83% agreement) and .83 for the improvement strategies (86% agreement). Disagreements were resolved through discussion. The percentage of response in each theme is presented in Table 1.

After delineating issues and strategies in Study One, we wished to determine the relationships among the issues, communication improvement strategies, type of conversation (satisfying or dissatisfying), and the individual difference variables of geography, age, gender, family income and ethnic identity. Unfortunately, the New York sample was small and some of the questionnaires pertaining to dissatisfying conversations were incomplete and not usable. Consequently, for analyses relevant to geography, only the data from Arizona and California were used. Age and family income were split at the mean. The average ages of the high and low groups were 45.9 and 21.3 respectively, and the average incomes for the high and low groups were $43,500 and $14,083, respectively.

The relationships among the variables were tested by means of hierarchical log linear analysis. First, a saturated model was examined using all variables and allowing all interactions. The test that k-way effects are zero was examined to determine the most efficient level of interaction. Successive analyses were then used to identify the best fitting model. In these analyses, we were restricted to 10 total variables due to a limitation of the program (SPSSX).

Results

Communication Issues

First, the relationship between the issues and satisfaction was examined. In the saturated model, the seven issues and satisfaction were entered. The likelihood ratio chi square (L^2) for the one way (297.54, df = 8, p = .00) and two-way (54.31, df = 28, p = .00) effects were significant. Next a model including satisfaction and each of the issues (e.g., satisfaction and negative stereotyping, satisfaction and acceptance, etc.) was examined. The L^2 value (86.06, df = 245, p = 1.00) indicated a significant relationship. The likelihood ratio chi square change for the satisfaction by negative stereotyping (5.17, df = 1, p = .02) and satisfaction by acceptance (5.15. df = 1, p = .02) effects were significant. Examination of the frequency tables indicated that when negative stereotyping appears it is associated with dissatisfaction and when acceptance appears it is associated with satisfaction. The significant effect for the overall model confirms that the issues are salient to communication satisfaction.

Second, we sought to determine if the relationship between the issues and satisfaction was independent of the individual difference variables (age, gender, income, geography, and ethnic identity). This was accomplished through five separate analyses. Each individual difference variable was added separately to the model. For example, age, the 7 issues, and satisfaction were examined simultaneously in one analysis. A significant three-way interaction might indicate an interaction among an issue, age and satisfaction. In the absence of a three-way, the relationships between the issues and satisfaction must be independent of age. Next, gender was examined with the issues and satisfaction, and so on until all 5 individual difference variables had been entered into the model. This procedure was necessitated due to the SPSSX restriction on the number of variables that can be simultaneously entered into the model. Small cell sizes for certain of the variables reduced the power of the tests. However, the main problem encountered when utilizing this statistical test occurs when *expected* frequencies are zero in one or more cells (Knoke & Burke, 1983), and all of the categories were large enough to avoid this. Further, SPSSX corrects for this problem by following Knoke and Burke's suggestion to substitute .5 for any void cell. Since none of the three-way interaction L^2 values was significant, it was concluded that the relationship between satisfaction and the issues was independent of age, gender, income, geography, and ethnic identity.

Finally, the relationship between each individual difference variable and the issues was examined. Again, 5 separate analyses were computed, with each individual difference variable used with all 7 issues. Again, the saturated model was examined first, followed by testing lower-order models. The two-way and higher order interaction effects for income and geography were nonsignificant, indicating that the issues were independent of these variables. Second-order interactions were indicated for the analyses involving ethnic identity, age, and gender.

The L^2 value (109.79, df = 371, p = 1.00) indicated a significant relationship between ethnic identity and the issues, with significant L^2 changes for negative stereotyping (6.31, df = 2, p = .04) and understanding (9.29, df = 2, p = .01). Examination of the frequencies indicated that respondents labeling themselves

Black American were most likely (24%) to feel negatively stereotyped. Those labeling themselves Black were second most likely (11%), whereas those using the label Afro-American were unlikely (3%) to feel this way. Black Americans were also the most likely group to see understanding as an issue (32%), followed by Afro-Americans (16%) and Blacks (5%).

Age was significantly associated with the issues ($L^2 = 109.77$, df $= 317$, $p = 1.00$), with significant changes in the L^2 value for authenticity (7.75, df $= 1$, $p = .01$) and goal attainment (3.95, df $= 1$, $p = .05$). Older respondents were more likely to see authenticity as an issue (22%) than younger respondents (4%), whereas younger respondents were more likely to report goal attainment as an issue (21%) than their older counterparts (7%).

Finally, the L^2 value (78.12, df $= 246$, $p = 1.00$) indicated a relationship between gender and the issues. The chi square change value for expressiveness was significant (4.40, df $= 1$, $p = .04$), with women reporting this as an issue (29%) more frequently than men (10%).

Conversational Improvement Strategies

The relationship between satisfaction and the strategies was examined next. The analysis of the saturated model indicated that only two-way interactions need be considered. The L^2 value (129.29, df $= 370$, $p = 1.00$) indicated that such a relationship does exist. Significant L^2 changes were observed for the interactions between satisfaction and open-mindedness (9.20, df $= 2$, $p = .001$) and between satisfaction and avoidance (24.04, df $= 2$, $p = .001$). Frequencies indicated that dissatisfying conversations could be improved by either being more open-minded or by avoiding the topic or the entire conversation. These findings indicate that improvement strategies are related to satisfaction.

Next, we sought to discern if this relationship was independent of the individual difference variables (age, gender, income, geography, and ethnic identity). As before, each individual difference variable was added separately to the saturated model and the interaction terms examined. Since none of three-way interactions was statistically significant, we concluded that the relationship between satisfaction and the

communication improvement strategies was independent of age, gender, income, geography, and ethnic identity.

We also examined the relationship between the individual difference variables and strategies exclusive of satisfaction. Each individual difference variable was included with the 7 strategies in tests of the saturated model. In this manner five separate analyses (one for each individual difference variable) were calculated. Since none of the two-way or higher order interactions were significant for age, gender, and geography, we assume the strategies are independent of these variables.

However, the L^2 value of ethnic identity (197.60, df $= 1134$, $p = 1.00$) indicated a relationship with the strategies. Significant likelihood ratio chi square change values were observed for the interaction of ethnic identity with assertiveness (6.47, df $= 2$, $p = .04$), open-mindedness (10.72, df $= 2$, $p = .00$), and other orientation (6.83, df $= 2$, $p = .03$). The frequency tables indicated that Black Americans (32%) and Afro-Americans (25%) are more likely to suggest assertiveness to improve conversations than are those who label themselves as Black (6%). Finally, Blacks (27%) and Black-Americans (23%) are more likely than Afro-Americans to report that communication can be improved by exhibiting more other-orientation.

A relationship between income and communication improvement strategies also was indicated by the L^2 value of 187.34 (df $= 755$, $p = 1.00$). Examination of the changes in the likelihood ratio chi square values indicated significant interactions between income and interaction management (5.92, df $= 1$, $p = .03$), and between income and other orientation (4.54, df $= 1$, $p = .03$). People with family incomes below \$25,000 were more likely to suggest interaction management (29% vs 12%), whereas those with incomes above this mark were more likely to suggest increased other-orientation (21% vs 2%).

Issues and Improvement Strategies

Finally, the relationship between the issues and improvement strategies was explored in two phases. First, we examined the issues and improvement strategies which had been related to satisfaction in the previous analyses (that is, negative stereotyping, acceptance, open-mindedness, avoidance) and tested a saturated model which included these four plus satisfaction. This analysis indicated only two-way interactions were significant. We interpreted this to mean that the relationship between satisfaction and the issues was independent of the improvement strategies. This appears logical when one considers that the improvement strategies were suggestions for what *could have been done* rather than descriptions of what *was done.*

Next we examined the relationship between each issue and the seven strategies, seeking to determine if certain strategies were perceived as remedies for specific issues. These analyses indicated that acceptance, expressiveness, and goal attainment were not related to this set of communication improvement strategies. However, the L^2 value indicated a relationship between negative stereotyping and the improvement strategies. A significant change value was observed for avoidance (6.22, df = 1, p = .01), with frequencies indicating that respondents believed that if you were stereotyped you should avoid either the specific topic, or the conversation entirely.

A relationship was also indicated between authenticity and the strategies (L^2 = 113.29, df = 246, p = 1.00), with a significant change value for assertiveness (5.05, df = 1, p = .02). The frequency cross-tabulation revealed that assertiveness is never suggested as an improvement strategy if the issue is authenticity. In other words, if the other person is acting in an authentic manner, being more assertive will not improve the conversation.

The likelihood chi square (104.28, df = 245, p = 1.00) also indicated a relationship between understanding and improvement strategies. Significant changes in the L^2 values were observed for open-mindedness (7.82, df = 1, p = .01) and doing nothing (6.01, df = 1, p = .01). The frequency cross-tabulation tables revealed that respondents believe that if a person feels understood the conversation can be improved by being more open-minded, but if the person does not feel understood there is nothing they can do.

A relationship also existed between powerlessness and the strategies (L^2 = 113.88,

df = 246, p = 1.00). The frequencies revealed that if a respondent felt powerless, one way of improving the conversation was to give in to the other person.

Summary

The analyses replicated and extended the preliminary findings. The themes were significantly associated with satisfaction, and these relationships were independent of the individual difference variables. This independence is important because it partially supports the ethnic claim for the findings. Results indicate that while the entire model is associated with satisfaction for this sample, the most salient issues were negative stereotyping and acceptance, with the former associated with dissatisfaction when present and the latter associated with satisfaction. The most salient conversational improvement strategies were open-mindedness and avoidance. Both are suggested as strategies for improving dissatisfying conversations.

Results also indicate that the issues and improvement strategies are related to each other. Respondents seem to believe that someone who feels stereotyped can only improve the conversation by avoiding the topic or terminating the interaction. Respondents also believe that if they are being understood the conversation can be improved by being more open-minded, but there is nothing that can be done if the other person does not understand. Taken together, the picture emerges of extreme dissatisfaction with certain types of conversations and the feeling that little can be done to improve these interactions.

Although the relationships among the issues, improvement strategies, and satisfaction are independent of individual difference variables, those variables were related when satisfaction is not considered. These findings are suggestive of directions for future research.

The strongest of these factors appears to be ethnic identity, which is related to both issues and improvement strategies. Previous studies (Hecht & Ribeau, 1987, in press) concluded that those labeling themselves Black American lie between those selecting other labels in political activism and ethnic awareness. This group perceives a duality in their identity, incorporating the color consciousness of Blacks with the cultural root metaphor of Africanism. This perception is reflected in the current findings. Black Americans report negative stereotyping and acceptance as issues more frequently, and are more likely to suggest assertiveness and other-orientation as improvement strategies. Blacks, however, emphasize other-orientation most heavily and do not raise the other issues and improvement strategies to the same extent. Consistent with their position as the most politically aware group, Afro-Americans emphasize the need for assertiveness and open-mindedness if inter-ethnic communication is to improve.

Differences were also observed for the other individual difference variables. Age and gender were related to the issues, and income was related to the improvement strategies. These findings suggest that older respondents are more concerned with authenticity, while younger respondents focus on goal attainment. Consistent with previous gender research in mainstream culture (Tavis & Wade, 1984), Afro-American females were found to emphasize expressiveness more than their male counterparts. Finally, those with lower incomes tend to suggest interaction management to improve conversations, while those with higher incomes stress other-orientation.

STUDY TWO

Study Two was designed once again to provide informant feedback on the results of the previous studies. One method for qualitatively assessing the utility of findings is to present them to key informants for comment and evaluation.

Methods

Respondents and Procedures

Four key informants were recruited (two Afro-American females, two Afro-American males) for Study Two. All were selected for their ability to comment on ethnic relations in the United States, and each had lived in numerous regions, including at least one of those sampled in this paper. The interviews were unstructured, with the goal of eliciting informed judgments on the findings. To provide some

consistency, informants were presented with a list of the issues and improvement strategies, and the main conclusions from Study One. Given the results of Study One, the focus was on the issues rather than the improvement strategies. The informants' comments were invited. Interviews lasted between 45 and 90 minutes each.

Results

Not all informants commented on all issues and improvement strategies. They agreed, in general, that these themes were important for interethnic communication. Their specific comments are summarized below.

Negative Stereotyping

One Afro-American male commented that the introduction of Afro-American topics by whites is in the attempt to find common interests, but he labeled people who bring them up as "patronizing or unaware." For example, white people try to talk to him about basketball, but he doesn't play or have any real interest in that sport. He thinks about it [this type of stereotyping] and "believes that many blacks feel offended. More educated blacks feel patronized." He also said that when most blacks see disliked behavior or don't understand what a white person is saying "they label the other person as racist."

A female added that language is important here. Afro-Americans who speak nonstandard dialect are faced with more frequent stereotyping. She feels that many whites are "predisposed to see the negatives in blacks."

The informants agreed that stereotyping was a fact of interethnic life in the U.S. Afro-Americans seem very sensitized to indirect forms of stereotyping, and react with disdain and withdrawal.

Acceptance

A male commented that many Afro-Americans overcompensate for "cultural deprivation" and "talk rather than listen in order to cover up." Most feel that their opinions are not respected and this leads them to get "more talkative and flippant." He referred to this as "not being taken seriously" by whites.

A female remarked that acceptance may be a problem initially, but not after people get to know you. She said, "It depends on how you present yourself." She believes she has the upper hand if a white person does not accept her because she is comfortable with herself and lack of acceptance means the other person is fearful of her. She sees this as an advantage.

A second male pointed out that for the Afro-American male acceptance for each other is expressed nonverbally through actions such as similar dress and other signs of inclusion. Verbally, "he will stay cool" or act removed.

Thus, acceptance is an issue tied to a communication style of talkativeness, flippancy, and being cool. Two of the informants also tied this back to stereotyping, noting that Afro-Americans may try to preempt such behavior by controlling the conversation. Others may seek to avoid recognizing stereotyping when it occurs by this stylized interaction.

Expressiveness

According to an Afro-American male, whites will often see black males as removed from the conversation. He believes this results from "feeling threatened and an attempt to hide a lack of a certain type of knowledge." This leads black males to either withdraw or become even more talkative. Black females are more talkative, although often in a "flippant" manner. The informant believed that white expressiveness is a lesser issue, although their lack of expressiveness would be interpreted as "racist or standoffish."

One female stated strongly that black women don't encourage each other to be emotionally expressive. They have had to be so tough as the head of the household throughout history that now they tend to "talk tough and make fun of white women who are soft." She said that black men criticize black women for this and some give it as a reason for preferring white women. Both black men and women stress "being cool"—not letting the other know what you are thinking or feeling. The remark of the second Afro-American male under acceptance supports this conclusion. Both agreed that there is a lot of underlying anger.

A second female remarked that while expressiveness is important to her, this is not typical. "Talking tough" is a way of carrying oneself. White females see themselves as more delicate and innocent than black females. She agrees with the other female informant that black women historically have had to take charge, and this has led to strength.

To the second Afro-American male this theme meant saying what you feel: "talking from the heart, not the head." Expressiveness is valued: "getting things off your chest."

Thus there is disagreement among the informants as to the role of expressiveness, particularly emotional expressiveness. Clearly verbal expressiveness, whether in the stylized talk or more genuine discussion, is valued when it occurs. The appropriateness of emotional expressiveness seems very situational, would require a considerable trust, and would only occur after the barriers had been brought down. The interpretation of expressiveness seems tied to the next issue, authenticity.

Authenticity

All agreed that authenticity was a factor in interethnic communication. One Afro-American male commented that there are "so many phony conversations—white people try to impress blacks with their liberalness." Blacks may or may not see through this, some accepting the illusion of equality. In the south southern blacks can see through "authentic" conversations. The informant commented on patronizing behavior again, noting that "even a sincere effort may come across this way."

Both females agreed that this issue is valued highly by Afro-American women, and one commented that it is expressed in the phrase "being real." She continued, commenting that black women "describe people in terms of their authenticity regardless of status level." If people are "unpretentious" and "down-to-earth" they are "real." Black women will say "be real" to someone who acts in a pretentious manner. She cited Afro-American literature which discusses this, including Tony K. Bombari's *Gorilla Love, The Johnson Girls,* and Gloria Naylor's *Women of Brewster Place.* The second woman commented that because this authenticity is so important she "doesn't accept people too readily." Instead, she "listens carefully to understand and assess authenticity."

All commented at one stage of the interview or another on the Afro-American male style of self-presentation. One male noted that among Afro-American males "high talk and stylin' are valued. You dress as if you had money even if you don't." He noted that the symbol of the Cadillac is another example of this image. Not being the "real you" is accepted because the self has been demeaned by society for so long that it is acceptable to create another image. Authenticity may be a female category, reflect a preference in how the white communicator should behave, or emerge only after the other issues have been dealt with. This is consistent with the Study One finding that lack of authenticity is frequently associated with dissatisfaction.

The concept of "realness" pervaded these discussions. Some commented on how unusual it was to have this quality of genuineness in interethnic communication, while others associated a lack of realness with Afro-American male behavior. Their comments indicated that authenticity might be valued in a white conversational partner, particularly by Afro-American females.

Understanding and Goal Attainment

In the discussions the two issues of understanding and goal attainment seemed to merge. A female noted that differences in upbringing may cause problems. "If people don't share the same life experiences they can't be expected to truly understand each other. If whites haven't been exposed to blacks there will be a 'fear of the unknown.'" As a result, little is gained from the conversation (goal attainment).

Similarly, an Afro-American male noted that "blacks and whites may come away with different meanings from a conversation because concepts aren't defined in the same way. The members of the ethnic groups tend to think in a different manner. Most times blacks don't get a lot from conversations with whites, so when it occurs it is highly valued—'like the gates opening.'" He noted that good conversations, ones that are open and honest, are rare. As a result, blacks frequently come away from

conversations with whites feeling they have gained little.

These discussions emphasized the difficulty of mutual understanding. Without understanding, goals cannot be attained. Thus both qualities are illusive, but valued.

Powerlessness

One male commented that in conversations among Afro-Americans there is a lot that "whites would consider antagonistic or brutal. Whites would be shocked to see this." He cited playing "the dozens," a put-down game, as an example. Such assertiveness can be too powerful for white interactants. He said "Whites wouldn't know how to take you if you acted really assertively. They would feel threatened." Similarly, the second male informant commented that a better label for this issue would be "Mau Mauing"—a black power strategy of extreme assertiveness and confrontation. He suggested that the label powerlessness "may be putting things in white terms."

A female commented that success, in general, depends on the power relationship and language. If you can articulate what you want and have the power to get it you will get something out of the conversation. She suggested that one of these factors may be missing for many blacks in their conversations with whites.

Power and power dynamics play a major role in interethnic relations and provide a clear example of Afro-American code switching. Afro-Americans believe that if they practiced the same power strategies with whites they use with each other their behavior would be badly misinterpreted. Power was an important undercurrent in many of the previous discussions.

Improvement Strategies

One male did not see much hope for improving dissatisfying conversations. Described it as "bouncing off a brick wall," he said that most blacks look for keys in the beginning. If they "see signs of racism, patronizing behavior, or other put-downs, they turn off quickly." The importance of stereotyping and acceptance is stressed here. He also noted that after "the first few minutes of a bad conversation it is almost a lost cause."

A female opined that open-mindedness is not highly valued. Afro-Americans are more concerned with appearing strong rather than uncertain. She saw the latter as a white, middle-class female attribute, consistent with the Study One finding that open-mindedness is a strategy for the white interactant to invoke.

The Afro-American informants felt that the improvement strategies might work under certain circumstances. However, where stereotyping and acceptance are issues, they did not hold out much hope. When the other issues were salient, the informants felt that some of the strategies might work but cautioned against placing too much faith in any attempt by Afro-Americans where power is unequal. This is consistent with the findings in Study One which indicate that avoidance by the self and open-mindedness by whites are the two most salient strategies. Interaction management is seen here and in Study One as a means for improving already satisfying conversations.

CONCLUSIONS

This paper reports the results of two studies designed to identify an implicit theory of interethnic communication from an Afro-American perspective. We sought to articulate the themes which Afro-Americans find salient to their conversations with whites and understand how members of this cultural group believe such conversations can be improved. These studies identified seven issues and five conversational improvement strategies whose relationship to satisfaction proved independent of the individual difference variables of sex, geography, age, income, and ethnic identity. Further, these themes are more characteristic of Afro-American perceptions than white perceptions.

The themes seem closely tied to previous discussions of Afro-American style. Hecht and Ribeau (1984) reported that compared to whites, Afro-Americans place greater emphasis on deep, intimate involvement, which seems consistent with the present categories of authenticity and understanding. Hecht and Ribeau went on to report that Afro-Americans also place more stress on other-orientation and goals, similar to the present issues of acceptance and goal

attainment, respectively. Ickes (1984) reported that in interracial dyads whites display more signs of both interaction involvement *and* stress. This relationship is mediated by racial attitudes such that whites with positive racial attitudes display more signs of interaction involvement than Afro-Americans, whereas those with negative attitudes display fewer of these cues. The salience of other-orientation and authenticity in this study indicates that Afro-American interactants are aware of the "mixed messages" conveyed through involvement and stress and the role of these cues as reflections of racial attitudes.

Afro-Americans seem to adopt a unique communication style. Kochman (1982) describes the oral tradition of Afro-American culture which manifests itself in a spontaneous and verbally aggressive style. Smitherman (1977) described 'high talk,' a highly dramatic and stylized from of expression derived from African roots. The categories of expressiveness, powerlessness, authenticity, and understanding seem well within the described style. Expressiveness is required for the dramatic effect and produces part of the aggressiveness found in descriptions of powerlessness. Authenticity is derived from spontaneity and facilitates the stylized story telling of the oral culture. Understanding becomes an important value when one works hard to convey one's message.

When viewed in concert with previous research (e.g., Bachman & O'Malley, 1984; Collier, Hecht, & Ribeau, 1986; Hecht & Ribeau, 1984, 1987, in press), these studies indicate Afro-Americans are highly involved in topics, conversations, and their partners. This level of involvement may lead to an "all or nothing" approach to conversation. To improve interaction, the other person should become more open-minded, one should be more assertive about the topic, and the conversation should be regulated more smoothly through interaction management. Failure leads to blame: close-mindedness or avoidance.

The question may still be asked if these themes constitute a uniquely Afro-American perspective on communication effectiveness. An answer to this question is not directly available from these data and was not the primary goal of the present study. Study One findings suggest that the relationship between the themes and satisfaction is independent of individual difference variables. In addition, the informants in Study Two cautioned that Afro-Americans, whites, and other ethnic groups do not have the same interpretation of the world. Even when the same label (e.g., power) is provided by both groups, it will mean something very different to Afro-Americans. There are, however, some indications that some of these issues are shared at least partially by other ethnic groups not in the dominant strata of society.

First, a similar analysis of Mexican-American conversational descriptions (Hecht, Ribeau & Sedano, in press) produced some overlap of issues. Both groups shared concern for negative stereotyping, acceptance, and emotional expressiveness. However, the indirect forms of stereotyping were not commented on by Mexican-Americans, expressiveness was less centered on emotional issues for Afro-Americans, and the other issues appear unique to the Afro-American experience.

Second, some of these themes have been discussed separately in mainstream communicative competence (e.g., Bochner & Kelly, 1974; Spitzberg & Cupach, 1984; Wiemann, 1977) or interethnic effectiveness (Abe & Wiseman, 1983; Gudykunst & Hammer, 1987; Hammer, Gudykunst & Wiseman, 1978) literature. Ruben (1976) suggests that being judgmental, self-centeredness, and turn-taking are key factors in all cross-cultural communication effectiveness. These factors are similar to the strategies of open-mindedness, other-orientation, and interaction management, although the current strategies have implications and meanings not implied in Ruben's original formulation. For example, one can avoid self-centeredness without communicating other-orientation, and interaction management includes aspects other than turn-taking (e.g., the length of the conversation). Further, Afro-Americans limited interaction management to the improvement of already satisfying conversations, whereas open-mindedness is seen as a strategy for the other to use, and then only after understanding has been achieved. As noted above, interpretations of the categories seem to differ for the respondents in our samples.

The similarities where they exist may reflect the effects of acculturation or generalizable themes based on human social needs of acceptance, self-worth, and bonding. The results of this study indicate that where such overlap exists the categories are both experienced and expressed differently in each culture. More direct cross-cultural comparisons await future research.

Third, the categories of powerlessness and negative stereotyping may be characteristic of many low-power groups. Power is a pervasive issue in race relations in the United States, and power differences have long existed between mainstream white culture and most other ethnic groups. Such groups are denied access to traditional sources of power, and this position frequently becomes institutionalized. At the same time, any 'out-group' is stereotyped when its members are treated categorically rather than as individuals. Separation of groups tends to deny the mainstream, high power group access to the out-groups expect through limited media contact. As a result, powerlessness and stereotyping become salient issues for interethnic communication.

Recent studies (Pettigrew, 1985; Zatz, 1987) suggest that racism in the United States now tends to be expressed less directly. For example, Zatz concludes that the effect of race on court sentencing is moderated by variables such as bail status. While van Dijk (1987) finds direct expression of prejudice in topics of conversations (e.g., minorities as criminal, lazy, etc.), less direct expressions are found in argument forms (e.g., arguments about immigration, affirmative action, learning English).

The sense of powerlessness among Afro-Americans, however, may differ from that of other groups. Lessing, Clarke, and Gray-Shellberg (1981) argue that Afro-Americans lack the in-group loyalty needed for a successful power struggle in the United States. Otto and Featherman (1975) note that early life cycle patterns influence feelings of powerlessness. Matineau (1976) points out that Afro-American neighborhood instability detracts from a sense of powerfulness and, further, this pattern is different for white and Afro-American populations. Thus, the meaning of powerlessness may differ for this group as a result of both historical and sociological trends.

The present study supports this interpretation. While traditional stereotyping was manifested, the less direct expression of stereotyping through the introduction of "Afro-American topics" was also prevalent. Other forms of "over-accommo-dating" or 'trying too hard' to adjust" (Gallois, Franklin-Stokes, Giles, & Coupland, 1988) are similarly interpreted as indirect stereotyping. White interactants' modification of their own behavior may appear so strained or extreme that it invokes a feeling of forced behavior or artificiality, "trying too hard." This interpretation is supported by the account of the white respondent who was pleased that her Afro-American conversational partner accepted her into her group. If such acceptance is over-emphasized, over-accommodation is likely. Interviews with Afro-Americans confirm this interpretation. These informants were able to provide numerous examples of this less direct form of stereotyping. This interpretation of "trying too hard" as stereo-typing is certainly unlikely among whites and will be expressed and interpreted differently among other ethnic minorities in the U.S.

The paper presents an Afro-American perspective on interethnic communication. It reflects the reality of being Afro-American, a product of an ethnic cultural background and pressures to assimilate into the American mainstream. The eminent scholar W.E.B. Du Bois has called this phenomenon "dual consciousness." Expressive forms such as music, dance, and communication style link Afro-Americans to their cultural tradition while formal education, the media, and the need for economic survival exert pressure towards the mainstream. To balance these competing forces Afro-Americans, like other under-represented groups, often live in two worlds. One conforms to the categories, labels, and norms of the dominant group; the other interprets reality from an ethnic cultural filter/perspective.

The findings of this study reflect this duality. Some of the labels used to categorize the themes are shared in common with other groups. Informants note differences in interpretations and actions. The seven communication issues identified in these studies may be shared by other nondominant groups but they merge into a cluster which describes Afro-American experience. The findings indicate that stereotyping and acceptance must be dealt with first before the other categories become salient. This reflects the ever-present cloud of racism that hovers above these interethnic encounters and permeates Afro-American interpretations. These categories poignantly illuminate the rejection and demeaning treatment of Afro-Americans, which are the legacy of slavery and which must be resolved before effective communication is to take place. Resolution brings to the front the issues of understanding and goal attainment, power, expressiveness, and authenticity.

Other questions also have yet to be addressed. The results identify improvement strategies for only some of the issues. Future research should attempt to specify the strategies more precisely and uncover a broader repertoire.

In addition, we must consider the role of individual difference variables. In these studies the primary purpose for including these variables was to test the independence of the relationships among the issues, strategies, and satisfaction. Subsidiary analysis indicated some of these factors may be related in other ways. In particular, the findings emphasize the importance of ethnic identity. However, in this study only the *type* of identity was measured. Research suggests that the divergence is more likely when there is a greater *degree* of in-group identification. Accordingly, it will be important for future research to address this issue.

Similarly, we might ask how the introduction of relational variables (e.g., type of relationship, degree of intimacy) would influence the findings. Are certain issues more prevalent among acquaintances? Are others more salient among friends? Are certain factors more salient for self or other?

In conclusion, then, the study achieved its primary goal of identifying an Afro-American perspective on interethnic communication. Future work is needed to elaborate this basic system.

DISCUSSION QUESTIONS

1. According to Hecht, Ribeau, and Alberts, what does it mean to have *satisfying communication*?

2. Compare and contrast potential rationales for speech convergence among Blacks and Whites.

3. What is a *failure event* and how do they occur?

4. In Hecht, Ribeau, and Alberts's study, how does communication satisfaction differ between Blacks and Whites?

5. Explain three of the seven communication issues that resulted from the study.

Reading 3.2

INTERRACIAL DATING

The Implications of Race for Initiating a Romantic Relationship

TINA M. HARRIS AND PAMELA J. KALBFLEISCH

Research indicates that attitudes toward interracial romantic relationships are complex; however, minimal attention has been given to motivating factors for involvement in such relationships. Public opinion polls (Romano & Trescott, 1992) and self-reports (Murstein, Merigihi, & Malloy, 1989) indicate that external pressures are ever present, and, consequently, relational partners are expected to dissolve these relationships for a myriad of "reasons." Currently, two theories exist that articulate why most individuals might become involved in an interracial romantic relationship. Kouri and Lasswell (1993) used the structural theory and the racial motivation theory to better understand these motivations. The structural theory posits that demographics (i.e., socioeconomic status, education, occupation, residence) and mutual attraction contribute to the initiation, development, and maintenance of an interracial marriage. Conversely, the racial motivation theory hypothesizes that interracial marriages occur *because* of racial difference, whereby at least one partner finds the racially different other more appealing *because* of her or his race.

In their in-depth interviews with interracial couples (African Americans and European Americans), Kouri and Lasswell (1993) found that 44 of the 46 interviewees were attracted to their partners due to similar values and interests, or overall compatibility (structural theory). Seven African Americans (1 female and 6 males) and 9 European Americans (7 females and 2 males) reported being attracted to each other strictly on the basis of their partners' physiological makeup (racial motivation theory). In essence, these participants seemed to exoticize the other race because their external beauty and skin color are reportedly the primary factors contributing to perceptions of attractiveness and the (interracial) mate selection experience.

In an earlier study by Murstein et al. (1989), 20 interracial couples were interviewed about the relationship between partner physical attractiveness and relational commitment. Findings

From Harris, T. & Kalbfleisch, P. (2000). Interracial dating: The implications of race for initiating a romantic relationship. *Howard Journal of Communications, 11*, 49-64.

reveal that partners were attracted to their mates for intrinsic reasons as well as physical attraction; however, the judges in the study observed that partner physical attractiveness for both races outweighed other criteria for mate selection. Judges also found that African American partners were much more attractive than their European American partners. Using the social exchange theory, Murstein et al. (1989) explained that "in a racially prejudiced society, African Americans would have to offer more to European Americans than vice versa to participate in an interracial romantic relationship. It was hypothesized and confirmed that African Americans would exceed their European American partners in physical attractiveness" (p. 334). Based on data analysis, Murstein et al. (1989) surmise that individuals involved in interracial romantic relationships are sometimes forced to "normalize" the relationship and justify its existence to themselves, family, and a race-consumed society. This concern is behaviorally manifested when partners choose a racially different partner whose physical beauty compensates for the "racial disparity" in the relationship.

The Future of Interracial Dating

By the year 2000, it has been predicted that the demographic makeup of the U.S. population will consist primarily of people of color (Masini, 1993). With these increased numbers of people of color in the workplace, schools, and all others aspects of life, and higher levels of interpersonal contact, the potential for interracial relationships is inevitably going to rise. Such proximity creates a unique dichotomy. For those consumed with the social significance of race, such relationships are often perceived as a threat to the racial social order. For others, this increased proximity and potential for interracial relationships is perceived as a positive interpersonal experience. As an extension, these individuals welcome the increased likelihood that interracial romantic and marriage relationships will develop. In either case, the potential and inevitability of such relationships forces individuals to reexamine their value systems and beliefs about interracial friendships and romantic relationships.

Despite this increased racial and cultural diversity, limited research exists that explores the role communication plays in the initiation of interracial romantic relationships and understanding the motivating factors that influence communication behaviors used in this context. As Orbe demonstrates (1995, 1996, 1998), racial and cultural identities influence the communicative process. In describing his model of co-cultural theory, Orbe (1998) provides six factors that he observes as influencing co-cultural communication, or communication between marginalized groups and dominant society members. These factors include: (1) preferred outcome for the relationship, or (un)conscious thought about the effects communication behaviors have on relationships with dominant group members; (2) field of experience, which is the lived experiences of co-cultural group members; (3) abilities, which refers to a person's skill at using different communication practices; (4) situational context, which involves the influence of the setting (i.e., work, home, school, social places) on the interaction; (5) perceived costs and rewards of co-cultural communication; and (6) communication approach, wherein a person chooses the appropriate communication strategy for that co-cultural interaction (i.e., nonassertive, assertive, and aggressive). Depending on the communicator, her or his characteristics, and the situational and relational factors present in the communication context, communication strategies utilized within each intercultural interaction will vary. Within an interracial context, both communicators enter this interpersonal interaction with anxieties and expectations based on their fields of experience. Because apprehensions exist, interracial interactions become more complex when both communicators have differing expectations. In either case, the cultural identities of the communicators greatly affect their interpersonal interactions and the communicative process.

As previously noted, little communication research explores the role of communication within interracial romantic relationships. In his research, Orbe (1998) observes that the situational context and preferred outcome, among other variables, influence the communication strategies used within a co-cultural context.

Using this general premise, it is the goal of this study to examine the degree to which communicator racial identity influences the verbal communication strategies hypothetically favored to initiate same-race and interracial dates within a hypothetical communication context.

In a pilot study that attempted to achieve this same research goal, Harris (1994) extended the work of Mongeau, Hale, Johnson, and Hillis (1993) and measured hypothetical verbal date initiation strategies that African Americans and European Americans (college students) reported they would (or would not) use in an interracial and interracial context. Results reveal that when the target of their romantic interest was of a different race (interracial dating), 65% of the participants were more likely to change behaviors and use more indirect verbal strategies (i.e., hinting, waiting) as compared with their same-race initiations. While the findings reveal a relationship between verbal strategy and race, attempts to generalize are minimized due to the exploratory nature of the study. In order to further address these initial findings, the present study has been designed to extend and address the dearth of research on this topic. Because so little research has explored interracial dating, it is the goal of this study to understand the degree to which the racial identity of a potential romantic partner (target) influences the verbal strategies used to initiate an interracial romantic relationship, and, on a smaller level, the decision to enter (or not) an interracial romantic relationship.

Rationale for Hypotheses

Research in the area of interracial communication has focused on how interaction expectations of European Americans negatively affect communication with and perceptions of African Americans (Leonard & Locke, 1993; Weitz & Gordon, 1993); therefore, it is reasonable to assume that African Americans have interaction expectations and perceptions of European Americans as well. As a result, mutual expectations of African Americans and European Americans may cause individuals to change their behavioral patterns when interacting interracially (Fitzpatrick & Hwang, 1992). Because of longstanding racial stereotypes and the

history of race relations in the United States, it is highly understandable why interracial interactions are perceived and received with high levels of communication apprehension.

Hypothesis 1 is designed to test whether behavioral change is influenced by target race and the expectation of dating a person of a different race (Harris, 1994; Orbe, 1998; Weitz & Gordon, 1993). Research indicates that racial group members use multiple forms of communication as they interact with ingroup members and outgroup members (Suzuki, 1998). When communicating with ingroup members, fewer psychological barriers are present that interfere with the communicative process; however, when there are interactions with outgroup members, perceptions and interaction expectations take on greater significance. To compensate for these perceptions, individuals will adapt their communication strategies for each group (Suzuki, 1998). With ingroup members, verbal communication is used to promote group solidarity and cohesion. Conversely, outgroup communication may be more formal and restricted due to communicator apprehension and stereotyping. When these interactions become more romantic, however, communication strategies have the potential to become more accentuated. Because such relationships have traditionally been perceived as "taboo," it is logical to assume that more passive date initiation strategies will be used to avoid social judgment from ingroup members. Therefore, individuals, regardless of gender, are predicted to employ passive (avoidant) strategies that compensate for racial difference in the initiation of an interracial romantic relationship. The following hypothesis articulates this prediction:

H1: Both African American and European American men and women will report a change in their communication strategies when initiating a date with a person from a different race.

The assessment process one engages in during strategy selection is a cognitive activity that allows individuals to select verbal strategies they are most comfortable using to initiate social relationships. When a person brings her or his racial identity into the communicative experience, however, it is reasonable to assume that racial difference will influence the interpersonal skills used when interacting with members of one's own race and members of other races.

Hypothesis 2 explores the influence gender has on verbal date initiation strategies used within same-race and interracial dating contexts. In their study of trust between African Americans and European Americans, Duncan and Kalbfleisch (1996) found that European Americans had a higher level of mistrust of African Americans. This element of mistrust becomes magnified when individuals are challenged to examine their own attitudes toward interracial romantic relationships. Recent research on attitudes toward interracial dating and marriages indicate that men, the young, and European Americans had more positive attitudes toward interracial dating than did women, the old, and African Americans (Todd, McKinney, Harris, Chadderton, & Small, 1992). Conversely, Paset and Taylor (1991) found that European American women favored interracial marriage more so than African American women, suggesting that "African American women perceive interracial marriages of African American men and women as substantively more threatening to their personal and racial welfare than do white women" (p. 754). These findings imply an existing level of mistrust as experienced by African American women, which mirrors the levels of mistrust found for European American men and women alike by Duncan and Kalbfleisch (1996).

Research has also been contradictory in its inquiry of attitudes toward interracial dating and marriage. Some have found that African American women are more threatened by interracial marriages between African American men and European American women, or other non-African American women (Todd et al., 1992) although others reveal that African American women are least threatened by this interracial pairing (Dickson, 1993). In terms of the latter, African American women have themselves become more involved in relationships with European American males to remedy the discrepancy (Dickson, 1993). In either event, there are two possible reasons for mixed reports regarding African American women's attitudes toward interracial dating. First, African American

women may resent interracial marriages between African American men and European American women because it places them at a relational disadvantage due to the lack of available African American men. Second, African American women who recognize this rising trend in interracial marriages are becoming more open to interracial relationships themselves for that very same reason. Given that women in general are more relationship-focused than men, it is reasonable to assume that African American women with higher education and fewer marriageable partners (Dickson, 1993; Weitz & Gordon, 1993) and European American women with increased interracial interactions will be more accepting of interracial romantic relationships than African American and European American men. Hypothesis 2 is designed to determine if any gender differences will emerge as participants select verbal date initiation strategies in same-race and interracial hypothetical contexts.

> H2: Men and women will experience a change in their communication strategies when initiating a date with a person from a different race.

The hypotheses guiding this study are designed to explore the various dimensions of interracial dating and the external factors influencing the development and pursuit of such a relationship. The methods and research design measure the influence of those factors on the initiation of interracial romantic relationships.

METHOD

Research Participants

Participants in this study were 120 students from a large southern university. Sixty of the participants were African American and 60 were European American, with equal numbers of men and women in each racial group. The research participants were contacted through introductory communication courses, Greek organizations, campus student organizations, resident advisor courses, and from referrals made by other participants in the study.[1]

Research Methodology

Q-sort methodology is the primary methodology used in this study to explore the influence of race and gender on date initiation strategies in same-race and interracial contexts. Q-sort methodology was designed by social scientist William Stephenson as a tool to better understand individual subjectivity (Stephenson, 1953). As a measure of social behavior, Q-sort attempts to understand the behaviors of the individual by identifying the person's subjectively held pattern of beliefs, attitudes, intentions, and the like. Instead of following the rule of the single characteristic referenced to many people, Q-sort proposes the rule of the single case referenced to many characteristics (Stephenson, 1953). Focusing on the relative significance of characteristics within an individual enables the researcher to understand how those judgments and beliefs influence a person's behavior.

Procedure

At the onset of data collection, research participants were reminded that participation was voluntary and that the goal of the study was to gain a better understanding of dating relationships. Participants then signed a consent form and were given a set of Q-sort items developed by Harris (1994), which was composed of 36 index cards containing one primary tactic reflective of either a (1) waiting, (2) hinting, (3) direct, or (4) third-party intervention dating strategy. With the Q-sort items at hand, research participants were asked to imagine that they have met a person of their same race with whom they would like to start a romantic relationship. With this condition of instructions in mind, participants were guided through the two-stage sorting process. In the first stage, they were instructed to sort their cards into three different piles: (a) tactics they would most likely use, (b) tactics they would least likely use, and (c) tactics they were unsure about using. Each participant read verbal strategies that specifically related to a cross-sex context from their gendered perspective. In the second stage, these decisions were refined by asking that the tactics be further sorted into a quasi-normal forced

distribution of 9 ranks. After sorting the cards, participants recorded their responses and were then asked to complete the same task and sort the cards as if they were attracted to a person from another race and wanted to start a romantic relationship with this person. After completing the Q-sort tasks, participants were asked to respond to an open-ended question about their future likelihood of being involved in an interracial relationship. This question provided participants the opportunity to briefly explain the motivations behind the verbal strategies chosen in both dating contexts.

RESULTS

Q-Sort: Same-Race Type Descriptions

Factor analysis of the same-race Q-sorts identified 3 distinct tactical patterns, or strategies, used by study participants. As with any z-score used in quantitative research, the z-score in Q-methodology generally ranges from +3 to –3, with a mean of 0 and a standard deviation of 1. Positive z-scores are interpreted as dating tactics that would most likely be used and negative scores are dating tactics that would least likely be used by those participants.

TYPE 1, STRATEGIC ACTIVE

The cluster members in Type 1 demonstrate a strong preference for using hinting strategies to initiate a same-race romantic relationship. The average z-score across the 9 tactics for the postulated strategy of hinting was 70. The cluster members include 15 African American males, 21 African American females, 24 European American males, and 19 European American females ($N = 79$), accounting for 66% of the participants. The hinting strategies positively endorsed by these participants allow them to subtly communicate interest in a romantic relationship with the target. The date initiation strategies include: (1) discussing mutual interests and related events, (2) determining target availability, (3) mentioning a group activity, (4) mentioning an event and asking the target to go, (5) inviting the target to study and get something to eat afterward, and (6) flirting with the target by letting her know he finds the target attractive. These tactics are passive yet somewhat direct hints used to convey interest and attraction; however, a great deal of subtlety was preferred. As indicated by the verbal content of their strategy, these participants appear to be establishing common ground or similarity with the target.

TYPE 2, STRATEGIC ASSERTIVE

The second type that surfaced in the same-race sort consisted of 21 participants (5.7% of participants), including 14 African American males, 2 African American females, 4 European American males, and 1 European American female. These cluster members are very different from the Strategic Active participants. Unlike the Strategic Active type, the Strategic Assertive participants prefer direct strategies (.983) to initiate a romantic relationship, followed by hinting (.699). The 9 most strongly endorsed assertive (stereotypically masculine) tactics, including 6 from the direct strategies, are (1) asking the target out on a specific night, (2) finding out the target's availability by asking if she is dating someone, (3) asking if the target is interested in dating someone and if the target is interested in the initiator, (4) getting to know each other better, (5) calling the target on the phone to ask her out, (6) asking the target if she wants to go out, (7) mentioning a certain event and then asking the target to go, (8) flirting with the target and letting her know he finds the target attractive, and (9) asking the target to study and get a bite to eat.

These cluster members hypothetically appear to have no reticence toward asking a person out on a date. It can only be inferred that there is a preference to communicate romantic interest to their target while being fully aware of the potential risks this behavioral pattern could create. This observation is supported partially in this cluster's strong rejection of waiting (−1.00) or having a third-party intervene (−.67). Because the self-reported behaviors demonstrate possible real-life tactics used to initiate a same-race romantic relationship that were very direct in nature, these behaviors may reflect gender role

expectations that males and females experience as they develop into adulthood and dating relationships.

TYPE 3, STRATEGIC PASSIVE

Members of the final cluster in the same-race sort prefer to wait for the target to initiate or indicate romantic interest in them. By engaging in waiting behaviors, Strategic Passives avoid using any strategies that denote interest in becoming involved in a romantic relationship. These cluster members are 1 African American male, 7 African American females, 2 European American males, and 10 European American females who all preferred to wait. Each of the 6 most strongly endorsed tactics are drawn from the postulated waiting strategies, which include: (1) letting the target ask her out, (2) waiting for the target to indicate interest, (3) talking to friends but not mentioning interest, (4) hoping the target would ask her out, (5) strategically placing herself where the target will be, and (6) talking about mutual interests and a related event. As evidenced by their choice in strategy, these cluster members appear determined to avoid behaviors that would reveal their attraction to the target.

The participants in this cluster are primarily female (17/20), which may further explain their self-reported behaviors and preference for waiting strategies. Because dating scripts for heterosexual romantic relationships have taught women to engage in passive behaviors while the male actively initiates the date, it is possible that the cluster members for Type 3 are comfortable waiting for the male to initiate. Given that 3 males prefer waiting strategies as well, it is plausible that their behaviors may be attributed to interpersonal characteristics and qualities (i.e., shy, introverted, fearful of rejection).

Q-Sort: Interracial Type Descriptions

Factor analysis of the interracial Q-sorts identified 4 distinct tactical patterns, or strategies, used by study participants. These accounted for 56% of total variance or 99% of trace.

TYPE 1, STRATEGIC PASSIVE

The first of the 4 types that surfaced in the inter-racial sort, Strategic Passive, consists of 54 participants (11 African American males, 20 African American females, 7 European American males, and 16 European American females) who prefer to use waiting strategies to initiate an interracial date. Seven of the most preferred tactics represent a waiting strategy: (1) waiting for the target to ask him or her out, (2) letting the target flatter him or her, (3) waiting for the target to indicate interest in him or her, (4) trying not to let the target know about his or her interest in the target, (5) discussing mutual interests and an event, (6) just hoping the target asks him or her out, and (7) flirting with the target about his or her attractiveness but avoiding direct date initiation.

The strongly rejected tactics are direct in nature and specifically communicate romantic interest. As their strategy choice indicates, there appears to be little desire for cluster members to communicate attraction. It is plausible that their preference for waiting instead of using a direct strategy is an attempt to conceal interest in an interracial relationship because of external factors (i.e., family, society) and the taboo nature of such relationships, or a lack of interest in dating an outgroup member. By waiting for the target to indicate interest, the participants appear to be purposely avoiding any attempt to communicate romantic interest to a person from a different race.

TYPE 2, STRATEGIC CONTEXTUAL

The next type to surface demonstrates a preference for using hinting and direct strategies. These 35 cluster members (7 African American males, 3 African American females, 13 European American males, 12 European American females) prefer to communicate attraction by creating social interactions where they are (1) discussing mutual interests, (2) inviting the target to an event and hoping the target expresses interest in going, (3) mentioning a group activity to the target, (4) mentioning an event and inviting the target to go, (5) inviting the target to study and get a bite to eat, (6) calling the

target to say hi, (7) asking the target out on a particular night, and (8) asking if the target is currently dating anyone.

The verbal content of these tactics is neutral in communicating romantic interest in the target. The Strategic Contextual participants appear careful in determining the target's level interest before asking for a date. These cluster members may demonstrate a preference for these strategies in an effort to create a communication climate conducive for the two to get to know each other without ego threat taking place. The Strategic Contextual participants develop their strategy by drawing on some hinting tactics and some direct tactics, while strongly rejecting other hinting and direct tactics, and some waiting and third-party strategies. The majority of the rejected direct strategies appear to be hypothetical overt displays of romantic interest, which does not fulfill the purpose of initiating a date with the target.

Given that this study was conducted at a predominantly European American institution, it is reasonable to assume that the European American students have had limited interracial contact. Therefore, when they were asked to initiate an interracial date, participants may have been hesitant to use direct strategies due to communicator apprehension within an interracial context. It is also possible that stereotypes and negative attitudes toward interracial romantic relationships may directly influence the use of passive verbal strategies.

TYPE 3, STRATEGIC FLEXIBLE

The Strategic Flexible participants consist of 8 African American males, 5 African American females, 9 European American males, and 1 European American female. These participants prefer using both hinting and direct strategies to initiate an interracial date, which may be indicative of openness to dating interracially or approaching someone from a different race "on the surface." The most preferred tactics are (1) hinting about the target's attractiveness, (2) asking the target out on a specific night, (3) inquiring about the target's availability, (4) inviting the target to study and get a bite to eat later, (5) asking if the target is presently dating anyone and would he like for the two of them to get to know each other better, (6) discussing mutual interests and an upcoming event, and (7) telling the target she has been watching the target for a long time.

As the items indicate, these cluster members appear flexible in their use of date initiation strategies, which may be attributed to the participants' comfort or personal experience with interracial interactions. Such flexibility may be grounded in positive past experiences or their repertoire of communication skills as influenced by social context. The strategic verbal behaviors chosen by these cluster members connote a preference for conveying romantic interest to their target.

TYPE 4, STRATEGIC INTERVENTION

The final cluster in the interracial dating sort is different from the others. Although they are few in number ($N = 7$), these cluster members are distinct because they prefer using a third-party, particularly a friend, to initiate an interracial date. These 4 African American males, 2 African American females, and 1 European American male most prefer (1) talking to friends about interest and wait for a response, (2) mentioning interest to a friend and hope the target would initiate, (3) flirting by letting the target know the respondent finds her attractive, (4) having a friend arrange a double date, (5) having a friend mention the respondent's interest to the target and wait for the target to initiate, (6) having a friend mention the respondent's interest and then ask the target out himself, and (7) waiting for the target to ask him out.

Reliance on the friend to coordinate or advise about the development of the relationship may be indicative of the high level of trust the participants have in the friend's judgment of their dating behaviors. By using a third-party, participants may be attempting to provide a buffer in the even they are rejected. The third-party may minimize the emotional trauma of direct rejection by acting as a go-between for both initiator and target. The initiator may perceive such rejection as a greater ego threat since they may be rejected by a person from a different race, thus compounding the feelings of rejection.

Hypothesis 1

The primary objective of the current study was to determine if both African American and European American men and women will experience a change in their date initiation strategies when initiating a date with a person from a different race. To test this relationship, the strategic patterns discovered in the same-race sort were correlated with those found in the interracial sort. Responses to the open-ended question about future likelihood of becoming involved in an interracial romantic relationship were used to probe these groups further. Because participants were forced to choose verbal strategies in both hypothetical situations, the researchers did not want to assume attraction when participants could not realistically visualize themselves dating a person from a different race. Participants were not asked to explain and compare their behaviors across both contexts; therefore, our interpretations are limited to assumptions based on behavioral patterns observed across dating contexts.

No or minimal influence of race on date initiation strategy

There are 3 combinations of strategies that are highly similar. Same-Race Strategic Actives correlate with Interracial Strategic Contextuals at $r = .929$; the Strategic Assertives from the same-race sort correlate with the Strategic Flexibles from the interracial sort at $r = .883$; and the Strategic Passives from the Same-race sort correlate with the Strategic Passives from the interracial sort at $r = .865$. There are 41 participants in these combinations, who represent 35% of the sample.

Of these 41 participants, 25 are in the Strategic Active/Strategic Contextual, 6 are in the Strategic Assertive/Strategic Flexible combination, and 10 are in the Strategic Passives/Strategic Passive combination. Participants in this behavioral pattern include 7 African American males, 7 African American females, 14 European American males, and 13 European American females. In both dating situations, participants utilize the same hinting strategies to initiate a date. Participants in the Strategic Passive/Strategic Passive combination prefer to wait on the target to initiate a date in the same-race and interracial dating contexts.

Although similar approaches to initiating a date are used in both the same-race and interracial dating context, several cluster members ($N = 23$) briefly shared that the likelihood of them dating interracially in the future was very slim, which may be attributed to the lack of availability of other-race persons in their usual circles. As explained in their open-ended response, participants would not date interracially due to "obvious" racial differences, stereotypes they had come to believe, not finding another race attractive, complexities associated with interracial relationships, social perceptions of interracial dating as taboo, and finding only members of their own race attractive.

Moderate influence of race on date initiation style

The majority of the participants (61, or 50%) were moderately influenced by race, including 14 African American males, 21 African American females, 13 European American males, and 13 European American females. There are 5 combinations of strategies that are moderately similar. Same-Race Strategic Actives correlate with Interracial Strategic Passives at $r = .582$; Strategic Assertives from the same-race sort correlate with Strategic Contextuals from the interracial sort at $r = .492$; Strategic Actives from the same-race sort correlate with Strategic Intervention from the interracial sort at $r = .441$; and Strategic Passives from the same-race sort correlate with Strategic Intervention from the interracial sort at $r = .521$.

Of those 61, there are 39 participants who conform to more passive date initiation strategies when approaching a person from a different race. Those in Strategic Active/Strategic Passive combination ($N = 34$) prefer to hint in the same-race context and to wait for the target to initiate in the interracial context. The remaining 5 participants, however, are Strategic Assertive/ Strategic Contextuals and resort to hinting with a person from a different race instead of being direct as they were in the same-race dating scenario. The shift in date initiation strategy is moderate yet may imply that the race of the

target does influence verbal tactics used to initiate a date.

Of the remaining 22 participants, 16 sub-group members changed from using hinting to direct strategies across dating contexts. Strategic Active/Strategic Flexible, may presumably have fewer apprehensions about and more comfort in approaching a different-race target. Similarly, Strategic Active/Strategic Intervention ($N = 5$) and Strategic Passive/Strategic Intervention ($N = 1$) combinations, respectively, went from hinting and waiting to third-party intervention. Involvement of a third party is a strategy that allows the participants to communicate attraction through an external "participant." This approach may be interpreted as an attempt to avoid appearing too forward or aggressive.

The behavioral patterns present suggest that the interracial manipulation for some participants is an unrealistic expectation, which causes them to resort to unconventional behavior that is less direct. The other participants, however, may perceive the interracial condition as a possibility or a realistic expectation. The preference for using somewhat direct strategies via a third party to initiate a date may be reflective of an increased desire to communicate interest without deviating from their reported conventional dating strategies.

Dramatic influence of race on date initiation strategy

The final category describing the behavioral changes occurring among participants is extreme change, or any behavior that significantly deviates in directness or hesitancy across same-race and interracial contexts. Within this category, there are 17 other participants (14% of the sample) whose behaviors seem to be influenced by the race of the target, which has resulted in a dramatic change in date initiation strategy.

These participants are 9 African American males, 1 African American female, 3 European American males, and 4 European American females. There are 4 combinations of strategies that are drastically different from each other. Same-Race Strategic Assertives are negatively correlated with Interracial Strategic Passives at $r = -.237$; Strategic Assertives from the same-race sort are correlated with Strategic Intervention from the interracial sort at $-.117$; Strategic Passives from the same-race sort are correlated with Strategic Contextuals from the interracial sort at $r = -.282$; and Strategic Passives from the same-race sort are correlated with Strategic Flexibles from the interracial sort at $r = -.300$.

Participants in the Strategic Assertive/ Strategic Passive combination and Strategic Assertive/Strategic Intervention ($N = 11$) engage in less-direct behaviors by either waiting for the target to initiate or having a third-party intervene. The inactive strategies of Strategic Assertive/Strategic Passive are possibly reflective of the participants' desire to avoid involvement in an interracial romantic relationship. According to their brief responses to an open-ended question about the likelihood of becoming involved in a real-life interracial relationship, the participants who prefer to use passive strategies in the interracial sort ($N = 7$) report opposition to interracial dating, thus potentially influencing the use of passive verbal strategies.

Conversely, participants in the behavioral patterns of Strategic Passive/Strategic Contextual and Strategic Passive/Strategic Flexible ($N = 50$) chose more direct approaches in the interracial sort. This increased directness may be the result of the participants' expectations that their target would be direct; therefore, they adapt their own behaviors to mirror the targets' behaviors. While participants in both combinations prefer to wait with a person from the same-race, there is a change to hint (Strategic Passive/Strategic Contextual) and use a third-party (Strategic Passive/Strategic Flexible) in the interracial dating context.

Synopsis of Results for Hypothesis 1

Hypothesis 1 predicted that both African American and European American men and women would experience a change in their date initiation strategies when initiating a date with a person from a different race. As their behavioral patterns indicate, 65% of the participants (45 African Americans and 33 European Americans) experienced either moderate or dramatic change in date initiation strategies between dating contexts. For these participants, dating strategy changed when target race was changed, thereby providing support for Hypothesis 1.

Although some of the same strategies were offered in both contexts, most participants engaged in more direct verbal strategies to initiate a date with a person from a different race. Such behavioral change may be attributed to apprehensions about dating interracially for those participants using ($N = 11$) less direct strategies within the interracial dating context. Conversely, participants using more direct strategies ($N = 50$) may have greater attraction toward or fewer inhibitions about dating a person from a different race.

Hypothesis 2

Hypothesis 2 predicted that men and women will experience a change in their date initiation strategies when initiating a date with a person from a different race. Findings reveal that 65% of the men ($N = 39$) and 65% of the women ($N = 39$) did change their verbal strategies when they were expected to demonstrate interest in an interracial dating relationship. The behavioral changes were moderate or dramatic in comparison with the verbal strategies utilized in the same-race context. Further, it was found that the males ($m = 2.137$) have slightly more reservations about interracial dating than do females ($m = 2.221$). This difference may be attributed to women generally being socialized to be relationship-focused, thus minimizing their apprehension of or disapproval of interracial romantic relationships.

In evaluating their open-ended questions regarding the likelihood of an interracial relationship, 56% of the African American females ($N = 17$) were open to dating a European American male and 44% of the European American females ($N = 13$) would not consider such a relationship. An overwhelming 87% of the African American males would not consider dating a European American female ($N = 26$) and only 13% would consider such a relationship ($N = 4$). Thus, approximately half of the African American female college students participating would consider an interracial relationship, while fewer than one-seventh of the African American males students would do so.

CONCLUSIONS AND DISCUSSION

As the findings indicate, the race of a potential romantic relational partner directly affects the verbal strategies a person uses to initiate a date. Whether it is due to stereotypes, attitudes about interracial relationships, or personality characteristics, the verbal strategies used within the context of dating were purposely chosen by participants for a variety of reason. By focusing on the centrality of race within interracial romantic relationships, the findings serve as an appropriate framework for understanding the degree to which the communicative process is affected by race.

While participants were forced to imagine themselves being attracted to and initiating a date with a person from a different race, they definitely adjusted their communicative behaviors when they were expected to initiate a date with a racial outgroup member. Q-sort items did not allow participants the opportunity to choose whether they would initiate such a date in reality; however, Mongeau et al. (1993), Mongeau, Yeazell, and Hale (1994), and Mongeau and Carey (1996) have found that the general content of an item is appropriate for same-race date initiation in a hypothetical context.

Open-ended questions allowing participants to explain whether or not they would actually date a person from a different race reveal that forced strategy selection did not influence their attitudes toward the topic of interracial dating. Participants did provide several reasons for why they would either avoid or be open to involvement in an interracial romantic relationship. Although a few participants attributed this to lack of attraction to members of the other race, others cited external factors as being primary deterrents to the initiation of such relationships. Examples include fear of upsetting or being disowned by parents or both, losing their job and limiting career advancement opportunities, fear of what friends will think, and the negative reactions they will receive in public from strangers, to name a few.

Participants did not articulate their reservations specifically through strategy choice. Open-ended answers, however, indicate that socialization on the issues of race, race relations, and interracial communication influences whether or not an interracial romantic relationship is even an option. According to some participants, family and society as external factors have communicated that romantic relationships between African Americans and European Americans remain socially "taboo," despite the antimiscegenation laws of 1964.

The current study is exploratory in nature. Although consistent with previous research conducted on date initiation strategies (Mongeau & Carey, 1996; Mongeau et al., 1993; Mongeau et al., 1994), the methodology used in this study is unique in its investigation of the verbal date initiation strategies used within same-race and interracial contexts. Instead of using traditional quantitative scales to measure date initiation behaviors, Q-sort provides an alternative methodology that does not conform to interpersonal research methods. Participants are grouped together by the verbal strategies they individually feel are most appropriate for achieving the goal of initiating a date or communicating romantic interest in another person. The Q-sort tasks challenged participants to intensely use critical thinking skills by reading 36 index cards twice as they imagine a hypothetical interpersonal interaction in two distinctly different contexts. By engaging in two sorts, the researchers reduce participant sensitivity to the overall intent of the study.

Orbe (1998) suggests that co-cultural communication research be extended by using qualitative instead of quantitative research methods, thus deviating from traditional approaches to social science inquiry. The use of Q-sort contributes to this reform by marrying both methodologies. Providing 36 verbal communication strategies (quantifying) allows for Q-sort analysis of the item groupings (qualitative) and descriptions of participants without making generalizations to similar populations of study. Instead, individual choice and content facilitate understanding of date initiation strategies and participant perceptions of what strategies are individually appropriate for initiating same-race and interracial dates. In either context, participants' choices reflect some change in strategy across dating scenarios.

As has been previously noted, limited research exists beyond the current study that explores communication strategies used to initiate interracial romantic relationships. Although not conclusive, findings are revealing as they reflect racial attitudes of a small sample of young adults in Western society. Strategy choices of participants reveal that the desire to maintain social distance between racial groups may become accentuated when the relationship has romantic connotations. The centrality of racial issues within the context of interracial romantic relationships demonstrates the intensity of race relations as they are today. Despite the end of slavery, the inception of civil rights, and the eradication of antimiscegenation laws, the findings further demonstrate society's resistance to challenging and deconstructing the existing racial and social order in the United States.

As an extension of previous research conduced by Mongeau et al. (1993, 1994) and Mongeau and Carey (1996), the current study was designed to explore and extend date initiation strategies that may be used within same-race and interracial contexts. While Mongeau et al. (1993) found a direct correlation between premarital interaction norms and perception, this study illustrates that when race is introduced in the dating context, norms and perceptions (i.e., stereotype, attitudes) remain critical factors in influencing strategy choice in the date initiation process.

DISCUSSION QUESTIONS

1. What is co-cultural communication?

2. How do the communication strategies differ among Black and White men when initiating a date with a person of a different race?

3. Why did Harris and Kalbfleisch select the Q-sort methodology for their study as a way of analyzing the data?

4. Compare and contrast the *strategic passive* and *strategic contextual* personality types.

5. Do you agree with Harris and Kalbfleisch that interracial romantic relationships remain taboo in the U.S.?

Reading 3.3

The Changing Influence of Interpersonal Perceptions on Marital Well-being Among Black and White Couples

Linda K. Acitelli, Elizabeth Douvan, and Joseph Veroff

Interpersonal perceptions (Kenny, 1994; Laing et al., 1966; Sillars & Scott, 1983) have important consequences for marital partners' everyday interactions and their satisfaction with the relationship. At the most elementary level, marital satisfaction has been demonstrated to relate more to perceived similarity than to actual similarity (e.g. Levinger & Breedlove, 1996). It is clear, however, that marital well-being hinges on any number of complex interpersonal perceptions (e.g. Acitelli et al., 1993; Oggins et al., 1993).

The present study asks two basic questions: (1) Do interpersonal perceptions of married couples change over the first three years of their marriages, and (2) do these perceptions have different effects on marital well-being over the same time period? A pervious study (Acitelli et al., 1993) had shown that spouses' perceptions of both their partners' and their own reactions to conflict in the first year of marriage correlated in systematic ways with how happy husbands and wives felt about their marriages at that time. The present study extends this work by relating first year perceptions to third year marital well-being. In so doing we scratch the surface of an enormously complex question of how marriages develop in the early years.

The theoretical basis of our work is formed mainly from the literature on social cognition and interpersonal perceptions in close relationships. As Sillars (1985) indicated, theories and findings about the significance of interpersonal perceptions may vary for different referents and contexts. While there are many other referents (e.g. preferences, attitudes) and contexts

From Acitelli, L., Douvan, E., & Veroff, J. (1997). The changing influence of interpersonal perceptions on marital well-being among Black and White couples. *Journal of Social and Personal Relationships, 14*(3), 291-304.

(e.g. dating, friendships) for considering interpersonal perceptions, we are raising questions about the effects of interpersonal perceptions of marital conflict behaviors only.

The context of conflict is critically important for understanding relationship development and negotiation, especially in the early years when the marital relationship is in its formative stages (Crohan, 1992; Fincham & Bradbury, 1991). Indeed, Gottman's (1995) research and cascade model of conflict demonstrate how spouses' momentary perceptions during conflict can lead to lasting cognitions about the marriage. Precisely how this happens and when such consolidation takes place have not been spelled out. It is generally thought, however, that difficulties in resolving conflicts stem not only from seeing events and situations differently, but also from seeing each other's attempts to resolve differences in different ways. What one partner intends to be a constructive attempt to resolve differences may be perceived by the other as irrelevant or even destructive. A common destructive pattern for a marriage is one partner confronting a problem while the other withdraws (e.g. Christensen & Heavey, 1990; Markman et al., 1993). There is little doubt regarding the incongruity of what a husband and wife perceive each other as doing or thinking in such situations.

In the first year study (Acitelli et al., 1993), married couples were asked to think of their last disagreement and to report on their own and their spouses' behaviors during that disagreement. Spouses were asked to rate statements with regard to how true they were of themselves (e.g. 'I calmly discussed the situation') and their spouses (e.g. 'My spouse calmly discussed the situation'). These perceptions of spouse and partner may be related in several ways, but we focused on three that, as a group, will be referred to as *perceptual congruence* variables: when both partners' self-perceptions were congruent, partners were said to be *similar;* when one person's perception of the self and other were congruent, this was termed *perceived similarity;* and when a partner's perception of the other partner corresponded with the other partner's self-perception, this was called *understanding.* (Researchers have not settled on a consistent set of terms for these concepts, as

Duck, 1994 has detailed.) Results of the earlier study (Acitelli et al., 1993) supported the long-standing finding that perceived similarity is greater than actual similarity and is more strongly related to first year marital well-being than actual similarity is.

Findings from the earlier study also indicated that the perceptual congruence variables were more predictive of wives' marital well-being than of husbands' marital well-being. Of particular salience to wives' marital well-being was wives' understanding of their husbands' constructive and destructive conflict behaviors. Husbands' marital well-being was more strongly related to both spouses' own self-reported behaviors. In addition, destructive conflict behaviors were understood better and related more strongly to marital well-being than were constructive ways of dealing with conflict. A major goal of the present study is to see how and if these findings change from the first to the third year and is reflected in our research questions.

Our first question was: *Do interpersonal perceptions of married couples change over the first three years of their marriages?* In general, a growing consensus of perspectives on how each partner handles conflict is expected to emerge over the first years of marriage and be associated with positive changes in marital well-being. Several scholars have noted the importance of consensus or congruence in developing a shared reality in marriages or families (Berger & Kellner, 1964; Deal et al., 1992; Duck, 1994). According to Berger & Kellner (1964), partners become more similar to one another over time, so partner differences in perception should decrease over time. Although this theory suggests a testable hypothesis, there is no clarity regarding when perceptions stabilize.

The initial development of norms for interpersonal perception in a marriage may very well take place early on and not fluctuate much beyond the initial period. Nevertheless, we expect some shifts toward increased congruity with regard to actual or perceived similarity in the way a couple reacts to conflict, and in the degree of understanding that spouses might have of how their partners see themselves reacting to conflict. Such congruence is also expected to be positively related to marital well-being. Couples who do not easily arrive at such congruence in the early period may have special difficulties in their relationship, and so we expect that indices of congruence of interpersonal perceptions of conflict will be even more related to marital happiness in the third year than in the first year.

These ideas lead us to a second question: *Do these perceptions have effects on third year marital well-being that are different from their effects on first year marital well-being?* While the overarching expectation is that congruence of interpersonal perceptions is beneficial for a marriage, the specific reactions assessed, responses to conflict, may be open to interpretations. In the study of the first year of marriage, destructive behaviors were more accurately perceived (or understood) than were constructive behaviors. This result is supported by the literature on social cognition in personal relationships demonstrating that negative behaviors are more easily noticed and more accurately recalled (e.g. Fletcher & Fitness, 1990). The constructive behaviors are not as vivid, or novel, and do not command as much attention. This finding is consistent with the idea that these 'constructive' behaviors are affectively neutral or ambiguous (Sillars, 1985; Wyer, 1973) and thus more subject to varying interpretations than the destructive behaviors. Fincham & Bradbury (1991) demonstrate that positive behaviors can be interpreted as negative, and Sher & Baucom (1995) emphasize that identical behaviors can have different meanings for a marriage. In extending schema theory to close relationship settings, the research of Fletcher & Fitness (1990) suggests that negative attributions of one's relationship partner will be more resistant to change than will positive attributions. Therefore, as partners approach the third year of marriage, we expect the meanings which constructive behaviors have for marital well-being to be more variable over time than the meanings of destructive acts.

Some of our thinking about the impact of interpersonal perceptions on marital well-being over the first three years has to consider ways in which the impact may be different far black couples and white couples. Our longitudinal data set is unique in that it has a substantial number of both black couples and white couples, while most longitudinal research on marriage is based on white samples. Even though the positives for outweigh the negatives, our sample composition is a mixed blessing in that, on the one hand, we have the valuable opportunity to compare marriages between groups that are rarely compared in the same sample (Broman, 1993). But, on the other hand, the rarity of such samples makes predictions difficult to make. We have very few data (except from our own project) from which to base predictions. In fact, an exhaustive review of the longitudinal research on marriage (Karney & Bradbury, 1995) demonstrated that only 8 percent of the samples used in these studies were drawn from both black and white populations. (Most were white, middle-class couples.) Of those that included black populations, the Veroff et al. (1993a) project was the only one that included both husbands and wives in the sample.

The ethnicity factor played a minor role in our analysis of the correlation of interpersonal perceptions and first year marital happiness primarily because there were not many differences between groups with regard to these associations. However, we kept ethnicity in the present analysis, since Veroff et al. (1995) and Hatchett et al. (1995) found that some of the determinants of marital stability are discrepant for black couples and white couples. They find that the stability of marriages for all couples depend on nurturant wives, relatively independent-feeling husbands, sound social networks, and harmonious interactions. They also find that unlike stable white marriages, stable black marriages depend on wives preserving a sense of independence in their marriages at the same time that they reassure their husbands about their acceptance. Their findings suggest that actual similarity in perceptions of how conflict is managed, while important for black marriages, may be somewhat less critical as long as black wives can maintain some separation and still reassure their husbands about their husbands' adequacy in spite of conflict. Thus, in black marriages, wives' understanding may be a more important factor than actual similarity.

METHOD

Data are obtained from the Early Years of Marriage (EYM) project, a 7-year longitudinal study of 373 newlywed couples conducted by Veroff et al. (1993a) of the Institute for Social Research at the University of Michigan. This is largely an urban sample that is heterogeneous with regard to socioeconomic status and educational background. Black couples were oversampled so that reliable race comparisons could be made. In approximately 40 percent of the couples, at least one partner said he or she could not think of a disagreement or that they never disagreed or argued. This reduced the size of the group for this analysis to 236 couples (116 black and 120 white). Missing data further reduced the sample to 219 couples. For more details on the sample used for this study, see Acitelli et al. (1993).

Spouses were interviewed separately in their homes for about an hour and a half on various aspects of married life between 5 and 8 months after their marriage and then again in their third year of marriage. (Shorter telephone interviews were conducted in the second and fourth years.) The race of the interviewers was matched to the race of the respondents.

Spouses were separately asked to think of the last time the couple had disagreed or argued about something in the past month or so and were then asked to report perceptions of self and spouse during the disagreement. Each question was asked twice, once for the respondent's own behavior and once for the respondent's perception of the spouse's behavior. For example, each spouse would indicate on a 4-point scale how true the following statements were: 'I calmly discussed the situation,' and 'My wife/husband calmly discussed the situation,' or 'I yelled or shouted at my wife/husband' and 'My wife/ husband, yelled or shouted at me.' The measures we utilize in this study were derived from 12 pairs of items. Six of the pairs are labeled constructive (i.e. calmly discussing the situation, listening to each other's point of view, finding out what the other is feeling, saying nice things, trying to compromise, suggesting a new way of looking at things) and six are labeled destructive (i.e. yelling/shouting, insulting or calling each other names, threatening, bringing

the spouse's family into the argument, bringing up things that happened long ago, having to have the last word) to the handling of conflict. Earlier studies on these data have shown that these items cluster together as separate factor (Oggins et al., 1993). Cronbach alphas were computed separately for husbands' and wives' reports of constructive behaviors (husband's alpha = .71; wives' alpha = .70) and destructive behaviors (husbands' alpha = .68; wives' alpha = .69) and demonstrate adequate, though not high, internal consistency.

Indices of similarity, perceived similarity and understanding were obtained for 12 pairs of items. For example, comparing what the husband said he did on a particular item to what he said his wife did would yield a measure of husband's *perceived similarity,* indicating the degree to which he thought he and his wife did the same thing. Comparing what the husband said his wife did to what the wife said she did would yield a measure of *understanding.* We derived *actual similarity* of response by comparing the husband's self-reported behavior to the wife's self-reported behavior. Note that we refer to actual similarity of response to the items which does not imply that we have a direct measure of actual similarity of behavior.

We obtained actual similarity, perceived similarity and understanding scores for each pair of items (e.g. 'I calmly discussed the situation' and 'My wife calmly discussed the situation'). Then we obtained averages for each of the three congruence measures on constructive and destructive items separately. Thus, we have perceived constructive similarity and perceived destructive similarity; actual constructive similarity and actual destructive similarity; and constructive understanding and destructive understanding. Although we are aware of the debate regarding discrepancy scores (e.g. Kenny, 1994), our measures are not discrepancy scores in the strictest sense of the term. They avoid the pitfalls of some scores having more than one possible meaning. For further detail on how these items were calculated, see Acitelli et al. (1993).

Marital well-being was measured by adding together standard scores of six items covering how happy, how satisfied, how equitable, and how stable the spouse feels the marriage is. Items were derived from Veroff et al. (1981) on happiness and satisfaction; Austin & Walster (Hatfield) (1974) on equity; Utne et al. (1984) and Booth et al. (1983) on stability. The items reflect general feeling states about the marriage, rather than specific characteristics of the marriage (e.g. communication, conflict), often found in popular marital adjustment scales (Spanier, 1976). Therefore, this measure avoids confounding independent variables that might be used to predict marital well-being (see Fincham & Bradbury, 1991; Glenn, 1990; and Johnson et al., 1992 for detailed discussions of this point). This 6-item measure has been demonstrated to be internally consistent (alpha = .83; Crohan & Veroff, 1989) and to have considerable construct validity (see Hatchett et al., 1995). Furthermore, we use the term marital well-being because the items tap into how happy, satisfied and stable the individual feels the relationship is, so it is an index of how the spouse thinks and feels about the relationship in general, much like an individual well-being measure asks the individual to rate feelings about life in general. Thus, our measure is not an adjustment or quality of marriage measure. All of the above measures were administered in both the first and third years of the respondents' marriages.

RESULTS

Results of analyses are presented in relation to the two research questions.

Q1: Do interpersonal perceptions of married couples change over the first three years of their marriages? Pairwise comparisons (accounting for the non-independence of scores) between the means of the perceptual congruence variables (actual similarity, perceived similarity, and understanding) in the first and third years were used. These revealed stability in both the constructive and destructive variables over the 2-year period. In only two groups—black wives and white husbands—was there significant change, and that occurred in only one constructive variable for each group. Black wives perceived themselves and their husbands as more similar in Year 3 ($M = 4.12$) than in Year 1 ($M = 3.85$, $t = 2.11$, $p < .05$) with respect to handling conflicts constructively. White husbands'

understanding of their wives was greater in Year 3 ($M = 3.88$) than in Year 1 ($M = 3.70$, $t = 2.26$, $p < .05$) with respect to handling conflicts constructively. The other two groups remained essentially the same on all of the congruence measures over the 2-year period. For the most part, neither blacks nor whites became more congruent in their perceptions over time.

Q2: Do these perceptions have effects on third year marital well-being that are different from their effects on first year marital well-being? Because the measures of perceptual congruence are complex variables, we kept our analyses relatively simple. Furthermore, the focus of our study is on the direct relationship between congruence variables and change in marital well-being, thus the testing of more complicated models is unnecessary for our purposes.

We tested the effect of congruence variables from the first year on marital well-being in the third year. We performed simultaneous regression analyses of the contribution of first year actual similarly, perceived similarity, understanding, and spouses' perception of their own behaviors to third year marital well-being. There were eight separate analyses—third year marital well-being regressed on constructive measures (Table 1) and on destructive measures (Table 2), each run separately for the four groups (white husbands, white wives, black husbands, black wives).

Congruence scores are entered simultaneously with the respondents' ratings of their own conflict behaviors. Because one component of all congruence scores is a spouse's self-report of conflict behavior, this analysis accomplishes two goals. First, when we find a significant association between a congruence score and marital well-being, we know it is due to the degree of congruence between variables rather than to the positivity or negativity of the behavior itself. The perceptions of the behaviors are in essence controlled for in this design. Second, we also account for the non-independence of the items that are different combinations of the same items. A careful inspection of the covariances between items also revealed no multicollinearity problems.

Other controls were entered into the equation simultaneously with the described variables.

Table 1   Betas from four multiple regression analyses predicting husbands' (H) and wives' (W) Year 3 marital well-being from perceptual congruence of constructive behaviors

	Husbands' marital well-being		Wives' marital well-being	
	Blacks	Whites	Blacks	Whites
W understanding H	.27***	−.31***	.19**	−.24**
H understanding W	−.10	−.06	−.03	−.22*
W perceived similarity	.12	−.06	.17*	−.16*
H perceived similarity	.05	−.05	−.11	−.17*
Actual similarity	−.36**	.10	−.52***	.29**
W self-perception	.02	.21***	.13	.08
H self-perception	.03	.23***	.09	.06
Year 1 marital well-being	0.3	.15	.29***	.35***
Parental status	−.31***	−.18**	−.09	−.07
Length of cohabitation	.06	.01	.07	−.02
Household income	.02	−.01	.03	.12
	$F(11,108)$ $= 2.87***$	$F(11,111)$ $= 2.45**$	$F(11,108)$ $= 5.34***$	$F(11,111)$ $= 2.57***$
	R^2(adjusted) $= .15$	R^2(adjusted) $= .12$	R^2(adjusted) $= .29$	R^2(adjusted) $= .12$

*$p < .10$; **$p < .05$; ***$p < .01$.

Table 2   Betas from multiple regression analyses predicting husbands' (H) and wives' (W) Year 3 marital well-being from perceptual congruence of destructive behaviors

	Husbands' marital well-being		Wives' marital well-being	
	Blacks	Whites	Blacks	Whites
W understanding H	.37***	.20	.13	−.01
H understanding W	.17	−.11	−.20	.12
W perceived similarity	.19	−.24*	.15	.09
H perceived similarity	.17*	−.09	−.02	−.12
Actual similarity	−.33**	−.06	−.26*	−.12
W self-perception	.06	−.45***	−.09	−.05
H self-perception	.10	−.08	−.06	−.26***
Year 1 marital well-being	−.06	.02	.31***	.23***
Parental status	−.25***	−.14**	−.01	.05
Length of cohabitation	.02	.03	.05	.07
Household income	.07	−.08	.12	.07
	$F(11,108)$ $= 2.80***$	$F(11,111)$ $= 2.29***$	$F(11,108)$ $= 3.09***$	$F(11,111)$ $= 2.49***$
	R^2(adjusted) $= .14$	R^2(adjusted) $= .10$	R^2(adjusted) $= .16$	R^2(adjusted) $= .12$

*$p < .10$; **$p < .05$; ***$p < .01$.

First year marital well-being was entered into the regression equation to control for the relationship between the first year perceptual congruence variables and first year marital well-being. Thus, we are assessing whether interpersonal perceptions in the first year can predict change in marital well-being from the first to the third year. Household income, parental status, and length of premarital cohabitation were also included as controls because these factors are related to the racial/ethnic co-cultures in this sample (Hatchett et al., 1995).

For black husbands and wives, actual similarity in the first year (in reports of constructive and destructive behaviors) is negatively related to marital well-being in the third year. Betas for black husbands and wives in the four analyses ranged from −.52 to −.26. In the first year analysis, the relation between similarity of destructive acts and wives' marital well-being was also negative. Although not significant, all of the associations between actual similarity and first year marital well-being were negative.

Our earlier report described the strong association between wives' understanding of husbands' constructive and destructive acts and wives' own marital well-being. Neither wives' understanding nor husbands' understanding was related to husbands' marital well-being in the first year.

For third year, wives' understanding predicts marital well-being in all four analysis groups in the case of constructive behaviors, and for black husbands with respect to destructive behaviors, as well (beta = .37, $p < .01$). Wives' understanding relates to marital well-being in very different—indeed opposite—way in black and white couples. For black couples, a wife's understanding her husband's constructive acts is positively related to her marital well-being (beta = .19, $p < .05$) and also to his (beta = −.27, $p < .01$) For white couples, on the other hand, a wife's understanding of her husband's constructive behaviors is *negatively* related to the both her marital well-being (beta = −.24, $p < .05$) and his marital well-being (beta = −.31, $p < .01$).

The same analyses (including the controls) predicting third year marital well-being from third year perceptual congruence variables yielded few significant results. Most constructive perceptual congruence variables in the third year did not relate significantly to third year marital well-being for any analysis group, except one. Black wives' third year perceived similarity was significantly associated with black wives' third year marital well-being (beta = .24, $p < .05$) and was marginally associated with black husbands' third year well-being (beta = .21, $p = .06$).

Also, most destructive perceptual congruence variables in the third year was not significantly related to third year marital well-being for any analysis group, except one. White husbands' perceived similarity was negatively associated with white spouses' third year marital well-being (husbands' beta = −.21, $p < .05$, wives' beta = −.37, $p < .001$), and actual similarity of destructive behaviors was positively related to white husbands' marital well-being (beta = .28, $p < .05$).

DISCUSSION

First, we consider findings that relate to our original research questions: *Do interpersonal perceptions of married couples change over the first three years of their marriages?* The perceptual variables are remarkably stable over the first three years of marriage. For the entire sample, there are no differences in perceptual variables. Only, when we analyze by sex and race do we find any changes. Black wives increase in perceived similarity and white husbands show increased understanding of their wives. Both of these changes occur in the context of constructive acts.

Because these specific results were not predicted, we must be cautious in our interpretations. Other analyses of the EYM data set prompt us to speculate that the change in black wives' perception relates to changes in the relative decision power of black spouses. In the first year of marriage black couples who say that the husband has the most say in decisions are also high on marital satisfaction and stability (Veroff et al., 1995). By the third year this association has decreased and, in fact, black husbands share roles (in things like household tasks and childcare) quite extensively with their wives (Veroff et al., 1995). This change—reflecting perhaps the black husbands' increased security in the relationship—may underlie the black wives' increased willingness to see that both spouses constructively handle conflicts in the same way.

The fact that black wives' third year perceived similarity was related to both black spouses' third year marital well-being, underscores the importance of the shift in black wives' perception. This shift is consistent with the Veroff et al. (1995) findings that black marital stability depended more than white marital stability on wives empathizing with and reassuring their husbands.

Reasons for the increase in white husbands' understanding of their wives' constructive acts are not as clear. We cautiously speculate that white men, who are generally accorded more power than women or blacks in our society, might be somewhat naive and untutored in taking the role of the other. Perhaps their wives gradually socialize them to attend to their behaviors, particularly during conflict situations, and thus increase the white husbands' understanding.

Overall, we are struck primarily by the stability of the perceptual congruence measures. This stability is important since it suggests that interpersonal perceptions in marriage and in perhaps any relationship are forged early in the commitment and remain relatively constant as the relationship progresses. There may be a critical period early in relationship development for the creation of these perceptions. As Duck (1994) states, developing a shared relational reality may be the most important process in relationship adjustment and satisfaction from the very beginning.

Do these perceptions have effects on third year marital well-being that are different from their effects on first year marital well-being? Just as in the first year analysis, wives' understanding of husbands is more important to the marital well-being of couples than is husbands' understanding of their wives. However, the effects of wives' understanding differs for blacks and whites and for positive and negative actions of the spouse. While wives' understanding of husbands predicted first year marital happiness significantly only for wives, wives' understanding, particularly regarding constructive acts, predicts third year happiness for both husbands and wives.

But the direction of effect is different for black and white couples. For black couples, the wife's understanding of her husband's constructive acts has a significant positive effect on her own and her husband's marital well-being as one may expect from our general congruence hypothesis. In the white marriages, however, the wife's understanding of her husband's constructive acts has a significant negative effect on her own and her husband's marital well-being.

How do we interpret this difference between the groups? The findings for black marriages—that the wife's understanding of her husband's behavior positively affects the couple's marital well-being—seems straightforwardly consonant with other findings indicating that the wife's sensitivity to her husband's needs and feelings (particularly to feelings of powerlessness caused by discrimination) is crucial for stability and happiness in black marriages (Hatchett et al., 1995). Indeed, we have noted in our first year analyses that the wife's understanding of her husband was more predictive of her marital well-being than was the husband's understanding of his wife, regardless of race. Thus the finding for blacks is consistent with our expectations and findings from the first year study. It is important to realize that wives' understanding continues to predict blacks' well-being in marriage even when partialling out the effects of first year marital well-being. For blacks, understanding in the first year paves the way for positive changes over the next two years.

But what about the findings for white couples—that wives' understanding of husbands predicts lower happiness for both husbands and wives? This means that the more a wife sees her husband as he sees himself, the less happy the couple becomes. Thus, more understanding of constructive acts predicts a decrease in marital well-being beyond the initial period.

These findings provide partial support for the idea that the meaning of constructive acts changes more than that of destructive acts, particularly for the white couples in this sample. The finding that the association between white wives' understanding of their husbands' 'constructive' behaviors and marital well-being changes from positive to negative from the first to the third year is consistent with the premise that positive behaviors are ambiguous and subject to varying interpretations (Fincham & Bradbury, 1991: Sillars, 1985). However, we can only speculate as to the specific form the varying interpretations take. Perhaps wives who once saw certain conflict styles in their husbands as constructive now see them as cool or patronizing (one more form of control). By the third year these wives may not be as happy about what they understood in the first year, recognizing it now as false, a kind of hood-winking, and may have communicated their distress to their husbands. Thus, a different 'understanding' may have gradually developed for some women. Regardless of the form the wives' interpretations take, the ambiguity of constructive behaviors can be problematic for analyses such as these. According to Sillars, ambiguous behaviors are the most problematic in determining meaning, and a spouse's under-standing of them may have negative correla-tions with marital satisfaction (Sillars, 1985; Sillars et al., 1990).

This intriguing finding is also consistent with the general supposition that a lack of consensus between spouses is detrimental to a marriage (e.g., Deal et al., 1992) even though it appears to indicate the opposite. Additional analyses showed that white husbands' and wives' per-ceptions of their own constructive acts do not correlate with each other ($r = -.05$, NS). Thus, the more wives understand their husbands, the more they may realize that their husbands are not reciprocal in the extent to which they deal with conflict constructively. In other words, white wives may perceive that the extent to which they are constructive does not at all relate to the extent to which their husbands are con-structive. Table 1 shows that similarity of con-structive behaviors predicts an increase in whites' marital well-being.

Thus, the more wives understand that the spouses are not similar, the more their marital happiness decreases.

Another finding supporting this interpreta-tion is that white wives' perceived similarity is negatively related to marital happiness. This finding contradicts a long-established associa-tion between perceived similarity and marital happiness (e.g., Levinger & Breedlove, 1966). Yet in light of the fact that white husbands and wives are not similar, the more similar a wife thinks the spouse is, the more inaccurate she is in her assessment of his behavior, and it is this inaccuracy that might relate to the decrease in marital well-being. Although we provide inter-pretations for these findings within racial/ethnic

groups, the reasons these links differ between racial/ethnic groups are not clear.

Two evident changes in findings for the third year compared to the first year are related to changes in the relative importance of destructive versus constructive acts, and in eth-nic differences which were not salient in the earlier study. Destructive acts, the locus of most of the findings in the first year, no longer seem to be the focus of findings in the third year. In the third year, most findings occur in the context of constructive acts. Gottman's (1993) balance theory of conflict suggests that positive behaviors have the capacity to negate the impact of negative behaviors over time. If so, then the number of positive associations between perceptions of constructive behaviors and marital well-being should increase from the first to the third year, as it did for black couples. For whites, however, the ambiguity of constructive acts may have set the stage for reinterpreting positive behaviors in a negative light.

Race differences, too scanty to report in the first year, are more significant in year three. We expected co-culture differences to become clearer as time went on. The romantic myth that dominates our larger cultural construction of early marriage ('the honeymoon period') might mask co-cultural differences among groups, particularly in the area of conflict. Thus time would be required to dilute the effect of the myth and allow co-cultural differences to emerge. Findings from these and other analyses from this data set consistently indicate that not only do there seem to be 'his' and 'her' mar-riages (Bernard, 1972), but that marriage is experienced differently, and perhaps the mean-ing of marriage is different for blacks and whites (Veroff et al., 1993b).

The results of our study in the third year sug-gest that there is both considerable continuity and change in the degree and effects of interper-sonal perceptions about conflict from the first to the third year. These interpersonal perceptions can become stabilized early in marriage, and yet there is some room for change. There are no simple answers regarding when to expect conti-nuity and when to expect change. The most provocative hypothesis generated from this study is that change occurs when couples are describing outwardly positive responses to conflict, and the underlying motivations for these responses are evidently more open to interpretation (than negative responses) as being either positive or negative.

DISCUSSION QUESTIONS

1. What is the difference between a constructive and a destructive act with respect to relationships?

2. What differences did Acitelli, Douvan, andVeroff find in marital satisfaction between the first and third years of marriage?

3. Are perceptual convergence and perceived similarity the same thing?

4. Do marriages benefit more from a couple sharing the same reality or establishing independent differences? (Explain what the authors say, then offer your own opinion.)

5. Why is it that Black wives' understanding is potentially more important to marital satisfaction than that of White wives?

Reading 3.4

"Let Us Go Into the House of the Lord"

Participation in African American Churches Among Young African American Men Who Have Sex With Men

Jeffrey Lynn Woodyard, John L. Peterson, and Joseph P. Stokes

Historians, sociologists, and theologians have documented the centrality of religious institutions in African American life from the enslavement period to the persent.[1,2] Today, African American churches retain a significant presence within nearly all African American communities.[3] The National Survey of Black Americans revealed that 84% of African American adults were in some way religious, 70% were members of an African American church, and 80% reported participating in prayer often, and an equal proportion (76%) was convinced that churches were very important institutions during their early childhood. No other African American institution garners this much support or has such an overwhelming influence.[4]

Lincoln and Mamiya's landmark study of churches in African American communities revealed that nearly three-fourths (71%) of these churches provide support services to their congregations and outreach to members of surrounding communities.[5] In almost every case, the sponsoring churches financed these efforts. Churches have been committed to providing social networks and support addressing membership needs throughout this century.[6,7,8,9] They are recognized as sites for delivering care to marginalized and under served populations.[10]

Despite a historic resolve to offer support to diverse populations within and beyond their congregations, the literature reflects no sustained effort to support church-going men who have sex with men (MSM) (We used the

From Woodyard, J. L., Peterson, J. L., & Stokes, J. P. (2000). "Let us go into the house of the Lord": Participation in African American churches among young African American men who have sex with men. *Journal of Pastoral Care, 54*(4), pp. 451-460.

rather clumsy term—men who have sex with men—to focus on relevant behaviors of having sex with other men rather than on self-identity as gay or bisexual. Not all African America MSM would see themselves as gay or bisexual.) Only recently has heterosexism in the church been identified as an evil to be eradicated.[11] Although present and very active in churches, MSM comprise a marginalized population that receives infrequent public discussion or acknowledgement. Generally, when these men are topics of concern for clergy and parishioners, little is discussed beyond perceived scriptural mandates against same-sex behavior. Cultural values such as theological positions and perceived biblical interpretations in African American churches contribute to the controversial nature of sexuality issues regarding MSM. These men, visible throughout African American communities, are seldom the targets for caring, nurturing, Christian ministry. The observations of Black theologian, James H. Cone, account for this potentially oppressive omission: "No theological issue is more potentially controversial in the Black Church and community than sexuality. Preachers and theologians tend to ignore it, apparently hoping homosexuals will go away or remain in the closet."[12]

Our study used qualitative methods to examine three questions surrounding church participation among young African American men who have sex with men: To what degree are they involved in African American churches? What are the effects of church involvement on their self-esteem? What impact does participation in churches have on their sexual behavior?

METHOD

Overview

This research was conducted in two cities, Atlanta and Chicago. The same methodology was used at both locations, and about half the data came from each city. The project used the Community Identification Process,[13] a qualitative assessment for hard-to-reach populations, and was conducted in three phases. First, we conducted in-depth, semistructured individual interviews ($N = 65$) with people who have either formal or informal relationships with young African American men who have sex with men (e.g., service providers, law enforcement personnel, bartenders, sex workers, family members, and friends). These interviews with "systems people" helped us to learn more about the various segments of young African American MSM, where they can be found, and how we might obtain their cooperation with this study.

Second, we conducted individual interviews with "key participants" ($N = 76$), 18–29 year old African American men who reported having had sex with a man in the past six months. These interviews constitute the data for the present study. In the third phase, interview transcripts were coded into predetermined themes and summarized by theme.

Procedures

To maximize the diversity of the sample, we recruited key participants from four sources: public parks where men cruise for male sex partners, clubs with largely gay and bisexual clientele, organizations in gay communities, and private parties. At each recruitment site, project outreach workers approached potential respondents and explained the nature of the study. After determining that the potential respondents met the eligibility criteria and were willing to be interviewed, in most cases the outreach workers either scheduled an appointment for an interview at one of the universities involved in the project or gave the participants a card with information about how to call to schedule an appointment. In some cases interviews were conducted immediately in a private area of a bar or club, or in a mobile van the project used during outreach.

The interview schedule consisted of a series of open-ended questions, with optional probes. Questions most relevant to this study included the following:

To what degree are men you know involved in the church?

How has the church affected how they see themselves?

How has the church affected their sexual behavior?

Interviewers in both cities were African American men who received extensive training.

Most of the interviewers themselves were gay identified. Despite their similarities to potential respondents and their familiarity with the communities, they had some difficulty recruiting respondents for the interviews. Respondents often had limited time and/or were suspicious of researchers in general.

The typical interview lasted between 60 and 90 minutes. Respondents were paid $35 and were not asked to identify themselves. Each interview was tape recorded and transcribed verbatim. Transcripts were proofread against the audiotape and corrected. Then, transcripts were coded into predetermined themes by multiple coders and summarized by theme using Tally 7 software for quantitative data.[14] Disagreements about how to code a particular section were resolved by discussion and consensus.

RESULTS

Church Involvement

Overall, young African American men who have sex with men reported consistently high levels of involvement in African American churches. Very few mentioned that they or other MSM averted religious affiliation. The data suggest that these men generally acknowledged no contradiction between being an African American MSM and being active in African American churches. This sentiment is reflected by one study participant who stated, "If you're gay, go to church." Another agreed: "Like I said, most of them [gay or bisexual men] go to church. "Still others spoke in terms of proportions, as this response indicates: "Most of the guys I know—I would say 80 percent of the people I know—are involved in the church." For these MSM the connection to churches was unquestioned, "You can find most gay men in church. [In] every church I have [gone] to, you can see . . . gay men there. So I would say religion and homosexuality are like peas and corn." Without question, "Black gay men have always been in the church."

Men we interviewed say there are two groups of MSM in churches, differentiated by their sexual/gender role. One group was men whose social behavior is commonly perceived as less masculine than heterosexual church-going males and who are thought to engage in receptive sexual roles with male partners. Their visibility promotes a view that many church affiliated gay or bisexual men are "queens" or "bottoms." A number of participants mentioned the presence of these men in church, often referring to them as "mama's boys" or "church queens." Another respondent asked: "What good 'sissy' is not in church every Sunday?" Another noted the presence in church of men who adopted aspects of explicitly feminine roles: "You have people coming to church in drag [looking] like Foxy [Brown]. You have several drag queens [in church]." Some young MSM may view church as a place to "perform" or act out their sexuality. They may see church as a place where they can be themselves and feel safe from the ridicule and torment they might face in other settings as a result of their lack of conformity to traditional notions of masculinity.

The second group of church-going MSM conform to masculine roles and are not easily detected. They "play the role" and their behavior is not distinguishable from heterosexual men: "Most of the men I know in church . . . even though they are married [and] they're sitting there with their wives . . . they have their [male] lovers probably sitting behind them or beside them.'' Another participant observed that the more stereotypically masculine MSM (those who are more "rough" or "tops") "tend to treat church like the average heterosexual African American male," that is, they don't go "unless forced."

Some men had detached from the church, either because they felt the church was not "a safe and friendly environment" for them or because they felt hypocritical going to church as a man who has sex with men. As one participant said, "I don't think I should [go to church] because I don't feel like I'm giving God my all. I'm going to church falsely, and I'd rather not go than to go to church thinking about going out partying the next day or going out to the club. . . . I just don't feel right about that." However, in general, participants sensed a dubious hospitality in African American churches. Clergy and members are aware of the range of sexual behaviors practiced by male congregants and have established traditions of acceptance that include a welcoming posture without public acknowledgment.

Despite church ambivalence toward them, men in our study reflected three primary reasons for maintaining church attendance. First, the churches fulfill a social role in the lives of African American MSM. They provide locations where these men can meet other gay or bisexual men without undue social pressure or scrutiny:

"If you know another man who wants a good man, tell him to go to church."

"Most of my friends I met through church."

"To me that [church] is another pick up spot."

"It's a very comfortable atmosphere in church. I think that's one of the most comfortable places you can be when you're gay. You'll be around other people who are gay and people in church who are not gay . . . accepting."

Since MSM presence is rarely publicly denounced or otherwise acknowledged, codified communication patterns facilitate the development of intricate social networks and communities. One man spoke about being able to identify other MSM: "They'll show you that they're gay just through their little signs that they have in the church."

A second justification for attendance was that churches were perceived as places where African American male identities are affirmed, particularly in response to multiple oppressions (*e.g.,* racial, economic, sexual) in the larger society. This is especially so for men with a history of religious affiliation since childhood:

"The church structure is the way to give a man confidence, especially black men, because the church has been the backbone to the north . . . as far as black men becoming stronger, teaching self-discipline . . . a very, very important part in gay . . . men . . ."

Still, a third motivation for church involvement has to do with opportunities for these men to bring their talents and skills to the service of African American communities. African American MSM comprise essential constitutive elements for weekly Christian ministry. They are active in music and preaching ministries. They serve as church ushers, on boards, and committees. They manage finances and are responsible for the spiritual and physical climates of their congregations:

"I know a lot of preachers, ministers, and deacons (who are) in-the-life. And all of these 'what we call kids' flounce in the clubs Saturday, go to church the next day, Sunday. Next thing you know they're back in the clubs Sunday night. So obviously, church is another meat market, another place to meet other guys."

"Even the preachers [can be gay] . . . we [MSM] are notorious for being in the choir. We'll sing like the angels or we might be in church with another man."

"I had relations with a guy who is a minister of music at a church."

"You find in your church choirs, a bunch of gays, choir directors. I've seen them out at the club."

"I got a couple friends who are gay [and] ministers."

"I'm just being honest. I have been in the church all of my life and have played for I don't know how many churches."

"I mean from the choir to ministers, to evangelists, pastors, . . . the whole shebang."

"If it wasn't for homosexuals in church, there would probably be [no] tenor section in the choir. Some of the baddest and hottest [gospel musical] groups out . . . most of the tenor section is gay."

"I have had [sex with] a lot of different pastors. A couple of pastors have approached me, you know."

Responses to Involvement of MSM

Young African American MSM church involvement presents challenges to Christian doctrine and orthodox biblical interpretations espoused in most African American churches. Generally, MSM reported that clergy preach against same-sex behaviour: "I get to church and [hear] 'Ain't no man should be sleeping with another man.'" A number of respondents echoed this sentiment: ". . . the pastor of our church is 100 percent against [homosexuality]." An immediate, constant and seemingly irreconcilable dynamic between perceived biblical teachings and the tradition of discreet hospitality toward these men often places them in precarious moments of psychological discomfort:

"It's very confusing, but it's basically just teaching people to hate themselves."

"You're being taught that this is wrong and an abomination and all that and . . . you sit there and you're hearing that and you just don't know you fit."

"It adds to the self-hatred, the self-loathing that you find in many homosexuals . . . , they have this whole self-loathing kind of psychotic episode."

"I think they go to church on Sundays . . . listen to the preacher and within themselves they know that they're gay so . . . they know that they're sinners. And so deep down inside I think they don't love themselves . . . they . . . enjoy church but then the preacher may say something about gay people . . . and I don't think they get a chance to really live totally free . . ."

As a function of their church involvement, most men in the study expressed feelings of guilt, condemnation, embarrassment, and alienation. Negative messages associated with church teachings appeared to do little to provide a sense of security and positive self-worth for MSM, despite their willful participation in religious activities. These men and the gay and bisexual men they know had internalized anti-same-sex messages:

"Once they have it [sex with men], then they feel guilty . . . the whole feeling of self-loathing just kind of comes back,"

"The black church does not embrace its gay children. They shun them. It's belittled them and made them feel less human."

"Your sin of being gay is enough to get you sent straight to hell . . . without a chance of . . . seeking redemption . . . the church has really done nothing more than to . . . alienate its gay members away. It makes us feel . . . as if we're not wanted. It makes us feel as if . . . we were born to be evil, and that we were born for the ultimate downfall. It doesn't matter if you never hurt anyone, it doesn't matter if you put money in the collection plate. It doesn't matter if you've . . . gone out into the community to help uplift the community. All that matters is that you're gay and you're going to hell. And it's as simple as that. There is no redemption for you."

"It's an abomination, you know. I've played for churches—I have sat in services where they have talked about homosexuals like dogs."

"I think the black church is really oppressive when it comes to [male] sexuality."

"It's really, really bad. You can't go to . . . heaven being gay. I believe God knows my heart and God knows this is the way I am. And I believe that you can't be gay going to heaven. I would like to see the other side—the gates of heaven."

Some study participants blame the church for being of no help to church-going MSM despite their consistently high levels of involvement. Many respondents are typified by this comment:

"I think it's turned off a lot of people . . . It's turned off people who have a lot to offer and the church could gain a lot from these individuals. But that's lost. And I don't know if it will ever be regained. And we've missed that opportunity to reach out and to help them, and I find that frightening. I mean if the church really has a true mission, they have failed. We have failed as a church community to address issues of our community."

A few (but only a few) churches have developed targeted ministries to foster MSM inclusion. One respondent who found affirmation from such a ministry stated:

"It's nice to see that . . . black men would be interested in a black gay Bible study group. It enables me—I think it enables black gay men to realize that there is a place for them in the Bible. And I think our study group enables us to identify where exactly we fit. And most of all, you have a lot of controversy about gays and the Bible and all those other types of things and I guess analyzing it through a homosexual perspective—I don't think there's really a place in the bible that says God condemned gays."

Another participant spoke of churches as spiritual resources for men "in-the-life" (those who participate in same-sex behaviors):

"You're on your last leg and you're down and out and you come to a point where you got tired of . . . all the cruising and tired of this world and sometimes you just give yourself to God and you go to church and pray."

Church efforts to conceal MSM involvement by discreetly and covertly welcoming these men without public acknowledgment were more common in the experiences of our study participants than those churches that appeared openly hospitable. Remarks about churches' covert acceptance of gay or bisexual men are typified by the following comment:

"It's like they know but it's really not mentioned and the people in church know, but it's like it's accepted . . . it's like a hush-hush thing. [Church members and clergy] know they're gay . . . Half the tenor section is gay."

Church resistance to a public embrace prompts a sense of rejection felt by a few of the men we interviewed:

"It ain't so much the sin that they're [MSM] doing, a lot of times, it's the sin that the church is doing. Their church is turning [its] back on them."

"They don't want to know the organist is gay. 'Oh, he sings too well to be gay. That brother is too sharp to be gay . . . He preaches too well to be gay . . .' They don't want to hear it."

Reconciling Church Tradition and MSM Experience

Most MSM we talked with have struggled with church tradition and have internalized negative messages about same-sex behavior as part of their sense of self. Generally, these men offered rationalizations that provide insight to these reconciling processes. In short, most study participants affirmed the notion that one's sexuality or same-sex preference is, in part, an element of created being. That is, since they have no recollection of "choosing" this status, it comes from God: "Well this is the way I was born. This is who I am. [I]f God would have wanted me to act differently, then he wouldn't have put this on me." Another participant stated: "I had no choice in the matter. It's just the way I was, it's my feelings and you have to go by your feelings. God knows the way I am . . . and I think it is accepted and God loves me the way I am now." Essentially, one respondent summarized a fundamental belief among church-going young African American MSM: "God understands."

Most study participants agreed that efforts to reconcile church involvement with orthodox teachings about same-sex behavior influenced both their attitudes and the frequency with which they had sex with other men. With very few exceptions, sexual activity with men was experienced in secrecy. Most also reported that church involvement decreased their number of same-sex contacts.

DISCUSSION

Young African American men who have sex with men perceive themselves as active participants in the life and ministry of African American churches. They are represented in pulpits, deacon and trustee boards, usher boards, and numerous committees and church auxiliaries. They provide churches and communities with the music and song that serve as core aspects of public ministry. Moreover, they fill church pews and are willful adherents to biblical teachings and church tradition. Almost every aspect of African American religion includes the presence of men who have sex with men.[15] Yet, MSM are marginalized within the churches to which they offer their devotion and services.[16,17] Perceived biblical interpretations and longstanding traditions of covert hospitality without public acknowledgement most often leave these church members wondering if they have a rightful place in the communion of the Christian institutions they help to build and sustain.[18]

In their own words, men we interviewed revealed an ambivalence about their relationship with these institutions and the central spiritual figures: God and Jesus Christ. They have internalized a God-concept who is at once loving and open to their humanness, yet condemns them because of the human sexual condition that they had never sought. They report being trapped in a repressive triangle constructed by African American religious rhetoric about sexual sin, a covert marginalizing tradition that disallows full group inclusiveness, and their own knowledge of significant MSM participation within institutions that cannot fully embrace them as brothers. These are the institutions to which nearly all segments of African American communities have pledged their faithfulness. Yet, MSM find little reward or comfort for their allegiance.

African American churches represent a major source of negative messages that these men incorporate into their sense of self.[19] These data suggest that churches have lasting and deep impact on the self-worth of MSM. Because of religious teachings that foster condemnation and church traditions of "underground" acceptance, ambivalence about relationships with God and issues regarding life after death provoke psychological discomfort in these African Americans. Moreover, our study reveals this intolerance persists although some clergy and other religious leaders, who are sources of anti-MSM rhetoric, participate in same-sex behaviors themselves.

Historically, African American churches emerged when free and enslaved believers sought to understand the biblical texts from oppressed perspectives.[20] Early church founders had a conception of a God whose primary reason for establishing relations with humans was to procure their deliverance from social, political, and economic oppression. A similar concept of God might be adopted by African American MSM.[21] In the tradition of liberation theology, scriptural bases for removing homophobic social and cultural discrimination toward these young men are more likely to emerge when churches adopt non-oppressive practices.

Several issues that transcend the scope of this research arise. These include questions central to understanding African American churches, particularly in light of the overwhelming evidence of active MSM participation. What aspects of African American church experiences account for this involvement in the face of vilification and concomitant erosion of self-esteem? How do these men cope with the dichotomous messages received from these churches?

Given the liberation tradition of African American churches, what is assumed about the nature of sexual desire? Is same-sexual desire as fundamental to the actual practice of African American Christianity as inter-gender desire is perceived to be in the biblical texts? What beliefs and teachings support levels of tolerance significant enough to afford the dubious hospitality among church-going African Americans? How can churches openly address the nature of sexual desire and assist their members to understand it despite anti-MSM biblical rhetoric? These and other concerns prompt further research and new conversations in African American churches.

Until careful and nurturing dialogue about MSM issues is initiated in African American churches, the struggles with self-esteem that these men experience may be expected to continue with possible negative psychological effects. There are indications that churches where MSM are likely to attend would be sites for discourse about MSM spirituality and other issues.[22] Such dialogue can only occur when clergy, other church leaders, and church-going MSM agree to honest communication about the following issues:

1. the use of perceived biblical mandates to foster homophobic marginalization against other African Americans,

2. the presence of MSM in nearly every area of church ministry,

3. the nature of MSM religious ambivalence,

4. the particular ministerial needs of religiously involved MSM, and

5. the development, of support for MSM from church congregations.

Dealing explicitly with these issues requires an approach to ministry that challenges covert traditions. Church leaders must clearly articulate what they know and are willing to know about these young men. They must provide leadership by example for congregations who have not reconciled the anti-MSM teachings with their ability to nurture these often-neglected members of African American congregations.

DISCUSSION QUESTIONS

1. What does *MSM* stand for?

2. Do all MSM consider themselves gay? Why or why not?

3. What is meant by *cruising* and how is that relevant to the study?

4. What are some of the concerns African American MSM have with the climate in Black churches?

5. When African American MSM have sustained involvement with Black churches, what strategies do they employ?

Part IV

COMMUNICATING AFRICAN AMERICAN GENDERED IDENTITIES

Very little communication research has explored African American gendered realities. Amazingly, much of what North Americans have come to understand about African American gendered relationships is that they are rife with pathology, which, of course, is no more present among African Americans than any other group. In this fourth part of the book, several essays appear that offer critical analyses of and insights into the lives of African American men and women.

As noted previously, interpersonal communication researcher Marsha Houston has been associated most with Black women's communicative experiences. In her lead essay presented here, she discusses Black women's varied perspectives on what can be characterized as "Black women's talk." With the premise that all discourse is culturally inscribed and that Black women's discourse is confounded by their double-jeopardy status, Houston initiates this study and thematically organizes 134 Black women participants' free descriptions of their style of discourse. She reported that 27 of the women evaded the question, and she shared their articulated rationales for not participating. She included these responses under a theme she labeled *evasion*. There were five remaining themes that emerged from the study: accommodation, celebration, wisdom, fortitude, and caring. She describes each, using the literature to help frame the participants' ideas. Subsequently, she concludes that Black women's metacommunicative perspectives on the style of their talk reveal some variance, but there was an overwhelming sense that Black women's talk is generally intelligent, assertive, compassionate, and warm, which are traits of what Patricia Hill Collins (1990) calls *an ethics of caring.*

Karla D. Scott, author of the next essay, addresses Black women's talk in intercultural interactions and discovers that "girl" and "look" are two expressions that mark Black women's code switching behaviors when conversing with Whites. Scott, like Houston, acknowledges that Black women's identities are an interlocking matrix of race, gender, and class, each of which is secured by its own sociocultural border concerns. As with any border, the boundary must be protected, especially when it is threatened. Unfortunately, Black women have experienced a history of race, gender, and class oppression, so the border is often policed. It is no mystery then that, when traversing the borders interculturally, Black women's discourses reflect identity negotiation. Scott's study of nine Black women's discourse included both participant observation and interviews. Her results indicated that when participants used the word "girl," it was followed by speech patterns specifically coded to identify the person about whom one is talking. For example, a certain vowel lengthening or intonation can be associated with a friendly ingroup greeting, and is not immediately connected to a shorter, more blunt articulation of the word "girl" that is engaged when speaking about Whites. As shown via Scott's examples, both style and dialect shifts take place. The style of speaking, again, is much more abbreviated and less nonverbally immediate when speaking to Whites; however, Black women were more likely to switch registers and begin speaking what sounded like Ebonics when they would say "girl" and "look" to other Blacks.

African American language use is also an important component of the next essay written by D. Soyini Madison. Madison recounts the oral narrative of an 80-something-year-old Black woman named Mrs. Alma Kapper, someone Madison met at a senior citizen daycare center in Chicago where she "spent six months interacting with elders." Using a theoretic framework comprised of Black feminist thought, nommo, kuntu, and rhythm, Madison explores the deep-structured talk of Mrs. Kapper, and Madison enriched her study by not only presenting her words poetically but also transcribing her talk using her actual phonemic structure and diction. Naturally, this was supported by her description of the Black oral tradition and its performative character. In this essay, Madison, like Joni Jones (also in this volume), sought to introduce to performance studies an alternative way of analyzing Black and gendered performance by enlisting the ideas of the African-inspired Black oral tradition.

With further attention to African American women's identities, Tina M. Harris critically assesses two Black films directed by Black men: *Waiting to Exhale* directed by Forrest Whitaker and *Set It Off* directed by F. Gary Gray. She contends that the cinematic portrayal of Black women in these films colludes with a sinister hegemonic discourse, which continually propagates Black female insecurity and poor decision-making. She labels these images caricatures that, at best, can be characterized as "sophisticated ghettoized images of African American female identity." Both movies have four Black female protagonists who share a friendship based on a common set of class and social struggles. *Waiting to Exhale* is the middle-class version and *Set It Off* is the working-class and ghettoized version, all enwrapped in strivings toward achieving success as measured by a capitalist American dream. Harris frames her study using Patricia Hill Collins's Black feminist standpoint, with particular attention paid to Collins's explication of four controlling images: the mammy, the matriarch, the welfare mother, and the Jezebel. Harris concluded that, while there was some space in each film lent to positive representations of Black femaleness, there were still images complicit with the stereotypical, degrading, and needy portrayals of Black women that foster harmful and annihilative cinematic effects on diversified audiences, not the least of which are Black women.

The final essay in Part IV was written by Celnisha L. Dangerfield and me. Nowhere in the communication literature will you find an essay theorizing about Black masculinity and manhood; this investigation is, therefore, groundbreaking. We distinguish between manhood and masculinity by defining manhood as a behavioral category in flux and masculinity as a perceptual category in flux. With these definitions, it is quite possible for females to be masculine, and we believe some females have masculine tendencies just as some males have feminine tendencies. Nonetheless, the article adopts a male masculine perspective. After describing three stereotypes of Black masculine bodies, we introduce a Black masculine identity theory comprised of five factors representing Black masculine positionality: community, recognition, independence, achievement, and struggle, all of which are affected by personal and cultural histories as well as one's sense of control over his life (i.e., self-efficacy). In introducing this theory, one of the most significant contributions is the plea to gender scholars to rethink masculinism as a term that is not necessarily pejorative.

Reading 4.1

MULTIPLE PERSPECTIVES

African American Women Conceive Their Talk

MARSHA HOUSTON

"Double jeopardy" (Beale, 1970) is often considered the fundamental insight into the lived experiences of African American women. African American feminist thinkers, from nineteenth-century orator Maria Stewart to contemporary cultural critic bell hooks, have pointed out that African American womanhood is experienced holistically. Black[1] women experience womanhood *in the context* of blackness; they do not experience their gender and ethnic identities as separate "parts" of who they are (Collins, 1990: Davis, 1981; hooks, 1981; 1984). The outcome of being African American *and* woman in a social order rife with both racism *and* sexism is that black women's experiences of womanhood may overlap with those of both white women and other women of color, but will also differ from them in important ways; and their experience of blackness may overlap with those of African American men, but will significantly differ from them as well. When the fundamental insight of "double jeopardy" is extended to other aspects of African American women's identities (e.g., socio-economic class, sexual orientation) the "multiple jeopardy" and "multiple consciousness"[2] that characterize African American womanhood become apparent (King, 1988).

For individual African American women, these twin concepts suggest both the risks of many sorts of disadvantage and marginalization and the possibilities of simultaneous, multiple, self- and group-affirming ways of seeing every aspect of human social life. For African American women as a social group, "multiple jeopardy" and "multiple consciousness" suggest a heterogeneity of social relationships, experiences, and outlooks that preclude essentializing black womanhood.

Any explanation of African American women's communication must, in some way, account for the heterogeneity of black women's lived experiences suggested by multiple jeopardy and multiple consciousness. In this essay, I

From Houston, M. (2000). Multiple perspectives: African American women conceive their talk. *Women and Language, 23*, 11-17.

endeavor to account for that heterogeneity by exploring three contrasting perspectives taken by African American women in response to my request that they write free descriptions of "black women's talk." One-hundred thirty-four middle-class professional women and aspiring middle class women (college students) responded to this request. This is not a report of the responses they gave, but an interpretation of the ways they approached the question, that is, the ways they conceived "black women's talk" as a distinct communication style or repertoire of styles. Some women evaded the idea of "black women's talk;" others saw style-switching as its central feature, but most celebrated one or more of three dimensions of black women's interpersonal style: wisdom, fortitude, and caring.

Hecht, Ribeau and Alberts (1989) suggest that cultural *speaking perspectives* are ways of thinking about and talking about talk that reveal the discursive forms a cultural group regards as ideal and perceives as typical of particular speakers and situations. Perspectives also reveal the personal qualities and types of interpersonal relationships that are valued by the group. My goal is to connect the three contrasting, gendered cultural perspectives African American women expressed about their talk to one aspect of "multiple jeopardy," the disparaging stereotypes that have formed the dominant consensus about black womanhood and black women's speech throughout most of U.S. history. These stereotypes are central elements of the discourse environment (van Dijk, 1987) in which African American women speak and develop their attitudes toward their own language and speaking styles. I suggest that each of the perspectives represents African American women's effort to positively conceive their talk in the face of the disparaging conceptions they routinely encounter in both the dominant and ethnic cultures that are the predominant settings for their communicative lives. In other words, I offer an inquiry into some of the socio-political bases for black women's conceptions of their communication styles. As Henley and Kramarae (1994) point out, feminist scholars recognize that descriptions of women's talk are of limited value unless they advance understanding of women's relationship to the social order.

THE PARTICIPANTS AND THE STUDY

I set out to gather and interpret qualitative data about how middle class and aspiring middle class African American women view their communication styles in relation to those of African American men and white women and men. I used a seven-item free-response questionnaire in which I asked, "How would you describe the following ways of speaking: 'women's talk,' 'black talk,' 'black women's talk,' 'black men's talk,' 'white talk,' 'white women's talk,' 'white men's talk?' The questionnaire was not intended as a quantifiable, "scientific" measure, but as a source of narrative descriptions.

The 134 African American women who responded to the questionnaire varied in age, socio-economic class, regional provenance, and the racial configuration of the neighborhoods in which they grew up. Most (104) were undergraduate students enrolled in introductory communication, English, sociology, and psychology classes at a black women's college located in the Southeast with a student body recruited from throughout the nation. The remainder (30) were professional women (aged 22 to above 50) who grew up in various regions of the U.S. and were currently working in the Southeast; their responses were solicited by students enrolled in an upper-level communication and gender seminar. Because all of the participants had or were acquiring college degrees and professional jobs, it is not surprising that most (110) self-identified as "middle class." Although 58 described themselves as growing up in "mostly black" neighborhoods, 72 described their neighborhoods as "mostly white" or "multi-racial" (the remaining 4 had lived in several different types of neighborhoods while growing up).

I encouraged participants to make their responses as lengthy or brief as they wished; the majority (109) were in the form of word lists, phrases or single sentences; 11 were narratives of two sentences or more. As I began a content analysis of the responses,[3] the most glaring, and troubling, results that emerged were that 14 of the women who completed the questionnaire chose not to describe "black women's talk," and another 13 wrote statements that suggested they resisted (or resented) the request to describe it. These resistant responses and non-responses came from women in all the demographic groups described above. Why would 20% of the participants in this study (27 African American women) evade the task of describing their own talk?

As a feminist scholar, I wanted to account for all responses in some manner, even the non-responses; to use a metaphor familiar to feminist researchers, I wanted to listen to all the voices in the text and to attend to the silences as well. It was reflection on the non-responses as well as the full range of written responses that led me to consider the perspectives participants took on the idea that "black women's talk" can or should be described as a distinct, identifiable style or repertoire of styles. In the remainder of this discussion, I describe what I have labeled the evasive, accommodating, and celebratory perspectives on black women's talk and their relationships to the socio-cultural milieus in which African American women routinely construct definitions of their talk and conduct their communicative lives.

Perspective on Black Women's Talk

Evasion

In this perspective I include the 27 women who either did not respond or who wrote responses that resisted the question, such as the following:

[Black women's talk] suggests nothing in particular.

[Black women's talk] is no different from women's talk in general.

I can't describe talking like a black woman because all black women don't talk alike; you can't generalize.

All written evasive responses were brief, that is, one sentence or phrase, such as those above; their tone was self-assured and sometimes vehement:

There is no description for talking like a black woman.

How would I describe black women's talk? I wouldn't!

Of the many possible reasons for evasive responses, I suggest the following two. First, Susan Ervin-Tripp has pointed out that it is often difficult for speakers to sufficiently objectify their own speech in order to discern its features (Ervin-Tripp, 1968). Both a non-response and a resistant response may be the result of a woman's inability to distance herself enough from her own talk on perceive its gendered cultural markings.

The second, more compelling, reason for evasive responses, I believe, has to do with how black women speakers and black women's speech is constructed in the U.S. American social order. Because the U.S. is a hierarchically structured, multi-cultural society in which marginalized groups have little control over the dominant consensus about any of their culture-based behaviors, some members of marginalized groups inevitably internalize dominant cultural evaluations of their ethnic language and communication style, even if those evaluations are overtly prejudiced (van Dijk, 1987). One black feminist scholar has described the dominant consensus about black women within U.S. American society in the following rather striking manner:

> Black women embody by their sheer physical presence two of the most hated identities in this . . . country. Whiteness and maleness . . . have not only been seen as physical identities but codified into states of being and worldviews. The codification of Blackness and femaleness by whites and males is contained in the terms 'thinking like a woman' and 'acting like a nigger.' . . . Therefore, the most prejorative concept in the white/male worldview would be that of thinking and acting like a "nigger woman" (Bethel, 1982).

There is abundant evidence of the "negative coding" of black womanhood in the U.S. Qualities the dominant culture defines as undesirable in women in general are frequently projected onto individual African American women (Manning-Marable & Houston, 1995) as well as onto African American women as a social group (Anderson, 1997). Historically, almost all the undesirable feminine qualities, from promiscuity to intellectual inferiority to outspokenness have been used to disparage black women (Collins, 2000; Essed, 1991; Guy-Sheftall, 1990; 1995).

In popular entertainment, for example, black women who were loud, smart-alecky, and/or ungrammatical speakers were stock characters in early nineteenth and early twentieth-century minstrel shows and continued to be reproduced in such mass media characters as "Sapphire" of the *Amos and Andy* radio and television programs, "Mammy" of the film *Gone With The Wind,* and "Florence" of television's *The Jeffersons* (Anderson, 1997; Merritt, 1997). When producers of pseudo-realistic daytime television talk shows encourage teenage and young adult black women guests to be particularly obstreperous, the long-standing stereotype that uncivil, ungrammatical, and traditionally unfeminine communication are central features of black women's talk is reinforced.

The mass media are not the only dominant cultural contexts in which black women's speech and black women speakers are coded negatively. In her study of black women's interpersonal interracial encounters, Philomena Essed (1991) demonstrates that any speaker or any discourse marked as black and female is likely to be pejoratively evaluated. Essed argues that racism and sexism are inseparable in interpretations of African American women's discourse, and that the dominant culture exerts tremendous pressure on African American women to assimilate by communicating in ways that are as non-black as possible. (See also Etter-Lewis, 1993; St. Jean & Feagin, 1998.)

But African American women not only encounter negative coding and an urge to assimilate in dominant cultural contexts. Members of marginalized groups do not develop speaking norms and values in isolation from those of the dominant group; thus some African Americans who recognize pragmatic reasons for not conforming to dominant cultural norms nevertheless valorize those norms as ideal behaviors

(Hannerz, 1970). This tension between ethnic and dominant cultural norms and behaviors is implied in the concept of multiple consciousness. For example, a black woman may recognize that black women's tradition of work outside the home has resulted in cultural expectations of egalitarian male-female relational communication (Ladner, 1971; Houston Stanback, 1985); nevertheless, she may idealize the more passive, submissive communication style considered traditional for white women. The valorization of dominant cultural norms for women's talk seems to underlie black men's portrayal of black women as domineering speakers, for example as "verbal castrators" (Abrahams, 1975; Bond & Peery, 1970; Rogers-Rose, 1980; Spillers, 1979), or as contentious "hard mouths" (Folb, 1980).

Nowhere was the tension between African American and dominant cultural linguistic norms more apparent than in the controversy over teaching "Ebonics" in the Oakland public schools which erupted in the national media in December 1996 (Locke, 1996). In her contribution to a special issue of *The Black Scholar* on "Ebonics," Rosina Lippi-Green (1997) summarizes the dialectical language attitudes of the masses of African Americans:

The greater African American community seems to accept the inevitability of linguistic assimilation to mainstream U.S. English in certain settings, but there is also deep unhappiness about the necessity in many quarters. . . . To make two statements: *I acknowledge that my home language is viable and adequate, and I acknowledge that my home language will never be accepted,* is to set up an unresolvable conflict (9).

I suggest that evasive responses are one way respondents to my study endeavored to resolve this conflict. Because African American womanhood and African American women's talk so often are maligned in both the dominant and ethnic cultures, the women who responded evasively, with silence or verbal resistance to the idea of *black* women's talk, may have conceived the question as a request for pejorative stereotypes of their language and speaking style (e.g., talking like a "nigger woman"). Those who had internalized the dominant consensus about "black women's talk" as linguistically unacceptable and stylistically unfeminine may have been unable to conceive a self-affirming way of describing their talk as black women except as singular (not generalizable to other *black* women) or as "no different" from the talk of women who are not black. When we consider the socio-political context in which respondents endeavored to describe their talk, evasive responses that appear to deny the existence of distinct black women's speaking styles can be more usefully understood as strategies for resisting racist and sexist stereotypes of those styles.

Accommodation

A small number (4) of the women who participated in the study took what I call the accommodationist perspective on black women's talk. This perspective is illustrated by the following response:

> If [a black woman] is around her friends, she will use slang . . . and if she is speaking with a group of business associates she will talk intellectually.

Rather than evading the idea of black women's talk, the woman who wrote this response valorized speakers who can use both an informal African American speaking style and a formal, mainstream American style.

By recognizing the need to switch styles, the women who took this perspective, like those who took the evasive perspective, indicated awareness of the dominant consensus that speech marked as "black" and "female" is inferior, lacking in prestige and social power. But they were more explicit about the components of their style, specifying an African American English lexicon, context sensitivity, and communicative flexibility as characterizing black women's talk:

> Talking like a black woman would depend on [the] social conditions and what education the woman had, but there could be talk about black men and how blacks, especially women, are treated.

> [Black women's talk is] anything [from what is] said between individuals living in a rural setting to communication that takes place in the world of

"high society" Blacks. It takes on many different forms given the scope of the topics and the situation. . . .

Respondents' descriptions of style-switching parallel those of language and communication scholars who also argue that style-switching is most often situation dependent, and that in order for African American speakers to alternate styles they must acquire a command of African American styles through socialization in African American speech communities, and of a mainstream style through formal education, or through a combination of education and modeling (e.g., by bi-stylistic parents) (Baugh, 1983; Nelson, 1990).

Like evasion, accommodation can be traced to the tension created by a social order that engenders multiple consciousness in African American women. Bi-cultural behaviors, such as communication style-switching, are one way of resolving that tension, especially for educated professional women whose lives require them to meet the communicative demands of both the ethnic and dominant cultural milieus (Bell, 1983; Bulcholtz, 1996; Dill, 1979; Rubin & Garner, 1984; St. Jean & Feagin, 1998).

Celebration

Most of the respondents (107) resisted and transcended stereotypic perceptions of black women's talk to offer alternative descriptions that spoke to the self-affirming interpersonal qualities that they considered central to their communication styles. This is the perspective that I call "celebratory." Celebratory responses were characterized by positive evaluations of black women's communication behaviors, including those that are often pejoratively stereotyped by others. The largest number of celebratory responses (49) focused on underlying social and interpersonal functions of talk, that is, on communication strategies and attributes of the speaker. Here are a few examples:

> [Black women's talk is] talking with intimacy [and] deep caring; [it is] highly intuitive, and charged with an other-worldly quality. It connotes that the conversation is humanistic, principled, and based on inner convictions . . .

A black woman's talk may be out of protest so she's going to be heard. Talking like a black woman also suggests that the conversation may be really down to earth.

[Black women's talk is] candidness, use of emphasis and intensity, "joaning,"[4] loudness; often entertaining and comical in her use of expressions ("honey," "child," "sugar"), especially characteristic of Southern black women. . . .

Three dimensions of black women's interpersonal communication style are suggested by the celebratory descriptions, each indicating the goals, strategies, and outcomes of talk that are valued by black women speakers: wisdom, fortitude, and caring.

Wisdom

Geneva Smitherman (1977) argues that communication scholars often place so much emphasis on the dynamic expressive style of black speakers, they ignore the high value blacks place on the substance of talk. Citing the criticism of dynamic but vacuous discourse in a once-popular soul song entitled, "Talkin' Loud, but Sayin' Nothin,'" Smitherman reminds us that through the "rich verbal interplay among everyday people, lessons and precepts about [black] life and survival are handed down from generation to generation" (p.73).

The ethnic cultural priority placed on the substance of talk is reflected in responses that describe what I term the wisdom dimension of black women's talk. The emphasis on wisdom and knowledge is one of two important distinctions between the stereotypes of black women's talk (as smart-alecky, domineering, obstreperous) and black women's own experience and understanding of their talk.

The women who took the celebratory perspective not only constructed black women's talk as substantive but constructed themselves as authorities. They described a variety of bases for their authority, including intellect, formal education, life experiences, common sense, moral principles, and intuition. While many responses described black women as generally knowledgeable, those that focused on the topics of black women's talk (30) give some sense of respondents' perceptions of the domains of black women's knowledge. Topical responses can be grouped into two major categories: talk about black men and talk about black women's personal and professional lives. The women referred to talk that criticized certain black male behaviors (e.g., infidelity) as well as talk that supported individual black men or empathized with the situation of black men as a social group. The majority of topical descriptors referred to talk about women's personal and professional lives, including "how black women are treated in the white patriarchal society," "sisterhood," "single motherhood," "being a working woman," "female strength and independence," and "bettering yourself."

Fortitude

In their study of black perspectives on interracial communication, Hecht, Ribeau and Alberts (1989) make several references to black women's talk as "tough;" their two black women informants told them that black women "have had to be so tough as the head of the household throughout history that they 'tend to talk tough and make fun of white women who are soft'" and that "'Talking tough' is a way of carrying oneself. . . . [B]lack females historically have had to take charge, and this has led to strength" (pp. 385–410). The word "tough" was never used by the women who responded to my questionnaire; however, they used a total of 27 other, more positively connoted words and phrases to describe what I term the dimension of fortitude in black women's talk. This was, by far, the largest number of descriptors used for any category; they included: "strong," "stern," "firm," "challenging," "with authority," "direct," "candid," "with assertion," and "says exactly what's on her mind."

In expressing fortitude, respondents frequently combined descriptions of strength and assertiveness. Unlike the African American women quoted by Hecht and his co-authors (1989), those in this study did not consider themselves to have been forced by circumstances to adopt a facade of strength. Instead, they constructed fortitude as a desirable quality in women communicators and women's communication. Their descriptions related fortitude to forthrightness ("getting down to the heart of the matter"), seriousness ("in-depth conversation"), sincerity ("meaning everything they say"), and the absence of pretension ("down to earth"). In addition, they often coupled descriptors related to fortitude (e.g., "powerful," "firm," "determined") with descriptors related to self-esteem (e.g., "self-assured," "confident," "speaks with pride and dignity"). The following are typical responses:

> [Black women's talk is the talk of] a strong woman with a lot of pride in who she is and what she believes in.

> [Black women's talk is] talking like you believe in yourself. You are speaking with strength.

> [Black women's talk is] assertive and proud talk.

This dimension of black women's talk is best understood when we keep in mind that it is realized and valued in the context of wisdom. Taken together, the two dimensions indicate that black women value speaking out and speaking strongly, but not without a basis in knowledge and experience. They do *not* value talking loud but saying nothing. In addition, we should not confuse fortitude or strength with dominance, an error that leads to stereotyping black women as domineering and obstreperous. An assertive speaker who conveys strongly held opinions and ideas is not necessarily one who wishes to exert undue control over the conversation, to silence others. My analysis of conversations among black women, between black and white women, and between black women and men demonstrates that black women do not engage in such dominance behaviors as monopolizing talk time, controlling topics, or interrupting more than they are interrupted by their conversational partners (Houston Stanback, 1983; Houston, forthcoming).

Caring

Collins (2000) emphasizes an "ethic of care" as a central element of black feminist epistemology and describes it as most often manifest in the high value placed on personal expressiveness and the interrelationship between cognitive and affective involvement in interaction. Earlier, I noted that the wisdom dimension was one important distinction between the stereotypes of black women's talk and black women's own experience of their talk. Their emphasis on caring is another important distinction. The relationship between expressions of caring and fortitude is illustrated in the following descriptions:

> [Black women's talk] reflects a warmth and sensitivity that is characteristic of their personalities; since they have to face so much in this society they are more nurturing to their families and husbands; caring.

> [Black women] will tell the truth if asked, even if it hurts (provided it's for the better).

The second response emphasizes the context-sensitive nature of black women's forthright speech. In contrast to whites who eschew confrontational talk (Foeman & Pressley, 1987), black women perceive forthrightness as caring, supportive discourse in some contexts, "if asked . . . [and] provided it's for the better." Most descriptors of the caring dimension of black women's talk were embedded in lists or narratives describing the other two dimensions as well; descriptors respondents frequently used were "concerned," "compassionate," "sensitive," "warm," and "humanistic."

Summary

Despite a discourse environment rife with racist and sexist stereotypes of their communication, both within and outside their own social group, most of the African-American women in my study constructed an alternative, self-affirming, celebratory vision of their talk that emphasizes speaking knowledgeably, assertively, and sensitively. This majority perspective stresses the social and interpersonal goals and strategies of talk. While the linguistic style-switching entailed in the accommodation perspective is dependent on socio-economic class and/or education (Seymour & Seymour, 1979; Nelson, 1990), the features of talk emphasized in the celebratory perspective are not necessarily linked to class or educational status. Further research is needed to determine whether the speaking perspectives of African American working class women are similar to those of the middle class (and aspiring middle class) women in this study, as well as whether there are class-related differences in African American women's ways of *expressing* wisdom, fortitude, and caring in interpersonal interactions.

Conclusion

Throughout their history in the United States, African American women have actively constructed alternative definitions of themselves and their behavior that defied the derogatory judgments of their intellectual abilities and, disproved the pejorative stereotypes of their moral character promulgated by the dominant culture (Collins, 2000; Guy-Sheftall, 1995). In this discussion, I have described evasion, accommodation, and celebration as three perspectives taken by African American women in describing their talk. Admittedly, speaking perspectives tell us how individuals think about talk, but not how

they use language in actual communication interactions. Yet they provide vital information about the communication behaviors speakers value and expect. In addition, perspectives suggest key elements of the frames speakers use to interpret talk.

The heterogeneity of African American women's lived experiences, suggested by the concepts "multiple jeopardy" and "multiple consciousness" (King, 1988), is reflected in the contrasting perspectives on their talk described in this discussion. Although a majority expressed the celebratory perspective, focusing on wisdom, fortitude, and caring as desirable features of their interpersonal style, a few chose to describe their talk as accommodating the language and communication demands of both the ethnic and dominant cultures, and others evaded the task of offering a specific description. Each of these ways of conceiving their talk demonstrated the respondent's struggle to positively construct her voice in the midst of a discourse environment that continues to disparage speech and speakers marked as black *and* woman.

Discussion Questions

1. Compare and contrast *multiple jeopardy* with *multiple consciousness*.

2. According to Houston, how is *Black Women's Talk* similar to the discourse of other women? Also, how is it culturally distinctive?

3. How have mass mediated images of Black women been negatively coded?

4. In what way can Black women's talk be considered accommodative?

5. What is meant by *an ethic of caring* and how is this exemplified in Black women's talk?

Reading 4.2

CROSSING CULTURAL BORDERS

"Girl" and "Look" as Markers of Identity in Black Women's Language Use

KARLA D. SCOTT

As noted by Black feminist theorists (Collins, 1991; hooks, 1981, 1989) an identity as Black and female is influenced by the interlocking nature of race, gender and class. However, issues of race and class have been virtually ignored in studies of women's communication (Carter and Spitzack, 1989; Ganguly, 1992: Houston, 1992; Rakow, 1992). Of particular interest to communication research is how the struggle to survive in contradictory worlds and multiple identities involves Black women's communicative behavior.

Those who inhabit multiple realities are forced to live in the spaces, places and positions in between categories and identities resulting in the consciousness of the borderlands (Anzuldua, 1987). Life in the borderlands requires the constant negotiation of identities across the borders that separate groups. Unfortunately, little research has been done in the area of Black women's communication practices, so it is difficult to even begin to conceptualize or discuss

the ways in which Black women use language, given that in everyday life they often cross the cultural borders of race, gender and (for many, if not most, Black women) class. The role of language in border crossings is the focus of this study, which examines the use of two words—"girl" and "look"—as markers of social distance in the talk of a group of Black women.

BLACK WOMEN'S LANGUAGE USE

The literature on Black language behavior largely neglects the unique communicative experiences of Black women. They early work of Claudia Mitchell–Kernan (1971) and Martha Ward (1971) on Black women and children's language is often overlooked in discussions of language within the Black community, where the focus often remains centered on male-dominated language performance studies conducted more than two decades ago (Kochman, 1972;

From Scott, K. (2000). Crossing cultural borders: "Girl" and "look" as markers of identity in Black women's language use. *Discourse and Society, 11*, 237-248.

Labov, 1970, 1972). Although the loud talking, signifying and marking identified by Mitchell-Kernan contain aspects of performance, they are rarely attributed to Black women. Largely overlooked as well is Abraham's (1976) study of Black women's presentation and maintenance of respect through communicative behavior, which also reveals the proficiency of Black women in verbal performance. That this omission has been sustained for so long is perplexing given that, as Marcyliena Morgan (1991) notes, studies of Black women's language behavior are imperative since it is Black women who are responsible for the language development of the children and ultimately of the community as a whole.

In more contemporary studies Black feminist scholars have drawn attention to the unique status of Black women as communicators. Marsha Houston's early groundbreaking work incorporates the impact of larger social structures on the gives of Black women, and of their language use, which is often characterized as assertive and outspoken (Houston Stanback, 1983). Such a description is counter to most characterizations of women's language, which is often described as more collaborative than men's, and focused on relationship maintenance (Kramarae, 1981). Houston takes up this discrepancy in her work on codeswitching where she argues that 'call and response,' identified as a distinct feature of Black women's communication, contains a similar nurturing characteristic associated with women's speech (Houston Stanback, 1983).

Such differences in Black and White women's language behavior can be attributed to the 'place' of Black women in larger society. Houston notes that the typical Black woman has a more complex communicative repertoire than the typical White woman, due to the history of Black women in roles both in and out of the home. This repertoire is displayed during interaction with White women, where Black women report that they used fewer features of Black Vernacular English when talking with White women in order to make conversations successful (Houston, 1985). In a challenge to further understanding the complex communicative behavior of Black women, Houston asserts:

Making women's ethnic culture the central organizing concept for feminist theory and research

means thinking of women as enculturated to a gendered communication ideal *within* specific ethnic groups, that is, learning how they should communicate as women in the context of a particular ethnic experience. (Houston, 1992, p. 53)

Recognizing the relationship of social context and language, studies of Black middle-class women illustrate the role of language in the negotiation of identity. Social and professional contexts require the incorporation of new norms and practices which include language behavior However, as the work of Gwendolyn Etter-Lewis (1993) reveals, many Black women maintain identification with cultural norms and practices of the Black community in the pursuit and attainment of professional and economic advancement. As a result of movement across social and cultural roles, language becomes a vehicle for marking identity in those various worlds.

Michele Foster's (1995) study of Black women teachers suggests that codeswitching as a 'deliberate and systematic practice intended to express the speakers' identities and influenced by the social relationships between participants' (p. 346) is an expression of solidarity and shared identity. Linda Nelson (1990) found that code switches from Standard English to Black English Vernacular 'mark the utterance with profundity or authority or indicate the narrator's solidarity with the elicitor' (p. 143). Making the connection of language and cultural identity even more explicit, she refers to one of her participants, who pointed out 'that "in order to talk about Black cultural experience" she needs the language created out of that experience, as opposed to the power code.'

In a discussion of Black women's discourse, Van Dijk et al. (1997) argue that cultural identities are 'expressed and reproduced by text and talk' (p. 145). The five discursive practices of Black women used for analysis include a discussion of the culturally-toned diminutive 'girl,' described by the authors as a 'highly visible, popular word used . . . to show solidarity and bridge social distance even when the females engaged in conversation are strangers' (p. 154). That "girl" continues to be used by Black women across ages, in both private and public contexts, indicates the importance of making shared identity through language.

Examining shared identity in text and talk is the focus of the present study. More specifically, it attempts to understand more about those language choices which Black women identify as being markers of identity, and what the strategies to employ such choices reveal about the shared identity of the speakers.

DATA COLLECTION AND ANALYSIS

The portions of talk presented and discussed in this study were produced by nine Black women attending undergraduate school in a large and predominantly White university in the midwestern United States. The ages of the participants who were attending sophomore, junior or senior classes in a variety of majors, ranged from 19 to 21 years. All participants were reared in the Midwest. One women was from a small college town she described as 'racially mixed.' Three of the women were from a suburban area of a large metropolitan area which they described as 'racially and culturally diverse.' Three participants identified their urban neighborhoods as 'all Black,' and one woman described her neighborhood as 'predominantly White.' When asked during individual interviews to describe their neighborhoods and their family socio-economic status, all of the women designated themselves as middle class.[1]

Data collection included 9 months of participant observation and interviews. Initial contact with participants was made during several residence hall social gatherings, and interaction in two undergraduate classes. Following several months of social interaction each woman was approached individually and asked about her interest in participating in a study about Black women's talk.

Semi-structured interviews were used to generate talk about the women's language use in everyday lived experiences. Initial individual interviews were held with each of the women. Three of the nine women only participated in the individual interviews. The remaining six also participated in two small group interviews, with three women in each group. The group interviews, designed to generate instances of talk among the women, were held within one week of the individual interviews.

During the individual and group interviews the women responded to questions pertaining to characterizations of Black women's talk. Both types of interview included similar questions, through the group schedule contained questions designed to elicit more examples from the women. The women were asked to define, identify and give examples of what they perceived to be a form of talk and language use that is often considered to be distinct to Black women. Individual interviews lasted an average of one hour. The two group interviews were both approximately 90 minutes.

Extra effort was taken to minimize the power dynamics in the interview, and to foster trust. Interviews were held in dormitory rooms, dormitory lounges or dining halls, all places familiar to the participants. In addition the researcher shared stories of language use and experiences at the university, and about being Black and female. A total of 20 hours of talk was generated during the interviews, all of which were recorded.

Each audiotaped interview was transcribed in its entirety. Analysis of audiotaped talk included many of the prosodic notations of conversation analysis (Heritage, 1984) to indicate characteristics of talk, but transcriptions were not to the microanalytic detail level of conversational analysis (Appendix A). During transcription, attention was given to changes and variations in prosody focusing on changes in register, pitch, and intonation. Though transcripts revealed linguistic variables of Black English Vernacular, such as morphology and syntax, the focus of analysis remains on prosodic cues and lexical items occurring in the talk.

RESULTS

Comparative analysis of the audiotaped talk reveals changes in prosody and the use of formulaic speech as contextualization cues used to signal change in the language of the women during interviews. The marking of identity with culturally-specific contextualization cues occurs in two forms: prosodic cues and formulaic speech (Hansell and Ajirotutu, 1982). Prosodic cues, concerned with rhythmical stress placement and intonation patterns, have three distinct forms: the shift of pitch register, a change in voice quality, and voice tensing, such as the use of falsetto or other forms of paralanguage. Prosodic cues can also be signaled through a marked use of vowel lengthening. Formulaic speech is more metaphorical, and occurs in context-bound situations where specific cultural knowledge is required for reference and understanding. Formulaic speech is often marked by a 'quotational style,' in which the speaker's voice quality further signals intent (Hansell and Ajirotutu, 1982, p. 86).

Analysis further reveals a pattern in the use of two particular words–"girl" and "look"–as discourse markers of a switch to another style of talk. As will be shown in the following discussion, both words are used consistently by the women prior to a switch in language style in both group and interview responses. The instances of the use of "girl" and "look" are included in larger portions of conversational interaction, or in the women's responses, in order to provide a context for the utterances. In the transcriptions talk which occurs following a contextualization cue signaling a switch in language style is underlined.

The Use of "Girl" as a Discourse Marker

The use of the word "girl" as a discourse marker in this study occurred a total of 40 times, both as reported speech and in actual discussions among the women during the audiotaped interviews. Regardless of whether it was reported or actual talk, the use of "girl" by the participants was always followed by a change in speech register that was identified by coders as different from the speech preceding it. Each of the women used "girl" in this way at least once, and some used it more than once. There are three distinct areas in which the use and subsequent switch occurred: 1) in discourse about differences between Black and White women's language use; 2) in discourse about being with other Black women, and 3) in uses of "girl" as a marker in discourse among participants during the interview.

When describing their perceived differences between the language use of Black and White women, respondents used "girl" as a discourse marker that signaled a switch in language style. The following examples are offered as representations of instances in which this occurred.

(1)

Andrea: Yeah you have to kind of censor yourself.

Mary: Be nice to them.

I : And how do you say it with the sisters?

Andrea: That is not cute, don't do it, I mean you can be blunt and say, *Girl don't do it.*
Mary: You can say, *Girl what's wrong with you? Don't even go there.*

Andrea: *Girl I don't care what you say.* ((laughter))

(2)

Mary: Well I think with White women they try to be polite or you know, it doesn't have anything behind it. It's like you know. ((lower volume, higher pitch)) "How are you dededede,'" It's nothing. But with Black women it's like a message, it's like, *Girl hey what's up?*, it's like friendliness, *Girl what's up? how you doing?*

In the following instances girl is used as a marker when the participants discussed their characteristic way of talking and using language when they are with their 'girls' who are described as the other Black women who are close friends or someone who they believe shares their cultural experience

(3)

Janice: Everytime I say, I say, "Hey Yvonne how you doin?" she's like "Gl:: rl let me tell you" you know. And she always tells me cause I know, like, I never say fine thank you I'm always like "Oh Lord I wish I wasn't here."

(4)

Laura: It's such entertainment for them they LOVE IT. Cause I can go to my [White] boss and I can say, ((lower volume, higher pitch)) "Ella should I do this this way should I organize this this way?" And five minutes later [to Black co-worker who is a close friend] *Gl: rl let me tell you what he said to me dadadada and she [White boss] looks at me like I have a split personality, honestly and she's like* ((lower volume, higher pitch)), "Wow Laura I didn't even know you were like that."

In the following excerpts Mary provides multiple instances of how "girl" is used prior to style switching when discussing interactions with other Black women at the university, and in her explanation of what it means to her to have other Black women to talk to in a predominantly White university:

(5)

Cause when you're around Black people they will keep you where you belong on the ground like, you know, "Girl please who you think you trying to be?" You kind of leave thinking you all that and you come back and they're like "I don't THINK so, who told you that? Somebody been lying to you."

(6)

Mary: It's uhm, comforting when you sit down and talk to someone who knows exactly where you're coming from. It's like, "yeah somebody understands me." It feels good to have somebody understand you and where you're coming from and when you're talking to them you don't have to explain everything you're saying and they're like. "But I don't understand." You can say, ((sucks teeth)) *"Gi: rl I had a rough day." "gi: rl I know exactly what you mean," "gi: rl my boyfriend"* and she's like, *"girl I know, I know exactly you're like, "Mama know girl, Mama know."*

While "girl" was used most often in instances of the women's reported and constructed speech, it also occurred in actual talk among interview participants. The first instance occurs in one of the small group interviews, as the three women are struggling to find words to describe what they consider a primary difference in the way Whites and Blacks use language:

(7)

Janice: There's a vibe you get,

Laura: A, a Black

Janice: That vibe you get

Laura: Yes, yes, ((laughter and hand slapping)) *GIRL, GIRL I'm not sure what.*

Janice: But it's that vibe

Laura: *YOU KNOW what I'm talking about.*

In the next instance Mary uses "girl" as she talks with two other interviewees, describing an incident in class where a White student was confronted by another Black woman in the class about his perception of Blacks:

(8)

Mary: Do you want to be poor? You think you wake up in the morning. "Oh let's have eight kids and let's be poor?" He was like, "I guess so." And she [the other Black woman in class] was like–you know, *Gi.:rl, she was about to get up and just smack him cause it was so stupid* ((laughter)).

The previous instances of "girl" as a discourse marker are provided as evidence that a switch in language style occurs in both the reported and naturally occurring talk of the women in this study There are no times in these interviews when "girl" is not followed by a change in prosody. This switch includes rhythmical stress placement and marked intonation patterns. This type of switch involves a culturally-specific contextualization cue, which still allows the one who switches to embed an in-group message and signal identity.

"LOOK" AS A DISCOURSE MARKER

In this study the word look was also used as a marker preceding a switch in style of talk. Each of the women used "look" in this way at least once, and some more than once. There were a total of 36 instances of "look" used as a discourse marker in reported speech.

The instances of "look" used preceding a switch occurred exclusively in three areas of the interviews: (1) in discussions and descriptions of talking like a Black woman versus White women's talk, (2) in the women's reports of interactions with Whites, both male and female, and (3) in the women's reports of interactions with

Black men. The first set of examples illustrates the use of "look" when the discussion centered on what the women perceived to be characteristics of Black women's ways of using language.

(1)

Mary: What do you want me to say ((lower volume, higher pitch)) "Oh dear, you're getting on my nerves" ((sucks teeth)) it's like *"Look, you're bothering me and I'm tired of you..."*... She's a calm person like, ((lower volume, higher pitch)) "Well I think maybe." I'm like, *"Look, you're bothering me and I'm tired so leave me alone."*

(2)

Andrea: [I]t's automatic, it's automatic. It's like, *"Look,"* *That's how people know you mean business.*... Like I was saying, in my meetings I may be speaking, you know, and all of a sudden somebody says something really dumb or something that is non-relevant and I'm just like, *"Look what is the problem with you, you know, are we on this subject or are we on this subject, you know what's the prob...?"* It's incredible the reaction you get.

In the next instances, Mary uses "look" in her discussion of interactions with Black men, which focuses on 'reading' a man. The women described this term as a way of telling a man very bluntly and directly about problematic areas in his life or in their relationship.

(3)

Mary: I'm like, "Oh no, you don't want to talk to me right now buddy, just let the door swing, just leave." I haven't talked to him in two weeks. Thank God cause I'm like *"Look, I don't have time either you gon be a man or be a boy, make up your mind. Cause I don't have time to wait for you to come to that level cause I'm already there. And when you catch up to me you give me a call."*

(4)

Chandra: Yeah because a Black man will relax when you read him they will relax, *"Look I'm gonna read you right now. What's*

wrong with you get it together or get out." And the Black woman sees it as liberating. They see it as it shows power. I'm like *"look you."* It's a defense mechanism because when we say something like, *"Look I'm not gonna tolerate this OK, I'm just not gonna deal with this."*

(5)

Alison: Right, you have to get on them about everything from head to toe, "Look, the real Black woman." I have, I think that Black women are just naturally, it's a level of respect that we are just due, you know. At least that's what I've seen in my family, that Black women are just due respect.

Instances of "look" also occurred frequently in the women's discussions of attractions with Whites.

(6)

Alison: But a true sister will be able to correlate and put it all together, "Look, you know I'm Black too, and maybe if I changed my language then you'll understand where I'm coming from."

(7)

Kim: Like if I'm talking like this and someone's gonna say. "Well you people" and "I don't understand," then I have to come closer to them, be demonstrative and explain to them, *"Look, you don't understand. In the Black community,"* you know. You raise your voice tone and you have to be very firm with them, especially when you're talking about something you know about and it's a very touchy subject. Anything dealing with Black people to me is a touchy subject, so whenever White people say anything like, I'm always up ((snaps fingers)).

(8)

Alison: When you have to break it down. "Look I'm Black" ... sometimes I want to break it down to TA's [teaching assistants] "Look" you know, in a sisterly way.

Unlike the use of the word 'girl,' all of the instances of the use of "look" recurred in discussions of reported speech. There were no instances of "look" used in actual interview talk among the participants.

DISCUSSION

Code switching encodes the dual identities of a speaker who switches between languages in order to identify with each of the two groups (Scotton, 1990). Underlying this argument is the premise that speakers make the choices they do because they are negotiating interpersonal relationships. The switch the women perform in this study is a switch from a more Standard American spoken speech to what they describe as "talking like a Black women" with distinct prosodic features—a choice that also encodes the dual identities they perceive when crossing cultural borders.

When analyzing the context of the utterances that follow "girl" and 'look,' what becomes apparent is that these two words mark a way of seeing self and other in the context of the inter-action. "Girl" becomes a mark of solidarity when used to discuss how one interacts with other Black women, in particular those who are closest to the speaker. Janice's description of her interaction with a friend illustrates this:

Janice: Every time I say, I say, "Hey Yvonne, how you doin?" she's like "*Gi: : rl, let me tell you,*" you know. And she always tells me cause I know, like, I never say, "fine thank you." I'm always like. "*Oh Lord I wish I wasn't here.*"

Like many of the other instances of 'girl,' Janice's use of the word marks her sense of shared understanding with her friend. The concept of shared understanding lends some comfort to the women, who are participants in a world that they perceive as not being wholly their own. Janice's reported use of "I wish I wasn't here" in response to her Black friend's question as they ride the bus on a predominantly White campus, appears to illustrate the importance of connecting with someone who is like you when cultural borders have been crossed. As the women's responses consistently illustrate, when one is with one's 'girls,' a feeling of comfort is evoked. Mary's description of

importance of comfort and of being understood illustrates the theme of solidarity that was present in many of the women's responses:

Mary: [I]t's uhm, comforting when you sit down and talk to someone who knows exactly where you're coming from. It's like, yea somebody understands me. It feels good to have somebody understand you and where you're coming from, and when you're talking to them you don't have to explain everything.

Just as the word "girl" is used by the women to mark solidarity with another Black woman, and a sense of shared understanding, their use of "look" emerges when they are talking about themselves in relationships with Black men, or in predominantly White situations where they feel a need to distance themselves from the other person in order to call attention to differences in identity, and be recognized.

Alison: Right, you have to get on them about every-thing from head to toe, "*Look, the real Black woman,*" I have, I think that Black women are just naturally, it's a level of respect that we are just due, you know. At least that's what I've seen in my family, that Black women are just due respect.

That same level of respect due is also com-manded through the use of "look" when the women discussed interactions with Whites.

Kim: Like if I'm talking like this and someone's gonna say, "Well you people" and "I don't understand," then I have to come closer to them, be demonstrative and explain to them. "*Look, you don't understand. In the Black community.*" You know you raise your voice tone and you have to be very firm with them, especially when you're talking about some-thing you know about and it's a very touchy subject. Anything dealing with Black people to me is a touchy subject, so whenever White people say anything like, I'm always up ((snaps fingers)).

The use of "look" is of particular importance when discussing interactions in predominantly White environments, where the women in this study have indicated that they don't feel recognized or understood. It appears that this use of "look" then becomes a marker to resist the racelessness that Signithia Fordham (1988, 1991, 1993) says many Blacks encounter when they are in predominantly White environments, particularly educational settings. As Fordham notes in her work, ignoring race might be preferable to the White majority, but it would not satisfy the Black students, who feel a need to retain and even assert identity. In the women's talk in this study, the word "look" appears to distance 'self' from 'the other' in order to call attention to self, and to assert an identity that is different from that of the other person.

CONCLUSION

In this study the words "girl" and "look" are used by the women as they describe their language use across cultural borders. The identification of a pattern in the use and context of these two words appears to indicate the women's shared recognition that in markedly different cultural worlds their language use is connected to identity. In one world, the world shared with other Black women, the word "girl" is used to mark not just identity but also solidarity with other Black women whom they perceive as sharing that same identity, and an understanding of that identity. Their explanations of language behavior offer further insight into why "girl" continues to be a marker of shared identity for Black women.

However, in a world that is predominantly White, in interactions with Black men the women perceive a need to mark identity in a different way. They report that it is when they are in this other world that they feel invisible and raceless. In their responses and reported speech the use of the word "look" illustrates the women's need to assert identity in a world where it is not shared or understood: "look" says 'I am different from you, you don't understand.' As a marker of social distance it functions in the same way as 'girl,' which says 'I am like you and understand.'

As revealed in the text and in the talk of these women, language is perceived as a marker of identity. Empirical studies such as this one offer a better understanding of communicative behavior in the lives of Black women by illuminating the motivations and implications of language use. The findings of this study suggest that these young Black women recognize the multiple worlds in which they live, move and have their being, and understand the critical role that language plays in the negotiation of identities across the cultural borders of those worlds.

Appendix A: Transcript Notations

Transcript notations are a modification of Heritage (1984).

Italics: Italics indicate some form of emphasis, which may be signaled by changes in press through pitch or amplitude.

Lengthening: Colons indicate that the sound just before the colon has been noticeably lengthened. The length of the row of colons indicates the length of the prolongation.

Increased volume: Capitals, except at the beginning of lines, indicate increased volume and loud sounds relative to the surrounding talk.

Comments: Double parentheses enclose material that is not part of the talk being transcribed. For example, a comment by the transcriber if the talk was spoken in some specially. These are the author's descriptions rather than transcriptions.

Punctuation: Punctuation marks are used to indicate intonation rather than grammar. Commas are used to indicate continuing intonation with pauses within portions of talk. Periods are used to indicate a fall in intonation upon completion of a portion of talk, is not necessarily the end of a sentence.

Question mark indicates that a question has been asked.

Discussion Questions

1. What does Scott define as the link between the "borderlands" and Black women's identities?

2. What are prosodic cues and how are they integral to Scott's study?

3. How was "girl" examined as a discourse marker of Black women's identity? (Give two examples.)

4. How was "look" examined as a discourse marker of Black women's identity? (Give two examples.)

5. When does Scott say the Black women in her study feel most like they are "invisible and raceless"?

Reading 4.3

"THAT WAS MY OCCUPATION"

Oral Narrative, Performance,
and Black Feminist Thought

D. Soyini Madison

Oppressed people resist by identifying themselves as subjects, by defining their reality, shaping their new identity, naming their history, telling their story.

—bell hooks
Talking Back: Thinking Feminist, Thinking Black

The voices of women fill most of my childhood memories: gossip, songs, testimonies, lyrical praise, and insults. I remember how these women talked, their voices rising and lowering in colorful tones and rhythms. Sometimes they would speak through cautious whispers and at other times through robust declarations. Sitting together in the kitchen, they told stories to entertain and to survive. These stories were sometimes set in laughter and sometimes in tears, but they never stopped. I remember most clearly the stories my mother told me about how to be a woman, when I should be wary of life and when I should not. Gloria Anzaldúa and Cherríe Moraga have called such stories "theories of the flesh" that "bridge the contradictions of our experience" (23)—those root metaphors that keep us centered and sane.

Theories of the flesh means that the cultural, geopolitical, and economic circumstances of our lives engender particular experiences and epistemologies that provide philosophies about reality different from those available to other groups (Collins, "Social Construction" 300). Particularly for people of color, life lived, whether on the concrete pavement of inner-city streets or in the backwoods of a rural southern community, is the root of our beginnings and the root of our understandings. The early quotidian experiences of the people we knew were our "first sight," and it is through them that we began to name and theorize the world.

Theories of the flesh privilege agency and interrogate notions of the "lethargic masses" or

From Madison, D. S. (1993). "That Was My Occupation": Oral narrative, performance, and Black feminist thought. *Text & Performance Quarterly, 13*(3), 213-232.

"voiceless victims." The question, "Where do theories come from?" is answered by honoring the "extraordinary in the ordinary" indigenous analysis, expressions and meditations of what bell hooks refers to as "homeplace." Speaking specifically of black women, hooks describes homeplace as the "folks who made this life possible." She states:

> Though black women did not self-consciously articulate in written discourse the theoretical principals of decolonization, this does not detract from the importance of their actions. They understood intellectually and intuitively the meaning of homeplace in the midst of an oppressive and dominating social reality, of homeplace as site of resistance and liberation struggle. (*Yearning* 45)

When we speak from theories of the flesh we are speaking from homeplace and, in turn, naming the location from which we come to voice (146).

Theories of the flesh mark black feminists' primary ways of knowing, but the second level of knowledge, what Patricia Hill Collins calls "specialized knowledge" and what hooks calls abstract, critical thought, initiates a balancing act to present alternative ways of producing and validating knowledge (Collins, "Social Construction" 298). I hear these questions from black women consistently across the country: how do my articulations that are wrapped in scholarly theory really represent the collective of black women who speak a different language and to whom I am committed? How do I justify writing about the experiences of black women in academic journals which the majority of my people will never read?

Collins discusses the relationship between black feminist thought and theories of the flesh that reflect the lived realities of the masses of black women: black feminist thought articulates and makes accessible the knowledge and collective philosophy of Black women, but it also creates new epistemologies and creates new dimensions for describing experiences and for liberation" ("Social Construction" 302). Collins's assertions about black feminist thought are congruent with interventionist and post-colonial criticism that advances merging the "text with the world" (Strine 194). However,

cultural criticism has always been part of black artistic and intellectual traditions, as hooks states:

> Cultural criticism has historically functioned in black life as a force promoting critical resistance, one that enabled black folks to cultivate in everyday life a practice of critique and analysis that would disrupt and even deconstruct those cultural productions. That were designed to promote and reinforce domination. (*Yearning* 3)

Collins and hooks are concerned with issues of historical and cultural significance related to the collective of black women and to those with specialized knowledge engaged in interpreting black women's experiences. The conjoining of theories of the flesh and specialized knowledge may be examined in four points made by Collins. First, she contends that the collective of black women telling their stories has carved out from their particular condition unique spaces to interpret and portray their lives that are distinctive in form ("Social Construction" 322). Second, she discusses two levels of thought. At the first level is the everyday taken-for-granted knowledge that is often unreflexive, the nuances of which are often foreign to others, yet ingrained in the language and experiences of the masses of black women. At the second level is the extended and more specialized knowledge furnished by experts who are part of the group—the two levels are interdependent ("Social Construction" 302). Third, Collins asserts that theory and abstract knowledge claims are obligated to the concrete experiences of daily life to be valued and judged (*Black* 26). Finally, she argues that traditional techniques and tools of dominance cannot be used unreflexively and unself-consciously to analyze disenfranchised people (*Black* 34).

Collins's ideas address questions about hierarchies of knowledge, power, and the honoring of tellers' experiences through critical and interpretive frameworks that serve to unite the text with the world. Women, particularly those marginalized by race and social class, create and invent spaces where they depict and interpret their concrete and imagined experiences. Traditional and certain popular techniques of analyses must be critically and self-reflexively extended when applied to the distinctive forms of these women's expressions. In examining these forms and spaces, indigenous thought and practice emanating from the tellers' language, history, and traditions will guide alter, add to, and adjust dominant analyses. In oral narrative analysis two symbol systems (teller and interpreter) are brought together where they each inform the other, but more importantly and unlike the conventional case study approach, the teller's symbol system uses its own theories of itself to tell us what it means (Gates, *signifying Monkey, x*)—it is not only "doing something in culture"; it is engaged in an on going Self-reflexive analyses and critique about what it is doing.

Specialized knowledge then enters to articulate, that is, to translate and unveil extant philosophical systems to those who (without this knowledge) are unable to locate them. While this specialized knowledge centers upon indigenous theory to tell us what it is we are observing as well as what it means, we may choose to go beyond the role of translator to the role of critic (as do Collins and hooks) to create new epistemologies and descriptions of experience and liberation. It is at this point that the teller's experience is illuminated, made accessible and available as an advocacy discourse for social change and/or affirmation. In turn, the theory and specialized knowledge of the interpreter is given greater relevance, legitimacy, clarity, and a larger purpose through the guiding force of human experience.

In the following oral narratives from the life history of Mrs. Alma Kapper, a black woman from Mississippi who worked as a sharecropper and domestic, the indigenous theories that inform her life experiences in the past events of the told (the "said" or narrated event) and the emergent event of the telling ("saying" or narrative event) most poignantly arise from performance traditions.[1] These performance traditions, or theories of the flesh, are then articulated primarily through the specialized knowledge, or scholarly discourse of people of color. As a result, the authority of knowledge, and therefore power, that comes with being a critic is now directed by the formal and informal theories of the cultural subjects themselves. This analytic choice was deliberate, but with no

intention to shut out other perspectives or claim this choice should be the rule. Addressing the marginalization of black scholarship as analysis and critical discourse, particularly regarding issues of culture and difference, hooks states: "It must be remembered that black studies programs have explored issues of race and culture from the moment of their inception," and ". . . it can be disheartening when new programs focusing on similar issues receive a prestige and acclaim denied black studies" (*Yearning* 124–125). My purpose is to make a contribution against the great imbalance of scholarly work that ignores black indigenous and intellectual traditions as critical and theoretical constructs that can guide and determine the analysis of texts and performances.[2]

THE POETIC TRANSCRIPTION APPROACH

Dennis Tedlock writes, "Once the audible text is in hand, there is the question of how to make a visible record of its sounds" (5). With this question in mind, I have recorded the narratives using a poetic form of transcription (Conquergood; Fine; Tedlock). Sound, as well as the literal word, creates the experience of the oral narrative, and in many moments pure sound determines meaning. Mikhail Bakhtin refers to sound as intonation "contaminated by rudimentary social evaluations and orientations" (231). Collins describes the significance of sound: ". . . it is nearly impossible to filter out the strictly linguistic-cognitive abstract meaning [sound]" (319). The poet Etheridge Knight states: "The sounds themselves evoke feelings; that's the way you are touched" (12).[3]

Black people, lettered and unlettered, have traditionally emphasized the sound and rhythm of black language when writing poetry or when recording speech. Locating and representing the range of sounds more than the literal word was "the signifying difference that made the difference," the distinction between how black folks described the world and how others described it (Gates, "Blackness" 47). From the Negritude movement, to the Harlem Renaissance, to the Black Arts Movement of the 1960s, many black artists and scholars did not wholly and consistently embrace European poetry and prose forms but chose to arrange words on a page that reflected the intonation, mood, tone, and rhythm of black speech (Smitherman; Jones [Baraka]). This preoccupation with sound was part of a West African inheritance (Senghor; Harrison; Jahn). In West African cultures, concrete expression was inseparably interwoven with meaning and *rhythm.* "Rhythm activated the word; it was its procreative component; only rhythm gave the word its effective fullness" (Jahn 110). It is *muntu,* the word that lives in *kuntu,* its mode of existence which is rhythm (Jahn 164). Therefore word and rhythm make sound indispensable in understanding the meanings of speech. Without the sound, which in West African cosmology is the rhythm, the identifying context with its social and historical distinctions becomes opaque and the "signifying difference that makes the difference" loses its profundity.

My choice in using a poetic text is consistent with the black tradition of acknowledging that words are alive with sounds that condition their meanings. By placing words on a page to resemble the rhythm of the human voice and the speaker as a social-historical being that colors each word based on that existential fact, the text comes closer in capturing the depth inherent in the indigenous performance of black speech. In the next section I present poetic transcriptions of four episodes from the oral narrative of Mrs. Alma Kapper and analyze their theories of the flesh using insights of black feminist thought and the performance paradigm.

THE ORAL NARRATIVE OF MRS. ALMA KAPPER

Mrs. Alma Kapper was born in a small town in the black belt of Mississippi at the turn of the century. Delivered by a midwife and having no birth records that she could remember, she believes she is in her mid-eighties.[4] Most of her life has been spent working as a sharecropper and domestic worker. She is a widow, but she demanded that her abusive husband leave the house and never see her again many years before his death. Later, when she began having problems with her eyes, she moved to Chicago, Illinois, to live with her brother and his family.

Glaucoma has caused partial blindness in both eyes.

I met Mrs. Kapper while doing field work at a social agency in Chicago; one of the programs was the senior citizen daycare center where I spent six months interacting with the elders. Arriving in the morning, I would spend the time singing with them their favorite songs, role playing, and enacting memories and characters from their past. Although there were several extraordinary people that I had met, I was drawn to Mrs. Kapper's flamboyant spirit, her quick wit, and the experiences of her life as a sharecropper.

Mrs. Kapper and I worked together on her oral narrative in the afternoons after all the formal sessions were over. The interviews took place in what we called "our private room" which was located down the hall from the seniors' activity room; it was quiet there and we could be alone and undisturbed. The episodes included in this article are taken from various sections of the complete oral narrative. On the days these episodes were recorded, Mrs. Kapper was sitting in a very large old chair next to the open window like she did just about everyday. She said that was her "place" because she could hear the birds, listen to the children playing, and feel the warmth of the spring sun against her face. I could only see a trace of Mrs. Kapper's eyes behind her large, dark glasses. Unlike her hands that worked Mississippi fields and kitchens, her face and body seemed untouched by decades of labor and struggle. Her face is small, smooth, and delicate; her body is thin and quick. About 115 pounds and about 5′5″ tall, she wears a curly black wig that frames shiny thread-like waves around her caramel colored complexion.

As she sat in the chair in her cotton skirt and blouse that always appeared freshly ironed with sharp creases at the sleeves and pleats, she was turned slightly toward me with both hands resting on the straps of her handbag. Mrs. Kapper wore her handbag around her neck because she felt that wearing it in this way assured her that her "blessings" would not be disturbed by the "thieving" hands of others. The previous week we had talked about her family and her extended family, and how she felt so secure in their love. I asked her if she could tell me about a time or a particular incident in her childhood when she remembered feeling this love, a time she could not forget.

"The WORD Spoke To Me"[5]

Member one day
it twas ah Sat'day
all the other chil'ren went off tuh play
well
I was on the porch by myse'f
I was jus' stittin' on the porch
Mama was in the bed
I thought 'bout all I did
wokin' in the fiel'
takin' care ah Mama an' all lika that
an' all the res' ah the chil'ren
goin' off havin' fun on Sat'day
so I say "I caint go/I caint go!!!"
||Jus' talkin' tuh myse'f||
an'
(sits up in her seat straight and tall)
the WORD spoke tuh me
the WORD say
GO WHEN YO' CAIN AN' WHEN YA'
CAINT
MAKE YO'SE'F SATISFIED!!
that was the spirit talkin' tuh/me
(she spoke with great confidence)
Make yo'se'f satisfied!!
An I got pleased right then
an' I never did get worried no mo'
and that next Sunday . . . the folks started
comin'
an' lettin' me go.
That's the honest truth!
(she leans into me and turns her head)
See that was the Lawd spoke tuh me
(Points her finger)
he tol' meh that
MAKE YO'SE'F SATISFIED
GO WHEN YO' CAIN
AND WHEN YO' CAINT
MAKE YO'SE'F SATISFIED.
And it fell off ah me
jus' lika that.
(brushes her hands back)
I go pleased an' happy
right then.
(points her finger in my direction)
That nex' Sunday evenin'

our door-neighbor came by an' ass' me
wouldn' I like tuh go tuh church that
evenin'
I say "yes Mam if I could?"
she say
I'll sit wit yo' mutha' sos you can go tuh church
I say "yes Mam I'll go."
From then on the peoples started
comin' an lettin' me go.
(she speaks very slowly and leans back)
I think that was mighty fine__.

As Mrs. Kapper begins speaking, her demeanor is stately and authoritative; her back is tall and straight against the chair; her hands are clasped together on her lap, and it appears as though she is looking directly at me through her dark glasses. Her voice is confident and controlling, yet tender like a mother about to teach an important life lesson to her child. She continues to speak with gentle authority until she says "the WORD spoke to me," and at this point her confidence rises into gestures and expressions of joy and excitement. As she speaks of the "Lawd" she leans over toward me, smiling big and bright. She points her finger and waves her hands, her head moving back and forth to the rising pitch and volume of her voice. She is having a good time, and the whole room is full of the joyful presence of Mrs. Kapper. On the last line, "I think that was mighty fine__," as she leans back against her seat, her voice and gesture begin to soften and slowly quiet down. Mrs. Kapper has performed a memory, an experience from her past, that brings to light the tradition of black women and the "ethics of caring" ("Social" Collins 318).

In the narrative of young Alma, homeplace as a site of resistance is manifest in her dedication to her mother. It was her mother who was the guide and teacher for what it meant to be human, to resist, and to live life. For young Alma, the mother and extended-mothers were the carriers of culture and the caretakers, but they were also the examples of lives based upon invention. Under the poverty and inequity of a sharecropping system in the black belt of Mississippi, it was the mother as the initial protector, the first source of knowing and the primary architect of identity who profoundly shaped the inventiveness and creativity required not only to survive but to construct a personhood and create a community. The young Alma, in the tradition of women as caretakers and as managers of homeplace, assumes her position in domesticity and becomes simultaneously mother and daughter to her own mother. Moreover, as nurturer-creator, she assumes her position within the network of extended-mothers that will come to her aid allowing her to further conjoin the woman-centered environment of the black church.

The moment on the porch is both a revelation and a transcendence of faith that draws from black gospel tradition and the traditional West African philosophy of *nommo*—*nommo* meaning the power of the word to create or bring into existence all entities, to set forth the "generative power of the community" (Asante, 48) and to transcend the physical world (Harrison). Framing young Alma's experience on the porch as gospel emanating from African and African-American traditions is a way of getting at that which is both ordinary and extraordinary about it.

For the young Alma, her revelation was unforgettable. She passed from one life experience into another through a performative act of speech or *nommo* that evoked communitas (Turner), celebration, and transformation. It all begins with a young girl alone and in despair sitting on a porch who breaks the silence of the summer night by naming her feelings and giving voice to the dilemma of being a child but having to live as an adult. Her feelings are materialized in the voice, words, and sound of a young girl calling out in the night. The ceremony takes shape and enters African and African-American performance tradition when the call, ironically spoken to herself, is met with a response. The act of speaking, motivated by a young girl's need and desire, culminates in breath and voice that is then heard by greater powers, greater than the nature of the problem itself. But for her to know that she had been heard there must be a sign, and the sign came back to her in voice, in words that she in turn heard. Through *nommo,* the call was served by the response. Through the dialogue of faith in the gospel tradition, when word evokes word and question evokes answer, a transformation takes place, and this transformation is always joyous (Wilmore; Edit; McIntyre).

In black gospel tradition as in the concept of *nommo,* the divine answer brings transformation that is manifested by an uplifted spirit, a celebration in knowing that the existential call brought forth one of the most human and most desired needs, a response. In addition to transformation and spiritual uplift, gospel performance and *nommo* affect and alter the situation of the real world. When Alma hears "the word" it speaks specifically to her, directing her in reconciling her material conditions. The gospel does not transform the spirit without a connection to the reality of the caller. The call is motivated by this reality and the divine response is believed to affect that reality. When this power beyond all powers instructs, this is the guidance that affects the life world, "an" 'I nevah did get worried no mo."[6]

But in order for there actually to be an impact on existence, the gospel must have another moment—the communal moment. We observe this moment in Alma's narrative when she says "an' the folks started comin' an' lettin' me go." When the young Alma set the gospel and *nommo* in motion through her call that night on the porch, it would follow that the community would be the major factor in Alma's transformation by solving her problem of loneliness and confinement, as well as by initiating the direction of her spiritual enlightenment. The community "folks came" in keeping with African and African-American tradition, for there can be no transformation and no healing without their initiatives, guidance, and affirmation. This communal coming forth reflects the West African saying "I am because we are, and we are because I am."[7]

When the joy came to lighten Mrs. Kapper's burdens, it was simultaneously a moment of community; the "spirit" and the "folks" conjoined as the force that transformed Mrs. Kapper's life and soul: "got pleased and happy right then." However, the gospel performance in Mrs. Kapper's narrative does not conclude with her going out on Saturday nights playing with other children, but going to church every Sunday. It is going to church that becomes the resolution of this gospel on the porch—the house of the divine spirit, and where community is not only brought together but where the very nature of the coming together is a celebration.

As profound as the tradition may be with its sustained impact upon black life, can the charges that the black gospel tradition has historically impeded empowerment and promoted passivity among the masses of black people be ignored? Social critics are disposed to point out the ways that structures of power operate, are sustained, dismantled, and disguised (Wallace; B. Smith; V. Smith). Black feminists also interrogate styles and structures that reinscribe oppression (Ladner; Christian; Davis). When Alma enacts the gospel motif and the word comes, "Make yo'se'f satisfied/Go when yo' cain/and when yo' caint/make yo'se'f satisfied," is it suggestive of Christian complacency? Is the contented church-goer passive to social injustice, believing that "God will find a way?" Critics of the tradition have argued that when the oppressed are at the brink of despair or outrage over their condition, this moment has the potential for the greatest consciousness, and as a result, the chance for greatest resistance against the exploitative forces. Instead, some argue, it becomes a moment of acceptance, of inaction, and of passivity when the call to a mystical force directs the oppressed to divert their salvation away from the struggle for empowerment and liberation in the material world. When this happens they strengthen the very forces of their oppression.

History has revealed the gospel tradition to be a complex and contradictory phenomenon in the way it impacts upon the values, beliefs, and experiences of black people. When gospel is simply labeled "counter-revolutionary" or supportive of a form of Christian complacency, how does one account for Fannie Lou Hamer, Ella Baker or Amy Jacques-Garvey, to name a few? The gospel tradition has contributed both to liberation and to reinscribing oppression. Therefore, it cannot be solely examined by theories based on political economy, defining human action purely in terms of power stratifications, that do not consider the feeling-sensing ambivalence of daily living. Nor can it be examined by a social theology that ignores or undermines these experiences. The cultural critic Cornel West, describing himself as a "non-Marxist socialist," points to Christian tradition and Marxist theory in terms of the relevance of these discourses in the daily lives of black people:

My Christian perspective—mediated by the rich traditions of the Black Church that produced and sustains me—embraces depths of despair, layers of dread, encounters with the sheer absurdity of the human condition, and ungrounded leaps of faith alien to the Marxist tradition. (xxvii)

What concerns West is not that the Marxist tradition is Eurocentric, but that it is "silent about the existential meaning of death, suffering, love, and friendship owing to its preoccupation with improving the social circumstances under which people pursue love, revel in friendship, and confront death" (xxvii).

The gospel tradition remains a contradiction simultaneously profound, beautiful, regressive, confusing, and liberating. For Alma Kapper, gospel evoked both peaceful compliance, "MAKE YO'SE'F SATISFIED," as well as the inspired volition to move beyond her mother's house and interact with the larger community. Gospel is consistent only in that it has always been present within African-American culture be it on a slave plantation, at a rock concert, or over seventy years ago as the young Alma calls out in the night on her porch in Mississippi.

"Few of Them Livin'"

The following episode was recorded the same day. Further on in the narrative Mrs. Kapper mentioned the absence of white children from the "colored schools." She then described how the white children went to school every day for longer hours and through most of the year, while the "colored" children were only allowed to attend school for a much shorter time because they had to work in the fields. As she spoke about the white children "knowing everything," she quickly defined this knowing as "scheming." She was adamant as she described how the parents of these children taught them, at an early age, the custom of scheming against the sharecroppers. In the excerpt below Mrs. Kapper describes an encounter with the landowner.

> Selling they cotton an' stuff.
> ||When they sell ah bail of cotton
> (whispering)
> ya' nevah would know what they get ah pound
> fo' it!||

||An' when they come back wit the ticket . . .
they say "well_ we_ couldn'_ get_ but_
35 cents_ fo'_ it_ ah_ pound_ this_ time_ "||
He got that deed ticket
but ya' would nevah know it
an' if he say
he didn't get no mo' than that fo' the nex' bail
he sol'
he would settle wit ya' fo' that 35 cents ah
pound
he keep those big tickets an' ya' would nevah
know it!
An ah tol' one ah them that once!
ah sho' did!
he say "Alma who tol' ya' all that"
I say I got sense enough tuh know it myse'f
nobody tol' me nothin'!!
They cheat the peoples
(very cautiously, very quietly)
I don' wont them tuh/do nothin' tuh me now
them that's livin'
(whispering)
||few of them livin'||
they souf' people but some of them
livin'
I don' wont them tuh do nothin' tuh meh.
no jus' in the souf
they was all doin' it
every which-a-way
'cause they didn' have nothin'
the colored people I mean
they didn't have nothin'
they couldn' live off the grass

In this episode Mrs. Kapper recounts how the landowner cheated the workers by misrepresenting the price of the deed ticket. She presents an interesting tension and contrast—the two contrasting performance modes in the simultaneous enactments of the telling and the told. She is forthright and bold in confronting the landowner within the told, or narrated event. She breaks through what is implied as the accustomed silence of the sharecropper, and then she bravely and proudly confronts the fraud: "An' ah tol' one ah them that once!/ah sho' did!" Her eyes widen and they appear stern and piercing with anger; her courage diminishes the aura of the exploitative landowner. In contrast to Mrs. Kapper's performance mode within the told experience of fieldworker and landowner,

in the telling, or narrative event, she speaks in a cautious whisper as if the landowner were some omnipotent force transcending space and time hearing her as she spoke to me miles away in a little room in the senior citizen daycare center. She whispers cautiously and contemptuously almost every word of this episode. The years of resentment and fear embodied in her voice were present at this performative moment whispering at points where I could barely hear. The fear and disdain for the landowner, projected in performance, marked a change in what had been her performance mode up to this point from a strong projected movement and voice to a contained, tense, almost rigid body and voice.

The performance encompassing the sensibility of the sharecropper talking to the landowner in the told, and the performance encompassing the sensibility of Mrs. Kapper talking to me in the telling, dramatically overlaid one another; they exemplify different realities, and we can observe here the importance of not isolating the performative representation of either, nor of reducing the representation to one mode or the other. To record only the words of this episode, focusing on the told as representative of Mrs. Kapper's personal experience without including the performance dynamic of her whispers and gesture in the telling, would render a misleading account.

This episode also reflects the function of storytelling as an empowering act. Since in the story-world we are in control of who we are and of what happens to us, in this world of our own design we may be queens, warriors, poets, or unafraid of white folks. Mrs. Kapper's performance in the told conveys her opposition to the landowner; she is implicitly boasting in the told. But we understand the boasting presented in the told is contradictory to her persona in the telling. Nevertheless, the tensions between Mrs. Kapper's telling and her told illuminate a broader performance tradition in African-American culture, a tradition where the contradictions and tensions in performance were a matter of survival—the "mask," or presentation of self, constructed for white people.

When literature, history, and contemporary experience demonstrate the roles black people perform for the benefit of whites—ranging from the obsequious Uncle Tom, the happy, harmless

Negro, the dignified stoic, the lascivious whore or buck, the refined intellectual, the frightful street hood, and the uncompromising black militant—we see these types have traditionally been played out for a variety of purposes: to achieve certain ends or gains, for protection and security, or because performing them was the only effective or acceptable way to be seen and heard. We may argue they are more than performances for white people; they are social behaviors, internalized and sometimes unconscious, enacted throughout black life whether whites are present or not. To say they are "genuine" social behaviors, or traditional performances consciously and deliberately constructed for white people, or simply stereotypes is consistent, on all three counts, with the ways these types (and others) are played out in black history and culture.

However we choose to focus on the dynamics of these types, Mrs. Kapper's narrative specifically addresses the complexity involved in the presentation of a "black self" before a hostile and untrustworthy, white, dominating presence. Because this dominating and untrustworthy presence required blacks to perform certain roles in their encounters with whites, these performances were a source of shame. To repress the will and the dignity of personhood in order to perform a role complicitious with oppressive forces was at times an act of cunning and clever guile; however, when performed out of fear and powerlessness it brought feelings of disgust and resentment. In the latter case, it may be understood in the black community as something black folks do from time to time, but the dishonor does not disappear. As a result, stories abound about getting back at, getting over on, and telling off white folks. If one cannot indulge the performance through cunning or by reversing control so the dominating presence becomes the butt or fool of your pretense, then there is another alternative. One can reconstruct the event and aim to claim dignity in a story. It is in this meta-performance, the performance of the performance, where one might finally get satisfaction.

Mrs. Kapper's performance in the told presented the brave woman who stood up for herself and others against the oppressive landowner. It was this boast within the told that strained against the years of fear and resentment manifested in the whispered telling. The two performances are evident in Mrs. Kapper's narrative: she tells off the land owner, "sho' did!" and at the same time—after more than 60 years, a distance of thousands of miles, in the safety of a public daycare program and in the privacy of our little room behind closed doors—she still felt she had to whisper.

"My Mutha Had Ah Time"

This excerpt was recorded the following day. Mrs. Kapper had arrived early and was alone in our room sitting next to the open window humming "Amazing Grace." I walked over to her and said hello. She smiled and said she wanted to talk about her mother, and she wanted to share a family story concerning her mother and a black farmer. She is sitting with her hands resting on her purse during this entire section; there is only an occasional move of her head.

My mutha had ah time
My older sista' tol' me
Mama had ah hard time
she say Mama was stayin' wit one colored man
he bring her
5 pounds ah lard each mont
5 pounds ah meal
|what else she say he give her|
I didn't' member
Mama got so po' till she jus' couldn' hardly walk
she say she an' my olda' brotha' would go out there in the fiel'
an' be so glad when the peach tree start tuh comin'
an' the peaches start tuh fallen
they go out there an' eat them half green peaches
an' they would pick them peas
an' carry them home an' put them in salt an' wata'
an' they was staying wit colored people too
my sister say that man give his chil'ren ah ear ah co'n
that man was about tuh starve my Mama tuh deaf.
Jus' give his chil'ren ah ear ah co'n.
An' his wife would get up an' fry ham
an'

make coffee an' eat that good ol' ham an'
biscuits an' thangs.
An'_ his_ chil'ren_ gone_ tuh_ the_ fiel's_
an'—
Gone_tuh_work_
off uh that
hard co'n.
But when she got able an' foun' somewhere.
The chil'ren grows up
she done very well
|fo' the few yeahs she was up|.
then ah was bo'n
then it fell tuh
me tuh take care
of mama
I would tend tuh mah cows an'thangs
but ah would tend tuh her first.
I would get up in the mornin'
make the fire in the stove
get the wata' an' wash Mama
I'd fix her breakfas' an' thangs
an' feed her an' then I get through wit cleanin'
her
afta' she got through wit eatin' I'd go back tuh
the kitchen

As she narrates this episode of her mother's life, her hands are clasped together, palms down on her purse across her chest. Her mood is pensive, without the graphic gestures or vigorous intensity of the previous episodes. Although she is less animated and theatrical, she is nonetheless dramatic. Her stillness is almost inalterable as it enhances, underscores, and intensifies the strength of her deep, thick, commanding voice. The authority and richness of her voice against the dramatic stillness of her body brings sounds, smells, and texture to the scene of the peach tree, cooked ham and biscuits, her mother's frailty, and the children having to work in the field hungry. Without one lean of her body, wave of her hand or toss of her head, this economy remained one of the most compelling of her performance modes.

As she describes the farmer, her body is almost perfectly still and quiet without any gestures that may indicate anger, resentment, or despondency—she is stoic. Only this time in the entire life history is Mrs. Kapper so "unmoving," as though her body is weighted down not only with her mother's hard times but also with

the all too familiar telling of "what one of our own has done to us." Only her intonation reveals the range of meanings and attitudes she holds for her mother and the farmer. When she talks about the farmer her voice is lower and more intense; there are fewer pauses and her lips are tight as though she is forcing the words. Not until she begins to discuss her mother leaving the clutches of the farmer—"but when she got able an' found somewhere/the chil'ren grows up/she done very well"—does her voice soften, and a note of tender affection loosens the harsh tightness of the performance. At this point, she seems to come back to the present moment of the narrative event. She then makes eye contact with me, unlocks the tight grip she had on her purse, and gently places her hands on her lap.

The events in this episode, between her mother and the black farmer, took place before Mrs. Kapper was born. Passed down by her mother, her older sisters, and her brothers, the narrative is a significant episode in their collection of family stories. The memory of her mother's life as a sharecropper is reminiscent of the South African saying: "our struggle is also a struggle of memory against forgetting." This history cannot be forgotten because to forget it means black women cannot know their mothers' struggles. To know their mother, they must know her past, what she did there and how she lived through it. This history is her life and tells them who she is. She is a woman who fought hunger, poverty, sexual abuse, loneliness, sickness and survived it. The narrative is the record and the proof of who this woman is, and to tell her story is to celebrate her life among them, as well as to celebrate more than 80 years of pride in being her daughter.

Yet it was the perception of Mrs. Kapper's mother as woman and as black woman that influenced the material conditions of her life and the farmer's treatment of her. And although black women of a different social class were redefining a "true womanhood" that was still ultimately based upon Victorian notions of good manners and a partriarchal morality, and although precepts regarding any notion of a "true womanhood" are regressive in the light of women's diversity and freedom, for better or worse, these women recognized that being black and being a woman carried with it fallacious and injurious perceptions that led to the abuse and disrespect of black women.[8] Uneducated, unprotected, isolated, ill, and sexually exploited, Mrs. Kapper's mother worked the land and cared for her children. "True womanhood," in the times of which she lived, was antithetical to her experience. Mrs. Kapper's mother was not endowed with social graces and genteel civility, nor was it her preoccupation to maintain a home of beauty, charm, and high-browed morals of her husband and children; she did not work to create an appearance of delicate beauty and feminine fragility nor was she treated as a woman of purity and chastity—unapprochable for carnal sex. Mrs. Kapper's mother was reminiscent more of the slave woman than the "true woman," and the black farmer more of the master than the mate.

The episode illustrates the very complicated forms of mistreatment when racial difference is not the factor but when racial homogeneity is; and, when being of the same race but of a different gender and class results in situations as painfully disempowering and oppressive as racism (Fanon). This black farmer in the late 1800s is representative of those members of a disenfranchised community who have adopted the oppressor's gaze, an objectification of individuals within their own community. The mother was "less" and therefore not expected to need, desire, or deserve that which sustains the dignity and well being of those viewed as fully human. Beyond her blackness and poverty, her gender objectified her even more, therefore she became less equal and less human by virtue of being female. And living in the shadow of slave tradition where "slave owners controlled black women's labor and commodified black women's bodies as units of capital" (hooks, *Ain't* 51) the black farmer, although a member of an oppressed group, functioned as both "target and vehicle" of hegemony and power (Foucault 170). While the farmer may have held his wife more in line with "true womanhood," complying with Victorian or southern gentry notions of wife, the narrative reveals that Mrs. Kapper's mother was positioned in such contrast to "true womanhood" that in terms of work, chastity, and civility, she was regarded as non-woman. Her non-woman positioning then becomes part of the justification for her abuse.

The irony is that is positioning of her as non-woman was the impetus for her exploitation that was unequivocally gendered. Her body, labor, and even children were exploited because she was a woman devalued as a non-woman.

"Our struggle is a struggle of memory against forgetting" is also manifest in Mrs. Kapper's embellishment of the story and her revisioning of her mother's sacrifice through descriptions of her own life. This embellishment and revisioning is made clear in hooks's reference to "struggle of memory" as she points to it as a "politicization of memory that distinguishes nostalgia, that longing for something to be as once it was, a kind of useless act, from that remembering that serves to illuminate and transform the present" (*Yearning* 147). Mrs. Kapper tells the story of her mother and then adds her own experiences of work and nurturing. She positions herself in the story as the one who must now sacrifice for her mother; she is now mother to her own mother. The historical experience of the subject/mother augmented by the contemporary experience of the teller / daughter persents an added heroine, and "like mother, like daughter," she will overcome hard times and do what needs to be done for her family and then pass the story along, as we see in the final narrative.

"That Was My Occupation"

This episode follows the preceding one by a few lines.

> I'd get my milk an' thangs ready tuh go milk the cows
> feed my hogs
> that was my occupation
> (smiling)
> throw ah little stuff out tuh my chickens
> I could raise some chickens!
> (proudly, waving her hands)
> in them times.
> Sometimes I'd have as many as 40 fryers at ah time on my yard
> at one time!
> (pointing her finger)
> an' I set my hens in
> the early winter an' they would hatch
> an' when she would quit the nes' an' I couldn' make

her stay on them long' nough
tuh hatch
all them eggs—
I would get me an ol' somthin'/or/other
an' bring the eggs in them an' put them down
front the fire
laka that
(She mimes nurturing the egg)
if it started tuh break
laka it started tuh hatch an' didn' do it
I'd get me a rag
(rubs the egg)
ah little warm wata' an' dampen it all way
'round an' make it sof'
(rubs all around the egg)
so that blood would get sof' an'
I would watch it
an' when I'd go back sometime
that shell be done bust on down laka dat
an' I'd wet it some mo'
when I knowed anythin'
that shell done bust
wide open
an' the little chicken layin' in
there
(points to "chicken")
I'd he'p him
pull loose.
They say I wasn'
nothin'
but ah
granny!
(laughing, waves her hands in the air.)

We are witness to the transformative power of Mrs. Kapper's performance through the inseparable act of *nommo,* "all magic is WORD magic" (Asante 49), and *kuntu,* meaning and rhythm. Since rhythm is the modality of the word, and since the word and its modality of rhythm and meaning are inextricable, it is rhythm/meaning/word that we may understand as performance. The Senegalese writer, Leopold Sedar Senghor writes:

Rhythm is the architecture of being, the inner dynamic that gives it form, the pure expression of the life force. Rhythm is the vibratory shock, the force which, through our sense, grips us at the root of our being. It is expressed through corporeal and sensual means; through lines, surfaces, colours, and volumes in architecture, sculpture or painting; through accents in poetry and music, through movements in the dance. But, doing this, rhythm turns all these concrete things towards the light of the spirit. In the degree to which rhythm is sensuously embodied, it illuminates the spirit. (60)

It was rhythm—the act of performance—that transcended time, illuminated meaning, created form and embodied the spirit of Mrs. Kapper as nurturer and healer; this performance is her "occupation." As she nurtures and heals in bringing life forth in the narrative performance of the told, she nurtures and heals in bringing her self-defined identity forth in the narrative performance of the telling. She scoots to the end of her chair as she begins to enact the hatching of the baby chick. With the "egg" in hand, her facial expressions, gestures, and focus are on this little fragile thing she holds. As the imaginary egg hatched, she brought those long ago years to this present moment in time through performance. It was at this moment where she crossed the threshold and became the woman on the farm, nurturing her very own cows, hogs, and chickens—her true occupation.

We observe the value of what Mrs. Kapper describes in this episode as something more than work; for her, it is an occupation. She has worked and known the labor of her mother and others as something outside their own control, something largely diminishing and without self-fulfillment. Work is a site of repression dissociated with creativity and prideful productivity. It is through her occupation that she is in control, empowered, independent, creative and where she can take pride in ownership. In owning the site of her own labor, she has ownership of herself. Because she is finally master of her own work, her work becomes an act of creation. And because there is a connection between what one does and how one thinks, she is euphoric in this new labor of creativity and self-possession through performance.

It was through the transcendence of performance where she was able to re-live the sense and feelings of being "granny" again. It was the emergent performance of granny—what granny told us and what granny did—that demonstrated it is the work we do that largely defines our existence and contributes to our cultural and self identity; it is in our work where we are fulfilled only to the extent that we believe we are creating something "through our transforming labor" (Freire 141). Mrs. Kapper is thrilled by being granny again. Her head rolls back in laughter as she positions her wig and opens her purse for a handkerchief to wipe the tears under her dark glasses.

CONCLUSION

The thrust of this essay has been to illuminate the oral narrative of Mrs. Alma Kapper through black feminist thought, black vernacular, and black intellectual traditions. These discourses interwoven with the performance paradigm advanced certain points.

First, distinctive interpretations of the world are carved out of the embodied, historical, and material reality of a group's life experiences— theories of the flesh—and they offer different perspectives, cast here as different traditions, expressions, and forms than those of groups outside that particular experience and reality. The collective of black women have used distinctive approaches, although varying and divergent, in interpreting, producing, and validating knowledge from their borderland status. Black women are diversely and complexly positioned inside and outside domains of race, class, and gender oppressions. To assert that black women create distinct theories and interpretations is not to essentialize black women as one monolithic group. The collective of black women's experiences is dialectic; the interpenetrating dynamic of racism, sexism, and classism cannot be reduced as though one "ism" at all times is dominant over the others or that they affect all uniformly. Black women's theories of the flesh arise not out of essentialist notions but out of the fact that black women live a shared history, race, and sex with certain shared experiences, traditions, and cultural meanings and values— however relative or divergent they may be. This is the contradiction and the paradox of the outsider/insider—of living on the borderlands.

Second, these theories of the flesh, or "repositories of a people's theories of themselves" (Gates, *Signifying* x), have been problematic for some to locate or understand as self-theorizing.

But as we move toward the performance paradigm, we are guided to their location, as well as their meaning and function for their creators. Through performance Mrs. Kapper unveiled what Collins refers to as taken-for-granted knowledge or "standpoint" and what hooks refers to as the concrete life experiences of black women. Framing this self-theorizing in performance helps to identify where and how people are giving name to themselves and their experiences, as well as the embedded meanings within them. Mrs. Kapper's performed narrative makes accessible what Kristin M. Langellier describes as the "'fit'—conjunction or disjunction—of person and his or her world-as-experienced" (271).

Third, these theories of the flesh and the "fit" unveiled and made manifest in performance are taken to the next step of specialized knowledge, the knowledge by "experts" who express the group's standpoint (Collins, "Social Construction" 302). This specialized knowledge is interdependent with theories of the flesh, re-articulating them and moving them beyond the argument that black women can produce independent theory. By infusing elements and themes of black women's culture and traditions with critical interventionist thinking, this specialized knowledge provides black women with new tools of resistance. Specialized knowledge functions as a counter-hegemonic discourse in providing epistemologies, grounded in sociocultural practices, that critically interrupt cultural productions that promote and reinforce dominance. Black feminism goes a further step by contending that these practices of rearticulating theories of the flesh for the purposes of providing tools of resistance, as well as critically intervening upon hegemonic conceptions of the world, must be followed by discussions and elaborations of black women as subjects. As bell hooks states, "opposition is not enough. In that vacant space after one has resisted there is still the necessity to become—make oneself anew . . . That space within oneself where resistance is possible remains. It is different then to talk about becoming subjects" (*Yearning* 15).

And finally, the combination of these four points—the process of recognizing "the repositories of a people's theories of themselves" carved out of everyday life; specialized knowledge as re-articulation for resistance; countering dominance through critical intervention; and finally, affirming subjectivity—are where black feminist thought, black discourse, oral narrative, and performance intersect. In narrating her remembrances, it was through performance, as the culmination and materialization of experience, that Mrs. Kapper's life, past, and culture came most forcefully and poignantly into being. Performance was then manifest as both ideology and experience, bringing to life and location the fit of world-as-experienced at that temporal moment, and leading, as Dwight Conquer-good writes, "from performance as Agency to performance as ultimate Scene" (190).

To illuminate this performance of Mrs. Kapper through a critical praxis that recreates "the bonds between the text and world" (Strine 198), an intersection of the intellectual traditions of black discourse and black feminist thought with the performance paradigm was required. The performance paradigm is congruent with and enriched the method and purposes of these discourses. As Conquer-good states, "The performance paradigm privileges particular, participatory, dynamic, intimate, precarious, embodied experience grounded in historical process, contingency, and ideology" (187).

In seeking to intersect performance, narrative, black feminist thought and black intellectual traditions, I remained mindful of the challenge involved in the process of interpreting any text—of naming it and struggling to be self-reflexive as meanings are proposed. This challenge comes to mind again when I remember the instructions of one elderly black women in domestic work who said to me: "If you want to write about what I'm telling you, don't put any flowers on my story, just tell the truth straight out!"

Discussion Questions

1. What are *theories of the flesh*?

2. What is the function of theories of the flesh?

3. Why did Madison consider oral narrative to be the most effective method for her study?

4. How is the Poetic Transcription Approach useful?

5. What does this approach suggest about African American culture?

Reading 4.4

INTERROGATING THE REPRESENTATION OF AFRICAN AMERICAN FEMALE IDENTITY IN THE FILMS *WAITING TO EXHALE* AND *SET IT OFF*

TINA M. HARRIS

In the past twenty years or so, members of Western culture have become consumed by a myriad of popular culture artifacts designed to entertain, educate, or inform. Such artifacts as film, television, and theater are primary mediums through which these needs are met. While the images constructed within these mediums are created essentially for the purpose of entertaining, they are often central to the (de) construction of race, class and gendered identities. More specifically, these images are critical in constructing and/or challenging lived reality and perceptions of that reality.

Research has discovered the critical role the mass media play in shaping our attitudes, beliefs, and perceptions; however, little inquiry has been made into the dialectical tensions associated with racialized gender identities in cinema. Victims of cinematic annihilation are African American women, whose cinematic caricatures typically perpetuate and rarely challenge longstanding stereotypes ascribed to them via film and television. These images of Jezebel, mammy, prostitute, maid, and welfare queen, among others, have adapted to the changing times; however, they have only evolved into "sophisticated ghettoized" images of African American female identity.

Few would argue against the observation that popular culture has become integral to life in

From Harris, T. (1999). Interrogating the representation of African American female identity in the films *Waiting to Exhale* and *Set It Off*. *Popular Culture Review*, *10*(2), 43-53.

America. Unfortunately, limited discourse has evolved regarding how film as a visual artifact articulates a dilemma for marginalized communities, particularly the African American community. Social scientists have observed a double standard in popular culture. While films and television programs that appeal to mainstream society give the opportunity to strictly entertain their audiences, a double standard exists to which African American television programs and movies are held (Tucker, 1997; Inniss & Feagin, 1995; Merritt, 1991; Poussaint, 1988). Instead of solely "entertaining" for the sake of entertainment, which we have come to assume is the goal of most Hollywood films, films featuring predominately African American casts are expected to possess a moral fiber that pricks our social consciousness. Whether it is to address racism, sexism, or classism within a political framework, films that capture and express racialized experiences and Blackness (Gray, 1996) are criticized as devaluing the very people they are embracing because the films fail to present an assimilated image of racial identity within a Western framework.

In order to address this dialectical tension as it relates to racialized gender identity in film, the current essay explores the mediated messages embedded within the films *Waiting to Exhale* and *Set It Off*. Each film is a visual (mis)representation of African American women's experiences with love and life in the 1990's. Each film presents character experiences that reflect real life experiences for some African American women, yet a dialectical tension emerges when the consequences of entertaining result in the perpetuation of negative stereotypical images. In their own right, each film embodies life for African American women from two distinct socio-economic classes. It is through the context of friendship, or sisterhood, that we understand the multidimensional aspects of African American female identity. The tension becomes more apparent as the movies are juxtaposed and examined for their contributions to (de)constructing racialized gender identity as it relates to African American women.

Waiting to Exhale is based on Terry McMillan's novel of the same name and explores the sisterhood between four African American women as they share with the audience the frustrations experienced in maintaining balance between their personal and public lives.

Similarly, *Set It Off* is a screenplay centering around four African American women who are in search of a "better" life as they deal with classism, sexism, and racism. In either case, both sets of friends capture the multidimensional aspects of identity and the centrality of female friendship in understanding one's self and her position in society.

The films *Waiting to Exhale* and *Set It Off* were selected because of their popularity, although undocumented, within the African American community and their shared attempts to address the centrality of sisterhood (emotional/spiritual) between the character as they survive and /or cope with their life circumstances. It is through their sisterly relationships that we understand how the characters negotiate and deal with pressures from mainstream society to achieve the "American Dream." As each film evolves, we are able to further understand how these pressures influence the individual and collective decisions made by the characters. Although each film presents a unique dilemma for its characters, both films collectively speak to a societal dilemma regarding representation and racialized gender identity. The images communicated from these visual texts create contradictory images that challenge our perceptions, constructions, and ideas of what it means to be an African American woman in the 20th century.

This critical essay will engage in a textual analysis of the films and how these storylines/plots, which are commonly found within mainstream films, present a dialectical tension that challenges the movies to entertain yet educate the audience as they reconstruct long-held notions of "the African American woman." As a conceptual framework, Black Feminist Thought will be used to understand the media's role in creating multiple, contradictory meanings that succeed in deconstructing or reconstructing the multiple identities of African American women.

BLACK FEMINIST THOUGHT: UNDERSTANDING CINEMATIC REPRESENTATION

As construction of knowledge varies across people and individuals, it is essential that a framework be used that embraces difference and provides a unique perspective from which this difference may be understood. By using Black Feminist Thought (Collins, 1996a; 1993) for the present study of *Waiting to Exhale* and *Set It Off*, voice will be given to two popular culture artifacts that position marginalized experiences and voices in the forefront for both African American and mainstream audience members (Hine, 1992). Such a standpoint provides a consciousness for an oppressed people and provides a platform for sharing gendered and racialized experiences too often excluded from dominant discourse (hooks, 1996; Phillips & McCaskill, 1995; King, 1988).

According to Collins (1996a), Black Feminist Thought offers African American women a Voice or a "self-defined collective women's standpoint about black womanhood." Inquiries into such experiences have provided African American women with a conceptual framework that challenges stereotypical images of American women (Collins, 1993), thus creating a consciousness of systematic oppression from all fronts. In her extensive investigation of Black Feminist Thought, Collins (1993) has described four controlling images that create a distorted image of African American women. These four controlling images are "the mammy–the faithful obedient house servant" (p. 71), the matriarch, who is "central to the interlocking system of race, gender, and class oppression," (p. 74), the welfare mother (breeder woman) who is dependent on the welfare state for survival, and the Jezebel, also referred to as "the whore or sexually aggressive woman" (p. 75). Collins further demonstrates that these images individually and collectively work to maintain the oppressive system within which racism, and classism work to denigrate the private and public being of all African American women.

Movies as Texts: Storylines of *Waiting to Exhale* and *Set It Off*

In a qualitative study of movies and their portrayals of African American women, Harris and Hill (forthcoming) found that African American women as an interpretive community (Bobo, 1995) observe a dialectical tension existent in *Waiting to Exhale*. They found that while the film was perceived as an appreciated visual text providing a multidimensional perspective of African American female identity, *Waiting to Exhale* is noted as perpetuating the very stereotypes and controlling images that oppress all African American women. Therefore, it is the purpose of this critical essay to provide a descriptive analysis of the controlling images within the movies *Waiting to Exhale* and *Set It Off*.

If we are to fully understand the dialectical tensions inherent in racialized representation in the media, a description of each movie's storyline must be provided. *Waiting to Exhale* is a visual text that captures the friendship of four middle- and upper-middle class African American women as they deal with balancing their single and professional lives. Each of the four women is searching for relationship satisfaction as she attempts to maintain her gender and professional identities. Given her own circumstance, each character battles for "centeredness" as she searches for a "complete" life involving family, relationship and career. Bernadine gave up her career to become a homemaker, only to later be divorced by her husband and left to raise their two children on her own. Gloria is a divorced, self-sacrificing mother and business woman who feels empty when her son leaves home. Her only solace comes from sporadic sexual encounters with her bisexual ex-husband. The two never-married characters, Robin and Savannah, are successful professional women who continually make bad choices in their relational partners, which ultimately lead to self-imposed heartache. On several occasions, however, both women are willing to compromise their standards in order to fill the empty void of loneliness. Savannah becomes involved with a married ex-boyfriend, while Robin settles for sexual relationships lacking emotional intimacy.

Conversely, the four characters in *Set It Off* are dealing with more complex issues relative to their low-income status. Instead of focusing on romantic relationships, the women are playing a game of survival in their everyday lives. Unfortunately, the characters experience classism, racism, and sexism on their journey. For one reason or another, each character ultimately is "forced" to compromise her integrity, which results in their collective decision to resort to a life of crime to absolve their financial woes and achieve the American Dream. The characters occupy a social position of oppression that creates barriers which hinder success. Level-headed Stoney is the moral compass of the group who takes on the role of mother as she nurtures her brother and friends through life. When she resorts to prostitution to save her brother from the streets, Stoney compromises her integrity but holds onto her dream of marriage, family, and living in suburbia. Frankie is the most successful of the group, as she has gone to college and has a professional job in a bank. Her dreams of receiving promotions and raises dissolve when she is accused by her White employers of conspiring with Black bank robbers from her neighborhood to rob the bank.

Unlike Stoney and Frankie, Cleo is the stereotypical "masculine" lesbian, and has little to dream about as she walks aimlessly through life with little ambition beyond just making it in the 'hood. Throughout the movie, we see Cleo become more resigned to a life of mediocrity, poverty, and oppression. The final character, Tee-Tee, is a single-mother trying to take care of her child as she searches for full-time employment. This task becomes overwhelming as Tee-Tee has no other means of providing childcare for her son and has limited employment opportunities due to her lack of education beyond high school. It is through their individual and collective economic oppression that the women establish a solidarity that surpasses the legal consequences of their actions.

WAITING TO EXHALE, SET IT OFF, AND AFRICAN AMERICAN FEMALE IDENTITY

In order to fully understand the degree to which each movie challenges the controlling images traditionally held of African American women, this critical analysis will examine each movie independently and then provide a comparative analysis of the overall impact such movies have on the social construction of African American female identity.

The movie *Waiting to Exhale* has been held in high regard as a positive visual text that provides an alternative image of African American women. Upon closer examination, however, one can observe a dialectical tension that challenges such observations. The movie is positive in that the women are presented as successful women of the 1990's; unfortunately, their relationship choices further preserve the very controlling images the African American community aims to dismantle. The preeminent images that demonstrate this tension and are integral parts of understanding cinematic portrayals of African American women are the matriarch and Jezebel.

As previously noted, Collins (1993) describes the matriarch as being "central to the interlocking system of race, class and gender oppression" (p. 71). This image is typically perceived as resultant of role reversal in the African American community whereby males and females (husbands and wives) exchange roles for the purpose of maintaining the family. In the absence of the male, however, the female takes on the role of father and mother for the sake of her children. According to Collins (1993), this role reversal stems from the systemic and purposeful destruction of the African American family through the slave system of Africans in the U.S. The matriarch is often perceived as a superwoman possessing incredible strength that enables her to effectively maintain her multiple roles within the family.

Unfortunately, the very qualities that exemplify her strength and character have been manipulated to construct an image of an overbearing, controlling woman committed to emasculating the African American man. The character that typifies this contradictory image is Gloria, a single mother and successful business owner of a beauty salon. As a parent, Gloria is very caring and attentive, yet when her son begins to mature, Gloria's role as mother and caregiver becomes more pronounced. She exhibits very controlling behaviors in that she attempts to heavily monitor her son's school and extracurricular activities as well as his sexual escapades. Though the reality of such parental obligations is magnified by her status as a single mother, the physical attributes and qualities of the character further support this perception of the matriarch. The matriarch is often presented as unattractive, overweight, and devoid of sexual identity. Throughout the movie, we observe Gloria's preoccupation with food, thus contributing to the overweight identity, and her feelings of low self-esteem which is quite evident in her choice to engage in meaningless, unfulfilling sex with her bisexual ex-husband. In comparison to the other characters, Gloria is presented as having less sex appeal, thus contributing to the asexual image of the matriarch.

A second and very disturbing controlling image in the movie is the image of the Jezebel. Although the movie is centered around the characters' search for relational satisfaction, the sexual encounters of the various women in *Waiting to Exhale* perpetuate the image of the sex-crazed African American woman. Characters Savannah and Robin sacrifice relationship for sexual encounters with men who are either commitment-phobic or not "marriage material." Instead, the characters experience a total of four sexual encounters with four men throughout the movie (two per character). While such brief escapades may appear mild or moderate in comparison to mainstream "relationship" movies, *Waiting to Exhale* is in a unique position as it is held to a double standard to which other movies are not. Thus, natural aspects of the male-female relationship are distorted and further perpetuate the allegations about African American men and women's "preoccupation" with pre-marital and adulterous sex. If a comparison were made, it is plausible that mainstream movies are the primary perpetrators of the very image that is typically ascribed to African Americans. Although the characters present various aspects of their individual identities as women balancing career obligations and their desires for satisfying romantic relationships, *Waiting to Exhale* encompasses a dialectical tension relative to realistic portrayals and entertainment as escape. Unfortunately, the controlling images of matriarch and Jezebel overshadow the relational component of their identities.

Set It Off, on the other hand, embodies the controlling images of matriarch, Jezebel, and welfare mother as it attempts to tell of class, race, and gender oppression through its four characters. Similar to *Waiting to Exhale, Set It Off* perpetuates the stereotype of the matriarch in subtle nuances embedded in the character

Stoney. On several occasions, Stoney takes on the role of mother as she provides nurturance for her younger brother after her parents' death and for her "sistahs" as they deal with their respective crises. Stoney attempts to provide emotional support as she bolsters her friends' self-esteem and security through their friendship. Though unspoken, Stoney serves as the moral guide for the women as they contemplate their decision to engage in criminal activities (i.e., bank robbing). Unlike Gloria in *Waiting to Exhale,* Stoney is very petite, physically attractive, and attuned to her sexual identity. This character possesses a quiet strength that is contrary to the stereotypic image of the matriarch ingrained in the psyche of many.

The controlling image of Jezebel is also contained in the character Stoney, specifically when she chooses to provide sexual services for a man in exchange for money so that her brother can attend college. After the exchange, Stoney's countenance changes as she acknowledges this moral compromise yet actively works to maintain her self-respect and dignity by keeping this indiscretion to herself. Similarly, the lesbian character Cleo is also perceived as an atypical form of the heterosexual Jezebel. Instead of being "preoccupied" with sex involving a male partner, Cleo's lesbian relationship is depicted as very sexual in one of the two scenes where her lover is present. It is in this scene where the sexual nature of their relationship supercedes all other aspects, thus perpetuating this construct of the Jezebel. This image is further compounded by the fact that Cleo has little inclination to rise above her circumstances; instead, she is happily resigned to a lazy life in the 'hood where she lives a commodified version of the American Dream.

As an extension, the controlling image of the welfare mother is inherent in *Set It Off*'s character Tee-Tee. In the beginning of the film, we observe Tee-Tee as a single mother dependent on social services to aid her in transition to motherhood. While she has no other familial unit to assist her with childcare, Tee-Tee is overly dependent on her "sistahs" to help her find employment. This perpetual cycle of economic oppression becomes more pervasive as Tee-Tee is fired from her job and her son is taken into foster-care until she can prove herself worthy of her parental responsibilities. Although this experience may be a reality for many young mothers, African American and otherwise, *Set It Off* unknowingly sustains the image of welfare mother which has been wrongly associated solely with African American women. As we observe Tee-Tee's evolution into motherhood and adulthood, it is quite obvious that her immaturity and naivete contribute to her inexperience with and apprehension of her newfound adult obligations. Thus, it is plausible to conclude that the financial trappings of single motherhood and limited education are obstacles also experienced by women of all racial and ethnic groups.

SIMILARITIES AND DIFFERENCES IN PORTRAYALS OF AFRICAN AMERICAN WOMEN

The current textual analysis indicates that the movies *Waiting to Exhale* and *Set It Off,* targeted to the African American community, contain controlling images historically and traditionally ascribed to African American women. The controlling image of the matriarch, as portrayed in both movies, presents the African American woman as provider of emotional and spiritual strength for others. *Waiting to Exhale's* character Gloria maintains this image by preserving the facade of the asexual (i.e., indiscriminant), overbearing, and overweight female. Conversely, *Set It Off's* Stoney is a pinnacle of strength and courage for her "sistahs," yet challenges this matriarch image through her petite stature and overall awareness of her feminine and sexual identities. Though many of the characters possess characteristics and qualities that are double-edged in their connotative meanings, it is the matriarchal characters' moral fiber in *Waiting to Exhale* and *Set It Off* that demonstrate positivity and "completeness" as experienced by some African American women. In Gloria's case, she is the only woman of integrity who deservedly wins the unconditional love of a divorcee committed to making her happy. As for Stoney, although she made a life-threatening decision to rob banks for a living, her escape at the end of the movie demonstrates her commitment to the vision she

set for herself. Of the four women, Stoney is dedicated to achieving a life beyond the four walls of the 'hood, despite the decision she made that temporarily compromised her integrity.

The second stereotype of the Jezebel was pervasive in both movies and re-introduced the image of the sexually promiscuous African American woman. The characters Robin and Savannah in *Waiting to Exhale* portrayed successful, professional African American women as self-serving sexual beings who were willing to sacrifice relationship for sexual relations. Such "amoral" decisions were evident in their decisions to become sexually connected with commitment-phobic men who were not considered "marriageable material." In essence, the women were willing to prostitute their bodies and souls in exchange for temporal relationship satisfaction. As previously noted, *Waiting to Exhale* is a visual text centered around relationships; therefore it would stand to reason that the portrayal of sexual intimacy is inherent in romantic heterosexual relationships. In *Set It Off,* only one character, Stoney, has a pronounced "traditional" sexual identity in her relationship with a male character. The underlying message revolving around her sexual encounters is that she is not solely defined by her sexual identity but also by her vision for a better life. Conversely, Cleo has a "nontraditional" sexual identity that perpetuates the Jezebel image from a divergent standpoint. As a lesbian, Cleo perpetuates the masculine lesbian image as well as the image of an African American woman being "preoccupied" with fulfilling her sexual needs and desires. In one of the two scenes where we observe Cleo interacting with her partner, there are strong sexual overtones that communicate to the audience the "true" a nature of their relationship. Despite Cleo's attempts to normalize their relationship, her partner's silence, or non-speaking presence, in each scene magnifies the sexual dimension of their defined relationship.

Despite this natural part of male-female relationships, the movies perpetuate the Jezebel stereotype. While the *Waiting to Exhale* characters engage in sex with only four male characters (two per female character) and *Set It Off's* Stoney remains sexually monogamous, these stereotypic depictions are further magnified due to the few opportunities African American screen writers, directors, and actors have to share these life experiences with the masses. In contrast, American audiences are bombarded with thousands of movies each year that feature predominately or all-White cast members who tell stories of romance, love, danger, humor, political warfare, and murder, among others. Although the characters engage in various sexual acts that are deemed "normal," rarely are the films individually and collectively scrutinized for perpetuating stereotypes that are historically ingrained in the psyche of their American audiences. Instead, various platforms are constructed to address a collective of social issues that are historically bound by race.

The final stereotype found in only one movie was that of the welfare mother in *Set It Off.* The character Tee-Tee personifies this stereotypic representation of African American women by her dependence on the welfare system to assist in her transition to motherhood and adulthood. She succumbs to the very oppressive force that has constructed her reality by choosing a life of crime to resolve her economic plight. The movie presents the welfare mother through a "victim of the system" framework which positions Tee-Tee as woman who has no control or will over her own destiny. Instead, this character is accustomed to a life of passivity, as this appears to be a part of her identity. The communication strategies used by Tee-Tee, including being passive, shy, even-tempered, and introverted, contribute to this persona, thus conveying to the audience that she is lazy and unable to find good work. Despite the fact that she only has a high school education and lacks a support system, Tee-Tee's efforts to find a job and provide a better life for herself and her son are minimized when she is deemed an unfit mother by social services, thus perpetuating the welfare mother stereotype. Her son is taken away from her and becomes a ward of the state, which ultimately serves as the catalyst for metamorphosis into an angry Black woman.

As the various images presented in *Waiting to Exhale* and *Set It Off* indicate, cinematic portrayals of African American women present a dialectical tension despite attempts made to capture their multidimensionality. For the characters in both films, their pursuit of relational satisfaction and overall happiness potentially becomes overshadowed by their "preoccupation" with sexual gratification (*Waiting to Exhale*) or getting out of the 'hood (*Set It Off*) by any means necessary. Despite the fact that sex and violence are primary components of most mainstream films, *Waiting to Exhale* and *Set It Off* are held to a different standard of credibility. While the characters' experiences may be reflective of reality for many African American women, the stereotypes of Jezebel and welfare queen have the potential to become pronounced as the viewer is exposed to these images on-screen. Instead of accepting sexuality, sexism, racism, and classism as a part of life for these characters, audience members stand the chance of perceiving these representations as confirmation of their beliefs about African American women as a whole.

In recent years, there have been a number of movies released specifically targeted to African American audiences. These visual texts create a dialectical tension in that they capture a myriad of "snapshots" of life for African Americans in the U.S. yet have the potential to distort reality through the perpetuation and/or maintenance of negative stereotypes. In order to fully understand the degree to which such tensions directly impact the socially constructed gender identities of African American women, this critical essay examined the portrayal of African American female identity as illustrated by the female characters and storylines present in the movies *Waiting to Exhale* and *Set It Off.*

It was found that while the African American female characters were telling stories of relationship (dis)satisfaction and race, class, and gender oppression, the same stories perpetuate controlling images that have become a mainstay in western culture. Instead of challenging the very negative depictions that such images epitomize, the various characters keep alive the matriarch, Jezebel, and welfare mother images traditionally associated with African American women. Both movies embody African American women's experiences from two distinct socioeconomic classes through the interpersonal context of friendship/sisterhood, creating an interesting dynamic in need of critical inquiry. Collins states that Black Feminist Thought offers African American women a voice or a "self-defined" collective black women's standpoint about back womanhood" (1996a). In turn, formal inquiries into such experiences have provided African American women a conceptual framework that challenges stereotypical images of American women (Collins, 1993), thus creating a consciousness of systematic oppression from all fronts.

In a recent qualitative study about perceptions of the cinematic representation of professional African American women in the movie *Waiting to Exhale,* Harris and Hill (1998) found that some women serving as members of an undervalued interpretive community experienced cognitive dissonance as they watched the characters develop on-screen. While there was satisfaction in seeing a somewhat realistic representation of life for themselves in the movie, most participants were disheartened to observe the subconscious debasing of African American women. Although they felt *Waiting to Exhale* was a positive attempt by African American film makers at providing creative space for the expression of

Blackness and femaleness, participants felt that it also perpetuated the matriarch and Jezebel stereotypes traditionally associated with African American women (Harris & Hill, 1998).

According to Collins (1993), African American women have experienced a particular oppression and misrepresentation, which has created unfavorable images that have been readily accepted as truth by the masses. Currently, some cinematic efforts have been made to challenge such manipulated constructs in an effort to redeem the beauty of all African American women. Using Black Feminist Thought as the conceptual framework, this essay explored a dialectical tension whereby attempts to portray African American women in the movies ultimately perpetuate stereotypes of matriarch, Jezebel, and welfare mother, which are historically and traditionally associated with African American women in Western culture. It is hoped that future inquiry into this tenuous state of cinematic annihilation will be explored to deconstruct and reconstruct the multiple identities of all African American women.

DISCUSSION QUESTIONS

1. What is meant by *Black feminist thought* as a conceptual framework?

2. What *controlling images* were present in each of the movies explored in this chapter?

3. How does the issue of class shift the stereotypes in each of the films?

4. What is a Jezebel?

5. What stereotype is most related to the *victim of the system* framework?

Reading 4.5

DEFINING BLACK MASCULINITY AS CULTURAL PROPERTY

Toward an Identity Negotiation Paradigm

RONALD L. JACKSON II AND CELNISHA L. DANGERFIELD

Black masculinist scholarship cannot afford to accept, approve, and adopt the same cultural, social, and political agendas as traditional white masculinist scholarship. The two areas of gender theory share some commonalities however there is a distinction that emerges at the intersection where gender meets culture.

—Jackson, 1997, p. 731

Theory, by its very nature, is something that can be proven wrong. It has voids because no one theory can possibly characterize all aspects of a given phenomenon. Communicologist Stanley Deetz (1992) explains: "A theory is a way of seeing and thinking about the world. As such, it is better seen as the 'lens' one uses in observation rather than as the 'mirror' of nature" (p. 66). The existing lenses used to explore Black masculinity, as a communicative aspect of gendered lives, require correction. Any time a body of theory, set of discoveries, or range of conceptualizations are no longer effective in explaining the phenomena or behaviors they purport to describe, a paradigm shift is needed.

After having reviewed the existing interdisciplinary literature and conceptualizations of Black masculinity, we feel we have read a set of foreign autobiographies, few of which pertain to the first author of this essay, a Black male. Married, middle-class, educated spiritual Black men, who are goal-driven, employed, competent, and non-criminal are missing from both the vast amount of literature and the constellation of media representations of Black males. The indisputable and tragic reality is that Black males have been pathologized and labeled as violent/criminal, sexual, and incompetent/uneducated individuals. This prevalent set of stereotypical depictions of Black masculinity as a stigmatized condition or of Black males as an

From Jackson, R. L., & Dangerfield, C. (2002). Defining Black masculinity as cultural property: An identity negotiation paradigm. In L. Samovar & R. Porter (Eds.), *Intercultural communication: A reader* (pp. 120-130). Belmont, CA: Wadsworth.

"endangered species" makes it extremely difficult to theorize Black masculinities in the same ways as White or other marginalized group masculinities. Black masculinities are first and foremost cultural property communicated in everyday interaction as manifestations of Black identities.[1]

Traditionally, the impulse among gender theorists in many disciplines including communication has been to interpret the incendiary nature of masculinity studies in the specter of the European American experience. The assumption made is that all masculine persons function in homogeneous ways.[2] However, a growing contingent of Black writers, including bell hooks, Clyde Franklin III, Patricia Hill Collins, Richard Majors, Michelle Wallace, Philip Brian Harper, Naim Akbar, Haki Madhubuti, Earl Ofari Hutchinson, and others, have proposed that Black masculinities are cultural property, and that they are ritualistically, explicitly, and implicitly validated by communities within everyday interactions. We agree with bell hooks' (1992) assertion about scholarship pertaining to Black masculinities. She writes:

> [The literature on black masculinity] does not interrogate the conventional construction of patriarchal masculinity or question the extent to which Black men have internalized this norm. It never assumes the existence of black men whose creative agency has enabled them to subvert norms and develop ways of thinking about masculinity that challenge patriarchy. (p. 89)

Essentially, the literature presupposes complicity with hegemony and never questions whether Black men have been affected by their own exclusion from the mainstream to the extent that they have constructed their masculinities differently. In assuming that all masculinities are the same, one presupposes that all men should completely share the burden of U.S. White male patriarchal allegations without sharing the licenses to White male privilege, Black men to be the "endangered species" and still function in a position of privilege, hence with the same sensibilities as White men. So, we are persuaded by hooks' argument that social depictions of Black masculinities as dominant are "fantastical" and "narrow" (p. 89). While introducing a Black masculine paradigm, this article issues a challenge to rethink how cultural particularity influences the existing range of Black masculinities, which significantly diverge from culture-generic characterizations of what it means to be masculine.

Feminist thinkers, who encapsulate and hold liable negative masculine tendencies for the American fixation on power, competition, greed, control, and institutionalized exclusion, have inspired a large segment of critical masculinity scholarship. Consequently, the versions of masculinity that are described are often culturally generic, fragmented, and aloof. Very few gender studies depict masculinities as positive, healthy, mature, productive, and balanced identities, but these masculinities do exist. The gender descriptors "masculinity" or "masculinist" usually refer to antagonistic, puerile, insecure, very unaware, and chaotic male identities. It is true that masculine, like feminine, persons enact a wide range of behaviors on a daily basis, from dysfunctional to quite functional. So, theorizing masculinities, in terms of a gendered continuum ranging from healthy to unhealthy and positive to negative self-definitions, is both necessary and revolutionary.

As mentioned previously, the everyday existence of healthy and productive human beings is not so new, which means that some gender theories have slipped with respect to how they account for healthy masculinities. This near absence of critical gender commentary on cultural masculinities only accents the inseparable link between power, ideology, and the politics of representation. It is the intent of this essay to address this void in gender thinking and offer a paradigm that may serve as some basis for explaining productive and counter productive masculine behaviors, while accenting culture as a means of understanding masculine realities.

This article is organized into four parts. First, the article begins by defining the terms *masculinity* and *femininity* and then discussing male and female sex and gender role stereotypes. Second, we provide a brief overview of three prominent social and racial stereotypes of Black masculinities. Third, a theoretic paradigm of Black masculine identities is introduced. Finally, the essay concludes with implications of the Black masculinity studies and suggestions for future research.

DEFINING MASCULINITY AND FEMINITY

Clearly, masculine and feminine mystiques socially dominate how we see the world. It only takes a quick survey of child-rearing practices among parents and mass-mediated reinforcements of sex and gender role stereotypes to see that these images are sharply divided. When writers speak of masculinities and femininities, we often assume we know what the terms mean, and we also presume that these universal categories are reasonable ways to conceptualize lived realities. Rather than totally discard the terms, we recommend that the terms be redefined as perceptual categories in flux. In order to discuss definitions of masculinity and femininity, it is appropriate to return to the distinctions between sex and gender. The contemporary conversation concerning sex and gender is similar to that of race and ethnicity. The first term in each pair refers to biologically conceived characteristics of an individual, whereas the latter pertains to social ascriptions and prescriptions.

Sex Roles

Just as one may be able to determine another's sex and/or race by observing optic markers, such as the hair, skin, lips, eyes, musculature, and so on, he or she may also be able to determine one's sex by the same means. This is what we call "preverbal communications," the communication that occurs via physiognomic markers before the talk begins. When we speak of sex roles rather than sex, expectations emerge. Sex roles are the biological prescriptions about what males and females should to with their bodies. For example, one female role is to procreate. Male are expected to talk with a deep voice. Although it is generally easier to visually identify a male or a female, gender identities are more intricate.

Gender Roles

Gender roles refer to ways women and men are socially and culturally assigned feminine and masculine behaviors. For instance, men are socially expected to actively pursue women for a dating and mating relationship. Women are socially expected to be more nurturing and affectionate than men. These gender roles are socializations that begin at birth. Family and friends purchase products that are blue for newborn boys. Purchased newborn gifts are typically pink if for girls, and if you don't know the sex of the baby, green is appropriate. A family would probably find it insulting to receive a baby boy's gift that is pink. Another gender role is seen with boys, who are normally socialized to play with trucks, whereas girls are typically encouraged to play with Barbies. This supposedly keeps the presumptions of what constitutes masculinity and femininity intact.

This social logic inspired both Toys 'R' Us and FAO Schwarz to come up with Boys' World and Girls' World in 1999. It must have sounded like a great idea at the time, until Toys 'R' Us received negative feedback about their discriminatory and sexist toy lines in the Girls' World section. Toys like Barbies, cookware, cleaning supplies, phones, and so on were placed in Girls' World, and trucks, cars, tools, monsters, race tracks, and video games were placed in Boys' World. This arrangement lasted for all of about two days as consumers complained that Toys 'R' Us was promoting stereotypes by suggesting that boys should have all of the fun while girls stay in the house, cook, clean, and talk on the phone. This short-lived fiasco with Toys 'R' Us escaped much of the national media's attention.

FAO Schwarz was a bit more strategic in its placement of toys. They divided toys by color. So, both sections had almost the same exact toys, except that the girls' section had pink, orange, yellow, and green toys and the boys' section had blue, black, purple, and green toys. They have somehow managed to reduce the negative feedback level significantly. The description of "FAO Girl," however, is still stereotypical. It reads:

Introducing FAO Girl. Because girls just wanna have fun. And fun stuff. This great new line will take your FAO Girl from homeroom to her room in style with a huge selection of hair accessories and jewelry, plush toys and pillows and cool gadgets—everything every girl can't do without. FAO Girls are filled with glamour, giggles and guts! (www.fao.com)

Body politics theorist Moira Gatens (1996) provides a valuable commentary concerning this problem of social stereotyping. She states:

Masculinity and femininity as forms of sex-appropriate behaviors are manifestations of a historically based, culturally shared phantasy [sic] about male and female biologies, and as such sex and gender are not arbitrarily connected. The connection between the female body and femininity is not arbitrary in the same way that the symptom is not arbitrarily related to its etiology. Hence, to treat gender, the symptom, as the problem is to misread its genesis. (p. 13)

Gatens' conceptualization is insightful with regards to the dual functions of gender—body and role. Majors & Billson (1992) contend that gendered beings are not merely socially characterized, however, but in the case of males, are also forced to "attain masculinity" by "being responsible and being a good provider for the self and family" (p. 30). In other words, masculinity is earned and achieved, rather than socially prescribed. We concur with Majors & Billson that masculinity is not necessarily natural or innate as is implied by Gatens' references to biologies; rather, it is learned.

Clearly, the intellectual analysis of the link between sex roles and gender stereotypes is nonunique. Sigmund Freud explored this issue in the early 1900s, and countless gender theoreticians comment on this phenomenon on a daily basis. But, are these academic assessments parochial? Have we redefined masculinities in such a way that they are no longer recognizable to the general population? It seems that socially understood conventions about masculinity include the medieval image of the "man as protector of his woman and family" to the more commonplace "man as the head of the household" and "primary breadwinner" motifs. Gender scholars' discussions of sex role orientations and gender stereotypes are often

antiquated conceptualizations that have outlived their epistemological utility. This is not to say that social discourse has completely discarded these notions, but that we must move forward because the analyses are stale. In an effort to do so, we recommend analyses of gendered relationships as behavioral institutions confined by context-based realities. With this in mind, masculinities are not to be understood as a singular or unitary reality, but as multiple masculinities, pluralized to accent an anti-essentialist perspective, which accounts for variegations resulting from culture, class, sexual preference, religion, and other axes of difference.

For the purposes of this chapter, *masculinity* is defined as a perceptual and cosmological category in flux. It is composed and validated by culturally particular behavioral tendencies that are consonant with personal, social, and communal expectations. Although women may have masculine tendencies, we will discuss masculinity as a perceptual category that is male-centered.

Thus far, we have discussed the voids and inconsistencies in masculinity research and provided some insights about sex and gender role stereotyping. Stereotypes are important information as indicators of problems within a given social context. Moreover, stereotypes inhibit social relationships and often offer inaccurate and damaging perspectives about others. Because stereotypes of all kinds are dangerous yet instructive, we would be remiss in discussing Black masculine identities without some discussion of the social stereotypes that make them problematic and inhibit them.

STEREOTYPING BLACK MASCULINE BODIES

Ribeau, Baldwin & Hecht (1997), in their studies of satisfying Black-White communication, indicated that the primary issue of concern to the Black participants they studied was *negative* stereotyping. They defined *negative* stereotyping as "the use of rigid racial categories that distort an African American's individuality" (p. 149). Negative stereotypes can be both racial and social. Racial stereotypes coupled with sex role stereotypes produce a rather interesting pastiche because discussions of the dual function of role and body are elicited. The public narratives pertaining to Black men's lives comply with several racialized social projections about the Black masculine body as (1) violent, (2) sexual, and (3) incompetent. These descriptors have been used to degrade and stigmatize black males and are considered projections because of what they imply about the insecurities, fears, and anxieties *society* has about Black males.

Black Masculine Body as Violent/Criminal. The media have helped to portray the black man as a violent person who often becomes ensconced in a life of crime. Nightly newscasts parade criminal offenders, the likes of which appear to represent a disproportionate number of non-white offenders. According to Entman and Rojecki (2000):

> The FBI estimated that 41% of those arrested for violent crimes in 1997 were Black (and 57% were White); 32% of those arrested for property crimes were Black. . . . Public [mass-mediated] perceptions exaggerate the actual racial disproportion. . . . By a 1.5:1 (241 to 160) ratio, while victims outnumber Blacks in news reports. . . . The average story featuring Black victims was 106 seconds long; those featuring white victims, 185 seconds long. (pp. 79–81)

These authors have illustrated that the public portrayals of Blacks as violent are often misguided and unjustly framed. Several recent studies have confirmed that the media tend to reinforce racial stereotypes, social deviancy, and delinquency of black males (Dixon & Linz, 2000; Entman, 1992; Entman and Rojecki, 2000; Gray, 1997; Heider, 2000). For example, Dixon & Linz (2000) analyzed local television news programming in Los Angeles to uncover whether Blacks, Latinos, and Whites were equally represented as lawbreakers. Their results indicated that televised crime stories presented on Los Angeles news stations were biased in their coverage. Blacks were found to be almost 2.5 times more likely to be portrayed as felons than Whites. Also, with an actual arrest rate of 21% in Orange Country, California, the televised coverage showed Blacks as perpetrators of crime 37% of the time. Dixon & Linz argue that biased coverage of this sort solidifies the

perception that Black males are habitual lawbreakers, much more so than Whites or any other cultural group. The reality, in Los Angeles and Orange Country, was that Blacks were arrested less frequently than Whites and Latinos. This stereotypical portrayal of Blacks as criminals is political. The politics of race and black masculine identity have produced a peculiar anxiety in the United States. This is also evidenced in the perception of the black masculine body as a sexual object.

Black Masculine Body as Sexual. Notwithstanding the myths of Black sexual prowess and phallus size, there is historical significance to the "Black Masculine Body as Sexual" stereotype. Historically, when white slave owners wanted to penalize the black male for acts of aggression or disobedience, they would perform one of two activities: emasculation or a picnic. Emasculation refers to cutting off the penis. This removal of the phallus symbolized the denial of black masculinity. Essentially, this would prevent the black male's body from performing its normal sexual reproductive function and eliminate the threat of miscegenation. This was only one form of lynching. Another form was the picnic. The social etymology of the term *picnic* is "pick a nigger." Picnics were festivals and family gatherings in which white slave owners would bring their children, wives, and friends to witness the hanging of a black slave who was deemed disobedient. For example, Cunningham (1996) recounts that Emmett Till, a 14-year-old black boy, was lynched in Mississippi for whistling at a white girl. This was done at a picnic. Till's death became the signpost of Black racial misery throughout the South.

These acts of aggression against blacks signified prohibition and assimilation. The slave master's narrative suggested that Black male bodies were lynched when they did not comply. The truth is that the slave's body was at once an object of disgust and admiration; hence, his body was seen as a threat (Best, 1996). His body was used as an object of labor, and in the process, his body became very muscular. This was especially threatening because it attracted white women, who were forbidden from contact with Blacks.

Black Masculine Body as Incompetent/Uneducated. Several deficit/deficiency models of black masculinity have proposed a pathologized version of these identities. Oliver (1989) contends that: "Blacks are disproportionately represented among Americans experiencing academic failure, teenage pregnancy, female-headed families, chronic unemployment, poverty, alcoholism, drug addiction, and criminal victimization" (p. 15). These social problems, presumably caused primarily by Black males, have led to perceptions of black masculine incompetence as a result of a process of inferiorization. It is not that some black males intrinsically sense they cannot achieve, but rather that the social conditions and mass media reinforcement of stereotypes remind and convince the Black male population that they will experience struggle. It is inevitable. For example, Entman & Rojecki (2000) assert:

> More generally, television's visuals construct poverty as nearly synonymous with "Black," and surveys show Whites typically accept this picture, even though poverty is not the lot of most Black people and more Whites are poor than Black. . . . In this sense news images encourage the sense of the prototypical Black as poor and the prototypical poor person as Black. (p. 102)

The media links Black poverty with Black crime, incompetence, and poor education. These false media images seem almost insurmountable. Eventually, images of this sort will affect anyone's worldview. This is not to suggest that black male delinquency or deviancy is excusable, but that not all Blacks or Black males are delinquent. Sociologist Manning Marable (2001) asks:

> What is a Black man in an institutionally racist society, in the social system of modern capitalist America? The essential tragedy of being Black and male is our inability, as men and as people of African descent, to define ourselves without the stereotypes the larger society imposes upon us, and through various institutional means perpetuates and permeates within our entire culture. (p. 17)

These social conditions and stereotypes coupled with cultural expectations for black males can be overwhelming. Besides the social idea of black macho rigidity (or the tough guy image), cultural mandates on Black masculinity have historically been centered on being a good provider. As a result, a Black male who cannot take care of his family almost immediately loses his "rights to manhood" or is viewed as not being a man. If the stereotypes of Black male incompetency and/or uneducability were true, Black manhood would be easily surrendered. Adaptative and protective behaviors are often employed to counter these stereotypes and have created a dual sensibility with respect to how Black masculinity is defined in Black versus White communities.

The three stereotypes just discussed are powerful statements that tremendously influence how Blacks define this perceptual category of masculinity and negotiate their masculinities in light of how they are socially and communicatively perceived. That negotiation of identity within varying contexts produces the "in flux" nature of Black masculine identities. This vacillated or dual consciousness is characteristic of the communicative process of negotiating identities. Identity negotiation refers to the win, loss, or exchange of one's ability to maintain one's own cultural worldview. It is, by nature, an act of resilience to outside pressures to constrict self-definitions and consequently self-efficacy. As Marable (2001) suggests, Black masculine identity development is impossible without acknowledging and countering the stereotypes that threaten the survival of Black masculinity.

BLACK MASCULINE IDENTITIES PARADIGM

Percepts to the Paradigm: Negotiating Black Masculine Identities

We choose to theorize Black masculinities rather than culturally generic or universal masculinities because the latter are foreign to me. One's behaviors are potent enactments of one's worldview coupled with cultural sensibilities. Additionally, the cosmological trivium of communication, history, and identity is culturally inscribed on the canvas we call the Self. Human beings are informed and transformed by the intricate *labyrinth* of agony, desire, pleasure, power, and difference. This labyrinth is literally the means by which we gauge self-efficacy and attachment to our personal and relational histories. As masculine persons, however, we establish positions that grant agency to the self and limit access to "Others." *Agency* is a power-laden term that presupposes that people are defensive about how they will control their lives. It is about authority, permission, boundaries, and rules, and by establishing these things, it enables the Self to make choices and explore the world without inhibitions. But, because identities are co-defined in everyday interactions with others, agency is sometimes negotiated and ends up resting externally with the "Other." This is the juncture at which the *labyrinth* becomes heightened, and therefore most visible. As Audre Lorde (1984) cautions: "For Black women as well as Black men, it is axiomatic that if we do not define ourselves for ourselves, we will be defined by others—for their use and to our detriment" (p. 45). The frustration of a displaced agency causes the "I" (i.e., masculine person) to struggle to reacquire stability and control over his choices, worldview, and life possibilities. The "Other," in the previously described scenario, can be anyone from another Black masculine person to another Cultural feminine person. Incidentally, both may be males.

Can Manhood Be Revoked?

The entire process of removing the agency of masculine persons is often referred to as *emasculation* or "revoking one's manhood." Three obvious assumptions are being made with this reference. The first is that men are the only ones who qualify as masculine, which of course is false. The second is that all men are masculine and all masculine persons are *men;* yet, some may be males or boys.[3] Masculinity is a perceptual category that attends each stage of self-development—boyhood, maleness, and manhood. Third, another assumption is that manhood can be revoked. Manhood is a category of being. Rationally, it does not seem possible to revoke a person's sense of being, but because being a man is highly significant among masculine persons, boys and males must

define it so that it is achievable. Boys and males define *manhood* as a subconscious extension of the self that is externally presented and licensed. Being on the exterior, manhood is more likely to be seized.

When it is defined this way, it is worn like paraphernalia; consequently it can be undressed relatively easily. Manhood, in its purest manifestation as defined by men, cannot be revoked, partly because it is internalized. It is not a standpoint or position that is defined solely or even primarily by a "way of knowing," but rather a way of being. It is a life-force that is achieved after reaching a level of spiritual, emotional, mental, and ontological maturity, consciousness, and balance and having one's manhood coextensively and relationally validated by one's community. One who has achieved manhood is aware of the ontological spatial boundaries and functions along the borders between himself and others to achieve desired ends, but is conscious of not "losing himself" in the identity negotiation process. "Losing himself" is always a threat because of the exhaustive code switching mandate as he attempts to coordinate his actions with others, as well as the possibility that his masculine identity may become anonymous, silenced, suppressed, and accessorized. So, he must always be cognizant of the effects of identity negotiation; this is accomplished through policing and maintaining surveillance over his identity. Keeping oneself in balance is the goal of masculine behaviors. It also defines struggle, the centerpiece of Black masculine identities (see Figure 1).

Explaining the Black Masculine Identities Paradigm

Masculinities in general are perceptual categories in flux; therefore, defining black masculine identities requires that black masculine perceptions are taken into account. Stuart Hall (1997) asserts that identities are the labels given to the different ways interactants are positioned by and position themselves in past and present social narratives. Essentially, all definitions of *masculinity* are a matter of positionality.

Black masculine social positionings are primarily communication phenomena. Positioning is the axis of ontological difference among

Figure 1   Black Masculine Identity Model

separate, but often overlapping, masculine identities. That is, positions facilitate how masculinity is understood and enacted at any given moment. If any of the following factors is threatened, the perceptual position can shift from positive to negative as an instinctive protective response; hence masculinities are not stable, predictable forces. They are as fluid as one's perceptions.

Five factors affect Black masculine positionality: *struggle, community, achievement, independence,* and *recognition.* These factors offer some explanation for how masculinities are selected and enacted. It is important to remember that masculinities vary with respect to conditions, maturity, and positionality. Masculinity, as with all behavioral manifestations, can be conceptualized along the twin registers of self-efficacy and symbiosis. *Self-efficacy* refers to the degree to which an individual feels he or she has control over his or her life. *Symbiosis* refers to the attachment one has to a certain life-space and/or relational history that is partly defined by a different, foreign, or asymmetrical cultural experience, such as the case with *African Americans.* So, a person who has a strong Black cultural identification and is militant may hate Whites because of what he has learned about slavery, yet he is forced to interact with Whites if he wants to be employed. He becomes

unavoidably attached to an American culture that has become synonymous with whiteness, while attempting to maintain a commitment to an African ancestral heritage.

This historical symbiosis may cause him to behave negatively toward anyone who looks White. On the other hand, a Black person who has a strong Black identification may feel self-efficacious, and therefore have little problem initiating and maintaining relationships with Whites despite what he knows about slavery. Both persons function this way for a variety of reasons. The factors of positionality offer some explanation for how masculinities are selected and enacted. As stated previously, it is important to remember that masculinities vary with respect to ontological condition, maturity, and positionality.

Struggle and the Mandala

Psychoanalyst Carl Jung contended that the self, as an archetype, is naturally motivated to move toward growth, perfection, and completion. The ultimate symbol of the self, he argues, is the mandala, a diagram that contains a circle inside of a square or vice versa. The dialectic between the shapes is consistent with the conscious, subconscious, and unconscious elements of the self; hence, the combination of the three represents the total self, which is in constant pursuit of balance and wholeness. It is particularly interesting that Jung applies the second law of thermodynamics, the principle of entropy, to explain his interpretations of dreams. This law is also an important component of chaos theory. The actual principle states that when hot and cold objects merge, the hotter flows into the colder to create a sense of equilibrium. No matter what conceptual label is used to describe entropic behavior, it refers to the degree to which disorder in a human or object-centered system may be managed. Because we, as human beings, are naturally incomplete, we often strive toward perfection and balance, and sometimes this is done on a most subconscious level.

So, it may appear on the surface that one may be stagnated or polarized in a certain life-stage; we often behave in ways that are meant to evoke recognition, approval, and validation. Black masculine persons do this by taking agency in defining the "spaces" where they live. Place, space, home, and territory are metaphors often used in postmodern research to describe positions of the self in society. Home is a particularly useful metaphor because of its implicit property of privacy, self-protection, shelter, and comfort. Place, space, and territory are much more public terms that fuse the constitutive features of adjacency, interconnectedness, isolation, possession, yet fragmentation. In both cases, something clearly accents a void that needs to be filled. The motivation to do so characterized struggle, but the behavioral quest is about human possibility and growth. This is why struggle is at the center of the mandala. To speak of achievement and independence, for instance, one must at some point address the issue of potentiality and ask: "What are the possibilities of my achievement, or of my being independent?"

On a psychic level, struggle can be understood as the effort to seek out portions to fulfill our (self-observed) conscious needs and desires. The peculiar operation of conscious behavior in the social domain is that it nourishes and reproduces subconscious motivations, but the social domain initially constitutes these self-understandings. Consciousness, by nature, is fragmentary and an enactment of self-recognition. The fascinating dimension of consciousness is how it gets perpetuated on a daily basis via communicated identities.

Recognition. Human beings clearly coexist, and consequently we coordinate our behaviors so that human activity is somewhat synthesized and rule-governed. Michael Walzer (1997) offers an interesting approach to managing social diversity by rethinking coordination as toleration. His central thesis is that difference can be tolerated if humans can recognize how we are basically alike and dissolve commitments to group localities. He supports this thesis by expounding on what he names "regimes of toleration," which are multinational instances of submerged difference for the sake of human totality. Although intriguing, Walzer's analysis oversimplifies human difference and proposes an alternative the mimics "the melting pot" concept; however, Walzer is correct in suggesting that human difference makes social coordination problematic for those who find the activity of recognition to be a hassle. The discourse humans use to capture the thoughts we have about the Other is significant.

As Chandra Mohanty (1994) points out: "The central issue, then, is not one of merely acknowledging difference; rather, the more difficult question concerns the kind of difference that is acknowledged and engaged" (p. 146). Personhood is founded on what the Canadian philosopher Charles Taylor coins the "politics of recognition." The entire concept of masculinity is predicated on recognition. Therefore, the natural progression of gender relationships depends on this social process. Taylor asserts that a politics of recognition requires that "Others" recognize and identify the authentic "I," and offer it permission to proceed with a given behavior.

So, self-authenticity is discovered within the dynamics of human interaction; meanwhile the "Other" serves the function of recognizing and validating that construction. In cases where the "Other" fails to recognize or refuses to validate masculine behavior, then either the masculine person discontinues the behavior or suffers social penalty, which is sometimes more punitive than any other kind. Certainly, people can and often do present themselves differently to different people. This is but another facet of recognition politics. This perceptual factor, which affects positionality, is explained by Ribeau, Baldwin & Hecht (1997) as understanding "the feeling that there was a genuine exchange of thinking, feeling and caring" (p. 150).

Independence. Independence is about self-authorization, autonomy, and freedom of self-expression. All human beings seek it at some point in their lives, often as teenagers. As one matures, the manner and mode of self-expression often becomes more sophisticated. It is then more about transformation of the self. When scholars merge Black masculinities and independence in their conversations, they often evoke notions of resistance to dependence, control of situations, and ultimately deviancy. Independence does begin with self-assertion but does not need to end with abnormality or delinquency. Perhaps the best method of pursuing this phenomenon is to theorize *male* masculinities as spaces that are attached to behavioral modes of existence, so that a male's (based on Akbar's distinctions) masculinity will be perceived differently than a boy's or a man's. For example, a male's masculine quest for independence may be read as an unwillingness to commit himself to a relational partner, whereas a man's masculine assertion of independence may be related to self-development. That is, he may find it necessary to separate himself in order to understand himself better, as a separate entity rather than a dependent pair. The healthiest relationships are interdependent; in these exchanges, there is some balance between autonomy and dependence.

Achievement. At first glance, achievement may appear to reflect only acquisition, but its real concern is with accomplishment of personal and collective goals. Personal goals may range from materialistic items such as owning a BMW to the spiritual goal of being at peace and one with God. The personal impinges directly on the collective. The content of and progress toward one's aspirations of achievement automatically affect the success and survival of the collective. This is reflected in the African-American affirmation "I am because we are, and because we are, therefore, I am." This is much different than the quote representing the individualist, competitive, survival-of-the-fittest nature of Cartesian thought—"I think therefore I am." Masculine behavior cannot be substantiated as an intricate identity matrix if the only achievement concerns are with an individual's materialistic bread-winning capabilities. The cultural community to which he belongs is also critical. The commitment to the immediate and extended family, the church, and to the preservation of African-American culture is critical.

The discussion of achievement cannot ignore the reality of cultural identity *negotiation* among Black males. Roberts (1994) maintains:

> African American men must negotiate two cultural models of human relationships. . . . The Euro-American model emphasizes values such as competition, individualism, and domination as central to the human condition. The African model for human relationships, conversely, stresses the importance of group and community needs over individual aspirations, cooperation over competitive relationships, as well as interconnectedness among people. (p. 384)

In seeking to achieve one's goals, both cultural modes of behavior may be enacted in rapid succession such that they appear to be simultaneously engaged. The real danger is when Black masculine persons cease from embracing indigenous African-centered values, hence negotiating African cultural aspects of their identities. Staying grounded in one's cultural worldview, while functioning within a "Euro-American model," is difficult when switching back and forth between two modes of consciousness; however, this activity is important. This is what is meant by the popular phrases in the Black community—"stay Black" and "keep it real." They are admonitions to remain aligned with one's culture as one pursues his aspirations rather than relinquishing or negotiating aspects of the cultural self in the process.

Community. It is impossible to define one's self alone while living in a community of persons who must validate one's presence. Here, Black manhood is achieved ritualistically and behaviorally, while Black masculinity is perceptually reaffirmed. So, Black manhood is the behavioral category and Black masculinity is the perceptual category. Essentially, by this definition, *manhood* is relationally discovered via one's actions. The community not only affirms but also contractualizes the behaviors of Black men via interaction. The value of Black manhood is what it gives to the rest of the community. If one is unproductive, then the community must question his value. Manhood is both an agreement and social, political, and/or cultural assignment contractually arranged. As a result of the contract, Black men are figuratively bound to the community, which is the co-author of normative masculine behavior.

Black manhood is a behavioral category in flux developing with age, experience, stability, cultural consciousness, self-comfort, and spiritual awareness, and affirmed by the community. The "community" can be defined broadly as in a global or diasporic "family" and/or locally as in the neighborhood in which one lives. Therefore, it is increasingly difficult to agree on universal criteria for Black manhood because communities change and are often diverse. Nonetheless, the community affirms one's masculinity, no matter whether one is homosexual or heterosexual, fatherless or not, employed or unemployed, male or female. The composite cultural community may not be the adjudicates of masculinity or manhood; sometimes, those that affirm are persons who function similarly to the adjudicated individual. Nonetheless, the community plays a viable role in how masculinities are constituted and positioned.

These five factors that affect Black masculine positionality—struggle, community, achievement, independence, and recognition—are important aspects of repositioning Black masculinities to counter pathological depictions of Black masculinity. These factors offer some explanation for how masculinities are selected and enacted but also facilitate the redefinition of Black masculinity as cultural property.

IMPLICATIONS OF BLACK MASCULINIST RESEARCH

Black masculine identities are deployed and negotiated with struggle at the center of the exchange. Recognition, independence, achievement, and community are four factors that affect masculine positioning. So, you might ask: What are the implications for females or homosexuals? In conceptualizing masculinities, it is my attempt to be critical, yet inclusive. Based on the definition of *masculinity* given in this essay, both sets of persons can be masculine, although we have diverged at times from a unitary gender framework to a male conception of masculinity in order to accent unique concerns of that group of masculine persons. We are aware that class is a dominant and interceding factor of masculine realities as well. It is not discussed here because of the scope and nature of this essay. Clearly, many scholars have combined race, class, and gender, rationalizing that these terms are inseparable, especially as we write about the intersection of power and social formations. Likewise, it could be argued that sexual preference, physical ability, and a host of other ontological facets cannot be disjoined. Difference as a pillar of identity must be constituted, grounded in critical examinations of everyday experiences. These experiences and personal histories are numerous and must be deconstructed in order to better understand the formation and maturation of self-definitions.

The study of Black masculinities is an effort to recombine the African-American gender community. That should remain the goal. Theorizing masculinity as cultural, ontological, historical, communicative, and gendered is one progressive formula to achieve this goal. Extant gender research purviews the communicative, sociological, and psychological dimensions of male behavior. That should continue, and it should be culturally specific. If Black masculine theory is described as a set of explanations that stipulates a defining relationship between Black males and their environment, then certainly communication scholars should continue to create, develop, and sustain this circuit of inquiry. Empirical studies should explore this barren terrain. If Black masculine theory's primary function is to illustrate its opposition to feminine ways of knowing, however, then the venture is counterproductive. There are truly unique concerns that Black men share about their masculinities. This article begins that dialogue in the discipline of communication.

Discussion Questions

1. Define *theory*.

2. What are the five parts of the Black Masculine Identity Theory?

3. What is the difference between sex and gender?

4. What are the three stereotypes about Black masculine bodies that are explored in this chapter?

5. What do Jackson and Dangerfield mean by *agency*? How is that related to liberation?

Part V

African American Communication and Identity in Organizational and Instructional Contexts

Within organizational and instructional communication contexts, African American identities flourish and are negotiated. Certainly, African Americans, like all others, have cultural perspectives and values that enrich the workplace and the academy. However, many organizational communication scholars who investigate issues of culture have asserted that organizations too seldom embrace the cultural differences of their employees. So, rather than value their employees' culturally different work and leadership styles, many company leaders structure work in a culturally homogeneous manner, which scholars contend may have potentially harmful effects on productivity and morale. Devaluation of culture also has adverse effects in instructional contexts. This may occur as a result of perceived credibility or simply lack of diversity or mature perspective. In Part V, the essays cover these issues and more.

Brenda J. Allen's study of organizational diversity leads this section. In this conceptual-theoretic essay, Allen investigates race-ethnicity as a missing core component of organizational communication research. She identified the voids and negative consistencies in the literature and discovered that a central theme emerged: "organizational members' experiences, attitudes, and behaviors are often influenced by race-ethnicity." This theme was uncovered as she examined communication issues as they relate to stereotypes, cultural norms, and diversified workplaces. She completes her review by noting methodological issues that may complicate organizational studies.

Patricia S. Parker sustains this discussion of race and culture in organizations by presenting the perspectives of 15 African American women executives who work throughout the Unites States within dominant-culture organizations. She contends that one of the greatest limitations of a workforce that will gradually include a more richly diversified set of employees is dismissal of the multicultural perspectives reflective of their unique heritages. Rather than ask White executives their opinions about how to enhance the current masculine model of leadership to embrace difference, Parker focused on the leadership styles of African American women with an accent on leadership socialization and communication strategies. Using a multiple case study approach, she directly observed 12 of the women and conducted several semistructured individual interviews with each of 15 Black women in senior and upper middle management positions. These two research activities were supported by additional archival research. One of the unique features of Parker's study was her interviews with at least one subordinate who directly reported to each executive and also several other interviews with four of the executives' immediate supervisors. This offered a more holistic portrait of her analysis. She explained the results and reported that Black women executives' leadership styles tend to be more direct, inclusive, communicatively open, and boundary-spanning.

Similar to Parker and Allen's studies, Katherine Grace Hendrix points out a conspicuous void within the instructional communication literature—inattention paid to the issue of student and professor perceptions of instructor credibility within the context of predominantly White educational environments. Hendrix examines how credibility is communicated in the classroom and how race influences student perceptions of it. The study consisted of three parts: nonparticipant observation of six professors, administration of surveys to 28 students, and follow-up interviews with 19 of the 28 students. All of the student participants were taking only one class from one of the six professors. Painfully, some students' comments revealed their self-reported tendency to scrutinize Black professors more than White professors. In order for a Black professor to be deemed credible, many of these students expected more educational credentials and greater latitude in curricular materials. Several students had greater expectations of competency for Black professors in ethnic studies and English courses. Overall, however, Hendrix noted that the students welcomed the opportunity to be taught by Black professors, which may or may not have been affected by the fact that the interviewer is Black. The students seemed aware that limited contact with non-Whites would enhance the credibility of Black professors.

The final essay in Part V is a conceptual-theoretic essay concerning the limited academic credibility assigned to African Americans and the overall devaluation of African American intellectualism, and, hence, a product reflective of African American identities. The essay also provides several suggestions for transforming perceptions and development of African American communication scholarship and also African American identity negotiation. More specifically, I explain the harmful dismissal of paradigms produced by African Americans and its incumbent effect on the state and condition of communication research. The fact that paradigms such as Molefi Asante's afrocentricity and Mark McPhail's complicity theory are excluded from communication textbooks speaks negatively to who we are as a communication discipline. Yet, there are several contributing causes to this predicament, and I explore these using a nascent paradigm I have developed called *cultural contracts theory*. After explaining the three contract types (ready-to-sign, quasi-completed, and co-created), I offer examples of the ways in which African American communication scholarship has assimilated (ready-to-sign) traditional White perspectives, accommodated (quasi-completed) scholarship that refuses to acknowledge Black people's communicative experiences, or developed a space (co-created) in which their scholarship can be valued for what it represents and and how it appreciates other perspectives. The essay concludes with several prescriptive visions and suggests a full embrace of African American intellectualism and identities.

Reading 5.1

"DIVERSITY" AND ORGANIZATIONAL COMMUNICATION

BRENDA J. ALLEN

"Diversity" is a buzzword in popular organizational literature. Articles abound on how to manage and/or value heterogeneity among employees (Boyer & Webb, 1992; Coleman, 1990; Lewan, 1990; Ownby & Cunningham, 1992). Increased attention to diversity stems partially from a report (funded by the U.S. Department of Labor) which predicts that by the turn of the century, five-sixths of new workers in the United States will be women, African Americans, Hispanics and immigrants (Johnston & Packer, 1987). In addition, population projections indicate that by the year 2000, almost one in every three persons in the U.S. will be African American, Hispanic, Asian or Native American. These dramatic changes in the composition of society and the workforce will introduce tensions because "differences in cultural norms and values among ethnic groups in the United States will manifest themselves in different work-related behaviors" (Cox, Lobel, & McCleod, 1991). Furthermore, traditional Western management techniques may not be as effective with culturally diverse work groups (Coleman, 1990; Zak, 1994).

Increasing diversity in the workplace engenders practical as well as theoretical implications for persons who study organizational communication. Practitioners need to determine how communication contributes to the effective integration of a diverse workforce and to develop communication strategies to promote both integration and equality in the workplace (Corman, Banks, Bantz, & Meyer, 1990).

Scholarly attention to diversity might expedite the move toward a newer, "meaning centered," approach which analyzes dynamic, processual, and constitutive functions of organizational communication (see, for example, Mumby, 1993). Researchers also could generate richer theories by moving beyond Eurocentric

From Allen, B. J. (1995). "Diversity" and organizational communication. *Journal of Applied Communication Research, 23,* 143-155.

viewpoints (Hecht, Collier, & Ribeau, 1993). And, investigators who understand diverse interaction styles might develop fresh perspectives on traditional organizational communication issues.

This essay urges organizational communication scholars to incorporate diversity issues into their research. Doing so is especially important for applied researchers because they "can make a significant difference in the world by proposing viable solutions to difficult problems within important social contexts" (Kreps, Frey, & O'Hair, 1991, p. 82). As an African American scholar who studies organizational communication, I believe that conducting research about race-ethnicity would allow us to confront a momentous social issue, while also providing insight and direction for developing and refining theory about organizational communication processes.

The essay unfolds in the following sequence: first, I explain the parameters of this discussion. Then I explore reasons for the dearth of studies on race-ethnicity and organizational communication. Next, I review relevant literature. Finally, I discuss theoretical and methodological issues entailed in research on diversity.

The Scope of Diversity

Diversity in the workforce encompasses a variety of personal and social bases of identiy, including race-ethnicity, gender, age, socioeconomic status, religion, sexual orientation, country of origin, etc. Although all of these influence organizational communication, I concentrate in this essay on race-ethnicity, while acknowledging that no single factor accounts for communication attitudes and behaviors.

Race-ethnicity is salient because it usually is physically observable, its roots lie in affirmative action/equal employment opportunity programs, and it references the fastest rising groups to enter the workplace, particularly in non-traditional roles. Furthermore, "ethnic and racial discrimination [e.g., differential hiring and promotion, racist slurs, lower pay, etc.] in both the work force and the corporate domain is still widespread" (Van Dijk, 1993, p. 116). And, most diversity initiatives within organizations center around people of color and women (Kossek & Zonia, 1994).

I use the hyphenated term, race-ethnicity, in order to account for classifications based on real or presumed biological differences (race) as well as cultural differences (ethnicity) among groups. In addition, I concentrate on predominant "minority" groups within the U.S.: African Americans, Chicana/os, Chinese Americans, Japanese Americans, Filipina/o Americans, Native Americans, and Puerto Ricans (see Amott & Matthaie, 1991, for population statistics). To refer to the collectively of these groups, I use the term "people of color."

Why the Dearth?

Relatively few organizational communication studies (from the past 15 years) concentrate on race-ethnicity issues. However, organizational communication textbooks and readers have begun to broach the topic (see, for example, Conrad, 1994; Corman et al., 1990; Eisenberg & Goodall, 1994; Pepper, 1995; Triandis & Albert, 1987). Most information on race-ethnicity comes from disciplines other than communication (e.g., anthropology, sociology, psychology, organization behavior, and human resource management). In this section I explore possible reasons for the paucity of organizational communication research about race-ethnicity.

The omission of race-ethnicity as a central component of early studies is somewhat understandable, given the field's traditional managerial bias and the relative scarcity of people of color in the upper ranks of most organizations. The current oversight is a result of numerous other developments. Within the United States, many persons seem to believe that legislation such as the Civil Rights Act and equal employment opportunity (EEO) initiatives has ended racial problems and inequities in the workplace (Marable, 1990). This sentiment is evident, for example, in a tendency among white research subjects to deny that race is an issue in organizational settings (Alderfer, 1990; Fernandez, 1981; Jones, 1986; Van Dijk, 1993; Wharton, 1992). Moreover, as Thomas (1989) notes, because EEO posits the goal of a color-blind society, it may reinforce taboos which impede studying (or even discussing) the impact of color on interaction.

In academia, studies about organizations have tended to be race neutral (Nkomo, 1992). Scholars have used knowledge about one group (white males) to generalize to all groups, thereby evoking a type of monism in which the dominant group is accepted as *the* reference group (Nkomo, 1992, p. 489; also see, Minnich, 1990). Due partially to these monocultural assumptions, race-ethnicity is viewed as a marginal topic, and/or as a domain for minority scholars (T. Cox. 1990; Moses, 1989; Nieves-Squires, 1991). Several writers provided quotes from journal editors or doctoral advisors which attest to this idea: "Why have you chosen to put yourself in a research ghetto?"; "Blacks can't get tenure and do work on race"; and, "No established person has expertise or interest in this area" (T. Cox, 1990, p. 8).

Numerous methodological impediments further constrain efforts to study race-ethnicity. For instance, since race may be a taboo topic in many corporate settings (Jones, 1986), some administrators do not support research about it. Also, participants may be concerned about reinforcing stereotypes and prejudices or about being seen as spokespersons for their racial-ethnic group (Hecht et al., 1993). Or, they may be skeptical about the purpose of the research and worried about anonymity (Cannon, Higginbotham, & Leung, 1988). Numerous other misgivings also may arise; managers may be concerned about their own reputations, as well as their employees' reactions and welfare; white employees may fear being labeled as racist; persons of color may resent being singled out for study; and members of all racial-ethnic groups might question the validity of exploring the topic. This type of research also piques a profound social desirability issue: How many of us would be willing to acknowledge behavior or attitudes that might seem racist?

Finally, researchers often must face the consequences of reporting disparaging findings. Jones (1986) relates the story of a white investigator who was ostracized after reporting survey results which corroborated black managers' charges of discrimination at a large company. Despite these and other hindrances, some researchers have studied race-ethnicity, and their work provides a starting point for organizational communication scholars.

REVIEW OF RELATED LITERATURE

From existing literature, as well as my own experiences, a central theme about race-ethnicity emerges: *organizational members' experiences, attitudes, and behaviors in the workplace are often influenced by race-ethnicity.* To explore this theme, I will describe and interpret the literature that reflects it. Although the body of work to which I refer is not exhaustive, it is representative of research on communication and related areas of study (such as, organizational behavior, human resource management, and sociology).

Stereotypes and Communication

Many scholars have reported racially-based differences in attitudes and behaviors that may influence interpersonal communication (see, for example, Daniel & Smitherman, 1976; Giles & Johnson, 1986; Hecht, Ribeau, & Alberts, 1989; Kochman, 1981; Pennington, 1979; Wolfram, 1977). Their work applies here because "communication between individuals is a major component of organizational behavior at every level," (Harris, 1993, p. 283). Furthermore, I believe that most interethnic interaction occurs in organizational settings (e.g., student-teacher; client-service provider; customer-clerk; patient-doctor; interviewee-interviewer, etc.).

Individuals often hold stereotypes about persons whose race-ethnicity differs from theirs. A group of black and white college students reported negative, differing stereotypes of one another: Blacks said that whites were "demanding" and "manipulative," while whites said that blacks were "loud" and "ostentatious" (Leonard & Locke, 1993). Referring to Gibb's (1961) work on supportive versus defensive climates, the authors conclude that stereotypes help to create defensive climates during interethnic interaction.

An experimental study illustrates how racial stereotypes may manifest themselves. Johnson and Buttny (1982) asked white college students to rate a black speaker who either "sounded white" or "sounded black." Participants responded more negatively when the speaker sounded black as she talked about an intellectual topic than when she sounded white. However, they attributed no differences to speech style when the speaker sounded black *or* white during a speech whose content was narrative or experiential. Thus, whites may selectively bias their evaluations about people of color according to cultural stereotypes. Sometimes after I give a presentation or speech, a white person will exclaim, "You are so articulate!" What seems to me to be left unsaid is, ". . . for a black person."

Black college students on white campuses reported that many white students seem to see black students as "all alike": they are assumed to be athletes, to receive financial aid, and to be unintelligent (Feagin, 1992). Similarly, white faculty and students often assume that faculty of color are under-qualified and /or were hired to meet quotas (see, for example, C. E. James, 1994; Kossek & Zonia, 1994). Within corporate settings, whites often assume that Mexican-American and African-American managers have been promoted because of their race (Fernandez, 1981).

Other prevailing stereotypes include assumptions that persons of color are experts on issues pertinent to their race (Hecht et al., 1993; Jones, 1973, 1986), and that they have experienced racism and are thereby qualified to discuss race relations, discrimination, etc. (C. E. James, 1994). In educational contexts, students of color report that instructors and white classmates often expect them to "speak for" their race or culture during class discussions (Feagin, 1992). In the corporate world, African American managerial employees often are consulted about any issue that has anything to do with blacks, whether it is within their area of expertise or not (Jones, 1986). I have experienced this mindset: a woman from my university's contracting office asked me for advice about how to obtain bids from minority-owned businesses.

Most research focuses on how whites stereotype people of color (usually blacks), or how people of color think that whites stereotype them. Exceptions include Leonard and Locke's (1993) study, and an African American female's personal account of childhood beliefs and stereotypes about whites (e.g., "most whites . . . cannot be trusted," p. 46) that emerged from family stories about race (N. C. James, 1994).

Race-ethnicity-based stereotypes and expectations, as well as outright prejudice, can influence formal and informal interethnic interactions. For example, during formal performance evaluations, white raters tend to weight social behavior skills (e.g., friendliness, acceptance by others, sensitivity) more heavily for black ratees than white ratees (Cox & Nkomo, 1986; Feagin, 1991; Kraiger & Ford, 1985). Because they often encounter stereotypes, blacks tend to be more consciously aware than whites of how others may perceive and evaluate their behaviors (Foeman & Pressley, 1987; also see, Royce, 1982). This perception may inhibit open communication within a variety of formal contexts (e. g., team meetings, job interviews, sales consultations, etc.). Racial dynamics also affects mentoring activities, often inhibiting authentic collaboration in cross-racial relationships (see, for example, Thomas, 1989).

Blacks reported that whites often engage in "indirect stereotyping" (e.g., talking about "African American" topics such as music or sports) during interethnic exchanges (Hecht et al., 1993). Here's a personal example: As the only African American at a university–sponsored party for faculty a few years ago, I was appalled when a white professor (whom I had just met) asked me to sing a Negro spiritual. Although whites who engage in this type of discourse may be making genuine attempts to "relate," some blacks view them as patronizing or insensitive.

Value Systems and Cultural Norms

Differing value systems and cultural norms also influence interethnic interactions. A study of women's expectations of talk revealed racial-ethnic distinctions: black women concentrated on interpersonal skills, strategies and attributes, while white women focussed on language style (Houston, 1994).

Race-ethnicity-based differences in cultural norms resulted in disparate behaviors in the prisoner's dilemma exercise (Cox et al., 1991). Using Hofstede's (1980) value dimension of individualism-collectivism, the researchers found that members of cultural groups from collectivist traditions (Asians, African Americans, and Hispanics) tended to engage in more cooperative strategies than persons from individualistic cultural traditions (Anglo-Americans) (also see, Knouse, Rosenfeld, & Culbertson, 1992). Similarly, Triandis and Albert (1987) report that Hispanics within a school setting focused on interpersonal relations more than the task during group interactions, while Anglo-Americans favored the opposite.

Interethnic interactions also may be influenced by differences in conceptions of morality, In a critique of Kohlberg's (1971) theory of moral development, and based upon interviews with Chicano, black, Asian, and white research subjects, Cortese (1990) concludes that modes of moral reasoning may vary according to ethnic background. For instance, concerns about care and responsibility were more common among Chicanos, blacks, and women than whites.

Organizations may benefit from racial–ethnic differences in cultural values, language behaviors, and social perspectives. Conrad (1994) maintains that valuing diversity in the workforce (e.g., recognition, being treated with respect, quality of life, and financial security) will help American firms compete successfully in a global economy. And, Foeman and Pressley (1987) assert that African Americans' propensity toward a strong group orientation may correspond with a high sense of responsibility and personal standards.

A dissertation project provides partial support for this idea. Marcus Cox (1983) designed a Black Identification Questionnaire (BIQ), based on Cheney's (1983) Organizational Identification Questionnaire (OIQ) and administered both instruments to faculty and staff members of three midwestern universities. Although white staff members had higher organizational identification scores than blacks, black employees who identified most highly with their organizations tended to score highest on black identification scores. Thus, as Tompkins and Cheney (1985) conclude, "blacks who identified highly with their university of employment were not 'Uncle Toms.' . . . they also tended to identify with their black 'brothers' and 'sisters' within and outside the organization" (p. 199). In a later project, Marcus Cox (1988) found gender-related differences among black employees in identification and communicator style.

Communication in Diversified Workplaces

Researchers have begun to assess relationships between organizational communication and workforce diversity. Kossek and Zonia (1994) found that race and ethnicity were significant indicators of faculty members' attitudes towards diversity programs at a large university; whites were less positive than people of color. Using a deductive approach, Hopkins and Hopkins (1994) proffered a model which contends that initial level of diversity in an organization and rate of change in workforce composition affect communication effectiveness among employees, which in turn impacts productivity.

Finally, an ethnography entitled "It's Like a Prison in There" (Zapk, 1994) depicts communication problems that may plague newly-diversified organizations. After complying with equal employment directives, a vehicle maintenance unit became more demographically heterogeneous (by race-ethnicity, class, and gender), leading veteran employees (primarily white males) to assert their power through "symbolic actions and language patterns [horseplay and shoptalk], traditionally used to establish and maintain hierarchy in that workplace" (p. 281). In response to the verbal and physical exchanges that consequently erupted between newcomers and oldtimers, management stepped up control and enforced punitive policies, thereby creating a fragmented, dysfunctional organization.

Zak claims that this outcome stemmed from managements' failure to foster "communication processes through which sufficient shared or negotiated meaning and agreed-upon language and behaviors appropriate to the new workplace could be constructed" (p. 282). Her data indicate that race-ethnicity helped to account for differences in language and behaviors among employees, although it was not the only influencing attribute (e.g., gender also played a role).

In sum, differences in employees' racial-ethnic backgrounds can affect formal and informal organizational communication processes: stereotypes and expectations based upon others' race–ethnicity may impede effective interaction; and, differences in value systems and cultural norms may influence attitudes, expectations, perceptions, and language behaviors. I invite organizational communication scholars to address these issues as they conduct research, and to incorporate their findings into teaching and practice.

THEORETICAL/CONCEPTUAL IMPLICATIONS

Scholars should develop rigorous conceptual frameworks or theories to address workforce diversity. I recommend that organizational communication scholars base research about race-ethnicity on frameworks which strive to understand human interaction and social systems, and which give "voice" to participants (as contrasted with perspectives that privilege the researcher's voice (see Foss & Foss, 1989; Wood & Cox, 1993).

Moreover, as Wood (1993) observes, we should go beyond merely including neglected groups in our research. As an example, we might apply *standpoint theory,* which "uses marginalized lives as the *starting point* from which to frame research questions and concepts, develop designs, define what counts as data, and interpret findings" (Wood, 1993, p. 12). Although Wood discusses standpoint epistemology in relationship to gender, she notes that it also can be applied to other social constructions, e.g., race and class (also see, Harding, 1991). This perspective compels researchers to recognize commonalities among group members' experiences. It also requires investigators to "discover the conditions that structure and establish limits on any particular person or group of people. Following that, researchers may inquire into how those conditions are understood and acted upon by various individuals" (Wood, 1993, p. 15).

Critical approaches seem particularly fitting because they would compel researchers to analyze issues of power and control that inhere racism in our society. We could explore race-ethnicity and dynamics of power and domination during specific communication events

(e.g., job interviews; performance reviews; newcomer socialization; decision-making). These endeavors could help to fulfill a need to systematically examine organizational actors' "micropractices" (Foucault, 1970; Mumby, 1993).

Furthermore, we need to assess dynamics of power from an organizational/structural perspective (Limaye, 1994). This approach seems timely as increasing numbers of people of color enter the workplace, because successfully managing diversity depends on the "willingness by a group to share power" (Limaye, 1994, p. 361). For instance, Zak's (1994) study suggests that authoritarian management strategies may engender power struggles among ethnically-diverse workers.

Zak's ethnography also illustrates the interaction between micro and macro issues of power, an issue which Essed (1991) explores in her theory of "everyday racism." Her model "connects structural forces of racism with routine situations in everyday life" (p. 2). Scholars might employ Essed's model to conduct critical studies of organizational communication. (Also see Limaye (1994) and Nkomo (1992) for discussions about paradigms that might be employed to study race and power in organizations.)

The application of approaches that recognize diversity is likely to promote re-assessment of traditional perspectives on organizational communication. For example, existing research and my own experiences imply a need to study *organizational socialization* or *assimilation,* the process by which newcomers "learn the ropes" of their job (see, for example, Jablin, 1987; Van Maanen & Schein, 1979). As more persons of color enter the workforce and strive to advance, interethnic interactions often will form the basis of socialization experiences. Regardless of employees' race-ethnicity, power distinctions inevitably pervade socialization processes as newcomers and veterans grapple with issues of hierarchy, territoriality, tenure, etc. And, research has shown that persons of color tend to have limited access to social networks, to experience blocked mobility, and often do not have mentors or sponsors (Jones, 1986; Nkomo & Cox, 1989: Thomas, 1990, 1993).

Traditional perspectives on socialization focus more on how the organization acculturates the individual than vice versa, though some writers have addressed the latter issue. (For instance, Van Maanen and Schien (1979) discuss ways that a newcomer may "innovate" his/her role by seeking "to improve, make more efficient or less corrupt the existing practices by which given ends are collectively sought" (p. 228).) Moreover, people of color have been expected to check their race at the door, to become assimilated.

Currently, however, due to diversity initiatives, persons of color in modern organizations sometimes are expected to "help the organization" deal with diversity. As a new faculty member, due to stereotypes and expectations that I can (and even *should*) provide "the minority perspective," I have been asked to give guest lectures on race-ethnicity and communication, to advise colleagues about how to interact with black students, and to offer input about a variety of diversity issues as a member of university committees. Persons of color often are expected to fulfill these types of responsibilities, even as they are expected to learn the ropes of their job, and even as others may view them as under-qualified to execute their formal organizational role.

Thus, I believe that race-ethnicity-based stereotypes and difference (in values, norms, work ethics, etc.) further complexify an already-complicated process. Studying race-ethnicity and socialization may advance our understanding of organizational socialization processes, while shedding light on the role of race-ethnicity in organizational communication. In addition, since socialization experiences probably interact with one's ability and willingness to identify fully with the organization, we also might study identification and its flip side, alienation, perhaps by extending M. Cox's (1983, 1988) work on relationships between race, gender and organizational identification.

METHODOLOGICAL ISSUES

While designing research to study race-ethnicity and organizational communication, scholars should address a variety of methodological concerns. For example, researchers should consider employees' attitudes toward the topic, race-ethnicity. Recent attention to diversity within organizations could inhibit and/or enhance research endeavors because some employees may welcome the opportunity to share their experiences, others may feel more threatened than ever, while others may be tired of talking about diversity because they do not believe that the talk will lead to constructive outcomes.

One way to address this problem is to gather extensive background information that may be relevant to research questions. Zak (1994) assessed demographic change and population growth in the area surrounding the organization that she studied. In addition, she collected, categorized, and reviewed race and discrimination charges that had been filed against the organization. Accordingly, she constructed interview and focus group questions which reflected her understanding of situational variables, and which may have facilitated interaction with the participants. The background data also provided insight for her analyses of findings.

Researchers also should consider the potential impact of their race-ethnicity on research outcomes. Taylor Cox (1990) suggests that we strive to use multi-racioethnic, gender balanced teams (also see Cannon et al., 1988). This strategy can abet data collection efforts by fostering a sense of identification between interviewers and participants. For example, Zak (1994) assigned consultants to focus groups according to similarities in gender and ethnicity. However, researchers should not assume that employees will respond more openly to people who share their racial-ethnic background. It is probably more important to use well-trained and/or experienced researchers who are open-minded, than to match investigators and respondents according to race-ethnicity.

Using multi-ethnic teams also might strengthen analytical processes. Alderfer (1990), explains:

> . . . . the research will be most effectively done if it involves collaboration among race-and-gender balanced teams of people who can accept and work with (that is, not deny) their own and their partners' racial and gender identities in the conduct of the research. (p. 495)

When selecting research participants, we should not treat race-ethnicity as a monolithic variable. Organizational studies about race-ethnicity have tended to focus on African Americans (Cox & Nkomo, 1990). We need to study other racial-ethnic groups, because organizational experiences often differ across groups (e.g., blacks, Asians and Chicanos may be victims of stereotyping, but the stereotypes vary significantly). And, as Conrad (1994) cautions, we should remember that "white people have a race" (p. 495), and we should include their perspectives (about their racial-ethnic identity and about others') in our research endeavors.

We also should discern intragroup differences. Combined with contextualizing our findings, reporting differences within groups should deter us from perpetuating stereotypes about how "all" members of certain racial-ethnic groups behave. These measures also should preclude the propensity to provide generic prescriptions for how to interact with members of certain racial-ethnic groups.

To analyze the role of race-ethnicity in organizational actors' social construction of reality, data collection efforts should maximize the depth and quality of input from participants by obtaining their own accounts of their subjective experiences. Numerous qualitative research methods could achieve these objectives (e.g., ethnographic analyses, case studies, non-directed interviews, focus groups; see, Herndon & Kreps, 1993).

This is not meant to rule out quantitative methods. Experiments and surveys represent alternative methods for giving employees "voice." In fact, combining quantitative and qualitative strategies might render more comprehensive findings than relying upon only one technique.

As we report and analyze results, we should contextualize and qualify findings, recognizing that race-ethnicity may only partially explain our observations. We must remember that race is only one component of a "complicated web of socially constructed elements of identity formation" (Nkomo, 1992). Researchers often describe a need to simultaneously study race and gender because investigators often overlook women of color: research on race-ethnicity tends to focus on men: while gender studies usually concentrate on white women (see, for example, Bell, 1992; Collins, 1990; Moses, 1989; Nieves-Squires, 1991; Rothenberg, 1988; Spelman, 1988).

Finally, as we report findings, must be careful to protect participants' privacy, a challenging task in situations where it is easy to identify someone due to scarce numbers of persons of color.

In conclusion, recent and projected changes in workplace demographics constitute a complex web of issues that surely will impact organizational communication. Although "diversity" encompasses numerous individual characteristics, race-ethnicity embodies a critical aspect of how organizations are being transformed, and research indicates that race-ethnicity influences how organizational actors communicate with each other. My suggestions and examples are not meant to be exhaustive; I offer them to illuminate issues which, though part of my everyday reality, may not be visible to individuals who are members of majority social groups in the United States.

DISCUSSION QUESTIONS

1. What does Allen give as reasons for limited research on race and ethnicity in organizational communication?

2. What is meant by *indirect stereotyping*?

3. What is *standpoint theory*? How is that concept useful for the study of race and ethnicity in organizations?

4. Discuss one of the methodological issues Allen explores in this chapter?

5. Why, according to Allen, is race–ethnicity salient in organizations?

Reading 5.2

AFRICAN AMERICAN WOMEN EXECUTIVES' LEADERSHIP COMMUNICATION WITHIN DOMINANT-CULTURE ORGANIZATIONS

(Re)Conceptualizing Notions of Collaboration and Instrumentality

PATRICIA S. PARKER

Whom should we study to learn about leadership in organizations of the 21st century? In the past, the defining group for conceptualizing leadership communication, as well as other organizational theories and constructs, has been White[1] men (Nkomo, 1992). More recently, as organizational researchers began to study women in management, the focus still has been limited to predominantly one group, White women (Nkomo, 1988). In the new millennium, as Johnston and Packer's (1987) forecast of an increasingly diverse workforce becomes a reality, organizations would benefit from (re) conceptualizing leadership from the multicultural perspectives of the workforce. Indeed, studying diverse perspectives of leadership communication forces us to take seriously the claim that with organizational diversity comes fresh perspectives on traditional organizational communication issues (Allen, 1995) and a richer pool of resources for creating desired outcomes. The purpose of this article is to call attention to one underrepresented leadership perspective—that of African American women executives.

From Parker, P. (2001). African American women executives' leadership communication within dominant-culture organizations. *Management Communication Quarterly, 15*(1), 42-81.

DEFINING LEADERSHIP

The idea that leadership perspectives vary is not new. In the vast body of literature on organizational leadership accumulated over the past century, definitions and meanings of leadership are numerous, conflicting, and sometimes even absent altogether (Rost, 1991). My view of leadership is grounded in my own experiences as an African American woman and as a leadership scholar. From that vantage point, I find it difficult to view leadership as a set of universal constructs derived from a select few and generalized to all groups because those generalizations often do not fit my experiences as a Black woman within dominant-culture institutions. Rather, I see leadership as a localized, negotiated process of mutual influence that would theoretically accommodate multiple view-points and diverse situational challenges. Smircich and Morgan's (1982) definition of leadership effectively describes this perspective as one of social construction:

> Leadership . . . is the process whereby one or more individuals succeed in attempting to frame and define the reality of others. . . . Leadership, like other social phenomena, is socially constructed through interaction (Berger & Luckmann, 1966), emerging as a result of the constructions and actions of both leaders and led. It involves a complicity or process of negotiation through which certain individuals, implicitly or explicitly, surrender their power to define the nature of their experience to others. (p. 258)

This socially constructed view of leadership is reflected in current research trends emphasizing meaning-centered approaches to leadership (for a review, see Fairhurst, 2000). Grounded in the symbolic interaction perspective (Blumer, 1969; Mead, 1934), meaning-centered approaches view leadership as a symbolic, inter-active process through which meaning in organizations is created, sustained, and changed. The meanings of *organizational leader* held by individuals and groups are rooted in cultural norms and values and have high symbolic importance (Biggart & Hamilton,

1984; Rost, 1991). Organizational members come to expect leaders to look, act, and think in ways that are consistent with the socially constructed meanings of *organizational leader* and *leadership.*

Within dominant-culture organizations, the expectations associated with leadership traditionally have been in conflict with individuals' stereotypical assumptions about African American women. When White, middle-class cultural forms and values are the norm to which organizational members are expected to adapt, African American women's leadership communication may be socially constructed as deviant and negative and generally devalued (Lubiano, 1992; Parker & ogilvie, 1996; Weitz & Gordon, 1993). For example, directness is often used in a pejorative sense to describe African American women's communication behavior (e.g., Hecht, Ribeau, & Roberts, 1989; Shuter & Turner, 1997). However, these negative connotations are products of the Eurocentric, patriarchal discourses that define masculine communication as direct, control oriented, and competitive (i.e., instrumental, Eagly, 1987) and feminine communication as nondirective, noncontrol oriented, and noncompetitive (i.e., collaborative, Helgesen, 1990). Within this dichotomy, directness associated with Black women's communication may be viewed as deviant or not feminine, even though femininity and masculinity are socially constructed and highly political terms that exist as taken-for-granted descriptions of men's and women's communication. Thus, the subjective meanings of communication in Black women's experiences are typically left undervalued or unexamined (for notable exceptions, see Allen, 1996; Bell & Nkomo, 1992; Houston, 1997; Shuter & Turner, 1997).

In this article, I challenge the hegemonic discourses that limit African American women's access to the meaning-making process in leadership theory by placing Black women at the center of analysis. In voicing the viewpoints of a previously muted group (Orbe, 1997), I join the efforts of other communication scholars (Allen, 1996; Bell, 1997; Bullis, 1993b; Buzzanell, 1994; Fine, 1991; Gonzalez, Houston, & Chen, 1997; Marshall, 1993) who took issue with the trend of "privileging some voices into the academic domain . . . and failing to include others" (Vande Berg, 1997, p. 89). However, I also deconstruct the Eurocentric patriarchal discourses that silence Black women's voices. As Michelle Fine (1994) emphasized, following Bhavnani (1992), it is important to analyze "not just the decontextualized voices of Others, but the very structures, ideologies, contexts, and practices that constitute Othering" (p. 70).

A fundamental goal of this research, then, is to focus attention on the contradictions inherent in the lives of people marginalized by dominant-culture ideologies and practices and to affirm the knowledge—in this case, leadership knowledge—gained as they work through those contradictions. In doing so, I hope to provide insight to scholars and practitioners interested in developing a broader understanding of leadership communication. Toward those ends, I present a grounded qualitative analysis of leadership communication from the perspectives of 15 African American women executives and their coworkers within dominant-culture U.S. organizations. The following research question guided the study: What are salient elements of African American women executives' leadership communication as described by the executives and their coworkers within dominant-culture organizations?

I begin with a Black feminist/standpoint perspective (Collins, 1990, 1998a; hooks, 1981; Hull, Scott, & Smith, 1982; Lorde, 1984), which provides an analytical framework for viewing leadership communication as an outcome of Black women's resistance to systems of race, gender, and class oppression. Next, I offer a critical review of the gender and leadership literature, demonstrating how notions of instrumental and collaborative communication are socially constructed through hegemonic discourses that privilege White cultural perspectives, creating gendered, institutionalized theories of leadership. Then, I present my research on leadership communication, which is grounded in the experiences of 15 African American women executives within dominant-culture U.S. organizations, followed by a discussion of some practical and theoretical implications of this research.

A Black Feminist Perspective for Studying African American Women as Organizational Leaders

A Black feminist perspective (cf. hooks, 1981; Hull et al., 1982; Lorde, 1984) directs attention to Black women as self-defined, self-reliant individuals who confront race, gender, and class oppression (Collins, 1990) and stands in opposition to the economic, political, and ideological systems of oppression that suppress Black women's ideas (Collins, 1990). A useful analytical framework for exploring Black feminist perspectives is standpoint theory (Collins, 1986, 1990, 1998a; Harding, 1987, 1991; Hartsock, 1987; Smith, 1987). Standpoint theory provides an epistemology that focuses on the production of knowledge that leads to emancipation from oppressive social conditions (Allen, 2000; Harding, 1987).

A fundamental tenet of standpoint theory is that women and others marginalized by intersecting systems of oppression (i.e., race, class, gender, age, sexual orientation, and national origin), occupy societal positions from which they are able to see, not only their own positions, but the dominant system as a whole. This view from the margins is often referred to as the "outsider within" perspective (Collins, 1986, 1990, 1998a). Outsiders within the dominant culture are assumed to be able to provide a more complete and less distorting social perspective (Harding, 1987) than is possible from the point of view of the insiders or more privileged group members (usually White middle-class men).

Like other research applying standpoint theory to the study of dominant-culture organizations (Allen, 1996; Cockburn, 1991; Ferguson, 1984; Marshall, 1993), the present study focuses on women's experiences as legitimate and important sources of knowledge about organizing. Collins (1986, 1990) argues that from the vantage point of the outsider within, African American women have created an independent, viable, yet subjugated knowledge concerning our own subordination. I would argue that from that vantage point, Black women also have created knowledge about leadership that historically has been ignored or devalued.

At the intersection of racist and sexist ideologies created during the era of slavery and perpetuated throughout U.S. history, Black women have been denigrated as "Mammies," matriarchs, super-women, castrators, and "Sapphires" (Christian, 1980; Morton, 1991; Walker, 1983), or most recently in the news media as "welfare queens" and overachieving Black ladies (Lubiano, 1992). African American women must negotiate and reconcile the contradictions separating their own internally defined images of self as African American women with identities that are (re)produced through patriarchal systems of domination and subordination (Collins, 1990).

The process of negotiating and reconciling identities contributes to the contours of Black women's voice (Collins, 1998a) and informs a Black feminist standpoint. Black women's standpoints are a valuable resource for understanding leadership. If organizational leadership is understood as a process of negotiating meanings within contradictory and paradoxical situations to forge viable solutions, then we would do well to listen closely to what the experiences of Black women leaders can reveal.

MANAGING THE TENSIONS OF THEORIZING WOMEN'S EXPERIENCE

Emphasizing a collective "women's experience" is problematic because it produces a tension between avoiding essentializing women's experiences on one hand and highlighting women's experiences as a critique of hegemonic discourses on the other (Alvesson & Billing, 1997; Mumby, 1993). Standpoint theorists responding to critiques of essentialism (i.e., Allen, 1996; Buzzanell, 1994) assert that rather than essentializing the category *woman,* feminist standpoint theory encourages researchers to solicit stories from many types of women. Others (i.e., Ferguson, 1984; Fletcher, 1994) suggested that what is most important is listening closely to women's experience as a way of developing alternatives to hegemony.

Although I also believe that it is important to listen closely to women's experience, I agree with Alvesson and Billing (1997) that in theorizing women's experience, it is equally

important to "explain which women and which experiences, and to address the problems and possibilities of generalization" (p. 35). African American, Hispanic, Native American, and Asian American women have criticized the feminist movement and its scholarship for being overly concerned with white middle-class women's issues (Andolsen 1986; Collins, 1990; Dill, 1983; Moraga & Anzaldua, 1983). White women's values are often put forth as representative of all women's values.

My focus on African American women executives' leadership communication within dominant-culture organizations situates my study within a particular group of Black women. On one level, this research challenges the depiction of "women in general," which usually refers to White middle-class women (hooks, 1984). However, on another level, I recognize that among the women in my study, there are multiple experiences of Black identity (hooks, 1990), worked out at the intersections of race, gender, class, and perhaps other socially constructed categories, such as sexual orientation, region of the country, urban or rural residence, color, and hair texture. Therefore, I do not intend to offer a "final vocabulary" (Rorty, 1989) on Black women's leadership communication, which would then be generalized to all Black women. Rather, with this study, I advocate drawing attention to Black women's voices in an ongoing dialogue about what counts as leadership knowledge. I argue, following Collins (1990, 1998a), that research that starts from a shared group standpoint—our common (but not uniform) location in hierarchical power relations in the United States—is necessary for such advocacy and for political action.

THEORIZING GENDER AND LEADERSHIP; DECONSTRUCTING (WHITE) "MASCULINE" AND (WHITE) "FEMININE" LEADERSHIP

In her critique of organizational communication theory development, Judi Marshall (1993) observed that "theory making is essentially an ideological process, an exercise of power that can privilege certain social groups, certain points of view" (p. 139). Marshall urged theorists to be explicitly aware of the fact that in male-dominated cultures (patriarchies), this exercise of power is inevitably gendered, such that "female forms are relatively devalued, underdeveloped, and muted" (p. 125).

I argue that, in addition to being gendered, the exercise of power in theory making is also "raced." That is, Western society has emphasized White middle-class values, and "'White' as a category is 'raced' in the same way that men as a category are gendered" (Frakenberg, 1993, as cited in Rowe, 2000, p. 65). Scholars tend to conceptualize organizations as race neutral, taking a dominant few (White middle-class men and women) as the inclusive group and the ideal for humankind (Nkomo, 1992). This race-neutral view-point is evident in theorizing about organizational leadership.

In the mainstream gender and leadership literature, two competing models of leadership are discussed, which were developed based almost exclusively on studies of White women and men but which are presented as race-neutral (Parker & ogilvie, 1996). One model is based on the notion of masculine instrumentality, and the other is based on the notion of feminine collaboration. Both models are grounded within perspectives that privilege White middle-class cultural norms and values and are reinforced through gender symbolism that operates as the universal depiction of men and women across cultural and class boundaries.

The masculine model of leadership emphasizes a hierarchical approach in which leaders initiate structure while demonstrating autonomy, strength, self-efficacy, and control (Bem, 1974; Eagly, 1987; Loden, 1985). The masculine model of leadership is theorized as representative of male values (Marshall, 1993) and is most often associated with men's socialized communication patterns (Tannen, 1990; Wood, 1998). According to this perspective, men use more instrumental communication—unilateral, directive, and aimed at controlling others—which is consistent with their learned view of talk as a way to assert self and achieve status (Eagly & Karau, 1991). Distance and detachment are common communication themes associated with male values (Marshall, 1993). Common symbolic representations of the masculine leadership model include characteristics such as aggressiveness, independence, risk

taking, rationality, and intelligence (Collins, 1998b; Connell, 1995).

The feminine model of leadership emphasizes a relational approach in which leaders show interpersonal consideration through relationship building, empathy, and interdependence (Bem, 1974; Eagly, 1987). The feminine model of leadership is associated with female values (Marshall, 1993) and viewed as a reflection of women's socialized patterns of communicating (Tannen, 1990; Wood, 1998). According to this perspective, women leaders use collaborative communication, which is viewed as supportive, participative communication that enables others (Helgesen, 1990, Lunneborg, 1990; Rosener, 1990). Common symbolic representations of this model include characteristics such as nurturance, compassion, sensitivity to others' needs, and caring (Collins, 1998b; Grant, 1988).

BEYOND WHITE CULTURAL LEADERSHIP: CONSTRUCTIONS OF THE FEMININE IN BLACK WOMEN'S EXPERIENCES

When the above descriptions of feminine and masculine leadership are treated as universal gender symbols, as they often are within dominant-culture institutions (Collins, 1998b), Black women's experiences are excluded, as are the experiences of other women of color, men of color, and non-middle-class White women and men. Collins (1998b) makes this point:

> Aggressive Black and Hispanic men are seen as dangerous, not powerful, and are often penalized when they exhibit any of the allegedly "masculine" characteristics. Working class and poor White men fare slightly better and are also denied the allegedly "masculine" symbols of leadership, intellectual competence, and human rationality. Women of color and working class and poor White women are also not represented [by universal gender symbolism], for they have never had the luxury of being "ladies." (pp. 217–218)

Such exclusionary thinking ignores the subjective meanings that individuals develop for themselves and limits the range of possibilities for leadership practice. For example, for African

American girls and women, constructions of the feminine are accomplished at the intersection of race, gender, and class and may take the form of resistance to the taken-for-granted definitions of femaleness (i.e., White middle-class womanhood). Ladner's (1971) pioneering research on African American girls' expectations about their adult sex-role behavior revealed that, in spite of what was then the popular Anglo-dominated image of womanhood—to be glamorous and carefree—the girls in her study expressed difficulty justifying this image as a legitimate one. Instead, the girls most frequently identified with an image of a strong, resourceful, hardworking, and economically independent African American woman.

More recent research (Fordham, 1993; Gilligan et al., 1992) indicated that African American girls may use communication behavior as a way of resisting images of White womanhood. Using data obtained from an ethnographic study of academic success in a predominantly African American urban high school, Fordham (1993) argued that loudness reflects the efforts of the Black girls in the study to subvert the consuming images of White middle-class womanhood. Similarly, in a 3-year ethnographic study of 33 Black, White, Hispanic, and Portuguese girls in the Midwest, Gilligan and her colleagues (1992) found that the Black girls in the study are "encouraged to be outspoken in the world . . . and to not suppress what they are thinking" (p. 128). The researchers argued that Black girls hold "cultural conventions of Black womanhood that may help an adolescent girl to stay in relationship with herself and her community and be a source of personal self-esteem and pride" (p. 130).

When viewed form White cultural standpoints, African American women's communication is often seen as deviant and negative, and it is generally devalued (Parker & ogilvie, 1996; Weitz & Gordon, 1993). For example, Weitz and Gordon (1993) surveyed 256 White non-Hispanic undergraduates about their perceived images of Black women. They concluded that (a) Anglo students assign different emotional evaluations to the same trait depending on whether they are characterizing women in general or Black women, and (b) Anglo students believe that Black women are generally characterized by a different and substantially more negative set of traits than women in general.

Like Marshall (1993), I advocate theorizing that embraces multiple points of view on leadership theory and practice, including the viewpoints of African American women.

Marshall emphasized "unmasking and contradicting the male positive/female negative values of this world" (p. 126). I believe it is equally important to unmask and contradict the White positive/non-White negative value orientation. To move beyond negative patterning, we must sometimes "create environments and forms in which women's meanings, and female values can be expressed, voiced, and explored as part of an evolving process of discovery" (Marshall, 1993, p. 139). It is in that spirit that I explore Black women's meanings of leadership.

METHOD

Research Design

The research reported here is part of a larger study that examined African American women executives' leadership socialization, communication strategies for managing dominant-culture constraints and opportunities, and leadership communication (Parker, 1997). The data analysis for the leadership communication portion of that study is reported in this article. The research followed a field-study design (multiple-case method) and used qualitative methods.

Sample

The research sample included 13 African American women executives in senior management positions, 2 African American women executives in upper-middle management, one or more of each executive's subordinates, and in four cases, the executives' supervisors. The African American women executives participating in the study were chosen based on the following sampling criteria: (a) they were employed at a dominant-culture organization at the time of the study, (b) they were at the level of director or above, (c) they had line responsibility, and (d) they had supervisory responsibilities.

These criteria are consistent with those used by other researchers interested in top management leadership by women (Mainiero, 1994; Rosener, 1990). Because of funding limitations, sampling was limited to the western, southern, and southeastern regions of the United States. The final sample consisted for 15 African American women executives who were interviewed in five states and in Washington, D.C. Six executives worked at organizations in the southern region of the United States (Arkansas, Louisiana, Tennessee), six were in the southeast (Georgia and Washington, D.C.), and three were in the Pacific southwest (California).

In addition to regional diversity, the African American women who participated in the study varied in terms of socioeconomic background, age, and tenure, as well as organizational type and industry.[2] The industries represented in the sample were insurance, communications, education, and state and federal government.

Data Collection

Data were collected using interviews, direct observation, and archival research. Face-to-face interviews were conducted with each executive. One or more of each executive's direct reports were interviewed, and in four cases, the executive's supervisor was interviewed, for a total of 42 face-to-face interviews and 1 telephone interview. Among the 15 participants, the interactions of 12 were observed. Four of the executives hold high-profile positions, and some instances of their interaction were taken from media sources (such as radio and television interviews, newspaper accounts of their activities, and public messages). Archival data were collected from each executive and included samples of internal and external forms of communication such as publications, memos, speeches, daily schedules, corporate media, logos, and emblems.

Interviews followed semistructured interview protocols (one each for the executive, subordinate, and supervisor interviews) based on topics related to the research question. Because I was interested in understanding leadership communication as the management of meaning, the questions for all three protocols were designed to solicit descriptions of the executives in interaction with coworkers, subordinates, and clients. In developing the questions, I focused on communication-based aspects of leader behavior described in the literature (Yolk, 1989), including the executives' leadership philosophy and stated mission, conflict management approach, influence strategies for employee performance, and methods for handling employee resistance. Most interviews lasted about an hour; they ranged from 45 minutes to 2 ½ hours.

The subordinate and supervisor interviews lasted an average of 30 minutes. All of the executives' supervisors were White men. The direct reports were predominantly white men and women but also included African Americans and Hispanics.

I used field notes to record descriptions of the leadership contexts, summarize the archival data, and document my direct observations and preliminary analyses of the leaders in interaction. Participants were asked to suggest activities that involved them in interaction with subordinates, peers, superiors, or clients (e.g., meetings, employee forums, and teleconferences). The direct observation times ranged from 30 minutes to 4 hours. When possible, I cross-checked my interpretations with those of the people being observed.

Data Analysis

Data for analysis were derived from transcripts of 43 interviews (with the 15 executives and 28 of their coworkers), field notes, and summaries of archival data. Grounded theory procedures and techniques, as outlined by Strauss and Corbin (1990), were used for data analysis. Consistent with the multiple-case-study method, each case was coded in turn. A case consisted of the executive interview and the corresponding supplemental interviews (i.e., supervisor and subordinates), fieldnotes, and archival summaries. I coded the case transcripts using constant comparative analysis in which data were assigned to an emergent open coding scheme (Strauss & Corbin, 1990). As an internal validity check, I recorded propositions and hypotheses that emerged as I made comparisons among and between the cases. As an additional cross-check, I compared the observational data and archival summaries from my field notes with the reports of the interviewees.

After all the data were coded, two researchers trained in qualitative analysis reviewed the coding scheme and coded data. These researchers played the roles of devil's advocate and questioner. During this final stage of analysis, no new categories were formed, but two categories were renamed to better fit the thematic descriptions.

RESULTS

Five themes related to leadership communication were revealed in the narratives and observations of the 15 African American women executives who participated in this study and in the descriptions provided by their coworkers. The themes are (a) interactive communication; (b) empowerment through the challenge to produce results; (c) openness in communication; (d) participative decision making through collaborative debate, autonomy, and information gathering; and (e) leadership through boundary spanning (see Table 1). These broad themes and their related subthemes are described below.

Interactive Leadership

This theme represents the central dimension of the African American women executives' leadership approach, because it forms the basis of their overall approach to communicating leadership. The women's leadership can be characterized as interactive, meaning that they are very much involved in negotiating the space between employees' needs and values and organizational needs and values. Their leadership is practiced primarily through face-to-face interaction. When face-to-face interaction is not possible, the executives said they use voice mail and telephone conference calls as a means of staying connected with their employees. The executives used written communication as a follow-up to oral communication. However, none of the executives said they used written communication as much as oral modes.

None of the executives are micro-managers who insist on having tight control over employee activities. Instead, the data revealed an interactive leadership approach characterized by the following subthemes: (a) knowing the business, its mission, and its goals and being able to communicate that knowledge clearly, directly, and consistently; (b) being accessible to staff and customers; and (c) modeling effective behavior. Each of these subthemes represents a form a leadership intended to facilitate both personal and organizational growth and learning.

Communicating knowledge about the business. One way the executives demonstrated interactive leadership was through knowing the business, its mission, and its goals and being able to communicate that knowledge in ways that directly engaged employees, clients, and other organizational constituents. One executive, who had left her post in senior management just prior to the interview, described her strategy for communicating her vision in this way:

> I was always out there painting my vision. I was really talking to people. I managed, if you will, by walking around. You know, whatever their piece was, I really went to paint the vision them of what their piece contributed to our getting up here. Let's say the clerks that answered the phone. I told them, "You're the ears for this entire [organization]. People call in and talk to you, and if you don't make them feel that they're wonderful, then they start talking about how horrible we are. They don't remember what I am or what I do. . . . It's you." And then all of a sudden they start feeling, "well our job is the most important job in the [organization]."

Similarly, another executive says she coaches her employees on how to communicate about the business:

> One of the things that I told my managers in some meetings, months ago [was] . . . when somebody asks you how's it going, you tell them "Great! This month, my group alone contributed $320,000 to the market area!" or "So far this year, our whole office has already done $4.3 million for the company!" And, so, I said that's the only thing people really respect, is numbers, dollars, and what is going on. And so, it's how you present it in a positive way. If you're like, "Well you know, we've got some people who aren't coming to work on time." So what? The point is most [units] in this company

Table 1   Descriptions of African American Women Executives' Leadership Communication Within Dominant-Culture Organizations

Leadership Communication Theme	*Description*
Interactive leadership	Knowing the business, its mission, and its goals, and being able to communicate that knowledge clearly, directly, and consistently Being accessible to staff and customers Modeling effective behavior
Empowerment of employees through the challenge to produce results	Expecting high performance, based on the executive's confidence in the person's ability to deliver Setting specific goals for producing high quality results
Openness in communication	Bringing important issues into the open Making sure voices (including their own) that need to be heard on a certain issue get that opportunity Having no hidden agendas
Participative decision making	Collaborative debate: dialectic inquiry that involves one-to-one argument and explicit agreement and refutation for the purpose of collaboratively reaching decisions Autonomy: trusting employees and pushing control of the organization to the lowest levels Information gathering: staying aware of multiple points of views
Leadership through boundary-spanning communication	Connecting the organization to the Black community in positive ways Articulating the organization's mission and purpose

don't generate money. They do servicing. They make sure the [services] are OK. You've got to have those, those organizations so that you can sell and so that you can get things in. But, I'm like, "You need to be proud. Hey, you are generating money for the company." . . . When I was in external affairs, I didn't generate money for the company. I gave money away. But I didn't generate it.

By engaging employees directly and frequently about their vision, the executives served as an important reference point for interpreting the organization's goals. One staff member commented.

> She is very good at molding her vision and goals into most all of her communications, whether they be one-on-one, whether they be group discussions with small groups, or in general communications with the organization as a whole. . . . She has an ability to fold [her vision and goals] in and keep them out front and visible to everybody so they always have that longer term sight of what those goals are.

One measure of effectiveness in communicating an organizational vision is consistency among organizational leaders and their followers in articulating a vision as it relates to the organizational mission and goals (Schein, 1985). In this study, I observed high consistency among the executives and their staff in the descriptions of the organizational mission and goals.

Accessibility. Another expression of the interactive leadership theme is accessibility. Several of the direct reports described their executive as "approachable" and as a good listener, revealing an overall tendency toward accessible leadership. For example, one staff member gave this account to describe her executive's approachability and listening effectiveness:

> Her calendar is usually really, really tight, but she makes it a point that once she's out there she comes and personally interacts with the service reps, gets to know who they are. . . . I'll give you an example. . . . One of my reps and her sister

[were] in another office and [had] been trying to transfer [here]. And, this young lady walked up to [the executive] and she said, "Oh hi, I understand I just got my transfer, I'm over here now." And [the executive] said, "Great, great!" She goes, "And you know, I'm still trying to get my sister over here." Well, [the executive] came to my area last week, and she walked up to her and said "Hi, [says the employee's name correctly] right? Listen, any luck getting your sister here yet?" She said, "As a matter of fact, yes, her transfer just came through," And [the executive] said, "Oh great!"

So, people know that [the executive] communicates with them, because she listens to what they say. . . . So I think people see how hard she works, and they work just as hard. I think, it's, you know, leadership by example.

Modeling. The executives themselves viewed modeling effective behavior as central to their leadership approach. One executive explained how behavior modeling serves as a powerful motivational tool:

> So my leadership style is personal involvement. Earlier this year, I felt that my sales teams needed additional sales training. I personally . . . found a consultant, met with the consultant, told him what I wanted him to do in the class. The first class [I attended] with my managers. I said, "I'm going to take this class. Y'all better show up. It's going to start on Sunday afternoon and it's going to go through Friday." I was there. And I stayed in the class the entire 6 days, which means, "You can't walk out of this class. If I'm in here and you're not in the classroom . . . I'm going, 'Well, I guess you don't need this, huh?'" I get directly involved with them. I don't ask them to do anything I won't do. I didn't ask my managers to go to the class if I wasn't going to go to the class.

Collectively, the descriptions, informing the interactive leadership theme reveal an emphasis on personal involvement that reinterprets the notion of control as interactive and personal rather than as distant and competitive. The executives' interactive style of control does not stifle employee autonomy. Indeed, staff members talked about feeling quite autonomous and even empowered as a result of their executive's

interactive leadership approach. This process of empowerment points to the second theme related to the African American women executives' leadership approach.

Empowerment of Employees Through the Challenge to Produce Results

From the perspective of these executives, a key tool for motivating employees is expecting high performance, based on the executive's confidence in the person's ability to deliver, and then setting specific goals for producing high-quality results. This approach informs a strategy for empowerment that is simultaneously directive and nondirective. It is directive in the sense that there is a clearly initiated structure within which employees are expected to operate; and it is nondirective in that the employees are encouraged to exercise a great deal of freedom within the initiated structure. The most persuasive evidence of employee empowerment is provided by staff comments. For example, one staff member commented,

> I think when she has trust in a person's substantive knowledge and judgment, she, you know, wants you to be out there doing what [needs to be done]. . . . She's very focused; never wants to have a meeting for the sake of the meeting. Wants an outcome on everything that happens. Wants assignments to come out of there. Wants people to come back with their assignments done. For example, during meetings, she turns to her staff and says, "You own that; that's your responsibility; do it." Every meeting that's what happens. [And if, for some reason, someone doesn't own a task effectively], she will get on the phone and say, "You haven't delivered." She believes in interacting directly with people.

Along similar lines, another executive's staff member commented,

> I think she's very people oriented, but understanding that she also wants action. She wants things moving in a positive direction. She's not happy with the status quo, as I told you before. But she balances it with the people, you know, she's very caring to the people. [The executive] looks out for our best interest. But understand that

people know that if they're not accountable, she will step up to doing what she needs to do. I mean, there is no question. She holds people accountable . . . if you're not doing your job, you may not be here.

In addition to the staff members' accounts, the executives' supervisors also commented about empowering employees through the challenge to perform. One executive's supervisor said,

I think she's very direct. I think if you talk to the people who work in the organization, it is all business. That doesn't translate to any lack of humanism . . . I think she is very compassionate. She really goes to bat for people, particularly if she believes that they're trying to improve and that they're working hard at it. I think she's going to drive and lead and expect, you know, people to perform. On the other hand, everybody is not at the same place at the same time. And it's OK to struggle, and you don't have to be at the same place at the same time, but you had better be improving. And she's not sympathetic for someone who's less than committed.

Indeed, the executives themselves described their approach to developing employees in terms of empowerment through encouraging autonomy.

What stands out among these accounts is the paradoxical notion that the employees feel a sense of autonomy that is, to a certain extent, mandated by the executive. Tensions reproduced by this paradox of structure (Stohl & Cheney, 2001) are managed by communication practices that emphasize a kind of openness that is redefined from Black women's standpoints.

Openness In Communication

The third leadership theme emerged from descriptions of the executives as direct communicators. Data from the executives' staff members and supervisors revealed words and phrases such as direct, straightforward, "shoots it straight," demanding, "all business," precise, focused, and dynamic to describe the women's leadership. Moreover, each of the executives described herself in terms such as direct, to the point, opinionated, or focused. When asked to elaborate on these words or phrases, the interpretation of directness that emerged was openness in communication not meant to intimidate but to negotiate.

Directness is a label that is often associated with African American women's communication (McGoldrick, Garcia-Preto, Hines, & Lee, 1988), although the interpretation is often negative (Hecht et al., 1989; Shuter & Turner, 1997; Weitz & Gordon, 1993). From the standpoint of these African American women executives and their coworkers, directness is interpreted positively. Here, directness means (a) bringing important issues into the open, (b) making sure voices (including their own) that need to be heard on a certain issue get that opportunity, and (c) having no hidden agendas. The data revealed that this directness through openness is accomplished not only at the interpersonal level but also at the group and organizational levels. Here is how one executive described her strategy for raising important issues and getting the 140,000 members of her organization involved in a dialogue that created their strategic mission:

It is very important to get everybody [in the entire organization] clear . . . to get everybody focused on what we do. And people were unclear about what we did. You know, people who worked in [one particular] program thought we do [tasks connected to that specific program]. But they didn't see their ties to the [core activities of the organization] . . . So I have worked very hard to engage people for almost 9 months in this debate as we shape where we are going for the 21st century. So I look 100 leaders in the organization—union, non-union, labs—each one of these . . . probably these people didn't know what the other guy did. And we banged away at it for 3 1/2 days. We came back 6 months later and came up with, you know, this [pointing to the pictorial model of the organization's mission statement].

The pictorial model the executive described was displayed prominently in the foyer of her office and served as a symbol of the executive's style of open engagement. Approaching the executive's suite of offices, one passes through a long hallway lined with the larger-than-life portraits, in muted colors, of her predecessors, who were all White and male. On entering the foyer that leads into the executive's suite of offices, there is an explosion of color. Covering one wall is the pictorial model of the organization's mission statement, depicted as a large, playful mural in bright red, yellow, white, and blue. On the opposite wall there are large, contemporary photographs of the executive at work sites around the country, with children in laboratories, and with prominent business and world leaders. The bulletproof doors and armed guard that served past executives were ordered removed by this executive. Clearly, the executive promoted an open style of communication with the members of her organization. More fundamental, however, is the way in which this openness is constructed symbolically through the executive's direct emphasis on her presence as a Black woman among her White predecessors.

Interviews with two of the executive's staff members confirmed the above description of her tendency toward openness and the effect on the organization. One staff member said that a major outcome of the executive's efforts is that the amount of communication within the organization has increased since the executive has been in charge. The other staff member reasoned that organizational members had the opportunity to be much clearer about how they contribute to the organization's goals.

In another example of bringing important issues into the open, another executive's supervisor extolled the value of her ability to promote openness at the interpersonal level:

I think she really practices what she preaches in that area [of being open with employees] very much. She is, of course, very, very honest with her management, her employees; she doesn't try to manipulate people or try to take a situation that's difficult and make it sound better than what it is. She went through a reorganization here very recently where she did some outsourcing of a lot of employees. And it was handled, I think, as well as any we've done in the company, because she was just very up-front and at the very beginning told everybody what the problems were and what solutions we were looking at, which included potentially outsourcing. And she was very sensitive to their . . . to the employees' needs.

Another subtheme related to openness is making sure voices that need to be heard get that opportunity. The primary practice here is making sure that status differences do not thwart efforts to invite organizational participation by all levels of employees. The executives used a number of tactics to reach employees, including interacting directly and in meaningful ways with employees in positions at lower levels of the organization. For instance, one executive reported.

Someone in [one of the field offices] told me that by the time a letter is sent to me, got to me and gone through all of these bureaus, they couldn't even identify the note that they sent. So, as the director, I don't call the people below me to answer questions; I call the folks where I want to talk with them and talk with them directly about whatever the issues are. I spend a lot of time going out to the local field units, doing speaking engagements and talking with them and answering questions for them.

Other tactics to ensure all employees' voices have the potential to be heard include convincing employees that their jobs are directly tied to the organization's effectiveness, "going to bat" across departmental and hierarchical boundaries to secure employees' and departmental interests, and recognizing employees for their work. Employee recognition seemed to be particularly salient among the 15 executives. In the following example, one executive explains how acknowledging employees' efforts is central to motivation, thereby inviting organizational participation:

I show appreciation for what they've done. . . . And, it's not money; it's not giving them more money, even though we have a responsibility to pay people for what they do. I think the motivation comes from within. It's making people feel good about the type of service they're providing and what they're doing and to show that you truly appreciate what they do, all levels. And that is the challenge I think we have with the corporation. . . . That's one [practice] I see that we need to spend a lot of time doing. [Since] coming over here the last several months . . . some people have told me—I mean not some, *lots* of people have said, "You know, as long as I've worked here I've never had anybody to tell me that they appreciate what I do. I feel appreciated because I feel like I can see my results but no one has taken the time to say that." And they have just thanked me for recognizing what they've done.

The final subtheme related to openness in communication is having no hidden agendas. The most common expression of this theme was in the staff members' and supervisor's observations that they are always sure where the executive stands. In one instance, an organizational newcomer commented,

I really wasn't expecting it to be like this. But she's a very dynamic person. She's always straightforward. I think most of the time, and by most of the time, I mean 99% of the time. I come out of a meeting knowing where things are, and what her objectives are and her goals, and that sort of thing.

Another executive's supervisor provided a similar description of what it means to have no hidden agendas in communicating leadership:

[I am impressed with] the ability she has to take a problem and get the issue on the table, in other words, you don't sit there trying to listen to a statement and wonder, "What's she really saying?" . . . She doesn't make people mad or anything about doing it; she is very good as far as getting the issues [on the table] and let's get 'em resolved and get on to the next thing.

In sum, the openness in communication theme reveals a form of communicating that emphasizes inclusion (i.e., issues and voices) and trust (i.e., no hidden agendas) as important outcomes. What is interesting, however, is how the executives achieve these outcomes through proactively seeking to animate multiple voices in the leadership context. The process of engaging multiple voices is central to employee empowerment and to the participative decision-making practices that inform the fourth leadership theme.

Participative Decision Making Through Collaborative Debate, Autonomy, and Information Gathering

The data revealed that all the executives used some form of participative decision making enacted through collaborative debate, autonomy, and information gathering. Several of them used a collaborative debate structure. The term *collaborative debate* is used to refer to the process of dialectic inquiry in which employees who are likely to disagree with prevailing opinions are invited to give input via one-to-one argument and explicit agreement and refutation (Kennedy, 1980) for the purpose of collaboratively reaching decisions. One executive, who described the kind of decision making on important issues she does *not* value, shows a clear example of the collaborative debate tactic in this passage:

I don't want a serial debate on this issue, where the people who are a little pro come to see me, the people who are a little con come to see me. I would like to debate with everyone in the room. I really do want everybody at the table with varying points of view in this intellectual and technical debate with the yea-sayers and the nay-sayers. Let's hear this debate. But, where this boils down when we talk to real people is in language so they can understand this. So, let's have this debate in clear, concise language, because we're going to have it with the American public. And that presumes, first of all, to come with a brand new and a very fresh point of view.

In addition to bringing together diverse or conflicting groups, participative decision making also was revealed in descriptions, such as the following, of an executive simply pulling together the groups necessary to move forward on a project that had been stifled by indecision and disagreement. A staff member explained.

What happens sometimes is that it becomes difficult to get people to agree around the state, so they drop it. [The executive] is like, "I don't accept status quo, we need to move this for the business, and who is it we need to call or whatever and get this going." And [the executive] got involved and said, "Well, why was it dropped?" You know,

"We need to pick this back up, because I think it is the right thing to do for the business." And she's started to move it, meaning getting in touch with the right people. She has held meetings with the [various groups from around the state] and stepped up to that, where it was kind of just dropped.

Decision autonomy is another decision-participation tactic revealed in the data. Employee accounts showed evidence that the executives encouraged departments to be autonomous in making decisions, for example, bringing the executive "in the loop," as one employee phrased it, only when necessary:

Today on the conference call from 3 to 4 we will review [a proposed performance plan] and we will discuss what we feel are the right things. Then, we'll put it in place. Now probably, at some point, we'll bring [the executive] into the loop. But, [until we make a decision, the executive] says, "Here's your revenue, here's your cost, and here's what you need to look like. How you measure the people to get that, that's your call."

In another example of decision autonomy, an executive described how she was restructuring her organization to increase localized decision making:

I think empowering people means trusting them and pushing the control of the organization as low as we can. How in God's creation can I tell this person what to do at the local county, when their finger is on the pulse of things, not mine? I think I look at it from the bottom-up approach not from a top-down approach.

Other examples of participative decision making demonstrate an information-gathering approach. Several staff members talked about expecting their opinions to be heard on issues, although on some issues, the executive would ultimately make her own decision. One staff member observed,

[The executive] really pays attention to the people who are in the trenches. She gives everybody an opportunity to speak [her or his] piece. And I think she gathers all that information. She utilizes

people that are around her to their utmost, because, you know, I think there's strength in what she does, in the way that she does that, it adds to the outcome.

Collectively, the executives' approaches to decision making revealed a reluctance to accept the status quo. However, there was no evidence that this tendency to challenge the status quo was grounded in a need for competition. Rather, the data revealed that these women saw themselves as a conduit through which the diversity of viewpoints could be brought together, negotiated, and enacted.

Leadership Through Boundary Spanning

The African American women executives in this study demonstrated a mastery of boundary-spanning communication. According to the four executives' supervisors interviewed, boundary spanning is an important function performed by the African American women executives who report to them. Although a central theme seems to be that the women are good at connecting the organization to the African American community in positive ways, the supervisors emphasized how effective the executives are in articulating the organization's mission and purpose across organizational boundaries, as the following example demonstrates:

When we brought to the board the need for a major curriculum redirection, that meant that we almost had to take the "road show" out to the people. And [the executive] and I brought that in a number of public forums that we had this year, and we did it in a number of presentations to civic and other groups, sometimes together, sometimes separately. . . . I'm proud knowing what community reaction to her is going to be. It's always very, very favorable because it is quite evident that she translates this kind of self-assuredness. And where we're going is interpreted by the people out there that the district's in good hands.

The executives themselves view boundary spanning as an important function. For example, one executive said that establishing rapport with other units that affect her organization is the key to her leadership effectiveness.

Staff members also expressed the importance of the boundary-spanning function. In their accounts, the predominant theme is how the executives are able to represent the staff members' interests to important others within the organization. Other subordinates describe their executives as skilled extraorganizational communicators:

> We went up in February to this meeting discussing a rather complex issue about combining certain programs, and it was pretty heated. And from what I saw—her speaking before a rather large group of people about something that is as controversial as this—she was very good. She was calm and she seemed to sense the divisiveness in the air. And some of the people that I talked to who were with her at board meetings commented on her ability to reach compromises and express herself well.

In summary, the leadership communication themes above represent one current interpretation of leadership practices grounded in the experiences of African American women executives within dominant-culture organizations. The themes reveal the commonality in the executives' leadership communication, depicting a proactive approach to leadership. Consistent with the goals of feminist-standpoint theory, these themes can be seen as movement toward valuing Black women's experiences. They are representative of leadership meanings and values that emerge from a particular vantage point—that of Black women executives within dominant-culture organizations—and that have been excluded or devalued in leadership theorizing. In the next section, I discuss how these themes and the analytical perspective developed earlier in this article can contribute to an ongoing process of leadership-theory building in the 21st century.

(RE)CONCEPTUALIZING COLLABORATION AND INSTRUMENTALITY

The purpose of this research was to describe leadership from the standpoints of 15 African American women executives within dominant-culture U.S. organizations. Using a Black feminist standpoint perspective in this research provided a framework for (a) questioning the hegemonic discourses that have suppressed Black women's ideas and (b) focusing instead on the leadership meanings and values that emerge from listening closely to their experience. Despite differences in age, organizational tenure, socioeconomic background of their family of origin, and the organizations and industries in which they worked, I noticed striking similarities in the ways the women enacted leadership, as revealed in the five leadership communication themes. I argue that underlying these themes is the influence of a Black woman's standpoint, which emerges through the struggle against oppression and the controlling images of Black womanhood (Collins, 1990). "Adding in" Black women's meanings to established theoretical frameworks (Marshall, 1993) can broaden our conceptualization of collaborative and instrumental leadership.

The results of this study can be used as a basis for reenvisioning traditional notions of collaborative leadership as nurturing and caring and instrumental leadership as directive and controlling. The five leadership themes reveal collaborative leadership as a negotiated and dynamic process that combines the redefined elements of instrumentality, control, and empowerment. Symbolic images of women as master collaborators (Helgesen, 1990; Loden, 1985) reflect an emphasis on collaboration as an alternative to control, where control is defined in terms of distance, detachment (Marshall, 1993), and competition. However, from the perspective of the African American women executives in this study, collaboration is worked out at the intersections of control and empowerment, where control is redefined as personal and interactive. Directness and control become a means of collaboration. The focus is on the other, not as a means of affirming the other person—although that may be an outcome—but as a way of assessing points of view and levels of readiness to perform. The women used personal involvement and attention as a medium for initiating structure, identifying places of struggle or conflicting viewpoints, and encouraging employee autonomy.

As a leadership strategy, this view of collaboration emphasizes the paradoxical practice of direct engagement (i.e., constraint/structure), which creates routes for individual empowerment (i.e., creativity/process). It contradicts the *either/or* thinking of traditional notions of collaboration and instrumentality and more accurately captures the *both/and* nature of organizational leadership (Fairhurst, 2000; Marshall, 1993).

Instumentality as a leadership strategy is often characterized as direct—unilateral, competitive, and aimed at controlling others—consistent with views of White, middle-class, masculine communication (Eagly, 1987; Rosener, 1990). In this study, the African American women executives' communication is described as direct, but the interpretations are positive and proactive. Grounded in the experiences of the executives and the people with whom they interact, the notion of directness is (re)defined as a type of openness in communication designed to invite dialogue and personal growth. In this study, instrumentality is (re) conceptualized as both direct and relational (Fairhurst, 2000). It is direct in terms of the strategic framing and transmission of messages (Fairhurst & Saar, 1996) and relational in terms of the emphasis on dialogue and meaning construction. This view broadens the concept of instrumentality to include processes associated with transformational leadership—being charismatic, engendering inspiration, providing intellectual stimulation, and showing individualized consideration (Avolio & Bass, 1988; Bass, 1985). In addition, with the dual emphasis on strategic message transmission and dialogue, this expanded view of instrumentality casts both leaders and followers as active agents in the creation of organizational meaning.

The (re)conceptualized notions of collaboration and instrumentality reported in this study counter the hegemonic discourses that have suppressed Black women's ideas and expand traditional views of organizational leadership. By placing Black women at the center of analysis, we can begin to see the both/and quality of Black women's voices (Collins, 1990), Behavior deemed as controlling, conflictual, or acquiescent through a White cultural framework is understood here as the capacity by Black women to see the infinite possibilities of individual characteristics through a lens of constructing a solution. Situated at the intersection of race, gender, and class oppression within dominant-culture society, the contours of Black women's voices are simultaneously confrontational (in response to different interests) and collaborative (in response to shared interests; Collins, 1998a). The result is a process of leadership that produces what Collins (1998a) terms *contextualized truth.* Based on Henderson's (1989) metaphor of "speaking in tongues," contextualized truth emerges through "the interaction of logic, creativity, and accessibility" (Collins, 1998a, p. 239). Implicit in the discourses of producing contextualized truth is the willingness and ability to construe knowledge and values from multiple perspective without loss of commitment of one's own values (Bruner, 1990). This kind of thinking about leadership, as exemplified by the African American women executives in this study, should be added alongside traditional thinking about leadership.

IMPLICATIONS FOR THEORY, RESEARCH, AND PRACTICE

The primary implication of this study for leadership theorizing is that we should continue to seek diverse sources of knowledge. For the past several decades, leadership researchers have been implicitly guided by the question, what can we learn about leadership from the perspective of assumed White privilege? What I have demonstrated in this research is that it is fruitful to learn about leadership from the perspective of people who struggle against race, gender, and class oppression. More research is needed that explores the leadership communication of other cultural groups, such as African American men, Asian Americans, Native Americans, and Latina/o Americans. Rather than reproducing the hierarchical view-points that have dominated leadership theorizing, it is more revealing to study groups in their own right and to see the relationship of all groups to the structure of race, class, and gender relations through society (Andersen & Collins, 1992).

Communication scholars (cf. Allen, 1996; Allen, 2000; Bullis, 1993b; Buzzanell, 1994; Houston, 1988, 1997; Wood, 1993) are at the forefront of advancing intersectionality in organizational studies. However, more research of this kind is needed. Only recently have we begun to take gender into account in theorizing about organizational communication (Bullis, 1993a; Marshall, 1993; Mumby, 1993), and rarely do we treat race as an analytic variable in organization studies (Nkomo, 1992), or as a central, constitutive feature of organizing. Research focusing on the influence of class is virtually nonexistent in organizational communication theorizing (for a recent exception, see Gibson & Papa, 2000). Studies are needed that address these gaps.

Another implication of this study is that we should continue to (re)conceptualize leadership in the 21st century in ways that shift away from mainstream leadership theories that are grounded in what Rost (1991) referred to as the leadership mythology of the industrial paradigm, for example, having one person take charge and directing from a distance (in the tradition of a John Wayne character or General George Patton). Rost argued that industrial narratives may have served their purposes since the 1930s, but leadership scholars need to develop a new leadership narrative grounded in values associated with the postindustrial paradigm, such as common good, diversity and pluralism in structures and participation, client orientation, and consensus-oriented policy-making process.

Several scholars have issued similar calls for this kind of redirection in leadership theory and research, offering alternatives to the hegemonic discourses of structural functionalism. Burns's (1978) concept of transformational leadership led to a completely new understanding of leadership. Also, Robert Greenleaf's (1977) model of servant leadership proposed a "new moral principle" in which individuals will not casually accept the authority of existing institutions but "will freely respond only to those individuals who are chosen as leaders because they are proven and trusted as servants" (p. 10). Finally, feminist critiques of structural functionalism have challenged the leadership theories of the dominant paradigm (see Calas & Smircich, 1998, 1991; Kellerman, 1984; Sayre, 1986), arguing against the closure imposed by organizational research and theory on what can be said

to be organizational knowledge. Future research should continue this trend of challenging the values of the industrial paradigm, constructing theories and models of leadership that address the wants and needs of people in a post-industrial society (Rost, 1991).

Finally, a third implication of this research relates to the way we view the leadership process. I propose that leadership theorizing should reflect the interplay and struggle of the multiple discourses that will likely characterize 21st-century organizations. The contemporary workplace is becoming increasingly multivocal and ambiguous in terms of organizational stakeholders' interests and values, the expectations associated with corporate social responsibility, and the challenges of meeting customer needs within the context of volatile global markets (Deetz, 1995; Eisenberg & Goodall, 1997). An important role of leadership is most certainly to animate (i.e., bring to the foreground) and then facilitate this multivocality. In the present study, this process is revealed in an interactive approach to leadership in which the executives see themselves as a conduit through which a diversity of viewpoints could be brought together, negotiated, and enacted. We should continue to explicate theories of leadership that acknowledge the facilitation of multivocality as a central process. Smircich and Morgan's (1982) approach to leadership as the management of meaning provides a good example of this kind of theorizing, as does Weick's (1978) notion of the leader as medium.

There are also practical implications of this research. First, this study serves an emancipative function by helping to give voice to a tradition of knowledge and communication practices grounded in Black women's experiences. In asking the women in this study to speak for themselves—to be self-defining—this research helps to shatter the controlling images of Black women that are created through racist and sexist ideologies (Christian, 1980; Lubiano, 1992; Morton, 1991; Walker, 1983). This study adds to the growing body of research that looks at traditionally marginalized people from their own viewpoints, giving voice to previously muted cultural traditions (Allen, 1996, 1998, 2000; Gonzalez et al., 1997; Hecht et al., 1989; Orbe, 1997; Shuter & Turner, 1997).

In addition, this research serves as a basis for promoting cultural sensitivity within contemporary organizations. Fine (1995) defines cultural sensitivity in terms of three components, with each building developmentally on the previous component: (a) recognition of cultural differences, (b) knowledge about cultural differences, and (c) suspension of judgment about cultural differences. This study provides important cultural information—grounded qualitative descriptions of African American women executives' communication—that might benefit people who work with African American women executives, encouraging them to reject their preconceived images of Black women, which may be based on stereotyping. Fine (1995) argued that developing multicultural literacy, which emerges from an attitude of cultural sensitivity, is essential for survival in a multicultural society. Similarly, Shuter and Turner (1997) point out, "With diversity growing in corporate America, it is important that culturally driven stylistic differences are understood and appreciated by managers and employees" (p. 92). I hope this research contributes to increased multicultural understanding.

DISCUSSION QUESTIONS

1. How does Parker define *leadership?*

2. What is meant by the *outsider-within* perspective?

3. How does Parker draw attention to Black women's voices in this chapter?

4. Compare and contrast the masculine and feminine models of leadership.

5. How does interactive leadership charcteize Black women's leadership styles in dominant-culture organizations?

Reading 5.3

STUDENT PERCEPTIONS OF THE INFLUENCE OF RACE ON PROFESSOR CREDIBILITY

KATHERINE GRACE HENDRIX

Teacher communication is sometimes referred to as the interface between knowing and teaching. Two major instructional goals include the acquisition of knowledge and the ability to transfer the knowledge learned in one context to new situations. The behavior of teachers can result in positive classroom outcomes because teachers can serve as catalysts who motivate students to achieve the cognitive and self-esteem goals associated with an academic environment (Brophy, 1979). Two factors influence a teacher's ability to affect the self-concepts of students: (a) credibility and (b) self-esteem. Teacher credibility is formed in "the minds of students," and teacher self-esteem is personal and internal (Bassett & Smythe, 1979, p. 179). The credibility construct, when applied to teachers, has been defined by McCroskey, Holdridge, and Toomb (1974) as consisting of five dimensions: character, sociability, composure, extroversion, and competence.

The communication discipline has devoted much attention to identifying speaker characteristics associated with credibility (O'Keefe, 1991). These studies, however, have typically focused on public speaking or public figures with whom the audience possessed limited, if any, direct contact. Of 99 studies with the term *credibility* in the title, only 5 examined ways in which teachers established, maintained, and lost credibility, or the effect of teacher credibility on learning (Beatty & Behnke, 1980; Beatty & Zahn 1990; Frymier & Thompson, 1992; McCroskey et al., 1974; McGlone & Anderson, 1973). None of the 5 teacher credibility studies employed a qualitative method despite the complexity of the classroom as evidenced by educational research within Shulman's (1986) classroom ecology paradigm.[1] Thus, the depth and texture normally associated with qualitative approaches were missing.

In addition to the absence of extensive research exploring teacher credibility, communication and

From Hendrix, K. (1998a). Student perceptions of the influence of race on professor credibility. *Journal of Black Studies, 28*, 738-763.

education researchers have overlooked the classroom experiences of teachers and professors of color. In particular, the experience of being a member of a subordinate minority (Fordham & Ogbu, 1986) functioning as a professional within a predominantly White educational environment has escaped the interest of the White social scientist (Foster, 1990; Weinberg, 1977). Yet, Black teachers and professors do exist.

Black teachers have contributed to the education of children and adolescents in the United States for 2 centuries. With the onset of desegregation, most Black teachers and principals were dismissed or demoted at the same time Black students were being enrolled in previously all-White schools (Coffin, 1980; Smith & Smith, 1973). According to Banks (1986), parents in the Northern cities were often as violently opposed to desegregation as their Southern counterparts. White flight to the suburbs was another means of avoiding desegregation under the guise of desiring neighborhood schools. At present, public schools in the United States (a) are becoming increasingly non-White and Poor and (b) are segregating a disproportionate number of White students from the rest of the student body by assigning them to academically gifted courses (Delpit, 1995; Ladson-Billings, 1994).

At the collegiate level prior to 1900, teaching positions for Blacks were confined to land grant colleges rather than to privately supported institutions. Only two Blacks, besides Dr. W.E.B. Du Bois, held teaching positions within predominantly White colleges prior to 1900 (Moss, 1958). According to Guess (1989), a U.S. Equal Opportunity Commission Report revealed that in 1985, 90% of the full-time faculty was White, whereas only 4.1% was Black. The number of Black professors has only increased slightly over the past two decades. *The Chronicle of Higher Education* (Magner, 1996) reported that Black faculty represented 4.4% of the senior faculty members at U.S. institutions and 5.4% of the new faculty hires.

Given the (a) restricted interactions between Black teacher/professors and White students, (b) negative tenor of race relations within the United States (Guess, 1989; "For the Record," 1996; Frisby, 1994), and (c) continued expression of alienation by Black faculty (Cook, 1990; Lopez, 1991), it is logical to speculate that a classroom of predominantly White students may present particular challenges to building credibility and acceptance (and promoting student learning) for the Black teacher and professor.

Black teachers and professors are expected to motivate students and to cultivate learning while also instilling a sense of appropriate and inappropriate behavior; yet, the classroom experience of these educators have not been carefully analoged. In view of the gaps in the extant literature regarding the (a) way teachers establish, maintain, and lose credibility; (b) classroom experience of Black teachers and professors; and (c) extensive reliance on quantitative research methods to identify and assess the impact of credibility, I developed four research questions to investigate the credibility of Black and White professors teaching at a predominantly White postsecondary institution (see Hendrix, 1994, 1997).

The investigation, grounded in a review of the literature as well as my professional experience, addressed four research questions relative to student and professor perceptions regarding how (a) credibility is communicated in the classroom and (b) race influences student perceptions of professor credibility.[2] This article details the research methods I used to investigate the credibility of six male professors and provides a brief overview of the students' definitions of professor credibility. However, the focal point of this article is not what was revealed in response to the original four research questions but, rather, what Black and White student participants revealed about credibility beyond direct responses to the research questions.

This article explores the underlying motivations leading students to look and listen for particular cues when enrolled in courses taught by Black professors.

RESEARCH METHODS

Research Site

Nonparticipant observation occurred in six undergraduate courses at a large 4-year research institution in the Northwest reflecting a predominantly White student enrollment. The university was selected as the site of the investigation because the percentage of Black faculty and Black student enrollment was consistently small. The fall 1993 student enrollment at this research institution was as follows: Native American Indian, 1.1%; Black, 3.2%; Hispanic, 3.3%; Asian, 16.1%; and White, 76.3%. Thus, out of a student body of 34,000, only 3.2% (1,088) of the students were Black. Yet, according to the 1990 federal census records, 10.1% of the metropolitan area's residents were Black. Black faculty represented 1.5% (60) of the 3,986 faculty, whereas White faculty represented 89.6% (3, 573).

Professor Participants

The participants in this study represented a "purposeful rather than random" sample (Miles & Huberman, 1984, p. 36). Six professors (two in Phase 1, four in Phase 2) were selected using the following criteria: (a) race, (b) gender, (c) age, (d) teaching experience, and (e) departmental affiliation. My goal was to obtain the participation of male dyads reflecting professors who worked in the same division and possessed comparable years of teaching experience at the collegiate level. However, three of the professors would be Black and three would be white.

This study reflected the beginning stage in a series of planned investigations on this topic. Thus, it was important to keep the level of complexity to a minimum. The study findings and their interpretation would have been complicated by the use of both male and female professors—especially considering the small number of professor participants. Using all male professors allows the study to be replicated at a future date with all female professors and, thereby, will allow for a comparison between the data sets. Thus, the criteria were developed to keep constant those variables that might otherwise account for differences (Nisbett & Ross, 1980) in perceived credibility (e.g., gender).

Dyads (using fictitious names) were created that consisted of two professors teaching in the same division within a particular college of the university. The three dyads represented the social sciences (Professors Bryan and Wyatt), performing arts (Professors Bell and Wilson), and an undergraduate professional program (Professors Blair and Webb). Professors Blair and Webb taught within a structured undergraduate professional program. The program admitted approximately 50 competitively selected undergraduate students each year into a structured series of courses taught over a 2-year period. The professional program prepared students for immediate entrance into the job market, and students moved through the curriculum sequence as a class. The remaining professors taught undergraduate courses with enrollments ranging from 100 to 400.

Student Participants

A total of 28 students enrolled in one of six courses under observation participated in this study. Data were gathered from 9 students in Phase 1 and 19 students in Phase 2. In Phase 1, on the 3rd week of the quarter, a Professor Credibility Survey was disseminated in the classes taught by Professors Bryan and Wyatt. Student volunteers (those providing identifying information allowing for follow-up contact) were separated by class standing (i.e., sophomore, junior, etc.), race, and major (in the same field as the professor or in another field). Student interviewees were then randomly selected from a volunteer pool within each category. In the second phase of data collection, the selection procedures were adapted. Due to the limited number of students who volunteered to make themselves available for in-person interviews, data collection in the second phase was adjusted to ensure a diverse pool. Because of the small number of students of color who volunteered, all were accepted. The students who were selected from the volunteer pool and assigned fictitious names are summarized in Table 1.

Data Collection Procedures

Three different methods were used in this study: (a) nonparticipant observation (Spradley, 1979, 1980), (b) semistructured interviews (Ginsburg, Jacobs, & Lopez, 1992) of students and professors, and (c) open-ended questionnaires.

Findings were triangulated across these three methods (Erickson, 1986; Mathison, 1988).

Nonparticipant observation schedule. In Phase 1, observations occurred on a daily basis during the 1st week of the quarter. Observations of one class period were also made during the 2nd, 3rd, 5th, 7th, and 10th weeks of the quarter. In the study's second phase, the communicative behavior of four professors and their interaction with students were noted during 7 weeks in a 10-week quarter.

Semi-structured student interviews. Student interviews occurred several weeks after the distribution of an open-ended survey during class time. Student interviews that assessed the credibility of their professors were critical because the students were the target audience for the professors' efforts.

One interview was conducted with each of the 28 student participants. Most interviews occurred during Weeks 6 and 7 in the quarter and typically lasted close to 60 minutes. Interviews were generally conducted in the researcher's office. When a student arrived, the person was greeted and left alone for several minutes to review the Student Consent Form. The time alone was also designed to give each student a personal glimpse by seeing my space within the office, family photos, books, and so forth as well as those of my office mates. The artifacts functioned as one means of self-disclosure. My ultimate goal was to allow self-disclosure before (artifacts) and during the interview to build trust and elicit honest answers from both the students of color and White students.

Professor credibility survey. The term *credibility* was first used during Week 3 when the researcher addressed each professor's class to explain the research project, distribute the Professor Credibility Survey document to each student, and to persuade students to provide identifying information that would allow for follow-up appointments and interviews. In each case, the professor left the room.

Once at the front of the room, I introduced myself and explained my objective of investigating how professors communicate to build, maintain, and even lose credibility. I then explained that the triangulated design called for input from professors, students, and me. An overlay of Page 1 of the survey was placed on the overhead and the following three options were discussed: (a) do not complete the survey; (b) complete only the demographic and open-ended questions but leave Section B (name and phone number) blank; and (c) complete all sections of the survey, including identifying information.

Data Analysis

Student interviews. Most of the student interviews were conducted in my office. Students were asked to comment on their responses on the Professor Credibility Survey as well as additional questions. I listened to the participant responses and took handwritten notes while also audio recording the interview. When analyzing the data from student interviews, the audio recording was played while handwriting the student comments verbatim. The verbatim transcript was cross-checked against the written information provided by the student on the Professor Credibility Survey and the researcher's notes taken during the actual interview.

The transcription from each interview was reread with marginal and reflective researcher comments jotted in the left margin along with location of the comment on the audiotape. Key phrases or words within the transcript were occasionally circled or underlined. Marginal comments included noted areas of similarity with other respondents–including the professor participants. Matrices were then constructed to visually display the student's oral and written responses to the questions posed on the Professor Credibility Survey. In addition, student responses to a particular set of questions and my general impression of each interview were also reduced and placed within the matrix. Examples of interview questions include: (a) Why are you enrolled in this course? (b) Have you ever taken a class from a Black professor or teacher? and (c) Do you typically assess the credibility of your professors?

The visual display was constructed in a series of stages. Stage 1 entailed the construction of a checklist matrix that allowed quick comparisons between the male/female and White/non-White students within one particular professor's class.

Table 1   Student Interviewees

Fictitious Name	Race/Ethnicity and Gender	Year in School
Professor Bryan		
Allan	White male	Freshman
Carrie	Native American female	Senior
Jay	Pacific Islander male	Freshman
Marie	White female	Junior
Steve	Black male	Senior
Professor Wyatt		
Antoinnette	Black female	Sophomore
Bill	White male	Junior
Mark	Black male	Junior
Patricia	White female	Junior
Professor Wilson		
Martin	White male	Freshman
John	White male	Sophomore
Walter	White male	Junior
Pete	Black male	Junior
Kandy	White female	Freshman
Brenda	White female	Junior
Darlene	White female	Senior
Professor Bell		
Carl	White male	Freshman
Gary	White male	Sophomore
Brent	White male	Senior
Frances	Black female	Freshman
Sabrina	White female	Junior
Robin	White female	Junior
Cantrel	White female	Senior
Professor Blair		
Anthony	White male	Senior
Harriet	Asian female	Senior
Professor Webb		
Nathan	White male	Fifth Year
Kramer	White male	Senior
Dorothy	White female	Senior

As the data analysis proceeded (Stage 2), the checklist matrix grew class-by-class to allow an across class comparison of student responses. When the data from each of the six professor participants were added to the checklist matrix, it transformed into a role-ordered matrix as well as a checklist, which allowed multiple comparisons across professors and students. In Stage 4, the final stage, the matrix became a checklist by role over time as the visual display could be viewed as Phase 1 (Professors Bryan and

Wyatt) in contrast with the Phase 2 professors (Bell, Wilson, Blair, and Webb).

During the process of visually creating a grid of participant responses, interviews were listened to or reread to ensure that key points and depth were not lost during the process of reducing the data to fit in the matrix. In sum, professor and student interviews were transcribed from audiotapes with the characteristics associated with credibility and the influence of race given particular attention. Who (gender, race, class) perceived what (Hymes, 1972) was transferred from narrative form into matrices to examine possible relationships.

Professor credibility survey. I balanced the potential for providing socially desirable answers by contrasting the survey and interview responses of three groups of student participants. The responses of the students actually interviewed were compared and contrasted with those provided by volunteers who were not interviewed and nonvolunteers who completed the survey (but did not provide their names and phone numbers), all of whom were enrolled in the same course. Every student survey was read and coded then reread and coded again at another time in the quarter. Key words, themes, and perceived components of credibility associated with each survey question were noted across gender and race. Tallies of responses (e.g., yes, no, probably) were also compiled depending on the nature of the survey question to which students responded.

RESULTS: DEFINING CREDIBILITY

When defining professor credibility in general, without reference to a particular person, the student participants in this study defined credibility in two ways: (a) being knowledgeable or (b) being knowledgeable and a good teacher. For the second group of students, to say that a professor was credible was simply a confirmation of the person's knowledge of the subject matter (whether from academic or field experience) without attesting to his/her teaching ability.

However, in either case, knowledge was a critical foundation from which to build an image of being an effective teacher. Knowledge could be obtained both academically and experientially. Experiential knowledge was particularly important to the students enrolled in the professional program courses. The difference, however, between a good professor and a poor one was not necessarily the presence versus the absence of knowledge. The critical difference was the ability to translate one's knowledge into statements and explanations easily understood by the students enrolled in one's course.

Subject matter knowledge was consistently listed as one of the top three components of

professor credibility across all six classes. Work experience and good teaching techniques were listed as two of the top three components of professor credibility by students in four of the six classes. In addition, the ability to understand a professor's comments and explanations was listed as one of the top four components of credibility by students in four of the six classes (Hendrix, 1997).

RACE AND CREDIBILITY

Students' responses to Research Question 4 (RQ4) (see Note 2) actually revealed their underlying motivations that led them to look and listen for particular cues when a professor's race differed from the majority of the students' in a class. The nature of the institutional enrollment patterns focused this question on students of the Black professors. However, all interviewees were asked how they would assess the credibility of a Black professor.

When responding, the student interviewees provided answers that can be categorized as follows: (a) applying more stringent credibility standards to professors depending on a combination of professor race and subject matter, (b) the belief that Black professors worked harder than the White professors to earn their educational and professional status, and (c) the presence of favorable/fair attitudes toward Black professors once credibility had been established.

Applying more stringent credibility criteria to professors depending on race and subject matter. The majority of the students who were interviewed (19) indicated that race alone would not automatically establish a professor's credibility in the classroom. Unlike Patricia, who believed she would rate Black professors higher on credibility scales because she had not had the exposure, most of these student interviewees indicated they would typically use the same standards when assessing the credibility of both Black and White professors. And these students usually repeated the same criteria they had listed on the Professor Credibility Survey in response to Question 2—What does it mean to say a professor is credible? For instance, Carl mentioned that he based his assessment on the individual's educational background (as listed in the college catalog), classroom presence, and knowledge, whereas Dorothy said credibility assessment depended on "how they set it up. How I get a feel for what I need to do." However, one of the students, Cantrel, did note, "I think the White male has an advantage over everybody else just because of our bias in the culture. For me, I'm more sensitive to whether it's a man or a woman."

Even though the majority of the students indicated race alone would not automatically establish credibility and that they would not personally apply a different set of standards to their Black professors, the discussions regarding race and class subject matter revealed when credibility might be more readily questioned. Antoinnette spoke of, even as a Black person, struggling with not assigning negative stereotypes to Black professors teaching courses without an ethnic/racial component in them. The tendency to find credence in the comments of Black professors speaking about Blacks or subjects typically connected with Blacks (e.g., crime) was also reflected in the comments of seven other students. Student interviewees admitted they assigned more credibility to Blacks teaching "ethnic" courses or believed other students—in particular, Whites—would do so. For example, three of Professor Bell's students (Cantrel, Gary, and Frances) believed other students would perceive him differently if he were teaching a course with classical content only. As Cantrel talked, she stated the belief that for herself (and others), "the more removed from cultural identity, the more you have to figure out the fit . . . [like fitting] a square peg into a round hole." Thus, Professor Bell would have a more difficult time establishing his credibility if his Blackness could not be somehow linked to the subject and attributed as providing him with a unique understanding of the subject.

Two other students indicated they personally would assign more credibility to a Black professor teaching English (Brent) or ethnic studies courses (Sabrina). Brent explained that he would judge all of his professors based on how "they handle themself [*sic*] in front of the class . . . whether they are well-versed in the subject matter and how they articulate [their points]." However, he went on to say a Black professor who was able to teach standard English, given the distinctions between Black dialects and standard English, would be given "an extra plus."

Sabrina indicated that a White person teaching an ethnic studies course could be viewed as credible if he or she met her criteria of believability, truth, and experience. However, even a White person with experience living with particular minorities could only present a marginalized view—"They can only get so close"—versus obtaining the perspective of an actual member of the community. Sabrina went on to say, "I'd want a minority perspective . . . [but] I don't think I'd typify any other subject like that."

Finally, one of the Black student interviewees, Pete, introduced his expectations regarding White professors. Pete indicated he expected "more liberalism" from his professors depending on their disciplinary area. Thus, he did not speak of assigning more credibility to professors of color teaching race-related courses; rather, he spoke of a different system of dividing curriculum. Pete believed professors teaching courses in the social sciences would likely be more liberal and well-rounded in their world outlook than those in the hard sciences or disciplinary areas, such as math.

Although students stated they would not automatically favor one race over another, some of their discourse revealed that Black professors had to work harder to establish their credibility. Carrie and Mark (both people of color) were very aware that the qualifications of Black professors were often questioned by their White classmates. During their interviews, both students spoke of overheard comments and conversations in class as well as open challenges to the authority of Black professors during class lectures. And Professor Bryan's student, Allan, noted that he tried to "embrace differences," yet he also mentioned that given his homogeneous upbringing, the physical appearance of his professors did have an impact. Allan was unable to clearly delineate whether the impact was a bias in favor of his professors of color or a bias in favor of those professors of his same race.

In addition to scrutiny from White students, three Black interviewees noted their own critical review of Black professors. Even though

Antoinnette was Black, she revealed that she constantly fought the negative stereotypes (e.g., Blacks cannot do math) she had learned from American society when making judgments about her Black professors. A second student, Pete, said Black professors would not begin with an automatic advantage and, in fact, would be judged harder than his White professors. Pete indicated he had greater expectations of his Black professors and, as a result, would be more stringent in his evaluation of their capabilities and ability to meet his needs as a student.

Thus, ironically with these two students, negative stereotypes about the intelligence and academic preparation of Black professors coexisted with a positive belief that Blacks must be quite accomplished individuals to be employed as professors because they must work harder than Whites to achieve professor status. The view that Black professors must work harder was held predominantly by the students of color.

The belief that Black professors work harder to earn their academic positions. In Phase 1, all five of the students of color believed Black professors had to work harder to earn their academic degrees and to become employed at predominantly White educational institutions. Black professors were believed to deserve more respect because they experienced a "tougher" time earning their position and must "work twice as hard." Jay, a freshman of Pacific Islander descent, said he did not give professors of any particular race an automatic advantage. However, he acknowledged that his professors were judged "not just by sight" but, rather, by "what [they have] been through." Jay indicated he perceived "colored" persons, like Professor Bryan, as being more aggressive in their studies to reach the same status as their White counterparts.

Pete agreed with his counterparts and, as a result, indicated he was usually very impressed when he met Black professors—especially given Pete's more stringent expectations of them. Two White students, Brent and Robin, also noted their belief that Black professors face many more academic and workplace challenges than do White professors. Robin, interestingly, combined race and age as a criterion for a professor's credibility. She believed older Black professors and older female professors to have

"really been ahead" of their time to become successful prior to the passage of fairly recent antidiscriminatory legislation.

Favorable/fair attitudes toward Black professors once credibility has been established. These students indicated a desire to be exposed to Black professors based on positive experiences with Black professors, previous exposure to Blacks in general, the desire to rectify limited or no exposure to Blacks in the past, and the desire to increase their comfort level (as Black students) at a predominantly White institution.

Gary said he usually would give anyone a "fair shake" based on their personality and knowledge and would begin to form judgments about a professor's credibility after the first week. Gary indicated Professor Bell was his first Black professor and had "set a precedent" in his mind because he was definitely credible and a good teacher. The first exposure to a Black professor setting a precedent—a standard of expected performance—was also reflected in Walter's comments. Walter had been exposed to three Black professors during his community college education and noted that he realized, as we talked, that his criteria for assessing credibility were drawn from experiences with his Black female drama teacher. His criteria for judging credibility included (a) believability (reliability of the lecture material, clear explanations, and an ability to answer questions) and (b) approachability ("humanity").

As noted earlier, Cantrel indicated she had worked with Blacks and Asians but had not experienced Blacks within her inner-circle of friends. Cantrel openly admitted that she was concerned that her daughter did not mingle with people of color because she did not see her mother doing so. Allan, Marie, and Patricia (all White students like Cantrel) indicated a desire for exposure to a less homogeneous environment. One way of achieving this was to expose oneself to Black professors. Thus, these students were in agreement with Professor Bryan, who during his interviews, stated the importance of his presence for the benefit of White students as well as students of color.

Steve expected both Black and White professors to be knowledgeable; however, he gave the judgments he made about the capabilities of

Black professors greater weight. This decision was based on the tougher time he perceived Black professors to have experienced while earning higher degrees in an Anglicized educational environment.

A number of the student interviewees—Gary, Brent, Robin, Martin, Walter, and Kramer—had previous exposure to Blacks. The implication from the interviews is that they possessed less bias against Blacks in general due to having Black friends and role models. Brent said his "Black friends [gave] a more understandable, straightforward answer [than his White friends]" when he had problems and, thus, he expected the same would be true of his Black professors in the way they handle their classes—they would be more easily understood. Robin said, "White professors I don't really think much of. . . . They're common." She went on to say she also understood that among Black people, including professors, "there are wonderful ones [pause], crappy ones [pause]. . . . They're just people like everybody else." In other words, Robin believed she was capable of making fair assessments because undue stereotypes (positive or negative) were not applied to Blacks because she had been exposed to a range of personalities. The same was true of her counterparts Gary, Brent, Martin, Walter, and Kramer.

Martin, Anthony, Kramer, and Robin all indicated they would welcome a Black professor because they believed he or she would present a different worldview. Two Black student interviewees, Pete and Frances, indicated that being in the presence of Black professors increased their comfort level. These students represented 3.2% of the student body and stood out in obvious contrast to the number of White students enrolled at this research institution. The comfort level of Black students in a predominantly White environment (and of new Black professors in the same environment) was an area of concern that was acknowledged by all three Black professor participants during their interviews—Professors Bryan, Bell, and Blair.

DISCUSSION

The findings associated with student motivations are summarized here along with a discussion of (a) phenomena reflected in recurring patterns of the data, (b) study limitations, and (c) reflections from an outsider within.

Summary

The findings in this article evolved from a general discussion of verbal and nonverbal cues to internalized factors students consider to assess credibility. These factors contributed to situations where particular verbal (e.g., the use of standard English) and nonverbal cues (e.g., age) were emphasized. Most of the students who were interviewed did not personally believe any professor had an automatic advantage in establishing credibility based on race, yet they simultaneously discussed a different set of criteria for evaluating the credibility of their Black professors teaching particular subjects. When doing so, one of the students articulated her belief that there was a "cultural" or "societal" norm that would automatically favor the White, male professor before he even spoke.

Several of the students acknowledged that it may be more difficult for Black professors to establish their credibility in subject areas that were not linked to their race—for example, ethnic studies versus electrical engineering. Several noted that even though they would use the same criteria for a Black and a White professor teaching math and science, they believed their White counterparts would use more rigorous standards before assessing a Black professor as being credible.

Students typically seemed interested in Black professors because they were accustomed to Blacks (had friends, role models, or Black teachers/professors) or because they were tired of a homogenous, White upbringing and desired exposure to differing worldviews. Finally, students (especially students of color) acknowledged their belief that Black professors must work harder to achieve academically and perform successfully as professionals within Anglicized educational systems.

Recurring Phenomena

Researcher status and influence. Common experiences between the student interviewees and me (more specifically, being persons of color and/or women) made the interview process enjoyable and comfortable. My race and gender attracted most of the students to volunteer for the interview as well as for the opportunity to share their thoughts regarding appropriate teaching pedagogy. Two White males (one in Phase 1, one in Phase 2) can best be described as curious rather than attracted to any of my characteristics or the research topic. One possible explanation is that these two students may have been curious about my ability to design a research project and to conduct interviews professionally.

The professors (or their research assistants) could have been asked to explain and distribute the survey, or a written statement could have been attached in the form of a cover letter; however, I believed it was critical that I appear personally in front of the students. To generate interest in the research and in volunteering for interviews, it was critical that the students see and hear me. The students needed to see my gender, age, clothing, and my brown skin. The students needed to hear my voice tone, volume, articulation, speech pattern, and my sense of humor. Showing myself to the students was consistent with Allen, Heckel, and Garcia's (1980) belief that new Black researchers "must chart an insightful course for those who will follow" (p. 770). For this researcher, that means using a combination of my formal academic training and my daily life experiences.

Student self-protection of identity. None of the student participants sat near, waved at, or approached me before, during, or after the class. A student interviewee would occasionally smile but it was a ritualistic salutatory greeting that they executed with others entering the class as well. Most students appeared comfortable and forthright in my office. Yet if a student and I completed an interview and walked together to a course designated for observation, it was common for the student to sit in a different location rather than sitting next to me or even in the same row. Students protected their identity as study participants from their classmates and professors and communicated nonverbally that they expected me to do so as well.

Study Limitations

The absence of interviews over time. Extra credit could not be offered to student participants because no other extra credit was offered by these professors, therefore making it impossible to camouflage the activity. Given that students were not being compensated, their time commitment to the study was minimized. Thus, I requested one interview from each student participant rather than two. I balanced the potential for providing socially desirable answers by contrasting the survey and interview responses of the interviewees with those provided by volunteers and nonvolunteers enrolled in the same class.

The nature of the data collection site. This research was conducted in a geographic area in the United States where 10.1% of the population in the metropolitan area was Black, whereas only 1.5% of the faculty, and 3.2% of the student body were Black. The tolerance of racial differences and exposure to Blacks in one's community may vary in other geographic areas.

Reflections from an Outsider Within

I approached this study from the particular vantage point of what Collins (1991) refers to as the *outsider within.* I was a Black female investigating cases in a predominantly White educational institution. Before concluding, a few reflections are noted here to provide a glimpse into the psyche of an outsider within and to suggest the direction of future research.

First, most of the 28 student interviewees were positively disposed toward the six professors in this study. The students viewed their professors as knowledgeable and, in most cases, as good teachers. These student interviewees likely reflect a minority perspective rather than that of the majority. It is critical to acknowledge and give credence to the Black professors' beliefs that generally White students (and even some Black students) assess them according to a more stringent standard (Hendrix, 1994). In addition, we should remember the organizational communication research of Foeman and Pressley (1987), which revealed that Black employees possessed a heightened awareness of the influence of race on their interactions with their White peers. The positive orientation of White student interviewees in this research is likely atypical of many Whites in the classroom.

Second, White confederates were not used to assist in the interview process. In my view, the use of White confederates denies (a) the commonplace position of underlying racial tension in everyday interaction within the United States settlement; (b) creates a second-order, contrived reality; (c) eliminates an opportunity for Black researchers to refine disciplined subjectivity in such a communicative event; and (d) diminishes the importance of the reality associated with Black/White encounters. According to Allen et al. (1980), "the journey outside the fishbowl for neophyte black researchers will be fraught with obstacles and pitfalls, for it is they who must chart an insightful course for those who will follow" (p. 770).

Third and finally, most of the student interviewees were attracted not only to the research topic (classroom communication and professor credibility) but to me, as the researcher, as well. Students came to participate in the study and to (a) commiserate with another woman they admired somewhat for my level of academic accomplishment, (b) commiserate with another person of color within the oasis of my office, and (c) seek advice about how to approach a Black classmate and/or make Black friends on campus.

When the interview progressed to a discussion about the credibility of Black professors, some White students also chose to discuss their ideas about race relations in general, noting that they appreciated the opportunity to talk out loud with someone. They apparently viewed me as a safe person and my office as a nonthreatening environment.

As a researcher, I was aware of the need to balance my roles and their corresponding responsibilities. It was necessary to anticipate what roles I would perform (researcher, person of color, confidant, advisor, etc.), what behavior each role entailed, and how the roles could be executed without sacrificing the integrity of the research. As noted by Allen et al. (1980), I was charting a course while conducting this research. And in my effort to chart a course through unexplored territory, I consciously chose to be guided by both my (a) formal academic training and (b) intuitive sense of human interaction between and among races (gained from my daily lived experience as a Black woman in America).

A parallel can easily be drawn between the multiple roles of this Black female researching in a predominantly White (and male) academic environment and the three Black male professors teaching within the same environment; even though the professors were male, we all functioned as outsiders within, performing our requisite tasks and recognizing additional responsibilities and obligations as well.

CONCLUSION

According to Rose (1966), universities reflect the ills of society rather than serving as agents for change. Although many classroom studies have been conducted over the past 40 years that assess teachers' effectiveness in the classroom, few have investigated how teachers establish and maintain their credibility and even fewer have addressed the experiences of Black teachers and professors. Instructional communication and education literature are incomplete as the classroom perspective and pedagogical knowledge of Black professors and teachers has often been overlooked.

Research findings indicate that (a) perceived source competence is the most consistent predictor of the selective exposure of receivers, and (b) highly ego-involved receivers are less likely to change attitudes and assign positive credibility ratings (Tucker, 1971; Wheeless, 1974a, 1974b). A research curiosity should naturally arise regarding parallel behavior on the part of highly prejudiced students. In other words, if highly ego-involved receivers are less likely to change attitudes and assign positive credibility ratings, can similar behavior be expected from highly prejudiced students in the classroom of Black professors? In my study, students revealed that the competence of Black professors was more likely to be questioned depending, in part, on the subject matter they taught.

Given the results of this study and the selective exposure research, it is likely that the classroom experiences of Black teachers and professors do not completely parallel those of their White counterparts, yet they are expected to motivate and teach students as well as meet promotional requirements (e.g., tenure). Considering the pivotal role of teachers and professors within the educational system and the differing student perceptions and expectations of professors based on race, as reflected in the findings of this study, it is imperative that additional research be conducted. We must add to our body of knowledge by incorporating the educational experiences of teachers and professors of color (male and female) and the perspectives and experiences of their students.

We must also investigate academe as an organization and research racial communication patterns (Foeman & Pressley, 1987). The key to addressing some of the critical issues associated with credibility and race undoubtedly lay with the students who chose to remain silent in this study. This knowledge may increase the (a) successful classroom and career experiences for professors of color; (b) cognitive, behavioral, and affective development of students; and (c) the level of interracial understanding and respect between Black and White inhabitants of the United States.

DISCUSSION QUESTIONS

1. According to Hendrix, how is teacher credibility formed?

2. In what two ways did student participants in the study define credibility?

3. To what degree is race a factor in teacher credibility in Hendrix's study?

4. What stereotypes or biases interfere with student perceptions of Black teacher credibility?

5. What are the personal and professional implications of these biases on Black professors' teaching practices and their identities? Would these effects change if the professor were teaching at a Predominantly White University (PWU) versus a Historically Black College or University (HBCU)?

Reading 5.4

EXPLORING AFRICAN AMERICAN IDENTITY NEGOTIATION IN THE ACADEMY

Toward a Transformative Vision of African American Communication Scholarship

RONALD L. JACKSON II

One of the first articles by an African American communicologist I remember reading was written by Molefi Asante (1988) as an opening chapter in his book *Afrocentricity.* I read this in 1992 while in my master's program at the University of Cincinnati. I was alarmed, engaged, and somewhat scared for him as I thought, "Can he say that? Can he talk about African ancestral legacies and linguistic continuities in the context of the United States with such force and agency without being censored?" I was already familiar with scholars such as Frances Cress Welsing, Leonard Jefferies, and Chiekh Anta Diop, who were being ostracized by their respective disciplines for antagonizing established European-centered epistemologies. They were censored for having the audacity to resist "traditional"

interpretations and replace them with well-researched and well-articulated African-centered paradigms. For at least the next two years. I was still baffled, vigilant, and somewhat curious about what appeared to me to be Asante's intellectual insurgency. Subsequently, I read books like Marimba Ani's (1994) *Yurugu,* which thoroughly deconstructed the incomplete nature of Whiteness and oppressive knowledge forms. Then I was awestruck by English professor bell hooks's (1994) *Outlaw Culture,* which had a very graphically titled opening chapter, and I finally answered my own question with, "I guess Asante *can* take such agency, Ani, hooks, and many others have." I began to think that it was not necessarily common, but acceptable to vociferously interrogate patriarchal tendencies wherever they might be discovered as a way to

From Jackson, R. L. (2002). Exploring African American identity negotiation in the academy: Toward a transformative vision of African American communication scholarship. *Howard Journal of Communication, 12*(4), 43-57.

take agency in defining my own identity and reclaiming access to the value of my humanity. I admired the three of them for boldly standing up to refute the denial of their humanity and intellectuality. I was just as proud of them as I was of Maria Stewart, Audre Lorde, Angela Davis, James Baldwin, The Combahee River Collective, Richard Wright, and Ralph Ellison. Each sought institutional change and was willing to fight for their beliefs.

The brands of critical scholarship espoused by Asante, Ani, and hooks gave me hope that I could contribute to the transformation of knowledge about culturally particular communicative patterns and experiences among African Americans without reservation or threat of censure. I entered my master's program and eventually the discipline with visions of hope and renewal. I write this article with that same spirit of hope and transformative vision.

As we begin the new millennium, African American intellectualism remains subordinated within the communication discipline, which institutionally refuses to acknowledge the importance of non-White ways of knowing. With that refusal comes a dismissal of African can American identities, which are enveloped in African American communication research. Essentially, many African American communicologists are being forced to negotiate their identities on a daily basis in academe no matter what their area of research inquiry. We tend to function with a Du Boisian (1903) "double consciousness"—"two souls, two thoughts, two unreconciled strivings in one dark body whose dogged strength alone keeps us from being torn asunder" (p. 12). Within such a climate, it is extremely difficult to maintain complete alliances to African American epistemologies and ontologies; hence, identity negotiation ensues.

This is not to say that all African American communicologists study African American communication and culture, nor is it to say that all who study African American communication and culture are African Americans. There are many non-African Americans who have substantial research commitments and investments in the study of African American communication and culture and they are invited to share in this conversation. At times in this article, I speak directly about and to African Americans

who conduct African American communication research as well as to non-African American communication researchers; however, I am writing most directly to an audience of African American intellectuals in the discipline of communication. Keep in mind this essay argues in favor all African American intellectual products regardless of one's area of study. It is interesting to note that this preambulatory act of naming audiences and locating intellectual placement is exemplary of the kind of identity negotiation of which I speak in this article.

The roles and functions of African American communication research can best be explained by using what I have coined as the cultural contracts paradigm, an offshoot of Stella Ting Toomey's identity negotiation theory. Ting Toomey asserts:

> The identity negotiation theory focuses on the motif of identity security-vulnerability as the base that affects intercultural encounters. . . . It explains how one's self-conception profoundly influences one's cognitions, emotions and interactions. It explains why and how people draw intergroup boundaries. (1999, pp. 26–27)

Everyone has a cultural contract or implicit agreement to coordinate his or her relationships with cultural others; however there is a unique set of corners that promote African American identity negotiation. Despite the present intellectual revival emerging among young African American communication scholars, a new brand of coping has developed. It is the result of an intensively inquisitive and politically savvy set of scholars who have learned from much more experienced African American communicologists such as Orlando Taylor, Melbourne Cummings, Jack Daniel, Geneva Smitherman, Molefi Asante, and many others. They have not only acquired a new understanding of the politics and process of performing communication research, but also ways to self-authorize and legitimate their lines of culture-centered inquiry.

Within this article, I have three simple objectives: to explain (1) where we are as African American communication researchers, (2) how we arrived at this point, and (3) where we should go from here. This will be followed by implications for future research. In explaining where we are, I will assess the state of African American communication research. Then I will introduce the cultural contracts paradigm to facilitate strategies of transformation and gradual agency over the politics of identity, which continue to restrict African American communicology. Finally, I will discuss both my visions and an agenda for the future of African American communication research.

WHERE WE ARE: THE STATE OF AFRICAN AMERICAN COMMUNICATION RESEARCH

While it would be wonderful to offer only optimistic millenarian projections for African American communication research, I would be remiss if I did not recognize the current predicament that plagues this area of social scientific and humanistic inquiry. Within the discipline of communication, diversity is celebrated less frequently than it ought to be. As a result, the state of African American communication research, as one form of diversified scholarship, needs enhancement. There are four areas of grave concern as I think about the state of African American communicology; low presence of African American researches, limited diversity among disciplinary editors, limited diversity among disciplinary leaders, and disciplinary dismissal of African American theoretic legacies.

First, there are absolutely too few African American communication researchers. In 1996, approximately 1,200 communication departments and programs were invited by the National Communication Association (NCA) to participate in a national survey concerning racial and ethnic diversity in the twenty-first century. The results were published in 1997 (Morreale & Jones, 1997). Of the 304 departments of communication who participated, there were only 106 African American doctoral students and 426 African American master's students. This indicates that African American in these programs make up 7% of all doctoral students and 9% of all master's students specializing in communication studies. Of those that remain in academia, many are being hired as instructors and professors in comprehensive liberal arts institutions and four-year colleges. Among the

"big ten" schools alone, which produce many of the Ph.D.s from research institutions in the discipline, there are a mere 10 tenure-line professors. These numbers are dismal and awefully telling as we consider the future directions of African American communication research.

Second, in the history of the discipline, there has *never* been an African American scholar who has served as editor of any of our 17 association-sponsored publications from the following organizations: International Communication Association (ICA), NCA, Eastern Communication Association, Western States Communication Association, Southern States Communication Association, Central States Communication Association, and the World Communication Association. In their report, "The Status of Research Productivity in Communication: 1915–1995," Hickson, Stacks and Bodon (1999) listed the top 100 active researches of communication studies, none of whom were African American. It is not that African Americans are not publishing, but that many are publishing in noncommunication journals. In a follow-up article, Bodon, Powell, and Hickson (1999) listed the top 50 book authors in the discipline, none of whom were African American. Naturally, given these numbers, one might think that there are no qualified African Americans to serve as editors of our most prestigious journals. It is illuminating to reflect on the blatant omissions in the research of Hickson and associates and other scholars who do not take into account the research productivity of African American communicologists within and without the discipline. One prime example is Molefi Asante, formerly known as Arthur Smith. With more than 40 books and 200 articles, he has single-handedly published more than any scholar in communication and yet his accomplishments continue to go unrecognized by the discipline with the exception of a "distinguished lecture" given at an NCA convention of a few years ago. The point is that there are qualified African American communicologists to fill the roles as editors of the previously mentioned journals, but they are very rarely being considered for these opportunities. This fosters a climate of African American distrust toward communication organizations' processes of selecting editors. As a result, many African American scholars choose to publish outside of the discipline such as in the *Journal of Black Studies,* where they feel secure about receiving a fair and equitable blind review. Every area of the discipline suffers when there is an absence of diversity. This is especially true because new knowledge is often limited to culturally homogenized analyses and paradigms: hence that is what students are required to read and know as they familiarize themselves with the literature and concepts of communication research.

Third, among the associations mentioned above, there have been three African American presidents, one of whom is Orlando Taylor, who has been the only African American president of the NCA in its 86-year history. There has never been an African American president of the International Communication Association, which is considered to be a prestigious multidisciplinary organization that attracts many of the most well published scholars in the field.

There is a tremendous need to have a more diverse leadership among our major organizations. Diversity cannot continue to simply mean an increase in more women as leaders of our profession. Women should be applauded for their most thorough leadership and we should continue to recruit and retain women in leadership positions. Likewise, we should also expand the entryways for other marginalized group members to serve in these capacities. The message is loud and clear; the discipline of communication rarely values diversity. This is only one telltale sign of a discipline bereft of multiculturalism. At first glance, diversity and multiculturalism seem synonymous; however, they are vastly different. Diversity merely suggests the presence of difference. This is easily accomplished by simply recruiting someone who looks different, but does not necessarily see the world differently. Multiculturalism refers to the existence and embrace of multiple cultural perspectives cohabitating within the same context. So, simply appointing a journal editor or association president who is African American or non-White does not advance our discipline. That may satisfy the uncritical observer; however, persons who bring a unique perspective that accents cultural particularities best facilitate advancement of the communication field.

Finally, as I have written elsewhere (Jackson, 2000), there is almost no recognition of African American communication research or theoretic paradigms in the literature of the discipline. There are virtually no textbooks that mention McPhail's complicity theory or Asante's metatheory of Afrocentricity, the latter of which has been celebrated in practically every other liberal arts discipline. I am dumbfounded by this explicit disregard for critical approaches developed by African Americans. It is reminiscent of the sentiment that African American consumer products and services are inferior to "mainstream" consumer products and services. One example of this in academe is the average research institution's attitude toward publishing in culture-centered journals such as the *Journal of Black Studies,* even if one does culture-centered research. The *Journal of Black Studies* is the premier journal in African American studies. It would be logical that if one specializes in communication and African American studies, this would be both an appropriate and ideal venue for such work. However, there is tragic devaluation of African American intellectual products, theoretic paradigms, and cultural relevancies in the discipline of communication.

Additionally, contemporary African American communication research concerns me in that there are still relatively few emergent revolutionary theoretic interventions that have shifted extant paradigms. With the exception of Asante's metatheory of Afrocentricity, McPhail's complicity theory, Daniel and Smitherman's reconnaissance of linguistic carryovers, and a small minority of other scholars' works, there is a lacuna of innovative thinking about our multiple communicative experiences. Every study and every line of research inquiry is a direct commentary on the cultural identities of the author(s) that produced it. That is, no matter how eccentric the topic may be, researchers can only investigate that which they know directly or vicariously, and these topics are chosen as conscious or subconscious iterations, reaffirmations and reproductions of the cultural self. Consequently, researches who study African American communication and culture must attune themselves to theories and research that reaffirm African American ontological experiences.

Stuart Hall (1992) insightfully contends identities are the ways we characterize who we are with respect to the past. The link between naming identities and identifying antecedent realities has transformative potential because of the power we have as African Americans to reshape and recenter our intellectual legacies and to legitimize our experiences without waiting for the discipline to do it for us or without assimilating to "mainstream" disciplinary trajectories as though we do not belong to the mainstream. Meanwhile, as we renegotiate our cultural contracts with the discipline, we must be ever mindful of how we arrived at our present state and condition. The cultural contracts paradigm facilitates understanding of how we can strategically transform our peripheralized positioning and identities.

UNDERSTANDING HOW WE GOT HERE: CULTURAL CONTRACTS PARADIGM AND IDENTITY NEGOTIATION

The cultural contracts paradigm suggests that at any given point in time human beings are coordinating relationships founded upon assimilation (ready-to-sign contract), adaptation (quasi-completed contract), or valuation of one another (cocreated contract). By understanding what kind of contract(s) you have, as an African American communicologist, and determining when and why you signed it, it is possible to deconstruct your relational position in the academy and renegotiate your contract(s). The tragic reality is that most people do not understand the contracts they have signed much less the implications of having signed them. In this section, I try to offer several examples of the kinds of cultural contracts that exist. Cultural contracts can manifest themselves within and among persons, institutions, and cultures. There are certainly numerous culturally constructed meanings and ways of behaving that permeate the roles and relationships of scholars, and these constitute implicitly negotiated agreements to behave in conformity with social, cultural, and institutional standards. Naturally, the nature of these contracts shifts as we mature, discover new approaches, and/or find identity shifting so exhausting that we select one contract as a means of stabilizing our lives.

Before going further, it is important that I explain how the identity negotiation process occurs (Jackson, 1999) via three cultural contract types: ready to sign, quasi-completed, and cocreated. *Ready-to-sign* cultural contracts are prenegotiated and no further negotiation is allowed. "Signing" or relational coordination may or may not be the goal. A White faculty member, for example, may not even be aware that his or her Whiteness is a marker of normality and privilege and that that might affect his research, pedagogy, and service. If a professor of an intercultural communication course refuses to acknowledge that his Whiteness is politically advantageous, then he may not realize that although the selected course texts affirm his existence, they may not affirm everyone else's. Essentially, he is asking that his students "sign" his ready-to-sign cultural contract, affirming the importance of White epistemologies and centrality. This contract type suggests that "I am not going to change who I am, so if you want this relationship to work, you must act like me." As mentioned previously, there is no such thing as not having a contract. To say that one has no cultural contract is to say that one has neither a culture nor understanding of how to function in the culture where he or she lives. In the prior examples, the cultural contracts were defined by someone's interest in maintaining White privilege, but they may also manifest themselves intraculturally.

Quasi-completed cultural contracts are partly prenegotiated and partly open for negotiation. The people with quasi-completed cultural contracts are not ready to fully value the other's cultural worldview because of the effects they think that might have on maintaining their own worldview. They "straddle the fence" in terms of their commitment to reorder privilege. With the ready-to-sign contract, privilege is implied because assimilation is required. Although you may not be the one with privilege, your "signature" verifies your participation in facilitating the maintenance of it. With quasi-completed contracts, there is recognition that there is something fundamentally wrong with assimilation and something equally wrong with polarity. So, this contract type suggests, "In order for this relationship to work, we both have to negotiate part of our identities." For example, if an African American communicologist always adopts European-centered paradigms to study African artifacts, then he has most likely "signed" a quasi-completed contract, which may imply that he will use nonindigenous paradigms if it will more likely lead him to publication. This is perhaps the least effective and least long-lasting contract because of the strain and tension of monitoring one's degree of commitment. However, many African American scholars are stuck in this modality their entire professional careers as they codeswitch before and after work.

Finally, *cocreated* cultural contracts are fully negotiable, with the only limits being personal preferences or requirements. This is often perceived as the optimal means of relational coordination across cultures, since the relationship is fully negotiable and open to differences. If a cultural contract is cocreated, there is an acknowledgment and valuation of cultural differences by all parties involved. In a discipline that seldom celebrates African American intellectual legacies, cocreated contracts can only be envisioned and actualized on an individual basis. Some African American scholars experience intellectual appreciation, while the masses of scholars tend to not have their work considered significant enough to include in mainstream disciplinary conversations.

With a cocreated cultural contract, cultural differences are not ignored, yet they do not become the only reason the two relational partners are together. The emphasis is truly on mutual satisfaction rather than obligation. Cocreated cultural contracts are most often discovered among interactants of the same culture, where there are minimized differences. When there is little to no value placed on African American intellectualism, it is difficult to decipher whether the reason is that the scholarship is poor or the attitude toward the scholarship is poor. The cocreated cultural contract assures interactants that there is optimal respect for the individual such that the scholarship is most likely to be the concern and not the attitude toward the person. This contract type suggests, "I am comfortable with and value you for who you are, and I am not interested in changing you in any way." Metaphorically, each contract type is a result of how identities have been personally and socially constructed and explored.

Generally, identity negotiation refers to a conscious and mindful process of shifting one's

worldview or cultural behaviors or both. During this process, cultural patterns of communicating and ways of seeing the world are at stake. A shift in anyone or any part of one of these aspects of identity constitutes the "signing" of a cultural contract.

Everyone has "signed" at least one cultural contract in his or her life, and with every significant encounter, one or more of those cultural contracts is negotiated. I coined the term "cultural contract" to mean an agreement between two or more interactants who have different interpretations of culture and who have decided whether to coordinate their relationship with one another so that the relationship is deemed valuable to both (Cronen, Chen, & Pearce, 1988). The term "cultural contracts" refers to the end product of identity negotiation; hence, every "signed" or agreed-upon cultural contract has a direct impact on one's identity. Two points of clarity must be offered here. First, this definition allows for the possibility of intracultural contracts. Second, unlike some previous research (Hecht, Ribeau, & Alberts, 1989), the definition does not assume that the relationship is mutually satisfying, only that it is deemed important. It is critical to mention this, since it is quite possible that a person is forced to sign a cultural contract, at work for example, in order to preserve their livelihood. Although this may not have been the preferred choice, it is deemed valuable because it is necessary for survival. As with all negotiations, power is often a constitutive feature of cultural contracts and cannot be ignored.

The effects on identities, whether it is a shifting or solidifying move, depend upon the nature of the identity negotiation process or the significance of the incident that initiated the negotiation. For example, an African American graduate student who is advised to use Fisher's narrative approach rather than an Africological paradigm to frame her study of African American proverbs will most likely be conditioned to believe that Africological approaches are substandard and likely to obstruct the possibilities of getting published. That one cognitive shift will eventually have an effect on her cultural self-perception and her understanding of disciplinary publishing. If she is not culturally conscious and does not receive any counterclaims, she is likely to be dissuaded from using culture-centered approaches in her research. In her willingness to comply with using only widely accepted disciplinary paradigms, she will have "signed" a ready-to-sign cultural contract requiring her to assimilate her ideas.

The word "cultural" in cultural contracts is deliberate. It is impossible to exist without culture. Even if one is unable to articulate the particularities of the cultural value system to which he or she subscribes, there are still cultural patterns of interaction, rules, and norms that guide everyday behavior (Calloway-Thomas, Cooper, & Blake, 1999). So, with this cultural contracts paradigm, there is no such thing as a noncultural or culturally generic contract, and everyone has at least one cultural contract.

Everyone has identified or aligned him or herself with others throughout his or her life. This alignment can be behavioral, cognitive or both. The cultural contracts paradigm is most concerned with sustained alignments, whether short or long term. As mentioned previously, one may choose to align oneself with our discipline's traditions and accepted epistemologies by adopting a Burkean paradigm rather than Afrocentricity to achieve desired ends, such as getting published in one of our discipline's journals. One may not agree with, question, or even like the biased standards of some journals; however, one will continue to publish with a given journal in order to meet institutional expectations. Consequently, one has sustained and coordinated the relationship (Jackson, Morrison, & Dangerfield, in press) because the perceived ends outweigh the means. Essentially, one will have agreed to a ready-to-sign cultural contract, and in doing so, one has placed a portion of one's cultural values, norms, and/or beliefs aside.

As with any negotiation, one can either abide by an existing contractual arrangement, change the terms of the contract if permissible, or choose another contract. Although the concept of identity negotiation is simple, it is not always clear what is being negotiated, especially since identities are nonmaterial. The cultural contracts paradigm is being introduced to make sense of what is actually being negotiated. Hecht, Collier, and Ribeau (1993) contend that identities are relational and negotiated in everyday interaction with others. Specifically, they assert, "Identity is defined by the individual and is co-created as people come into contact with one another and the environment. As people align themselves with various groups this co-creation process is negotiated" (p. 30).

Professional identities are constantly attached to cultural epistemologies and ontologies. The way we learn to coordinate our cultural identities and perspectives so that they are aligned with other cultural identities and perspectives is perhaps one of the world's most intricate balancing acts, and everyone who is employed must participate in it. This activity is complicated by the negotiation of identity as evidenced in identity conflicts. A conflict is usually understood to be the result of incompatible goals and interests, so when identities are unaligned, there is said to be an identity conflict (Roloff & Cloven, 1990). An example of this is the limited recruitment of students of color in the communication major. The conflict is most obvious in the disciplinary conversation about diversity; some scholars are concerned with diversity, while others are not. The goals and interests are not only incompatible, but they also lead to marginalized identities by politically situating White identities at the center of recruitment and curricular efforts. The cultural contracts approach facilitates mapping of the kinds of choices. African American communicologists have made to date. In order to shift the direction in which we are going, we must renegotiate those cultural contracts that limit our progress.

WHERE DO WE GO FROM HERE? TRANSFORMATIVE VISIONS AND AN AGENDA FOR THE FUTURE

Recent African American communication research has shown signs of an evolution, a renegotiation of outdated cultural contracts. Many scholars are not as preoccupied with artificially linking their cultural experiences with those of European Americans. For example, Karla Scott's (in press) essay in Houston and Davis's anthology explores the intersection of culture, gender, and language by examining Black women's everyday talk. She accomplishes this while utilizing the work of Marsha Houston and Geneva Smitherman. Her analysis is rightfully rooted in African American theoretic traditions. There is a revived sense of autonomy developing among African American communicologists that self-authorizes scholarship about African American communicative experiences using African American paradigms as the theoretic framework and/or inviting African American participants or coresearchers to take part in a study about their own experience. The fact that there are more indigenous African-centered paradigms and concepts that are being logged into the range of epistemologies communication scholars adopt to capture the logic of their investigations is promising. I maintain five prescriptive visions as I ruminate about where African American communication research must go and what we must do as African American communicologists in the years to come.

Vision 1

Those of us who study African American communicative practices must be unafraid to place African- and African American-centered paradigms at the center of our analyses of Black diasporic experiences. Many African American communicologists seem to be fearful of the real possibilities of not getting published when they use literature that is foreign to many Whites. For example, I have never read a communication study presented in essay form that used the conceptual work of Chiekh Anta Diop, Linda James-Myers, Maulana Karenga, Theophile Obenga, Marcelle Griaule, Amos Wilson, Haki Madhubuti, Jawanza Kunjufu, or Marimba Ani, all of whom are well-respected scholars in African American studies. We are much more prone to using non-Black scholars outside of the discipline such as Michel Foucault, Gayatri Spivak, Clifford Geertz, Carolyn Ellis, Roland Barthes, Julia Kristeva, and Elizabeth Grosz. If we can use Burke's pentadic analysis to study rap music, we can also use Asante's Afrocentricity or Diop's cosmological triad. Although one paradigm may suffice within a given study, this is not to say that one must replace the other or be introduced at the exclusion of the other. Another option is to triangulate theoretic approaches so that theories produced to explain African American culture, epistemologies, and communicative behaviors may be juxtaposed with

theories that were produced to accent European American culture, epistemologies, and communicative behaviors. This functions as a cocreated contractual arrangement where cocultural standpoints are valued equally.

Vision 2

We must be unafraid to cite one another's work. Rarely do we as African American scholars critique and engage one another's ideas, but even in the absence of public debate, we still implicitly suggest that our own paradigms and studies are unworthy of consideration by not acknowledging their existence. In this way, we become, as McPhail (1991, 1994) might contend, complicitous with hegemonic devaluations of African American intellectual production. There is a common saying among African Americans that advises people not to "air their dirty laundry" and, unfortunately, I think this axiom has facilitated a restrictive intellectual atmosphere. Many intellectuals find it impermissible to critique another scholar's work unless one has a vendetta against that scholar. Nonetheless, I am convinced that positive, good-willed criticism of African American paradigms will lead to more recognition of approaches and theories produced by African Americans.

As Hickson and associates have illustrated via their study of research productivity in the communication field, citation indexes are critical instruments used for measuring productivity and peer recognition. Naturally, there is a limited set of journals and publication outlets that count within the indexes; however, as scholars who study African American communication see fit, it is necessary to quote and cite African American scholars who have made significant contributions in one's respective areas of inquiry. In this way, we cocreate and affirm an intellectual presence in the field. Without personal efforts to acknowledge the work of African American intellectuals, the bevy of African American intellectual products remains unnoticed.

Vision 3

We must form research collaboratives and alliances. The 25 most active producers of communication research amassed the prolific records they have today due to their willingness to collaborate. Many of them accomplished 50% or more of their research collaboratively. There is still a consistent tendency among African American scholars to publish alone. Many of us have been taught to function as islands, detached and autonomous. The danger in this can be illustrated with numbers alone. A person such as Professor X who has more than 100 manuscripts to his credit might publish eight to 15 articles in a year, none of which are single authored, which means he always has a set of ongoing projects even when he is not writing much. He is working smarter, not harder. On the other hand, Professor Z has about 40 publications to his credit, and in any given year he has three to six articles published. He is still quite prolific; however, his output is less and he is probably working harder. Which model would you choose?

The reality is that even if one has a magnum opus, that one work alone probably will not help one earn tenure, but suppose one is already tenured; then what is the benefit of collaborating? The dearth of knowledge about African American communication requires that research constantly be generated. One concern some African Americans have is that there are non-African Americans researching African American communication. For that, I have two responses. First, this is not new. People of other cultures have always studied other civilizations and cultural patterns and in some ways it is a compliment. If scholars choose to conduct fair and balanced studies of your experience, recognizing that they do not have all of the answers, then that shows they have some value of your culture. Second, why complain if you are not doing the work others are? We cannot blame others for theorizing about African American communicative experiences, especially if we are not doing that work. There is a plethora of themes that have barely been examined in our discipline, including, but not limited to, Black masculinities, Black aesthetic forms of expression, Black homosexuality, African diasporic orature, and nonverbal subtleties indigenous to African American and African cultures. Additionally, we have a limited range of studies concerning the confluence between African American culture, discourse and art, architecture, science, spirituality, philosophy, and history. Collaborating will produce such knowledge more rapidly and efficiently.

Keep in mind that there are six caveats to doing collaborative research. First, if one is on tenure track, one must publish several manuscripts either alone or as first author to establish oneself as a scholar who is capable of intellectual rigor. Second, when comparing social scientific research versus humanistic studies like rhetorical criticism, collaborations tend to be with fewer coauthors and, overall, they are less frequent. Third, one should try to be first or second author more often than not. Fourth, collaboration is not always productive on every project, so select collaborators and collaborative projects carefully. Fifth, every friend is not a good collaborator, and every good collaborator is not your friend. Sixth, collaboration can be stressful unless all research partners are accountable, punctual, energized, goal directed, organized, and competent.

Eventually, establishing African American research collaboratives and alliances in the discipline may lead to expanding the boundaries of thinking about communicative experiences and/or founding another professional organization that meets the needs of marginalized group members. As our interests and possibilities expand, so will our need to be openly validated, valued, and recognized by the discipline and its associations. Just as the discipline of psychology underwent a radical change in the 1970s with the implementation of a "school" of Black psychologists, likewise Black communicologists may need to do likewise. For some people, this may be interpreted as a move toward separatism. In fact, it would be a move toward the acknowledgment of a diversified human experience. There will still be those who participate in NCA, ICA, and the regional associations, but their primary allegiance would be to the organizational body that appreciated their scholarship.

Vision 4

We must participate in recruitment and retention efforts at every level of postsecondary education. This can be strenuous given the other demands on one's time in research, teaching and service-related activities. However, longstanding evidence suggests that faculty tend to be retained when they feel supported and surrounded by people with similar interests and backgrounds. It is professionally healthy to have people who share perspectives, experiences, and directions.

Obviously, the major problems with ensuring student cultural diversity are recruiting and maintaining African Americans and non-Whites in the discipline. Personality, I had no plans of staying in academia, because the environment did not seem conducive for me, and although I saw that as my problem, I did not see it as my battle to fight. Now, I see it as my battle, because when I read the flurry of communication textbooks and articles emerging from varying publication vehicles, I still see few studies that tell of my cultural experiences. Obviously, the more students are retained, the more likely they are to pursue a terminal degree and stay within the profession and discipline, which, of course, potentially leads to a wider range of positive, liberatory voices in our disciplinary literatures.

Although recruitment of diverse student and faculty scholars may seem external to one's present responsibilities, it is only so because communal responsibility has been arrested within the academy and often is treated as secondary to the university mission. "Town and gown relations" is a buzz phrase used in the academy to signify a rejoinder or detachment from the community, depending on how one perceives it. For a collective people, detachment is not an option to be exercised for any length of time lest we subscribe to a ready-to-sign cultural contract that abandons community in favor of personal interests.

Community connectedness does not always translate into physical presence at a community center; one form of community connectedness may also mean empowering a community by participating as an institutionally situated community advocate for recruitment and retention of culturally diverse students and faculty.

Vision 5

We must speak to, with, and regarding our own communities, and they are varied. Some of us have grown up in lower-class ghettos, some

in class-varied rural enclaves, others in middle- and upper-class neighborhoods. Each of these experiences is different and worthy of examination. West (1993) speaks of organic intellectualism as a return to home and a commitment to the communities in which we have lived. African American scholars cannot afford to disengage ourselves from our communities, because of our collective nature. Mbiti (1990) suggests the old adage, "I am because we are and because we are, I am." It is our obligation to return. In doing so, we may locate issues or problems that confront the communities and offer strategies and methods to resolve or assist in resolving the conundrums. For example, there is a great program in Cincinnati, Ohio, which began in the early 1990s, called the 'Summer Incentive Program.' This grass-roots tough-love program for preteen adolescent males is structured to emphasize cultural awareness, communicative competency, educational achievement, familial respect, and social responsibility. It was designed to help low-income, at-risk children confront and resist the pressures of academic, personal, and eventually professional failure. Programs like this for boys and girls, men and women may target community concerns regarding safety, homelessness, starvation, and employment to financial investment and community banking. For ideas that represent such a transformative vision, see Amos Wilson's (1998) latest book, *Blueprint for Black Power.*

These five visions offer a path for future African American communication research. It is imperative that each of these prescriptions be filled if we are to effectively advance the research of African Americans in the discipline.

IMPLICATIONS

Where do we stand as African American communicologists at the birth of the new millennium? We are in a precarious position. On the one hand, we are fortunate not to be in the post civil rights era when scholars were distracted by the inhumane acts of violence perpetrated by federal, state, and local authorities as well as centralized hate groups. On the other hand, we are still stunted by our limited collective visions. I am confident African American communicologists will transcend the machinery of race. This does not mean we will be unfazed by it; rather, we will not be consumed by it to the extent that it hinders our progress. Admittedly, the intellectual landscape in the discipline for African Americans is often overwhelming, but there is hope. This was evident as we celebrated Orlando Taylor as the first African American president of NCA. Likewise, we have celebrated other African Americans who have been leaders of our regional associations. Carolyn Calloway-Thomas and Deborah Atwater have presided over the Central States Communication Association and Eastern Communication Association, respectively. More African American and non-White scholars are needed to serve as professional leaders of our major associations, including, but not limited to, the ICA. Likewise, we need African Americans to serve as editors, researchers, and in every other facet of our discipline so that our identities are not continually marginalized.

Identities are perhaps the most dynamic feature of human communication behavior. As human beings, we have the fascinating ability to shape, position, and reconstitute dimensions of ourselves throughout time, space, and interactions, even in repressive climates such as that which we have in our discipline. Critical studies scholars such as postmodernists, feminists, Afrocentrists, and postcolonialists suggest that the power differentials among interactants interrupt harmonious and equitable relationships even when assimilation occurs. This is an important point, because often-times within inequitable relationships, artificial congruence in opinion and behaviors seems awfully real. If a subordinate in a supervisor—subordinate relationship enacts codeswitching properly, for example, then on the surface everything may appear intact. But, beneath the surface, the identity negotiation that has taken place has inhibited freedom of expression and negatively impacted the subordinate's identity by lowering his or her self-efficacy (Houston, 1983). This is only one possible identity effect among African American communicologists.

Here are two of the implicit questions we must ask ourselves as African American communicologists: Who controls how we define ourselves culturally and to what degree is power an intermediating variable in how African American research is shaped and understood? While the cultural contracts approach helps us to understand how we arrived at our current disciplinary condition and whether we are persistently signing ready-to-sign cultural contracts, we still have the ability to take agency in how new knowledge concerning African American communicative experiences is constructed within the discipline.

Within the racially and culturally oppressive disciplinary climate in which we professionally exist, it is extremely difficult to independently explore the communicative nuances of African American lives without reference to hegemony. Often we feel compelled to investigate Whiteness in order to access our Blackness. On the surface, this seems problematic, because it suggests that understanding Blackness is contingent upon understanding Whiteness. Bodunrun (1991) insightfully asserts,

> Philosophers cannot afford to expend all their energies on the often unproductive and self-stultifying we-versus-you scholarship. Africans must talk to one another. We are likely to have a more frank debate that way. (p. 84)

Often, we are afraid to engage one another's scholarship, but in failing to do so, we limit the multiple ways we can conceptually frame our own experiences. I remember hearing Molefi Asante's distinguished lecture at the 1995 NCA convention in San Antonio, Texas. He was using Egyptological and other African texts and concepts with which I was quite familiar, but I was sure he had lost half the audience. At first, I was a bit uneasy about it because of what I have learned about audience analysis and not alienating one's audience. It appeared that he was not concerned about how or whether they received the information. As I reflected more, I realized that this was not his intent. He was affirming the cultural uniqueness of African-centered intellectual legacies without making reference to Europe. This was unique for me, because in my training, Europe had always been the center around which other legacies were required to orbit. I remember thinking that this set of emotions I initially felt when hearing Asante's lecture was exactly how I felt throughout my undergraduate and master's degree education. I understood the jargon, but I still felt alien to the experience. For years, professors, students, and other researchers were not talking to me; they were talking among themselves about communicative experiences they could relate to most. They did not seem to be the least bit concerned about my level of comfort or the way in which I received the information. Suddenly, I felt myself cheering Asante once again for teaching me that it is okay to investigate my own ancestral epistemologies and cosmological forms of expression. As Bodunrun suggests in the above quotation, we must talk to one another via our research and reshape the discussion of African American particularities so that it reflects the fullness of African American culture.

DISCUSSION QUESTIONS

1. What is a *cultural contract*?

2. What are the cultural contracts types?

3. What cultural contracts do Black scholars "sign" in academia?

4. Explain three of the five transformative visions for African American communication scholarship.

5. How are identities both tied to and divorced from Black scholarship?

Part VI

AFRICAN AMERICAN IDENTITIES IN MASS MEDIATED CONTEXTS

The field of mass media and popular culture covers the range of venues from television, radio, print, computer, and film media. Of all of the areas studied in communication, this may very well be the most broad and the most well-known. Mass media studies have explored audience and producer intentionality and effects. The studies are historical, social, political, and ecological. Nearly all of the studies presented in Part VI focus on institutionally driven images about African Americans. The exception is Catherine Squires's essay, which is much more about how audiences co-construct and resonate with news content by, for, and about their communities. In this final section of the book, we explore television, film, and radio.

The first essay is written by Melbourne Cummings and is a landmark piece in the communication literature. Although not the first to talk about mass media images, her essay is one of the more poignant commentaries on the evolution of Black family depictions on primetime television. She begins with *Amos and Andy* and proceeds by analyzing subsequent shows such as *Julia, Sanford and Son, The Jeffersons, Good Times, Gimme a Break, Webster, The Cosby Show, 227,* and *Diff'rent Strokes.* Pointing out recurrent themes of poverty, chronic joblessness, boisterous behaviors, malapropisms, self-deprecating servitude, inescapable immaturity, and adolescent behaviors, Cummings asserts that, although more positive images have been inserted into the roles of Black television actors, there is still a long way to go in dissolving the "comforting images" of Black family life.

Still being attentive to televisual images of Blacks, Herman Gray, in this excerpt from his book *Watching Race: Television and the Struggle for Blackness,* broadens the scope of his analysis to include representations of Black bodies as the "hyperspace of identity" throughout American popular culture, especially within music. In a unique exploration of Black youth culture, Gray also hones in on how Black hair, dance, language, music, and dress communicate "Black sensibilities." He opines that rhythm is the centerpiece of Black youth culture. Furthermore, he contends,

> Television (especially music videos, television ads, situation comedies, comedy-variety programs, and sports) is made up of cultural zones and social spaces of mediation, contestation, and circulation among groups that are differently positioned socially and differently organized culturally.

This essay is significant in part because of what it says about the social and material forces at work in a capitalist-driven economy and an industry set on presenting commodifying images of Blackness.

The presence of Cummings's and Gray's essays is complemented by an excerpt from Donald Bogle's book *Toms, Coons, Mulattoes, Mammies, and Bucks: An Interpretive History of Blacks in American Films*. Bogle is perhaps the leading Black film historian in the United States, with this particular book the first in a four-part series that includes *Brown Sugar, Blacks in American Films and Television,* and *Primetime Blues.* In this monumental excerpt, he introduces what he calls the *pantheon*, comprised of the following stereotypical images: The Tom, The Coon, The Tragic Mulatto, The Mammy, and The Brutal Black Buck. Explanations and examples of these stock characters have been recycled in almost every essay and book written on depictions of African Americans in film. Bogle explains and exemplifies each stock type by pointing out their presence in films up until the 1920s and the deficiencies inherent in the villainous, cunning, obsequious, or vociferous nature of each character.

Although she does not address mass media images per se, Catherine Squires's essay explores another area of African American identities in the mass mediated context of radio. Again, as in the rest of the essays in this section, this study examines the degree to which the needs and concerns of Black audiences are addressed in the media. Moreover, the study seeks to explain how nonsyndicated local radio, which has experienced decreased support by audiences introduced to new media, is a very useful venue for expressing and responding to communal concerns. Her study included ethnographic observation, interviews with staff and listeners, and completed surveys received from 232 listeners. Squires's triangulated investigation of WVON, an African American owned and operated radio station in Chicago, revealed that listeners remain loyal to the station because they trust that the station will represent a distinct Black public sphere divergent from a more mainstreamed White public sphere, and, hence, there is more of a commitment to community enhancement facilitated by the station. In fact, Squires likens the role of stations like WVON to the early Black press that supported and advocated the needs of Black citizens while promoting an institutional discourse reflective of political action initiatives important to the economic viability and sustenance of Black communities.

Reading 6.1

THE CHANGING IMAGE OF THE BLACK FAMILY ON TELEVISION

MELBOURNE S. CUMMINGS

Historically, black people have been given roles in the media that have tended to strengthen and perpetuate the negative stereotypical images that white people have created. Despite how blacks had been depicted in the popular media of film and radio previously, however, television was maintained as the medium of the future which would reverse the misinformation that had surrounded blacks.

When they were shown in films and radio broadcasts, black people were maids, janitors, shoe shine boys, cooks, waiters, wet nurses, all, of course, with distorted racial characteristics. They shuffled, rather than walked; they popped and rolled their eyes; they giggled, never laughed or smiled. These were the characteristics that talented Black actors and actresses were called upon to portray because white audiences found these traits lovable, enjoyable, funny, entertaining, and controllable. And if these actors were to practice their art and find their livelihood in these media they had to perform as they were told, no matter how demeaning the role or unflattering the image that was made.

During the beginning years, television promised to be color-blind; that any programs treating race would do so with dignity and objectivity; and that racial types would not be depicted in a manner that would ridicule or demean.[1]

But as time progressed, gradually, variety shows like *Ed Sullivan's, Toast of the Town,* and *Steve Allen's Tonight Show,* blacks indeed were given equitable, non-stereotypical, unbiased "roles" to play. They displayed their musical and comedic talents along with their white counterparts. Later, on quiz shows, they were allowed to show their intelligence as they won large sums of money for answering challenging questions.

When television showed blacks in situation comedies or dramas where they had supporting roles they were given roles that supported the stereotypical images created from fiction, movies and radio. The roles of (a) the black mammy on shows like *Beulah* and *Make Room For Daddy,* and (b) the handyman on shows like *The Jack Benny Program* and *Trouble With Father* did nothing to portray realistically black

From Cummings, M. S. (1988). The changing image of the African American family on television. *Journal of Popular Culture, 22,* 75-85.

people as they lived in American culture. Many of the portrayals, in fact, were detrimental to all that Nat King Cole, Steve Allen and Ed Sullivan attempted to do on their respective shows.

In practically all instances except one, blacks were shown on a continuing basis when they worked in a white household or were a regular on a variety show. They never had a steady companion or a friend of substance or never a sustained, intelligent conversation. The one exception was the "Amos 'n Andy Show," a television show which definitely highlighted Black talent and showed that indeed Black people lived full and rewarding lives. It demonstrated further that they did not all live in slums and ghettos; that Blacks had jobs other than those of cleaning, cooking and taking care of white people's babies; and that they could be sensitive, warm and caring parents. These positive images, however, were shown very seldomly and were often profoundly overshadowed by the negative and racist imagery projected by the series.

The series, *The Amos 'n Andy Show,* was a patronizing picture of Black America. The characters were treated as immature children synonomous with pranks, malapropisms, and weak imitations of white society. It was a highly false interpretation of the Black reality, for it unfairly fulled whites into complacency and reduced Blacks to a position of inferiority, causing them to continue to perpetuate myths.[2]

The series perpetuated the myth of the Black matriarch, the castrating black female, the domineering, overpowering Black woman. These characteristics were portrayed by Sapphire, Kingfish's wife, and her mother, Mama, who lived with them and who found every conceivable thing wrong with her daughter's husband. These two women were caricatures of Black femininity. Though Sapphire was portrayed by a very attractive Black woman, Ernestine Wade, she was made to look and act shrewish and overbearing.

The men were classic minstrel types. Not one spoke grammatically. Their mispronunciations illustrated their basic and deep-seated ignorance about everything. They were constantly being devastated by abusive women. The men were never shown working, even though it was a show with at least two Black families. The

closest thing to working that we were shown was Amos in his taxi (always without a fare) and Calhoun the lawyer, helping kingfish swindle money from Andy or some other unsuspecting soul.

Neither were there role models in the women. They were all unsalaried housewives. The only professional represented in the cast was Calhoun, but his use of the English language was as ungrammatical or maybe worse than that of Lightning, the janitor, who spoke so slowly and inaudibly that it was often difficult to understand him.

This first Black television family lived in the ghetto, but its members did not receive welfare nor were their surroundings blighted. It was easy for whites to watch for there was never a racial, social, economic, or political issue discussed. No one was discriminated against, and no one was hungry or complaining about not working or working in unchallenging, unfulfilling jobs. They were all apparently "satisfied" with their conditions.

An interesting side about the Amos 'n Andy Show relative to its long lasting impact is that it was only produced for two seasons, 1951–1953. However, the show continued in syndication until 1966 after years of litigation by Black people and their organizations to have it removed from the airways.[3]

Hadn't there been newsworthy items that captured the attention of the news media, it is fair to note, the image of Black people would have been totally distorted, one dimensional and without any redeeming human value.

During the time that the Civil Rights Movement and African National Independence Movements were going on, no other show was aired on a continuous basis until *Julia.* Instead, this series focused on the day to day life of a single professional, self-supporting mother who lived in a sterile world. The fact that her husband had been an officer in the armed forces and had been killed in combat gave the show a quality of credibility to white audiences, but received a great deal of criticism from the Black community.

Julia only continued to aggravate the racial stereotype of the Black matriarch because she never encountered racial prejudice at work nor in the integrated, well kept, very middle class apartment building in which she lived. At another level, the show seemed to have been designed to subvert the aims and purposes of national civil rights activists. It was meant, some argued, to assuage white consciences and to make President Richard Nixon's militant actions toward the people of the Black ghettos more palatable.[4]

The *Julia* series was such a "white wash" that even white people began to feel uncomfortable with this patronizing portrayal of how Black life could be if Blacks did not riot, but wait their turn, and work within the capitalist system. The networks countered these criticisms by saying that television is an entertainment medium; that the show was not meant to be socially and politically relevant.

Despite the conflicting pressures, *Julia* was well received by viewers, after all it was the first Black Family show since *Amos 'n Andy*—and what a difference it was! *Julia* showed on a weekly basis that Black people did not all live in the ghetto; that they went to professional jobs every day; that they could have fewer than five children in a household; that they could speak impeccable English; could wear attractive clothes without being a prostitute or royalty; and that they could have dilemmas that had nothing to do with white folks. *Julia* was a positive role model. The problem was that her character was so positive that she was implausible.

Although Blacks remained on television in mainly supporting roles during the 1970s, the next television family created was *Sanford and Son*. With this production, we witnessed a return to the Black minstrels, for throughout the 1970s we were assaulted with variations on this theme in terms of Black families on television. We were shown *The Jeffersons, Good Times, What's Happening,* and *Diff'rent Strokes.*

Each of these shows had very wide appeal, all enjoying top ratings variously from 1972 until 1983. These shows highlighted Black talent in a way that had never been done before. Blacks were stars of their shows, but the quality of the characterizations compromised many of the goals of the Civil Rights Movement. They portrayed the "coon"—that is, those characters who were loud, conniving and ostentatious. This image was portrayed in the show *The Jeffersons* by Sherman Hemsley in the character

of boisterous George Jefferson for ten years and by Jimmy Walker as grinning J. J. in the production *Good Times* for five years. We also had the loud but lovable "mammy" types as shown in the character of Louise Jefferson and Florence the maid of *The Jeffersons,* and Aunt Esther, a very loud, overbearing, purse swinging, swearing character created by LaWanda Page in *Sanford and Son.*

The most disgusting of these "mammies" is the role Nell Carter played, discussed below, as the maid/momma to three white teenagers (and before his death, their father), a white boy and a white grandfather. Defenders of shows of this type claim that the difference between these comedies and those of years past, such as *The Amos 'n Andy Show,* is that these shows had socially relevant themes and that the comedy format made the substantive issues that were raised more palatable to the general public and easier for them to be accepted.

It is true that these situation comedies dealt with issues like rape, mastectomy, venereal disease, racism, poverty, welfare, unemployment, and did it in such a way that some consciences were raised, but it also brought to the forefront long forgotten stereotypes and introduced to a generation of Blacks and whites an era of racism, racial slurs and racial images that would have been best forever lost.

With the 1970s situation comedies on the black family, we were told once *again* that all Blacks lived in the ghetto, were poor, lazy, unemployed and if not on welfare, were living from hand to mouth. Those who were industrious like the father and mother on *Good Times* and Mama Thompson on *What's Happening* would lose their jobs and find it difficult to get another. Those who were lazy and not really looking for work could find jobs easily and were not satisfied with them, like J. J. of *Good Times* and Lamont's friend on *Sanford and Son.*

To counter the negative stereotypes of poverty created by *Sanford and Son, Good Times,* and *What's Happening,* we were given *The Jeffersons,* a self-made, self-sufficient millionaire with a loving wife, a well behaved, intelligent son, and a wise-cracking maid. George Jefferson owned several dry-cleaning stores; employed blacks and whites; contributed (through his wife) time and money to worthy causes; and extolled (through his son) black consciousness. For every positive feature of *The Jeffersons,* the character of George had at least two negatives. He was not only loud and boisterous, he was ostentatious, ignorant, and a bigot, and a chauvinist.

In these black series, there was usually enough of a mixture of the ridiculous and the serious to keep something of a balance, fragile through it was. With *Good Times,* however, the ridiculous simply outweighed the serious concerns that were attempted in the production. J. J., the loud mouthed, grinning "coon" of a son on the show received too much attention from the writers and therefore considerable negative criticisms from the public.

The co-star, John Amos, was among the loudest critics. He was a highly principled actor who cared a great deal about how black people were portrayed on television. He understood, moreover, the power of television and how difficult it is to erase an image from the public's mind, especially one which supports a stereotype. J. J. was simply a younger version of Kingfish of *Amos 'n Andy* fame. He had a trademark saying, "dyn-o-mite" that was reminiscent of Kingfish's "holy Mack 'I'" that was so often heard on *The Amos 'n Andy Show.* The J. J. character also popped his eyeballs a lot and showed a huge toothy grin often at inappropriate times.

Despite the strong, proud, determined image of the father and the loving, respectful, supportive mother figure, it was hard to counter J. J.'s image. John Amos left the show as he noticed more and more buffoon and coon parts for J. J. Esther Rolle who played the role of the mother left a short time later. The show was finally canceled in 1979, five years after it was first aired.

Sadly, the 1980s continued perpetuating negative stereotypes, while at the same time pretending to be responsive to demands for more black programming and more black actors. Television became more blatant with assertions that if blacks were to be successful, well educated, properly brought up in a supportive, nourishing middle class environment, it was necessary for there to be white people at the head of each of the households.

Different Strokes was created as an example of this theory. This show centered around the antics and life situations of two young black boys, orphaned by the housekeeper of a rich man who lived his young daughter on New York City's Park Avenue. The maid gets her boss to promise that he will take care of her children after she dies. He complies and we have another patently stereotypical situation comedy with the great benevolent white father showering good cheer, wisdom, wealth and a problem-free, healthy home environment on two black ghetto children.

Arnold, the central characters, and his brother, Willis, are virtually a rehash of the little pickaninnies.[5] Willis is straight man to Arnold's jokes. Arnold is, as J-J., a classic Kingfish with his stock response of "wha'cha talkin' 'bout, Willis?" The Arnold character is smart alecky, prankish, and egocentric. The role is that of a small child, but a teenager was chosen to play it. That in itself is a negative commentary on the ability of young Gary Coleman, who plays Arnold, to act his age, or to be considered anything other than a kind of 'freak.' This theme is played out in another series as noted below.

If there is anything that is well known about the culture of black people, even in the United States, it is the importance of the extended family. The only times these boys were visited by relatives was when these family members wanted to "con" Mr. Drummond, the white benevolent father of the series, out of a large sum of money. Naturally, the boys exposed their relatives for what they were and Mr. Drummond acted in the fashion of a big hearted, benevolent great white father and forgave them all.[6]

Such is a familiar theme in the series *Webster,* another show which capitalizes on the unfortunate growth problems of a Black teenager and casts him as a younger child. He even has friends who are intelligent white children who are cast at their chronological ages. However, the main character, Webster, acts like and is given parts to speak as if he is a child of about nine years old.

Webster was orphaned by his professional football star father and his wife who had asked George Pappadopalous, his closest friend on the team, to be their child's godfather. George is simply carrying out his responsibility as a godfather, raising Webster, together with his wife, to the best of his ability with lots of love.

Webster, too, has an extended family. As a matter of fact, the young boy has a very loving uncle, yet the uncle also decides that Webster is somehow much better off living with this white "mom ("ma'm") and dad." However, since the story lines are not at all socially relevant, and the problems Webster encounters are no different from other kids, there is really no reason why his adoptive parents could not have been black.

And then we were given the classic, the oldest stereotype in the history of America: The black "mammy" to "massa's three little children." *Gimme A Break* stars Nell Carter, a robust, happy, musical, loud, self deprecating maid in an all-white household . When this show was introduced and later flourished in the ratings, many critics felt that television no longer even attempted to be socially responsible.

It seems that as far as television is concerned, there will always be one ethnic group. Every other group has mixed, mingled and become a part of humanity, but not black people.[7]

It was not until 1984 that television began to seriously address black families on a continuing basis. There was no longer *one* show or series on which all the burdens of the race must be heaped.

There were now three black television families. *The Cosby Show, Charlie and Company,* and *227,* all starting between 1984 and 1986. The three families were from different socio-economic backgrounds, although two were very similar. Neither of the three deals with overt racism and neither is blatantly different in substance from any other series which focuses on the family. There are, of course, subtleties which give one show the edge on the other two. But basically these shows were about any family and its daily life situations.

Of the three series, *Charlie and Company* was the weakest. The casting, for example, was done poorly, so the elder son did not seem to belong to the family unit. The scripts were usually thin as they attempted to show off the comedic talents of its star, Flip Wilson, a stand-up comic. The acting talents of the children exceed those of the mother and father, who were in fact novices—the character of the mother was played by a popular singer, Gladys Knight.

The family was middle class, with the father employed by the Transportation Department of the City of Chicago; the mother was a public school teacher, and they lived together with their children in their home. The father was shown often at his office which he shared (mostly joked) with four other employees, one a Hispanic. The show provided wholesome entertainment, using several cultures to interact.

227 is a situation comedy about a Black family who lives in Washington, D.C. They are lower middle class and are able to live comfortably–even share their resources at times with their neighbors. They rent their apartment and share the usual problems encountered by renters of an old building in a neighborhood that is beginning to cater to condominiums for young upwardly mobile whites (or Yuppies). The family is a more traditional family unit in that the father clearly is the head of the household and he is a construction worker foreman. The mother does not work outside the home, but primarily cares for her budding teenage daughter, leaving the more serious problems, however, for her husband to handle when he gets home. She is, however, very civic-minded, often taking the lead in community concerns.

This family also does not live in a social vacuum, for much of the focus of the show is with the neighbors, who are primarily a single woman-parent, an elderly retired woman who is raising a young teenage grandson, and Sondra. All of these, however, live as well as Mary, the central character and her family. The only other person besides Lester, Mary's husband, who is gainfully employed, is Sondra, the brunt of all the conversations because she is single and attractive, and her clothes, walk, voice and general demeanor say that she is 'available'; moreover, she gets lots of male attention and she flaunts it.

The problems Mary deals with are problems that all mothers and wives sooner or later must face: her daughter wanting to date before the family is ready; the attention paid her daughter by a particular older teenage boy; children defying their parents; the seeming interest of her husband in another woman; the husband taking her for granted; whether or not to leave a note of identification on a parked car that she accidentally struck, etc. All her predicaments make for good, light, wholesome entertainment. She does not have to act a buffoon to get a laugh, and she does not emasculate her husband or berate his family. Though she and her friends are a little bit jealous of Sondra, they never resort to speaking of her as a prostitute or a "loose woman." Sondra is respected as a person.

The Children of *227* sometimes prefer, in fact, to speak to Sondra about their "problems" and though she may go a bit overboard, the children's parents know they can trust her to be responsible in her advice. The series does not carry the weight of the entire black world; it is not angry; it does not espouse a particular political point of view. No one grins or wisecracks unnecessarily or shuffles aimlessly. The production may or may not be an award winner or top the Neilson charts, but it will not be criticized for its failure to address black concerns or for its emphasis on minstrelsy.

The ultimate black family television production to date is *The Cosby Show*. It has all the elements necessary for a successful production. It has excellent script writers, high priced and respected sponsors, a superb production crew–several members of which are black, seasoned directors, and a well educated, highly trained, experienced, attractive, "all-American" black cast, hand-picked by the star of the show, Bill Cosby.

The Cosby Show is about a black upper middle class family. The husband is a medical doctor; the wife is a practicing attorney; their five children are bright, witty and full of mischief. The family did not just appear from nowhere–it has historical roots. The audience is told where the family came from: grandparents are a part of the show–on a continuing basis; we are introduced to family friends and teachers, and occasionally, to the parents' co-workers. The children are not perfect: they fight; they take things without first asking permission; they make bad grades in school, sometimes; they pretend to study; the son keeps an atrociously dirty room; they abuse privileges; and they talk back, with various results, to their parents, but they love and respect each other–and their love is effusive.

The series is black not because it deals with racial issues or prejudice, or because there are poor people on the shows, or because it

espouses a particular political point of view. It does none of these things. The series is unmistakably black because of the *Symbols* associated with it. The main character, Cliff Huxtable, wears sweat shirts from black colleges and universities; black paintings fill his home; famous black people appear on the shows; and black teachers, among others, who represent strong role-models are introduced.

On Dr. Martin Luther King's National Birthday Celebration, there was not a lesson on the Civil Rights Movement, but in the final scene of the show, and after a particularly angry fight scene between two of the daughters, everyone, including a youthful visitor, silently watched the television set as it displayed the 1964 March on Washington and King's extraordinary Speech. Moreover, during the height of the Free South Africa demonstrations around the United States, an Anti-Apartheid poster was prominently displayed in the Huxtable residence.

Dr. Alvin Poussaint, the noted psychiatrist, has pointed out that it is unnecessary and racist to always place all the burdens and problems of the black race on the shoulders of black people and black television shows. It sets these shows up for certain-death and predictable negative criticism.[8]

Naturally, *The Cosby Show*, as one of the top ranking continuing series on television today, has its critics. Mostly these critics discuss aspects of the same topic: it is not black enough; it is not relevant enough; and it is not true to the life of the black family. The debates and discussions will continue for as long as there is more than one lifestyle which characterizes *the* black family.

Marketability has always been the central concern for any television show. If the shows disturb the innate sensibility of the viewing audience, they will not be viewed. And if no one watches, production companies and television stations lose money.

Shows like *The Jeffersons* appealed to the public, for it was a top rated show for years. For blacks, it showed an upwardly mobile couple going from 'rags to riches.' Though George Jefferson was a loud-mouthed buffoon, at least he did not shuffle; he *strutted*. He did not scratch his head and bow in deference to white folks; he showed that blacks found them as distasteful as they found blacks. To whites, there was the ease of observing blacks in a setting that said if they behaved and worked hard, they could live like whites. The show catered to whites' stereotypical image of black people. On a whole, it said that black people were different; they are separate and distinct from other Americans; that no matter what the political, social, and economic situation, they just are not regular human beings.

At a National Conference in 1980 on the image of black television families, Tony Brown and Lester Strong, individually, asserted that shows like *The Jeffersons, Good Times, Diff'rent Strokes, Amos 'n Andy,* and *Sanford and Son* were appealing precisely because these images do not disturb or dispute the overall view of black people generally held in the minds of the viewing American audience. Images that are incongruent with established beliefs cause mental tensions. Correct and strong images would be inconsistent with the reasons people watch television: to escape from the sameness of everyday life, and escape to fantasy. Black families, therefore, became "narrow, negative, stereotypical portrayals designed to reflect what television producers and distributors believe the majority of the American market/public imagines black families to be."[9]

The theory of the "comforting image" has emerged now among scholars in their effort to analyze and offer explanations for the continuing stereotypical images which characterize American television regarding black family life.[10]

This continuing negative portrayal of black people is disconcerting now both to whites and black people, finally. It appears that people are beginning to realize that their neighbors regardless of their skin colorations are much like themselves. They share many of the same experiences, laugh and cry at many of the same atrocities, react similarly to negative and positive influences. Black people, however, are overdue for fair treatment and a change of image in television, as in real life.

The Cosby Show and *227* are well on the way to making an impact and to changing the stereotypical image of the Black family on television in the United States.

DISCUSSION QUESTIONS

1. Distinguish the role of the *mammy* from that of the *sapphire.*

2. How was *Julia* a "white wash" according to Cummings?

3. Discuss the way in which Black families were portrayed in the following three shows: *The Jeffersons, Cosby Show,* and *Good Times.*

4. What show(s) discussed in this chapter depicted Black men as buffoons?

5. How do the mass mediated images of Black family life look today?

Reading 6.2

JAMMIN' ON THE ONE!

Some Reflections on the Politics of Black Popular Culture

HERMAN GRAY

We live in a consumer culture where we seem to have unlimited choices in how we construct ourselves in the realm of public life. In a media-saturated consumer culture such as the United States one can, momentarily at least, locate a person or group socially through personal style—hair, dress, tastes, music, movements, and talk. Through personal (and collective) style we endlessly invent and reinvent, position and reposition ourselves in public life.

Although feminist scholars have gone to some length to point out the oppressive and denigrating impact of consumer culture on women and young girls, the body, nevertheless, seems to reign as the preeminent site for the expression of individual imagination and collective cultural identity. From the demarcation of gang territory through the use of dress, colors, and hand signs to radical rejections (and celebrations) of beauty myths through markings, tattoos, and mutilation, obsessions with the body in places like Los Angeles, Miami, and San Francisco have transformed the body into a hyperspace of identity.

We use adornment and inscription to camouflage, even parody, our social locations in a world of increasing social control, surveillance, and social inequality. At the same time the body has become a major site for individual and collective expression of identity, the (re)organization and circulation of identities, including the literal bodies on which they hang, constitute a major enterprise of modern consumer culture industries, including fashion, health and fitness, music, and advertising.

By emphasizing the dual nature of this process of self-construction and representation and the role of consumer culture in its production and circulation, I want to foreground the constructed and contested nature of black expressive youth culture and the politics of culture it enacts. Often the expressive styles of black youth labor to reproduce, in commercial culture at least, the terms and processes of marginalization, control, and domination; but just as often the expressive styles of black youth serve as points of intervention and struggle over claims about black youth (Lipsitz 1994).

From Gray, H. (1995). Jammin' on the One! Some Reflections on the Politics of Black Popular Culture from *Watching Race: Television and the Struggle for "Blackness"* (pp. 147-161). Minneapolis: University of Minnesota.

As one important terrain for the representation and circulation of black youth style, the media, especially television, music video, popular music, and film, operate as sites and resources through which and with which black youth construct, invent, and situate themselves in public spaces. I regard black youth styles as an expressive attempt by these youth to reposition themselves and in the process reconfigure and disrupt those political, cultural, and moral discourses that constantly police, contain, and otherwise discipline them (Lipstiz 1994; Rose 1994).

By framing the representation of black youth in terms of the relations among various systems of meaning (moral, cultural, political and commercial), representation (media and consumer culture), and subsequent struggles over them, I want to situate black youth subjectivities at the center of popular cultural analysis.[1] Any cursory examination of contemporary music, video, television, and advertising would suggest that such a repositioning is historically warranted and, furthermore, consistent with Cornel West's (1993) reminder that we are experiencing the African Americanization of American popular culture. Such a repositioning also necessarily reconfigures the center, especially in terms of the politics of representation.

Indeed, given the level of saturation of the media with representations of blackness, the mediascape can no longer be characterized accurately using terms such as *invisibility*. Rather, we might well describe ours as a moment of "hyperblackness." The emphasis on struggles or contests over representations in the media highlights the need for a look at the complexity and vitality of black youth culture, especially the important discursive role it plays in enacting and reconfiguring claims on and representations of blackness in the media. My argument, then, is that, multiply structured as they are by social class, education, gender, and region, black youth cultures and the social positions they articulate and mobilize can never be completely marginalized, appropriated, and absorbed. Rather, as enacted through black expressive forms, black youth subjectivities are constantly produced, made, and remade.

Within the mediascape of contemporary consumer culture, black youth constantly use the body, self-adornment, movement, language, and

music to construct and locate themselves socially and culturally. These, I believe, are the sites of some of the most complex and imaginative practices in black popular culture. These constructions of identity within and through commercial popular culture also represent significant and strategic interventions and cultural struggles in a world that is, for black youth, often hostile and suspicious. Although the various constitutive elements of black youth style often operate within separate discursive spaces, they also constitute a certain kind of coherence. It is a coherence, as Dick Hebdige (1979) shows in the case of British youth, that forms a kind of bricolage constructed of elements traditions, refuse, and practices of contemporary culture.

Using the case of contemporary rap music, Tricia Rose (1994) and Robin D. G. Kelley (1994) show, for example, how the musical practices of black youth signify meanings within the context of social locations and circumstances that often deny, block, and negatively sanction access by black youth to the material and status rewards offered by U.S. society. Rose (1994) carefully details how black (and latino) youth in the Bronx combine technology, oral traditions, vernacular language, dance, and graffiti writing to construct complex counter representations. The elements that came to be called hip-hop and rap emerged in the midst of the fiscal and social crisis of New York City in the late 1970s that produced massive social and economic dislocation for large numbers of black and latino youth. Kelley (1994) brilliantly connects the emergence (and appeal) of the genre of gangsta rap in Los Angeles to the structural deindustrialization and subsequent social reconfiguration of Los Angeles. These structural changes and social processes (ethnic and racial dislocation, competition and territorialization expressed most dramatically in the form of gangs), together with the cultural impress of Hollywood's image machine, Kelley suggests, help to explain and contextualize the salience, glorification, and centrality of the figure of the outlaw and the gangsta in the Los Angeles rap scene.

Both Kelley and Rose are extraordinarily careful not to use factors like social context or cultural significance to explain away or excuse the nihilism, violence, misogyny, and homophobia so often associated with black male youth culture. Instead, by carefully attending to the complex relationship of cultural and social forces at play in producing these practices, both are able to grapple with the complex and contradictory character of rap as a leading edge of African American youth culture. Their exemplary analyses of black popular culture avoid a zero-sum (dismissal/celebration) approach to popular culture, especially rap.

The terms, representations, and claims operating in the ensemble of inscriptions that characterize black youth culture, then, are socially situated and culturally produced. It is in this continual process of cultural invention that we can glimpse something about how individuals, groups, and communities struggle against and reproduce forms of domination in their attempt to make a world for themselves.[2]

I take as my major texts for this exploration the representations of urban black youth found in mass media and popular culture as they circulate through the mass entertainment system of American commercial television.[3] Following the theorizations of Rose and Kelley, I focus on this dynamic process of cultural invention by African American youth to highlight their claims on blackness and their engagement with such media forms as music, video, advertising, and television.

JAMMIN' ON THE ONE! ELEMENTS OF BLACK YOUTH POPULAR STYLE

Black youth styles are expressed through a number of distinct but related forms that constitute an ensemble of cultural practices. The expression of black youth styles, articulated through body, hair, language, music, and dress, produces a dynamic dialogue (Lipsitz 1990b) with African American cultural traditions, a coherence that Paul Gilroy (1991a, 1993), following Amiri Baraka (1991), has aptly described as "the changing same." Negotiating between discourses of blackness as a fixed or absolute essence and blackness as a radical social construction, Gilroy sees blackness as a socially situated production that is constantly invented and reinvented from tradition. Using popular music as his analytic trope, Gilroy accepts the existence of different black Atlantic

Diasporic traditions, but avoids essentializing, reifying, or fixing them. He 'is critical of approaches that do, as well as of those that posit a blackness as always made a new without regard for the social locations and traditions in which they are embedded.

By theorizing blackness in this way, Gilroy forces us to see black expressive forms in different parts of the black Atlantic as related social processes of invention, travel, interruption, and remaking (see also Hall 1989). Thus, for Gilroy, African American cultural expressive popular forms are not fixed, essential, and unchanging, as some cultural guardians of black (for Gilroy, African American) cultural traditions would have it. Indeed, Gilroy's larger project and more general discussion of the black Atlantic seems heavily staked in disarticulating specific claims by African Americans from what he regards as their hegemonic status relative to blackness in the Caribbean and England.

Although I would quarrel with Gilroy's particular construction and representation of black American claims on blackness as hegemonic (together with Lipsitz's, 1990b, notion of dialogue), I do find productive his conceptualization of blackness in terms of the notion of the "changing same." This view of blackness as a cultural trope is alert to, but not blinded by, the socially constructed character and context in which different notions of blackness are made and made meaningful. African American, black Atlantic, and African traditions do survive and exist in popular forms and practices through which they are socially organized and made culturally meaningful. But they are not, as some neonationalists and Afrocentric advocates would have it, frozen in time in some original from to be preserved and revisited and resurrected as a source of authentic affirmation and guidance. Rather, traditions are differently structured, constantly invented and reinvented, appropriated, modified, and transformed within specific historical, social, and cultural conditions. This is the condition of the changing same, a condition that must be constantly situated and theorized and not assumed in the manner of either essentialism (ethnic absolutism) or radial social construction.

The use of music, dance, dress, language, and the body as sites for the articulation of certain decidedly black sensibilities is neither recent nor specific to black youth. Punks, hippies, and rastas (and before them black nationalists) have used hair, for example, as a site to express identity and identifications that distinguished them from those outside of their social formations. The point, as Lipsitz (1990b) shows with Chicanos in Los Angeles and the Mardi Gras Indians in New Orleans, is that marginalized and subordinated communities have creatively transformed and used popular cultural artifacts and practices such as music, costumes, parades, traditions, and festivals to transgress their particular locations, to express their visions, and to invent themselves. What characterizes black youth culture in the 1990s and therefore warrants careful attention is the central role of the commercial culture industry and mass media in this process. I want to try to capture some of the flavor—the dialogue and hybridity—of black youth practices and inventions, especially their circuits and manifestations of mass media and commercial culture. Hence, I want to take a closer look at two of the less obvious elements of the expressive style of black youth—hair and dance.

Without claiming that my discussion is definitive, I want to appreciate and hence foreground that fact that aurally, kinetically, and visually rhythm emerges as the central thread that unifies contemporary black youth culture (Rose 1989, 1994; Snead 1990). That is, rhythm (through the play and endless reconfiguration of repetition) is imaginatively deployed and constantly recombined in the language and wordplay of rap; in the insistent movement and expression of bodies in contemporary popular dance; in the angles, curves, and lines of contemporary hairstyles worn by both men and women; and, of course, in the scratches, spaces, bass lines, and grooves (especially funk) that are so central to most contemporary black popular music.[4] Rhythm and repetition, in other words, are common elements that organize the multiple and syncretic practices of contemporary black youth styles.

Hair

In many public arenas (streets, shopping malls, television programs, schools, playgrounds, movie theaters, concert halls) throughout America's major cities, one can see a wide range of hair textures, shapes, sizes, and colors among black youth: jerri curls, dreadlocks, extensions, braids, parts, crowns, and intricate designs cut into the hair. Kobena Mercer (1990) reminds us that for blacks in various locations within the black Atlantic, hair has long been one of the sites in which black youth identity has been expressed. One's hairstyle can be used to locate one's personal taste and cultural outlook (e.g., processes in the 1950s, Afros in the 1960s, braids in the 1970s, jerri curls in the 1980s, extensions in the 1990s).

Mercer (1990) suggests that the endless variations in black hairstyles might be understood as a kind of inventive reworking and expression of blackness rather than as some pathological imitation of whiteness. That is, black hair is a place where the particular sensibilities of various black cultural experiences are symbolically inscribed. Rather than reading the expressions of black hairstyles as a kind of internalized psychological state (e.g., assimilation) or authentic black essence (nationalism), Mercer argues instead that they are the continual inventions and articulations of black cultural imaginations played out on the material and symbolic surface of the body. By simply inscribing these surfaces and spaces with various icons, shapes, and figures, black youth literally use their bodies to construct their identities (see Bakhtin 1984).

Following Mercer, we can locate historically and socially the discourses that shape and inform these bodily inscriptions of blackness. The contemporary hairstyles that adorn the heads of black youth engage a rich and imaginative amalgam of contemporary and historical influences: commercial consumer culture (e.g., Batman insignias, Mercedes-Benz and BMW logos, sports logos, black superstars), Africa and Afrocentricity (hairstyles that reproduce and emulate crowns and various forms of headdress), urban street life (e.g., parts, geometric designs, and bald heads), middle-class entrepreneurial spirit (crew cuts, fades), the Caribbean (e.g., dreadlocks), and contemporary African American cultural and political neonationalism informed by the philosophies of Malcolm X, the Nation of Islam, and the Black Panther Party (e.g., Afros, fades, boxes, jerri curls).

These shifting hairstyles incorporate elements from different historical and contemporary periods that are constantly reinvented and reassembled to produce new forms and meanings. Thus, although the figure of Michael Jordan, a Batman insignia, or the logo of BMW cut into the hair of a black male may explicitly suggest identification with materialist aspirations of a hedonistic consumer culture, it might just as easily indicate the fertile imagination of black youth playing with a storehouse of readily available images and meanings from commercial consumer culture. (For an interesting theoretical elaboration of this point, see Sawchuk 1988). The use of parody, irony, and, yes, irreverence (in this case toward the body and commercial culture) as both affirmation and spectacle should not be lost. (Think, for example, of NBA star Dennis Rodman, whose hair color changed in one season from red to blond, or sitcom star Sinbad, who once sported a blond "do.") It shows, I believe, active intervention, appropriation, and participation in an environment dominated by consumer commodities that have displaced, taken over, and now compete with values and mores that have traditionally defined and guide African American communities. Following Cornel West's concerns about rampant nihilism among black youth, I would prefer to read the centrality of consumer commodities in the iconography of black youth as an expression, rather than the cause, of the breakdown of civility and morality in the black public sphere. Perhaps we should read the inscriptions on the bodies and heads of black youth as forceful and direct expressions of the seduction and power of consumer capitalism. (After all, how different are these emblems of identity and self-expression from "buppie," "chuppie," and "yuppie" preoccupations with badges and emblems of status that come in the form designer labels and national brands as signs of quality in consumer goods?)

Whatever political and moral conclusions one draws, in the broader discourse of representation and the politics of identity, using the body as a site of inscription and representation is simply one of a number of imaginative ways in which youth with limited resources and power not only get noticed, but express themselves in their own voices and on their own terms (Lipsitz 1994).[5]

Movement/Dance

As in the past, popular dance, performance, gesture, gesture, and pose remain among the most dynamic and expressive cultural forms through which black youth express and authorize their own subjectivity (Hazzard-Gordon 1990). Contemporary black youth continue to select, recycle, and embellish body movements from different groups and periods, inflecting them with new meanings.

Body movements, given coherence by the centrality of rhythm in the black music tradition, express the imagination and experience of life in modern urban spaces (for an interesting discussions of the vitality of such spaces, see Whyte 1989). In the video explosion of the 1980s, movement and dance in the videos of artists such as Paula Abdul, Heavy D. and the Boyz, Big Daddy Kane, Hammer, Janet Jackson, Quincy Jones, and Salt-N-Pepa expressed the authority and imagination of a generation of black youth whose preoccupation was to be noticed and taken seriously on their own terms and at almost any cost.

No doubt, many of the dance styles that turn up in contemporary black youth style have long traditions in the social and cultural rituals of various parts of Africa, the United States, Latin America, and the Caribbean. In addition to being held together and punctuated by black music, these movements are marked by polyphonic and independent movements of various body parts—legs, arms, head, and trunk. They are at once, cybernetic, athletic, and erotic in their incorporation of traditional and contemporary elements.

This imaginative incorporation of aesthetic and social elements in the service of contemporary cultural invention by black youth can be seen in two popular dances from the 1980s, the cabbage patch and the running man. The running man in particular might be read as metaphor for the urgency and velocity of life in urban America. This dance and its poignant name express the character of life in large urban areas, where black youth (especially males) are the objects of surveillance, control, and pursuit by the police, gangs, and the criminal justice system. The running man is not only an expression of the dynamism and immediacy of life in the city but also a major survival strategy for urban youth.[6]

Not at all bashful, or for that matter imaginative, about preoccupations with sex, young black men and women also incorporate suggestive and literal sexual movements and accents as central elements of popular dance styles. Bumps, grinds, and thrusts of the hips, butt, and entire lower body graphically mark the place of sensuality and the erotic in the popular music and dance of black youth.[7] As youth preoccupations with sex have become both more explicit and more intense, they have also become more central and graphic in the popular dance styles of black youth. And for many adults they have also become more disturbing and troublesome. This disturbance is not so much about the place of the erotic and the sexual in black popular culture, especially dance; black popular forms of music and dance have always erected and maintained a public place for the sensual and the erotic. Rather, both this sexual preoccupation and the disturbance it produces are made particularly meaningful in relationship to recent moral panics, the crisis of AIDS, and the epidemic rates of teen pregnancy and violence in the black community. Many policy and moral debates explicitly target popular music, music video, and dance in relation to social, cultural, and moral debates about increased violence against women, increased homophobia and gay bashing, and increased teen pregnancy (Grossberg 1992; West 1993).

For many, some of the most offensive and troubling expressions in contemporary popular music and dance are primarily, but not limited to, masculine movements and styles incorporated from sports, notably street basketball, gymnastics, and exercise culture. (Many of the celebration routines performed by black athletes in highly organized team sports, such as basketball and football, incorporate clear elements of popular black dance styles to express their individuality.)

In the culture of rap and contemporary dance, young men and women pose in defiant (and, for many, menacing) stances of authority and affirmation. These are simultaneously expressions of individual autonomy, the influence of the peer group, and distance from the culture of adult authority and control. Like rap

music samples, such comportment of the body is borrowed and remixed from urban street culture, Hollywood westerns and gangster films, and the military. This sense of authority is equally present in the performance of black male jazz musicians, where the body functions as an extension of the instrument or voice. As Miles Davis and many of his critics and admirers recount in his autobiography, for musicians and listeners alike, the body, dress, and general style of many musicians, especially during the 1950s and 1960s, served as a crucial means of expressing black passion, defiance, and authority (Davis and Troupe 1992; Tate 1992).

There are some correspondences, then, among the pose of the rapper, the stance of the jazz musician, the celebration rituals of the athlete, and the popular dances of black youth. They all operate on a plane of visceral and visual expression to articulate an individual and collective body positioned in a dynamic relationship to sexual, aesthetic, and physical sensibilities rooted in African American culture.[8]

Social, Historical, and Cultural Locations of Contemporary Black Youth Culture

In the popular American imagination, so much of which is profoundly shaped and institutionally structured by the popular media, especially television, black gangs, drug dealers, and unemployed and incorrigible blacks (especially black male youth) represent fear and menace. In television news accounts and newspaper stories, blacks, especially the black poor, are presented as victims of crime, perpetrators of crime, and the objects of white fear and suspicion. Recall, for example, Ronald Reagan's construction and strategic use of the black welfare queen, the Bush administration's reliance on the image of Willie Horton, and the blanket surveillance of black neighborhoods in Boston in search of black male suspects following Charles Stewart's murder of his wife.

Even in critically celebrated films put out by Hollywood's image machine, liberal treatments of black life remain, by and large, imprisoned by and dependent on the agency of whites. Black subjectivity and agency are framed and made possible at the behest of sympathetic whites such as the contentious but benign Miss Daisy in *Driving Miss Daisy,* the ambitious but dutiful young white officer in *Glory,* and the transgressive but loyal Idgie in *Fried Green Tomatoes.*[9]

Where personal and institutional constraints are not as explicit or rigid, black subjectivities are often framed in terms of individualism and exceptionalism. Here I have in mind television and press depictions of successful blacks who are constructed as exceptional. In this assimilationist discourse of positive images, the quality of exceptionalism organizes and drives media representations of personal success (e.g., the former chair of the Joint Chiefs of Staff, General Colin Powell; New York Mayor David Dinkins; Virginia Governor Douglas Wilder; Secretary of Commerce Ron Brown; and entertainers such as Oprah Winfrey, Bill Cosby, Michael Jackson, and Janet Jackson). This black exceptionalism, marked by individuality, separates these individuals from black collectivity or community.[10]

In many of the media representations of success and achievement, blacks appear as objects rather than as the subjects of their own construction. They are, as it were, inserted into a discourse of menace or benign acceptance within a larger American discourse of individual success and assimilation. In such stories moral, cultural, and behavioral accounts dominate as explanations for the state of various depressed sectors of black America, especially the disenfranchised and the poor.

These representations of black exceptionalism leave little room for complex collective (and individual) expression of black subjectivity and imagination. They depend on the notion of role models for their appeal—either positive (in the case of individual success) or negative (in the case of collective threat). In the negative case they tend to portray poor black youth as either victims or soulless predators who, because of fatal moral and character flaws, cannot possibly transcend the limits of their condition. These youth must be carefully and continually surveyed and contained (Lipsitz 1994).

But the very same images of threat and menace that underwrite television and media representations of black youth in the news have another cultural dimension, one of titillation, adoration, celebration, ad consumption (Jones 1991). There can be little doubt that the poses, stances, dances, and general body comportment of rappers that have become almost conventional in popular and campaigns for Nike and Reebock athletic wear, Gap jeans, and Calvin Klein underwear, to name only a few, originated in the very quarters of black youth culture that signal threat and menace to civic and moral order. In other words, while holding to my claims about the social locations and political salience of contemporary black youth expression, I do think it important to foreground the centrality of black youth expression for consumer commercial culture and hence black youths' travel through and transformation in the production and consumption circuit of consumer capitalism (Frith 1998).

As these traces and signs of black youth culture percolate through the commercial mainstream by way of advertising, film, and television, they labor discursively in several directions at the same time. As consumers and producers of their media images, black youth, in the manner of organic intellectuals, seem to understand implicitly and negotiate effectively the dual nature of their representations. For example, rap artists such as Ice-T, Ice Cube, Queen Latifah, Monie Love, Public Enemy, Boogie Down Productions, and Paris cleverly use the media, especially music video, to transform and reposition images of black menace and threat into expressions of affirmation and defiance (for an application and elaboration of this argument, see Hebdige 1989). These and other black rappers effectively stage their self-authored and authorized representations under the glare of the very spotlight that is also used to commodify, survey, contain, and marginalize black youth. They do so without apology or regard for the public codes of civility or the culture of politeness with respect to race that so saturates public discourse (Hebdige 1989).

When presented at the floodlit center of American commercial culture (e.g., fashion magazines, music video, advertising, commercial network television), the expressions of black youth are transported into a media hyperspace where they are magnified into a spectacle of hyperblackness. Transformed by the electronically shaped circuit of their production and travel, once in this floodlit center this hyper-blackness is repositioned yet again, not only in relation to social discourses and institutions of domination and containment, but in relation to commercial imperatives of spectacle, commodification, and objectification. Through the conventions, aesthetics, and structures of the concert tour, the television screen, the fashion spread, and cinema, the cultural expressions of black youth become accessible to much broader audiences. They are more available for and susceptible to transformation—including reinvention, modification, and appropriation. And, of course, because these very same conditions of production and circulation are also available to black youth, this same media space refracts these electronic images of blackness back to black youth, who in turn use them to engage, transform, modify, and reinvent blackness.

This complex status of black youth style as a meaningful cultural practice *and* cultural commodity is the source of its cultural power and commercial appeal. This commodity character, and hence the potential for commercial appropriation and commodification, is constantly present, especially for representations such as those in black "ghetocentric" (Jones 1991) cinema and television shows—for example, *In Living Color* or rap videos—that most directly and forcefully disrupt and subvert dominant constructions and representations of black youth.

Black popular practices, then, are deeply contradictory. This contradictory character is part of the condition of black cultural politics in commercial culture. As popular expressions and forms, including the sensibilities and subjectivities they articulate, ride the popular currents of commercial culture, they remain contested, contradictory, and constantly mediated by the social and political circumstances and dynamics that situate them.

The Cultural Politics of Black Youth Style

What is registered as counterhegemonic, reactionary, and affirmative in the complex ensemble of black youth style, then, can be analytically discerned only by situating the constitutent elements socially and then reading them relationally as an ensemble. To be sure, popular representations of black youth that appear on commercial and cable television are codified and frozen. One could even argue that these representations are institutionally mediated and intentionally constructed to maximize their commercial (read crossover) appeal. Such a reading is completely warranted, given that music video and advertising are first and foremost promotional and marketing devices designed to stimulate product sales. What is more, music videos and television commercials are structured by aesthetic and organizational conventions that are shared and negotiated by record executives, art directors, agents, producers, and artists themselves. Nevertheless, in relationships to the popular media and public spaces where such practices are generated and produced, representations of black youth styles in commercial and cable television are important precisely because of their constructed and mediated nature (Frith 1988; Goodwin 1992; Grossberg 1992; Hebdige 1989).

Television (especially music videos, television ads, situation comedy, comedy-variety programs, and sports) is made up of cultural zones and social spaces of mediation, contestation, and circulation among groups that are differently positioned socially and differently organized culturally. Television is an important space for the production, expression, and circulation of contemporary black youth identity. In short, an interrogation of television constructions and representations of expressive black youth culture can shed some light on the operation of television as a social space of cultural struggle.

As a commercial space, television also represents a vital public site of cultural contestation where different claims on and representations of blackness bump up against, compete with, displace, complement, and comment on each other. Thus, black representations of youth culture exist in the same cultural space as neoconservative demonizations, commodified appropriations, and innovative explorations. Although clearly different from the street or community of origin, television is nonetheless a shared site, another place in the popular imagination where multiple representations of black youth get framed and presented. Indeed, television, especially music television and advertising, is the common place where different and differently interested claims on blackness (ethnic, racial, corporate capitalist, suburban middle-class, nationalist, assimilationist, urban poor) meet, each borrowing from the others, each using the others for its own ends, each making meanings of the others in often different, conflicting ways. Let me be clear here: I do not mean to celebrate the presence of this borrowing and exchange in some pluralist interest-group sense, but I do want to underscore the fact that these different representations and claims on blackness, including television itself, are situated and structured by shifting and unequal relations of power (including class, gender, race, and sexuality).

The representations of black youth on music television, in TV advertising, and in comedy-variety, stand-up comedy, and situation comedy programs draw viewers, significant numbers of whom are black youth themselves. Thus, by treating these electronic and mass-mediated images as "representations" rather than as real(istic) reflections of certain kinds of black youth practices, we can avoid the burden of representation that weighs so heavily on popular commentary and analysis of black images on television. In commercial media representations and refractions of blackness, there are multiple levels of self-reflexivity operating, the most dominant of which is an organizational imperative underwritten by institutional and aesthetic conventions that define and structure television as a profit-making corporate enterprise. Again, processes of both self-representation and media commodification are at work. It is the play of both commercial imperatives and cultural desires that makes television such an important site of social and cultural struggles over the sign of blackness.

Television representations of blackness and the range of possible meanings that can be made from them are not completely open. How they are constructed and positioned within social and cultural discourse is what gives them meaning and significance, not the fact of their existence alone. Just as audiences are socially organized and structured, so too are representations of black youth culture. That is to say, such representations operate in and are structured by discourses of youth and race that are hierarchically arranged. These discourses and the social and material relations of power in which they are embedded (and that they also help to reproduce) are the terms within which responses and meanings are registered and made. I think that it is possible to view identifications and meanings generated from the margins (the production of black youth styles and expressions—rap music) and at the center (advertising, fashion, and language styles that emulate black youth styles) of the culture as evidence of the differential (and hierarchically ordered) registers of social responses to black youth.

Here Stuart Hall's (1981a) notion of popular culture as a site of struggle and contestation is appropriate (see also Kelley 1992). I have claimed that it is possible to understand the popular constructions and expressions of black youth as subversive attempts on the part of black youth to open social and cultural spaces in which to express themselves. Let me be clear about this. I am not speaking of these expressions and their content as necessarily involving politics or social movements in some intentional or programmatic sense. Instead, I mean to point to the process by which these representations enact discursive struggles in cultural and social spaces (including commercial media). The impact of these cultural expressions and the effects they produce in commercial media (especially the reactions they generate among agents, organizations, and institutions of social control) suggest something of the power of these representations. Consider, for example, the campaign of the Parents' Music Resource Center to label recorded music, or the condemnations in the press by police departments, police associations, the Federal Bureau of Investigation, and the general law enforcement community as a result of Ice-T's uncensored LP *Cop Killer* and public Enemy's video for their song "By the Time I Get to Arizona," which features staged attacks on various Arizona state officials (Gray 1989; Grossberg 1992).

That the dominant apparatus of representation (and circulation) has responded with attempts at incorporation, surveillance, marginalization, and control tells us something about the power and potency of these expressions. What the consequences of that power will be for the rearrangement of social and cultural relations and the distribution of power in society is socially and historically contingent, and therefore remains to be played out.

DISCUSSION QUESTIONS

1. What effect does music have on mass mediated depictions of Blackness?

2. Why is it that individuals must "struggle for Blackness"?

3. In what ways do the effects of televisual images differ from that of film?

4. How did videos transform perceptions of Blackness in the mass media?

5. Do media determine reality or does reality determine media?

Reading 6.3

BLACK BEGINNINGS

From Uncle Tom's Cabin *to* The Birth of a Nation

DONALD BOGLE

In the beginning, there was an Uncle Tom. A former mechanic photographed him in a motion picture that ran no longer than twelve minutes. And a new dimension was added to American movies.

The year was 1903. The mechanic-turned-movie-director was Edwin S. Porter. The twelve-minute motion picture was *Uncle Tom's Cabin.* And the new dimension was Uncle Tom himself. He was the American movies' first black character. The great paradox was that in actuality Tom was not black at all. Instead he was portrayed by a nameless, slightly overweight white actor made up in blackface. But the use of whites in black roles was then a common practice, a tradition carried over from the stage and maintained during the early days of silent films. Still, the first Negro character had arrived in films, and he had done so at a time when the motion-picture industry itself was virtually nonexistent. The movies were without stars or studios or sound. There were no great directors or writers. And the community of Hollywood had not yet come into being.

After the tom's debut, there appeared a variety of black presences bearing the fanciful names of the coon, the tragic mulatto, the mammy, and the brutal black buck. All were character types used for the same effect: to entertain by stressing Negro inferiority. Fun was poked at the American Negro by presenting him as either a nitwit or a childlike lackey. None of the types was meant to do great harm, although at various times individual ones did. All were merely filmic reproductions of black stereotypes that had existed since the days of slavery and were already popularized in American life and arts. The movies, which catered to public tastes, borrowed profusely from all the other popular art forms. Whenever dealing with black characters, they simply adapted the old familiar stereotypes, often further distorting them.

In the early days when all the black characters were still portrayed by white actors in blackface, there was nothing but the old character

From Bogle, D. (1993). Black beginnings: From *Uncle Tom's Cabin* to *The Birth of a Nation*, in *Toms, coons, mulattoes, mammies, and bucks: An interpretive history of Blacks in American films* (pp. 3-18). New York: Continuum.

types. They sat like square boxes on a shelf. A white actor walked by, selected a box, and used it as a base for a very square, rigidly defined performance. Later, when real black actors played the roles and found themselves wedged into these categories, the history became one of actors battling against the types to create rich, stimulating, diverse characters. At various points the tom, the coon, the tragic mulatto, the mammy, and the brutal black buck were brought to life respectively by Bill "Bojangles" Robinson, Stepin Fetchit, Nina Mae McKinney, Hattie McDaniel, and Walter Long (actually a white actor who portrayed a black villain in *The Birth of a Nation*), and later "modernized" by such performers as Sidney Poitier, Sammy Davis, Jr., Dorothy Dandridge, Ethel Waters, and Jim Brown. Later such performers as Richard Pryor, Eddie Murphy, Lonette McKee, Whoopi Goldberg, and Danny Glover also found themselves struggling to turn old stereotypes inside out. Often it seemed as if the mark of the actor was the manner in which he individualized the mythic type or towered above it. The types were to prove deadly for some actors and inconsequential for others. But try as any actor may to forget the typecasting, the familiar types have most always been present in American black movies. The early silent period of motion pictures remains important, not because there were any great black performances—there weren't—but because the five basic types—the boxes sitting on the shelf—that were to dominate black characters for the next half century were first introduced then.

THE TOM

Porter's tom was the first in a long line of socially acceptable Good Negro characters. Always as toms are chased, harassed, hounded, flogged, enslaved, and insulted, they keep the faith, n'er turn against their white massas, and remain hearty, submissive, stoic, generous, selfless, and oh-so-very kind. Thus they endear themselves to white audiences and emerge as heroes of sorts.

Two early toms appeared in the shorts *Confederate Spy* (c. 1910) and *For Massa's Sake* (1911). In the former, dear old Uncle Daniel is a Negro spy for the South. He dies before a Northern firing squad, but he is content, happy that he "did it for massa's sake and little massa." In *For Massa's Sake* a former slave is so attached to his erstwhile master that he sells himself back into slavery to help the master through a period of financial difficulties.

During the silent period, there were also remakes of the Harriet Beecher Stowe novel in which the tale of the good Christian slave was again made the meat of melodrama. The first remakes in 1909 and 1913 had little in style or treatment to distinguish them. But a fourth version, directed by William Robert Daly in 1914, distinguished itself and the tom tradition by starring the Negro stage actor Sam Lucas in the title role. Lucas became the first black man to play a leading role in a movie. Later in 1927, when Universal Pictures filmed *Uncle Tom's Cabin,* the handsome Negro actor James B. Lowe was signed for the leading role. Harry Pollard directed the Universal feature. Twelve years earlier, Pollard had filmed a version of the Stowe classic in which he portrayed the Christian slave in blackface. But for this new venture Negro Lowe was selected to fit in with the "realistic" demands of the times. Congratulating itself on its liberalism, Universal sent out press releases about its good colored star:

James B. Lowe had made history. A history that reflects only credit to the Negro race, not only because he has given the "Uncle Tom" character a new slant, but because of his exemplary conduct with the Universal company. They look upon Lowe at the Universal Studio as a living black god. . . . Of the directors, critics, artists, and actors who have seen James Lowe work at the studio there are none who will not say he is the most suited of all men for the part of "Tom." Those who are religious say that a heavenly power brought him to Universal and all predict a most marvelous future and worldwide reputation for James B. Lowe.

Although a "heavenly power" may have been with actor Lowe, it had little effect on his interpretation of the role. Tom still came off as a genial darky, furnished with new color but no new sentiments. Yet to Lowe's credit, he did his tomming with such an arresting effectiveness that he was sent to England on a promotional tour to ballyhoo the picture, thus becoming the first black actor to be publicized by his studio. The film also introduced the massive baptism scene, which later became a Hollywood favorite. Curiously, in 1958 this version of *Uncle Tom's Cabin,* although silent, was reissued with an added prologue by Raymond Massey. Because it arrived just when the sit-ins were erupting in the South, many wondered if by reissuing this film Universal Studios hoped to remind the restless black masses of an earlier, less turbulent period, when obeying one's master was the answer to every black man's problems.

The Coon

Although tom was to outdistance every other type and dominate American hearth and home, he had serious competition from a group of coons. They appeared in a series of black films presenting the Negro as amusement object and black buffoon. They lacked the single-mindedness of tom. There were the pure coon and two variants of his type: the pickaninny and the uncle remus.

The pickaninny was the first of the coon types to make its screen debut. It gave the Negro child actor his place in the black pantheon. Generally, he was a harmless, little screwball creation whose eyes popped, whose hair stood on end with the least excitement, and whose antics were pleasant and diverting. Thomas Alva Edison proved to be a pioneer in the exploitation and exploration of this type when he presented *Ten Pickaninnies* in 1904, a forerunner of the Hal Roach *Our Gang* series. During his camera experiments in 1893, Edison had photographed some blacks as "interesting side effects." In *Ten Pickaninnies,* the side effects moved to the forefront of the action as a group of nameless Negro children romped and ran about while being referred to as snowballs, cherubs, coons, bad chillun, inky kids, smoky kids, black lambs, cute ebonies, and chubbie ebonies. In due time, the pickaninnies were to be called by other names. In the 1920s and the 1930s, such child actors as Sunshine Sammy, Farina, Stymie, and Buckwheat picked up the pickaninny mantle and carried it to new summits. In all the versions of *Uncle Tom's Cabin,* the slave child Topsy was presented as a lively pickaninny, used solely for comic relief. When

the 1927 version of *Uncle Tom's Cabin* opened, the character was singled out by one critic who wrote: "Topsy is played by Mona Ray, a wonderfully bright youngster who seems to have the comedy of her part in extraordinary fashion . . . her eyes roll back and forth in alarm. She also evinces no liking for her plight when she is found by Miss Ophelia while dabbing powder on her ebony countenance." In her day, the character Topsy was clownish and droll and became such a film favorite that she starred in *Topsy and Eva* (1927), in which her far-fetched meanderings and her pickaninnying won mass audience approval.

Shortly after Edison introduced the pickaninny in 1904, the pure coon made its way onto the screen in *Wooing and Wedding of a Coon* (1905). This short depicted a honeymooning black couple as stumbling and stuttering idiots. Later the coon appeared in *The Masher* (1907), which was about a self-styled white ladies' man who is rebuffed by all the women he pursues. When he meets a mysterious veiled woman who responds to his passes, the hero thinks he has arrived at his blue heaven. And so finding success, he removes the veil only to discover that his mystery lady love is *colored!* Without further ado, he takes off. He may have been looking for a blue heaven, but he certainly did not want a black one.

Before its death, the coon developed into the most blatantly degrading of all black stereotypes. The pure coons emerged as no-account niggers, those unreliable, crazy, lazy, subhuman creatures good for nothing more than eating watermelons, stealing chickens, shooting crap, or butchering the English language. A character named Rastus was just such a figure.

How Rastus Got His Turkey (c. 1910) was the first of a series of slapstick comedies centering on the antics of a Negro called Rastus. Here Rastus tries to steal a turkey for his Thanksgiving dinner. Next came *Rastus in Zululand,* about a darky who dreams of going to Zululand in the heart of Africa. There he wins the affections of the chief's daughter. He is willing to flirt with the girl, but when asked to marry her, in true unreliable, no-account nigger fashion, he refuses, expressing a wish for death rather than matrimony. The savage chief (from the beginning, all Africans are savages) nearly grants that wish, too. *Rastus and Chicken, Pickaninnies and Watermelon,* and *Chicken Thief* were other shorts in the series, all appearing during 1910 and 1911. In some respects, this series and its central character simply paved the way for the greatest coon of all time, Stepin Fetchit.

The final member of the coon triumvirate is the uncle remus. Harmless and congenial, he is a first cousin to the tom, yet he distinguishes himself by his quaint, naïve, and comic philosophizing. During the silent period he was only hinted at. He did not come into full flower until the 1930s and 1940s with films such as *The Green Pastures* (1936) and *Song of the South* (1946). Remus's mirth, like tom's contentment and the coon's antics, has always been used to indicate the black man's satisfaction with the system and his place in it.

THE TRAGIC MULATTO

The third figure of the black pantheon and the one that proved itself a moviemaker's darling is the tragic mulatto. One of the type's earliest appearances was in *The Debt* (1912), a two-reeler about the Old South. A white man's wife and his black mistress bear him children at the same time. Growing up together, the white son and the mulatto daughter fall in love and decide to marry, only to have their relationship revealed to them at the crucial moment. Their lives are thus ruined not only because they are brother and sister but also—and here was the catch—because the girl has a drop of black blood!

In Humanity's Cause, In Slavery Days, and *The Octoroon,* all made around 1913, explored the plight of a fair-skinned mulatto attempting to pass for white. Usually the mulatto is made likable—even sympathetic (because of her white blood, no doubt)—and the audience believes that the girl's life could have been productive and happy had she not been a "victim of divided racial inheritance."

THE MAMMY

Mammy, the fourth black type, is so closely related to the comic coons that she is usually relegated to their ranks. Mammy is distinguished, however, by her sex and her fierce independence. She is usually big, fat, and cantankerous. She made her debut around 1914 when audiences were treated to a blackface version of *Lysistrata.* The comedy, titled *Coon Town Suffragettes,* dealt with a group of bossy mammy washerwomen who organize a militant movement to keep their good-for-nothing husbands at home. Aristophanes would no doubt have risen from his grave with righteous indignation. But the militancy of the washerwomen served as a primer for the mammy roles Hattie McDaniel was to perfect in the 1930s.

Mammy's offshoot is the aunt jemima, sometimes derogatorily referred to as a "handkerchief head." Often aunt jemimas are toms blessed with religion or mammies who wedge themselves into the dominant white culture. Generally they are sweet, jolly, and good-tempered—a bit more polite than mammy and certainly never as headstrong. The maids in the Mae West films of the 1930s fit snugly into this category.

THE BRUTAL BLACK BUCK AND *THE BIRTH OF A NATION*

D. W. Griffith's *The Birth of a Nation* (1915) was the motion picture to introduce the final mythic type, the brutal black buck. This extraordinary, multidimensional movie was also the first feature film to deal with a black theme and at the same time to articulate fully the entire pantheon of black gods and goddesses. Griffith presented all the types with such force and power that his film touched off a wave of controversy and was denounced a the most slanderous anti-Negro movie ever released.

In almost every way, *The Birth of a Nation* was a stupendous undertaking, unlike any film that had preceded it. Up to then American movies had been two- or three-reel affairs, shorts running no longer than ten or fifteen minutes, crudely and casually filmed. But *The Birth of a Nation* was rehearsed for six weeks, filmed in nine, later edited in three months, and finally released as a record-breaking hundred-thousand-dollar spectacle, twelve reels in length and over three hours in running time. It altered the entire course and concept of American moviemaking, developing the close-up, cross-cutting, rapid-fire editing, the iris, the split-screen shot, and realistic and impressionistic lighting. Creating sequences and images yet to be surpassed, the film's magnitude and epic grandeur swept audiences off their feet. At a private White House screening President Woodrow Wilson exclaimed, "It's like writing history with lightning!" *The Birth of a Nation,* however, not only vividly re-created history, but revealed its director's philosophical concept of the universe and his personal racial bigotry. For D. W. Griffith there was a moral order at work in the universe. If that order were ever thrown out of whack, he believed chaos would ensue. Griffith's thesis was sound, relatively exciting, and even classic in a purely Shakespearean sense. But in articulating his thesis, Griffith seemed to be saying that things were in order only when whites were in control and when the American Negro was kept in his place. In the end, Griffith's "lofty" statement—and the film's subject matter—transformed *The Birth of a Nation* into a hotly debated and bitterly cursed motion picture.

It told the story of the Old South, the Civil War, the Reconstruction period, and the emergence of the Ku Klux Klan. Basing his film on Thomas Dixon's novel *The Clansman* (also the original title of the film), Griffith focused on a good, decent "little" family, the Camerons of Piedmont, South Carolina. Before the war, the family lives in an idyllic "quaintly way that is to be no more." Dr. Cameron and his sons are gentle, benevolent "fathers" to their child-like servants. The slaves themselves could be no happier. In the fields they contentedly pick cotton. In their quarters they dance and sing for their master. In the Big House Mammy joyously goes about her chores. All is in order. Everyone knows his place. Then the Civil War breaks out, and the old order cracks.

The war years take their toll. In Piedmont, the Cameron family is terrorized by a troop of Negro raiders, and all the South undergoes "ruin, devastation, rapine, and pillage." Then comes Reconstruction. Carpetbaggers and uppity niggers from the North move into Piedmont, exploiting and corrupting the former slaves, unleashing the sadism and bestiality innate in the Negro, turning the once congenial darkies into renegades, and using them to "crush the white South under the heel of the black South." "Lawlessness runs riot!" says one title card. The old slaves have quit work to dance. They roam the streets, shoving whites off sidewalks. They take over the political polls and disenfranchise the whites. A black political victory culminates in an orgiastic street celebration. Blacks dance, sing, drink, rejoice. Later they conduct a black congressional session, itself a mockery of Old South ideals, in which the freed Negro legislators are depicted as lustful, arrogant, and idiotic. They bite on chicken legs and drink whiskey from bottles while sprawling with bare feet upon their desks. During the Congressional meeting, the stench created by the barefoot Congressmen becomes so great that they pass as their first act a ruling that every member must keep his shoes on during legislative meetings! Matters in *The Birth of a Nation* reach a heady climax later when the renegade black Gus sets out to rape the younger Cameron daughter. Rather than submit, the Pet Sister flees from him and throws herself from a cliff—into the "opal gates of death." Then the mulatto Silas Lynch attempts to force the white Elsie Stoneman to marry him. Finally, when all looks hopelessly lost, there emerges a group of good, upright Southern white men, members of an "invisible empire," who, while wearing White sheets and hoods, battle the blacks in a direct confrontation. Led by Ben Cameron in a rousing stampede, they magnificently defeat the black rebels! Defenders of white womanhood, white honor, and white glory, they restore to the South everything it has lost, including its white supremacy. Thus we have the birth of a nation. And the birth of the Ku Klux Klan.

The plot machinations of the Griffith epic may today resound with melodramatic absurdities, but the action, the actors, and the direction did not. The final ride of the Klan was an impressive piece of film propaganda, superbly lit and brilliantly edited. Indeed it was so stirring that audiences screamed in delight, cheering for the white heroes and booing, hissing, and cursing the black militants. *The Birth of a Nation* remains significant not only because of its artistry but also because of its wide-ranging influence. One can detect in this single film the trends and sentiments that were to run through almost every black film made for a long time afterward. Later film makers were to pick up Griffith's ideas—his very images—but were to keep them "nicely" toned down in order not to offend audiences.

Griffith used three varieties of blacks. The first were the "faithful souls," a mammy and an uncle tom, who remain with the Cameron family throughout and stanchly defend them from the rebels. By means of these characters, as well as the pickaninny slaves seen dancing, singing, and clowning in their quarters, director Griffith propagated the myth of slave contentment and made it appear as if slavery had elevated the Negro from his bestial instincts. At heart, Griffith's "faithful souls" were shamelessly naïve representations of the Negro as Child or the Negro as Watered-Down Noble Savage. But these characters were to make their way through scores of other Civil War epics, and they were to leave their mark on the characterizations of Clarence Muse in *Huckleberry Finn* (1931) and *Broadway Bill* (1934) and of Bill Robinson in *The Little Colonel* (1935) and *The Littlest Rebel* (1935).

Griffith's second variety were the brutal black bucks. Just as the coon stereotype could be broken into subgroups, the brutal black buck type could likewise be divided into two categories: the black brutes and the black bucks. Differences between the two are minimal. The black brute was a barbaric black out to raise havoc. Audiences could assume that his physical violence served as an outlet for a man who was sexually repressed. In *The Birth of a Nation,* the black brutes, subhuman and feral, are the nameless characters setting out on a rampage full of black rage. They flog the Cameron's faithful servant. They shove and assault white men of the town. They flaunt placards demanding "equal marriage." These characters figured prominently in the Black Congress sequence, and their film descendants were to appear years later as the rebellious slaves of *So Red the Rose* (1935), as the revolution-arise of *Uptight* (1969), and as the militants of *Putney Swope* (1969).

But it was the pure black bucks that were Griffith's really great archetypal figures. Bucks are always big, baadddd niggers, oversexed and savage, violent and frenzied as they lust for white flesh. No greater sin hath any black man. Both Lynch, the mulatto, and Gus, the renegade, fall into this category. Among other things, these two characters revealed the tie between sex and racism in America. Griffith played on the myth of the Negro's high-powered sexuality, then articulated the great white fear that every black man longs for a white woman. Underlying the fear was the assumption that the white woman was the ultimate in female desirability, herself a symbol of white pride, power, and beauty. Consequently, when Lillian Gish, the frailest, purest of all screen heroines, was attacked by the character Lynch—when he put his big black arms around this pale blond beauty—audiences literally panicked. Here was the classic battle of good and evil, innocence and corruption. It was a master stroke and a brilliant use of contrast, one that drew its audience into the film emotionally.[1] But in uncovering the attraction of black to white, Griffith failed to reveal the political implications. Traditionally, certain black males have been drawn to white women because these women are power symbols, an ideal of the oppressor. But Griffith attributed the attraction to an animalism innate in the Negro male. Thus the black bucks of the film are psychopaths, one always panting and salivating, the other forever stiffening his body as if the mere presence of a white woman in the same room could bring him to a sexual climax. Griffith played hard on the bestiality of his black villainous bucks and used it to arouse hatred.

Closely aligned to the bucks and brutes of *The Birth of a Nation* is the mulatto character, Lydia. She is presented as the mistress of the white abolitionist carpetbagger, Senator Stoneman. Through Lydia, Griffith explored the possibilities of the dark, sinister half-breed as a tragic leading lady. Although merely a supporting character, Lydia is the only black role to suggest even remotely genuine mental anguish. She hates whites. She refuses to be treated as an inferior. She wants power. Throughout, she anguishes over her predicament as a black woman in a hostile white world.

Lydia is also the film's only passionate female. Griffith was the first important movie director to divide his black women into categories based on their individual colors. Both

Lydia and Mammy are played by white actresses in blackface. But Mammy is darker. She is representative of the all-black woman, overweight, middle-aged, and so dark, so thoroughly black, that it is preposterous even to suggest that she be a sex object. Instead she was desexed. This tradition of the desexed, overweight, dowdy *dark* black woman was continued in films throughout the 1930s and 1940s. Vestiges of it popped up as late as the 1960s with Claudia McNeil in *A Raisin in the Sun* (1961) and Beah Richards in *Hurry Sundown* (1967). A dark black actress was considered for no role but that of a mammy or an aunt jemima. On the other hand, the part-black woman—the light-skinned Negress—was given a chance at lead parts and was graced with a modicum of sex appeal. Every sexy black woman who appeared afterward in movies was to be a "cinnamon-colored gal" with Caucasian features. The mulatto came closest to the white ideal. Whether conscious or not, Griffith's division of the black woman into color categories survived in movies the way many set values continue long after they are discredited. In fact, it was said in 1958 and 1970 that one reason why such actresses as Eartha Kitt in *Anna Lucasta* and Lola Falana in *The Liberation of L. B. Jones* failed to emerge as important screen love goddesses was that they were too dark.

Influential and detrimental as the Griffith blacks were to be for later generations, they were not meekly accepted in 1915. *The Birth of a Nation's* blackfaced baddies aroused a rash of hostilities. At the film's New York premiere, the NAACP picketed the theater, calling the movie racist propaganda. Later the Chicago and Boston branches of the NAACP led massive demonstrations against its presentation. Other civil rights and religious organizations were quick to protest. Race riots broke out in a number of cities. Newspaper editorials and speeches censured the film. Black critics such as Laurence Reddick said it glorified the Ku Klux Klan, and Reddick added that the film's immense success was at least one factor contributing to the great and growing popularity the organization enjoyed during this period. In the South, the film was often advertised as calculated to "work audiences into a frenzy . . . it will make you hate." In some regions, the ad campaign may have been effective, for in 1915 lynchings in the United States reached their highest peak since 1908. Ultimately, *The Birth of a Nation* was banned in five states and nineteen cities.

The anger and fury did not die in 1915 either. The film was reissued at regular intervals in later years. At each reopening, outraged moviegoers, both black and white, vehemently opposed its showing. In 1921, *The Birth of a Nation* was attacked as a part of a "Southern campaign to stimulate the Ku Klux Klan"—which it had already done. The Museum of Modern Art temporarily shelved the picture in 1946. Because of "the potency of its anti-Negro bias . . ." read the Museum's press announcement, "exhibiting it at this time of heightened social tensions cannot be justified."

The 1947 revival of the movie by the Dixie Film Exchange was blasted by the Civil Rights Congress, and the NAACP picketed New York's Republic Theatre where it was to be shown. "It brings race hatred to New York City," said NAACP Secretary Walter White, "and we don't want it here." The Progressive Labor Party led demonstrations against the film during the following year. In 1950, there were renewed outcries when word leaked out that a Hollywood company was to remake the movie in sound. The remake plans were quickly aborted, as were the 1959 proposals to present it on television.

Throughout the years, D. W. Griffith defended himself as a mere filmmaker with no political or ideological view in mind. Surprised and apparently genuinely hurt when called a racist, Griffith made speeches across the country, wrote letters to the press, accused the NAACP and its supporters of trying to bring about screen censorship, and even went so far as to issue a pamphlet titled "The Rise and Fall of Free Speech in America," all in an effort to squelch the controversy. As late as 1947, one year before his death and some thirty-two years after the movie's release, D. W. Griffith still maintained that his film was not an attack on the American Negro.

The Birth of a Nation has become one of the highest grossing movies of all time. (The amount it has earned has never been fully tabulated.) Eyeing its profits, a number of Hollywood producers undertook projects with similar anti-Negro themes. *Broken Chains* (c. 1916) and *Free and Equal* (filmed in 1915 but not released until 1925) were prominent imitations. The former failed miserably. The latter's release was held up for some ten years while the producer waited for the furor to cool down. For one thing was certain after *The Birth of a Nation:* never again could the Negro be depicted in the guise of an out-and-out villain. This treatment was too touchy and too controversial. Griffith's film had succeeded because of its director's artistry and technical virtuosity, but no studio dared risk it again. Consequently, blacks in Hollywood films were cast almost exclusively in comic roles. And thus even the great comic tradition of the Negro in the American film has its roots in the Griffith spectacle. Finally, many of Hollywood's hang-ups and hesitations in presenting sensual black men on screen resulted, in part, from the reactions to the Griffith spectacle. So strong was his presentation, and so controversial its reception, that movie companies ignored and avoided such a type of black character for fear of raising new hostilities. Not until more than a half century later, when Melvin Van Peebles' *Sweet Sweetback's Baadasssss Song* (1971) appeared, did sexually assertive black males make their way back to the screen. Afterward, when the box-office success of that film indicated that audiences could at long last accept such a type, the screen was bombarded with an array of buck heroes in such films as *Shaft* (1971), *Super Fly* (1972), *Slaughter* (1972), and *Melinda* (1972).

With *The Birth of a Nation* in 1915, all the major black screen types had been introduced. Literal and unimaginative as some types might now appear, the naïve and cinematically untutored audiences of the early part of the century responded to the character types as if they were the real thing.

As far as the audiences were concerned, the toms, the coons, the mulattoes, the mammies, and the bucks embodied all the aspects and facets of the black experience itself. The audience's deep-set prejudice against any "foreigners" accounts for the typing of all minorities in all American films. But no minority was so relentlessly or fiercely typed as the black man. Audiences rejected even subtle modifications of the black caricatures. When Jack Johnson became the first black heavyweight champion of the world in 1908, filmed sequences of him knocking out white Tommy Burns so disturbed the "racial pride" of white America that they were banned for fear of race riots. Thereafter, black boxers in films were invariably defeated by their white opponents. Similarly, when the first film versions of *Uncle Tom's Cabin* were released in the South, advertisements announced that the black characters were portrayed by white actors. Even at this stage, the evolving film industry feared offending its dominant white audience.

Once the basic mythic types were introduced, a number of things occurred. Specific black themes soon emerged. (The Old South theme proved to be a great favorite.) And the basic types came and went in various guises. Guises long confused many movie viewers. They were (and remain) deceptive, and they have traditionally been used by the film industry to camouflage the familiar types. If a black appeared as a butler, audiences thought of him a merely as servant. What they failed to note was the variety of servants. There were tom servants (faithful and submissive), coon servants (lazy and unreliable), and mammy servants, just to name a few. What has to be remembered is that the servant's uniform was the guise certain types wore during a given period. That way Hollywood could give its audience the same product (the types themselves) but with new packaging (the guise).

With the Griffith spectacle, audiences saw the first of the guises. The brutes, the bucks, and the tragic mulatto all wore the guise of villains. Afterward, during the 1920s, audiences saw their toms and coons dressed in the guise of plantation jesters. In the 1930s, all the types were dressed in servants' uniforms. In the early 1940s, they sported entertainers' costumes. In the late 1940s and the 1950s, they donned the gear of troubled problem people. In the 1960s, they appeared as angry militants. Because the guises were always changing, audiences were sometimes tricked into believing the depictions of the American Negro were altered, too. But at heart beneath the various guises, there lurked the familiar types.

DISCUSSION QUESTIONS

1. Who are the five characters that comprise the pantheon?

2. In what movie was Uncle Tom first introduced?

3. What is a pickaninny? (Give an example.)

4. Compare the *tragic mulatto* with the *mammy*.

5. What was the legacy left by the film *The Birth of a Nation?*

Reading 6.4

BLACK TALK RADIO

Defining Community Needs and Identity

CATHERINE R. SQUIRES

Although many researchers have investigated the negative impact of traditionally white-controlled mass media on white attitudes toward blacks[1] (see Entman 1992; Peffley et al. 1996), the question of how black-controlled mass media shape black public life has not been as rigorously investigated. As Michael Dawson notes, "How and to what extent the circulation of and participation in debates within social movements, indigenous organizations, and *Black media* and artistic outlets influence political attitudes of individuals is an empirical question" that has yet to be answered (Dawson 1994:217, emphasis added). Building on Dawson's suggestion, I explore the relationship between black mass media and black publics through a study of WVON-AM radio, the only black owned talk-radio station in Chicago. Results of a survey and an ethnographic research study suggest that WVON and its listeners create alternative conversational and physical public spheres in which members of the audience (also known as "the WVON family") circulate information and provide opportunities for community interaction and political involvement.

TALK RADIO

Most studies of talk radio either focus on nationally broadcast, celebrity hosts, such as Rush Limbaugh, or use large, random national samples to extract information about the talk-show audience and talk-show texts (Davis 1997; Hofstetter and Gianos 1997; Hollander 1997; Owen 1997). These approaches have resulted in a lopsided picture of the talk-show phenomenon: that is, that the shows are overwhelmingly enjoyed by white conservative males (often associated with the Gingrich "revolution") and that the content is also mainly conservative. Not surprisingly, this picture resonates with liberal politicians' and commentators' complaints about the "new" influence talk shows have on voters and the irresponsibility of political journalists. These studies do not fully explain the reemergence of talk-show popularity, nor do they encompass the wide range of hosts, formats, and audiences involved in this phenomenon. Their focus on and concern with the behavior of white conservative listeners has fueled the fire over "hate radio" without

From Squires, C. (2000). Black talk radio: Defining community needs and identity. *Harvard International Journal of Press and Politics,* 5(2), 73-95.

revealing the differences that exist across stations and audiences. By exploring local radio stations in addition to the national broadcasters, we will gain a more nuanced understanding of talk radio's function in both the lives of its audiences and its effects on political processes.

Black talk radio, largely ignored by media scholars, has been growing steadily around the country. In addition to the popularity of nationally syndicated host Tom Joyner, many local Black-owned stations have included talk programming for years. Earlier in the century, Blacks who were able to buy airtime in large cities, like Jack Cooper's pioneering efforts in Chicago, or who were hired at stations that played Black music created talk shows for their Black listeners (Cantor 1992; Newman 1988). However, these traditions in programming and African-American audience have been overlooked and underrepresented in national sample surveys and are rarely mentioned in editorial discussions concerning talk radio.

Below, I present some of the results of a long-term study of WVON-AM in Chicago, combining ethnographic and survey research methods to begin constructing a more diverse picture of the talk-radio phenomenon. Furthermore, I intend for my description of this particular audience to advance Susan Herbst's contention that studies of talk radio should attempt to discern why they are an attractive means of "discursive political participation" and how the talk show "illuminates debates about the nature of the public sphere" (Herbst 1995:264). At the end of her article, Herbst suggests that part of the attraction for the conservative white listeners is their distrust of mainstream media, creating the desire for an alternative forum. I find that Black listeners at WVON also distrust mainstream white media, but their attraction to an alternative sphere of discourse has other roots as well—roots that reach back to the birth of a separate (yet overlapping and interactive) Black public sphere.

THE PUBLIC SPHERE(S)

The translation of Jurgen Habermas's *The Structural Transformation of the Public Sphere* (1989) has inspired many scholars to rethink the idea of the public forum, the importance of public discourse, the nature of public opinion, and the role of the mass media in the production of all three. Habermas proposes the existence of a single public sphere where participants leave behind status markers in order to engage in rational critical discourse. His idealized conception, based in eighteenth-century Europe, does not echo Black experiences with public spaces or the media. African-Americans have had neither the luxury of leaving the status marker of race behind (unless they could "pass" for white), nor have they had access or been welcome to speak and participate in the dominant public sphere until very recently in American history. Hence, Blacks have created alternate forms of publicity in the face of a hostile and often threatening white public. Blacks made their own sequestered and semisequestered spaces for deliberation, resistance, and sustenance to survive in America. This history of African-Americans and the public sphere demands a more complex vision of public spaces and deliberation than Habermas's ideal type provides.

Like Dawson, I consider the Black public sphere to be closer to Nancy Fraser's vision of a subaltern counterpublic (1992). In her critique of Habermas, Fraser demonstrates that, rather than insisting upon the existence of a single public sphere, it is more useful to envision multiple public spheres coexisting, overlapping, and competing in stratified societies like the United States. There is a dominant public sphere that "will tend to operate to the advantage of dominant groups and the disadvantage of subordinates" (Fraser 1992: 122). However, subordinates are not rendered completely silent. Rather, they create their own discursive arenas, which Fraser calls "subaltern counterpublics." Dawson uses Fraser's general depiction of a subaltern counterpublic to create a specific operationalization of the Black counterpublic and its goals:

> The Black public sphere [is] . . . a set of institutions, communication networks and practices which facilitate debate of causes and remedies to the current combination of political setbacks and economic devastation facing major segments of the Black community, and which facilitate the creation of oppositional formations and sites. (Dawson 1994:197)

Dawson, like other Black political and cultural theorists, believes that the current state of the majority of Blacks in the United States necessitates an oppositional sphere. Counterpublics give oppressed and/or marginalized groups arenas for deliberation outside the surveillance of the dominant group. Here, they can

> invent and articulate counterdiscourses to formulate oppositional interpretations of their identities, interests and needs. . . . On the one hand, [subaltern counterpublics] function as spaces of withdrawal and regroupment; on the other, they function as bases and training grounds for agitational activities directed toward wider publics. (Fraser 1992: 123–24)

Daniel Brouwer provides three additional reasons for the existence and importance of subaltern publics: (1) when the standards for participation are perceived by marginal cultures to be restrictive or unfairly applied; (2) when official public forums are perceived "not to be adequate sites for the redress of sociopolitical or cultural grievances"; and (3) when the representations of subaltern publics produced by mainstream sources are "inaccurate, offensive, limiting, or dangerous" (Brouwer 1995). So, while African-Americans have made great legal gains in this society, there are still structural and cultural barriers to full equality (see Marable 1991; Omi and Winant 1994; West 1993). In addition, harmful narratives and images concerning blacks are still circulated in mainstream and other media (Dates and Barlow 1990; Entman 1992; Gilens 1996; Morrison 1992). Therefore, there is still a need for an alternate sphere (or spheres) for Blacks in the United States, as well as alternative black media.

However, Dawson concludes in his overview of the state of the Black community that such a sphere has not existed since the early 1970s. Furthermore, he questions whether there can be a single Black public sphere any longer, given division along class and gender lines. Hence his call for a new program of research into the institutions that undergird a counterpublic and investigations of Black public opinion to spur on the revitalization of such a public (or publics). In this article, I present evidence that the activities at a particular talk-radio station are

providing sites for the creation of communication networks and oppositional sites for political organization. WVON radio is an institution that serves a Black public sphere occupying a particular niche in the Chicago radio market at the frequency 1450 AM.

AUDIENCE AS (SUBALTERN) PUBLIC; AUDIENCE AS NICHE MARKET

James Webster and Patricia Phalen note that in American media policy debates, the public is conceived as a large collection of citizens, unknown to each other and unseen by the government—except, perhaps, as poll data. This concept of the public bears obvious similarities to the mass audience (Webster and Phalen 1994:21). Their observation is built on Susan Herbst and James R. Beniger's observation that, as politicians in the twentieth century increased their use of media to reach the public, the media audience became analogous for the publics they were trying to persuade. Because "mass media now transmit much of the information needed to formulate opinions . . .., publics might be viewed as bodies formed through communication" (Herbst and Beniger 1994:109, 97). In the age of mass media, the terms *audience* and *public* have become interchangeable.

Habermas, however, depicts modern mass media as distraction from rather than preparation for rational critical debate. This critique is based on the assumption that media are no longer produced by the public itself and are entangled in commercial interests which run counter to the ideals of public education and debate (Habermas 1989:188). Many scholars of media and democracy would agree with Habermas's critique that today's news media are debilitating rather than energizing the public sphere. Robert Entman, for instance, describes the media as heavily dependent on elites and politicians for information and focused on profit maximization rather than public service (1989). Others' accounts, whether they tend toward conspiracy (Chomsky 1992; Parenti 1993) or pragmatism (Bennett and Paletz 1994; Page 1996), also focus on the problematic relationships between political elites, news producers, and commercialism. However useful these analyses of mainstream media are, though, they operate within a singular public sphere model. To get a more complete look at how different sectors of the populace use media and discuss public issues, we use a model of multiple public spheres. One must then investigate each particular sphere's production and consumption of media (in addition to its relationship to the media of the dominant sphere) to ascertain the utility of the media to that particular public.

William Gamson states that "because media discourse is so central in framing issues for the attentive public, it becomes . . . 'a site on which various social groups, institutions, and ideologies struggle over the definition and construction of social reality.'" However, acknowledging this function of the media "doesn't tell us how and in what ways it operates on different parts of the audience. . . . Media practices both help and hurt social movement efforts in complex ways that differ from issue to issue" (Gamson 1992:71). I would amend Gamson's statement to add that media practices help and hurt social movement efforts in ways that differ from medium to medium, from public to public. In other words, one might hypothesize that media created by and for subaltern publics will operate differently than media created by and for dominant publics. The talk-show format, which allows the audience to participate in constructing social texts and assigning meanings, may assist the social and political goals of different publics in different ways. The management and production teams of WVON believe that the talk-show format is a catalyst for, not a hindrance to, its audience's political and social goals.

In the case of WVON, the distinctions between producer and audience are not as stark as with the mainstream commercial media firms critiqued by the authors mentioned above. First, WVON grounds itself in a community ethic and a commitment to disseminating information shared by its listeners. Second, the talk-show format itself is an opportunity for a dynamic process of joint creation of texts and reciprocal information sharing between audience, guests, and station staff. Through this particular media environment, the audience participates in a Black public sphere created in multiple ways: through the discursive space of the talk show,

the physical spaces of community forums sponsored by or announced by WVON, and membership in the WVON family, a subset of a larger Black collective.

From the publication of *Freedom's Journal* in 1827 to the ascendancy of the *Chicago Defender* in the 1920s, the role of the black media has been to "serve, speak, and fight for the black community" (Wolseley 1971:3). Not only has the black media spoken to and for black publics, presenting an alternate portrayal of black life, but it has also provided an alternative, autonomous discursive public sphere for Blacks from Chicago to the deep South (Suggs 1996; Washburn 1986).[2] Dawson calls for researchers to focus their attention on the importance of such institutions to a Black public sphere, noting that

> a multiplicity of Black institutions have formed the material base for a subaltern counterpublic. *An independent Black press,* the production and circulation of socially and politically sharp Black music and the Black church have provided institutional bases for the Black counterpublic since the Civil War. (Dawson 1994:210, emphasis added)

In the past, the black press and other media have enriched the Black public sphere, even though they targeted a wide swath of the black public and depended on subscriptions and advertisements for revenue (Squires 1999). Creating oppositional frameworks for African-Americans and rearticulating black identity, the Black press served as a site for grievances to be aired when even letters to the editor were segregated, spread the word for activists and scholars, and allowed blacks to use their expertise and modes of expression without as much censure from the dominant public.[3] Despite this historical legacy, little work has been done on the role of contemporary Black talk radio in black political discourse. Two studies of Black radio's educational impact on Black communities currently available (Johnson 1992; Johnson and Birk 1993) find that Black radio managers report a high level of community involvement. In particular, these studies by Phylis Johnson and her colleagues find that concern for the health and welfare of Black communities guides many decisions about promotions and special events put on by Black-owned stations.[4] In light of the history of Black-owned media and current activities in radio, it is not surprising to find WVON catering talk shows to a niche of the Black community in Chicago. This study suggests that WVON is continuing the legacy of the black press via radio, creating an institution with the potential to meet Dawson's criteria for a revitalization of the Black counterpublic. This article centers on the following issues and questions:

1. Does the programming on WVON provide useful information to listeners and staff in terms of critical debate and public action?

2. What relationships to the black community/public do listeners and station staff expect from black media?

3. How does the station imagine the Black public it serves, and how do audience members imagine that public?

METHODS

This article began with fieldwork at WVON in the summer of 1995. Through participant observation, interviews with staff and listeners, and analysis of broadcasts, I was immersed in its motives and history.[5] In this article, I share both the results of this ethnographic research and a 1996 survey that focused on audience members who reside in Chicago. The list of audience members was generated through WVON's first subscription drive of late 1995. From this database (WVON's only official listing of any of its listeners), I randomly selected 515 names. Fifteen were used to pretest the questionnaire,[6] and the remaining five hundred were sent surveys with return postage and mailing included. The response rate was 46 percent *(N = 232),* a rather high rate for a mail survey of this type. The questionnaire contained open-ended items, dichotomous choice questions, and Likert-scale-styled questions that required respondents to answer whether they strongly agreed or disagreed with statements about WVON and other media.

I also analyzed the conversations between hosts, listeners, and guests on the station. The excerpts related here come from a collection of tapes I recorded while I was a volunteer production assistant at the station. I worked two days a week at the station and recorded Cliff Kelley's drive-time show, *World Objectives,* each of those days (6 A.M. to 10 A.M.). In addition to those tapes, I also recorded shows that concerned historically important events (e.g., the O.J. Simpson verdict, the Million Man March) and interviews with important national figures (e.g., Jesse Jackson, Dick Gregory, former senator Carol Mosely-Braun). I then transcribed the tapes and read them closely for recurrent themes and controversies. I also listened to the tapes repeatedly to recall the tones of the conversations, vocal emphases, and the like to create better descriptions of the conversations I was transcribing. Through this close listening and reading, I was able to discern recurrent themes, concerns, and controversies that illuminated the station's role in its audience members' lives.

WVON AS A SITE FOR DISCOURSE AND FOR ORGANIZATION

WVON seems to have a high degree of utility for respondents. It seems to be living up to one of its slogans: "Bringing the community together," as demonstrated in Table 1.

A large majority of respondents have become involved with community events and organizations after listening to or participating in WVON's discussions. Beyond being a site for "just talk" on the airwaves, WVON provides links to other physical and discursive public forums. In addition to informing listeners about community happenings and organizations, WVON regularly sponsors its own community events: breakfasts with speakers, aldermanic debates, and panel discussions about issues ranging from economic renewal to affirmative action to male-female relationships. In addition, WVON's hosts and callers provide information about rallies, protests, seminars, and entertainment events in the Black community and in Chicago at large. Here, for example, are excerpts from the drive-time show on October 5, 1995, where a caller thanks Cliff for discussing the murder of a Black homeless man by a white Chicago policeman instead of concentrating on the O.J. Simpson trial.

Table 1   Community Involvement and Participation

| | Agree/Yes | |
Question	(%)	N
Have you attended events after hearing about them on WVON?	83	224
Have you met new people through WVON?	58	223
Have you become involved with a community organization after hearing about it on WVON?	61	228
Have you contributed money to a political campaign after hearing about it on WVON?	61	218
Have you volunteered for a campaign after hearing a candidate on WVON?	39	219
Does WVON inspire you to become involved in the community	78	221
Listening to WVON helps me get information on activities in the community I don't get from other media	96	228

Source: Mail survey of WVON audience (*N* = 232).

Note: The responses to these questions were either yes/no or a scale of "strongly agree" to "strongly disagree." In this table, "strongly agree" and "agree" responses are combined.

Cliff: Getting to other racial bombs . . . Becker, the off-duty pig—I mean, cop—who shot the homeless gentleman [Joseph Gould]. Judge John Brady yesterday refused to raise Becker's bond. . . . Now you know exact—this is why people don't have any faith in the system. Black people, that is. Because you know what would happen if Gould had shot Becker: There wouldn't be any bond. He'd be in jail—if he ever even got to jail. . . . That judge is a threat to justice. That's why we have to remember these names, folks. . . . 591–5990 is the number. We've got [Caller 1] with us now. How are you today?

Caller 1: I'm super, and that's because you addressed the Becker issue this morning and I was afraid people were getting away from it. We still need to keep the pressure on here because even if the trial comes up, this man can only be convicted of manslaughter. And that is not equal to the crime. . . .

Have you heard about the [push] to increase the charges to murder? Because justice will not be served unless we Black people jump on that band-wagon. . . .

Cliff: That [process of increasing the charges] is the sole responsibility of the county prosecutor, who you know is Mr. O'Malley, who many of you think—the only reason we have anything [a manslaughter charge]

is because of outside agitation. He claims, of course, that's not the case, but outside agitation needs to continue to achieve the goal you are speaking of. Otherwise it's not gonna happen.

Caller 1: I just got a letter from Telli Imani's organization, and I was very disappointed because it had a lot of [additional] riders on it. And I thought that, if we were gonna be effective, we need to be focused on increasing the charges and dealing with these judges, because . . . the only way you can remove them is during election time. . . .

Cliff: You're right. The only way to do it is during retention, which is—that's why I'm saying . . . what we will have to do is keep these names out front so people can remember. And I promise I will certainly be doing that when the election comes up.[7]

As this exchange shows, not only is the caller interested in learning new information about the Gould murder, but both he and Kelley are invested in continuing the community protests and increasing pressure on the Cook County state's attorney. And not only is protest deemed necessary, but Black involvement specifically. Finally, the caller mentions his contact with a particular organization headed by Telli Imani, which is organizing around the issue, and he gives his critique of their tactics.

On another show, listeners and politicians called in to respond to what they felt was a questionable endorsement of Dick Devine, a white candidate for state's attorney, over a Black candidate, Judge Eugene Pincham. The guest, Artensa Randolph, is the president of a Chicago Housing Authority (CHA) community group that registers voters and makes endorsements for Chicago elections.

Cliff: How are you, sir?

Caller: Fine, thank you. Good morning Miss Randolph!

Artensa: Good morning!

Caller: Listen! When I heard you say that you were supporting Devine, you scared the life out of me! I grabbed this phone quick! Listen! I can't think of anything worse than folks in the projects and CHA citizens voting for Devine. I can't. And I would hope that somebody from Judge Pincham's campaign would get in touch with you right away. . . .

Cliff: Well, let me say this, Reggie. Not only do I agree with you, and that's why I told Miss Randolph when she said nothing's in stone, and she said "at this point," Judge Pincham called in while we were off the air and said that he certainly wanted to meet with you. . . .

Another caller, Ann, calls in to voice her disapproval of the endorsement.

Ann: I hope that you turn your endorsement around because so many people look to you for leadership and guidance. . . .

Later in the show, Alderman Anna Langford calls in to remember when she and other activists went door-to door to get voters out at the CHA buildings represented by Randolph's organization:

Anna: We went to five of the buildings in Robert Taylor. We covered every floor and every door, until eleven o'clock that night. Ralph Metcalf won by about nineteen votes or something like that. We got those buildings out of it, so there's a voting strength in those buildings; it's very significant.

Artensa: Sure is!

Anna: However, and I'm glad that you got those five thousand people, but I would hate to think that those five thousand people are going to vote for the opposition and the enemy. Devine . . . has done a terrible disservice by having his law firm vote against remap. And we can't have that. And Judge Pincham I've known ever since he was practicing law.[8]

These sorts of exchanges happen daily on WVON as topics of the day and are brought up by host, guest, and caller alike. Thus it seems that the audience, as evidenced by the survey results and the exchanges above, are attending events, meeting people, circulating in the other public spaces WVON clues them in on. This social circulation is key to a healthy public sphere. The statistics on WVON audience involvement support the notion that "audience discussion programs . . . may offer a constructive experience which demands analysis rather than dismissal . . . [because] the programs have many unintended consequences which only audience research can discover" (Livingstone and Lunt 1994:2). On the talk show, listener involvement and feedback is immediate and required for the success of the show. Even those who do not personally call in may have their concerns aired by their peers in the audience who do choose direct participation. The studio audience, Livingstone says, in effect "becomes a joint author . . . to debate social, moral, and political topics" (Livingstone and Lunt 1994:4). Furthermore, as illustrated by the preceding conversation and survey responses, the callers and listeners do not stop at participation in political talk; they take the next step to connect themselves to opportunities for public action.

IMAGINING AND ADDRESSING A BLACK AUDIENCE

WVON serves as a locus both for information crucial to community activities and political education and for the formation and sustenance of a Black identity. Not only does WVON

Table 2   Reasons for Listening to WVON

Question	Strongly Agree (%)	Agree (%)	N
I relate to the topics and guests on WVON more so than on other talk shows.	69.8	26.8	221
People who call WVON voice similar opinions to mine.	27.6	63.2	219
There is a difference between black-owned and white-owned media.	77.6	21.9	228
WVON interviews Black guests I don't hear anywhere else.[a]	87.7	N/A	228
WVON voices a Black perspective that isn't available on other stations.[a]	95.6	N/A	228
The talk on WVON sounds like conversations I have with friends.	33.3	57	218
I find WVON's talk shows informative.	79.8	18	224

a These responses were given as reasons why the listener responded positively to the statement, "There is a difference between black-owned and white-owned media."

speak to "Black issues," it also seeks to address all issues with a Black framework. There are many reasons for this. There is a great distrust of mainstream/white media, both among listeners and staff. Looking to audience responses in the questionnaires, WVON listeners discern a need for Black media in their lives and in the life of the larger Black collective. More evidence of this desire for an independent Black media comes in the form of financial contributions during the station's yearly subscription drives. Begun in 1995, subscription drives at WVON have brought in more than $180, 000 over the last three years. As the following quotes from the survey reveal, most listeners who answered the open-ended questions felt that white-owned and mainstream media sources continue to misconstrue the Black community, whether through ignorance, malice, or neglect, while WVON gives a fairer view of their communities.

> Unlike white-owned media, you can count on WVON to inform and inspire its audience with truth on all issues discussed, especially those issues Afro-Americans need to hear (e.g., improve their economic standing, their educational pursuits, etc.).

> The white-owned media is not at all objective in its assessment of what is news in the Black community. It appears they almost always focus on the negative, or that which demeans us. . . . WVON fights back!

> Community issues are discussed in depth. WVON serves as a forum for the Black perspective [which is] rarely understood by whites.

> WVON is more relevant [to Blacks].

As this testimony illustrates, the white-owned media fall short of these listeners' expectations. In addition to the free-responses, Table 2 illustrates that respondents also overwhelmingly agreed that the station did a better job than mainstream media in reflecting their concerns and giving a broader view of Black opinions and life.

WVON provides a wide range of topics and guests to its listeners, week in and week out. Local and national Black elected officials, leaders, artists, authors, scholars, and activists are interviewed and talk with listeners on a regular basis. But more important, these participants come from varied ideological backgrounds and support bases. For instance, representatives from the Nation of Islam, the Rainbow Coalition, the Urban League, the National Black Gay and Lesbian Leadership, and the NAACP have all been guests. Local grassroots activists like Conrad Worrill, as well as national figures like Reverend Jesse Jackson, have been interviewed and have called in to participate in discussions or to spread the word about events or important issues. Elected and appointed officials also populate the WVON landscape. Here is a sampling from the September 1997 schedule:

Katy Meaker Menges, National Centre for Policy Analysis

Hedy Ratner, Women's Business Symposium

Roland Burris, gubernatorial candidate

Dr. Earl Ofari Hutchinson

Eleanor Chapman, Africa Travel Advisors

Alderman Robert Shaw, Chicago City Council Black Caucus

Asia Coney, Million Woman March co-organizer

Prime Minister Hage Geingob, Republic of Namibia

Haki Madhabuti, founder of Third World Press

Erayne Gee, NAACP student organizer, University of Texas at Austin

Philip Jackson, chief of staff, Chicago Public Schools

Theresa Welch, housing organizer, South Austin Coalition

The Christian Explainers, a South African Choir

Renae Ogletree, People of Color Coalition

Through its talk programs, WVON airs views from the mainstream to the underground. Callers, hosts, and guests together create a spectrum of opinions and ideas that run the gamut from socialism to nationalism to neoconservatism. Talk is not restricted to traditionally defined politics, such as elections. WVON addresses social trends, economics, health issues, scholarly and popular literature, and entertainment in its discussions, and the political implications of issues related to these are often revealed in the discussions that occur.

For the guests listed above, topics included local electoral politics; COINTELPRO; travel in Africa; public school policies; fair housing laws; AIDS and health care; supporting Black businesses; and current political and economic trends in African nations. Many of the topics aren't just "Black" topics, as defined by the mainstream media, or complaints about white oppression. Producer Keisha Chavers explains:

I guess one thing that the [greater Chicago] community needs to know about us is that we don't spend our time dealing with white—you know, dogging white people. We try to get, we try to become issue oriented. . . .

They'll poll us if it's a racial or if it's a, you know, criminal issue, something of that matter. But they won't come and poll us when it's regarding health care or when it's regarding some of the other items that, you know, that the mainstream community is talking about. They won't come and poll us.

So I think that we are able—I mean in my capacity as a producer at WVON—I'm able to offer the programming you know, for members of our community just to call in and discuss as they would at WLS. Medicare, education, politics, today we did the piece on the environment. You know what I'm saying? And those are the types of things that the mainstream [media] don't come, they don't come to our community just to discuss it with us until it becomes a racial issue.[9]

In the mainstream public sphere, Black, like other nonwhite groups, are considered "special interest," not included in the category or everyday citizens. Hence, conversations concerning issues that are pertinent to the entire body politic are often considered relevant only to members of the class considered "typical" citizens: whites.[10] In addition, the pool of experts consulted regularly by mainstream media outlets is predominantly white. Getting a Black expert on economics on CNN is largely unheard of, unless the topic is somehow coded "Black." WVON allows the community to hear a larger range of Black expertise on civic topics than mainstream information sources. Furthermore, WVON given listeners and opportunity to speak with these people—most of whom are rarely interviewed in mainstream venues—and they hear them talking one-on-one with black people. This makes a huge difference to the audience and to the staff. As producer Keisha Chavers told me when I asked her why she tries to book Black experts,

Outside the obvious that we're a Black radio station, the other thing is that, in the mainstream, what do you see? You know, nothing but white experts, unless it's a racial issue or even a criminal issue. . . . The criteria I've set is to get the black expert first, the one who could talk about it as well as a white expert, who could relate it to our community. . . .

Host Cliff Kelley and Lu Palmer reiterate the need for Blacks to provide information for Blacks to compensate for the omissions and misrepresentations in mainstream media.

> It is the only Black talk radio in the city. We give Black people a method of communication we wouldn't have otherwise, because many stations would not even have the people that we have on. They wouldn't recognize them as important.[11]

> You have to understand also that I've always been what's called an advocacy journalist. See, you're taught in school that you are supposed to be objective and never advocate any cause. . . . All crap. And that's all that is, crap, because it's impossible to be objective.[12]

According to these responses, WVON is fulfilling the task of the traditional oppositional Black press, presenting Blacks in a different light than the mainstream media, as well as compensating for the omissions in the dominant press. Given the history of representation of African-Americans in the American mainstream media, this is no surprise. But the impetus to provide "in-house" information has other motives as well. Listeners and staff feel that information regarding specific Black events and concerns is rarely given airtime or column space in the mainstream media. Hence, WVON provides them with information and encouragement they cannot rely on or trust the white press to present.

Listeners and staff expect Black media to perform many tasks. First, they expect Black journalists to undo the damage done by their white counterparts. Second, they demand coverage of Black issues and Black accomplishments. Third, they expect the Black press to advocate Black progress. It is this last aspect where important differences within the Black public arise. What the next or best strategy is for the Black public is a matter of debate based on one's vision of Black identity and political ideology. Listeners and staff have strong views about black loyalty that echo Dawson's depiction of one problematic aspect of the Black public sphere: an insistence on race loyalty that can serve to suppress oppositional or diverse viewpoints and squelch certain attempts to build bridges outside of the black sphere (Dawson 1994:215; West 1993). President and general manager Melody Spann sums it up concisely here:

> Some [Black journalists] are just plain lazy. They're not gonna go beyond the call of duty to help you. . . . But I think they need to have a commitment to enhance anything that is owned by anybody who looks like them. And when they lose sight of that commitment, they might as well not be Black and working in the industry.[13]

The accusation of effectively losing one's blackness if one is not committed to a particular vision of Black advancement is extended to Blacks who disagree with certain views and policy preferences. Although this is not a constant feature of WVON's programs, it exists in proportion to the larger Black collective's debates over identity and politics. Although WVON's management and hosts follow the ideal of "agree to disagree" when addressing listeners and guests who are ideologically dissimilar, this credo becomes more or less strained, depending on the issue at hand. For example, affirmative action is a volatile issue at WVON, as it is across the nation. During the show on February 9, 1996, a white author of a book opposing affirmative action was taking calls with Cliff Kelley. When this caller chimed in, one could hear some animosity between host and caller as they try to engage in egalitarian debate.

Caller 1: What this gentleman [the guest] is saying is, to make things equal, everybody has to be playing by the same rules. And it is time for us as Black Americans to start playing by the same rules as everybody else. And affirmative action ain't doing us any favors. And I'd like to point out that when the gentleman is trying to make a point, Cliff, that you should let him finish his sentence, and don't interrupt him. It would be easier for all of us to understand what he's saying.

Cliff: Well it would be nice if we both did that, but you're right. . . . I think I do a good job at that [Caller 1] . . .

Caller 1: I think there's more truth in what he's saying that we as Black people are willing to admit.

Cliff: Thanks for your call. I disagree with you, but I appreciate your call. [Hangs up on Caller 1.] [Caller 2], you're on with Attorney Stratton.

Caller 2: Good morning, Mr. Kelley. . . . He [the first caller] is in the minority. As for the gentleman who just called, when he is swiped from the shelf, then people will have a different attitude.

Cliff: Well, you know, there are some people, when the master dies, they go out and the first thought is, "Where's the next master?" . . . There are people who are psychologically crippled who believe anything someone says as long as they are of a lighter hue.

Caller 2: Right, right. . . . And that's the most dangerous weapon they [white people] have is the pen and paper, the twisting and turning of language and phrases. See, they can take something and turn it right around and make it something other than what it actually meant.

While Kelley certainly tries to remain civil to the first caller, he is very obvious in his agreement with and approval of the second caller's views. They assert a view of what Black concerns should be, which clashes with the first caller's, questioning his race loyalty and fitness in the process. Kelley and the second caller use a metaphor of slavery's varied effects on the psyche of Blacks and find some to be brainwashed and subservient (the first caller) and others (themselves) resistant to white trickery. Callers and hosts feel free to label other listeners, political figures, and others along these lines. For example, Senator Carol Mosely-Braun and Clarence Thomas have been labeled race traitors or too close to whites on air by staff and listeners. Vernon Jordan was subject to the same judgment during an interview with June Cross, a Black television producer.

Cliff: I think he was talking to some people I know [laughter].

June: Yeah, we all know those people.

Cliff: When you talk about him going out and trying to mentor some young black children in the inner city, or going out to help somebody get elected, they look at you like you're nuts. . . .

June: Oh God, I heard a great quote last night, if I would remember what it is. Everything in this country comes down to race, even things that don't appear to be of that race; and when we start to talk about race, we talk about everything except race!

Cliff: You know, that's very true.

June: And I think it does kind of come down to that. Um, it is an American problem. It's always been an American problem, and I think a part of what we're seeing is that there's a certain group of Black Americans who've been admitted to the club of Americans, you know? Like Brother [Vernon] Jordan is an American now, he's not a Black American anymore [both laugh at this], at least he was until he got caught up with Bill in this thing. So now they're going to separate him out again, because he got caught with Bill covering up this thing. . . .

And, you know, there is a question that we hope the documentary raises and starts people thinking about, is, do we want to become Americans if the cost of becoming an American is that we become self-centered people who don't care about anybody else.

Cliff: Yeah, particularly our own.[14]

The station's staff believes (with much evidence, I think) that its audience is not only intelligent but politically aware and committed to Black advancement. Survey results, interviews, as well as caller exchanges on the air support their vision of the listening public. In addition to assuming a level of commitment to Black struggles, listeners and staff assume a common memory among the WVON family. Listening to any broadcast takes not only basic knowledge of current events, but familiarity with Black history and black cultural forms. If you aren't in the know, many exchanges on the air, as well as the texts of some station identifications and advertisements, will be opaque. References to slavery, use of Black vernacular, and excerpts from famous jazz, blues, and funk songs are constantly woven through broadcasts, flavoring the discourse for the insider. During the Million Man March broadcast, for example, we played key James Brown and Aretha Franklin tunes to fade in and out from commercials.[15] In addition, many callers linked the march to important events and figures in black history as they celebrated or critiqued the march. One caller used prophetic language, comparing the march to the return of Nat Turner. Others invoked the legacy of Rosa Parks, Ida B. Wells, and other strong Black women to counteract the assumptions that Black women were acquiescing to the desires of Black men.[16] Other callers and guests just took some time out to reminisce, "drop some science," or remark on the music played for intros, as this caller did: (Voices are talking together at times, overlapping.)

Caller: Hi Cliff!

Cliff: Hi, how are you?

Caller: . . . and Ahmad Jamal?

Cliff: Hey hey! You've got it!

Caller: [Jamal is] the greatest. You're dating yourself—

Cliff: I love it! I love it, too.

Caller: Israel Crosby, you remember him?

Cliff: Yes!

Caller: Yeah . . .

Cliff: Absolutely!

Caller: I learned a lot from him. . . .[17]

This guest included a little Black history lesson in his commentary:

Caller: So [the term] *African-American* is not new. Actually, you can go back to T. Thomas Fortune, who was a famous black journalist in the 1890s, with the Afro-American, and the National Afro-American Council, which had in its very name the term *Afro-American*. So, a lot of these terms come out of our struggle and our attempt to define ourselves. . . .[18]

These exchanges reveal the assumption of a shared cultural background or the shared cultural interests of Black folks. These bits of talk and information that underscore a shared Black heritage allow Black listeners to feel secure that the station and the community of listeners "talk their talk."

Conclusions

This study suggests that (1) the audience and WVON have constructed a community of listeners within the public spheres produced by the station and members of the audience; (2) the community of listeners and the staff view WVON as an important source of information and perspectives relevant to Black public life; and (3) WVON provides an institutional basis for Black discourse and links to certain forms of political action and organization. From this study of a specialized audience, I argue that commercial media can play a positive role in forming and sustaining serious discourse within a subaltern public sphere, especially through a small-market or niche format like WVON's. By constructing and attracting a dedicated "family" of media consumers, WVON and its listeners have created a media environment whose commercial and community goals overlap. Cultivating such an environment, WVON has produced a community/commodity to show advertisers. At the same time, listeners, activists, and community leaders can use the interactive discursive space provided by the station to effectively distribute information and ideas to other active members of the community.

However, my analysis thus far has not sufficiently addressed a key question posed both by Dawson and by other scholars: How can a single counterpublic serve all of its constituents when within itself exist its own cleavages along class, gender, and generation lines? Even if WVON provides institutional support and discursive opportunities, how can it address this issue of dealing with disagreements within, let alone relations to non-Black publics? As for the first concern, the affirmative action debate excerpted above raises a key issue: How can a Black political discourse (or any minority discourse) be constructed without stifling differences under oppressive, convenient essentialisms and "race traitor" accusations? The discourses surrounding Anita Hill and Clarence Thomas, Mike Tyson, and Marion Berry all serve as examples of the dangers of what Cornel West terms "racial reasoning," but can we really expect to find a racial politics devoid of a sense of some shared identity?[19] The second concern is linked to the first: How can coalition politics be fostered more successfully? After a century of ebbing and flowing cross-racial partnerships, how can we construct new ways of approaching the discourse within and across public spheres to facilitate more cross-cultural understanding and political organization? As Melody Spann said in a conversation concerning the white financial investment in Spike Lee's film *Get on the Bus,* "You can't do anything in this society without dealing with white people!" While this blanket statement may certainly be disproved in various contexts, the message is clear: In a pluralist society, one will eventually have to deal with one's adversaries, as well as one's allies, who have healthy disagreements with one's position. Again we return to the question, How can one support the notion of ethnic or racial solidarity without subsuming the identities of individuals and particular subgroups under an oppressive form of essentialism?[20] In addition to concerns about the implications of inter- and intragroup politics for public spheres, this project leads me to further question the definition of the audience. What are the main distinctions between audiences and publics in modern mass-mediated society? Although I agree with Herbst and Beniger's statement that publics today are more likely to be composed of audiences, are the two truly synonymous in all cases? And if they are interchangeable, how durable is this audience/publics? When are they merely "imagined communities," as described by Benedict Anderson (1991), and when are they truly organized and interactive toward political ends?

Rather than add to the debate over whether talk is truly political action, I propose we speak of multiple publics that take on different modes of discursive and political actions, depending on social and political conditions. So we can speak of a public *enclaving* itself, hiding its antiestablishment ideas and strategies to avoid sanctions, but internally producing lively debate and planning; we can also imagine a public *oscillating* to engage in debate with outsiders, to test ideas. A public that engages in mass actions to assert its needs would be a *counterpublic,* using traditional social movement tactics (boycotts, civil disobedience) to make demands on the state. Finally, we can envision a public working in conjunction with other publics on equal footing enjoying a *parallel* status. With these four labels, I hope to offer scholars a more flexible and descriptive vocabulary to employ when analyzing the various actions of a particular public or group of publics.[21]

As regards to WVON, we can see how this talk-radio station could be—and is—useful to the Black public sphere in all of these modes. Although the station is broadcast and can be heard by anyone, its African-American staff and majority Black listenership make callers feel comfortable that they are safer from sanction than in other forums (enclave). Through interviews with non-Black guests, ideas can be exchanged, and concerns can be aired to those in power outside the Black public sphere (oscillating). WVON also serves as a mobilizing tool, announcing and facilitating community meetings that may result in social movement-type actions, such as the protests in response to the Joseph Gould murder (counterpublic). As for parallel activities, the station could facilitate similar meetings with members of other publics if the opportunity arose. In these examples and in this study, we see how WVON's audience can be transformed into an active public in the traditional sense as well as being a talking public and an imagined public. Membership in "the WVON family"—both of fellow listeners and the larger imagined black community—serves as a strong bond for listeners. This bond compels them to participate in the talk and activities made available through WVON, as well as linking them to other community sites, cultural events, and political activities. Notions of shared black culture and identity and political interests serve as bonds beyond media exposure. Hence, even after one's exposure to the station ends, one still feels like a part of a larger Black collective with more complex cultural ties than the traditional notion of audiences connected only through common media exposure.

To get a more nuanced picture of how the media influence public spheres, we should use a model of coexisting, multiple spheres, which can describe various activities and roles in their interactions with the state and other publics. We must also examine how different publics create, consume, and use particular media products. As the WVON case demonstrates, a commercial media enterprise does not necessarily create the contradictions between public goods and private gain that Habermas and Entman lament. Rather, WVON exists in response to the poor public service Blacks feel they receive from mainstream media providers. Its commercial success rests on listener loyalty, which can only be had through public-minded programming, awareness, and celebration of black culture and through a commitment to community service.

DISCUSSION QUESTIONS

1. Describe Jurgen Habermas's notion of the public sphere.

2. What is the difference between Habermas's notion of the public sphere and what Squires calls the *Black public sphere*?

3. What is meant by the *subaltern status* of Blacks?

4. How does Squires differentiate the terms *audience* and *public*?

5. How does radio station WVON respond to community needs?

NOTES AND REFERENCES

Reading 1.1 /
HOW I GOT OVER /
JACK L. DANIEL & GENEVA SMITHERMAN

Notes

1. Throughout the paper, we will use the terms Black, Afro-American, and African-American interchangeably to refer to Americans of African descent.

2. This paper is anchored in the life-long experiences of Jack L. Daniel at Mt. Sinai Baptist Church, Johnstown, Pennsylvania, and Geneva Smitherman at Tennessee Baptist Church, Detroit, Michigan. Both are Traditional Black Churches. For a detailed analysis of the Traditional Black Church, see Melvin D. Williams, *Community in Black Pentecostal Church: An Anthropological Study* (Pittsburgh: Univ. of Pittsburgh Press, 1974), and Henry Mitchell, *Black Preaching* (New York: J. B. Lippincott, 1970).

3. Eugene A. Hammel, "The Myth of Structure Analysis: Levi-Strauss and the Three Bears," Addison-Wesley Module in Anthropology (Module XXV, 1972), p. 3.

4. Joseph R. Washington, *Black Sects and Cults* (New York: Doubleday, 1973), p. 20.

5. Williams, p. 183.

6. E. Franklin Frazier, *The Negro Family in the United States* (Chicago: Univ. of Chicago Press, 1966). p. 21.

7. Robert Farris Thompson, *African Art in Motion* (Los Angeles: Univ. of California Press, 1974), pp. 5–45.

8. Daryll Forde, ed., *African Worlds: Studies in the Cosmological Ideas and Social Values of African Peoples* (New York: Oxford Univ. Press, 1954), p. x.

9. For a good summary of the underlying similarity of thought found among diverse African people, see George Balander and Jacques Maquet,

Dictionary of Black African Civilization (New York: Leon Amiel, 1974), pp. 276–78.

10. Forde, p. X.

11. E. G. Parrinder, *African Traditional Religion* (London: Hutchinson House, 1954), pp. 20–28.

12. K. A. Busia, "The African World View," In Jacob Draker, ed. *African Heritage* (New York: Crowell-Collur, 1963), pp. 146–51.

13. Fela Sowande, "The Quest of an African World View: The Utilization of African Discourse," in Jack L. Daniel, ed., *Black Communication: Dimensions of Research and Instruction* (New York: Speech Communication Association, 1974), p. 76.

14. John S. Mbiti, *African Religions and Philosophies* (New York: Doubleday, 1969), p. 20.

15. Balander and Maquet, p. 277.

16. Sowande, p. 76.

17. Mbiti, p. 3.

18. Washington, p. 31.

19. Ibid., p. 30.

20. Adolf E. Jensen, *Myth and Cult Among Primitive People* (Chicago: Univ. of Chicago Press, 1951), p. 9.

21. C. Eric Lincoln, "Foreword," in Leonard E. Barrettt, *Soul-Force* (New York: Anchor Books, 1974), p. viii.

22. Melville J. Herskovits, *The New World Negro* (New York: Minerva Press, 1969), p. 13.

23. Sowande, pp. 67–88.

24. Barrett, p. 17.

25. Pierre Erny, *Childhood and Cosmos: The Social Psychology of the Black African Child* (Rockville, Md.: Media Intellectic, 1973), p. 15.

26. Mbiti, p. 20.

27. Ibid., p. 141.

28. Ibid., p. 174.

29. Erny, p. 149.

30. Ibid., p. 149.

31. For a detailed discussion of African and Black American temporality, see Dorothy Pennington,

Temporality Among Black Americans: Implications for Intercultural Communication, Diss. Univ. of Kansas 1974.

32. Oliver Jackson, "Preface," *Kuntu Drama.* ed. Paul Harison (New York: Grove, 1974), pp. ix-xiii.

33. Leonard Doob, *Communication in Africa* (New Haven: Yale Univ. Press, 1961), p. 79.

34. Thompson, p. 27.

35. Richard Wright, *The Long Dream* (New York: Ace Books 1958), pp. 259–97.

36. Ralph Ellison, "Mister Toussan," in *Black American Literature: Fiction,* ed. Darwin Turner (Columbus: Charles E. Merrill, 1969), pp. 98–99.

Reading 1.3 /
COMPLICITY /
MARK LAWRENCE MCPHAIL

References

Asante, M. (1974). Theoretical and research issues in black communication. In J. L. Daniel (Ed.). *Black communication: Dimensions of research and instruction.* New York: Speech Communication Association.

Awkward, M. (1988). Race, gender, and the politics of reading. *Black American Literary Forum. 22,* 5–27.

Baldwin, J. (1974). *If Beale Street could talk.* New York: Dial Press.

Baudrillard, J. (1988). On seduction. In M. Poster (Ed.). *Jean Baudrillard: Selected writings.* Stanford: Stanford University Press.

Chisolm, R (1966). *Theory of knowledge.* Englewood Cliffs, NJ: Prentice Hall.

Christian, B. (1987). The race for theory. *Cultural critique,* New York: Telos Press.

Crapanzano, V. (1985). *Waiting: The whites of South Africa.* New York: Random House.

Dobris, C., & White, C. (1989). *Rhetorical constructions of self and identity: Toward a genre view of feminist identity discourse.* Paper presented at the Speech Communication Association Convention.

Freeman, K. (1977). *Ancilla to the pre-socratic philosophers.* Cambridge: Harvard University Press.

Gates, H. L., Jr. (1984). Criticism in the jungle. From *Black literature and literary theory.* New York: Methuen.

Gearhart, S. M. (1979). The womanization of rhetoric. *Women's Studies International Quarterly, 2,* 195–201.

hooks, b. (1984). *Feminist theory: From margin to center.* Boston: South End Press.

Kress, G., and Hodge, R. (1979). *Language as ideology.* Boston: Routledge & Kegan Paul.

Laclau, E. (1977). *Politics and ideology in Marxist theory.* London: New Left Books.

Laclau, E., & Mouffe, C. (1989). *Hegemony and socialist strategy.* London: Verso.

Lanham, R. (1976). *The motives of eloquence.* New Haven: Yale University Press.

Norris, Christopher. (1984). *The deconstructive turn: Essays in the rhetoric of philosophy.* New York: Methuen.

Pirsig, R. (1985). *Zen and the art of motorcycle maintenance.* New York: William Morrow.

Radhakrishnan, R. (1987). Ethnic identity and post-structuralist difference. In *Cultural critique.* New York: Telos Press.

Radhakrishnan, R. (1988). Feminist historiography and post-structuralist thought: Intersections and departures. In E. Messe and A. Parker (Eds.). *The difference within: Feminism and critical theory.* Philadelphia: John Benjamins.

Valesio, P. (1980). *Novantiqua: Rhetorics as a contemporary theory.* Bloomington: Indiana University Press.

Whitson, S. (1988). The *Phaedrus* complex. *PRE/TEXT: A Journal of Rhetorical Theory, 9,* 9–25.

Woolf, V. (1978). *A room of one's own.* London: The Hogarth Press.

Young, R. E., Becker, A. L., & Pike, K. L. (1970). *Rhetoric: Discovery and change.* New York: Harcourt.

READING 1.5 /
IMPROVISATION AS A
PERFORMANCE STRATEGY FOR
AFRICAN-BASED THEATRE / JONI L. JONES

Notes

1. For a more detailed description of *Egungun* masquerades, see Henry John Drewal and John Pemberton's discussion in *Yoruba: Nine Centuries of African Art and Thought.* In addition to the commentary on the *Egungun.* Drewal also provides a clear analysis of a Yoruba world view which helps situate *Egungun* in its cultural context.

2. Joel A. Adedeji gives a full account of the formation of what he calls *Alarinjo* Theatre in "'Alarinjo': The Traditional Yoruba Travelling Theatre." Kacke Götrick in *Apidan Theatre and Modern Drama* prefers the term *Apidan* to *Alarinjo* because of the negative connotatins associated with *Alarinjo* performers. The term *Alarinjo* acquired negative associations as performers came to be known as

tricksters; this may have to do with the very nature of their performances in which they often transform themselves before the participant observers. *Apidan* translates as "one who performs tricks," making this not only an accurate, but also untainted title for these performers (255).

3. The most extensive information on Ogunde is found in Ebun Clark's biography of this playwright, director, actor, film maker in *Hubert Ogunde: The Making of Nigerian Theatre.* Clark gives important details about Ogunde's work; however, only excerpts from his dramas are presented. Ogunde's manuscripts remain in Yoruba and therefore unavailable to non-Yoruba speaking scholars.

4. *Nommo* is a Dogon word which means "word force." Several scholars use the word *nommo* even when referring to other African cultures, perhaps following Janheinz Jahn's lead in *Muntu.* Jahn argues that it is possible to apply a word from one African culture to the philosophy of another because of the cultural unity of Africa (27). Paul Carter Harrison uses *nommo* when describing the culture of African-Americans. In *The Drama of Nommo* Harrison discusses the potency of *nommo* and its various manifestations "on the block" and in theatres (xi–xxiv). Harrison's and Jahn's usage allows me likewise to take a Dogon word and apply it to another culture, the Yoruba.

5. For a more detailed discussion of this analysis, see "The Development of an African-based Dramatic Structure," Joni L. Jones, Ph. D. Dissertation, New York University, 1993.

6. The Spring 1991 issue of *Black American Literature Forum* is devoted to an analysis of the relationship between African-American church services and African-American theatre. In that issue, of particular interest is the work of Gale Jackson and Winona Fletcher. Also, Ulysses Duke Jenkins's *Ancient African Religion and the African-American Church* notes continuities of content and form from Yoruba religious practices found in African-American Baptist churches.

7. Both events were so controversial among African American they each elicited written responses from prominent African-American writers. Haki R. Madhubuti edited a series of essays by African Americans entitled *Confusion by Any Other Name.* His book was an attempt to diffuse the impact of Ali's work. Toni Morrison edited a collection of essays by African Americans entitled *Rac-ing Justice, En-gendering Power* in response to the Hill-Thomas hearings.

8. The graduate students who performed were Brenda Cotto-Escalera, Lisa Jo Epstein, Harley Erdman, Beth Glenn, Kirsten Kern, Dan Modaff, and Joe Rice. Their performances and insights significantly contributed to my understanding of how the nine features of Yoruba performance can best be used in creating African-based dramaturgical/performance paradigms.

9. Viola Spolin's *Improvisation for the Theatre* offers suggestions about the use of improvisation for building characters and for developing scenes. The suggestions are based on determining and fulfilling an objective that is typically at odds with the objective of the other characters in the scene. This establishes conflict as the foundation for much of Spolin's work.

References

Adedeji, Joel A. "'Alarinjo': The Traditional Yoruba Travelling Theater." *Theatre in Africa.* Ed. Oyin Ogunba and Abiola Irele. Ibadan, Nigeria: Ibadan UP, 1978.

Ali, Shahrazad. *The Black Man's Guide to Understanding the Black Woman.* Philadelphia, PA: Civilized Publications, 1989.

Black American Literature Forum. Spring 1991, Vol. 25, No. 1.

Boal, Augusto, *Theatre of the Oppressed.* New York: Theatre Communications Group, 1985.

Clark, Ebun. *Hubert Ogunde: The Making of Nigerian Theatre.* Oxford, England: Oxford UP, 1979.

Clark, John Pepper, "Aspects of Nigerian Drama." *Drama and Theatre in Nigeria: A Critical Source Book.* Ed. Yemi Ogunbiyi, Lagos, Nigeria: Nigeria Magazine, 1981: 57–74.

Coker, Jerry. *Improvisation Jazz.* Englewood Cliffs, NJ: Prentice-Hall, 1964.

Drewal, Henry John and John Pemberton. *Yoruba: Nine Centuries of African Art and Thought.* New York: Center for African Art, 1989.

Drewal, Margaret Thompson. "Performers, Play, and Agency: Yoruba Ritual Process." Diss. New York U, 1989.

Gates, Jr., Henry Louis. *The Signifying Monkey: A Theory of African-American Literary Criticism.* New York: Oxford UP, 1988.

Götrick, Kacke, *Apidan Theatre and Modern Drama.* Stockholm, Sweden: Almqvist and Wiksell International, 1984.

Harrison, Paul Carter. *The Drama of Nommo.* New York: Grove P, 1972.

Jahn, Janheinz. *Muntu: The New African Culture.* New York: Faber and Faber, 1961.

Jenkins, Ulysses Duke, *Ancient African Religion and the African-American Church.* Jacksonville, NC: Flame International, 1978.

Jones, Joni L. "The Development of an African-based Dramatic Structure." Diss., New York U, 1993.

Madhubuti, Haki R. *Confusion by Any Other Name: Essays Exploring the Negative Impact of the Black Man's Guide to Black Women.* Chicago, IL: Third World, P, 1990.

M'Biti, John. *African Religions and Philosophy.* 2nd ed. Portsmouth, NH: Heineman, 1990.

Morrison, Toni., ed. *Rac-ing Justice, En-gendering Power,* New York: Random House, 1992.

Ogunba, Oyin. "Traditional African Festival Drama." *Theatre in Africa.* Ed. Oyin Ogunba and Abiola Irele. Ibadan, Nigeria: Ibadan UP, 1978. 3–26.

Ogunbiyi, Yemi. "Nigerian Theatre and Drama: A Critical Profile." *Drama and Theatre in Nigeria: A Critical Source Book.* Ed. Yemi Ogunbiyi. Lagos, Nigeria: Nigeria Magazine, 1981.

Pennington, Dorothy. "Time in African Culture." *African Culture: The Rhythms of Unity.* Trenton, NJ: African World P, 1990, 123–139.

Schechner, Richard. "From Ritual to Theatre and Back: The Structure/Process of the Efficacy-Entertainment Dyad." *Educational Theatre Journal.* 26.4 (1974): 455–480.

Spolin, Viola. *Improvisation for the Theatre.* Evanston. IL: Northwestern UP, 1963.

Teer, Barbara Ann. "Appendix H." In "The Development of an African-Based Dramatic Structure." Diss. Joni Lee Jones. New York U, 1993.

Thompson, Robert Farris. *African Art in Motion: Icon and Act.* Los Angeles, CA: U of California P, 1974.

Turner, Victor, "Are There Universals of Performance in Myth, Ritual, and Drama?" *By Means of Performance.* Ed. Richard Schechner and Willa Appel. New York: Cambridge UP, 1990, 8–18.

wa Thiong'o, Ngugi, *Decolonizing the Mind: The Politics of Language in African Literature.* Portsmouth, NH: Heinemann, 1986.

Reading 2.1 /

A DILEMMA OF BLACK
COMMUNICATION SCHOLARS /
DEBORAH F. ATWATER

References

Asante, M. K. (1980) Afrocentricity: The Theory of Social Change. Buffalo, NY: Amulefi——and A. S. Vandi [eds.] (1980) Contemporary Black Thought: Alternative Analyses in Social and Behavioral Science: Beverly Hills, CA: Sage.

Becker. S. (1974) "Rhetorical scholarship in the seventies," in W. R. Fisher (ed.) Rhetoric: A Tradition in Transition. East Lansing: Michigan State Univ. Press.

Ben-Jochannan, Y. (1978) Black Man of the Nile and His Family. New York: Alkebu-an.

Black, E. (1980) "A note on theory and practice in rhetorical criticism." Western J. of Speech Communication 44 (Fall): 331–336.

Booth, W. C. (1979) Critical Understanding: The Powers and Limits of Pluralism. Chicago: Univ. of Chicago Press.

Braden, W. (1980) "The rhetoric of a closed society." Southern Speech Communication J. 45 (Summer): 333–351.

Brown, W. R. (1982) "Attention and the rhetoric of social intervention." Q. J. of Speech 68 (February): 17–27.

Brummett, B. (1980) "Symbolic form, Burkean scapegoating, and rhetorical exigency in Alioto's response to the 'Zebra' murders." Western J. of Speech Communication 44 (Winter): 64–73.

Calloway-Thomas, C., and R. G. Smith (1981) "Images of leadership: Black vs. white." Southern Speech Communication J. 46 (Spring): 263–277.

Cummings, M. S. and J. L. Daniel (1980) "Scholarly literature on the Black idiom," pp. 97–144 in B. E. Williams and O. L. Taylor (eds.) Working Papers: International Conference on Black Communication, Bellagio, Italy, 1979, New York: Rockefeller Foundation.

Davis, G. and G. Watson (1981) Black Life in Corporate America. Garden City, NY: Doubleday.

Diop, C. A. (1978) Cultural Unity of Black Africa, Chicago: Third World Press,

Harrison, P. C. (1972) The Drama of Nommo. New York: Grove.

Haskins, W. A. (1981) "Rhetorical vision of equality: analysis of the rhetoric of the southern Black press during reconstruction." Communication Q. 29 (Spring): 116–122.

James, L. B. (1980) "The influence of Black orality on contemporary Black poetry and its implication for performance." Southern Speech Communication J. 45 (Spring): 297–312.

Lerner, G. (1972) Black Women in White America. New York: Pantheon.

Logue, C. M. (1981) "Transcending coercion: the communicative strategies of Black slaves on antebellum plantations." Q. J. of Speech 67 (February): 31–46.

Mc Farlin, A. S. (1980) "Hallie Quinn Brown: Black woman elocutionist." Southern Speech Communication J. 46 (Fall): 72–82.

McWorter, G. A. (1981) Guide to Scholarly Journals in Black Studies. Chicago: People's College Press.

Niles, L. (1980) "Comment," pp. 145–150 in B. E. Williams and O. L. Taylor (eds.) Working Papers: International Conference on Black Communication, Bellagio, Italy, 1979. New York: Rockefeller Foundation.

Nwankwo, R. L. (1982) "The methodology of social science and the future of communication equality." Still Here (published by the School of Communications, Howard University, Washington, D. C.), February.

Oravec, C. (1982) "Where theory and criticism meet: a look at contemporary rhetorical theory." Western J. of Speech Communication 46 (Winter): 56–71.

Pennington, D. (1980) "Guilt-provocation: a strategy in Black rhetoric," pp. 111–125 in M. K. Asante and A. S. Vandi (eds.) Contemporary Black Thought: Alternative Analyses in Social and Behavioral Science. Beverly Hills, CA: Sage.

Richards, D. (1980) "European mythology: the ideology of 'progress,'" pp. 59–79 in M. K. Asante and A. S. Vandi (eds.) Contemporary Black Thought: Alternative Analyses in Social and Behavioral Science. Beverly Hills, CA: Sage.

Ritter, K. (1980) "American political rhetoric and the jeremiad tradition: presidential nomination acceptance addresses 1960–1976." Central States Speech J. 31 (Fall): 153–171.

Sidran, B. (1971) Black Talk. New York: Holt, Rinehart & Winston.

Simmons, R. (1982) "An Afrocentric reorientation of communication research." Still Here (published by the School of Communications, Howard University, Washington, D. C.), February.

Smitherman, G. (1973) Black Language and Culture: Sound of Soul. New York: William Morrow.

Stanbeck, M. H. and W. B. Pearce (1981) "Talking to 'The Man': some communication strategies used by members of 'subordinate' social groups." Q. J. of Speech 67 (February): 21–30.

Zarefsky, D. (1980) "Lyndon Johnson redefines 'equal opportunity': the beginnings of affirmative action." Central States Speech J. 31 (Summer): 85–94.

Reading 2.2 /

African American Ethos and Hermeneutical Rhetoric /

Eric King Watts

Notes

1. Steven Watson, The Harlem Renaissance: Hub of African American Culture (New York: Pantheon Books, 1995).

2. Michael J. Hyde, "Hermeneutics and Interpretation," in Encyclopedia of Rhetoric, ed. Thomas O. Sloane (New York: Oxford University Press, 2001), 329-337.

3. Houston Baker, Jr., Modernism and the Harlem Renaissance (Chicago: University of Chicago Press, 1987), 56.

4. David Levering Lewis, When Harlem Was in Vogue (New York: Oxford University Press, 1979).

5. Baker, Modernism and the Harlem Renaissance.

6. Eric K. Watts, "Re-fashioning a Reasonable Aesthetic: A Case Study in the Transformation of American Modernism Through Argument in African American Art," in Argumentation and Values, ed. Sally Jackson (Annandale: Speech Communication Association, 1995), 237-241.

7. Lewis, When Harlem Was in Vogue, 170.

8. Bruce Tyler, From Harlem to Hollywood: The Struggle for Racial and Cultural Democracy, 1920-1943 (New York: Garland Press, 1992).

9. Arna Bontemps, The Harlem Renaissance Remembered (New York: Dodd, Mead & Co., 1972).

10. George S. Schuyler, "The Negro Art Hokum," The Nation 122 (1926): 662-663.

11. Nathan Huggins, Harlem Renaissance (New York: Oxford University Press, 1971).

12. Lewis, When Harlem Was in Vogue.

13. Abby Johnson and Ronald Johnson, Propaganda and Aesthetics: The Literary Politics of African-American Magazines in the Twentieth Century (Amherst: University of Massachusetts, 1991).

14. Tyler, From Harlem to Hollywood, 13.

15. Walter Jost and Michael J. Hyde, eds., Rhetoric and Hermeneutics in Our Time: A Reader (New Haven: Yale University Press, 1997), 1.

16. Michael J. Hyde and Craig R. Smith, "Hermeneutics and Rhetoric: A Seen and Unobserved Relationship, Quarterly Journal of Speech 65 (1979): 347-363.

17. Michael J. Hyde, "The Call of Conscience: Heidegger and the Question of Rhetoric," Philosophy and Rhetoric 27 (1994): 374-396.

18. Hyde and Smith, "Hermeneutics and Rhetoric," 347.

19. Roger Scruton, The Aesthetic Understanding: Essays in the Philosophy of Art and Culture (Manchester: Carcanet Press, 1983), 139-142.

20. Scruton, Aesthetics Understanding, 139.

21. Scruton, Aesthetics Understanding, 142.

22. M.M. Bakthin Toward a Philosophy of the Act, ed. Michael Holquist and Vadim Liapunov (Austin: University of Texas, 1993). 7

23. Scruton, Aesthetic Understanding, 147–143.

24. James Risser, Hermeneutics and the Voice of the Other: Re-reading Gadamer's Philosophical Hermeneutics (Albany: State University of New York Press, 1997), 14.

25. Hans G. Gadamer, Truth and Method (London: Sheed and Ward, 1975).

26. Jost and Hyde, Rhetoric and Hermeneutics in Our Time, 24.

27. Jost and Hyde, Rhetoric and Hermeneutics in Our Time, 19.

28. Jost and Hyde, Rhetoric and Hermeneutics in Our Time, 16.

29. Thomas Rosteck and Michael C. Leff, "Piety, Propriety, and Perspective: An Interpretation and Application of Key Terms in Kenneth Burke's Permanence and Change," Western Journal of Speech 53 (1989): 327-341.

30. Hyde, "The Call of Conscience," 376.

31. Bakthin, Toward a Philosophy of the Act.

32. Scruton, Aesthetic Understanding, 142.

33. Craig R. Smith and Michael J. Hyde, "Rethinking 'The Public': The Role of Emotion in Being-with-Others," Quarterly Journal of Speech 77 (1991): 446–466.

34. Michael C. Leff, "Hermeneutical Rhetoric," in Rhetoric and Hermeneutics in Our Time: A Reader, ed. Walter Jost and Michael J. Hyde (New Haven: Yale University Press, 1997), 196-214.

35. Leff, "Hermeneutical Rhetoric," 203.

36. Eric King Watts, "Voice and Voicelessness in Rhetorical Studies," Quarterly Journal of Speech 87 (2001): 179–196.

37. Leff, "Hermeneutical Rhetoric," 203.

38. Risser, Hermeneutics and the Voice of the Other, 14.

39. Richard A. Long, "The Genesis of Locke's The New Negro," Black World 25 (1976): 14-20.

40. Winston Napier, "Affirming Critical Conceptualism: Harlem Renaissance Aesthetics and the formation of Alain Locke's Social Philosophy," Massachusetts Review 39 (1998): 96.

41. Baker, Modernism and the Harlem Renaissance, 85.

42. Lewis, When Harlem Was in Vogue, 91.

43. By progressivism I refer to the belief in the modern perfection of society and to the ways that this belief affected black intellectualism. See Adolph Reed, Jr., W.E.B. Du Bois and American Political Thought: Fabianism and the Color Line (New York: Oxford University Press, 1997).

44. Lewis, When Harlem Was in Vogue, 91.

45. Langston Hughes, The Big Sea: An Auto-biography (New York; Hill & Wang, 1940).

45. Tyler, From Harlem to Hollywood, 11.

47. Hughes, The Big Sea, 223.

48. Long, "The Genesis of Locke's The New Negro," 15.

49. Watson, The Harlem Renaissance.

50. Long, "The Genesis of Locke's The New Negro," 16.

51. Houston Baker, Jr., Afro-American Poetics: Revisions of Harlem and the Black Aesthetic (Madison: University of Wisconsin Press, 1988), 5.

52. In a January 1926 review of the anthology in the Crisis, Du Bois criticized Locke for asserting that black artists should create strictly "for the sake of art." This apparent endorsement of a pure aesthetic troubled Du Bois because he was concerned about the effect such a dictum might have on "The New Negro Movement."

53. Napier, "Affirming Critical Conceptualism."

54. William James, Pragmatism and Four Essays from the Meaning of Truth (New York: Meridian Books, 1955/1907).

55. Adolph Reed, Jr., W.E.B. Du Bois and American Political Thought: Fabianism and the Color Line (New York: Oxford University Press, 1997).

56. Alain Locke, "Pluralism and Intellectual Democracy," in The Philosophy of Alain Locke: Harlem Renaissance and Beyond, ed. Leonard Harris (Philadelphia: Temple University Press, 1942/1989), 51-66.

57. Alain Locke, The New Negro: An Interpretation (New York: Arno Press, 1968/1925), 3. Subsequent citations from this work will be indicated in parentheses in the text.

58. Houston Baker, Jr., Long Black Song: Essays in Black American Literature and Culture (Charlottesville: University Press of Virginia, 1972).

59. Baker, Long Black Song, see also Henry Louis Gates, The Signifying Monkey: A Theory of Afro-American Literary Criticism (New York: Oxford University Press, 1988).

60. Baker, Long Black Song.

61. Dale E. Peterson, "The African American Dialogue with Bakhtin and What It Signifies," Bakhtin in Contexts: Across the Disciplines, ed. Amy Mandelker (Evanston: Northwestern University, 1995), 96.

62. Baker, Modernism and the Harlem Renaissance.

63. Alain Locke, "Values and Imperatives," in American Philosophy, Today and Tomorrow, ed. Horace M. Kallen and Sidney Hook (New York: Lee Furman Inc., 1935), 313-333.

64. Alain Locke, "Unity Through Diversity," in The Philosophy of Alain Locke: Harlem Renaissance and Beyond, ed. Leonard Harris (Philadelphia: Temple University Press, 1936/1989), 133-138.

65. Kirt H. Wilson, "Toward a Discursive Theory of Racial Identity: The Souls of Black Folk as a Response to Nineteenth Century Biological Determinism," Western Journal of Communication 63 (1999): 193-215.

66. Locke, "Pluralism and Intellectual Democracy."

67. Ross Pognock, Color and Culture: Black Writers and the Making of the Modern Intellectual (Cambridge: Harvard University Press, 1998), 27.

68. Locke, "Unity Through Diversity," 135.

69. Locke, "Pluralism and Intellectual Democracy," 57.

70. Locke, "Values and Imperatives," 319.

71. Locke, "Values and Imperatives," 328.

72. Leff, "Hermeneutical Rhetoric," 203.

73. Risser, Hermeneutics and the Voice of the Other, 17.

74. Locke, "Pluralism and Intellectual Democracy," 56.

75. Locke, "Unity Through Diversity," 135.

76. Locke, "Unity Through Diversity," 136.

Reading 2.3 /

PLAYING THE DOZENS /
THURMON GARNER

Notes

1. Playing the Dozens is also referred to as joaning, mining, cracking, sounding, screaming and talkin' 'bout yo' mamma.

2. For perspectives which view folklore as communicative and socially oriented see Roger D. Abrahams, "Introductory Remarks to a Rhetorical Theory of Folklore," *Journal of American Folklore,* 31 (1968) 143-58, and "A Rhetoric of Everyday Life: Traditional Conversational Genres," *Southern Folklore Quarterly,* 32 (1968), 44-59; Dan Ben-Amos, "Toward a Definition of Folklore in Context," *Journal of American Folklore,* 34 (1971), 3-15; E. Ojo Arewa and Alan Dundes, "Proverbs and the Ethnography of Speaking Folklore," *American Anthropologist: Special Publication,* 66 (1964), No. 6, Part 2, 70-85; and Richard Bauman, "Differential Identity and the Social Base of Folklore," *Journal of American Folklore,* 84 (1971), 31-41.

3. John Dollard, "The Dozens: Dialectic of Insult," *American Imago,* 1 (1939), 3-25.

4. Roger D. Abrahams, *Deep Down in The Jungle* (1963; rpt. Chicago: Aldine Publishing Company, 1970), pp. 38-54; For other examinations see Lee Rainwater, *Behind Ghetto Walls* (Chicago: Aldine Publishing Company, 1970), p. 277; David A.

Schultz, *Coming Up Black* (New York: Prentice-Hall, 1969), pp. 67-68; Allison Davis and John Dollard, *Children of Bondage* (1940; rpt, New York: Harper and Row, Publishers, 1965), p. 83; John H. Rohrer and Munro S. Edmonson, *The Eighth Generation Grows Up* (New York: Harper and Row, Publisher, 1960), p. 162; Ulf Hannerz, *Soulside: Inquiries into Ghetto Culture and Community* (New York: Columbia University Press, 1969), pp. 129-138; Boone Hammond, "The Contest System: A Survival Technique" (St. Louis: Washington University Masters Essay in Sociology, 1965), p. 27 (mimeographed); and Amuzie Chimesie, "The Dozens: An African-Heritage Theory," *Journal of Black Studies,* 6 (1976), 401-419.

5. J. Dan Rothwell, "Verbal Obscenity: Time for Second Thoughts," *Western Speech,* 35 (1971), pp. 231-242.

6. For a description and analysis of the real but fictitiously named "Tattler" community, see Thurmon Garner, "Tattler: Environmental Influences on Patterns of Communication in a Black Community," Diss. Northwestern University 1979, pp. 46-91.

7. The theoretical framework used here is based on essays by Roger D. Abrahams. See "Personal Power and Social Restraint in the Definition of Folklore," *Journal of American Folklore,* 84 (1971), 16-30; "Introductory Remarks," pp. 143-58; and "A Rhetoric of Everyday Life," pp. 44-59. Abrahams' rhetorical approach to folklore developed long after his initial analysis of the dozens.

8. Abrahams, "Introductory Remarks," p. 149.

9. Ibid., p. 146.

10. See Abrahams, *"Deep Down,"* pp. 35-54; Dollard "The Dozens," pp. 3–5; and William Labov, "Rules for Ritual Insults," in *Studies in Social Interaction,* ed. David Sudnow (New York: The Free Press, 1972), pp. 120-169. Remarkably the game, as played in Tattler, has retained those characteristics identified by Dollard, Abrahams, and other researchers. The only recognizable difference appears to be that themes reflect modern events, situations, or views rather than past ideas. This historical similarity attests to the longevity of the game as a folkloric event.

11. The examples used in this essay were from men since they provided the majority of the data. This researcher observed women playing the dozens with men in public settings, but informants did not consider them representative of how females played with females. Yet, young women of different social backgrounds reported playing the dozens to make other girls "break down" or "crack up." They admitted that their play was often as nasty and as dirty as was the play of men. The themes they addressed were of homosexuality, sexual promiscuity, and immorality.

12. Abrahams, "Introductory Remarks," p. 148.

13. Roger D. Abrahams, "Joking: The Training of the Man of Words in Talking Broad," in *Rappin and Stylin Out: Communication in Urban Black America*, ed. Thomas Kochman (Chicago: University of Illinois Press, 1972), pp. 215-39.

14. Roger D. Abrahams, "Negotiating Respect: Patterns of Presentation Among Black Women," *Journal of American Folklore*, 88 (1975) 64.

15. See H. Rap Brown, *Die Nigger Die!* (New York: Dial Press, 1969), pp. 25-31 for similar kinds of responses used by teenagers.

16. Abrahams, *Deep Down*, p. 48.

17. Molefi K. Asante, "A Metatheory for Black Communications," *The Journal of Black Psychology*, (1975), 30-41.

18. Abrahams, "A Rhetoric of Everyday Life," p. 58.

19. Paul D. Goodwin and Joseph W. Wenzel, "Proverbs and Practical Reasoning: A Study in Socio-Logic," *Quarterly Journal of Speech*, 65 (1979), 303.

Reading 2.4 /
BLACK STREET SPEECH /
JOHN BAUGH

Notes

1. Turner was strongly influenced by Herskovits and Kurath, who developed American dialect atlases.

2. I would especially like to thank William Labov and Ralph Fasold for pointing me in the right direction with their pioneering studies.

Reading 3.1 /
AN AFRO-AMERICAN
PERSPECTIVE ON INTERETHNIC COMMUNICATION /
MICHAEL L. HECHT, SIDNEY RIBEAU, &
J. K. ALBERTS

References

Abe, H., & Wiseman, R. (1983). A cross-cultural confirmation of the dimensions of intercultural effectiveness. *International Journal of Intercultural Relations, 7*, 53–67.

Agar, M., & Hobbs, J.R. (1982). Interpreting discourse: Coherence and the analysis of ethnographic interviews. *Discourse Processes, 5*, 1–32.

Andersen, P.A., Lustig, M.W., & Andersen, J.F. (1987). Regional patterns of communication in the United States: A theoretical explanation. *Communication Monographs, 54*, 128–144.

Antaki, C. (Ed.) (1981). *The psychology of ordinary explanations*. London: Academic Press.

Asante, M.K., & Noor-Aldeen. H.S. (1984). Social interaction of black and white college students. *Journal of Black Studies, 14*, 507–516.

Bachman, J.G., & O'Malley, P.M. (1984). Yea-saying, nay-saying, and going to extremes: Black-white differences in response styles. *Public Opinion Quarterly, 48*, 491–509.

Ball, P., Giles, H., & Hewstone, M. (1985). Interpersonal accommodation and situational constraints: An integrative formula. In H. Giles & R. St. Clair (Eds.), *Recent advances in language, communication & social psychology* (pp. 263–286). London: Lawrence Erlbaum.

Baxter, J.C. (1970). Interpersonal spacing in natural settings. *Sociometry, 33*, 444–456.

Baxter, L. (1986). Gender differences in the heterosexual relationship rules embedded in break-up accounts. *Journal of Social and Personal Relationships, 3*, 289–306.

Baxter, L.A., (1987). Symbols of relationship identity in relationship cultures. *Journal of Social and Personal Relationships, 4*, 261–280.

Baxter, L., & Bullis, C. (1986). Turning points in developing romantic relationships. *Human Communication Research, 12*, 469–493.

Beebe, L.M., & Giles, H. (1984). Speech-accommodation theories: A discussion in terms of second-language acquisition. *International Journal of the Sociology of Language, 46*, 5–32.

Berger, C.R., & Douglas, W. (1982). Thought and talk: Excuse me, but have I been talking to myself? In F.E.X. Dance (Ed.), *Human communication theory* (pp. 42–60). New York: Harper & Row.

Bochner, A.P., & Kelly, C.W. (1974). Interpersonal competence: Rationale, philosophy, and implementation of a conceptual framework, *Speech Teacher, 23*, 279–301.

Bourhis, R.Y. (1985). The sequential nature of language choice in cross-cultural communication. In R.L. Street, Jr. & J.N. Capella (Eds.), *Sequence and pattern in communicative behavior.* London: Edward Arnold.

Carbaugh, D. (1988). Cultural terms and tensions in the speech at a television station. *Western Journal of Speech Communication, 52*, 216–237.

Capella, J.N., & Planalp, S. (1981). Talk and silence sequences in informal conversations III: Interspeaker influence. *Human Communication Research, 7*, 117–132.

Cody, M.J., & McLaughlin, M.L. (1985). Models for the sequential construction of accounting episodes: Situational and interactional constraints on message selection and evaluation. In R.L. Street & J.N. Capella (Eds.), *Sequence and pattern in communicative behavior* (pp. 60–69). London: Edward Arnold.

Collier, M.J. (1988). A comparison of intracultural and intercultural communication among acquaintances: How intra- and intercultural competencies vary. *Communication Quarterly, 36,* 122–144.

Collier, M.H., Ribeau, S., & Hecht, M. L. (1986). Intercultural communication rules and outcomes within three domestic cultural groups. *International Journal of Intercultural Relations, 10,* 439–457.

Dodd, C.H. (1982). *Dynamics of intercultural communication.* Dubuque, Iowa: William C. Brown.

Douglas, W. (1983). Scripts and self-monitoring: when does being a high self-monitor really make a difference? *Human Communication Research, 10,* 81–96.

Duncan, B.L. (1978). The development of spatial behavior norms in black and white primary school children. *The Journal of Black Psychology, 5,* 33–41.

Fisher, D.V. (1986). Decision-making and self-disclosure. *Journal of Social and Personal Relationships, 3,* 323–336.

Folkes, V.S. (1985). Mindlessness or mindfulness: A partial replication and extension of Langer, Blank and Chanowitz. *Journal of Personality and Social Psychology, 48,* 600–604.

Gallois, C., Franklin-Strokes, A., Giles, H., & Coupland, N. (1988). Communication accommodation in intercultural encounters. In Y.Y. Kim & W.E. Gudykunst (Eds.), *Theories in intercultural communication.* Newbury Park, CA: Sage.

Geertz, C. (1973). *The interpretation of cultures.* NY: Basic Books.

Geertz, C. (1983). *Local knowledge.* NY: Basic Books.

Giles, H. (1973). Accent mobility: A model and some data. *Anthropological Linguistics, 15,* 87–105.

Giles, H., Bourhis, R.Y., & Taylor, D. (1977). Towards a theory of language in ethnic group relations. In H. Giles (Ed.), *Language, ethnicity and intergroup relations.* London: Academic Press.

Giles, H., Mulac, A., Bradac, J.J., & Johnson, P. (1987). Speech accommodation: The first decade and beyond. In M. McLaughlin (Ed.), *Communication Yearbook 10* (pp. 13–48). Beverly Hills, CA: Sage.

Gudykunst, W.B., & Hammer. M.R. (1987). The influence of ethnicity, gender, and dyadic composition on uncertainty reduction in initial interaction. *Journal of Black Studies, 18,* 191–214.

Hammer, M.R., Gudykunst, W.B., & Wiseman, R.L. (1978). Dimensions of intercultural effectiveness: An exploratory study. *International Journal of Intercultural Relations, 2,* 382–393.

Harré, R. (1979). *Social being.* Oxford: Blackwell.

Hecht, M.L. (1984). Satisfying communication and relational labels: Intimacy and length of relationship as perceptual frames of naturalistic conversations. *Western Journal of Speech Communication, 48,* 201–216.

Hecht, M.L., Andersen, P.A., & Ribeau, S. (in press). The cultural dimensions of nonverbal communication. In M.K. Asante & W.B. Gudykunst (Eds.), *Handbook of intercultural communication.* Newbury Park, CA: Sage.

Hecht, M.L., & Ribeau, S. (1984). Ethnic communication: A comparative analysis of satisfying communication. *International Journal of Intercultural Relations, 8,* 135–151.

Hecht, M.L., & Ribeau, S. (1987). Afro-American identity labels and communicative effectiveness. *Journal of Language and Social Psychology, 6,* 319–326.

Hecht, M.L., & Ribeau, S. (in press). Socio-cultural roots of ethnic identity: A look at Black America. *Journal of Black Studies.*

Hecht, M.L., Ribeau, S., & Sedano, M.V. (in press). A Mexican-American perspective on interethnic communication. *International Journal of Intercultural Relations.*

Ickes, W. (1984). Compositions in black and white: Determinants of interaction in interracial dyads. *Journal of Personality and Social Psychology, 47,* 330–341.

Jaffe, J., & Feldstein, S. (1970). *Rhythms of dialogue.* New York, NY: Academic Press.

Jones, S.E. (1971). A comparative proxemics analysis of dyadic interactions in selected subcultures of New York City. *Journal of Social Psychology, 84,* 35–44.

Katriel, T. (1988). Rhetoric in flames: Fire inscriptions in Israeli youth movement ceremonials. *Quarterly Journal of Speech, 73,* 444–459.

Katriel, T., & Philipsen, G. (1981). What we need is communication: "Communication" as a cultural category in some American speech. *Communication Monographs, 48,* 301–318.

Kendon, A. (1967). Some functions of gaze direction in social interaction. *Acta Psychologica, 71,* 359–372.

Kitayma, S., & Burnstein, E. (1988). Automaticity in conversations: A reexamination of the mindless hypothesis. *Journal of Personality and Social Psychology, 54,* 219–224.

Knoke, D., & Burke, P.J. (1983). *Log-linear models.* Beverly Hills: Sage.

Kochman, T. (1982). *Black and white: Styles in conflict.* Chicago, IL: University of Chicago Press.

LaFrance, M., & Mayo, C. (1976). Racial differences in gaze behavior during conversations: Two systematic observational studies. *Journal of Personality and Social Psychology, 33,* 547–552.

Langer, E.J. (1978). Rethinking the role of thought in social interaction. In J.H. Harvey, W. Ickes, & R.F. Kidd (Eds.), *New directions in attribution research* (Vol. 2). Hillsdale, N.J: Erlbaum.

Leiter, K. (1980). *A primer on ethnomethodology.* NY: Oxford University Press.

Lessing, E.E., Clarke, C.C., & Gray-Shellberg, L.G. (1981). Black power ideology: Rhetoric and reality in a student sample. *International Journal of Intercultural Relations, 5,* 71–94.

Levine, L. (1977). *Black culture and black consciousness.* NY: Oxford University Press.

Martineau, W.H. (1976). Social participation and a sense of powerlessness among Blacks: A neighborhood analysis. *The Sociological Quarterly, 17,* 27–41.

Maslow, A. (1954). *Motivation and personality,* NY: Harper.

McLaughlin, M., Cody, M.J., & O'Hair, H.D. (1983). The management of failure events: Some contextual determinants of accounting behavior. *Human Communication Research, 9,* 208–224.

Miller, G., & Steinberg, M. (1975). *Between people.* Chicago, IL: Science Research Associates.

Morris, G.H. (1985). The remedial episode as a negotiation of rules. In R.L. Street, Jr. & J.N. Capella (Eds.), *Sequence and pattern in communicative behavior* (pp. 70–84). Arnold.

Otto, L.B., & Featherman, D.L. (1975). Social stratification and psychological antecedents of self-estrangement and powerlessness. *American Sociological Review, 40,* 701–719.

Pearson, J.C. (1985). *Gender and communication.* Dubuque, Iowa: Wm. C. Brown.

Pettigrew, T.F. (1981). Race and class in the 1980's: An interactive view. *Daedalus, 110,* 233–255.

Pettigrew, T.F. (1985). New Black-white patterns: How best to conceptualize them? *American Sociological Review. 11,* 329–346.

Rawlins, W. (1983). Openness as problematic in ongoing friendships: Two conversational dilemmas. *Communication Monographs. 50,* 1–13.

Rogers, C.R. (1961). *On becoming a person.* Boston: Houghton-Mifflin.

Ruben, B. (1976). Assessing communication competence for intercultural adaptation. *Group and Organizational Studies, 1,* 335–354.

Schonbach, P. (1980). A category system for account phases. *European Journal of Social Psychology, 10,* 195–200.

Smith, R.C., & Eisenberg, E.M. (1987). Conflict at Disneyland: A root-metaphor analysis. *Communication Monographs. 54,* 367–380.

Smitherman, G. (1977). *Talkin' and testifyin': The language of Black Americans.* Boston: Houghton-Mifflin.

Spitzberg, B.H., & Cupach, W.R. (1984). *Interpersonal communication competence.* Beverly Hills, CA: Sage.

Spitzberg, B.H., & Hecht, M.L. (1984). A component model of relational competence. *Human Communication Research, 10,* 575–600.

Tavis, C., & Wade. C. (1984). *The longest war: Sex differences in perspective* (2nd Ed.). NY: Harcourt Brace Jovanovich.

Thibaut, J.W., & Kelley, H.H. (1959). *The social psychology of groups.* NY: John Wiley.

van Dijk, T.A. (1987). *Communicating racism: Ethnic prejudice in thought and talk.* Newbury Park. CA: Sage.

Webb, J.T. (1972). Interview synchrony: An investigation of two speech-rate measures in the automated standardized interview. In A. W. Siegman & B. Pope (Eds.), *Studies in dyadic communication.* Oxford: Pergamon Press.

Wiemann, J.M. (1977). Explication and test of a model of communicative competence. *Human Communication Research, 3,* 195–213.

Wood, J. (1982). Communication and relational culture: Bases for the study of human relationships. *Communication Quarterly, 30,* 75–83.

Zatz, M.S. (1987). The changing forms of racial/ethnic biases in sentencing. *Journal of Research in Crime and Delinquency, 24,* 69–92.

Reading 3.2 /

Interracial Dating /

Tina M. Harris & Pamela J. Kalbfleisch

Note

1. Researchers used snowball sampling techniques to increase the number of African American partuicipants in the study.

References

Collins, P. H. (1990). African American feminist thought: Knowledge, consciousness, and the politics of empowerment, New York: Routledge.

Dickson, L. (1993). The future of marriage and family in African American America. Journal of African American Studies, 3(4), 472–491.

Duncan, V. J., & Kalbfleisch, P. J. (1996). Patterns of trust and distrust across race and gender. Challenge: A Journal of Research on African American Men, 7(4), 5–28.

Fitzpatrick, K. M., & Hwang, S. S. (1992). The effects of community structure on opportunities for interracial contact: Extending Blau's macrostructural theory. Sociological Forum, 7(3), 517–536.

Harris, T. M. (1994). Date initiation: A q-sort analysis of dating behaviors in same race and interracial romantic relationships. Paper presented at the annual Speech Communication Association conference, New Orleans, Louisiana.

Kouri, K. M., & Lasswell, M. (1993). Black-White marriages: Social change and intergenerational mobility. Marriage and Family Review, 19(3–4), 241–255.

Leonard, R., & Locke, D. C. (1993). Communication stereotypes: Is interracial communication possible? Journal of Black Studies, 23(3), 332–343.

Masini, E. B. (1993). Future studies and the trends toward unity and diversity. International Social Science Journal, 45(3/137), 323–331.

Mongeau, P. A., & Carey, C. M. (1996). Who's wooing whom II? An experimental investigation of date-initiation and expectancy violation. Western Journal of Communication, 60(3), 195–213.

Mongeau, P. A., Hale, J., Johnson, K. L., & Hillis, J. D. (1993). Who's wooing whom? An investigation of female initiated dating. In P. J. Kalbfleisch (Ed.) Interpersonal communication: Evolving interpersonal relationships (pp. 51–68). Hillsdale, NJ: Lawerence Erlbaum.

Mongeau, P. A., Yeazell, M., & Hale, J. L. (1994). Sex differences in relational message interpretations on male- and female-initiated first dates: A research note. Journal of Social Behavior and Personality, 9, 731–742.

Murstein, B., Merigihi, J. R. & Malloy, T. E. (1989). Physical attractiveness and exchange theory in interracial dating. The Journal of Social Psychology, 129(3), 325–334.

Orbe, M. (1995). African American communication research: Toward a deeper understanding of interethnic communication. Western Journal of Communication, 59(1), 61–78.

Orbe, M. (1996). Laying the foundation for co-cultural communication theory: An inductive approach to studying "non-dominant" communication strategies and the factors that influence them. Communications Studies, 47, 157–176.

Orbe, M. P. (1998). From the standpoint(s) of traditionally muted groups: Explicating a co-cultural communication theoretical model. Communication Theory, 8(1), 1–26.

Paset, P. S. & Taylor, R. (1991). Black and white women's attitudes toward interracial marriage. Psychological Reports, 69, 753–754.

Romano, L., & Trescott, J. (1992). Love in black and white, Redbook, 178(4), 88–94.

Stephenson, W. (1953). The study of behavior: Q-technique and its methodology. Chicago, IL: University of Chicago Press.

Suzuki, S. (1998). In-group and out-group communication patterns in international organizations. Communication Research, 25(2), 154–182.

Todd, J., McKinney, J. L., Harris, R., Chadderton, R., & Small, L. (1992). Attitudes toward interracial dating: Effects of age, sex, and race. Journal of Multicultural Counseling and Development, 20, 202–208.

Weitz, R., & Gordon, L. (1993). Images of African American women among Anglo college students. Sex Roles, 28,1/2 19–33.

Reading 3.3 /

THE CHANGING INFLUENCE OF INTERPERSONAL PERCEPTIONS ON MARITAL WELL-BEING AMONG BLACK AND WHITE COUPLES / LINDA K. ACITELLI, ELIZABETH DOUVAN, & JOSEPH VEROFF

References

Acitelli, L. K., Douvan, E. & Veroff, J. (1993) 'Perceptions of Conflict in the First Year of Marriage: How Important are Similarity and Understanding?,' *Journal of Social and Personal Relationships* 10: 5–19.

Austin, W. & Walster (Hatfield), E. (1974) 'Reactions to Confirmations and Disconfirmations of Expectancies of Equity and Inequity,' *Journal of Personality and Social Psychology* 30: 209–16.

Berger, P. & Kellner, H. (1964) 'Marriage and the Construction of Social Reality,' *Diogenes* 46: 1–24.

Bernard, J. (1972) *The Future of Marriage,* New York: World Publishing.

Booth, A., Johnson, D. & Edwards J. (1983) 'Measuring Marital Instability,' *Journal of Marriage and the Family* 45: 387–94.

Broman, C. L. (1993) 'Race Differences in Marital Well-Being,' *Journal of Marriage and the Family* 55: 724–32.

Christensen, A. & Heavey, C.L. (1990) 'Gender and Social Structure in the Demand/Withdraw Pattern of Marital Interaction,' *Journal of Personality and Social Psychology* 59: 73–81.

Crohan, S. E. (1992) 'Marital Happiness and Spousal Consensus on Beliefs about Marital Conflict,' *Journal of Social and Personal Relationships* 9: 89–102.

Crohan, S. E. & Veroff, J. (1989) 'Dimensions of Marital Well-Being among White and Black Newlyweds,' *Journal of Marriage and the Family* 51: 379–83.

Deal, J. E., Wampler, K. S. & Halverson, C.F. (1992) 'The Importance of Similarity in the Marital Relationship,' *Family Process* 31: 369–82.

Duck, S. W. (1994) *Meaningful Relationships: Talking, Sense, and Relating.* Thousand Oaks. CA: Sage.

Fincham, F. D. & Bradbury, T.N. (1991) 'Marital Conflict: Towards a More Complete Integration of Research and Treatment,' in J. Vincent (ed.) *Advances in Family Intervention, Assessment, and Theory* (Vol. 5). London: Kingsley.

Fletcher, G. J. O. & Fitness, J. (1990) 'Occurrent Social Cognition in Close Relationship Interaction: The Role of Proximal and Distal Variables,' *Journal of Personality and Social Psychology* 59: 464–74.

Glenn, N. (1990) 'Quantitative Research on Marital Quality in the 1980s: A Critical Review,' *Journal of Marriage and the Family* 52: 818–31.

Gottman, J. M. (1993) 'The Roles of Conflict Engagement, Escalation, and Avoidance in Marital Interaction: A Longitudinal View of Five Types of Couples,' *Journal of Consulting and Clinical Psychology* 61: 6–15.

Gottman, J. M. (1995) 'A Theory of Marital Dissolution and Stability,' *Journal of Family Psychology* 7: 57–75.

Hatchett, S., Veroff, J. & Douvan, E. (1995) 'Factors Influencing Marital Stability among Black and White Couples,' in B. Tucker & C. Mitchell-Kernan (eds) *The Decline of Black Marriages,* Newbury Park, CA: Sage.

Johnson, D. R., Amoloza, T. O. & Booth, A. (1992) 'Stability and Development Change in Marital Quality: A Three Wave Panel Analysis,' *Journal of Marriage and the Family* 54: 582–94.

Karney, B. R. & Bradbury, T. N. (1995) 'The Longitudinal Course of Marital Quality and Stability: A Review of Method, Theory, and Research,' *Psychological Bulletin* 118: 3–34.

Kenny, D. A. (1994) *Interpersonal Perception.* New York: Guilford Press.

Laing, R. D., Phillipson, H. & Lee, A. R. (1966) *Interpersonal Perception: A Theory and a Method of Research.* New York: Springer.

Levinger, G. & Breedlove, J. (1966) 'Interpersonal Attraction and Agreement,' *Journal of Personality and Social Psychology* 39: 367–72.

Markman, H. J., Silvern, L., Clements, M. & Kraft-Hanak, S. (1993) 'Men and Women Dealing with Conflict in Heterosexual Relationships,' *Journal of Social Issues* 49: 107–25.

Oggins, J., Veroff, J. & Leber, D. (1993) 'Perceptions and Marital Interaction among Black and White Newlyweds,' *Journal of Personality and Social Psychology* 65: 494–511.

Sher, T. G. & Baucom, D. H. (1995) 'Marital Communication: Differences among Maritally Distressed, Depressed, and Nondistressed-Nondepressed Couples,' *Journal of Family Psychology* 7: 148–53.

Sillars, A. L. (1985) 'Interpersonal Perception in Relationships,' in W. Ickes (ed.) *Compatible and Incompatible Relationships,* New York: Springer.

Sillars, A. L., & Scott, M. D. (1983) 'Interpersonal Perception between Intimates: An Integrative Review,' *Human Communication Research* 10: 153–76.

Sillars, A. L., Weisberg, J., Burggraf, C. S. & Zietlow, P. H. (1990) 'Communication and Understanding Revisited: Married Couples' Understanding and Recall of Conversations,' *Communication Research* 17: 500–22.

Spanier, G. (1976) 'Measuring Dyadic Adjustment: New Scales for Assessing the Quality of Marriage and Similar Dyads,' *Journal of Marriage and the Family* 38: 15–27.

Utne, M. K., Hatfield, E., Traupmann, J. & Greenburger, D. (1984) 'Equity, Marital Satisfaction and Stability,' *Journal of Social and Personal Relationships* 1: 323–32.

Veroff, J., Douvan, E. & Hatchett, S. (1993a) 'Marital Interaction and Marital Quality in the First Year of Marriage,' in W. Jones & D. Perlman (eds) *Advances in Personal Relationships.* London: Jessica Kingsley.

Veroff, J., Douvan, E. & Hatchett, S. J. (1995) *Marital Instability: A social and Behavioral Study of the Early Years.* Greenwich, CT: Greenwood.

Veroff, J., Douvan, E. & Kulka, K. (1981) *The Inner American,* New York: Basic Books.

Veroff, J., Sutherland, L., Chadiha, L.A. & Ortega, R. M. (1993b) 'Predicting Marital Quality with

Narrative Assessment of Marital Experience,' *Journal of Marriage and the Family* 55: 326–37.

Wyer, R. S. (1973) 'Category Ratings as "Subjective Expected Values": Implications for Attitude Formation and Change,' *Psychological Review* 80: 96–112.

Reading 3.4 /
"LET US GO INTO THE HOUSE OF THE LORD" / JEFFREY LYNN WOODYARD, JOHN L. PETERSON, & JOSEPH P. STOKES

Notes

1. Albert J. Raboteau, *Slave Religion: The Invisible Institution in the Antebellum South* (New York, NY: Oxford University Press, 1978).

2. C. Eric Lincoln and Lawrence H. Mamiya, *The Black Church in the African American Experience* (Durham, NC: Duke University Press, 1990).

3. Andrew Billingsley and C. Caldwell, "The Church, the Family and the School in the African American Community," *Journal of Negro Education,* 1991, Vol. 60, NO. 3, pp. 427–440.

4. Andrew Billingsley, *Climbing Jacob's Ladder: The Future of African American Families* (New York, NY: Simon & Shuster/Touchstone, 1992).

5. C. Eric Lincoln and Lawrence H. Mamiya, *The Black Church in the African American Experience* (Durham, NC: Duke University Press, 1990).

6. A. Wüst and J. Flack, "A Church-Based Cholesterol Education Program," *Public Health Report,* 1990, Vol. 105, pp. 381–387.

7. E. Eng, J. Hatch, and A. Callan, "Institutionalizing Social Support through the Church and into the Community," *Health Education Quarterly,* 1985, Vol. 12, No. 1, pp. 81-92.

8. J. Levin, "The Role of the Black Church in Community Medicine," *Journal of the American Medical Association,* 1984, vol. 76, pp. 477-483.

9. Benjamin Mays and J. Nicholson, *The Negro's Church* (New York, NY: Russell & Russell, 1969).

10. Stephen B. Thomas and Sandra C. Quinn, "The Characteristics of Northern Black Churches with Community Health Outreach Programs," *American Journal of Public Health,* 1994, Vol. 84, No. 4, pp. 575-579.

11. James H. Cone, "General Introduction," in James H. Cone and Gayraud Wilmore (Eds.), *Black Theology: A Documentary History, Volume Two: 1980-1992.* (Maryknoll, NY: Orbis, 1993), pp. 1-11.

12. *Ibid.*

13. Donna Higgins, "Using Formative Research to Lay the Foundation for Community Level HIV Prevention Efforts: An Example of the AIDS Community Demonstration Projects," *Public Health Reports,* 1996, Vol. 111, No.1. Suppl., pp. 28-35.

14. J. W. Bowyer, *Tally: A Text Analysis Tool for the Liberal Arts* (Dubuque, IA: Brown, 1991).

15. Elijah Farajaje-Jones, "Breaking Silence: Toward an In-The-Life Theology," in James H. Cone and Gayrand Wilmore (Eds.), *Black Theology: A Documentary History, Volume Two: 1980-1992* (Maryknoll, NY: Orbis. 1993), pp. 139-159.

16. Charles I. Nero, "Toward a Black Gay Aesthetic: Signifying in Contemporary Black Gay Literature," in Essex Hemphill (Ed.) *Brother to Brother: New Writings by Black Gay Men* (Boston, MA: Alyson, 1991), pp. 229-252

17. Ron Simmons, "Some Thoughts on the Challenges Facing Black Gay Intellectuals," in Essex Hemphill (Ed.), *Brother to Brother: New Writings by Black Gay Men* (Boston, MA: Alyson, 1991), pp. 211-228.

18. James Tinney, "Why a Black Gay Church?" in Joseph Beam (Ed.), *In the Life: Black Gay Anthology* (Boston, MA: Alyson, 1986), pp. 70-86.

19. Elijah Farajaje-Jones, "Breaking Silence: Toward an In-The–Life Theology," in James H. Cone and Gayraud Wilmore (Eds.), *Black Theology: A Documentary History, Volume Two: 1980-1992* (Maryknoll, NY: Orbis, 1993), pp. 139-159.

20. Albert J. Raboteau, *Slave Religion: The Invisible Institution in the Antebellum South* (New York, NY: Oxford University Press, 1978).

21. James H. Cone, "General Introduction," in James H. Cone and Gayraud Wilmore (Eds.), *Black Theology: A Documentary History, Volume Two: 1980-1992* (Maryknoll, NY; Orbis, 1993). Pp. 1-11

22. A. M. Somlai, T. G. Heckman, J. A. Kelly, G. W. Mulry, K. E. Muthauf, "The Response of Religious Congregations to the Spiritual Needs of People Living with HIV/AIDS," *The Journal of Pastoral Care,* 1997, Vol. 51, No. 4, pp. 415-426.

Reading 4.1 /
MULTIPLE PERSPECTIVES / MARSHA HOUSTON

Notes

1. Throughout this discussion the terms "black" and "African American" will be used interchangeably.

2. "Multiple consciousness" is an extension of the concept "double consciousness" developed by the

African American sociologist W. E. B. Du Bois (1937) to describe the social outlooks of blacks in the United States.

3. Content analysis was done by the author using a combination of repeated manual searches of the responses and the list-processing computer program PC-File III (Button, 1984). Details can be found in Houston (1992, April), obtainable from the author.

4. "Joaning" is one contemporary term for those African American speech events that involve using teasing or kidding to criticize or "talk about" another (e.g., "signifying" (Smitherman, 1977; Garner, 1983), "loud-talking" and "marking" (Mitchell-Keman, 1972).

References

Abrahams, R. D. (1975). Negotiating respect: Patterns of presentation among black women, *Journal of American Folklore, 88,* 58–80.

Anderson, L. M. (1997). *Mammies no more: The changing image of black women on stage and screen:* Lanham, MD: Rowman & Littlefield.

Baugh, J. (1983). *Black street speech.* Austin, TX: University of Texas Press.

Beale, F. (1970). Double jeopardy: To be black and female. In T. Cade (Ed.), *The black woman.* New York: Signet, pp. 90–100.

Bell, M. J. (1983). *The world from Brown's Lounge: An ethnography of black middle class play.* Urbana, IL: University of Illinois Press.

Bethel, L. (1982). This infinity of conscious pain: Zora Neal Hurston and the black female literary tradition. In G. T. Hull, P. Bell Scott, & B. Smith (Eds.), *All the women are white, all the blacks are men: but some of us are brave.* Old Westbury, NY: The Feminist Press.

Bond, J. C. & Peery, P. (1970). Is the black male castrated? In T. Cade (Ed.), *The black woman* (pp. 101–110). New York: Signet.

Button, J. (1984). PC-File III [Computer program]. Bellevue, WA: Buttonware.

Bucholtz, M. (1996). Black feminist theory and African American women's linguistic practice. In V. L. Bergvall, J. M. Bing & A. F. Freed (Eds.), *Rethinking language and gender research: theory and practice* (pp. 267–290). London: Longman.

Collins, P. H. (2000). *Black feminist thought: Knowledge, consciousness, and the politics of empowerment.* Rev. Ed. New York: Routledge.

Davis, A. Y. (1981). *Women, race, and class.* New York: Random House.

Dill, B. T. (1979). The dialectics of black womanhood. *Signs, 4,* 543–57.

Du Bois, W. E. B. (1937). *The souls of black folk* (21st ed.). Chicago: McClug.

Ervin-Tripp, S. (1968). An analysis of the interaction of language, topic, and listener. In Joshua Fishman (Ed.), *Readings in the sociology of language* (pp. 192–211). The Hague, Netherlands: Mouton.

Essed, P. (1991). *Understanding everyday racism: An interdisciplinary theory,* Newbury Park, CA: Sage.

Etter-Lewis, G. (1993). *My soul is my own: Oral narratives of African American women in the professions.* New York: Routledge.

Foeman, A. K. & Pressley, G. (1987). Ethnic culture and corporate culture: using black styles in organizations. *Communication Quarterly, 33,* 293–307.

Folb, E. (1980). Gender. *In her Runnin' down some lines: The language and culture of black teenagers* (pp. 193–98). Cambridge, MA: Harvard University Press.

Garner, T. (1983). Playing the dozens: Folklore as strategies for living. *Quarterly Journal of Speech, 69,* 47–57.

Guy-Sheftall, B. (1990). *Daughters of sorrow: Attitudes toward black women,* 1880–1920. New York: Carlson Publishing.

Guy-Sheftall, B. (1995). Introduction: The evolution of feminist consciousness among African American women. In her *Words of fire: An anthology of African American feminist thought* (pp. 1–24). New York: New Press.

Hannerz, U. (1970). The notion of ghetto culture. In J. F. Szwed (Ed.), *Black America* (pp. 99–109). New York: Basic Books.

Hecht, M., Ribeau, S., & Alberts, J. K. (1989). An Afro-American perspective on interethnic communication. *Communication Monographs, 56,* 385–410.

Henley, N. & Kramarae, C. (1994). Gender, power, and miscommunication. In C. Roman, S. Juhasz, and C. Miller (Eds.), *The women and language debate: A sourcebook* (pp. 383–406). New Brunswick, NJ: Rutgers University Press.

hooks, b. (1981). *Ain't I a woman?: Black women and feminism.* Boston: South End Press.

hooks, b. (1984). *Feminist theory: From margin to center.* Boston: South End Press.

Houston, M. (1992, April). Listening to ourselves: African-American women's perspectives on their communication style, Paper presented to Gender Studies Division, Southern States Communication Association, San Antonio, TX.

Houston, M. (Forthcoming). Triumph stories: Caring and accountability in African American women's conversation narratives. In M. Houston & O. I. Davis (Eds.), *Centering Ourselves: African American Feminist and Womanist Studies of Discourse.* Cresskill, NJ: Hampton Press.

Houston Stanback, M. (1983). Code-switching in black women's speech (Doctoral dissertation, University of Massachusetts). *Dissertation Abstracts International, 84* (01), 105 (University Microfilms No. TX1–384–886).

Houston Stanback, M. (1985). Language and black woman's place: Evidence from the black middle class. In P. A. Treichler, C. Kramarae, and B. Stafford (Eds.), *For alma mater: Theory and practice in feminist scholarship* (pp. 177–93). Urbana, IL: University of Illinois Press.

King, D. K. (1988). Multiple jeopardy, multiple consciousness: The Context of a black feminist ideology. *Signs, 14* (Autumn), 42–72.

Ladner, J. (1971). *Tomorrow's tomorrow: The black woman* Garden City, NJ: Doubleday-Anchor.

Lippi-Green, R. (1997). What we talk about when we talk about Ebonics: Why definitions matter. *The Black Scholar, 27* (2), 7–11.

Locke, M. (22 December 1996) Debate over Black English heats up: Critics call it an insult to students. *The New Orleans Times-Picayune,* p. A24.

Manning-Marable, C. and Houston, M. (1995). Toward an understanding of agenda-building discourse by African American Women: The case of Lani Guinier. *Women and Language, 18* (1), 34–36.

Merritt, B. (1997). Illusive reflections: African American women in primetime television. In A. Gonzalez, M. Houston, & V. Chen (Eds.), *Our voices: Essays in culture, ethnicity, and communication* (2nd Ed.) (pp. 52–60). Los Angeles, CA: Roxbury.

Mitchell-Kernan, C. (1972). Signifying, loud-talking, and marketing. In T. Kochman (Ed.), *Rappin and stylin' out,* (pp. 315–355). Urbana, IL: University of Illinois Press.

Nelson, L. W. (1990). Code-switching in the oral life narratives of African American women: Challenges to linguistic hegemony. *Journal of Education, 172* (3), 142–55.

Rogers-Rose, L. (1980). Dialectics of black male-female relationships, In her *The black woman,* (pp. 251–264). Newbury Park, CA: Sage.

Rubin, D. and Garner, T. (1984, November). Middle class blacks' perceptions of dialect and style switching. Paper presented to Speech Communication Association, Chicago, IL.

Seymour, H. & Seymour, C. (1979). The symbolism of Ebonics: I'd rather switch than fight. *Journal of Black Studies, 9,* 367–82.

Smitherman, G. (1977). *Talkin' and testifyin': The language of Black America.* Boston: Houghton Mifflin.

Spillers, H. (1979). The politics of intimacy: A discussion. In R. Bell, B. Parker, and B. Guy-Sheftall (Eds.), *Sturdy black bridges: Visions of black women in literature* (pp. 87–106). New York: Anchor.

St. Jean, Y. & Feagin, J. R. (1998). *Double Burden: Black Women and Everyday Racism.* Armonk, NY: M. E. Sharpe.

van Dijk, T. A. (1987). *Communicating racism: Ethnic prejudice in thought and talk.* Newbury Park, CA. Sage.

Reading 4.2 /
CROSSING CULTURAL BORDERS/
KARLA D. SCOTT

Note

1. No attempt was made to obtain participants based on their socioeconomic status. Social class was not omitted because it is considered to be unimportant, but rather because its complex nature is far too difficult to attempt here. This study foregrounds language and cultural identity, while acknowledging that class always serves as a backdrop of sorts for the participants. For Black women, social class is not sorted as neatly as one would like it to be. It is also becoming even more problematic, as more Black women find themselves moving into or out of certain classes (Collins, 1991).

References

Abrahams, R. (1976) *Talking Black.* Rowley, MA: Newbury House.

Anzuldua, G. (1987) *Borderlands/La Frontera: The New Mestiza.* San Francisco, CA: Aunt Lute Books.

Carter, K. and Spitzack, C., eds (1989) *Doing Research on Women's Communication.* Norwood, NJ: Ablex.

Collins, P.H. (1991) *Black Feminist Thought: Knowledge, Consciousness and the Politics of Empowerment.* New York: Routledge.

Etter-Lewis, G. (1993) *My Soul is My Own: Oral Narratives of African-American Women in the Professions.* New York: Routledge.

Fordham, S. (1988) 'Racelessness as a Factor in Black Students School Success: Pragmatic Strategy or Pyrrhic Victory?,' *Harvard Educational Review* 58(1): 54–84.

Fordham, S. (1991) 'Racelessness in Private Schools: Should we Deconstruct the Racial and Cultural

Identity of African-American Adolescents?' *Teachers College Record* 92(3): 470–84.

Fordham, S. (1993) 'Those Loud Black Girls: (Black) Women, Silence and Gender "Passing" in the Academy,' *Anthropology and Education Quarterly* 24(1): 3–32.

Foster, M. (1995) ' "Are you with me?" Power and Solidarity in the Discourse of African American Women,' in K. Hall and M. Bucholz (eds) *Gender Articulated: Language and the Socially Constructed Self,* pp. 330–50. New York: Routledge.

Ganguly, K. (1992) 'Accounting for Others: Feminism and Representations' in L. Rakow (ed). *Women Making Meaning: New Feminist Directions in Communication,* pp. 60–79. New York: Routledge.

Hansell, M. and Ajirotutu, C.S. (1982) 'Negotiating interpretations in interethnic settings,' in J.J. Gumperz (ed.), *Language and Social Identity,* pp. 85–94. New York; Cambridge University Press.

Heritage, J. (1984) *Garfinkel and Ethnomethodology.* Cambridge: Polity.

hooks, b. (1981) *Aint I a Woman? Black Women and Feminism.* Boston: Southend Press.

hooks, b. (1989) *Talking Back: Thinking Feminist, Thinking Black.* Boston: Southend Press.

Houston Stanback, M. (1983) 'Codeswitching in Black Women's speech,' doctoral dissertation, University of Massachusetts.

Houston, M. (1985) 'Language and Black Woman's Place: Evidence from the Black Middle class,' in P.A Treichler et al. (eds) For Alma Mater: Theory and Practice in Feminist Scholarship. Chicago: University of Illinois Press.

Houston, M. (1992) "The Politics of Difference: Race, Class and Women's Communication," in L. Rakow (ed.) *Women Making Meaning: New Feminist Directions in Communication,* pp. 45–59. New York: Routledge.

Kochman, T. (1972) *Rappin' and Stylin Out.* Champaign-Urbana: University of Ilinois Press.

Kramarae, C. (1981) *Women and Men Speaking: Framework for Analysis.* Rowley, MA: Newbury House.

Labov, W. (1970) *The Study of Nonstandard English.* New York: Columbia University.

Labov, W. (1972) *Sociolinguistic Patterns.* Philadelphia: University of Pennsylvania Press.

Mitchell-Kernan, C. (1971) *Language Behavior in a Black Urban Community.* Monograph of the Language Behavior Laboratory. No. 2. Berkeley: University of California Press.

Morgan, M. (1991) 'Indirectness and Interpretation in African American Women's Discourse,' *Pragmatics* 1(4): 421–51.

Nelson, L. W. (1990) 'Codeswitching in the Oral Life Narratives of African American Women: Challenges to Linguistic Hegemony,' *Journal of Education* 173 (3): 142–55.

Cotton, C. M. (1990) 'The Negotiation of Identities in Conversation: A Theory of Markedness and Code Choice,' *International Journal of Social Language* 44: 115–36.

Van Dijk, T., Ting Toomey, S., Smitherman, G. and Troutman, D. (1997) 'Discourse, Ethnicity, Culture and Racism,' in T. Van Dijk (ed.) *Discourse as Social Interaction,* pp. 144–80, London: Sage.

Yard, M. (1971) *Them Children: A Study in Language Learning,* New York: Holt, Rinehart & Winston.

Reading 4.3 /
"THAT WAS MY OCCUPATION" /
D. SOYINI MADISON

Notes

1. The "narrated event" and "narrative event" are drawn from Richard Bauman's discussion in his introduction to *Story, Performance, and Event.* Although there are other terms and classifications for the reported or past events *inside* the story and the immediate act of *saying* the story, my own sensibilities draw me toward "telling" and "told" because these two terms have more of an identification with orality, as well as having more cultural familiarity.

2. Traditions of color are abundant in the many ways they theorize themselves, and black artists and scholars have been asserting this in very emphatic and formal discussions, particularly since the Harlem Renaissance in the 1920s with the classic work by Alain Locke in *The New Negro.*

3. Knight goes on to describe the materiality of language: "I believe language is not only physical, it's a living thing, a living organism. It's informed by the physical environment, by how we breathe, and our speech patterns. . . . That's the side of the language where nuance and inflection come in; we have to agree what the lifting of a voice means . . . it is the language of nuance, coloring, tone, not necessarily the literal meaning of the words. Sometimes the major meaning of a word is not even in the literal sense of the word so much as in the rhythms and rhymes" (13–16).

4. Mrs. Kapper's narrative was recorded in 1988.

5. As John Van Maanen suggests in *Tales of the Field: On Writing Ethnography,* when the researcher

does her own transcription—re-remembering and re-listening to the voice—the interpretation is enhanced because one discovers new nuances by revisiting the performance. Although sitting through the tapes can be tedious and time consuming, I think it is imperative with the poetic approach to recapture the performance event that only involved the researcher and the teller—the account will be more honest and the interpretation more studied.

The symbol_indicates a dramatic *lowering* of the voice; the symbol indicates the voice has risen to a *higher pitch;* a slash/indicates two words were *spoken together* as one word with hardly a pause between them. Words written in CAPITAL letters were spoken with great *volume* and *intensity;* the symbol ‖ ‖ indicates a *whisper.* The lines were broken according to the pause and rhythm of the voice: if there was a one or two second pause, another line was started. If the rhythm was generally slower, the break would come at two or three seconds. If the pause was greater, then it was noted.

6. The theologian Gayraud S. Wilmore elaborates: "From the beginning the religion of the descendants of the Africans who were brought to the Western world as slaves has been something less and something more than what is generally regarded as Christianity. Under the circumstances, it could not have been otherwise. The religious beliefs and rituals of a people are inevitably and inseparably bound with the material and psychological realities of their daily existence" (1).

7. Asante describes African-American spirituality coming out of an African centered consciousness that knows and acknowledges the "WE are": "We can reach our own transcendence, but never without the help of others. If I run to the sea alone, my solitude finds me searching for new ways to come together with others. I know myself only in relation to others, without whom I am a Piagetian egocentric. We say that we can never truly know ourselves without the knowledge of others; or more precisely, in the productive engagement with the other we truly experience our own harmony" (188–89).

8. For a detailed analysis of black women's contestation of the "cult of true womanhood," see Giddings.

References

Anzaldúa, Gloria, and Cherríe Moraga, eds. *This Bridge Called My Back: Writings By Radical Women Of Color.* New York: Kitchen Table, 1983.

Asante, Molefi Kete. *The Afrocentric Idea.* Philadelphia: Temple UP, 1987.

Bakhtin, Mikail. *The Dialogical Imagination: Four Essays by M.M. Bakhtin.* Ed. Michael Holquist. Trans. Caryl Emerson and Michael Holquist. Austin: U of Texas P, 1981.

Bauman, Richard. *Story, Performance, Event: Contextual Studies of Oral Narrative.* Cambridge: Cambridge UP, 1986.

Christian, Barbara. *Black Feminist Criticism.* New York: Pergamon, 1985.

Collins, Patricia Hill. "The Social Construction of Black Feminist Thought." *Black Women in America.* Ed. M.R. Malson, E. Mudimbe-Boyi, J.F. O'Barr, & M. Wyer. Chicago: U of Chicago P, 1988. 297–325.

——. *Black Feminist Thought: Knowledge, Consciousness, and The Politics of Empowerment.* Boston: Unwin Hyman, 1990.

Conquergood, Dwight. "Rethinking Ethnography: Towards A Critical Cultural Politics." *Communication Monographs* 58 (1991): 179–194.

Davis, Angela Y. *Women, Culture, and Politics.* New York: Random House, 1989.

Edit, Edna. "One Hundred Years of Black Music." *The Black Scholar* 7.10 (1976): 38–48.

Fanon, Frantz. *Black Skin, White Mask.* New York: Grove, 1963.

Fine, Elizabeth C. *The Folklore Text: From Performance to Print.* Bloomington: Indiana UP, 1984.

Foucault, Michel. *Discipline and Punish: The Birth of the Prison.* Trans. Alan Sheridan. New York: Random House, 1979.

Freire, Paulo. *Pedagogy of the Oppressed.* New York: The Continuum Corporation, 1986.

Gates, Henry Louis. *The Signifying Monkey: A Theory of Afro-American Literary Criticism.* New York: Oxford UP, 1988.

——. "The Blackness of Blackness: A Critique of the Sign and the Signifying Monkey." *Black Literature and Literary Theory.* Ed. Henry Louis Gates. New York: Methuen, 1984.

Giddings, Paula. *When and Where I Enter: The Impact of Black Women on Race and Sex in America.* New York: Bantam Books, 1984.

Harrison, Paul Carter. *The Drama of Nommo.* New York: Grove P, 1972.

hooks, bell. *Ain't I a Woman? Black Women and Feminism.* Boston: South End P, 1981.

——. *Talking Back: Thinking Feminist/Thinking Black.* Boston: South End P, 1989.

——. *Yearning: Race, Gender, and Cultural Politics.* Boston: South End P, 1990.

Jahn, Janheinze. *Muntu: African Culture and The Western World.* New York: Grove P, 1990.

Jones, LeRoi (Imamu Amiri Baraka). *Blues People.* New York: William Morrow and Company, 1963.

Knight, Etheridge. "On The Oral Nature of Poetry: A Talk by Ethridge Knight." *Painted Bird Quarterly,* 32/38 (1988): 12–17.

Langellier, Kristin M. "Personal Narratives: Perspectives in Theory and Research." *Text and Performance Quarterly* 9 (1989): 243–276.

Ladner, Joyce A. *Tomorrow's Tomorrow: The Black Woman.* New York: Double Day, 1971.

Locke, Alain. *The New Negro: An Interpretation.* Ed. Alain Locke. New York: Albeit Boni, 1925.

McIntyre, Charshee Sharlott Lawrence. "The Double Meanings of the Spirituals." *Journal of Black Studies* 17 (1987): 379–401.

Senghor, Leopold Sedar. *Chants d'Ombre.* Trans. Marjorie Grene. West Germany: Eugene Diederichs Verlag, 1945.

Smith, Barbara. "Toward a Black Feminist Criticism." *All the Women Are White, All the Blacks Are Men, Some of Us Are Brave: Black Women's Studies.* Ed, Gloria T. Hull, Patricia Bell Scott, and Barbara Smith, New York: The Feminist P, 1982. 157–175.

Smith, Valerie. "Black Feminist Theory and the Representation of the "Other." *Changing Our Own Words.* Ed. Cheryl A. Wall. New Brunswick: Rutgers UP, 1991. 38–57.

Smitherman, Geneva. *Talkin and Testifyin: The Language of Black America.* Boston: Houghton-Mifflin, 1977.

Strine, Mary S. "Critical Theory and 'Organic' Intellectuals: Reframing the Work of Cultural Critique." *Communication Monographs* 58 (1991): 195–201.

Tedlock, Dennis. *The Spoken Word and the Work of Interpretation.* Philadelphia: U of Pennsylvania P, 1983.

Turner, Victor. *From Ritual to Theatre: The Human Seriousness of Play.* New York: Performing Arts Journal Publications, 1982.

Van Maanen, John. *Tales of the Field: On Writing Ethnography.* Chicago: U of Chicago P, 1988.

Wallace, Michele. "A Black Feminist's Search for Sisterhood." *All the Women Are White, All the Blacks Are Men, But Some of Us Are Brave: Black Women's Studies.* Ed. Gloria T. Hull, Patricia Bell Scott, and Barbara Smith. New York: The Feminist P, 1982. 5–12.

West, Cornell. *The Ethical Dimensions of Marxist Thought.* New York: Monthly Review P, 1991.

Wilmore, Gayraud S. *Black Religion and Black Radicalism: An Interpretation of the Religious History of Afro-American People.* New York: Orbris Books, 1973.

Reading 4.4 /

INTERROGATING THE REPRESENTATION OF AFRICAN AMERICAN FEMALE IDENTITY IN THE FILMS *WAITING TO EXHALE* AND *SET IT OFF* / TINA M. HARRIS

References

Bobo, J. (1995). "The Color Purple: Black Women as Cultural Readers." In G. Dines and J.M. Humez *Gender, Race, and Class in the Media,* 52–60. Thousand Oaks, CA: Sage Publications.

Collins, P.H. (1996). "Sociological Visions and Revisions." *Contemporary Sociology,* 25(3), May, 328–331.

Collins, P.H. (1993). *Black Feminist Thought: Knowledge, Consciousness, and the Politics of Empowerment.* Routledge: New York.

Gray, H. (1995). *Watching Race: Television and the Struggle For "Blackness."* Minneapolis: University of Minnesota Press.)

Harris, T.M & Hill, P. (1998). "Waiting to Exhale' and 'Breath(ing) Again': A Search for Identity, Empowerment, and Love in the 1990's." *Women and Language.* 9–19.

Hine, D.C. (1992, Summer). "The Black Studies Movement: Afrocentric-Traditionalist-Feminist Paradigm for the Next Stage." *Black Scholar,* 22(3), 11–17.

hooks, b. (1996, Summer). "Sisterhood: Beyond Public and Private." *Signs: Journal of Women in Culture and Society,* 21(4), 814–829.

Inniss, L.B. & Feagin, J. (1995, July). "*The Cosby Show:* The View from the Black Middleclass." *Journal of Black Studies,* 25(6), 692–711.

King, D.K. (1988, Autumn). "Multiple Jeopardy, Multiple Consciousness: The Context of Black Feminist Ideology." *Signs: Journal of Women in Culture and Society,* 14(1), 42–72.

Merritt, B. (1991, Spring). "Bill Cosby: TV Auteur?" *Journal of Popular Culture,* 24(4), 89–102.

Phillips, L. & McCaskill, B. (1995, Summer). "Who's Schooling Who? Black Women and the Bringing of the Everyday into Academe, or Why We Started the Womanist" *Signs: Journal of Women in Culture and Society,* 20(4), 1007–18.

Poussaint, A. (1988, Oct.). "The Huxtables: Fact or Fantasy?" *Ebony,* 43(12), 72–74.

Tucker, R. L. (1997, Winter). "Was the Revolution Televised: Professional Criticism about *The Cosby Show* and the Essentialization of Black Cultural Expression." *Journal of Broadcasting and Electronic Media,* 42(1), 90–108.

Reading 4.5 /
DEFINING BLACK MASCULINITY AS CULTURAL PROPERTY /
RONALD L. JACKSON II & CELNISHA L. DANGERFIELD

Notes

1. We purposefully use the term "Black" instead of African American for two reasons: (1) to accent the body politic inherent in seeing the color black during interracial interaction and (2) to make the point that "Black" refers to peoples throughout the Diaspora who are Black, from Brazil to Trinidad to the United states and beyond. These Black masculinities share the common positionalities and overall struggle discussed in the Black masculine identity theory.

2. Incidentally, these are often the same people who believe that all humans share the same desires, interests, needs, and motivations.

3. According to Nakim Akbar (1991): "A male is a biological entity. . . . One need not look beyond the observable anatomical characteristics to determine that he is a male. Maleness is also a mentality that operates with the same principles as biology. It is a mentality dictated by appetite and physical determinants. This mentality is one guided by instincts, urges, desires, and feelings. He is in this mentality a whining, crying, hungry, and dependent little leech. The next stage in the transformation from the biologically bound definition of 'male' is the development of the 'boy.' The movement is determined by the development of discipline. Once the mind has become disciplined, the boy is in a position to grow into reasoning. . . . When the primary use of your reason is for the purpose of scheming or lying then you are fixated in the boyish mentality. . . . The thing that transforms a boy into becoming a man is knowledge." (pp. 3–12).

References

Best, S. M. (1996). "Stand by your main": Richard Wright, lynch pedagogy, and rethinking black male agency. In M. Blount & G. P. Cunningham (Eds.), *Representing black men* (pp. 131–154). New York: Routledge.

Collins, P. (1991). *Black feminist thought: Knowledge, consciousness, and the politics of empowerment.* New York: Routledge.

Cunningham, G. P. (1996). Body politics: Race, gender, and the captive body. In M. Blount & G. P. Cunningham (Eds.), *Representing black men* (pp. 131–154). New York: Routledge.

Deetz, S. (1992). *Democracy in an age of corporate colonialization: Developments in communication and the politics of everyday life. Albany:* SUNY Press.

Dixon, T., & Linz, D. (2000). Overrepresentation and underrepresentation of African Americans and Latinos as lawbreakers on television news. *Journal of Communication, 50(2),* 131–154.

Entman, R. M. (1992). Blacks in the news: Television, modern racism and cultural change. *Journalism Quarterly, 69(2),* 341–361.

Entman, R. M., & Rojecki, A. (2000). *The Black image in the White mind: Media and race in America.* Chicago: University of Chicago.

FAO Girl. (2000). Available: *www.fao.com.*

Gatens, M. (1996). *Imaginary bodies: Ethics, power, and corporeality.* New York: Routledge.

Gray, H. (1997). *Watching race: Television and the struggle for the sign of blackness.* Minneapolis: University of Minnesota Press.

Hall, S. (1997). *Representation: Cultural representatives and signifying practices (culture, media, and identifiers).* Thousand Oaks, CA: Sage.

Heider, B. (2000). *White news: Why local news programs don't cover people of color.* Mahwah, NJ: Lawrence Earlbaum Associates.

hooks, b. (1992). *Black looks: Race and representation.* Boston: South End.

Jackson, R. L. (1997, July). Black "manhood" as xenophobe: An ontological exploration of the Hegelian dialectic. *Journal of Black Studies 27(6),* 731–750.

Lorde, A. (1984). *Sister outsider.* Freedom, CA: Crossing Press.

Madhubuti, H. (1990). *Black men: Obsolete, single, dangerous?* Chicago: Third World Press.

Majors, R., & Billson, J. (1992). *Cool pose: The dilemmas of Black manhood in America.* New York: Lexington Books.

Marable, M. (2001). The Black male: Searching beyond stereotypes. In M. Kimmel & M. Messner (Eds.), *Men's lives* (6th ed.). Boston: Allyn & Bacon.

Mohanty, C. (1994). On race and violence: Challenges for liberal education in the 1990s. In H. Giroux & P. McLaren (Eds.), *Between borders: Pedagogy and the politics of cultural studies.* New York: Routledge.

Oliver, W. (1989). Black males and social problems: Prevention through Afrocentric socialization. *Journal of Black Studies, 20(1),* 15–39.

Ribeau, S., Baldwin, J., & Hecht, M. (1997). An African American communication perspective. In L. Samovar & R. Porter (Eds.), *Intercultural communication: A reader* (8th ed., pp.147–153). Belmont, CA: Wadsworth.

Roberts, G. (1994). Brother to brother: African American modes of relating among men. *Journal of Black Studies, 24(1),* 379–390.

Walzer, M. (1997). *On toleration.* New Haven, CT: Yale University Press.

Reading 5.1 /
"DIVERSITY" AND
ORGANIZATIONAL COMMUNICATION /
BRENDA J. ALLEN

References

Alderfer, C. P. (1990). Reflections on race relations and organizations. *Journal of Organizational Behavior, 11,* 493–495.

Amott, T. L., & Matthaei, J. (1991), *Race, gender and work. A multi-cultural history of women in the United States.* Boston, MA: South End Press.

Bell, E. L. (1992). Myths, stereotypes and realities of black women: A personal reflection. *The Journal of Applied Beahvioral Science, 28,* 363–376.

Boyer, E. P., & Webb, T. G. (1992). Ethics and diversity: A correlation enhanced through corporate communication. *IEEE Transactions on Professional Communcation, 35,* 38–43.

Cannon, L. W. ., Higginbotham, E., & Leung, M. L. A (1988). Race and class bias in qualitative research on women. *Gender and Society, 2,* 449–462.

Cheney, G. (1983). The rhetoric of identification and the study of organizational communication. *Quarterly Journal of Speech, 69,* 143–158.

Coleman, T. (1990). Managing diversity at work: The new American dilemma. *Public Management, 72,* 2–6.

Collins, P.H. (1990). The social construction of black feminist thought. In M. Malson, E. Mudombe-Boyi, J.O' Barr, & M. Wyer (Eds.), *Black women in America (*pp. 94–120). Chicago: University of Chicago Press.

Conrad C. (1994) *Strategic communication: Toward the twenty-first century,* Third Edition. Fort Worth, TX: Harcourt, Brace and Jovanovich.

Corman, S. R., Banks, S. P., Bantz., C. R., & Mayer M. E. (1990). *Foundations of organizational communication: A reader.* New York: Longman.

Cortese. A. (1990). *Ethnic ethics: The restructuring of moral theory.* Albany, NY: State University of New York Press.

Cox, M. (1983). The effectiveness of black identification and organizational identification on communication supportiveness. Ph. D. dissertation, Purdue University.

Cox, M. (1988). The impact of sex and black identification or evaluations of communicator style: Implications for organizational sense-making. In L. B. Nadler, M. K. Nadler, & W. R. Todd-Mancillas (Eds.), *Advances in gender and communication research* (pp. 317–348). Lanham, MD: University Press of America.

Cox, T. (1990). Problems with research by organizational scholars on issues of race and ethnicity. *The Journal of Applied Behavioral Science, 26,* 5–23.

Cox, T., Lobel, S. A., & McLeod, P. L. (1991). Effects of ethnic group cultural differences of cooperative and competitive behavior on a group task, *Academy of Management Journal, 34,* 827–847.

Cox, T., & Nkomo, S. (1986). Differential performance appraisal criteria. A field study of black and white managers, *Group & Organizations Studies, 11,* 101–119.

Daniel, J., & Smitherman, G. (1976). How I got over: communication dynamics in the black community. *Quarterly Journal of Speech, 62,* 26–39.

Eisenberg, E. M., & Goodall, H. L. (1994). *Organizational communication: Balancing creativity and constraint.* New York: St. Martin's Press.

Essed, P. (1991). Understanding everyday racism: An interdisciplinary theory. Newbury Park, CA: Sage.

Feagin, J. R. (1991). The continuing significance of race: Antiblack discrimination in public places. *American Sociological Review, 56,* 101–116.

Feagin, J. R. (1992). The continuing significance of racism: Discrimination against black students in white colleges. *Journal of Black Studies, 22,* 546–578.

Fernandez, J. P. (1981). *Racism and sexism in corporate life.* Lexington, MA: D. C. Heath and Company.

Foeman, A. K., & Pressley, G. (1987). Ethnic culture and corporate culture: Using black styles in organizations, *Communication Quarterly, 35,* 293–307.

Foss, K. A., & Foss, S. K. (1989). Incorporating the feminist perspective in communication scholarship: A research commentary. In K. Carter & C. Spitzack (Eds.), *Doing research on women's communication: Perspectives on theory and method* (pp. 65–91). Norwood, NJ: Ablex Publishing Co.

Foucault, M. (1980). *Power/knowledge.* G. Gordon. (Ed., Trans.) New York: Pantheon.

Gibb, J. R. (1961). Defensive communication. *Journal of Communication, 11,* 141–148.

Giles, H., & Johnson, P. (1986). Perceived threat, ethnic commitment and interethnic language behavior. In Y. Y. Kim (Ed.), *Interethnic communication: Current research* (pp. 91–116). Beverly Hills, CA: Sage.

Harding, S. (1991). *Whose Science? Whose knowledge?: Thinking from women's lives.* Ithaca. NY: Cornell University Press.

Harris, T. E. (1993). *Applied Organizational Communication: Perspectives, Principles, and Pragmatics.* Hillsdale, NJ: Lawrence Erlbaum Associates.

Hecht, M. L., Collier, M. J., & Ribeau, S. A. (1993). *African American communication: Ethnic identity and cultural interpretation.* Newbury Park, CA: Sage.

Hecht, M. L., Ribeau, S. A., & Alberts, J. K. (1989). An Afro-American perspective on interethnic communication. *Communication Monographs, 56,* 385–410.

Herndon, S. L., & Kreps, G. L. *Qualitative research: Applications in organizational communication* Cresskill, NJ: Hampton Press, Inc.

Hofstede, G. (1980). *Culture's consequences.* Beverly Hills, CA: Sage.

Hopkins, W. E., & Hopkins, S. A. (1994). Impacts of diversity on communication effectiveness: A proposed typology. *Journal of Business and Technical Communication, 8,* 335–343.

Houston, M. (1994). When black women talk with white women: Why dialogues are difficult. In A. Gonzalez, M. Houston, & V. Chen (Eds.) *Our voices: Essays in culture, ethnicity, and communication* (pp. 133–139). Los Angeles: Roxbury Publishing Co.

Jablin, F. (1987). Organizational entry, assimilation, and exit. In F. M. Jablin, L. L. Putnam, K. H. Roberts, & L. W. Porter (Eds)., *Handbook of organizational communication* (pp. 679–740). Newbury Park, CA: Sage.

Jackson, S. E., & Associates (1992). *Diversity in the workplace: Human resources initiatives.* New York: Guilford Press.

James, C. E. (1994). The paradox of power and privilege. Race, gender and occupational position. *Canadian Women's Studies, 14,* 47–51.

James, N. C. (1994). When miss America was always white. In A. Gonzalez, M. Houston, & V. Chen (Eds.) *Our voices: Essays in culture, ethnicity, and communication* (pp. 43–47). Los Angeles: Roxbury Publishing Co.

Johnson, F. I., & Buttny, R. (1982). White listeners' responses to "sounding black" and "sounding white": The effects of message content and judgments about language. *Communication Monographs, 49,* 33–49.

Johnston, W. B., & Packer, A. H. (1987). *Workforce 2000: Work and workers for the 21st century.* Hudson Institute, Indianapolis, IN. 33–49.

Jones, E. W. (1973). What it's like to be a black manager. *Harvard Business Review, 51,* 108–116.

Jones, E. W. (1986). Black managers: The dream deferred. *Harvard Business Review, 64,* 84–93.

Knouse, S. B., Rosenfeld, P. & Culbertson, A. M. (1992). *Hispanics in the workplace.* Newbury Park, CA: Sage.

Kochman, T. (1981). *Black and white styles in conflict.* Chicago: University of Chicago Press.

Kohlberg, L. (1984). *Essays in moral development: vol. II, the psychology of moral development.* New York: Harper & Row.

Kossek, E. E., & Zonia. S. D (1994). The effects of race and ethnicity on perceptions of human resource policies and climate regarding diversity. *Journal of Business and technical communication, 8,* 319–334.

Kraiger, K., & Ford. J. K. (1985). A meta-analysis of rate race effects in performance ratings, *Journal of Applied Psychology, 70,* 56–65.

Kreps. G. L., Frey, L. R., & O'Hair, D. (1991). Applied communication research: scholarship that can make a difference. *Journal of Applied Communication Research 19,* 71–87.

Leonard, R., & Locke. D. C. (1993). Communication stereotypes: Is interracial communication possible? *Journal of Black Studies, 23,* 332–343.

Lewan, L. S (1990). Diversity in the workplace. *HRMagzine, 35,* 42–49.

Limaye, M. R. (1994). Responding To work-force diversity: Conceptualization and search for paradigms. *Journal of Business and Technical Communication, 8,* 353–372.

Marable. M. (1990). The rhetoric of racial harmony: Finding substance in culture and ethnicity. *Sojourner, 15,* 14–18.

Minnich, E. K. (1990). *Transforming knowledge.* Philadelphia: Temple University Press.

Moses. Y. T. (1989). Black women in academe: Issues and strategies. Project on the Status and Education of Women, Association of American Colleges, Washington, D. C.

Mumby, D. K. (1993). Critical organizational communication studies: The next 10 years. *Communication Monographs, 60,* 18–25.

Nieves-Squires, S. (1991). Hispanic women: Making their presence on campus less tenuous. Project on the Status and Education of Women. Association of American Colleges. Washington, D.C.

Nkomo. S. M. (1992). The emperor has no clothes: Rewriting "race in organizations." *Academy of Management Journal, 17,* 487–513.

Nkomo. S. M., & Cox, T. (1989). Factors affecting the upward mobility of black managers in private sector organizations. *The Review of Black Political Economy,* 17, 39–57.

Ownby, A. C., & Cunningham, K. L (1992). Managing and teaching diversity in business communication. *Business Education Forum.*

Pennington. D. L. (1979). Black-white communication. In M. Asante, E. Newmark, & C. Black (Eds.), *Handbook of intercultural communication* (pp. 383–402). Beverly Hills: Sage.

Pepper, G. L. (1995). *Communication in organizations: A cultural approach.* New York: McGraw-Hill.

Plax, T. G. (1991). Understanding applied communication inquiry: Researcher as organizational consultant. *Journal of Applied Communication.* 19, 55–70.

Rothenberg, P. S. (1988). *Racism and Sexism: an integrated study.* New York: St. Martin's Press.

Royce, A. P. (1982). *Ethnic identity.* Bloomington, IN: Indiana University Press.

Smitherman, G. (1977). *Talkin' and testifying' The language of black America.* Boston: Houghton-Mifflin.

Spelman, E. V. (1988). *Inessential woman: Problems of exclusion in feminist though.* Boston: Beacon Press.

Thomas. D. A. (1989). Mentoring and irrationality: The role of racial taboos. *Human Resource Management,* 28, 279–290

Thomas, D. A. (1990). The impact of race on managers' experiences of developmental relationships (mentoring and sponsorship): An intra- organizational study. *Journal of Organizational Behavior,* 11, 479–492.

Thomas, D. A. (1993). Racial dynamics in cross-race developmental relationships. *Administrative Science Quarterly, 38,* 160–194.

Tompkins. P. K., & Cheney, G. (1985). Communication and unobtrusive control in contemporary organizations In. R. D. McPhee & P. K. Tompkins (Eds.), *Organizational communication: Traditional themes and new directions,* (pp. 179–210). Beverly Hills, CA: Sage.

Triandis, H. C., & Albert, R. D (1987).Cross-cultural perspectives. In F. M. Jablin, L. L. Putnam, K.H. Roberts, & L. W. Porter (Eds.) *Handbook of organizational communication: An interdisciplinary perspective,* (pp. 264–296). Newbury Park, CA: Sage.

Van Dijk, T. A. (1993). *Elite discourse and racism.* Newbury Park, CA: Sage Publications.

Van Maanen. J., & Schein. E. H. (1979). Toward a theory of organizational socialization. *Research in Organizational Behavior, 1,* 209–264.

Wharton, A. S. (1992). The social construction of gender and race organizations: A social identity and group mobilization perspective. *Research in the Sociology of Organizations, 10,* 55–84.

Wolfram, W. (1977). Black-white speech differences revisited. In W. Wolfram & N. H. Clark (Eds.) *Black-white speech relationships* (pp. 139–161). Washington, DC: Center for Applied Linguistics.

Wood, J. T. (1993). Gender and moral voice: Moving from woman's nature to standpoint epistemology. *Women's Studies in Communication, 15,* 1–24.

Wood, J. T., & Cox, R. (1993). Rethinking critical voice: Materiality and situated knowledges. *Western Journal of Communication, 57,* 278–287.

Zak, M. W. (1994). It's like a prison in there. *Journal of Business and Technical Communication, 8,* 282–298.

Reading 5.2 /

AFRICAN AMERICAN WOMEN EXECUTIVES' LEADERSHIP COMMUNICATION WITHIN DOMINANT-CULTURE ORGANIZATIONS / PATRICIA S. PARKER

Notes

1. The terms *White* and *Black* are capitalized to emphasize the point that race structures the experiences of both groups in ways that significantly shape their identities (Dugger, 1991). I use the terms *Black* and *African American,* and *White, Anglo,* and *European American* interchangeably.

2. Please see Parker (1997) for detailed demographic information about the sample.

References

Allen, B. J. (1995). "Diversity" and organizational communication. *Journal of Applied Communication Research, 23,* 143–155.

Allen, B. J. (1996). Feminist standpoint theory: A Black woman's (re)view of organizational socialization. *Communication Studies, 47,* 257–271.

Allen, B. J. (1998). Black womanhood and feminist standpoints. *Management Communication Quarterly, 11,* 575–586.

Allen, B. J. (2000). "Learning the ropes": A Black feminist standpoint analysis. In P. M. Buzzanell (Ed.), *Rethinking organizational and managerial communication from feminist perspectives* (pp. 177–208). Thousand Oaks, CA: Sage.

Alvesson, M., & Billing, Y. D. (1997). *Understanding gender and organizations.* London: Sage.

Andersen, M. L., & Collins, P. H. (1992). *Race, class, and gender: An anthology.* Belmont, CA: Wadsworth.

Andolsen, B. H. (1986). *Daughters of Jefferson, daughters of bootblacks: Racism and American feminism.* Macon, GA: Mercer University Press.

Avolio, B. J., & Bass, B. M. (1988). Transformational leadership, charisma and beyond. In G. Hung, B. R. Balaga, H. P. Dachler, & C. Schriesheim (Eds.), *Emerging leadership vistas* (pp. 29–50). Elmsford, NY: Pergamon.

Bass, B. M. (1985), *Leadership and performance beyond expectations.* New York: Free Press.

Bell, E. (1997). Listen up. You have to: Voices from "women in communication." *Western Journal of Communication, 61,* 89–100.

Bell, E. L., & Nkomo, S. (1992). *The glass ceiling vs. the concrete wall: Career perceptions of White and African American women managers* (Working Paper No. 3470–92). Cambridge: Massachusetts Institute of Technology.

Bem, S. (1974). The measurement of psychological androgyny. *Journal of Consulting and Clinical Psychology, 42,* 155–162.

Bhavnani, K. (1992). Talking racism and editing women's studies. In D. Richardson & V. Robinson (Eds.), *Thinking feminist* (pp. 27–48), New York: Guilford.

Biggart, N. W., & Hamilton, G. G. (1984). The power of obedience. *Administrative Science Quarterly, 29,* 540–549.

Blumer, H. (1969). *Symbolic interactionism: Perspective and method.* Englewood Cliffs, NJ: Prentice Hall.

Bruner, J. (1990). *Acts of meaning.* Cambridge, MA: Harvard University Press.

Bullis, C. (1993a). At least it's a start. *Communication Yearbook, 16,* 144–154.

Bullis, C. (1993b). Organizational socialization research: Enabling, constraining, and shifting perspectives. *Communication Monographs, 60,* 10–17.

Burns, J. M. (1978). *Leadership.* New York: Harper & Row.

Buzzanell, P. (1994). Gaining a voice: Feminist organizational communication theorizing. *Management Communication Quarterly, 7,* 339–383.

Calas, M. B., & Smircich, L. (1988). Reading leadership as a form of cultural analysis. In J. G. Hunt, B. R. Baliga, H. P. Dachler, & C. A. Schriesheim (Eds.), *Emerging leadership vistas* (pp. 201–226). Lexington, MA: Lexington Books.

Calas, M. B. & Smircich, L. (1991). Voicing seduction to silence leadership *Organization Studies, 12,* 567–602.

Christian, B. (1980). *Black women novelists: The development of a tradition, 1892–1976.* Westport, CT: Greenwood.

Cockburn, C. (1991). *In the way of women.* London: Macmillan.

Collins, P. H. (1986). Learning from the outsider within: The sociological significance of Black feminist thought. *Social Problems, 33*(6), 14–32.

Collins, P. H. (1990). *Black feminist thought: Knowledge, consciousness, and the politics of empowerment.* Winchester, MA Unwin Hyman.

Collins, P. H. (1998a). *Fighting words: Black women and the search for justice.* Minneapolis: University of Minnesota Press.

Collins, P. H. (1998b). Toward a new vision: Race, class, and gender as categories of analysis and connection. In M. L. Anderson & P. H. Collins (Eds.), *Race, class, and gender: An anthology* (pp. 213–223). Belmont, CA: Wadsworth.

Connel, R. (1995). *Masculinities.* Cambridge, UK: Polity.

Deetz, S. A. (1995). *Transforming communication.* Albany: State University of New York Press.

Dill, B. T. (1983). Race, class, and gender: Prospects for an all-inclusive sisterhood. *Feminist Studies, 9,* 131–150.

Dugger, K. (1991). Social location and gender role attitudes: A comparison of Black and White women. In B. Lorber & S. Farrell (Eds.), *The social construction of gender* (pp. 38–55). Newbury Park, CA: Sage.

Eagly, A. H. (1987). *Sex differences in social behavior: A social-role interpretation.* Hillsdale, NJ: Lawrence Erlbaum.

Eagly, A. H., & Karau, S. J. (1991). Gender and the emergence of leaders: A meta-analysis, *Journal of Personality and Social Psychology, 60,* 685–710.

Eisenberg, E. M., & Goodall, H. L., Jr. (1997). *Organizational communication: Balancing creativity and constraint* (2nd ed.). New York: St. Martin's.

Fairhurst, G. T. (2000). Dualisms in leadership research. In F. M. Jablin & L. L. Putnam (Eds.), *The new handbook of organizational communication* (pp. 379–439). Thousand Oaks, CA: Sage.

Fairhurst, G. T., & Saar, R. A. (1996). *The art of framing: Managing the language of leadership.* San Francisco: Jossey-Bass.

Ferguson, K. (1984). *The feminist case against bureaucracy.* Philadelphia: Temple University Press.

Fine, M. (1991). New voices in the workplace: Research directions in multicultural communication. *The Journal of Business Communication, 23,* 259–275.

Fine, M. (1995). *Building successful multicultural organizations.* Westport, CT: Quorum Books.

Fine, M. (1994). Working the hyphens: Reinventing self and other in qualitative research. In N. K. Denzin & Y. S. Lincoln (Eds.), *Handbook of qualitative research* (pp. 70–82). Thousand Oaks, CA: Sage.

Fletcher, J. (1994). Castrating the female advantage: Feminist standpoint research and management science. *Journal of Management Inquiry, 3,* 74–82.

Fordham, S. (1993). "Those loud Black girls": Black women, silence, and gender, "passing" in the academy. *Anthropology and Education Quarterly, 24*(1), 3–32.

Gibson, M. K., & Papa, M. J. (2000). The mud, the blood, and the beer guys: Organizational osmosis in blue-collar work groups. *Journal of Applied Communication Research, 28,* 68–88.

Gilligan, C., Taylor, J. M., Tolman, D., Sullivan, A., Pleasants, P., & Dorney, J. (1992). The relational world of adolescent girls considered to be at risk. In *understanding adolescents: A study of urban teens considered to be at risk and a project to strengthen connections between girls and women* (Final report to the Boston Foundation). Cambridge, MA: Harvard Graduate School of Education.

Gonzalez, A., Houston, M., & Chen, V. (Eds.). (1997). *Our voices: Essays in culture, ethnicity, and communication* (2nd ed.). Los Angeles: Roxbury.

Grant, J. (1998). Women as managers: What they can offer to organizations. *Organizational Dynamics, 16*(1), 56–63.

Greenleaf, R. F. (1977). *Servant leadership: A journey into the nature of legitimate power and greatness.* Mawah, NJ: Paulist Press.

Harding, S. (1987). Introduction: Is there a feminist method? In S. Harding (Ed.), *Feminism & methodology* (pp. 1–14). Milton Keynes, UK: Open University Press.

Harding, S. (1991). *Whose science? Whose knowledge?* Ithaca, NY: Cornell University Press.

Hartsock, N. (1987). The feminist standpoint: Developing the ground for a specifically feminist historical materialism. In S. Harding (Ed.), *Feminism & methodology* (pp. 157–180). Milton Keynes, UK: Open University Press.

Hecht, M., Ribeau, S., & Roberts, J. K. (1989). An Afro-American perspective on interethnic communication. *Communication Monographs, 56,* 385–410.

Helgesen, S. (1990). *The female advantage: Women's ways of leadership.* New York: Doubleday.

Henderson, M. G. (1989). Speaking in tongues: Dialogics, dialects, and the Black woman writer's literary tradition. In C.A. Wall (Ed.). *Changing our own words: Essays on criticism, theory, and writing by Black women* (pp. 16–37). New Brunswick, NJ: Rutgers University Press.

hooks, b. (1981). *Ain't I a woman: Black women and feminism.* Boston: South End Press.

hooks, b. (1984). *Feminist theory from margin to center.* Boston: South End Press.

hooks, b. (1990). *Yearning: Race, gender, and cultural politics.* Boston: South End Press.

Houston, M. (1988). What makes scholarship about Black women and communication feminist communication scholarship? *Women's Studies in Communication, 10,* 78–85.

Houston, M. (1997). When Black women talk with White women: Why dialogues are difficult. In A. Gonzalez, M. Houston, & V. Chen (Eds.), *Our voices: Essays in culture, ethnicity, and communication* (2nd ed., pp. 187–194). Los Angeles: Roxbury.

Hull, G. T., Scott, P. B., & Smith, B. (Eds.). (1982). *All the women are White, all the men are Black, but some of us are brave: Black women's studies.* Old Westbury, NY: Feminist Press.

Johnston, W. B., & Packer, A. H. (1987). *Workforce 2000: Work and workers for the 21st century.* Indianapolis, IN: Hudson Institute.

Kellerman, B. (1984). Leadership as a political act. In B. Kellerman (Ed.), *Leadership: Multidisciplinary perspectives* (pp. 63–89). Englewood Cliffs, NJ: Prentice Hall.

Kennedy, G. A. (1980). *Classical rhetoric.* Chapel Hill: University of North Carolina Press.

Ladner, J. (1971). *Tomorrow's tomorrow.* Garden City, NY: Doubleday.

Loden, M. (1985) *Feminine leadership or: How to succeed in business without being one of the boys.* New York: Times Books.

Lorde, A. (1984). *Sister outsider.* Trumansberg, NY: Crossing Press.

Lubiano, W. (1992). Black ladies, welfare queens, and state minstrels: Ideological war by narrative means. In T. Morrison (Ed.), *Racing justice, engendering power: Essays on Anita Hill, Clarence Thomas, and the construction of social reality* (pp. 323–361). New York: Pantheon.

Lunneborg, P. (1990). *Women changing work.* Westport, CT: Greenwood.

Mainiero, L. (1994). Getting anointed for advancement: The case of executive women. *The Academy of Management Executive, 8 (2),* 53–68.

Marshall, J. (1993). Viewing organizational communication from a feminist perspective: A critique and some offerings. *Communication Yearbook, 16,* 122–143.

McGoldrick, M., Garcia–Preto, N., Hines, P. M., Lee. E. (1988). Ethnicity and women. In M. McGoldrick, C. Anderson, & F. Walsh (Eds), *Women in families* (pp. 169–199). New York: Norton.

Mead, G. H. (1934). *Mind, self, and society.* Chicago: University of Chicago Press.

Moraga, C., & Anzaldua, G. (Eds.) (1983). *This bridge called my back: Writings by radical women of color.* New York: Kitchen Table, Women of Color Press.

Morton, P. (1991). *Disfigured images: The historical assault on Afro–American women.* Westport, CT: Greenwood.

Mumby, D. (1993). Feminism and the critique of organizational communication studies. *Communication Yearbook, 16,* 155–166.

Nkomo, S. M. (1988). Race and sex: The forgotten case of the black female manager. In S. Rose & L. Larwood (Eds.), *Women's careers: Pathways and pitfalls* (pp. 133–150). New York: Praeger.

Nkomo, S. M. (1992). The emperor has no clothes: Rewriting race in organizations. *Academy of Management Review, 17,* 487–513.

Orbe, M.P. (1997).*Constructing co-cultural theory: An explication of culture, power, and communication.* Thousand Oaks, CA: Sage.

Parker, P.S. (1997). *African American women executives within dominant-culture organizations: An examination of leadership socialization, communication strategies, and leadership behavior.* Unpublished doctoral dissertation, University of Texas at Austin (University Microfilms Number 9802988)

Parker, P. S., & ogilvie, d. t. (1996). Gender, culture, and leadership: Toward a culturally distinct model of African-American women executives' leadership strategies. *Leadership Quarterly* 7(2), 189–214.

Rorty, R. (1989). *Contingency, irony, and solidarity.* Cambridge, UK: Cambridge University Press.

Rosener, J.B (1990). Ways women lead. *Harvard Business Review, 68(6),* 11–12.

Rost, J. C. (1991). *Leadership for the twenty-first century.* Westport, CT: Praeger.

Rowe, A. (2000). Locating feminism's subject: The paradox of White femininity and the struggle to forge feminist alliances. *Communication Theory, 10,* 64–80.

Sayre, S. (1986). *Leadership communication and organizational culture: A field study.* Unpublished doctoral dissertation, University of San Diego, CA.

Schein, E. (1985). *Organizational culture and leadership.* San Francisco: Jossey–Bass.

Shuter, R., & Turner, L. H. (1997). African American and European American women in the workplace: Perceptions of workplace communication. *Management Communication Quarterly. 11,* 74–96.

Smircich, L., & Morgan, G. (1982). Leadership and the management of meaning. *Journal of Applied Behavioral Science, 18,* 257–273.

Smith, D. (1987). *The everyday world as problematic: A feminist sociology* Boston: Northeastern University Press.

Stohl, C., & Cheney, G. (2001). Participatory processes/paradoxical practices: Communication and dilemmas of organizational democracy. *Management Communication Quarterly, 14,* 349–407.

Strauss, A., & Corbin, J. (1990). *Basics of qualitative research: Grounded theory procedures and techniques.* Newbury Park, CA: Sage.

Tannen, D. (1990). *You just don't understand: Women and men in conversation.* New York: William Morrow.

Vande Berg, L. (1997). Editor's introduction: special series on voices. *Western Journal of Communication, 61,* 87–88.

Walker A. (1983). *In search of our mothers' gardens.* New York: Harcourt Brace Jovanovich.

Weick, K. (1978). The spines of leaders. In M. W. McCall & M. Lombardo (Eds.), *Leadership, where else can we go?* Durham, NC: Duke University Press.

Weitz, R., & Gordon, L. (1993). Images of Black women among Anglo college students. *Sex Roles, 28,* 19–34.

Wood, J.T (1993). From "woman's nature" to standpoint epistemology: Gilligan and the debate over essentializing in feminist scholarship. *Women's Studies in Communication, 15,* 1–24.

Wood, J.T. (1998). *Gendered lives: Communication, gender, and culture (*2nd ed.). Belmont, CA: Wadsworth.

Yukl, G. (1989). Managerial leadership: A review of theory and research. *Journal of Management, 15,* 251–289.

Reading 5.3 /
STUDENT PERCEPTIONS OF THE INFLUENCE
OF RACE ON PROFESSOR CREDIBILITY /
KATHERINE GRACE HENDRIX

Notes

1. The credibility literature review spans the 80-year period from 1915 to 1996. The following journals were reviewed by the author from inception through 1996; *Association for Communication Administration Bulletin, Central States Speech Journal, Communication Education, Communication Monographs, Communication Quarterly, Critical Studies in Mass Communication, Human Communication Research, Journal of Communication, Philosophy and Rhetoric, Southern Communication Journal, Quarterly Journal of Speech*, and the *Western Journal of Speech Communication*. The researcher recognizes that the term *ethos* or the terms representing the specific dimensions of credibility (e.g., integrity and trust-worthiness) will undoubtedly reveal more studies. I chose to narrow the literature review to a manageable group of 99 studies by reading the research with the term *credibility* used in the title. Another useful summary of credibility research can be found in O'Keefe's (1991) text, *Persuasion: Theory and Research.*

2. The four research questions were originally worded as follows:

RQ1: What verbal and nonverbal communication cues do professors believe lead their students to perceive them as credible?

RQ2: What verbal and nonverbal communication cues exhibited by professors lead students to perceive their professors as credible?

RQ3: When the professor's race is not the same as the majority of the students' in the class, what verbal and nonverbal cues does the professor view as leading to student perceptions of credibility?

RQ4: When the professor's race is not the same as the majority of the students' in the class, what verbal and nonverbal cues do the students view as leading to perceptions of credibility?

3. The original document was two pages printed back-to-back to allow for writing space. Question 3 under Section C did not appear on the survey in Study 1.

References

Allen, S. S., Heckel, R. V., & Garcia, S. J. (1980). The Black researcher: A view from inside the goldfish bowl. *American Psychologist, 35* (8), 767–771.

Banks, J. A. (1986). Race, ethnicity, and schooling in the United States. In J. A. Banks & J. Lynch (Eds.), *Multicultural education in western societies* (pp. 30–50). New York: Holt, Rinehart, & Winston.

Bassett, R. E., & Smythe, M. (1979). *Communication and instruction.* New York: Harper and Row.

Beatty, M. J., & Behnke, R. R. (1980). Teacher credibility as a function of verbal content and paralinguistic cues. *Communication Quarterly, 9*(1), 55–59.

Beatty, M. J., & Zahn, C. J. (1990). Are student ratings of communication instructors due to "easy" grading practices? An analysis of teacher credibility and student reported performance levels. *Communication Education, 39,* 275–282.

Brophy, J. E. (1979). Teacher behavior and its effects. *Journal of Educational Psychology, 71,* 733–750.

Coffin, G. (1980). The Black principal—the vanishing American, *Professional Psychology, 11*(5), 39–44.

Collins, P. H. (1991). Learning from the outsider within: The sociological significance of Black feminist thought. In M. M. Fonow & J. A. Cook (Eds.), *Beyond methodology: Feminist scholarship as lived research* (pp. 35–59). Bloomington: Indiana University Press.

Cook, D. A. (1990). Alienation of Black college students on White campuses: University-centered and student-centered interventions. *Educational Considerations, 18,* 19–22.

Delpit, L. (1995). *Other people's children: Cultural conflict in the classroom.* New York: New Press.

Erickson, F. (1986). Qualitative methods in research on teaching. In M. C. Wittrock (Ed.), *Handbook of research on teaching* (pp. 119–161). New York: Macmillan.

Foeman, A. K., & Pressley, G. (1987). Ethnic culture and corporate culture: Using Black styles in organizations. *Communication Quarterly, 35*(4), 293–307.

For the record. (1996, November). *Klanwatch Intelligence Report: A Project of the Southern Poverty Law Center, 84,* 21–31.

Fordharn, S., & Ogbu, J. U. (1986). Black students' school success: Coping with the "burden of 'acting White.'" *The Urban Review, 18*(3), 176–206.

Foster, M. (1990). The politics of race: Through the eyes of African-American teachers. *Journal of Education, 172*(3), 123–141.

Frisby, M. K. (1994, March). Weathering the storm: Ron Brown's nightmarish year at the commerce department. *Emerge,* pp. 46–50.

Frymier, A. B., & Thompson, C. A. (1992). Perceived affinity-seeking in relation to perceived teacher credibility. *Communication Education, 41*(4), 388–399.

Ginsburg, H. P., Jacobs, S. F., & Lopez, L. S. (1992). Assessing mathematical thinking and learning potential. In H. P. Ginsburg, R. B. Davis & C. Maher (Eds.) *Schools, math, and the world of reality* (pp. 237–262). Boston: Allyn & Bacon.

Guess. J. M. (1989). Race: The challenge of the 90s. *Crisis, 96,* 28–30, 32–33.

Hendrix, K. G. (1994). *Is the classroom really like 'To Sir, With Love?' Case studies of professor credibility and race.* Unpublished doctoral dissertation, University of Washington.

Hendrix, K. G. (1997). Student perceptions of verbal and nonverbal cues leading to images of Black and White professor credibility. *The Howard Journal of Communication, 8,* 251–274.

Hymes. D. (1972). Models of the interaction of language and social life. In J. J. Gumperz & D. Hymes (Eds.), *Directions in sociolinguistics: Ethnography of communication* (pp. 35–71). New York: Holt, Rinehart, & Winston.

Ladson-Billings, G. (1994). *The dreamkeepers: Successful teachers of African American children.* San Francisco, CA: Jossey-Bass.

Lopez, T. R. (1991). *Some African-American and Hispanic voices from the University of Toledo: A monograph* (ERIC Document Reproduction Service No. ED 328153). Toledo, OH: University of Toledo.

Magner, D. K. (1996, February 2). The new generation: Study shows proportions of the female and minority professors are growing. *The Chronicle of Higher Education,* pp. A17-A18.

Mathison, S. (1988). Why triangulate? *Educational Research, 17,* 5–12.

McCroskey, J. C., Holdridge, W., & Toomb, J. K. (1974). An instrument for measuring the source credibility of basic speech communication instructors. *The Speech Teacher, 23* 26–33.

McGlone, E. L., & Anderson, L. J. (1973). The dimensions of teacher credibility. *The Speech Teacher, 22,* 196–200.

Miles, M. B., & Huberman, A. M. (1984). *Qualitative data analysis: A sourcebook of new methods.* Newbury Park: Sage.

Moss, J. A. (1958). Negro teachers in predominantly White colleges. *Journal of Negro Education, 27*(4), 451–462.

Nisbett, R., & Ross, L. (1980). *Human inference: Strategies and shortcomings of social judgment.* Englewood Cliffs, NJ: Prentice Hall.

O'Keefe, D. J. (1991). *Persuasion: Theory and research* (3rd ed.). Newbury Park, CA: Sage.

Rose, H. M. (1966). An appraisal of the Negro educator's situation in the academic marketplace. *Journal of Negro Education, 35*(1), 18–26.

Shulman, L. S. (1986). Paradigms and research programs in the study of teaching: A contemporary perspective. In M.C. Wittrock (Ed.), *Handbook of research on teaching* (pp. 3–36). New York: Macmillan.

Smith, J. W. & Smith, B. M. (1973). For Black educators: Integration brings the axe. *The Urban Review, 6*(3), 7–12.

Spradley, J. P. (1979). *The ethnographic interview,* New York: Holt, Rinehart, and Winston.

Spradley, J. P. (1980). *Participant observation.* New York: Holt, Rinehart, & Winston.

Tucker, R. K. (1971). Reliability of semantic differential scales: The role of factor analysis. *Western Speech, 35,* 185–190.

Weinberg, M. (1977). *A chance to learn: The history of race and education in the United States.* Cambridge, UK: Cambridge University Press.

Wheeless, L. R. (1974a). The relationship of attitude and credibility to comprehensive and selective exposure. *Western Speech, 33*(2), 88–97.

Wheeless, L. R. (1974b). The effect of attitude, credibility, and homophily on selective exposure to information. *Speech Monographs, 41(4),* 329–338.

Reading 5.4 /
EXPLORING AFRICAN AMERICAN IDENTITY NEGOTIATION IN THE ACADEMY / RONALD L. JACKSON II

References

Ani, M. (1994). *Yurugu.* Trenton, NJ: Africa World Press.

Asante, M. (1988). *Afrocentricity: A theory of social change.* Trenton, NJ: Africa World Press.

Bodon, J., Powell, L., & Hickson, M. (1999). An analysis of book versus article productivity based on top research careers. *Communication Research Reports, 16*(3), 213–222.

Bodunrun, P. (1991). The question of African philosophy. In T. Serequeberhan (Ed.), *African philosophy.* New York: Paragon.

Calloway-Thomas, C., Cooper, P., & Blake, C. (1999). *Intercultural communication: Roots and routes.* Boston: Allyn & Bacon.

Collier, M. J., & Thomas, M. (1988). Cultural identity. In Y. Y. Kim & W. B. Gudykunst (Eds.), *Theories in intercultural communication.* Newbury Park, CA: Sage.

Cronen, V. E., Chen, V., & Pearce, W. B. (1988). Coordinated management of meaning. In Y. Y. Kim & W. B. Gudykunst (Eds.), *Theories in intercultural communication* (pp. 66–98). Newbury Park, CA: Sage.

Du Bois, W. E. B. (1903). *The souls of black folk.* Chicago: A.C. McClurg.

Hall, S. (1992). What is this "Black" in Black popular culture? In G. Dent (Ed.), *Black popular culture.* Seattle: Bay Press.

Hecht, M. L., Collier, M. J., & Ribeau, S. A. (1993). *African American communication: Ethnic identity and cultural interpretation.* Newbury Park, CA: Sage.

Hecht, M. L., Ribeau, S., & Alberts, J. K. (1989). An Afro-American perspective on interethnic communication. *Communication Monographs, 56,* 385–410.

Hickson, M., Stacks, D., & Bodon, J. (1999). The status of research productivity in communication: 1915–1995. *Communication Monographs, 66,* 178–197.

hooks, b. (1994). *Outlaw culture: Resisting representations.* New York: Routledge.

Houston, M. (1983). *Codeswitching in Black women's speech.* Unpublished doctoral dissertation. University of Massachusetts, Amherst.

Jackson, R. L. (1999). *The negotiation of cultural identity.* Westport, CT: Praeger.

Jackson, R. L. (2000). So real illusions of Black intellectualism: Exploring race, roles, and gender in the academy. *Communication Theory, 10*(1), 48–63.

Jackson, R. L., Morrison, C. D., & Dangerfield, C. (In press). Exploring cultural contracts in the classroom and curriculum: Implications of identity negotiation and effects in communication curricula. In J. Trent (Ed.), *Promoting the success of students of color in communication.* Washington, D.C.: National Communication Association & American Association of Higher Education.

Mbiti, J. (1990). *African religions and philosophy* (2nd ed.). Portsmouth, NH: Heinemann.

McPhail, M. (1991). Complicity: The theory of negative difference. *Howard Journal of Communication, 3*(1/2), 1–13.

McPhail, M. (1994). The politics of complicity: Second thoughts about the social construction of racial equality. *Quarterly Journal of Speech, 80,* 343–357.

Morreale, S., & Jones, A. (Eds.). (1997). *Racial and ethnic diversity in the 21st century: A communication perspective.* Annandale, VA: National Communication Association.

Roloff, M., & Cloven, D. (1990). The chilling effect in interpersonal relationships: The reluctance to speak one's mind. In D. Cahn (Ed.), *Intimates in conflict: A communication perspective.* Mahwah, NJ: Lawrence Erlbaum Associates.

Scott, K. (In press). Conceiving the language of Black women's everyday talk. In M. Houston & O. Davis (Eds.), *African American women's communication: Rhetoric and everyday talk.* Hampton, VA: Hampton.

Ting Toomey, S. (1999). *Communicating across cultures.* New York: Guilford.

West, C. (1993). *Keeping faith.* New York: Routledge.

Wilson, A. N. (1998). *Blueprint for Black power: A moral, political, and economic imperative for the twenty-first century.* New York: Africa World Press.

PART VI: AFRICAN AMERICAN IDENTITIES IN MASS MEDIATED CONTEXTS / RONALD L. JACKSON II

References

Kern-Foxworth, M. (1994). Aunt Jemima, Uncle Ben, and Rastus: Blacks in advertising, yesterday, today and tomorrow. Westport, CT: Greenwood Press.

Turner, P. (1994). Ceramic Uncles & Celluloid Mammies. New York: Anchor Books.

Reading 6.1/

THE CHANGING IMAGE OF THE AFRICAN AMERICAN FAMILY ON TELEVISION, MELBOURNE S. CUMMINGS

Notes

1. *N B C Declaration of Standards and Practices.* Revised, 1951.

2. J. Fred MacDonald. *Blacks and White TV: Afro-Americans in Television since 1948.* Chicago: Nelson-Hall Publishers, 1983, p. 33.

3. *Op. Cit.,* p. 29.

4. *Ibid, p.* 117.

5. *Ibid.,* p. 198.

6. *Diff'rent Strokes.*

7. Robert MacKenzie. "Review: Gimme A Break", *TV Guide,* January 9, 1982, p. 23.

8. Alvin Poussaint. Personal Interview with Judi Moore-Smith. March 1, 1985, Cambridge MA.

9. Tony Brown. "Television and the Black Family: The Role of Government", in Anthony Jackson, editor. *Black Families and The Medium of*

Television, Ann Arbor: The University of Michigan, 1982, pp. 83–85.

10. Lester Strong, "Blacks, Television and Ratings," in Anthony Jackson, editor. *Black Families and The Medium of Television.* Ann Arbor: The University of Michigan, 1982, pp. 27–32.

Reading 6.2 /
Jammin' on the One! /
Herman Gray

Notes

1. This notion of cultural struggle implies, at the very least, the existence of access to various forms of power and the ability to implement them. Given the material constraints on black youth and their access to various forms and expressions of power, the location of struggles over meaning at the site of culture is of particular interest. The attempt of black youth to assert subjectivity and authority through the use of the body, language, music, dance, and so on represents an important moment and an attempt to bring a measure of equality to their unequal access and relationship to various quarters of the dominant culture. I thank Teshome Gabriel for bringing this point to my attention.

2. The observations in this section have greatly benefited from my discussions with Rosa Linda Fregoso.

3. In particular, my observations are drawn from representations found on Black Entertainment Television *(Video Soul, Rap City)* and MTV *(Yo! MTV Raps).*

4. This unity is detectable in the music of rap culture, the fusions and collaborations of Miles Davis and Quincy Jones, the dynamism of Janet Jackson and her calls for unity of the rhythm nation, and in Public Enemy's anthem, "Fight the Power." It is also expressed in the dance movement of Pee-wee Herman and the running man, and in verbal expressions such as "Jammin' on the one."

5. Like musical tastes, hairstyles represent one of the earliest and most important expressions available to youth for separating and distancing themselves from adult authority, institutional control, and social practices where they do not have a great deal of power, space, or voice.

6. I want to thank Rosa Linda Fregoso for pointing out the dual significance of this dance and its name. One of my students further complicated my reading of this dance by pointing out that it meant one thing prior to the commercial success and adoption of it by M.C. Hammer and Vanilla Ice and something quite different afterward. My thanks to Ryan Monihan for this important insight.

7. For an interesting and often amusing discussion of the institutional policing of the contemporary body by the state, see Kroker and Kroker (1988). See also Bakhtin (1984) and Hebdige (1989).

8. These expressions are not limited to the world of popular music performance or athletics. They are also expressed in the performance of the black minister and in the detectable leaks in the formal presentation and demeanor of the Wall Street banker or the college professor. I also think that traces of the kind I have described constitute one of the ways in which inscriptions of black cultural sensibilities are expressed in commercial television. Obviously, what is detectable as an expression of African American sensibilities has less to do with biology (black skin) than with performance and presentation through language and the body. Examples of these kinds of leaks and expressions can be seen in the character of Thelma on the series *Amen.* For an interesting discussion of this topic, see comments by South African pianist Abdullah Ibrahim (Dollar Brand) in a video titled *A Brother with Perfect Timing.*

9. Lisa Kennedy and bell hooks, among others, have recently made similar observations about black films. They charge that in black films the subjectivities of women are contained by black men *(Do The Right Thing)* and that the subjectivities of darker, working-class segments of the black community are subordinated and marginal to those of fairer and middle-class blacks *(House Party).* For more complete elaboration, see Kennedy (1990) and Wallace (1992a).

10. Another illustration of this set of discourses can be seen in two stories that appeared in the March 7, 1990, issue of the *Los Angeles Times.* One story, which appeared with a large photo, was a racial uplift story about the successful crossover of black radio (i.e., urban contemporary). This piece detailed the rise and successful bridging of black and white markets by black radio stations and programmers in major U.S. markets. (In the photo that accompanied the story, a respectable black businessman appeared in a tailored business suit.) To the immediate right of this story was another story about black music. This one, what I would call a problem story, reported the details of a Florida state investigation into a Miami-based rap group accused of presenting suggestive, pornographic, and otherwise unacceptable lyrics in their music. Headlined "2 Live Crew, Nasty as They Wanna Be," the piece detailed the intentions of a Florida state legislator who pushed to have the group's lyrics monitored and if necessary labeled as pornographic because they offend public sensibilities *(Los Angeles Times,* March 7, 1990, F1).

References

Bakhtin, M. (1984). *Rabelais and His World.* Bloomington: Indiana University Press.

Baraka, A. (1991). The Changing Same (R&B and New Black Music). In A. Baraka, *The Leroi Jones/Amiri Baraka Reader.* (pp. 186–209). New York: Thunder's Mouth.

Davis, M. & Troupe, Q. (1992). *Miles: The Autobiography.* New York: Simon & Schuster.

Frith, S. (1988). (Ed.). *Facing the Music: Pantheon Guide to Popular Culture. New York:* Pantheon.

Gilroy, P. (1993). *The Black Atlantic: Modernity and Double Consciousness.* Cambridge: Harvard University Press.

Gilroy, P. (1991a). Sounds Authentic: Black Music, Ethnicity, and the Challenge of a 'Changing Same.' *Black Music Research Journal 11*(2), 111–136.

Goodwin, A. (1992). *Dancing in the Distraction Factory: Music Television and Popular Culture.* Minneapolis: University of Minnesota Press.

Gray, H. (1989). Television, Black Americans and the American Dream. *Critical Studies in Mass Communication 6,* 376–87.

Grossberg, L. (1992). *We Gotta Get Outta This Place: Popular Conservatism and Postmodern Culture.* New York: Routledge.

Hall, S. (1989). Cultural Identity and Cinematic Representation. *Framework 36,* 68–82.

Hall, S. (1981a). Notes on Deconstructing the Popular. In R. Samuel (Ed.) *People's History and Socialist Theory.* London: Routledge & Kegan Paul.

Hebdige, D. (1988). *Hiding in the Light: On Images and Things.* London: Comedia.

Jones, J. (1991). The New Ghetto Aesthetic. In M. Diawara (Ed.) [special issue on Black Cinema]. *Wide Angle, 13(3&4),* 32–44.

Kelley, R. D. G. (1994). Kickin Reality, Kickin Ballistics: The Cultural Politics of Gangsta Rap in Postindustrial Los Angeles. In E. Perkins (Ed.) *Droppin' Science: Critical Essays on Rap Music and Hip Hop Culture.* Philadephia: Temple University Press.

Kelley, R. D. G. (1992). Notes on Deconstructing 'the Folk.' *American Historical Review 97,* 1400–1406.

Kennedy, L. (1990, March 13). Wack House: *House Party Is* Business as Usual. *Village Voice,* 67.

Kroker, A. & Kroker, M. (1988). (Eds.). *Body Invaders: Panic Sex in America.* New York: St. Martin's.

Lipsitz, G. (1994). We Know What Time It Is: Race, Class, and Youth in the Nineties. In A. Ross and T. Rose (eds.) *Microphone Fiends: Youth, Music, and Youth Culture.* (pp. 15–29) New York: Routledge.

Lipsitiz, G. (1990). *Time Passages: Collective Memory and American Popular Culture.* Minneapolis: University of Minnesota Press.

Los Angeles Times. (1990, January 12). FCC Considering Ending Cable TV Monopolies. *Los Angeles Times,* p. D2.

Mercer, K. (1990). Black Hair/Style Politics. In R. Ferguson, M. Gever, & T. Minh-Ha (Eds.). *Out There: Marginalization and Contemporary Cultures.* (pp. 247–65) Cambridge: MIT Press.

Rose, T. (1994). *Black Noise: Rap Music and Black Culture in Contemporary America.* Middletown, Conn.: Wesleyan University Press.

Rose, T. (1989). Orality and Technology: Rap Music and Afro-American Cultural Resistance. *Popular Music and Society,* 13(4), 35–41.

Sawchuk, K. (1988). A Tale of Inscription/Fashion Statements. In A. Kroker and M. Kroker (Eds.) *Body Invaders: Panic Sex in America.* (pp. 60–77). New York: St. Martin's.

Snead, J. A. (1990). On Repetition in Black Culture. In R. Ferguson, M. Gever, & T. Minh-Ha (Eds.). *Out There: Marginalization and Contemporary Cultures.* Cambridge: MIT Press.

Tate, G. (1992). *Flyboy in the Buttermilk: Essays on Contemporary America.* New York: Simon & Schuster.

Wallace, M. (1992). *Black Popular Culture: A Project by Michelle Wallace* (Gina Dent, ed.). Seattle: Bay.

West, C. (1993). *Race Matters.* Boston: Beacon.

Whyte, W. H. (1989). *City: Rediscovering Its Center.* Garden City, N. Y.: Doubleday.

Reading 6.3 /
BLACK BEGINNINGS /
DONALD BOGLE

Note

1. Lillian Gish's comments in the January 1937, issue of *Stage* verify the fact that Griffith was well aware of this contrast and that he used it to arouse his audience. Said Gish: "At first I was not cast to play in *The Clansman.* My sister and I had been the last to join the company and we naturally supposed . . . that the main assignments would go to the older members. But one day while we were rehearsing the scene where the colored man picks up the Northern girl gorilla-fashion, my hair, which was very blond, fell far below my waist and Griffith, seeing the contrast in the two figures, assigned me to play Elsie Stoneman (Who was to have been Mae Marsh)."

Reading 6.4 /
BLACK TALK RADIO /
CATHERINE R. SQUIRES

Notes

1. In this article, I use "Black," "African-American," and "black" interchangeably to reflect the use of all three of these terms by different peoples in Black communities.

2. The *Defender* was one of many Black northern newspapers that were circulated widely between urban and rural black publics both by subscription and by other means. In the days of Jim Crow, many copies of the *Defender* made their way South via Pullman porters who smuggled them to relatives who feared white repression if a *Defender* subscription was discovered (Senna 1993; Walker 1996).

3. Of course, in certain cases even the segregated newspapers did not provide safe haven. Ida B. Wells's offices were destroyed by a white mob; subscription agents for the *Defender* were beaten and threatened in the South; and Black publications were threatened with sedition charges for printing editorials about racism in the armed forces during World War II (Washburn 1986; Wolseley 1971).

4. Trade publications have also commented on the Black and "urban format" stations' community focus. See Walt Love, "WDAS Brings Philly Together: Twelfth Annual Unity Day Focuses on Community, Youth, and Family Fun," Radio and Records, September 27, 1991:50; Walt Love, "WVEE Wages War against Violence," Radio and Records, December 6, 1991: 36; and Brown 1990.

5. At the time of my research, WVON was a 1,000-watt station. WVON shared its frequency with WCEV ("Chicago's ethnic voice"), switching to WCEV from 1 P.M. to 10 P.M. Thus, WVON had the morning drive-time hours, a lucrative position in the Chicago market. The signal reached the south and west sides of the city and the southwest suburbs easily, thus covering most of the Black neighborhoods in the area. Reception was not as good on the north side of the city at that time, but a new transmitter installed in late 1998 cleared up that problem.

6. The pretest revealed that two ranking questions concerning the O.J. Simpson trial and the Million Man March were too confusing for respondents, so these were eliminated.

7. *World Objectives.* Broadcast aired October 5, 1995.

8. *World Objectives.* Broadcast aired October 4, 1996.

9. Keisha Chavers, executive producer, WVON-AM, interview, October 20, 1995, WVON studios, Chicago, Illinois. Tape recording.

10. Sec Michael Warner's discussion of the citizen body and the public sphere (1992). Warner contends that the historical position and privilege of white propertied males created a public sphere in which only some (white males) are allowed to take on the role of "citizen," and nonwhite males are marked noncitizen and biased by their particular racial, ethnic, ro gender differences. Hence nonwhites have the burden of being seen as pursuing "special interests" rather than the public good.

11. Cliff Kelley, talk show host, WVON-AM, interview, March 5, 1995, Nick's Restaurant, Chicago, Illinois, Tape recording.

12. Lu Palmer, talk show host, WVON-AM, telephone interview, March 8, 1995, Tape recording.

13. Melody Spann, president and general manager, WVON-AM, interview, October 18, 1996, WVON Studios, Chicago, Illinois, Tape recording.

14. *World objectives.* Broadcast aired February 9, 1998.

15. I use the pronoun *we* here because I was assistant producer on the *Sisters at Sunrise* broadcast and was active in the choice of music that day. However, this sort of musical call and response with show subjects is a regular attribute of the shows. Cliff Kelley's show, for example, is always introduced by jazz music, often the music of Gene "Jug" Ammons, which listeners name and comment on before making comments on the topic at hand. Also, in program identification spots, Cliff is often referred to as "Jug." A non-Black friend of mine who listened to the broadcast with me one morning asked me why Cliff would want to be referred to as a jug. For him, jug denoted "Jughead" from the Archie comic strip, not jazz music, saxophone players, and the like.

16. *Sisters at Sunrise.* Broadcast aired October 16, 1996.

17. *World Objectives.* Broadcast aired October 6, 1995.

18. *World Objectives.* Broadcast aired January 5, 1998.

19. Cornel West describes the skewed results of racial reasoning as decisions that subordinate common sense and compassion to the idea that all black "leaders" (especially black males) should be defended despite the potentially disastrous ramifications (1993). The classic example is the defense of Clarence Thomas in the face of his conservative stance on most civil rights issues.

20. Following the argument of Craig Calhoun, Gayatri Spivak, and others that there are many essentialisms that can be deployed strategically, I believe that essentialism in the service of solidarity can be useful in particular situations, just as it can stifle dissent in others (Calhoun 1994).

21.   These labels are taken from my dissertation on the Black public sphere and will be more fully explicated in a future paper excerpted from the dissertation.

References

Anderson, Benedict. 1991. *Imagined Communities.* London: Verso.

Bennett, W. Lance, and David L. Paletz, eds. 1994. *Taken by Storm: The Media, Public Opinion, and U.S. Foreign Policy in the Gulf War.* Chicago: University of Chicago Press.

Brouwer, Daniel C. 1995. "The Charisma of 'Responsibility': A Comparison of U.S. Mainstream Representations of Gay Men with AIDS in U.S. AIDS 'Zines." Master's thesis, Northwestern University.

Brown, Fred, Jr. 1990. "African American Broadcasters: The Link to Their Communities." *Pulse of Radio: Radio's Management Weekly* 5(46): 22–24.

Calhoun, Craig, ed. 1994. *Introduction to Social Theory and the Politics of Identity.* Oxford: Blackwell.

Cantor, Louis. 1992. *Wheelin' on Beale: How WDIA Memphis Became the Nation's First All-Black Radio Station and Created the Sound That Changed America.* New York: Pharos.

Chomsky, Noam. 1992. *Deterring Democracy.* New York: Farrar, Straus and Giroux.

Dates, Jannette L., and William Barlow, eds. 1990. *Split Image: African Americans in Mass Media.* Washington, D.C.: Howard University Press.

Davis, Robert. 1997. Introduction to the symposium "Understanding Broadcast Political Talk." *Political Communication* 14(3): 323–32.

Dawson, Michael. 1994. "A Black Counterpublic? Economic Earthquakes, Racial Agenda(s), and Black Politics." *Public Culture* 7(1): 195–224.

Entman, Robert. 1989. *Democracy without Citizens: Media and the Decay of American Politics.* New York: Oxford University.

Entman, Robert. 1992. "Blacks in the News: Television, Modern Racism, and cultural Change." *Journalism Quarterly* 69(2): 341–61.

Fraser, Nancy. 1992. "Rethinking the Public Sphere: a Contribution to the Critique of Actually Existing Democracy." In *Habermas and the Public Sphere,* ed. Craig Calhoun. Cambridge, MA: MIT Press.

Gamson, William. 1992. "The Social Psychology of Collective Action." In *Frontiers in Social Movement Theory,* ed. Aldon D. Morris and Carol McClurg Mueller. New Haven, CT: Yale University.

Gilens, Martin. 1996. "Race and Poverty in America." *Public Opinion Quarterly* 60: 515–41.

Habermas, Jurgen. 1989. *The Structural Transformation of the Public Sphere: An Inquiry into a Category of Bourgeois Society.* Trans. Thomas Burger. Cambridge, MA: MIT Press.

Herbst, Susan. 1995. "On Electronic Public Space: Talk Shows in Theoretical perspective." *Political Communication* 12:263–74.

Herbst, Susan, and James R. Beniger. 1994. "The Changing Infrastructure of Public Opinion." In *Audiencemaking: How the Media Create the Audience,* ed. James Ettema and D. Charles Whitney. London: Sage.

Hofstetter, C.R., and Christopher L. Gianos. 1997. "Political Talk Radio: Actions Speak Louder than Words." *Journal of Broadcasting and Electronic Media* 41(4):501–15.

Hollander, Barry A. 1997. "Fuel to the Fire: Talk Radio and the Gamson Hypothesis." *Political Communication* 14(3):355–70.

Johnson, Phylis. 1992. "Black/Urban Radio Is in Touch with the Inner City: What Can Educators Learn from This Popular Medium?" *Education and Urban Society* 24(4):508–18.

Johnson, Phylis, and Thomas A. Birk. 1993. "The Role of African American–Owned Radio in Health Promotion: Community Service Projects Targeting Young African Males." *Urban League Review* 16(2):85–94.

Livingstone, Sonia, and Peter Lunt. 1994. *Talk on Television: Audience Participation and Public Debate.* London: Routledge.

Marable, Manning. 1991. *Race, Reform, and Rebellion: The Second Reconstruction in Black America, 1945–1990.* 2nd Edition. London: University Press of Mississippi.

Morrison, Toni, ed. 1992. *Race-ing Justice, En-gendering Power: Essays on Anita Hill, Clarence Thomas, and the Construction of Social Reality.* New York: Pantheon.

Newman, Mark. 1988. *Entrepreneurs of Profit and Pride: From Black-Appeal to Radio Soul.* New York: Praeger.

Omi, Michael, and Howard Winant. 1994. *Racial Formation in the United States.* 2nd Edition. New York: Routledge.

Owen, Diana. 1997. "Talk Radio and Evaluations of President Clinton." *Political Communication* 14(3):333–54.

Page, Benjamin I. 1996. *Who Deliberates? Mass Media in Modern Democracy.* Chicago: University of Chicago Press.

Parenti, Michael. 1993. *Inventing Reality: The Politics of News Media.* 2nd Edition. New York: St. Martin's.

Peffley, Mark, Todd Shields, and Bruce Williams. 1996. "The Intersection of Race and Crime in

Television News Stories: An Experimental Study." *Political Communication* 13(3):309–27.

Senna, Carl. 1993. *The Black Press and the Struggle for Civil Rights.* New York: Franklin Watts.

Squires, Catherine. 1999. "Searching Black Voices in the Black Public Sphere: An Alternative Approach to the Analysis of Public Spheres." Ph.D. diss., Northwestern University.

Suggs, Henry L., ed. 1996. *The Black Press in the MiddleWest, 1865–1985.* Westport, CT: Greenwood Press.

Walker, Juliet E. 1996. "The Promised Land: The Chicago Defender and the Black Press in Illinois, 1862–1970." In *The Black Press in the Middle West, 1865–1985,* ed. Henry L. Suggs. Westport, CT: Greenwood Press.

Warner, Michael. 1992. "The Mass Public and the Mass Subject." In *Habermas and the Public Sphere,.* ed. Craig Calhoun. Cambridge, MA: MIT Press.

Washburn, Patrick S. 1986. *A Question of Sedition: The Federal Government's Investigation of the Black Press During World War II.* New York: Oxford University Press.

Webster, Jame and Pat Phalen. 1994. *The Mass Audience: Rediscovering the Dominant Model.* Unpublished manuscript.

West, Cornel. 1993. *Race Matters.* New York: Vintage.

Wolseley, Robert E. 1971. *The Black Press,* U.S.A. Ames, IA: Iowa State University.

INDEX

ABOUT THE EDITOR

Ronald L. Jackson II (Ph.D., Howard University) is Associate Professor of Culture and Communication Theory in the Department of Communication Arts & Sciences at Pennsylvania State University. He is author of *The Negotiation of Cultural Identity, Think About It!, African American Communication: Identity and Culture* (with Michael Hecht and Sidney Ribeau), and *Understanding African American Rhetoric* (with Elaine Richardson).

Forthcoming are four books: *African American Rhetoric(s): Interdisciplinary Perspectives* (with Elaine Richardson); *Scripting the Black Masculine Body: Intersections of Masculinity, Communication, Culture, and Identity,* and *Pioneers in African American Communication Research* (with Sonja Givens). Dr. Jackson's theory work includes the development of two paradigms coined "cultural contracts theory" and "black masculine identity theory."

ABOUT THE AUTHORS

Linda K. Acitelli (Ph.D., University of Michigan) is Associate Professor and Director of the Social Psychology program, University of Houston. Her major research interests are cognition and communication in relationships, specifically thinking and talking about relationships and the factors that determine their impact on individual and relationship well being. She intends to expand her research by investigating relationship dynamics within different contexts and ethnic groups. Recently, she has begun to examine the interpersonal challenge of being in a close relationship in which one partner has a chronic illness. The National Institute of Mental Health, USA, has supported her research program for several years, giving her the opportunity to become a research investigator at the Institute for Social Research, Ann Arbor, Michigan. In 1995, she received the Gerald R. Miller Award from the International Network on Personal Relationships for her early career achievements.

J. K. Alberts (Ph.D., University of Texas) is Professor and Chair of the Hugh Downs School of Human Communication and President of the Faculty Women's Association at Arizona State University. Her research appears regularly in academic journals, and in 2000, she co-authored *Adolescent Relationships and Drug Use* with Michelle Miller-Day, Michael Hecht, Melanie Trost, and Robert Krizek.

Brenda J. Allen (Ph.D., Howard University) is Associate Professor, Department of Communication, University of Colorado at Denver. She specializes in the study of organizational communication, social identity, and computer-mediated communication. Allen focuses her scholarship activities on organizational communication processes, with an emphasis on two areas of study that will impact organizations in the 21st century: social identity and workplace diversity and computer-mediated communication.

Molefi Kete Asante (Ph.D., University of California at Los Angeles) is Professor, Department of African American Studies, Temple University. He is the author of 47 books, including *The Afrocentric Idea, African Intellectual Heritage, The Egyptian Philosophers, African American Atlas,* and *African American History: A Journey of Liberation.*

Deborah F. Atwater (Ph.D., State University of New York at Buffalo) is former Head of the Department of African and African American Studies and Associate Professor of Speech Communication at Pennsylvania State University, where she teaches courses on cross-cultural communication and Black rhetoric. She has published in *Communication Education, Communication Quarterly, Journal of Black Studies, Western Journal of Black Studies,* and *Rhetoric Society Quarterly.* Her research interests include intercultural communication and African American rhetoric with an emphasis on African American women. Recently, she has traveled to South Africa, Russia, Finland, and Italy as part of cross-cultural communication exchanges.

John Baugh (Ph.D., University of Pennsylvania) is Professor of Education and by courtesy Linguistics, Stanford University.

Author of *Beyond Ebonics* (2000), Baugh specializes in studies of the relation of social stratification to linguistic diversity in the U.S. and elsewhere, along with related policy issues, primarily in education. Most recently he has integrated this work into studies of linguistic discrimination in the U.S. and South Africa. He is a founding member of the National Advisory Committee to the Social, Behavioral, and Economic Sciences within the National Science Foundation and past president of the American Dialect Society.

Donald Bogle, who lives in Manhattan and holds joint appointments at the University of Pennsylvania and New York University's Tisch School of the Arts, is one of the country's foremost authorities on African Americans in film. Additionally, he is the author of three prize-winning books. *Toms, Coons, Mulattoes, Mammies, and Bucks: An Interpretive History of Blacks in American Films* is considered a classic study of Black movie images. *Brown Sugar: Eight Years of America's Black Female Superstars* was adapted into a four-part PBS series.

Melbourne S. Cummings (Ph.D., University of California at Los Angeles) is Professor and Chair of the Department of Communication and Culture at Howard University. She teaches courses across the discipline in rhetoric, public address, nonverbal communication, and intercultural communication. Her publications span the areas of African American communications: rhetoric, poetry, song, comedy, and others. She has served on major planning, organizational, and policy boards in regional, national, and international communication associations, and has traveled extensively in Africa, Europe, and Asia as part of intercultural exchanges in communication, international education, and religion.

Celnisha L. Dangerfield (M.A., Pennsylvania State University) recently received her M.A. in intercultural communication and communication theory within the Department of Communication Arts & Sciences at Pennsylvania State University. She is a summa cum laude graduate of Clark Atlanta University and previous undergraduate summer fellow of both Brown University and NYU. Her research interests are related to cultural identity negotiation

as evidenced in varying contexts from mass media to interpersonal relationships. Ms. Dangerfield has also developed a paradigm she has coined "race shock,"which was the subject of her thesis.

Jack L. Daniel (Ph.D., University of Pittsburgh) is Professor of Communication and Vice Provost for Academic Affairs at the University of Pittsburgh. His research interests and publications include the study of African American rhetoric and African American families with a specific focus on African American males who grow up in female-headed, father-absent homes. He teaches African American Rhetoric as well as African Americans and the Mass Media.

Elizabeth Douvan (Ph.D., University of Michigan) is Professor Emerita in the Department of Psychology at the University of Michigan. Her research examines the relation of social organization to personality development and attitudes, sex and family roles, alternative dispute settlement, and multiculturalism.

Thurmon Garner (Ph.D., Northwestern University) recently retired as Associate Professor in the Department of Speech Communication at the University of Georgia. He graduated from the Department of Communication Studies at Northwestern University in Evanston, Illinois in 1979. His general area of study is in rhetorical communication, with an emphasis in rhetorical criticism and African American discourse. His publications have appeared in such outlets as *The Journal of Black Studies, The Quarterly Journal of Speech,* and the *Journal of Language and Social Psychology.*

Herman Gray (Ph.D., University of California, Santa Cruz) is Associate Professor in the Department of Sociology, University of California, Santa Cruz. He is author of *Watching Race: Television and the Struggle for Blackness* (1995) and has published widely on topics related to cultural studies, popular culture, mass communication, and minority discourse.

Tina M. Harris (Ph.D., University of Kentucky) is Assistant Professor in the Department of Speech Communication at the University of Georgia. She teaches undergraduate courses in the areas of interracial, intercultural, and interpersonal communication and graduate courses in interracial communication, mentoring and social support, and qualitative methods. Dr. Harris conducts research on interracial communication, interracial dating, race relations, racial representation and the media, and Christian identity.

Michael L. Hecht (Ph.D., University of Illinois) is Professor and Head of Communication Arts and Sciences and Professor of Crime, Law, and Justice at Penn State University. He has edited and authored books on prejudice and communication, adolescent relationships and drug use, nonverbal communication, and interpersonal communication and has authored numerous articles and chapters on topics such as communication effectiveness, interethnic communication, identity and communication, communication and emotion, and communication in a social context.

Katherine Grace Hendrix (Ph. D., University of Washington) is Associate Professor in the Department of Communication Studies at the University of Memphis. Author of numerous scholarly essays, Dr. Hendrix is an instructional communication scholar with a broad teaching range including argumentation, interpersonal and intercultural communication, and qualitative research methods. She is dedicated to the scholarship of teaching, and she studies professor and graduate teaching assistant (GTA) communication contributing to their classroom credibility. Dr. Hendrix has a particular interest in the pedagogical contributions of and challenges faced by professors and GTAs of color. She has been nominated for teaching awards at the University of Memphis and within her regional and national communication associations. Her career in postsecondary education includes teaching and administrative positions in both the community college and university educational systems.

Marsha Houston (Ph.D., University of Massachusetts) is Professor and Head of the Department of Communication Studies at the University of Alabama. Her work on African American communication and culture as well as women's language and social interaction has

been published in numerous journals and anthologies. She is co-author (with Alberto Gonzalez and Victoria Chen) of the award-winning anthology *Our Voices: Essays in Culture, Ethnicity, and Communication.* Her most recent book (with Olga Davis) is entitled *Centering Ourselves: African-American Feminist and Womanist Studies of Discourse* (2001).

Kenneth R. Johnson (Ed.D., University of Southern California, Los Angeles, California) retired as Professor of Education and Ethnic Studies at Chicago State University and still resides in Chicago, Illinois. He has done extensive research and published several volumes: a book on educating the disadvantaged, a reading series for grades 1 through 8, and a language series for grades 1 through 8. Moreover, he has published over 42 papers in scholarly journals on African American communication patterns and the influence of nonstandard dialects in learning to speak, read, and write standard American English. He has lectured at over fifty colleges and universities throughout the United States, and he has conducted numerous workshops on minority concerns, language patterns of African Americans, and methods of educating the disadvantaged.

Joni L. Jones (Ph.D., New York University) is Associate Professor of Performance Studies in the Department of Theatre and Dance, and Associate Director of the Center for African and African-American Studies at the University of Texas at Austin. She is an artist/scholar who is currently engaged in performance ethnography and videography around the Yoruba deity Osun. In Austin, Texas and Washington, D.C., she has received acting awards for her work in professional theatre. Her articles on performance and identity have appeared in *Text and Performance Quarterly, The Drama Review, Theatre Insight,* and *Black Theatre News.*

Pamela J. Kalbfleisch (Ph.D., Michigan State University) is Associate Professor in the Department of Communication and Journalism at the University of Wyoming. She specializes in personal relationships, interpersonal communication, persuasive communication, and quantitative research methodology. She has published in numerous journals some of which include the

Howard Journal of Communication, Resiliency in Action, Journal of Youth and Adolescence, and *Challenge: A Journal of Research on Black Men.* Currently, in press, "Similarity and Attraction in Business and Academic Environments: Same and Cross-Sex Mentoring Relationships" is to be published in *Review of Business.* Also, she is the co-editor of the book *Gender, Power, and Communication.* Her research interests are inclusive of mentoring relationships, issues of trust, and distrust in personal relationships.

D. Soyini Madison (Ph.D., Northwestern University) is Associate Professor in the Department of Communication Studies at University of North Carolina. Her published works focus on performance practices and the intersections between gender and critical race theory. Her teaching centers on myth and popular culture, performance ethnography, performance of literature for social change, and the political economy of performance. As a Fulbright Scholar, Madison has recently completed a visiting lectureship at the University of Ghana. Her current project is an examination of staging/performing local debates surrounding human rights and traditional religious practices as these debates are influenced by the global market and national development.

Mark Lawrence McPhail (Ph.D., University of Massachusetts, 1987) is Professor of Communication at Miami University in Oxford, Ohio. He is the author of *The Rhetoric of Racism Zen in the Art of Rhetoric: An Inquiry into Coherence,* and *The Rhetoric of Racism (Revisited): Reparations or Separation?* His work has been published in *The Quarterly Journal of Speech, Critical Studies in Mass Communication,* the *Howard Journal of Communications,* and the *American Literary Review.* His research interests include rhetorical epistemology, language and race relations, and Eastern philosophy and spirituality.

Patricia S. Parker (Ph.D., University of Texas) is Assistant Professor in the Department of Communication Studies at University of North Carolina. Her research and teaching interests include critical studies of gender, race, and culture in organizations. Her recent work focuses on the communication strategies and leadership behaviors of African American women executives within dominant culture organizations.

Sidney A. Ribeau (Ph.D., 1979, University of Illinois) is Professor of Interpersonal Communication and President of Bowling Green State University, positions he has held since 1995. He has published in a number of scholarly journals including the *Journal of Black Studies, Negro Educational Review,* and *International Journal of Intercultural Relations.* Ribeau writes regularly for periodicals and newspapers and has lectured at Chautauqua and the Smithsonian Institutes. He has taught courses on African American culture, public speaking, interpersonal communication, African American rhetoric, and intercultural communication.

Karla D. Scott (Ph.D., University of Illinois) is Professor in the Department of Communication Studies and Acting Director of the African American Studies Program at Saint Louis University. She is interested in teaching and writing in the areas of intercultural/interracial communication and in feminist approaches to social theory. An award-winning classroom teacher, she is also an experienced trainer, group facilitator, and consultant. Her scholarly research has been published in the journals *Linguistics and Education* and *Women and Language.* Scott is the 1996 recipient of the Cheris Kramerae Outstanding Dissertation Award presented by the Organization for the Study of Language, Communication, and Gender.

Geneva Smitherman (Ph.D., University of Michigan) is University Distinguished Professor of English and the Director of the African American Language and Literacy Program at Michigan State University. A linguist and educational activist, she has been at the forefront of the struggle for language rights for over 25 years. She is also the director of "My Brother's Keeper" in Detroit.

Catherine R. Squires (Ph.D., Northwestern University) is Assistant Professor in the Department of Communication Studies and The Center for Afro-American and African Studies at the University of Michigan. Her research interests include politics and media, history of African Americans, and multiracial identity issues.

Joseph Veroff (Ph.D., University of Michigan) is Professor Emeritus in the Department of Psychology at University of Michigan. His research interests include personality-role interaction, social incentives over the life span, subjective mental health, and marital adaptation.

Eric King Watts (Ph.D., Northwestern University) is Associate Professor in the Department of Communication at Wake Forest University. His articles on African American rhetoric and culture have been published in *Quarterly Journal of Speech, Rhetoric & Public Affairs, Critical Studies in Media Communication, Communication Studies,* and *New Media & Society.* Watts has received the New Investigator Award by the Rhetorical and Communication Theory Division of the National Communication Association.

Jeffrey Lynn Woodyard (Ph.D., Temple University) is a communication and diversity consultant who lives in DeLand, Florida. He received his Ph.D. in African American Studies at Temple University while focusing on African American communication and africalogical rhetorical studies. His research appears in several journals including the *Journal of Black Studies,* the *Journal of Pastoral Care,* and *The Griot.* He has written book chapters exploring afrocentric approaches to rhetorical studies.